Fodor's

IRELAND

**FODOR'S
TRAVEL PUBLICATIONS**

NEW YORK • TORONTO
LONDON • SYDNEY • AUCKLAND

WWW.FODORS.COM

74

CONTENTS

CONTENTS IRELAND

164

281

171

215

UNDERSTANDING IRELAND

Understanding Ireland is an introduction to the country, its geography, economy, history and its people, giving a real insight into the nation. Living Ireland gets under the skin of Ireland today, while The Story of Ireland takes you through the country's past.

UNDERSTANDING IRELAND

The most striking feature of Ireland is the legendary 40 shades of green that make up this Emerald Isle. You may have to put up with the unpredictable showers of its maritime climate, but your reward is the dazzling spectrum of colour on the lush pastures and rolling hills when the sun breaks through. Some 6 million visitors come to Ireland every year to see its prehistoric monuments, castles and high crosses, crumbling monasteries and stately homes. But although the island looks small on a map, don't assume you can tour it quickly. Its winding country roads and beautiful scenery demand a leisurely pace. Besides, it's almost a sacrilege to hurry in Ireland. Take time to chat with the locals, linger in the brightly painted coastal towns or vibrant cities, share a story or a song in a local pub. Through the people, as well as the places, you will discover the magic of Ireland.

WHAT IS IRELAND?

Officially, this North Atlantic island nation goes by its ancient name of Éire. Known in English as Ireland, it measures 84,421sq km (32,924sq miles) and is part of the British Isles. The independent Republic of Ireland comprises 26 counties, while the six northeastern counties that make up Northern Ireland are part of the United Kingdom. However, 20th-century political divisions cannot erase Ireland's strong ties to its united past. Its four provinces reflect the island's ancient kingdoms: Leinster in the east, Connacht in the west, Ulster in the north and Munster in the south. Even though they hold no official significance today, they are still important historically and culturally, featuring in regional literature, and often referred to in poetry and song as 'the four green fields'.

Ireland's landscape is varied. Much of the coastline is backed by a rim of mountains and sea cliffs, while a limestone plain spreads across the interior, where the terrain ranges from flat pasture to rolling hills, with winding rivers and lakeland. Much of the land is agricultural. The ancient oak forests are long gone, but there are still vast stretches of peat bog in the centre and northwest.

POLITICS

Although the violent clashes known as 'the Troubles' came largely to an end with the Good Friday Agreement of 1998 (▷ 40), peace in Northern Ireland remains the biggest political issue on the island. The problems of the province are often simplified by outsiders as being a religious conflict between Catholics and Protestants, but the reality involves more complex economic, social and political issues. About 60 per cent of the population of Northern Ireland are Protestant. Both the Unionists (who want union with Britain) and the Nationalists (who wish for Irish unity) have long historical ties to their positions.

The implementation of a devolved Assembly in Northern Ireland, with the main opposing parties sharing power, has been difficult. Since October 2002, the Democratic Unionists have refused to sit in government with Sinn Féin over concerns that a rogue branch of the Irish Republican Army—called the Real IRA—is still active. Talks on restoring devolution continue, but the Assembly remains suspended. When these issues are resolved, the Assembly will have legislative powers over social and economic policy in Northern Ireland.

The Republic is a parliamentary democracy. The Oireachtas (National Parliament) consists of the president and two houses: Dáil Éireann (House of Representatives) with 166 members (Teachta Dála or TDs), and Seanad Éireann (Senate), with 60 senators. Both are elected through a system of proportional representation.

The president is the head of state and is elected directly by the people for a term of seven years, with a limit of two terms. Although the president does not have an executive or policy-making role, he or she may still influence legislation. Mary Robinson, a lawyer who served as president from 1990 to 1997, championed civil liberties. Under her term of office, homosexuality was decriminalized and divorce was made legal, despite fierce opposition from the Catholic Church. She was succeeded by Mary McAleese, now in her second term.

The Head of the Government, or Taoiseach (pronounced 'tea-shook'), is nominated by the Dáil and appointed by the President. Bertie Ahern has served as Taoiseach since 1997. In May 2007, the general election, resulted in a coalition government of Fianna Fáil, the Green Party and the Progressive Democrats. The Republic of Ireland is a member of the European Union (EU).

ECONOMICS

Ireland joined the European Economic Community (EEC), forerunner of the EU, in 1973, and by the 1990s it was one of Europe's biggest success stories. The lowering of trade barriers expanded the market for Irish goods, while EU aid helped Ireland to modernize its economy. Between 1995 and 2002 it was the fastest growing economy in the industrialized world. Ireland became known as the Celtic Tiger, and for the first time in decades, young people no longer had to seek work abroad.

In the past decade, Ireland has prospered from foreign investment. Ireland's young, well-educated workforce is also highly attractive to overseas firms—more than 1,000 have moved here, nearly half of them from the US.

Around 70 per cent of Irish workers are employed in the services sector, which now accounts for half of the country's GDP. Electronics, pharmaceuticals, financial services and telemarketing are other leading industries. Tourism is one of the fastest growing economic sectors. Agriculture remains an important factor in the economy, particularly livestock production. Prosperity has also brought a boom in the construction industry, not only in Dublin but all around the country.

HERITAGE

Ireland's rich heritage stretches back to prehistoric times. Megalithic tombs, cairns, stone circles, ring forts and *crannógs* (artificial islands built on lakes) scattered throughout the countryside are testimony to an ancient and mysterious race.

Opposite *Lofty view over Derrynane on the Ring of Kerry*
Right *Crossing Carrick-a-Rede rope bridge*

Early Irish craftsmen were making weapons and exquisite gold jewellery as far back as the Bronze Age. These skills were enhanced by the Celtic people who came to Ireland from Europe in the sixth century BC. Celtic art features interlaced geometric patterns, and its motifs are still used in Irish arts and crafts.

The early Christian era gave Ireland some of its most striking architecture. The slender round towers, unique to the island, and tall, elaborately carved high crosses are key features of monastic sites around the country such as Glendalough and Clonmacnoise. From the seventh to the ninth centuries, while the rest of Europe was in the Dark Ages, art and learning flourished in Ireland's monasteries. Celtic arts reached their zenith in magnificent illustrated manuscripts such as the Book of Kells.

The Anglo-Normans brought Romanesque and Gothic churches, and monastic sites such as Jerpoint Abbey. In eastern counties, you can find the ruins of a few early Norman castles. Most of Ireland's 2,500 castles and fortified tower houses date from the late 12th to the 16th centuries and are in the west and southwest. During the 1700s and early 1800s, the aristocracy built neoclassical mansions such as Castle Coole and Bantry House, and Dublin's elegant Georgian squares.

The art, literature, music, theatre and culture of Ireland has been central to Irish life throughout the centuries and was particularly highlighted when Ireland was European Capital of Culture in 2005, hosted by the City of Cork.

THE IRISH

The Republic of Ireland is a nation of more than 4 million people. Its population is young, with about 37 per cent under the age of 25. About 1.7 million people live in Northern Ireland.

The official language of the Republic of Ireland is Irish. The second official language, English, is spoken almost everywhere (▷ 352).

Though attitudes are becoming more relaxed, many people remain deeply religious. In the Republic 88 per cent are Roman Catholic (around 40 per cent in Northern Ireland).

The Irish are famous for their humour and there's no better place to enjoy it than the pub, the hub of Irish social life. Come for the *craic*—the Irish word for fun. This often involves an impromptu session of Irish music, with everyone who is able joining in. Good conversation and tall tales flow as freely as the Guinness.

REGIONS OF IRELAND

DUBLIN

The Republic of Ireland's vibrant capital has lively pubs, restaurants and nightclubs, and numerous historical and contemporary attractions. Greater Dublin has a population of nearly 1.7 million. More than 40 per cent of the population of the Republic lives within 97km (60 miles) of Dublin.

THE EAST

Bordering the Irish Sea, the eastern counties contain some of the country's most visited attractions. North of Dublin, the ancient sites of the Boyne Valley lie in County Meath, while County Louth has outstanding monastic ruins. Inland along the border with Northern Ireland, Monaghan and Cavan are quiet lakeland counties. West of Dublin, Ireland's famous racehorses are bred in the rolling pastures of County Kildare, home of the National Stud. South of the capital are the Wicklow Mountains, with Powerscourt Gardens and the monastic site of Glendalough, leading south to Wexford and its wildfowl reserve. Inland are counties Carlow and Kilkenny, with a fine castle and medieval sites.

THE SOUTH

The bustling city of Waterford, along the south coast, is famous for its crystal glassworks, while the surrounding county has pretty harbours, fishing villages and market towns. Inland, bordering the Midlands and the East, County Tipperary is ringed by low mountains that form the backdrop to attractive river valleys, historic towns such as Clonmel and Caher, and the famous Rock of Cashel. Bordering the West is County Limerick, whose northern boundary is defined by Ireland's longest river, the Shannon. Limerick, Ireland's fourth-largest city and western international gateway, has a historic hub with fine churches, museums and galleries. Many castles, both ruined and restored, dot the rolling landscape that leads to lovely beaches on the coast. Inland are picturesque villages such as Adare, and the Stone Age settlement of Lough Gur. The dramatic scenery of counties Cork and Kerry in the island's southwestern corner makes them among the most visited regions of Ireland. Killarney and Kenmare make good bases for driving the famous Ring of Kerry, round one of several wild, rocky peninsulas that stretch into the sea. To the north, the Dingle Peninsula lies west from Tralee with rugged mountains, stunning seascapes, and fascinating ancient forts and beehive huts. Cork is Ireland's second-largest city, known for its art and music scene. Nearby is the famous Blarney Castle and the picturesque coastal town of Kinsale.

THE WEST

Bordered by the Atlantic Ocean, the South and the Midlands, the western counties have some of the most fascinating scenery in Ireland. North of the River Shannon, County Clare is home to the stark limestone plateau called The Burren and the towering Cliffs of Moher. Ennis is its largest town. County Galway's capital is lively Galway City, set on Galway Bay. Offshore are the largely Irish-speaking Aran Islands. Between here

Below *St. Fiachra's Garden evolving naturally in County Kildare, one of the eastern counties of Ireland*

and Clifden stretches Connemara, with its rugged sea coasts, mountains and heathlands. Westport is the main town in County Mayo, home to Croagh Patrick and the miraculous shrine of Knock. It is a large county of vast boglands, lonely headlands and dramatic sea cliffs. From Sligo Town visit County Sligo's picturesque coastline, mountains, lakes and forests that inspired the poet W. B. Yeats. There are also many prehistoric sites. Carrick-on-Shannon is the capital of nearby County Leitrim. County Donegal in the northwestern corner borders Northern Ireland. Donegal Town and Letterkenny are the biggest towns in this large but sparsely populated region. Its stunning Atlantic coastline is studded with rocky inlets, towering cliffs and deserted beaches.

THE MIDLANDS

The defining features of the landlocked Midlands are the many loughs (lakes) that dot the landscape and the vast stretches of bogland in counties Offaly and Laois. Clonmacnoise is one of Ireland's finest ecclesiastical sites. The Georgian town of Birr has delightful castle gardens. County Westmeath boasts the region's largest town, Athlone, and the country's largest castle, Tullynally. It adjoins counties Longford and Roscommon; in the latter is Strokestown Park and the Famine Museum.

NORTHERN IRELAND

Belfast is the province's capital, with attractive city buildings. The coast of County Antrim has some of Ireland's most spectacular scenery, including the famous Giant's Causeway with its dramatic cliffs and volcanic rocks, as well as quaint fishing villages and Carrickfergus Castle. The Mountains of Mourne rise along the coast in the southeast corner of County Down, which has several sites linked to St. Patrick around Downpatrick. The historic city of Armagh is in nearby County Armagh, as is the huge Lough Neagh. To the west is County Tyrone with the Ulster American Folk Park. Enniskillen is the main city of County Fermanagh, a lakeland county with many attractions set around Lough Erne. The walled city of Derry is in County Londonderry, which has a fine stretch of coast.

THE BEST OF IRELAND

DUBLIN

Book of Kells (▷ 91–92) This magnificent ninth-century illuminated manuscript in the Old Library at Trinity College represents the height of Celtic artistic achievement.

Christ Church Cathedral and St. Patrick's Cathedral (▷ 78 and 89) Dublin's two grand cathedrals are filled with monuments to historic figures, from Strongbow to Jonathan Swift.

Dublin Castle (▷ 74–75) In the historic heart of the city, the castle has Viking and Norman foundations and lavish State Apartments.

Guinness Storehouse (▷ 77) Drink a pint of Ireland's most famous brew while enjoying the view from the rooftop bar.

Howth Head (▷ 78) Take the cliff walk out beyond Howth Harbour for sweeping sea views over the bay.

Kilmainham Gaol (▷ 80–81) Learn the poignant history of the Irish fight for independence on a tour of the jail where Irish rebels were held and executed.

The National Museum (▷ 84–85) Marvel at the stunning gold jewellery and other treasures that make up the largest collection of Celtic objects in the world.

St. Stephen's Green (▷ 93) Do as the locals do—relax on a park bench and watch the passers-by.

THE EAST

Boyne Valley (▷ 120, 124 and 134) Drive through beautiful scenery to visit fine monastic sites and the seat of the High Kings at Tara.

Brú na Bóinne (▷ 117–119) Tour the mysterious passage tombs at Newgrange and Knowth, over 5,000 years old and among the world's most important prehistoric sites.

Glendalough (▷ 122–123) Set in a valley beside two lakes, this is one of Ireland's foremost and loveliest early Christian sites.

Kilkenny (▷ 128–130) After touring the magnificent cathedral, castle and Black Abbey, explore the medieval alleyways and lively streets of this delightful historic town.

National Stud and Japanese Gardens (▷ 126–127) Learn the secret of breeding Ireland's finest racehorses at the National Stud in Kildare, and enjoy the charming Japanese Gardens.

Powerscourt Gardens (▷ 132–133) Enjoy the superb view from the terrace, then wander through the beautiful gardens.

Wexford (▷ 124) See how early settlers lived at the Irish National Heritage Park.

Wicklow Mountains (▷ 136–137) Take a walk along the Wicklow Way in the Wicklow Mountains National Park.

THE SOUTH

Blarney Castle (▷ 161) Kiss the Blarney Stone at one of Ireland's most famous castles.

Cork City (▷ 164–165) Explore the picturesque lanes of the old French Quarter, in Ireland's second city.

Dingle Peninsula (Corca Dhuibhne) (▷ 166–169) Duck inside the curious beehive huts, among the many antique sites on this scenic peninsula.

Kinsale (▷ 171) Enjoy a seafood meal in one of the highly acclaimed restaurants in this pretty harbour town.

Ring of Kerry (▷ 191–196) Drive the most famous scenic route in western Ireland, but start early to avoid the many tour buses.

Rock of Cashel (▷ 176) Walk up to the top of this monumental fortress church, an impressive sight from above and below.

Sheen Falls Lodge (▷ 200) Relax at this former fishing lodge, now a beautiful luxury hotel on the banks of the Sheen River.

Take a sea cruise to the Skelligs (▷ 177) and spot dolphins and other wildlife along the way.

Waterford (▷ 178–179) Shop for a special piece of glassware at Waterford Crystal.

THE WEST

The Burren (▷ 210–211) Walk out across the limestone and look for the tiny wild flowers that brighten this barren landscape.

Carrowmore Neolithic Cemetery (▷ 207) See the passage graves, standing stones and other remains of one of Europe's oldest and largest prehistoric graveyards.

Cliffs of Moher (▷ 209) Enjoy the awesome view from the top of these coastal cliffs, but expect to share this prime beauty spot with the crowds.

Connemara (▷ 212–215) Mountains, lakes, boglands and a jagged coastline of rocky bays and islets make this one of the most scenic areas of the country.

County Mayo (▷ 230–231) Drive from stunning seascapes to remote mountains to lonely stretches of blanket bog that are amazing in their vastness.

Galway City (▷ 218) Bright shop-fronts and medieval buildings line the cobbled streets in this lively university town.

Glencolumbkille (Gleann Cholm Cille) (▷ 219) It's well worth the drive to this remote Gaeltacht village to see its excellent folk museum surrounded by beautiful scenery.

Glenveagh National Park (▷ 219) Stroll through the stunning gardens amid beautiful mountains and woodland.

Gregans Castle (▷ 242) Escape from it all at this hotel in the heart of The Burren and enjoy the views towards Galway Bay.

Sligo (▷ 222–224) Base yourself in this lively town, for music, the arts, and the landscape that influenced poet W. B. Yeats.

THE MIDLANDS

Birr (▷ 250) Admire the splendid gardens of Birr Castle, with plants from around the world, and see the Great Telescope.

Blackwater Bog (▷ 249) Take a narrow-gauge train for a close-up look at the boglands and learn how they were formed.

Above Two essentials at the Galway Oyster Festival
Opposite The majestic cliffs of Fair Head in County Antrim

Clonmacnoise (▷ 252–255) Admire the elaborate stone-carved high crosses, round towers and ruined churches at this important early Christian monastery.

Strokestown Park and Famine Museum (▷ 258–259) Visit the Famine Museum, where the tragedy of the famine years is movingly portrayed.

Water sports (▷ 257 and 265) Try a spot of fishing on Lough Ree or a canoe trip on the River Shannon.

NORTHERN IRELAND

Armagh (▷ 278) Two historic cathedrals grace the skyline of one of Ireland's oldest cities, founded in the time of St. Patrick.

Belfast (▷ 280–287) Attend a performance to see the lavish interior of the city's Grand Opera House.

Derry (▷ 189) Walk around the ramparts of the 17th-century town walls and admire the historic buildings.

Giant's Causeway (▷ 292–295) Walk along the volcanic stepping stones of Northern Ireland's most popular sight.

Glens of Antrim (▷ 291) Hike the scenic trails in the glacier-carved glens that wind up from the scenic Antrim Coast Road.

Lough Erne (▷ 298–299) Take a boat trip to White Island to see the strange carved figures on the old church.

Shu (▷ 319) Visit this chic Belfast restaurant and enjoy the relaxed atmosphere as you sample the eclectic menu.

Ulster American Folk Park (▷ 303) Relive the experience of Ulster immigrants to the New World during the famine years.

TOP EXPERIENCES

Attend a ceilidh where you can watch reels, jigs and other dances. Set dancing is big in the west and you can even join in!

Brush up on Ireland's literary history at The James Joyce Centre in Dublin (▷ 75), and visit the Dublin Writers Museum (▷ 73).

Drink Guinness with the locals in a pub, or tour the Guinness Storehouse and have a pint in the Gravity Bar (▷ 77).

Drive along the Antrim Coast, a spectacular scenic route that begins north of Belfast and runs all the way to the Giant's Causeway (▷ 292–294).

Eat some Galway Bay oysters, wild salmon or mussel soup—Ireland offers excellent fresh seafood.

Experience Ireland's famous passion for horses Attend a race meeting and maybe even place a small bet (▷ 335).

Get sporty Play a round of golf at one of Ireland's many courses (▷ 335), or visit Croke Park to watch a Gaelic football or hurling match (▷ 72).

Hop on a ferry to Achill Island (▷ 205) or to the Aran Islands (Oileáin Árann; ▷ 206) for the sense of tradition and timelessness.

Listen to live, traditional music; some of the best can be found in villages on the south and west coasts.

Marvel at the views Look out from the high ramparts of a castle tower and admire the view, such as that over the River Boyne from the castle at Trim (▷ 135).

Pack a picnic and head for a remote spot on the Beara (▷ 162), Mizen or Sheep's Head peninsulas (▷ 175). They're less busy but just as scenic as the Ring of Kerry.

Party on St. Patrick's Day or at one of the many other festivals around the country.

Seek out Ireland's prehistoric sites The remote, less-visited sites are often the most rewarding and retain a sense of ancient spirituality (▷ 70–93, 116–135, 156–179, 204–225, 248–259, 274–303).

Shop for traditional Irish goods such as Aran sweaters or Donegal tweed.

Take a hike From woodland strolls to cliff-top rambles along the coast, there are walks to suit everyone (▷ 94–97, 136–139, 180–181, 226–227, 260–261, 304–305, 308–309).

Trace your ancestors Every region has local offices that can help (▷ 356).

Watch a sunset from the Cliffs of Moher (▷ 209) or any number of scenic spots on Ireland's west coast.

Below *Walkers on Croagh Patrick mountain in the west of Ireland*

LIVING IRELAND

HIP HIBERNIA

As Ireland grows more confident and more prosperous, a distinctive sense of style has emerged. Dublin takes its cool image seriously, as a young, fashion-conscious and cash-rich generation demands chic bars, clubs, shops and hotels. In 21st-century Irish style, Celtic meets European with lots of Eastern and trans-Atlantic influences, and local designers are given every opportunity to impress. In Dublin, don't go north of the River Liffey if you want to follow the current style icons, mostly figures from the world of music, like Bono, The Thrills, Ronan Keating and Westlife. These are the new leaders of fashion, and the good causes, artists and restaurants they patronize are sure to be well supported. Organizers of big events in the young, sharp-edged capital will want A-list celebrities like actor Colin Farrell and Rugby Union star Brian O'Driscoll to be present, while ex-Formula One driver Eddie Irvine always attracts attention. Although Dublin likes to think it is the leader of fashion, Belfast and Cork also have boutique hotels, hip clubs, sleek restaurants and designer shops, which highlight local talent and demonstrate modern style. Customers may find them less pretentious and not as expensive as those in Dublin.

CASTLE ROCK

The dashing head of the Conyngham family, Lord Henry Mount Charles, plays host to the greatest stars of world music every summer at his picturesque estate at Slane Castle, the family home for more than three centuries. And he shares the occasion with 80,000 fans. Since 1981, the elegant Irish peer has brought mega-names to his estate on the banks of the River Boyne. U2, David Bowie, Bob Dylan, The Rolling Stones, Robbie Williams, Queen and Eminem have all played at Slane. In 2004 Madonna headed the bill, causing controversy by playing on a Sunday, a decision not welcomed by all residents in this quiet and religious, rural village. Celebrity guests have coveted invitations to watch the concerts from the castle battlements.

Clockwise from left to right *Belfast has a thriving nightlife scene; bright costumes feature in the St. Patrick's Day parades; models dressed in Paul Costelloe; a Robbie Williams concert at Slane Castle*

CELEBRITY AISLE

The Irish have been delighted and bemused at the number of celebrities who have chosen to marry in Ireland. Famously, Sir Paul McCartney married Heather Mills at romantic Castle Leslie in Glaslough, County Monaghan, in June 2002. Sir Paul explained that Monaghan was the chosen venue because his mother came from the county. The sleepy village was more than a little surprised by the glamorous extravaganza, and by the famous faces who attended. Host for the day was 84-year-old, Sir John Leslie, whose family have owned the property since the 17th century. The couple were married in the private St. Salvator chapel in the grounds and the lavish reception followed in giant lakeside marquees, with a pontoon and a luxury boat moored alongside.

RANKIN'S REVIVAL

When Paul Rankin and his Canadian wife Jeanne came to Belfast in the 1980s, they bravely opened their chic new restaurant Roscoff (which evolved into Cayenne and five years on Roscoff has been reborn in a new home) in a city not previously noted for gastronomy. Rankin acquired a reputation for stylish and adventurous cuisine, using the best local produce. The stylish restaurateur, now a television celebrity, has trained a generation of new chefs, including Robbie Millar of Shanks restaurant, who tragically died in a car crash in 2005, and his influence has made the Belfast area a gastronomic hub. His empire extends to airport cafés, Roscoff brasseries, a range of speciality Irish breads including wheaten bracks, potato bread and soda farls.

POP AND POLITICS

Many people in Ireland were intrigued in 2003 when the daughter of the Taoiseach (or prime minister), Bertie Ahern, married one of the stars of the Irish 'boy' band Westlife. Childhood sweethearts, Georgina Ahern and Nicky Byrne dressed down, wearing jeans and baseball caps, at a low-key civil ceremony that took place in Wicklow, to the south of Dublin, but four days later exchanged their vows in church followed by a lavish celebration. It was a glitzy affair, with friends of the couple from the worlds of showbiz and professional football, and entertainment provided by the likes of Ronan Keating. Despite the father of the bride's constitutional position, there was not a politician in sight. To the disappointment of many in Ireland, however, the wedding took place, not in a romantic Irish setting, but in a French château.

REAL WOMEN, REAL SUCCESS

Ireland's most famous fashion designer, Paul Costelloe, claims to get more pleasure from seeing his designs worn on the street than paraded on the catwalk. His clothes are made for 'real women', rather than wafer-thin supermodels, and his trademark, timeless elegance has made his clothes sought after in the most stylish stores around the world. The 'Costelloe' brand made a significant breakthrough when the late Diana, Princess of Wales, started to wear his creations. Subsequently, Ireland's first woman president, the stylish Mary Robinson, made a point of choosing the Costelloe label. Preferring fabrics which must be 'good and fluid', he has repeatedly turned to the special qualities of Irish linen for inspiration, and has based his factory shop at the Linen Green in Dungannon, Co. Tyrone.

SPORT: ANSWERING THE CALL

Players in the Irish rugby team come from both north and south of the border, and compete as a united country under the flag of the Irish rugby football union. A stirring anthem has been adopted which transcends political divides, and before the big international matches in Dublin members of the team lock arms and sing 'Come the day and come the hour, come the power and the glory, we have come to answer our country's call, from the four proud provinces of Ireland . . .' Many other sporting bodies, including boxing, hockey and swimming, also draw their international teams from both sides of the political border, but others, such as soccer, field individual teams from Northern Ireland and the Republic. The Gaelic sports of hurling and football for men and camogie for women, now thriving abroad, have keenly fought competitions within the country. Prepare to be amazed at the combative style of these intensely exciting, fast and physical Gaelic games—some played without the protection of padding or helmets. Tickets for the major international games and finals are hard to come by, but are easily available at interprovincial and county level.

SAM'S YOUR MAN
Don't be surprised if you hear many references to 'Sam' in Irish pubs through August and September. 'Sam' will be spoken of with reverence, affection and a good deal of nervous anxiety. The 'Sam' in question is the Sam Maguire Cup, the trophy for the All-Ireland final of the Gaelic football competition played among the 32 Irish counties (that is, those in both the Republic and Northern Ireland). The passion of the support is intense, and visitors can tell when they cross from one county to another by the change in the flags proudly flown throughout. The victorious county team will parade 'Sam' from village to village, and the trophy has become a bit battered from years of celebration, as serious partying follows every All Ireland success.

Clockwise from left to right *Ireland vs. Barbarians rugby match; Padraig Harrington on the 18th green at Westchester, New York; a young player kitted out for a hurling game; competitors in the biennial Round Ireland Race*

RACING THE TIDE

It was, they say, the idea of a local priest, in 1876, to start one of Ireland's most extraordinary horse-racing meetings, held each August or September at Laytown, about 46km (29 miles) north of Dublin. It is the only horse race in the world, organized under Jockey Club rules, that is held on a beach. The length of the course is an inexact science, laid out in haste as the tide goes out, but it's around one or two miles of an expansive strand. The finish line has a wonderful backdrop of foaming surf, so the going can never be said to be 'firm'. The grandstand is in the dunes, and the jockeys have to race not only the other horses, but often the tide as well!

STADIUM SAGA

A frustrating quest to build a national stadium for major events has so far failed because of financial problems, lack of agreement on sites and logistics, and the Gaelic Athletic Association's reluctance to share facilities with rugby and soccer, which they regard as 'foreign' games. Gaelic football games are currently staged in a first-rate stadium at Croke Park, Dublin, while rugby and soccer internationals always took place in an increasingly decrepit, but much-loved, stadium at Lansdowne Road. However, Six Nations Rugby internationals and football internationals will take place at Croke Park until 2010 while Lansdowne Road is given a massive makeover.

BULLETS

Despite its alarming name, the game of bullets is frightening only if you happen upon it unprepared. This traditional sport is really a form of road bowls. Played in counties Cork and Armagh (but not exclusively), contestants throw iron balls at great speed along country roads, which are often winding and hilly, for a distance of about 4km (2.5 miles). Half the fun lies in the antics of the partisan camp followers who support the contestants. The cry of 'wey-hay' (bullets' equivalent of golf's 'fore!') isn't much use to the unwary driver who happens to be coming in the other direction. The bullets season is in May and June, and local pubs are the best source for information.

LOCAL BOY WINS THE OPEN

Padraig Harrington was born in August 1971 in Ballyroan, south Dublin, and by the age of four was already swinging a golf club. In the early 1990s he played as an amateur for Ireland and in 1994 he won his first senior event, the West of Ireland Championships. In 1995 he clinched the Irish Open at Fota Island and the Irish Closed at Lahinch. He joined the European Tour as a professional in 1996 and over the next ten years won numerous prestigious titles, including the Spanish Open in 1996. In May 2007 he won the Irish Open and in July 2007 he netted the ultimate prize, the Open at Carnoustie, the first Irishman to win the event.

THE CRAIC

To Irish men and women, there is nothing like a bit of *craic*. It's hard to define: Good-natured and relaxed, it involves laughter, conversation and sometimes a drink or two. Stout with a whiskey 'chaser' traditionally fuels many a good night. In Ireland any excuse will do for a celebration; birthdays and weddings are examples, and at many Irish weddings guests are invited to entertain the gathering. *Craic* is very inclusive. 'Wetting the head' of a new baby is another good reason for a night out—usually a party of lads supporting the new father. The Irish tradition of a 'wake' is a strong one: Family and friends meet to celebrate a life that is over. The Irish are great at acclaiming a fine sporting victory in style, but they are just as good at 'drowning their sorrows' in defeat.

THE BANTER

A crucial element of Irish fun is 'the banter', and it's a form of humour that visitors can sometimes misinterpret. Essentially it's a type of teasing. In Ireland it's natural to engage casual acquaintances in conversation but beware of the seemingly innocent question, asked with an angelic smile, addressed to the unwary. The Irish, north and south, have developed a comprehensive vocabulary to identify potential jokers, including 'Are you having me on?,' 'taking the mick', 'jossing', 'messing' or 'gegging'. When Irish people 'banter', it can sometimes sound like outright abuse, but this humour is linked to a delight in the ludicrous. Just don't take it too seriously.

Clockwise from left to right *Traditional dance at Galway's Oyster Festival; an advert for Guinness; the pub is a popular part of Irish social life*

Lovely day for a GUINNESS

CAFÉ SOCIETY OR ALFRESCO FUN

Ireland has followed the lead of New York by imposing a total ban on smoking in public places, including bars and restaurants. One result of this is that traditional pub culture has spilled out into the streets, with many bar owners providing outside tables, Parisian-style, for those who feel they need a smoke. Although not quite the Champs-Élysées, the elegant Georgian streets of the capital lend themselves to boulevard merriment, and portable gas heaters are often provided to take the chill off the air. One enterprising publican attempted to dodge the ban by setting up a double-decker bus outside his premises, but officials insisted it was still contravening the law and had to be removed.

WHISKEY WITH AN 'E'

An essential element of Ireland's pub culture and the *craic*, Irish whiskey is different from Scotch, not only because it's spelled with an 'e'. Irish distillers claim that their whiskey is lighter and smoother than its Scottish counterpart. The Irish also claim to have the oldest licensed distillery in the world at Bushmills (note the word 'licensed': The tradition of distilling poteen, illegally, goes much farther back). Irish whiskey fans will also point out that its distilling process usually takes longer—why rush something so important? And finally, where would we be without Irish coffee? Visitors can decide for themselves in the rivalry between Scotch and Irish whiskey by taking one of the distillery tours and sampling the product.

SIN BIN

Irish Rugby legend Peter Clohessy earned an international reputation as an abrasive and pugnacious prop forward, affectionately known to colleagues and opponents alike as The Claw. He served his province, Munster, and Ireland gallantly for many years, but his unofficial activities in the thick of the game often led to a warning yellow card from the referee and banishment to the 'sin bin' at the side of the pitch. It was no surprise, then, that when he retired from rugby and opened a bar and nightclub in his native Limerick, that he called it The Sin Bin. As the affable proprietor he now hosts many visiting athletes and teams.

MEET YOUR MATCH?

A good way to be sure of finding some fun is to follow the trail to the Matchmaking Festival in the normally sleepy town of Lisdoonvarna, where, traditionally, single farming men and girls came to find a partner. Europe's largest matchmaking festival retains much of its original character and Ireland's last remaining matchmaker, Willie Daly, still presides over the proceedings, which take place in late summer (after the harvest), but much of the fun is tongue-in-cheek. Afternoon dances are one way to meet the right partner, although today's singles may prefer the organized speed-dating or music bars which go on late into the night.

Ireland's phenomenal economic success, which in the 1990s earned it the tag the 'Celtic tiger', continues, though at a less meteoric rate. Within the last decade the economy has grown by 80 per cent, bringing prosperity and national confidence. A major factor has been Ireland's policy of maximizing the advantages of EU membership. Unemployment, for so long a scourge throughout Ireland, has practically disappeared. The infrastructure of transport and telecommunications has improved and Ireland's education system is judged to be serving the demands of the new industrial and technological employers. A wealthy top tier of society has emerged and demands for a luxury lifestyle have pushed up prices. The price of housing has rocketed, which analysts see as a potential threat to future growth. There is still much hardship, however, and poverty and urban deprivation pose significant social problems. The republic's welfare and health benefits are improving, but sometimes still lag behind those in Northern Ireland.

THE SPIRE OF DUBLIN
The Spire of Dublin, in the city's principal thoroughfare, O'Connell Street, was erected in 2003 to replace Nelson's Column, blown up by extremists in 1966. As a monument to the millennium, it is regarded as a bold symbol of national confidence. A slim needle of light-reflective stainless steel, 120m (394ft) tall, 3m (10ft) wide at the base and tapering to 15cm (6in), it is designed to look stunning throughout the day. It is central to the rejuvenation of O'Connell Street. Dubliners have not lost the opportunity to poke fun at the monument and its environment. Mostly known colloquially as the 'spike', other nicknames include the 'skewer in the sewer', 'The North Pole', the 'Nail in the Pale' and the 'Stiffy on the Liffey'.

Clockwise from left to right *Waterfront Hall and the Hilton Hotel on Belfast's waterfront; the two huge cranes, 'Samson' and 'Goliath', in Belfast; the Dublin Spire occupies the site of the old Nelson pillar, blown up in 1966; Dublin's state-of-the-art Luas tram system*

TUNNEL VISION

Dublin's notorious rush-hour traffic congestion has been eased by the ambitious Luas tram system—continually being extended—which links the southern suburbs with the heart of the city. It supplies efficient public transportation for commuters. Another solution lies in people bicycling to work, and, with 200km (125 miles) of bicycle lanes, thousands of lock-up positions and a relatively flat city, it's estimated that 25,000 Dubliners now choose pedal power. A plan to 'hoover' heavy goods vehicles off the streets by siphoning them into the new and expensive Port Tunnel, opened in 2006, has run into a problem: Nicknamed the 'Leprechaun' tunnel, it is 25cm (10in) too low for the new generation of monster trucks, which have to be diverted.

TOWER BLOCK TURN AROUND

Ireland's new wealth has put into sharp contrast the country's acute social difficulties. The problems at Ballymun, a 1960s north Dublin housing estate, had reached crisis proportions by 1985. By then the available housing, including seven high-rise blocks, had become run-down and was used for housing homeless people in an area with few employment opportunities. The area's regeneration began with a community-led initiative, and now Ballymun Regeneration Ltd is building a new town due to be completed in 2013. It has demolished six tower blocks, and is building homes based on quality design, matched by sustainable local employment, links with the nearby Dublin City University, and community involvement.

RYDER RICHES

Nowhere is the new wealth of Ireland more evident than at the opulent K-Club in County Kildare. Owned by the Smurfit Group, founded by entrepreneur Michael Smurfit, it represents the last word in luxury, and hosted the 2006 Ryder Cup. This prestigious golf tournament between Europe and the United States came to Ireland for the first time, played on a course designed by international golf legend Arnold Palmer. Art meets affluence here in the Jack B. Yeats room, where a collection of paintings by Ireland's greatest 20th-century artist is displayed. The golf courses are dotted with luxury villas owned by celebrities, who no doubt must have appreciated not having to travel far to enjoy the 2006 golfing extravaganza.

TITANIC QUARTER

The skyline of Belfast is dominated by two huge bright yellow cranes, dubbed 'Samson' and 'Goliath' by the citizens of the northern capital. It is unlikely, however, that these monsters of the shipbuilding industry will be in use again, as the order book of Belfast's proud shipbuilding yards has emptied in the past decade. Small-scale refurbishments and work for the oil industry have replaced the proud tradition of ocean-going liners in the dry-docks of Harland and Wolff. The 'Titanic Quarter', however, named after the most famous ship to slide down the slipway, is an ongoing scheme to turn the decaying dockland into a vibrant new commercial and residential development, and will extend the urban renewal schemes along the River Lagan.

THE POWER OF THE PEN

It seems that the Irish have always had a gift for words. The Celtic saints, whose persuasive speech converted non-believers throughout medieval Europe, the bardic poets and the giants of modern literature all form part of a proud tradition in Ireland. Poets and writers are (nearly always) honoured in this country, although in the past, writers such as James Joyce and Samuel Beckett had to go into exile to create their best work. Most Irish writers now live here, encouraged by the tax benefits offered to those who create original works of cultural or artistic merit, and film-makers and screenwriters also favour the Republic. The Abbey Theatre, founded by W. B. Yeats, still holds a pre-eminent place, and there are good local theatres everywhere. The Dublin Theatre Festival is a lively event, and the works of Marie Jones, a Belfast playwright with a sharp, analytical sense of humour, regularly transfer to London's West End. Buildings associated with some of Ireland's great writers, however, have not been well preserved, and controversy has surrounded attempts to demolish the homes of W. B. Yeats, Seamus Heaney and C. S. Lewis.

JEDI OR NOT?
Ireland has a legacy of wonderful libraries, of which the finest is The Long Room at Trinity College, Dublin. Not only does it house the world-famous monastic manuscript, the Book of Kells, it also has the right to receive a copy of all material published in Britain and Ireland. Jonathan Swift, Oliver Goldsmith, Edmund Burke, William Congreve, J. M. Synge, Oscar Wilde and Samuel Beckett all studied here—but did the Jedi? Well, Thomas Burgh's 1732 architectural masterpiece bears an uncanny similarity to the Jedi Archive in *Star Wars: Attack of the Clones* (2002). Lucas Films have denied any replication, but the suggestion of the cloning of the Library has led College authorities to stock *Star Wars* items in the college shop.

Clockwise from left to right *Trinity College Library; writers Roddy Doyle and Seamus Heaney; Martin McDonagh poses with his Oscar for Best Live Action Short Film*

HOPE AND HISTORY

Seamus Heaney, who won the Nobel Prize for Literature in 1995, is hugely respected throughout his native Ireland. A dignified and self-effacing man, he has given generously of his intellect and time to the community. He comes from a farming family in south Derry and his early poetry reflects the rural society of Ulster, while his subsequent work is marked by rigorous analysis and restrained and sensitive beauty. Before moving to Wicklow, he taught at Queen's University, Belfast, where a major literary centre bearing his name has been opened. An excerpt from his translation of *The Cure at Troy* is often used as an evocation of a national aspiration for peace. He articulates the yearning that once in a lifetime 'hope and history rhyme'.

HELL'S KITCHEN— DUBLIN

Hell's Kitchen is familiar as an area of New York, but a leafy suburb of south Dublin also has a 'Hell's Kitchen' tag. Screenwriter and director of Academy award-winning films, Jim Sheridan named his Irish-based film company after the area in New York where he lived. It was the setting for his 2004 Oscar-nominated screenplay *In America* (2003), about the experiences of an immigrant family, which was to a large extent autobiographical and co-written with his daughters. Never afraid to be controversial, but with a keen sense of humanity, Jim Sheridan has made a number of films that have an Irish theme including *My Left Foot* (1989), *In the Name of the Father* (1993), *Some Mother's Son* (1996) and *The Field* (1990).

OSCAR WINNER

An exciting day for Ireland occurred on 5 March 2006, when the London-Irish playwright and film-maker Martin McDonagh won his first Oscar for the short film *Six Shooter*, which he also directed. The 27-minute black and bloody comedy was backed jointly by the Irish Film Board and the UK's FilmFour Lab and tells the tale of a sad older man journeying on a train after his wife has died. He meets a strange and somewhat psychotic oddball of a young man and bizarre developments ensue. The film has been described by critics as bloody, tasteless and very funny. McDonagh is no stranger to success, however, being among a growing new crowd of brash young playwrights storming both the Irish and international scene.

DOYLE'S DUBLIN

The vitality and pathos of life in a north Dublin suburb is captured with extraordinary accuracy by the perceptive writer, Roddy Doyle. The former teacher delights in letting his vividly real characters inhabit an unglamorous landscape of run-down estates, schools and shopping complexes. His books are funny and popular, and are also critically acclaimed. *Paddy Clarke Ha Ha Ha* was awarded the prestigious Booker Prize in 1993, while the film *The Commitments* (1991), based on Doyle's gritty and hilarious novel, wowed film audiences with its story of a working-class soul band taking on the Dublin music scene. Doyle's historical novel, *A Star called Henry*, features the Dublin city slum landscape of the War of Independence.

RURAL IDENTITY

The rural Ireland of picturesque thatched cottages and donkey carts, if it ever existed outside the film *The Quiet Man* (1952), has more or less disappeared. Today's Irish farmer is a combination of business executive, environmentalist and agricultural expert, as the demands of European and domestic legislation, landscape management and market forces make the job of farming more demanding. However, almost all farms in Ireland are still family concerns, and are relatively small in scale. Farming families have become skilled in diversifying, offering specialist food production, farmhouse bed-and-breakfast stays and leisure activities. Because of the history of land legislation and absentee landlords, the typical Irish farmer jealously protects his holding; the ties with the land are strong. Only a small proportion (around 9 per cent) of the land is farmed for crops; the vast majority of Ireland's countryside is devoted to grass for pasture. It's the predominance of pasture that explains Ireland's description as 'The Emerald Isle', an effect helped by the legendary amount of rain which waters its fields. Those green fields feed thriving herds of dairy and beef cows that produce top-quality meat, butter and cheese.

AGRI-GOURMETS

As the agricultural industry meets the challenges of a shifting economy, farmers have diversified to maintain their incomes. One of the most successful ventures has been the production of specialist cheeses, made on family farms, from the yield of superb dairy herds, and also from sheep's and goats' milk. Most of these delicious cheeses are handmade and wrapped on the farms, using skills that have been passed down through the generations. Look especially for the creamy Cashel Blue and the Camembert-style Cooleeney, which comes from Tipperary, and oak-smoked Gubbeen and Carrigaline Farmhouse from Cork. The taste of the award-winning Durrus reflects the salty conditions of the southwest tip of Ireland, where it is made.

TURF ACCOUNTS

As with many aspects of Irish life, rain made the difference. High rainfall and bad drainage are the primary causes of the formation of the distinctive native landscape: the peat bog. Now environmentalists are worried about the protection of this habitat. Country people have cut turf for burning for centuries, and neat piles of cut turf can be seen beside many farmhouses. The traditional cutting method used a specially designed turf spade but with mechanization, the disappearance of bogs increased dramatically. The demand for peat for horticultural use created an additional threat. Steps have been taken to stop the destruction, and visitors can learn the whole story at the peatland Nature Reserves.

THE URBAN HORSE

The Irish passion for horses goes back to pre-Christian times. Even in today's densely populated cities, horse-lovers hold on to this relationship with an amazing tenacity. It's not unusual to see horses in Irish cities. Right in the heart of Belfast, there's a small triangle of grass on which a horse is regularly tethered, and city traffic may have to slow down to the pace of a pony and trap. On the housing estates of Dublin, Limerick and Cork, young men will ride horses bareback with all the bravado and style of their motorcyclist counterparts. Horses are kept in cities for pulling tourist carriages or for competing in trotting races, but more often, just for the sheer love of the animal.

COUNTRY MEETS TOWN

The essence of rural Ireland can be experienced at the dozens of agricultural shows around the country in summer. But the best displays can be seen at the two major shows, the Balmoral in Belfast in May and the Royal Dublin Society (RDS) Show in August. The RDS is a venerable institution, established in 1731 to promote the development of agriculture, arts, science and industry. It still plays a significant role in Ireland's farming life. Both events showcase the latest farming technology alongside traditional crafts. The prize agricultural specimens are paraded, and Ladies' Day is a considerably stylish affair. The highlight of the Dublin Show is the day on which international show-jumping teams vie for the Aga Khan Trophy.

SALMON LEAP?

As well as the sport of angling for salmon, there are commercial sea fisheries, and locally smoked salmon can be bought in coastal villages. In County Antrim there is a remarkable fishery at Carrick-a-Rede, a tiny, craggy island called 'the Rock in the Road', where the salmon that swim between the rock and the mainland are caught in the nets. Each year the fishermen erect a rope bridge 18m (59ft) wide and 24m (78ft) above the sea, to enable them to cross to the island. The bridge used to be a precarious affair, constructed using rickety wooden slats to walk on and with only one guide rope, but it is now in the hands of the National Trust, and is much safer. People who want to cross it will still need to have a head for heights, however.

Opposite *Traditional rural houses often have spectacular views*
Above *Many Irish farms have been in the same family for generations*
Left top *A man with his cart and horse in Dublin*
Left bottom *Fáilte Ireland horse show*

GAELIC COUNTRY, EUROPEAN NATION

Geographically, Ireland may be on the edge of Europe, but it became integrated into the European ideal. Quick to adopt the euro as currency, the Republic readily embraced European institutions. Ireland is modern and cosmopolitan. It is also traditional and still essentially Gaelic, although the Anglo-Irish influence is evident everywhere, and Dublin's gracious architecture dates largely from the Georgian era. Great efforts have been made to nurture the Irish language, but although its use officially is comprehensive, only in the Gaeltacht in the far west and south is it used in everyday speech. Gaelic sport, dance and music are alive and well, though, and city streets and pubs everywhere echo to the sounds of traditional instruments. Ulster-Scots and Gaelic traditions are complementary in Northern Ireland. Here, European identity is less evident. The British pound is the official currency, but the euro is often accepted.

MILES OR METRES?

Visitors to the Republic of Ireland have often baffled by inconsistent distance measurements on signposts. One sign showing miles would be followed shortly down the road by one in kilometres, but now nearly all signage is made to conform to metric units. North of the border distances are measured in miles, and observers are concerned that the discrepancy in speed limit signs will cause confusion. Petrol pumps have been standardized to dispense in litres, not gallons, and although shops are required to label in multiples of grams, many customers still ask for goods in pounds and ounces. And a pint is still a pint, not 0.57 litres. In both Northern Ireland and the Republic motorists drive on the left, and there are no plans to change that—at least not for the foreseeable future.

CULTURAL CORK

The Republic of Ireland's second city, Cork, was selected as the European Capital of Culture in 2005, the smallest city (to date) ever to have been awarded this title. More than 100,000 people took to the streets of the city to celebrate the opening of the event on 8 January 2005. A high point of the city's events was the installation of a pavilion designed by Daniel Libeskind, the architect of the master plan for the rebuilding at Ground Zero in New York, and of the stunning Jewish Museum in Berlin. In another project, labelled 'Iris', the Daghdha Dance Company distributed 10,000 message-laden rings throughout the city. Each ring came with its own set of particular instructions, and when released 'Iris' took on a remarkable life of its own.

Above *Children celebrate Cork's installation as European Capital of Culture 2005*

THE STORY OF IRELAND

MYSTERY, MYTH AND RELIGION

About 10,000 years ago hunter-gatherers crossed a land-bridge linking Britain to Ireland. As the sea separated the two islands, Stone Age people settled along the Irish coasts and rivers. From the fourth century BC neolithic communities began clearing forests and planting crops. Among the few clues to their lives are traces of walled fields, unearthed from bogland at Céide Fields (▷ 209), and the decorated passage graves at Knowth and Newgrange (▷ 117–118). Trade links spread new technologies—first the bronze industry and then, from around 700BC, the Celts of southern and central Europe brought ironworking skills to Ireland. Last of the Celtic tribes to arrive were the Goidels, or Gaels, who enjoyed a culture of music, art and mythology, and whose settlements were grouped into small kingdoms, or *tuátha*. Ireland remained outside the control—though not free from the influence—of the Roman Empire. But the Celtic world was changing: By the late fourth century AD Christianity was replacing Druidic religion. In AD432 St. Patrick established the Christian Church in Ireland.

Above left *Finn McCool, hero of Irish legends*
Above right Children of Lir *statue in Dublin's Garden of Remembrance*

SACRED WATERS

According to Celtic legend, the River Boyne was once no bigger than a well—a holy well, surrounded by hazel trees which shed hazelnuts of knowledge and inspiration into the water every year. Only initiates were allowed to approach the well, but the goddess Boanna, lover of chief god Dagda Mór, let curiosity get the better of her. The waters promptly rose up and washed her away, and the resulting flood became the river that took her name. Water played a fundamental part in Celtic beliefs and similar stories were told about other rivers—such as the Shannon, which was said to have been created when the goddess Sionnain looked into a sacred well.

KINGS AND KINGDOMS

For many centuries Celtic society followed the same basic pattern. Each autonomous community, called a *tuátha*, was ruled by a *rí* (king), a worthy warrior chosen from among royal ranks. A *tuátha* was made up of scattered *ráths* (farming settlements), and a strict class system extended from slaves, at the bottom of the heap, to the learned and the royal, at the top. Throughout Ireland there were a hundred or so of these kingdoms grouped into five regions—Ulster, Munster, Leinster, Connaught and Meath—and lord of them all (in theory) was the *Ard Rí* (High King), who sat in state at Tara. Frequent and violent power struggles arose as royal dynasties vied for control of their own territories and, ultimately, of the whole land.

THE MIGHTY FINN

During the third century AD King Cumhal (Cool) was killed in a battle over leadership of the fearsome Fianna warriors. His son, Finn, was brought up in the wild and sent to a druid for instruction. One day the druid caught the Salmon of Knowledge in the River Boyne and gave it to his pupil to cook. In the process Finn burned his thumb and licked it, immediately acquiring great wisdom. He subsequently made his way to Tara, where a demon was wreaking nightly havoc after mesmerizing the townsfolk with enchanted harp music. Finn touched his forehead with the tip of a magic spear, thus blocking the music's effects, and slew the demon, earning the right to be Chief of the Fianna, the strongest and wisest king they ever had.

LANGUAGE OF THE GODS

Standing stones carved with intriguing lines and strokes are found all over Ireland, Britain and Europe and even in parts of America. These are no abstract decorations but inscriptions in Ogham, the Celtic language named after Ogma, god of literature. Ogham script was in use from the fourth century AD, but according to some theories had been part of Druidic ritual since the first century or earlier. The alphabet is simple but flexible: Straight or angled strokes are placed above, below or through a vertical line to represent 15 consonants and 5 vowels, each letter taking the name of a tree. Ogham script gradually gave way to the Roman alphabet, but some remote communities were still using it as recently as the 19th century.

ST. PATRICK'S ADVENTURES

Ireland's patron saint was born to Roman parents in Britain in around AD389. At 16 he was abducted and sold into slavery in Ireland, where he worked as a shepherd in County Antrim. After six years he escaped and was reunited with his family. During his captivity Patrick had developed a strong faith. He trained as a priest in France, and dreamed that the Irish called for his help, and this convinced him of his life's mission, so he returned to Ireland to lay the foundations of its Church. Legend has it that while preaching from Croagh Patrick in County Mayo (▷ 216) St. Patrick rang his bell and drove the country's snakes into the sea, a miracle that may symbolize the eradication of paganism.

Above left *Display in Adragl Heritage Centre*
Above right *Ogham script on the Brandsbutt Stone*

MONASTERIES AND MISSIONARIES

Christianity took root in Ireland and during the fifth and sixth centuries monastic communities sprang up. Missionaries ventured abroad to spread the word: Columcille (St. Columba) journeyed to Scotland to found the monastery of Iona; St. Brendan the Navigator may have reached American shores, and St. Columbanus developed communities in Belgium, Germany, Switzerland and Italy. Scholarship and art flourished in the Irish monasteries, but from AD795 people lived under the threat of Viking attacks. High round towers were built to keep watch for, and to provide refuge from, the plunderers. In 914 the Vikings launched an all-out invasion and established themselves in Ireland, building walled cities such as Dublin, Wicklow and Wexford. Meanwhile the rival Irish dynasties struggled for ascendancy. Brian Borúma (Boru), King of Munster, emerged as High King but was killed defeating the Danes at the Battle of Clontarf in 1014. Interdynastic wars simmered on, and in 1169 the exiled King of Leinster, Dermot MacMurrough, summoned to his aid an Anglo-Norman magnate, Richard Fitzgilbert de Clare, known as Strongbow. Troubled by Strongbow's military success, English king Henry II sailed for Ireland, and, backed by the Pope, declared himself its feudal overlord.

COLUMCILLE AND THE COPYRIGHT CASE

In 561 Columcille (St. Columba) set sail for Scotland, and established several important monastic communities. But it is thought that the journey may have been prompted by his part in a terrible battle. Columcille was an aristocrat who trained as a scholar and a monk under the tutelage of St. Finnian. The story goes that he copied the saint's book of psalms but refused to hand over his work. In the first recorded case of copyright, a court ruled that St. Finnian, as the original book's owner, had a right to its copy. The dispute was taken up by Columcille's relatives, and the two sides came to blows. As a penance for this horrific turn of events, Columcille went into exile with a dozen followers, and began his famous mission.

Above *Detail of stonework on St. Declan's well at Ardmore*

VIKING DUBLIN

In summer 2003 the remains of four Viking warriors were unearthed at South Great Georges Street in Dublin—members, perhaps, of the Norse invaders who sailed up the Boyne and Liffey in the early ninth century, meeting little effective resistance. By 841, Viking settlers were following in the warriors' wake. A thriving port evolved at Duiblinn (Dublin), and coinage was introduced. Within the town's walls the Vikings built houses of wattle and daub, designed to last about 15 years. Ships came and went, carrying animals, slaves, wool, fur, wine and gems. The townspeople went about their business in the latest Scandinavian fashions: shirts and long trousers for the men, aproned tunics and silk headbands for the women.

THE TRIALS OF CLONMACNOISE

The sixth-century monastic site of Clonmacnoise, on the River Shannon, suffered more than its fair share of disasters. After its foundation by St. Ciaran in AD545 the monastery earned a reputation for scholarship, but in the seventh century many students were killed in a bout of plague. The site was destroyed by fire three times during the eighth century, and in the ninth and tenth centuries it was frequently targeted by Viking raiders and rival Irish leaders. During his wars of expansion King Fedelmid MacCrimthainn of Cashel burned Clonmacnoise and slaughtered its monks in 832, 833 and 844. On the final occasion, it's said that St. Ciarán appeared and dealt Fedelmid a fatal blow with his staff.

THE BOOK OF DURROW

There's a touch of mystery to the Book of Durrow, now kept in Trinity College Library, Dublin. Created in AD675, it's Ireland's oldest surviving illuminated gospel and takes its name from Durrow Abbey, County Offaly, where it was said to have been made. But clues have emerged to cast doubt on its origins. Among the tints used is orpiment, a yellow mineral from the Mediterranean. Fragments of this dye were found during excavations of the hill fort of Dunadd in Argyll, Scotland. This has prompted speculation that the book was put together at Iona monastery, which was only 56km (35 miles) from Dunadd and whose monks would have had access to the town's imported goods.

LIFE OF BRIAN

Brian Boru was a name whispered with dread in 10th-century Munster. The younger brother of King Mahon, he had fled in protest at an alliance with the Vikings, and from a hideout in the woods he and his followers conducted vicious attacks on the Norse settlements. As Brian's fame grew Mahon sought him out, and together they expelled the Norse king. After Mahon's death Brian fought his way to ascendancy over all Ireland's kingdoms and ruled as High King for a decade until, in 1014, the King of Leinster and the Dublin Vikings joined forces against him at Clontarf. After a day of carnage, Brian emerged victorious, but was killed by a retreating Viking in his moment of glory.

Above *Illuminated page from seventh-century Book of Durrow*
Left *The 12th-century church of St. Finghin and its round tower*

NORMANS TO THE FLIGHT OF THE EARLS

Henry II failed to extend his authority beyond Dublin and a swathe of land around it known as the Pale. The Anglo-Norman invaders were gradually assimiliated into Gaelic culture and customs, and in the 14th century the Crown tried—unsuccessfully—to separate the two sections of the community with the Statutes of Kilkenny (1366), which forbade the English from taking Irish names, marrying into Irish families or even employing Irish balladeers. The most powerful Anglo-Irish families embarked on a struggle for supremacy; the Fitzgeralds, earls of Kildare, emerged victorious. When, in the 1490s, Henry VII determined to bring Ireland under his control, he used the Kildares as his agents. Royal deputy Sir Edward Poynings instigated Poynings' Law, requiring royal approval for the summoning of Irish parliaments. In the 1530s Henry VIII split from Rome and pronounced himself head of the English Church. Rebellion broke out in Ireland, led by the Kildares, and was ruthlessly put down. In the years that followed a steady trickle of Protestants arrived from England. Elizabeth I made concerted efforts to establish colonies, or plantations, in Munster and Ulster, provoking uprisings. In 1607 Irish aristocrats left for Italy in the Flight of the Earls.

Clockwise from left to right *Dunluce Castle set upon the cliffs; Archbishop of Armagh, Jacobus Usserius; the graveyard of Dunluce Old Church; exhibit from Dublin's Chief Herald Collection at the National Library; Irishmen attacking a tower*

MIXED MOTIVES
The conquest of Ireland served several purposes for Henry II, apart from reining in Strongbow's (▷ 30) ambitions. The King needed the distractions provided by an invasion. In December 1170 the Christian world had been shocked by the murder of Thomas Becket, Archbishop of Canterbury, by four of Henry's knights. Becket was canonized within a record two years and pilgrims flocked to his shrine. Faced with the wrath of the Vatican, Henry performed elaborate public penances. The invasion was, likewise, calculated to please, as the pope was anxious to bring the Irish monasteries to heel. Henry's Irish campaign was a way of simultaneously asserting power, distracting public attention and restoring himself in the papal good books.

BEYOND THE PALE

English royal authority was dwindling by the 1400s. Events of the previous century, which included the Black Death, had further weakened its hold. The only area loyal to the Crown was Dublin and a belt of land around it known as the Pale (or fortified boundary). This was defended by trenches, forts and guards, but Irish raiders from 'beyond the Pale' still managed to penetrate the area. In 1429 Henry VI offered every Englishman within the Pale £10 to build a castle measuring 5m (16ft) by 6m (20ft) and 12m (40ft) high. Within 20 years the authorities had to call a halt to the building work, as hundreds of castles sprouted across the countryside.

THE O'NEILL REBELLION

Hugh O'Neill (1550–1616) was brought up as an English gentleman, but his true ambition was to rule an independent, Catholic Ireland, and in 1595 he led a full-scale rebellion in Ulster. Reinforcements were sent by sea from Spain to help him in his quest, but violent storms and outbreaks of disease weakened the Spanish troops and in 1601 O'Neill was forced to surrender. He was later restored to his earldom but with only nominal status, and the English authorities continued to treat him with suspicion. In 1607 O'Neill joined several other disgruntled earls on a ship bound for Italy, where he died in exile nine years later.

GALLOWGLASS

In 1290 Turlba O'Donnell enlisted the help of mercenaries to overthrow his brother. Contemporary accounts include the first known use of the term 'gallowglass'—an anglicized version of *gallóglach*, Irish for foreign soldier. Between the 13th and 17th centuries, well-trained bands of mercenaries—some of Viking origin—fought for Irish and Scottish kings. Easily recognizable by their chain-mail or padded coats and cone-shaped helmets, they were skilled in the use of double-handed swords (claymores) and battle-axes. Some gallowglass families remained in service to the same dynasties for hundreds of years, but with the departure of the most prominent Irish nobles in 1607 these warriors disappeared from the scene.

FEUDING FAMILIES

There was constant animosity between Ireland's titled families, and evidence of one particularly stormy period is displayed in St. Patrick's Cathedral in Dublin. A fierce tussle for political power between the Butler family, earls of Ormonde, and the Fitzgeralds, earls of Kildare, erupted into violence in the 1490s. Gangs of their supporters clashed in the Dublin streets, and when the family heads and their bodyguards crossed paths in the cathedral nave more fighting broke out, forcing the Earl of Ormonde to take shelter in the chapterhouse. Eventually a truce was agreed and a hole was cut in the chapterhouse door so that the rivals could shake hands. The door and its hole can still be clearly seen in the south transept.

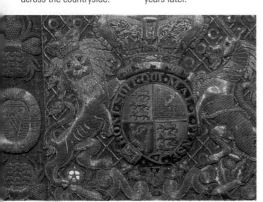

In the early 17th century land grants attracted some 100,000 Protestant immigrants from England and Scotland to Ulster and Munster. Sectarian conflict was rife in England, where enmity between the largely Protestant parliament and Charles I was escalating into civil war. Ireland's Catholic gentry took arms in the King's name, and during the 1641 uprising thousands of Ulster settlers were slain. Oliver Cromwell's Parliamentarian army gained ground in England, while the Catholic royalists had almost full control of Ireland. Charles sought their help, but baulked at their demands for independence. Soon after the King's capture and execution, Cromwell brought 12,000 troops to subdue Ireland; Drogheda and Wexford suffered terrible massacres. Within nine months Cromwell had crushed the opposition. Nearly half of Ireland's land was confiscated, and dispossessed Catholics were transplanted west of the River Shannon under the 1652 Act of Settlement. In 1685 James II, himself a Catholic, became king; three years later parliament invited a Dutch Protestant prince, William of Orange, to seize the throne. James escaped to Ireland and raised an army, but on 1 July 1690 William won a decisive victory by the Boyne and James fled to France.

Above *British cavalry at the battle of the Boyne*

BIRTH OF A DYNASTY

After the 1641 rebellion about a million hectares (2.5 million acres) of land were confiscated from the Catholics and snapped up by English Protestant adventurers. One was Richard Boyle (1566–1643), who, having arrived in Ireland with less than £100 to his name, took on the title Earl of Cork and increased his worth to £20,000 a year. His youngest son, Robert (1627–91), was a scientific pioneer, experimenting with air pressure and advocating the theory that matter was made up of atoms. Richard Boyle's grandson Charles (1676–1731), Earl of Orrery, continued the family's scientific interests and paid inventor George Graham to design a mechanical model of the planets—a device called an orrery to this day.

Above *Oliver Cromwell*
Top left *Ireland's oldest Quaker cemetery, at Mountmellick*
Bottom left *The Siege of (London)Derry*

AN UNSEEMLY SCUFFLE

The Irish parliament summoned in 1613 had a large Protestant majority. Its first task was the election of a speaker. The Protestant candidate was Sir John Davies; the Catholic choice Sir John Everard. When Davies' supporters filed out to vote, his Catholic opponents grabbed Everard and shoved him into the speaker's chair. On their return the indignant Protestants promptly heaved their own, rather stout man onto Everard's lap. During the ensuing fisticuffs Everard was ejected from the chamber, and the Catholic members walked out. But the incident made its mark—the number of rotten boroughs was cut drastically and several proposed anti-Catholic laws were withdrawn.

THE BOYNE MEDAL

Some 60,000 men took to the field in the Battle of the Boyne (1690) as William of Orange and James II fought over the right to rule. William won the battle and the throne, but events could have taken an entirely different direction. In the confusion of battle a Jacobite soldier had managed to reach William and almost pulled him off his horse. A certain Major Rogers galloped to the rescue. In gratitude the King commissioned an 18-carat gold medal, possibly the first to be awarded for an act of individual courage. A profile of William III decorated one face; the other depicted Enniskillen Castle, in tribute to the Major's company, the Royal Enniskillen Fusiliers.

LEADER OF THE GANG

Like most notorious outlaws in history, 'Count' Redmond O'Hanlon (*d*1681) is an enigmatic figure, whose story is a tangle of fact and myth. Starting out as a footboy, in 1670 he took charge of a gang of Ulster tories (from the Irish *toraighe*, or bandit). According to some historians O'Hanlon had been dispossessed of his land by Cromwell. O'Hanlon's men were feared throughout the counties of Armagh, Tyrone and Down, where they levied 'tributes' from the colonists. A price of £200 was put on O'Hanlon's head, but he evaded capture on several occasions before being tricked and shot by his foster brother, who was in the pay of the Earl of Ormond. O'Hanlon's head was removed from his body and ended up on the end of a spike, displayed at Downpatrick Jail.

THE GROWTH OF DUBLIN

By the mid-17th century Dublin was in a sorry state. Many Catholics were expelled after the civil war and in 1650 the plague struck. Dublin's population fell from 20,000 in 1640 to less than 9,000 in 1659. Lord Lieutenant James Butler, Duke of Ormonde, raised from earl to duke by the restored Charles II, commissioned a flurry of new developments. Phoenix Park and St. Stephen's Green were laid out. New institutions such as the Blue Coat School and the Royal Hospital were built, and brick and tile dwellings replaced thatched dwellings. Trade in wool and linen boomed, a second bridge was built across the River Liffey in 1670 and the city's quays were revamped. By 1700 the population had grown to 60,000, and the prosperity that continued into the Georgian era was under way.

FROM PENAL LAWS TO EMANCIPATION

After the Jacobites' defeat, Ireland was firmly under Protestant control. A series of measures passed in the late 17th and the 18th centuries—the penal laws—kept the Catholic majority out of power, forbidding them to hold public office, sit in parliament, vote, teach, inherit land from Protestants or buy land. Meanwhile trade flourished and Dublin became the hub of Anglo-Irish intellectual life. Protestant thinkers increasingly criticized Catholic persecution. Politician Henry Grattan called for equal rights and limited Irish independence and achieved some of his objectives, but not for long. In 1798 Wolfe Tone led an ill-fated uprising, and three years later the Act of Union brought Ireland under direct British rule. Ireland sent MPs to Westminster, but only Protestants could take their seats. Rebel Robert Emmet led an abortive attack on Dublin Castle in 1803, but the most effective campaign was Daniel O'Connell's peaceful movement for Home Rule and emancipation. O'Connell (▷ 38) was elected an MP in 1828; his faith excluded him from parliament, but his success had a major impact. The following year the Catholic Emancipation Act extended the vote to all Catholics with a £10 freehold—14,000 in all—and enabled them to sit in Parliament.

BATTLE OF THE DIAMOND
County Armagh was a powder-keg in the 18th century. Catholics and Protestants competing to control the growing linen industry formed armed gangs: the Peep O' Day Boys (Protestants) and the Defenders (Catholics). Both sides notched up a terrible tally of atrocities. In September 1795 a particularly vicious clash in a pub called The Diamond ended in the deaths of a dozen Defenders. To mark the event the victors formed an association and named it after William of Orange, pledging allegiance to the Crown and to Protestantism. In 1786, members of the Orange Order paraded in celebration of the Battle of the Boyne (▷ 34–35). The Orangemen's marches continue to this day and remain a contentious issue between the two communities.

Clockwise from left to right *Mussenden Temple built in the 18th century; Irish insurgents led by Father John Murphy; Jonathan Swift; a Georgian town house*

UNDERSTANDING | THE STORY OF IRELAND

THE SOUND OF MUSIC

Georgian Dublin was an affluent and fashionable city with a flourishing creative life. Among many musicians who came to enjoy its buzz were Italian violinist and composer Francesco Geminiani (1687–1762); Thomas Arne (1710–78), who wrote songs and oratorios; his son Michael (1740–86), an opera singer; and the musical superstar of his day, Georg Friederich Handel (1685–1759). Handel arrived at the invitation of the viceroy, who commissioned a new work for Dublin and within six weeks was presented with the *Messiah*. The oratorio was first performed on 13 April 1742 in the Charitable Musical Society's base, Neal's Music Hall in Fishamble Street. It was conducted by Handel himself, who stayed on in Ireland to take in the Dublin scene for a year.

HEDGE SCHOOLS

Under the penal laws, teaching in Irish and about the Catholic faith was banned, but rather than send their children to schools where only an English-language, Protestant curriculum was taught, many parents opted to support hedge schools. Under the law these schools were illicit gatherings—under hedges, on the roadside or in derelict buildings—where teachers passed on Irish history, legends and ballads and the tenets of Roman Catholicism to their pupils. An 1826 report estimated that of 550,000 children registered in schools, 403,000 of them attended hedge schools. By 1832 the laws had been relaxed and, as new schools became more open to recognizing Irish tradition and the Roman Catholic faith, the hedge schools died out.

THE FAILED REVOLUTION

Wolfe Tone (1768–98), a Protestant lawyer from Dublin, was a leading light of the United Irishmen, a society inspired by French revolutionary ideas. He hoped that, together, Catholics and Protestants could overcome the government's 'boobies and blockheads' and enjoy equal rights in an independent republic. After his implication in a plot to encourage a French invasion, Tone sailed first to America and then to France, where he persuaded the government to send troops to Ireland. One fleet was beaten by the weather; the second was defeated in 1798 at Lough Swilly. Tone was captured and convicted of treason. He requested a soldier's death—by firing squad—but on learning that he would be hanged, cut his own throat in prison.

A WAY WITH WORDS

The 18th century was a golden age for English-language Irish literature. Leading the pack was Jonathan Swift (1667–1745), who employed his acerbic wit in *Gulliver's Travels* and *Modest Proposal* (where the rich end poverty by eating the babies of the poor). George Farquhar (1677–1707) was an actor who took up writing after injuring someone in a stage fight. He had to borrow 20 guineas to write his last comedy, *The Beaux' Stratagem*, which brought him success at the end of his life. Other literary stars were playwright Richard Brinsley Sheridan (1751–1816) and Oliver Goldsmith (1730–74), whose unsentimental novel *The Vicar of Wakefield* broke new ground; its success saved him from imprisonment for debt.

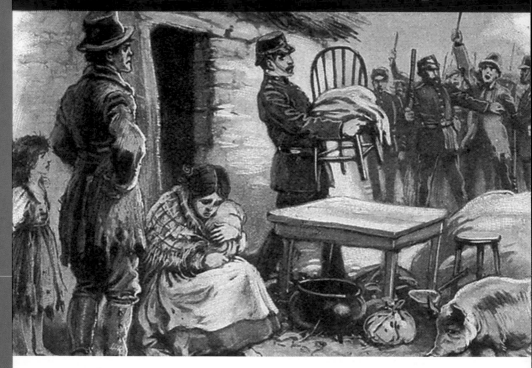

By the mid-19th century most of Ireland's 8 million inhabitants were rural poor, living mainly on potatoes. In 1845 and 1846 a fungus ruined the potato crop, and about a million died of starvation or disease. Government relief was slow and inefficient. Mass emigration followed, many thousands dying en route to the Americas. Meanwhile, landlords hiked their rents and evicted tenants unable to pay. The famine left a bitter legacy. In 1858 the Fenian movement was formed, advocating armed insurrection. Alternative strategies were pursued by MP Charles Stewart Parnell and his Home Rule Party, who kept Irish grievances in the spotlight in the House of Commons. A fragile alliance with Prime Minister William Gladstone fell apart in 1882 after the British Chief Secretary's murder in Dublin's Phoenix Park, and a few years later Parnell's reputation was destroyed by news of his affair with a married woman. A Home Rule Bill was eventually passed in 1912 but put aside when World War I broke out. Rival Unionist and Republican militias were formed, and on Easter Monday 1916, Republicans occupied Dublin's major buildings. Six days' fighting ensued before their capture. The ringleaders' execution created new martyrs for the Republican cause.

THE LIBERATOR
On 13 August 1843 a million people stood on the Hill of Tara to hear a 68-year-old lawyer. The crowd-puller was Daniel O'Connell (1775–1847), champion of emancipation, land reform and the repeal of the Anglo-Irish Union. The Tara gathering was the last of 40 held across the country. O'Connell was opposed to violence. His peaceful campaigns attracted widespread support, and a final meeting was planned on 8 October, but O'Connell was arrested and imprisoned, and was released six months later only after a national protest.

Above *Depiction of an all-too-common eviction*

ROUTE TO POWER

Among the emigrants occupying the Great Famine in 1848 was a 25-year-old brewer's cooper from Dungans-town, near New Ross. Patrick Kennedy came from a farming family which was facing eviction. Determined to try his luck elsewhere, he boarded the SS *Washington Irving* to Boston, and with his wife, Bridget, set up home in a tenement. They raised three daughters and a son before Patrick's death from cholera at 38. Bridget worked on, eventually buying a grocery store. Their son, Patrick Joseph, did well as a saloon-owner and grandson Joseph became ambassador to Britain. In 1961 Joseph's son John was elected President of the United States, little more than a century after his great-grandfather's departure from Ireland.

CURTAIN UP

Celtic legend and poetry and the political struggle were themes that injected new life and interest into the literature of the early 20th century. At the heart of this revival was Dublin's Abbey Theatre, headquarters of the Irish National Theatre Society. In 1903 Miss Ann Elizabeth Horniman bought the derelict theatre and the former morgue next door and converted them into the Abbey. Poet W. B. Yeats (▷ 41) and his friend Lady Gregory were closely involved in the project, and Lady Gregory wrote *Gods and Fighting Men* for performance there. In 1907 the theatre confirmed its reputation for staging controversial contemporary works with J. M. Synge's play *The Playboy of the Western World*, which sparked riots.

CITY OF SHIPS

Writer Stephen Gwynn (1864–1950) noted in 1911 that Belfast's ships were 'marvels of symmetry and strength'. Shipbuilding was at the heart of the city's success and on 31 May 1911 Belfast celebrated the launch of the mighty SS *Titanic*. Shipbuilders Harland & Wolff had employed hundreds of men on the building of the *Titanic*, which, along with her sister ship *Olympic*, was the biggest moving vessel of the time. Launched from the Queen's Island and cheered by a big crowd, she set off for sea trials in Belfast Lough. Her 1912 maiden voyage, from Southampton to New York, called at Queenstown, aka Cork, and carried many Irish emigrants. Three days later she struck an iceberg and sank, with the loss of 1,495 lives.

THE FIRST BOYCOTT

Charles Stewart Parnell's policy of ostracizing negligent landlords was responsible for coining a new phrase which soon became common parlance in the English language. One of its first targets was Charles Cunningham Boycott (1834–97), an ex-army captain employed to manage Lord Erne's estates in County Mayo. When supporters of the Land League refused to work for him, Boycott faced a ruined harvest and a ruined career. Volunteers from the Orange Order (▷ 36) were hastily brought in to do the work, but police and troops were needed to protect them from reprisals by the Land League as they gathered the crops. Within a month the term 'boycotting' was in use in the press, and the captain had earned his place in history.

Clockwise from left *John F Kennedy with Dublin's mace-bearer Jim Buckley in Dublin, 1963; a Dublin plaque commemorating Bram Stoker; the sinking of the Titanic in 1912*

THE 20TH CENTURY

At the 1918 general election the Republican Sinn Féin party virtually swept the board and set up its own Dáil (parliament) in Dublin. After two years of fighting between the Irish Republican Army and the Royal Irish Constabulary, reinforced by the notoriously ruthless Black and Tans, a motley band of mostly ex-soldier mercenaries, the Government of Ireland Act was passed, establishing one parliament for the 26 southern counties—the Irish Free State—and one for the six northern counties. The Free State left the British Commonwealth in 1949 and became a republic. The IRA remained active in Northern Ireland, and a pattern of attacks and reprisals was set. British troops were sent in after riots in 1969 and became targets for the splinter Provisional IRA group. On 30 January 1972—'Bloody Sunday'—soldiers opened fire during a civil rights demonstration in Derry (Londonderry) and 13 unarmed protesters were killed. 'The Troubles' escalated, and Northern Ireland's assembly at Stormont was suspended. Bombing campaigns, protests and riots marked the 1970s and 1980s. But tentative negotiation was under way and, in 1994 a ceasefire was declared by the IRA and the Loyalists. In 1998 the Good Friday Agreement proposed an elected assembly and the disarmament of all paramilitary groups.

COUNTESS MARKIEVICZ
One of the first orders to open fire on Easter Monday 1916 was given by Constance, Countess Markievicz (1884–1927), the deserted wife of a Ukrainian aristocrat and the daughter of Arctic explorer Sir Henry Gore-Booth. Countess Markievicz was a member of Sinn Féin and an ardent activist, who commanded a Republican contingent during the Easter Rising. For her part in the event she received a death sentence, but was subsequently reprieved. She went on to become the first woman ever to be voted into the British parliament, at the general election of 1918. She, like other Sinn Féin members, refused to take up her seat in Westminster. In 1919 the Countess served in the cabinet of the first Dáil, as Minister of Labour.

LOVE STORY

In his 1929 collection *Last Poems* William Butler Yeats (1865–1939) described Maud Gonne as 'Pallas Athene in that straight back and arrogant head'. He had first met the beautiful radical 43 years earlier, and his unrequited love for her was a constant theme from then on. Having refused the poet many times, Gonne married fellow revolutionary John MacBride, and in his next collection Yeats paid wistful tribute to his lost love. MacBride was executed after the Easter Rising and again Yeats proposed unsuccessfully, first to Gonne and then to her adopted daughter, Iseult. In 1917 he married Georgie Hyde-Lees, an old friend. Fascinated with the supernatural, Yeats found inspiration in his wife's talent for automatic writing.

Opposite *A Derry mural*
Top right *The Red Hand of Ulster, from a Shankhill Road mural*
Bottom right *Bono speaking at a Canadian Liberal Party conference*
Below *Eamon de Valera*

FAME AND FORTUNE

Rock band U2 was discovered by manager Paul McGuinness playing in a community hall behind the Clarence Hotel in Dublin. Now the band owns the hotel, along with a string of clubs, bars, media firms and other ventures contributing to its multi-million-euro empire. In 2004 the band was worth more than €680 million, making it the fifth richest company in Ireland. Earnings were helped by sales of 85 million albums over the past 23 years, each sale bringing in more than €4 in royalties, as well as the tax-free status granted to major Irish artists. Lead singer Bono (Paul Hewson) is a prominent campaigner on various Third World issues, and appeared alongside a host of international stars at the Live 8 concert in July 2005.

DE VALERA

Eamon de Valera (1882–1975), the only military commander to escape execution after the Easter Rising, became president of Sinn Féin in 1917. Months later he was imprisoned for treason, but escaped in 1919 and returned to lead the new Dáil. De Valera sent negotiators to London, but rejected the resulting Anglo-Irish Treaty. Civil war raged over the treaty until the 1923 ceasefire. De Valera founded Fianna Fáil, which took power in 1932. Éire's 1937 constitution reflected his ideal of a socially conservative, Gaelic-speaking, Catholic nation. In World War II his government maintained neutrality; consequently Éire was not admitted to the UN until 1955. Summing up his career, de Valera remarked that he should have been a bishop, rather than a revolutionary.

OMAGH

On 15 August 1998 the market town of Omagh, in County Tyrone, was busy with shoppers. At about 2.30pm police received a bomb warning by telephone. The middle of town was immediately evacuated. But there was confusion about the location of the bomb, and shoppers were actually directed into the danger area. When a car bomb exploded at 3pm, 29 people were killed and hundreds wounded. Sinn Féin leader Gerry Adams condemned the bombing, and chief negotiator Martin McGuinness described it as an appalling act, designed to stall the peace process. The Real IRA, a splinter group opposing the Good Friday Agreement, claimed responsibility and issued an apology; two weeks later it suspended military action, but later resumed bombing.

21ST-CENTURY IRELAND

IRELAND IN EUROPE

On 1 January 2004 Ireland took over presidency of the EU for the sixth time. Since its entry into the EEC in 1972, the Republic has enjoyed the benefits of regional grants and tax concessions contributing to a meteoric rise in its economy that earned it the name 'Celtic Tiger'. In 2001 the nation's commitment to Europe was underlined when the Irish punt was replaced with the euro. Not everyone is comfortable with the influx of international business and immigration, however. A referendum on the Nice Treaty, proposing increased European integration, produced a 'no' vote. Subsequently, a second referendum, held in 2002, reversed the earlier decision and approved the treaty.

The Republic of Ireland entered the third millennium with an impressive record of economic growth. The Dáil is dominated, as it has been since the 1930s, by the rival Fianna Fáil and Fine Gael parties, often relying for power on the support of smaller parties. Elections took place in June 2007 and the government was led by Bertie Ahern of Fianna Fáil with support from the Green Party and the Progressive Democrats. The Northern Ireland Assembly was suspended until 8 May 2007 when, following the acceptance of the St. Andrews Agreement, it was restored to form a new power-sharing Northern Ireland Executive headed by Ian Paisley of the Democratic Unionists and Martin McGuinness of Sinn Féin.

ARMS INSPECTIONS

The decommissioning of arms was a hotly debated part of the Northern Ireland peace process. Arguments about timing, definition and inspection of disarmament hampered negotiations and led to the suspension of the Assembly. In May 2000 the IRA announced its intention to put weapons beyond use, agreeing to the inspection of arms dumps by independent observers. The Independent International Commission on Decommissioning, headed by Canada's General John de Chastelain, oversaw the process, and in January 2006 a report stated that all arms have been decommissioned, although many Unionists remain sceptical.

HOT PROPERTY

By 2000 Dublin was capital of a booming economy and the second most expensive place to live in the EU. The average price of a Dublin house rose from €89,032 in 1996 to €468,273 in 2005, and new one-bedroom apartments in Smithfield Market were snapped up at €345,000. Nearly 50 new houses sold in a few days at Malahide, each one costing €750,000. Despite an international downturn in the economy and the average house price in Dublin falling to €395,096 in January 2008, building continues at a pace.

Top *Peace monument silhouetted against the Derry sky*
Above *Waterfront development at Lanyon May, Belfast*

ON THE MOVE

On the Move gives you detailed advice and information about the various options for travelling to Ireland before explaining the best ways to get around the country once you are there. Handy tips help you with everything from buying tickets to renting a car.

ARRIVING BY AIR

BY AIR TO THE REPUBLIC OF IRELAND

The Republic is well served by major airlines, and there are three international airports at Dublin, Shannon (near Limerick) and Cork. There are regional airports on the Aran Islands and in Donegal, Galway, Kerry, Knock, Sligo and Waterford. More than 30 airlines fly into the Republic from more than 55 cities, with an increasing number of budget airlines operating routes from various places in Europe, which means that if you reserve in advance on a low-cost airline, your flights need not be too expensive.

The national airline in Ireland is Aer Lingus; Ryanair, a privately owned Irish airline, is the largest low-cost airline in Europe.

You can fly into Dublin and Shannon airports from North America, but if you are coming from Australasia, you will have to connect in another city (for example, London), as there are no direct flights. For more information about flights within Ireland, ▷ 55.

Dublin Airport (DUB) is 11km (7 miles) north of the city. New facilities are on the way with the new boarding gates in place and a €2 billion investment to improve the airport.

In Departures there is a bureau de change, a pharmacy (open Mon–Thu 6.30–6.30, Fri–Sun 9am–11.30pm), a vending machine that sells stamps, a shoe shine and plenty of cafés.

In Arrivals there are car rental desks, a tourist information desk, CIE (state-run transport company) information desk, an ATM, a café, a bureau de change and a bookshop.

Airlines with flights to and from Britain include Ireland's own (and Europe's largest) low-cost carrier Ryanair. Others are Aer Lingus, bmi, bmi baby, Flybe and BA CitiExpress. Airlines with flights from Europe include Aer Lingus, Air France, Luxair, Alitalia, Austrian Airlines, Iberia, Lufthansa, Ryanair and SAS. Carriers from the US include Delta, Continental Airlines and Aer Lingus.

For general information about Dublin airport tel 01 814 1111; www.dublinairport.com

Cork Airport (ORK) is 8km (5 miles) south of Cork in the south of Ireland. Facilities in the main terminal building include a bank (Bank of Ireland) with a bureau de change, an ATM which dispenses euros and pounds sterling, an information desk, a mailbox, cafés and bars. Aer Arann, bmi baby, Loganair, Aer Lingus, Ryanair and easyJet fly in from Britain. Airlines with flights to and

GETTING TO THE CITY FROM THE AIRPORT

Airport (code)	Dublin (DUB)	Cork (ORK)
Taxi	Price: approx €20–€25 to downtown Dublin. Extra charges for luggage, pets, extra passengers and on Sundays and public holidays. Taxi stand on the right outside Arrivals hall.	Approx €12 to the middle of Cork.
Trains	None.	None.
Bus	For all buses, turn left outside the Arrivals hall. Aircoach (www.aircoach. ie) to O'Connell Street, Grafton Street, St. Stephen's Green. Frequency: every 15 min. Journey time: 30 min. Price: adult single €7, return €12. Airlink Express Bus number 747 or 748 (run by Dublin bus; www.dublinbus. ie) to O'Connell Street, bus station *(busáras)*, Heuston train station. Frequency: every 15 or 20 min 5.45am–11.30pm. Journey time: 30 min. Price: adult single €6, adult return €10, child single €3. Dublin Bus also operates several regular services (16a, 41, 41a, 41b, 230), which go from the airport to the downtown area, although there is not as much space for luggage as on designated airport services. Frequency: every 15–20 min. Journey time: 45 min. Price: adult single from €2.	The Air Coach (operated by Bus Éireann) goes to the bus station at Parnell Place in Cork City. Frequency: Mon–Fri from 7.50am. Between 10am and 8.45pm they run about every 30 min. Journey time: 25 min. Price: adult single €4, adult return €6.90.
Car	Take the M1 then the M50, following signs to City Centre and An Lár.	Take the N27 to Cork City.

from Europe include Centralwings, Skyeurope, W122 and Aer Lingus Cork airport does not have any flights from North America.

For general information about the airport tel 021 431 3131; www.corkairport.com

Shannon Airport (SNN) is 24km (15 miles) west of Limerick in the Shannon region in the west of Ireland. Scheduled flights from Britain are operated by Aer Lingus, Ryanair, easyJet and BA CitiExpress. Most European flights (Paris, Frankfurt, Brussels), are operated by Ryanair, although there are other airlines which run flights from destinations farther away, such as Minsk and Wroclaw. There are many flights from cities in the east of the US. Aer Lingus has flights from Boston, Chicago and New York (JFK), Continental Airlines flies from New York (Newark) and Delta has flights from Atlanta. Note that US immigration officials check your documentation at Shannon airport before you board your flight back to the US.

For general information about Shannon airport tel 061 712 000; www.shannonairport.com

BY AIR TO NORTHERN IRELAND

Northern Ireland is served by Belfast International Airport, George Best Belfast City Airport and City of Derry airport. Most of the scheduled flights to these airports are from Britain or the Republic of Ireland. There are a limited number of flights operating to the US and Canada from Belfast International Airport. For more information about flight operators and schedules within the island, ▷ 55.

Shannon (SNN)	Belfast International (BFS)	Belfast City (BHD)
There is a desk in the Arrivals hall where you can hire a taxi. Price: approx €32 to Limerick City or Ennis	Price: approx £25 to downtown Belfast.	Price: approx £6 to downtown Belfast. Almost all taxis are wheelchair-friendly.
None.	There are no rail services directly to the airport. The nearest station is at Antrim, 9km (6 miles) away.	There is a free shuttle bus service from Belfast City Airport to Sydenham train station every 30 min from 6.30am–11pm.
Service 343 goes to Limerick City bus station. Frequency: irregular service, but at least every hour from 7.15am–midnight. Journey time: 45 min. Price: adult single €5.30.The City Link (www.citylink.ie) coach goes to Galway via Ennis. There are four journeys a day leaving at 8.30, 11.15, 1.30, 8. Journey time: 90 min. Price: adult single €15, adult return €22. Service 344 goes to Ennis bus station (and there you can take bus number 051 on to Galway). Frequency: irregular service from 8am–11pm. Journey time: between 45 min and an hour. Price: adult single €5.70.	Airbus service 300 (www.translink.co.uk) goes to Templepatrick, The Chimney Corner Inn, Sandy Knowles Roundabout, Laganside Bus centre and Central Railway Station as well as Shangall Street Bus Station. Frequency: Mon–Fri every 10 min from 7.10am–6.15pm, then every 30 min until 10.20pm, Sat 7am–10.20pm every 20 min, Sun 9.15am–10.20pm every 30 min. Journey time: 30 min. Price: adult single £6, adult return £9.	Airlink number 600 (www.translink.co.uk) to Donegall Square and Europa Buscentre. Frequency: Mon–Sat every 20 min, between 6am and 9.50pm. Journey time: 12 min. Price: adult single £1.30, adult return £2.20, child single 65p, child return £1.10.
Take the N18 south to Limerick City or north to Galway.	Take the A57 then the M2 to the heart of the city.	Take the A2 Sydenham bypass to downtown Belfast.

Belfast International Airport (BFS) is 29km (18 miles) north of the city. Services in Departures include internet kiosks, a travel agency, a bureau de change, cafés, restaurants, shops and ATMs. In Arrivals there is an information desk (7am–11pm) that provides information on flights and public transport and a bureau de change. Most flights to the airport are from Britain on airlines such as bmi baby and Jet2. Budget carrier easyJet operates flights to the UK and also Amsterdam. There are a large number of charter flights in the summer to European holiday resorts.

For general information about Belfast International Airport, tel 028 9448 4848; www.belfastairport.com

George Best Belfast City Airport
(BHD) is 4km (2.5 miles) east of the heart of the city and is used mostly by business people from Britain. Airlines include British Airways, Flybe and bmi.

For general information about Belfast City airport, tel 028 9093 9093; www.belfastcityairport.com

BUDGET AIRLINES
The number of low-cost flights to and from Ireland has increased enormously in the last few years, making Ireland a popular weekend destination for visitors from Britain and Europe. One-way tickets to destinations in Ireland are sometimes advertised for as little as €5 (not including taxes) although you will need to reserve well in advance and be flexible about when you travel and at what time of day. The downside for passengers is that routes come and go fairly quickly. Flights are inexpensive because the airlines do not provide services such as accommodation or a refund if flights are severely delayed, for example. When you reserve a flight, always read the conditions of carriage of that airline carefully. Make sure you also know what identification the airline requires, as there have been cases of airlines refusing to allow passengers to board, because they did not have acceptable photo identification.

ARRIVING BY FERRY
Ireland has six main ferry ports with services from Scotland, England, Wales, the Isle of Man and France run by different ferry operators. Sometimes more than one ferry operator runs services on a particular route, so it pays to shop around. You should always check crossing times as there are fast and slow services, so if time is short you may want to sail on a faster, if more expensive, service. You should remember that the Irish Sea can sometimes be quite rough, which occasionally leads to crossings being cancelled. Many ferry operators run a reduced service in January, when ships have their annual refit. The information below is grouped under the name of the Irish port and includes details of which ferry operators have services to that port, where they sail from and how long the sailing takes. The section also includes details on how to get from the port to the middle of town.

REPUBLIC OF IRELAND
Cork
Swansea Cork Ferries sail from Swansea in South Wales to Cork in the south of Ireland in 10 hours. Brittany Ferries provide a crossing from Roscoff, Brittany, in the northwest of France, to Cork, and from Santander in Spain.

Dublin
Irish Ferries and Stena Line run services from Holyhead in North Wales to Dublin. The journey time is 3 hours 15 minutes on the Stena *Adventurer*. With Irish Ferries the journey takes around 2 hours on the fast service or 3 hours 15 minutes on the Cruise Ferry.

P&O Irish Sea and Norfolkline have Liverpool to Dublin services.

The Isle of Man Steam Packet Company has a service from the capital of the Isle of Man, Douglas, to Dublin, which takes 2 hours 50 minutes.

Dún Laoghaire (South of Dublin)
Stena Line has a high-speed service from Holyhead in North Wales

to Dún Laoghaire, (pronounced 'Dunleery') which takes 1 hour 40 minutes. From the port it's then only a 20-minute journey on the DART light railway to the heart of Dublin. A return ticket to Pearse station in Dublin costs €3.80.

Rosslare
Irish Ferries runs a service from Pembroke in South Wales to Rosslare which takes 3 hours 15 minutes. The company also sails to Rosslare from the French ports of Cherbourg and Roscoff. Stena Line sails from Fishguard in the southwest of Wales to Rosslare. The journey time is 2 hours on the fast Stena *Express* or 3 hours 30 minutes on the Stena *Europe*.

NORTHERN IRELAND
Belfast
Stena Line has a fast Stranraer (Scotland) to Belfast service which takes 1 hour 45 minutes (Stena HSS). There is also a slower service which takes 3 hours 15 minutes (Superferry). Norfolkline runs a ferry from Liverpool in the north of England to Belfast, with a journey time of 8 hours.

The Isle of Man Steam Packet Company runs a service from the Isle of Man to Belfast, which takes 2 hours 45 minutes. The Steam Packet terminal on Donegall Quay in Belfast is just a 5-minute walk from the Laganside Buscentre and taxis are available at the port.

Larne (North of Belfast)
P&O Irish Sea operates two services from the west of Scotland. The Superstar Express service sails from Troon to Larne in 1 hour 49 minutes and the Cairnryan to Larne service takes 1 hour on the *P&O Express* or 1 hour 45 minutes on the *European Causeway* or *European Highlander* superferries. Stena has a crossing from Fleetwood in Lancashire, in the north of England.

ON-BOARD FACILITIES
Generally, the bigger the ship, the better the facilities. All services have

the minimum on-board amenities, such as a café or restaurant, toilets and a shop, while larger ferries may have cabins with private bathrooms, a cinema, a children's play area, video games, a choice of restaurants and a bureau de change. If you want to be sure what facilities and diversions are available on board, ask when you reserve or have a look at the ferry operator's website.

BY LONG-DISTANCE BUS AND FERRY

You can travel by long-distance bus and ferry to Ireland with Eurolines (www.eurolines.com). Inter-city bus services in Britain are operated by National Express (www.nationalexpress.com) and in Ireland by Bus Éireann (www.buseireann.ie), and you can travel from major UK cities, such as London, Birmingham, Oxford, Glasgow, Edinburgh, Bristol and Cardiff. The ferry routes that are used by these services are Holyhead to Dublin Port, Holyhead to Dún Laoghaire, and Fishguard to Rosslare.

TRAIN AND FERRY

It's possible to purchase one ticket (known as 'Rail and Sail') which includes a train journey to a ferry port in England and a sailing with Stena Line and Irish ferries to a port in Ireland. For example, you can take a train from London (which stops en route at Birmingham, Leeds, Manchester, Liverpool and Chester) to Holyhead then sail to Dún Laoghaire on the Stena HSS. Alternatively, there's a service from London to the Welsh port of Fishguard (via Bristol, Cardiff and Swansea), from where you sail on the Stena *Europe* to Rosslare. For train information call National Rail Enquiries in England on 08457 484950 or see their website, www.nationalrail.co.uk. To make a reservation tel 08450 755755 and state that you are travelling by train.

FERRY OPERATORS		
FERRY COMPANY	TELEPHONE RESERVATIONS	WEBSITE
Irish Ferries	0818 300400 (Ireland), 08705 171717 (UK)	www.irishferries.com
Stena Line	08705 707070 (UK), 01 204 7777 (Republic) Ferrycheck numbers provide up-to-the-minute information on sea conditions and timetable changes: 01 204 7799 (Republic), 08705 755755 (UK)	www.stenaline.com
Swansea Cork Ferries	021 483 0000 (Ireland), 01702 466 116 (UK)	www.swanseacork ferries.com
P&O Irish Sea	01 407 3434 (Ireland), 0871 664 4999 (UK)	www.poirishsea.com
Isle of Man Steam Packet Company	0871 221333 (Republic and UK),	www.steam-packet.com
Norfolkline	01 819 2999 (Republic), 0844 499 0007 (UK)	www.norfolkline.com
Brittany Ferries	021 427 7801 (Ireland), 0870 907 6103 (UK)	www.brittany-ferries.com

BY ROAD

If you want to travel around the countryside, stopping in little villages, realistically you're going to need a car, as smaller places are not served by public transport. In both Northern Ireland and the Republic you drive on the left and speed limits (▷ 50) are observed and enforced. The main factor to consider, particularly when driving in the Republic, is time. On the map, distances may seem short, but a combination of country roads, less than comprehensive signage and some poorly maintained road surfaces can lead to journeys taking longer than you might anticipate. You can prepare for this by buying a detailed road map, allowing plenty of time to get to your destination and accepting the often slow speeds on Irish roads. Avoid taking a car into Dublin, particularly during the rush hour. For more information on driving and car rental, ▷ 49–51.

When several people are travelling together they may well find that taking a taxi is a sensible option for some shorter journeys. Taxis in Dublin, Belfast, Cork, Limerick and Galway have a meter. In other parts of the country you need to agree the fare with the driver in advance.

BY TRAIN

Getting around Ireland by train may not be as economical as using the bus, but it is fast—the maximum time for a long-distance journey will be less than 4 hours. There has been massive investment in improvements to major stations and in the railway network as a whole, although the network still does not cover the entire country. For example, there is no railway line which covers the west coast from north to south and no service at all in Donegal or the far southwest of the country. Getting from Dublin to Belfast is quick (2 hours) and easy, though, thanks to the excellent Enterprise

service (▷ 52–53 for more detailed information).

BY BUS

Most of Ireland is covered by some sort of bus service, although they can be somewhat haphazard, and on long journeys you will probably have to change bus at least once. Buses are still the least expensive way of getting around and if time is not pressing, they are a good way to see the countryside. If it's your intention to travel around the island by public transport, consider investing in a special pass, such as the Irish Rover, which gives you unlimited travel on buses in the Republic and Northern Ireland, or the Emerald Card, which covers unlimited travel both on long-distance buses and on trains. For more information, including details on the various bus passes that are available, ▷ 53 and 54.

FLIGHTS WITHIN IRELAND

Taking internal flights in Ireland is not usually necessary, as it is not a large country and you may find that if you take into account check-in time and the journeys to and from the airport, that it does not save you much time. If you do prefer to fly, there are nine regional airports (including one on the Aran Islands), which operate domestic flights of no more than 45 minutes, at a cost of between €35 and €70 one way. For information on routes, prices and airline contact details, ▷ 55.

MAPS

Local Tourist Information Offices can supply you with a free basic town map or directions to your hotel, although you will probably have to pay for a more detailed country map. Tourist Information Offices and book and magazine retailers such as Eason sell a wide variety of travel guides, street maps and road maps. If you are driving around the country, a map showing both major and minor roads is absolutely essential. For recommended maps, ▷ 51 in the driving section.

DRIVING IN IRELAND

Driving around Ireland is a good way to see the countryside and of getting to small villages that are not served by public transport. In recent years the volume of traffic on the roads has increased significantly and the peak visitor season of July and August sees a lot of traffic around the most popular places. The golden rule is always to leave yourself plenty of time, as your average speed is likely to be only 56–72kph (35–45mph) because motorways often have only two lanes, many main roads have only one lane each way, and there are box junctions and traffic lights instead of roundabouts (traffic circles).

SIGNPOSTS

In the Republic signage is erratic, which makes navigating tricky, even with a detailed road map. When there is a signpost, it may have up to eight arrow signs coming off it, so be prepared to read quickly! The transition from older black and white signs in miles to green and white signs in kilometres is nearly complete. In Northern Ireland signposts use miles.

BOX JUNCTIONS

Where you see this yellow diamond pattern painted on the road surface, you should not enter the box unless it is clear that you can exit on the other side.

CAR RENTAL

You'll find the larger well-known car rental companies as well as smaller rental firms at airports, ferry ports and in towns. It is always best to reserve a car in advance, from home if possible. The Car Rental Council of Ireland's website www.carrental-council.ie has information, although you can't actually reserve a car on this site.

» You must have a valid driver's licence, held for more than a year. An international licence is not acceptable.

» Many firms require a minimum age of 23, 24 or 25 and a maximum age of 70 so check when you reserve.

» Make sure you have personal insurance as well as Collision Damage Waiver (CDW).

» If you have any specific requirements such as an automatic transmission car, air-conditioning or a child seat, request these when you reserve. There is normally an extra fee.

» If you plan to rent in the Republic and drive into Northern Ireland, check that your insurance covers this. Most car rental firms in the Republic allow you to take rental cars into Northern Ireland.

CAR RENTAL COMPANIES

The first telephone number is for the Republic, the second number is for Northern Ireland/UK.

NAME	TELEPHONE AND WEBSITE
Argus	01 499 9600/0870 387 5670 www.argusrentals.com
Avis	1890 405 060/0870 606 0100 www.avis.ie /www.avis.co.uk
Budget	090 662 7711/0800 973159 www.budget-ireland.co.uk
County	01 235 2030 www.countycar.com
Dan Dooley	062 53103/0800 282189 www.dan-dooley.ie
Europcar	01 614 2800/028 9442 3444 www.europcar.ie/www.europcar.com
Hertz	053 915 2511 www.hertz.ie
National/Alamo	021 432 0755/0870 600 6666 www.carhire.ie
Sixt/Irish Car Rentals	1850 206088/00800 47474227 www.irishcarrentals.com
Thrifty	1800 515800/0800 783 0405 www.thrifty.ie

» Most cars use unleaded fuel; check before filling the tank.

RULES OF THE ROAD
» Drive on the left.
» You must wear seatbelts in the front and rear seats of the car.
» Drivers and passengers on a motorcycle must wear a helmet.
» Speed limits, unless a sign indicates otherwise, are: Northern Ireland 30mph (48kph) in built-up areas, 60mph (96kph) on the open road and 70mph (112kph) on motorways (expressways); Republic of Ireland: motorway (blue) 120kph (75mph), national (green) 100kph (62mph) (in some areas 80kph (50mph)), regional and local (white) 80kph (50mph), urban roads 50kph (31mph).
» Give way to the right at roundabouts (traffic circles) and always go left around them.
» There are tough laws against drinking alcohol and driving, and random breath-testing is carried out. Never drive under the influence of alcohol.
» In the Republic of Ireland and Northern Ireland, it is illegal to use a mobile (cellular) phone while driving. Drivers are routinely prosecuted for dangerous driving brought about by using a mobile phone while driving.
» If you are involved in a collision, you must stop, give your name, the name and address of the car's owner and the car registration number to others involved. If you don't give your details at the time of the collision, you must immediately report the incident to the police.

» In the Republic, the Gardaí can issue on-the-spot fines for parking and speeding offences.
» Northern Ireland rules of the road: www.highwaycode.gov.uk

BRINGING YOUR OWN CAR
Bringing your own car to Ireland from Europe is straightforward thanks to the car ferry services to Ireland from Britain and France. Contact your motor insurer at least a month before you travel to check that your car is covered in the Republic and/or Northern Ireland. As well as your passport, you'll need to bring a valid driver's licence, International Driving Permit (where necessary) and your motor insurance and vehicle registration documents.

FUEL
There is a network of petrol (gas) stations across Ireland, selling super unleaded, unleaded and diesel. Fuel is more expensive in the North than in the South—a litre of unleaded costs around €1.25 in the Republic and £1.20 in Northern Ireland.

PARKING
In Dublin and the Republic
Dublin is divided into five tariff zones, with the tariffs displayed on 'Pay & Display' machines. Zones are colour coded and you can tell the zone by the coloured strip on Pay & Display street signs and machines. The hourly rate varies from €1.02 in the blue zone to €2.50 in the yellow zone (heart of the city). The maximum parking time is 3 hours and fees apply from 7am to 7pm Monday

to Saturday and 2pm to 6pm on Sundays, although in some streets you have to pay after 7pm and at weekends. Signs and the ticket machine will give information for that street. Parking in a Dublin city centre parking area costs €3 an hour.

In other parts of the country, there are parking areas as well as disc parking schemes, where you buy a disc in a newsagents, scratch off the time, day, date and year and leave it on display inside your car. Discs are only valid in the area where they are bought.

IN BELFAST
» There are several NCP parking areas in Belfast (Castle Court, Victoria Centre, Montgomery Street and Great Northern) that charge about £1.50 an hour.
» If you park in the street, you have to put money in a meter (£1 an hour), and the maximum stay is usually only an hour. Evenings and Sundays are usually free but there are exceptions, so check the signs.

WHERE NOT TO PARK
» Parking is restricted where there is a single yellow line painted by the roadside and prohibited on double yellow lines.
» Do not park at a bus stop, in a bus lane, on a pedestrian crossing or where there are school entrance markings.
» If you are illegally parked, you risk a fine, having wheels clamped or the car towed away. If your car is towed, there's a release fee which can be as much as €125 (£280 in NI).

CAR BREAKDOWN AND ACCIDENTS
Emergency breakdown assistance is normally provided as part of a car rental, so check your documentation or the car key ring for the number to call. If you bring your own car to Ireland, check if membership of an automobile association in your home country entitles you to reciprocal assistance from a British or Irish organization.

BREAKDOWN ORGANIZATIONS

ORGANIZATION	TELEPHONE NUMBERS	WEBSITE
The Automobile Association of Ireland (AA) Republic—56 Drury Street, Dublin 2	01 617 9999 (general enquiries), 01 617 9977 (to become a member), 1800 66778 for 24-hour rescue assistance service	www.aaireland.ie
The Automobile Association (AA) Northern Ireland	0870 600 0371 (general enquiries), 0800 667788 (breakdown assistance)	www.theAA.com
The Royal Automobile Club (RAC) Republic—RAC House, 232 Lower Rathmines Road, Dublin 6	1800 805 498 or 01 412 5500 (to become a member)	www.rac.ie
The Royal Automobile Club (RAC) Northern Ireland	0870 572 2722 (general enquiries), 0800 828282 (breakdown assistance)	www.rac.co.uk

TRAFFIC INFORMATION

» Phone: AA Roadwatch Traffic Information line, tel 1550 131811 (Republic) or 09003 401100 (Northern Ireland). Calls cost €0.79/£0.60 per minute, www.aaireland.ie

» Website: www.aaroadwatch.ie Updated every few minutes, this site gives latest road conditions, parking availability and local weather, and has a route planner for Ireland, the UK and Europe.

» Radio: Traffic reports are on RTE1, 2FM, Lyric FM and Today FM.

TIPS

» Avoid driving into or out of Dublin during the rush hour.

» Invest in a detailed road map, particularly for the Republic. The AA produces three detailed road maps—the Touring Map of Southern Ireland (scale 1:250,000), the Road Map Ireland (scale 1:300,000) and the Road Atlas Ireland (scale 1:200,000), all of which are very clear.

» Allow plenty of time for your journey and be patient. Country roads can be narrow and may have slow-moving agricultural vehicles and few passing places.

» Don't overload your car. As well as being unsafe, it may invalidate your insurance.

» Ireland is generally safe but as always, do not leave valuables in your car.

» Dogs can be a small-town hazard—watch for them sleeping in the road.

» Sheep may stray onto the road on unfenced hills.

DRIVING DISTANCES AND JOURNEY TIMES

This chart below gives the distances in kilometres (green) and duration in hours and minutes (blue; hours are given in the larger number) of a car journey between key towns. The times are based on average driving speeds using the fastest roads. They do not allow for delays or rest breaks.

From \ To	Armagh	Athlone	Belfast	Cork	Derry/Londonderry	Donegal	Drogheda	Dublin	Dundalk	Dún Laoghaire	Galway	Kilkenny	Killarney	Larne	Limerick	Rosslare Harbour	Shannon Airport	Sligo	Waterford	Westport	Wexford
Armagh		222	049	516	142	202	112	150	047	205	333	329	542	117	409	407	415	210	357	334	354
Athlone	158		311	314	332	242	159	148	205	204	118	152	324	339	151	307	154	146	232	205	254
Belfast	66	224		539	136	232	135	213	110	228	423	351	618	030	444	429	504	240	420	405	416
Cork	395	218	425		643	548	408	338	429	348	302	207	119	606	134	256	153	451	152	416	244
Derry/Londonderry	114	233	115	449		107	247	325	223	340	400	501	652	142	517	542	507	200	530	324	529
Donegal	135	182	187	399	74		305	326	243	345	257	432	549	243	413	538	404	056	513	221	525
Drogheda	90	132	119	307	193	189		043	026	058	316	221	449	203	316	259	336	257	249	337	246
Dublin	139	125	168	261	242	219	50		104	019	305	151	420	241	246	218	306	302	220	338	205
Dundalk	53	150	83	342	159	179	36	85		118	322	242	508	137	335	320	354	240	310	341	307
Dún Laoghaire	149	140	178	266	252	229	60	10	95		320	200	428	255	255	205	315	317	223	353	152
Galway	241	91	307	206	278	205	226	219	244	233		232	304	451	128	402	118	200	312	118	350
Kilkenny	257	122	287	148	348	305	169	123	204	128	170		250	420	150	130	209	336	040	345	118
Killarney	385	228	436	90	459	408	354	309	353	314	216	195		646	136	351	155	453	247	418	339
Larne	100	259	36	460	120	182	154	203	117	212	341	327	471		512	457	532	308	447	433	444
Limerick	276	119	327	103	369	296	245	199	244	205	104	121	112	361		250	020	317	146	242	238
Rosslare Harbour	293	200	323	203	397	384	205	154	240	147	260	91	266	357	200		310	451	104	510	015
Shannon Airport	293	134	359	126	357	284	269	223	268	228	92	145	135	394	24	223		307	206	232	258
Sligo	147	118	202	335	137	64	200	214	169	228	141	241	344	236	232	320	220		416	124	438
Waterford	301	169	331	129	392	353	213	167	248	166	217	48	192	365	126	74	149	289		425	052
Westport	249	144	304	286	238	166	254	258	267	272	82	249	295	338	183	345	171	102	296		457
Wexford	279	186	308	189	382	370	190	140	225	132	247	78	253	343	186	16	210	305	61	331	

TRAINS

All train services in the Republic are run by Iarnród Éireann and by Northern Ireland Railways (Translink) in Northern Ireland. The network does not cover the whole country. For example, there is no railway line that covers the west coast, and no service at all in Donegal or the far southwest of the country, although the east coast of the island is well served. The good news is that journey times are short with almost all journeys less than 4 hours long.

REPUBLIC OF IRELAND

Over the last few years some €1.3 billion have been invested in the rail network in the Republic, operated by the national rail company Iarnród Éireann. This has resulted in the modernization of stations such as Heuston and Connolly in Dublin, which are now bright, airy and passenger-friendly. From Connolly station you can get trains to Belfast (▷ 53, The Enterprise Dublin–Belfast), Wexford, Rosslare Europort and Sligo and from Heuston there are services to such destinations as Galway, Limerick, Cork, Waterford and Westport.

BUYING A TICKET

Tickets can be purchased from the ticket office in the station, online at www.irishrail.ie or from one of the automatic ticket vending machines at Connolly, Tara Street and Pearse stations in Dublin. These machines have instructions in English, Irish, Spanish, German and French and accept cash and credit cards (Eurocard/Master Card, Laser and Visa). On most routes a day return costs the same amount as or only slightly more than a single, so avoid buying single tickets if you can. You can upgrade to first class on some services for an extra €10 for each journey.

Timetables and fares
Tel 01 836 6222 (Mon–Sat 9–6, Sun and public holidays 10–6).

Travel Centre
35 Lower Abbey Street, Dublin; www.irishrail.ie

NORTHERN IRELAND

Translink runs all of the public transport in Northern Ireland, including Northern Ireland Railways. There are four lines, all originating in Belfast, with services to Derry, Portadown

JOURNEY TIMES FROM DUBLIN		
The journey times below are approximate, and are for journeys from Dublin. All services are operated by Iarnród Éireann apart from the Dublin to Belfast route which is jointly run by Iarnród Éireann and Northern Ireland Railways.		
TO	**JOURNEY TIME**	**TIMETABLE INFORMATION**
Ballina	3 hours 45 min	01 805 4299
Belfast	2 hours 5 min	01 805 4277
Cork	2 hours 40 min	01 805 4200
Galway	2 hours 40 min	01 805 4222
Killarney/Tralee	3 hours 50 min	01 805 4266
Limerick	1 hour 40 min	01 805 4211
Rosslare Europort	3 hours	01 805 4288
Sligo	3 hours 5 min	01 805 4255
Waterford	2 hours 40 min	01 805 4233
Westport	3 hours 35 min	01 805 4244

(south of the capital), Bangor (east) and Larne harbour. All trains are totally non-smoking. The Belfast to Derry service takes about 2 hours and costs £9.80 for an adult single and £14 for a day return.

BUYING A TICKET
Tickets can be purchased from Great Victoria Street or Central stations, via the website www.translink.co.uk or by telephone 028 9089 9409.

CONTACT DETAILS
Translink timetable information
Tel 028 9066 6630; www.translink.co.uk (daily 7am–8pm).
First-class reservations only
Tel 028 9089 9409 (Mon–Sat 9–5).

THE ENTERPRISE
DUBLIN–BELFAST
The popular Dublin to Belfast route is jointly run by Iarnród Éireann and Northern Ireland's Translink. The service, known as the Enterprise, runs between Connolly station in Dublin and Central station in Belfast, and takes 2 hours and 5 minutes. From Dublin there are eight trains a day Monday to Thursday and Saturday, nine on Friday and five on Sunday. From Belfast there are 10 trains a day Monday to Friday, nine on Saturday and five on Sunday.

Standard adult tickets cost €36 for a single midweek, €38 for a day return midweek and €52 for an open return; you must use the return portion of your ticket within a month. You can pay a supplement of €27.50 or £20 to upgrade to first class (known as First Plus) on most trains. Tickets are not available on the train, and must be bought in advance from the ticket counter at either station, or from one of the automatic vending machines at Connolly station, which accepts cash and

credit cards. Your ticket also entitles you to travel on the DART in Dublin between Connolly and Tara Street or Pearse stations.

The entire train is non-smoking, and on-board facilities include a trolley service of snacks, hot and cold drinks and a restaurant car.

The train doors close up to 2 minutes before the train leaves, so allow enough time to find the platform and your carriage.

RAIL AND BUS PASSES	
Irish Explorer Rail	Valid on trains only, for 5 days' travel out of 15 consecutive days. Adult €138, child €70.
Irish Explorer Rail and Bus	8 days' travel out of 15 consecutive days. Adult €210, child €133.
Irish Rover (bus only)	Unlimited travel for 8 days out of 15 consecutive days on Bus Éireann and Ulster Bus. Adult €172, child €94.
Emerald Card	Valid on Intercity, DART and suburban rail, Iarnród Éireann, Northern Ireland Railways, Ulsterbus and Bus Éireann. 8-day ticket adult €248, child €124; 15-day ticket adult €426, child €213.
Freedom of Northern Ireland	Unlimited travel on all scheduled bus and rail services in Northern Ireland operated by Metro, Ulsterbus and Northern Ireland Railways. 1 day of unlimited travel £14, 3 days of unlimited travel out of 8 consecutive days £34, 7 days' unlimited travel £50.
Eurail Pass	This pass is available to non-European residents and should be bought before arriving in Europe (where the cost is 20% higher). It provides unlimited rail travel in 20 European countries, including the Republic of Ireland. Passes are available for periods of travel from 10 days to three months.
Inter Rail Pass	Available to European residents only, this pass gives up to 50% off trains in Ireland, but is only worth buying if you plan to travel by train in several European countries, and not just around Ireland. You can buy the pass at train stations in participating European countries; www.interrailnet.com

LONG-DISTANCE BUSES

All buses in the Republic, apart from buses in Dublin, are run by Bus Éireann. In Northern Ireland, cross-country services are operated by Ulsterbus, which is owned by Translink. Despite the fact that Ireland is relatively small, some bus journeys can seem disproportionately long (for example the Cork to Sligo journey takes 7 hours), because you have to change once or even twice. For this reason, if you are going any distance, investigate all of your options; it will be faster to take a train, an internal flight, or rent a car, although it will almost certainly be cheaper to go by bus. If you are getting around the island by public transport, consider buying a pass such as the Emerald Card which gives you unlimited travel on buses and trains in the Republic and Northern Ireland (▷ 53). Students who are holders of an ISIC card are entitled to a reduction.

Popular routes have several services a day: For example, there are 17 buses a day from Dublin to Galway and 13 from Dublin to Limerick; you can take a bicycle on many services for about €10.50.

MAIN BUS STATIONS

The bus stations below have a ticket office, information, refreshments, a newsagent, payphones, an ATM, toilets (at least one for people with disabilities) and a baby-changing room. Busáras also has luggage lockers. Neither of the Belfast stations has luggage facilities, but you can leave bags at the Belfast Welcome Centre on Donegall Place.

Dublin

Busáras: Store Street, Dublin Tel 01 836 6111 (timetable); ticket office open Mon–Sat 8.30–7, Sun 9–7.

Belfast

Europa Buscentre: tel 028 9066 6630 (timetable); ticket office open Mon–Sat 7.30–6.30, Sun 9.30–5.30.
Laganside Buscentre: tel 028 9066 6630 (timetable); ticket office open Mon–Fri 8.30–5.45.

Useful contacts

Bus Éireann: tel 01 836 6111; www.buseireann.ie
Ulster Bus (Translink): tel 028 9066 6630; www.translink.co.uk

BUS PASSES

» **Open Road:** (Republic) Bus only unlimited travel on all Bus Éireann services from 3- to 15-day periods from €49.
» **Irish Rover:** (all Ireland) Bus only 3-day Rover adult €76, child €44; 8-day Rover adult €158, child €87; 15-day Rover adult €255, child €138.
» **Irish Explorer:** (Republic) Rail and bus 8-day Explorer adult €210, child €133.
» **Emerald Card:** (all Ireland) Rail and bus 8-day Emerald Card adult €248, child €124; 15-day adult €426, child €213.
» **Freedom of Northern Ireland:** (NI) Travel on all Translink transport in Northern Ireland including city buses, long-distance buses and trains. Adult prices: 1 day £14, 3 out of 8 consecutive days £34, unlimited travel for 7 days £50.

BUSES TO BRITAIN

Bus Éireann operates occasional services to cities in Britain (Glasgow, Leeds, Manchester, Birmingham, London) in conjunction with the British long-distance bus company National Express (Eurolines).

To reserve, contact Bus Éireann (tel 01 836 6111; www.buseireann.ie) or Eurolines (tel 01582 404511; www.eurolines.ie).

An example is the 861 service, which leaves Dublin Busáras at 10am, sails with Stena Line ferries at 11.10am and arrives at London's Victoria bus station at 8.45pm.

Ticket prices start at €34, but phone or check the website for current information.

INTER-CITY ROUTES				
FROM	TO	JOURNEY TIME	ADULT SINGLE	ADULT MONTHLY RETURN
Belfast	Derry	1 hour 40 min	£9.00	£13.00
Cork	Dublin	4 hours 25 min	€10.50	€18.00
Cork	Limerick	1 hour 50 min	€13.20	€21.61
Cork	Sligo	7 hours	€22.50	€36.00
Cork	Waterford	2 hours 15 min	€14.40	€21.60
Dublin	Belfast	2 hours 35 min	€14.00	€20.00
Dublin	Derry	4 hours	€19.50	€26.00
Dublin	Donegal	4 hours 15 min	€17.50	€27.00
Dublin	Limerick	3 hours 40 min	€12.50	€20.50
Galway	Belfast	6 hours 40 min	€27.00	€40.50
Galway	Sligo	2 hours 30 min	€12.20	€19.80
Limerick	Galway	2 hours 20 min	€16.20	€26.60
Waterford	Wexford	1 hour	€10.80	€17.10

FLIGHTS WITHIN THE ISLAND

Ireland's compact size means that taking flights within the Republic or between the Republic and Northern Ireland is not usually necessary; Irish people generally drive or take some form of surface public transport between towns. When deciding on your transport options between towns, you should take into consideration the time and cost of getting to and from the airports at each end, and how far in advance of the flight you need to check in. It's quite possible that the total time will not be much less than the journey time on the train. A one-way ticket from Dublin to Donegal (flight time around 50 minutes) on Aer Arann costs about €40 including taxes. A one-way ticket from Dublin to Galway (flight time 45 minutes) costs from €35 including taxes.

AIRPORT FACILITIES

Facilities at regional airports are fairly limited, although usually include somewhere to eat, a taxi stand and an ATM. Regional airports benefit in particular from flights operated by budget airlines, and are increasing their facilities as passenger numbers grow. To find out more about the airports you are flying to and from, see the websites listed above right, or make enquiries when you make your reservation. See also ▷ 44–46.

FLIGHTS WITHIN THE ISLAND		
FROM	**TO**	**AIRLINE**
Dublin	Cork	Aer Arann
Dublin	City of Derry	British Airways (Logan Air)
Dublin	Donegal	Aer Arann
Dublin	Kerry	Aer Arann
Dublin	Knock	Aer Arann
Dublin	Galway	Aer Arann
Dublin	Shannon	Aer Lingus
Dublin	Sligo	Aer Arann
Connemara	Aran Islands	Aer Arann Islands

REGIONAL AIRPORTS		
AIRPORT	**TELEPHONE**	**WEBSITE**
Aran Islands	091 593034	www.aerarannislands.ie
Belfast City	0871 855 4274	www.belfastcityairport.com
City of Derry	028 7181 0784	www.cityofderryairport.com
Connemara	091 593034	www.aerarannislands.ie
Donegal	074 954 8284	www.donegalairport.ie
Galway	091 755 569	www.galwayairport.com
Kerry	066 976 4644	www.kerryairport.com
Knock	1850 672 222	www.knockairport.com
Sligo	071 91 68280	www.sligoairport.com
Waterford	051 846 600	www.flywaterford.com

AIRLINES OPERATING REGIONAL FLIGHTS		
AIRLINE	**TELEPHONE**	**WEBSITE**
Aer Arann	00 353 818 210 210 (International)	www.aerarann.ie
	0870 876 7676 (UK)/0818 210 210 (Republic)	
Aer Arann Islands	091 593 034 (Republic)	www.aerarannislands.ie
Aer Lingus	0870 876 5000 (UK)/0818 365 000 (Republic)	www.aerlingus.com
Logan Air (British Airways)	0870 850 9850 (UK)	www.ba.com/www.loganair.co.uk
Ryanair	0871 246 0000 (UK)/0818 303030 (Republic)	www.ryanair.com

FERRIES

You can take ferries to many of the islands off the coast of Ireland, to cross a lough (lake) or simply to cross a narrow stretch of water, saving yourself a long drive. Some of these services run only in the summer and may be disrupted in bad weather. For most journeys it's not necessary to reserve because you buy your ticket on board or on the quay. Prices range from €5 to €25.

FERRIES ON LAKES

» **Lough Derg:** Boats go from Mountshannon to Holy Island on Lough Derg; tel 061 921351.

» **Lough Erne:** Erne tours depart from Enniskillen at the south of Lower Lough Erne (May to September) and take in the monastic site on Devenish Island; tel 028 6632 3110; www.fermanaghlakelands.com

» **Lough Foyle:** Foyle Cruise Line runs day and evening tours on Lough Foyle; tel 028 7136 2857; www. foylecruiseline.com

» **Lough Neagh:** *Maid of Antrim* (tel 028 2582 2159; Apr–Oct) and Master McGrá Cruises (tel 028 3832 7573; Apr–Oct) offer trips on Lough Neagh.

FERRY SERVICES

TO	FROM	CONTACT DETAILS
Republic of Ireland		
Aran Islands (Oileáin Árann)	Rossaveal	Arandirect, 091 566535; www.arandirect.com
Aran Islands (Oileáin Árann)	Galway	O'Brien Shipping, 091 567676; www.doolinferries.com
Aran Islands (Oileáin Árann)	Doolin	Doolin Ferries, 065 707 4455; www.doolinferries.com
Arranmore Island (Árainn Mhór)	Burtonport (Ailt an Chorráin)	074 952 0532; www.arranmore.ferry.com
Ballyhack	Passage East	The Passage East Ferry Company, 051 382 480
Baltimore	Schull	West Cork Coastal Cruises, 028 39153; www.westcorkcoastalcruises.com
Bere Island	Castletownbere	Murphy's Ferry Service, 027 75014; www.murphysferry.com
Blasket Island (Na Blascaodai)	Dunquin (Dún Chaoin),	066 915 4864 Dingle (An Daingean)
Cape Clear Island	Baltimore	Cape Clear Ferry, 028 39159 or 086 346 5110; www.www.atlanticboat.ie/ferry-cape
Cape Clear Island	Schull	028 28278; www.capeclearferries.com
Clare Island (winter);	Westport	Clare Island Ferry 098 28288, 098 25212 www.clareislandferry.com O'Malley Ferries, 098 25045; www.omalleyferries.com
Garinish Island	Glengarriff	Blue Pool Ferry, 027 63333; www.bluepoolferry.com
Inishbofin Island	Cleggan	095 45903
Sherkin Island	Schull	Heir Island Ferries, 028 22001; www.heirislandferries.com
Tarbert	Killimer	Shannon Ferries, 065 905 3124; www.shannonferries.com
Tory Island (Toraigh)	Bunbeg (An Bun Beag)	Donegal Coastal Cruisers, 074 953 1320
Valencia Island	Cahersiveen	The Skellig Experience, 066 947 6141; www.skelligexperience.com
Northern Ireland		
Island Magee	Larne	028 2827 4085; www.johnmcloughlinshipping.co.uk
Magilligan	Greencastle	074 938 1901; www.loughfoyleferry.com
Portaferry	Strangford	028 4488 1637
Rathlin Island	Ballycastle	Caledonian MacBrayne, 08000 66 5000; www.calmac.co.uk

HORSE-DRAWN CARAVANS AND BICYCLING

HORSE-DRAWN CARAVANS

For a holiday with a slower pace and a traditional feel, a horse-drawn caravan offers a wonderful way to see the countryside. The caravans, although small, have cooking facilities and most sleep up to four people, but check what you can expect before reserving.

There are four operators in the Republic (in Co. Laois, Co. Galway, Co. Wicklow and Co. Mayo), but none in Northern Ireland. Visit www. horsedrawncaravans.com, ask in any Fáilte Ireland tourist information office or contact the Irish Horse-Drawn Caravan Federation (▷ below).

To rent a horse and caravan costs between €600 and €950 per week, the peak season being mid-July to the end of August. You will also have to pay a fee (approximately €15–€20 a night), to the owners of the place where you stop, which covers parking the caravan, grazing and use of shower facilities.

Before setting off, you plan your route with the caravan provider, who instructs you on care of the horse.

Clissmann's
Carrigmore Farm, Co. Wicklow
Tel 0404 48188;
www.clissmann.com/wicklow

Into the West 2000 Horse Drawn Caravans
Cartron House Farm, Ballinakill, Kylebrack, Loughrea, County Galway
Tel 090 974 5211;
email. cartronhouse@hotmail.com

Irish Horse-Drawn Caravan Federation
Kilvahan Horse-Drawn Caravans, Tullibards Stud, Coolrain, Co. Laois
Tel 057 873 5178;
www.horsedrawncaravans.com
email: kilvahan@eircom.net

Mayo Horse-Drawn Caravan Holidays
Belcarra, Castlebar, Co. Mayo
Tel 094 903 2054;
www.irishhorsedrawncaravans.com

BICYCLING

Bicycling is another great way to see the countryside as most of the country is relatively flat, the temperature is mild (if showery!) and there are plenty of quiet country roads. Tourist offices can give details on where to rent bicycles and have information about bicycle routes.

The Northern Ireland Tourist Board has an excellent free guide called *Cycling in Northern Ireland*, which lists routes, maps and details of nearby tourist information offices. It also publishes a *Walkers & Cyclists Accommodation Guide*, featuring places that provide extra services for walkers and bicyclists, such as secure, covered bicycle storage and a place to dry wet clothes. Tourism Ireland's *Cycling in Ireland* and *Belfast By Bike* brochures both have useful directories at the back.

In Northern Ireland there are two mapped and signposted National Cycle Network routes that follow minor roads and often cut through parks and along river and canal paths. Route 95 is from Ballyshannon to Ballycastle (298km/186 miles) and Route 93 is from Belfast to Ballyshannon (368km/228 miles). You can buy route maps (from £5.99 each) from bookshops or online at: www. sustrans.org.uk. Another long bicycle trail, the Kingfisher Trail in Co. Fermanagh, the first long-distance bicycle trail in Ireland, is 368km (230 miles) long.

ACCOMPANIED BICYCLE TOURS

Irish Cycling Safaris run week-long bicycling holidays all over Ireland from May to September where you bicycle about 48km (30 miles) a day and your luggage is transported to your accommodation for you. The company is based in Dublin at Belfield Bike Shop, UCD, Dublin 4; tel 01 260 0749; www.cyclingsafaris.com

BICYCLING TIPS

» It is a legal requirement that you have a white or yellow front light and a red rear light on in darkness.
» Don't bicycle on footpaths.
»You must have a red reflector clearly visible on the back of your bicycle.
» Lock your bicycle if you leave it unattended.
» Be seen—wear bright reflective clothes.
» Unleashed dogs can be a small-town hazard to bicyclists.
» In unfenced areas, sheep may stray onto the road.
» Take waterproof clothing with you.
» Some roads in the Republic are in a poor state; potholes at the edge of the road mean that you have to bicycle in the middle, which has safety implications.

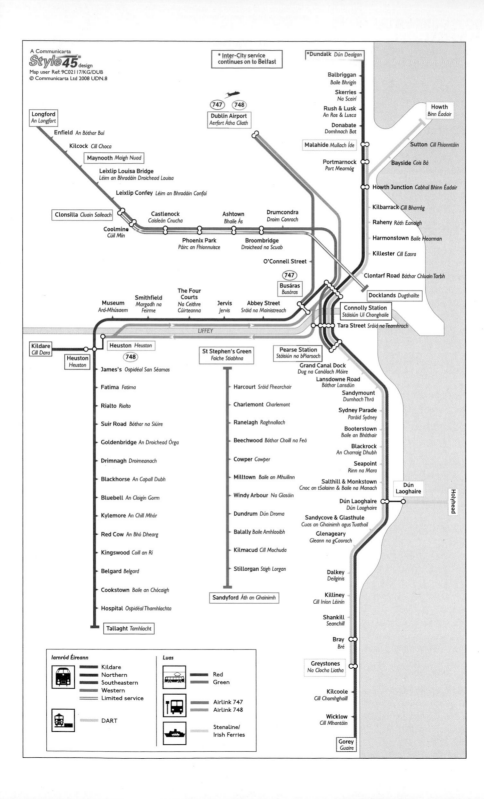

A Communicarta
Style45 design
Map user Ref: 9C02117/KG/DUB
© Communicarta Ltd 2008 UDN.8

*Inter-City service
continues on to Belfast

*Dundalk Dún Dealgan

747 748
Dublin Airport
Aerfort Átha Cliath

Balbriggan Baile Bhrigín
Skerries Na Sceirí
Rush & Lusk An Ros & Lusca
Donabate Domhnach Bat
Malahide Mullach Íde
Portmarnock Port Mearnóg

Howth Binn Éadair
Sutton Cill Fhionntáin
Bayside Cois Bá
Howth Junction Cabhal Bhinn Éadair
Kilbarrack Cill Bharróg
Raheny Ráth Eanaigh
Harmonstown Baile Hearman
Killester Cill Easra
Clontarf Road Bóthar Chluain Tarbh
Docklands Dugthailte

Longford An Longfort
Enfield An Bóthar Buí
Kilcock Cill Choca
Maynooth Maigh Nuad
Leixlip Louisa Bridge Léim an Bhradáin Droichead Louisa
Leixlip Confey Léim an Bhradáin Confaí
Clonsilla Cluain Saileach
Coolmine Cúil Mín
Castleknock Caisleán Cnucha
Ashtown Bhaile Ás
Drumcondra Droim Conrach
Phoenix Park Páirc an Fhionnuisce
Broombridge Droichead na Scuab

O'Connell Street

747
Busáras Busáras

Museum Ard-Mhúsaem
Smithfield Margadh na Feirme
The Four Courts Na Ceithre Cúirteanna
Jervis Jervis
Abbey Street Sráid na Mainistreach
Connolly Station Stáisiún Uí Chonghaile
Tara Street Sráid na Teamhrach

LIFFEY

Kildare Cill Dara
Heuston Heuston
Heuston Heuston
748
St Stephen's Green Faiche Stiabhna
Pearse Station Stáisiún na bPiarsach
Grand Canal Dock Dug na Canálach Móire
Lansdowne Road Bóthar Lansdún
Sandymount Dumhach Thrá
Sydney Parade Paráid Sydney
Booterstown Baile an Bhóthair
Blackrock An Charraig Dhubh
Seapoint Rinn na Mara
Salthill & Monkstown Cnoc an tSalainn & Baile na Manach
Dún Laoghaire Dún Laoghaire
Sandycove & Glasthule Cuas an Ghainimh agus Tuathail
Glenageary Gleann na gCaorach

Dún Laoghaire

Holyhead

James's Ospidéal San Séamas
Fatima Fatima
Rialto Rialto
Suir Road Bóthar na Siúire
Goldenbridge An Droichead Órga
Drimnagh Droimeanach
Blackhorse An Capall Dubh
Bluebell An Cloigín Gorm
Kylemore An Chill Mhór
Red Cow An Bhó Dhearg
Kingswood Coill an Rí
Belgard Belgard
Cookstown Baile an Chócaigh
Hospital Ospidéal Thamhlachta
Tallaght Tamhlacht

Harcourt Sráid Fhearchair
Charlemont Charlemont
Ranelagh Raghnallach
Beechwood Bóthar Choill na Feá
Cowper Cowper
Milltown Baile an Mhuilinn
Windy Arbour Na Glasáin
Dundrum Dún Droma
Balally Baile Amhlaoibh
Kilmacud Cill Mochuda
Stillorgan Stigh Lorgan

Sandyford Áth an Ghainimh

Dalkey Deilginis
Killiney Cill Iníon Léinin
Shankill Seanchill
Bray Bré
Greystones Na Clocha Liatha
Kilcoole Cill Chomhghaill
Wicklow Cill Mhantáin
Gorey Guaire

Iarnród Éireann
Kildare
Northern
Southeastern
Western
Limited service

DART

Luas
Red
Green

Airlink 747
Airlink 748

Stenaline/
Irish Ferries

GETTING AROUND IN DUBLIN

Dublin is a compact city, easily negotiated on foot and if you are visiting for a short time, you may find that you don't use public transport at all. However, if you do need to use transport, there's an extensive bus network, plenty of taxis, open-top bus tours, DART light railway and the Luas trams to get you about.

BUS

Buses in Dublin and its suburbs are operated by Bús Átha Cliath (Dublin Bus). Fares for adults within the city are between €1.05 and €2 (€0.75–€0.95 for children). If you plan to use the bus at least twice a day, a Rambler ticket covers unlimited city travel for varying periods: 1 day €6, 3 days €11, 5 days €17.30, 7 days €21. A family day ticket costs €8.50. Buy them from any news-agent displaying the sign *Dublin Bus Tickets*, from the Upper O'Connell Street office or online from www.dublinbus.ie or www.ticketmaster.ie. If you don't buy a prepaid ticket, you must pay the exact fare in coins (no notes) on the bus.

Dublin Bus
59 Upper O'Connell Street
Tel passenger information 01 873 4222 (Mon–Sat 8.30–6);
www.dublinbus.ie
Open: Mon 8.30–5.30, Tue–Fri 9–5.30, Sat 9–2, closed Sun and public holidays.

CITY BUS TOURS

The Dublin City Tour is an open-top bus tour that takes in all the main attractions, with a lively commentary from the driver. The buses, operated by Dublin Bus, are beige and dark green. Tickets are valid for 24 hours from when they are stamped in the machine on board, and you can get on and off as many times as you wish during that period. Tickets are €14 for adults and €6 for children under 14. There are 21 stops around the city and buses run every 10 minutes from 9.30 to 5, and every 15 minutes from 5 until 6.30 April to September. The rest of the year buses run every 15 minutes from 9.30 to 5.

DART

www.irishrail.ie
The DART (Dublin Area Rapid Transit) is a light railway system which runs along the coast, from Howth, northeast of Dublin, to Arklow to the south. You are most likely to use the DART if your hotel is outside the city, if you arrive on foot at Dún Laoghaire port, or for day trips to one of the attractions en route. You can catch the bright green DART trains from Connolly, Tara Street or Pearse stations in the city; purchase tickets from the ticket desk or a vending machine (instructions in English, Irish, Spanish, German and French) which accepts cash, credit cards (Eurocard/MasterCard or Visa) and debit cards (Solo). As an example, an adult return from Pearse station to Dún Laoghaire costs €3.20 and the journey takes 20 minutes. You need to validate your ticket by stamping it in the machine before you get to the platform on outward and return journeys. The DART can get crowded during rush hour.

LUAS

Opened in 2004, the Luas operates modern trams on two city-to-suburbia routes. The Red Line runs from Dublin Connolly station (where it links to the DART) west to Heuston, then to Tallaght. The Green Line links St. Stephen's Green with Sandyford. Tickets range from a single journey to an annual pass, plus combined Luas–bus tickets. There are ticket machines, taking coins, notes and credit cards, at Luas stops, or you can buy from ticket agents, Luas or Dublin Bus (for combined Luas–bus tickets only). Prices range from €1.50 to €2.20 for a single adult, €0.80 to €1 for a child. A one-day ticket costs €5 (child €2.60); a 7-day ticket costs €18 (child €7.50). There's park-and-ride parking at Redlow, Stillorgan and Balally (€4 per day; €2 per hour, free for disabled drivers); retain your Luas ticket for when you leave, or you'll pay an additional fee.

Luas

Connex/Luas Depot, Red Cow Roundabout, Clondalkin, Dublin
Tel 1800 300 604 (Mon–Fri 9–5) (1461 4910 outside Ireland);
www.luas.ie

DRIVING

Driving in Dublin is not fun, particularly during rush hour, and not necessary—the city is walkable, and there are plenty of buses to outlying attractions. In addition, city parking costs around €3 an hour. For information on car rental, ▷ 49.

BICYCLING

Dublin is a fairly flat, compact city and many Dubliners bicycle to work. The only place you can rent bicycles is outside the middle of the city—take bus number 46a to Belfield Bike Shop, University College, Dublin 4.

Irish Cycling Safaris
Tel 01 260 0749;
www.cyclingsafaris.com

TAXI

City taxis are metered and there are stands outside train and bus stations and at various points in the city. To call a taxi, try one of the companies listed below.

TAXIS	
COMPANY	TELEPHONE
NRC Taxis	01 677 2222
City Cabs	01 872 7272
Budget Cabs	01 459 9333
Pony Cabs	01 661 2233

GETTING AROUND IN BELFAST

The excellent public transport system in Northern Ireland, all controlled by Translink, consists of Belfast buses (Metro), long-distance buses (Ulsterbus) and the train network (Northern Ireland Railways). Translink has worked hard to provide an efficent and integrated network, and you can travel around the city and from the airports to the principal bus and train stations fairly simply.

The Metro bus in Belfast was launched in 2005 and Translink campaigns to encourage people to use their service rather than the car. By 2008, 500,000 passengers were using the service each week with 38,000 fewer cars on the city's roads.

BUS

Pink, grey and white Metro buses operate services that cover most of central Belfast, and blue and white Ulsterbuses cover most of the suburbs. Most buses leave from Donegall Square in the heart of the city. All services are operated by Translink.

You can buy tickets in some newsagents and also at the Metro kiosk on Donegall Square West, which is open Monday to Friday from 8am to 5.30pm. A ticket for a short distance (within Metro's inner zone) costs £1 for an adult single and 50p for a child single. A single cross-city journey costs £1.30 for an adult and 65p for a child.

A Smartlink top-up card is available for multiple journeys. Fares for single journeys can be paid to the bus driver on boarding, but Smartlink cards must be purchased at the Metro Kiosk in Donegall Square West.

» For timetable information, tel 028 9066 6630, 7am–8pm; www.translink.co.uk
» For people who are hard of hearing or deaf, textphone 028 9038 7505.
» For Lost Property enquiries (Metro), tel 028 9045 8345, Monday to Friday 8.45–5.30.

BUS TOURS

Belfast City Sightseeing (tel 028 9062 6888; www.belfastcitysight seeing.com), charges £11 (child £5, family £28) and runs tours in open-top buses from 9.30–4.30, departing every 30 minutes in summer; 10–4, departing every hour in winter, with commentary by highly trained guides. Minicoach tours (£8; tel 02890 246609; www.mimicoachni. co.uk), planned with the assistance of local historians, tour the city's landmarks, leaving at 12 noon every day from 22 Donegall Road.

TAXI

Taxis in Belfast are London-style black cabs, and you can find taxi stands at Central and Great Victoria Street train stations and in Donegall Square North. A reliable company is Value Cabs (tel 028 9080 9080; www.valuecabs.co.uk).

DRIVING

As in many cities, a car is often more of a hindrance than a help in Belfast, as there are many one-way systems, you have to pay for all parking in the centre (usually about £1.20 per hour) and the public transport system is efficient.

There are several multi-level parking areas in the city run by a company called NCP (National Car Parks), and the city authorities have plans to build more in the near future. For information on where to rent a car, driving and parking, ▷ 49–51.

BICYCLING

You can rent bicycles while you are in the city at Life Cycles (located opposite the rear entrance to Castle Court shopping mall), 36–37 Smithfield Market, Belfast, BT1 1JE; tel 028 9043 9959; www.lifecycles.co.uk

You may like to pick up the very useful brochures *Cycling in Northern Ireland* and *Belfast By Bike* from the Belfast Welcome Centre. For more information on bicycling in Northern Ireland ▷ 57.

VISITORS WITH A DISABILITY

Ireland's facilities for visitors with disabilities are improving, and any new buildings and public transport must have disabled access. With some advance planning most forms of transport are accessible, although older city buses are not accessible to wheelchair users.

AIRPORT BUSES
Airlink Express buses (numbers 747 and 748) run by Dublin Bus are all wheelchair accessible. You can reserve wheelchair space on the Airbus service 300 from Belfast International Airport to the city (tel 028 9033 7011).

BUSES
Wheelchair access to buses in the Republic is not good. Newer buses in Northern Ireland (Metro in Belfast and Ulsterbus) have low floors for wheelchair access, but these are not in use everywhere. Of the city centre Metro buses, 70 per cent allow for unassisted wheelchair access. The buses have been designed to assist with other disabilities such as poor vision.

TRAINS/DART
Republic of Ireland
Iarnród Éireann prefers 24 hours' notice from visitors with special needs so that they can arrange for assistance. Intercity and suburban trains are accessible only via a portable ramp. The DART is fully wheelchair accessible, with wide doors and a large open area on board. Guide dogs and hearing dogs are welcome, including in restaurant cars. To arrange assistance, call the station (Connolly 01 703 2358, Heuston 01 703 3299, Pearse 01 828 6000, Tara Street 01 828 6400) or call the Access & Liaison Office (tel 01 703 2634).

Northern Ireland
Trains run by Northern Ireland Railways have space set aside for wheelchair users in each train carriage (car). To arrange assistance before you travel, call the station directly. Belfast Central station 028 9089 9400, Great Victoria Street station 028 9043 4424.

FERRIES AND AIR TRAVEL
Check with the ferry company before you make a reservation. For longer crossings, cabins adapted for passengers with limited mobility are available. If you are arriving by air, advise the airline when reserving if you will need help. Larger airports such as Dublin, Belfast International and Shannon have suitable facilities, such as adapted toilets and wheelchairs to use; smaller airports have fewer facilities.

GETTING AROUND CITIES
In central Dublin, many pedestrian crossings have a beeping noise to indicate when it is safe to cross the road. Some also have a screen counting down the seconds to when pedestrians can cross. Some taxi firms have accessible taxis such as NRC Taxis in Dublin (tel 01 708 9282) and black cabs in Belfast.

HELPFUL GUIDES
» Iarnród Éireann's *Guide for Mobility Impaired Passengers*, with details of access and facilities in stations in the Republic, is available free at stations or by post from Access & Liaison Office, Room 213, Iarnród Éireann, Connolly Station, Dublin 1; tel 01 703 2634.
» *Belfast City Centre Access Guide* gives access information about public buildings, shops and banks for people with a disability. Pick up a copy at bus and train stations or the Belfast Welcome Centre.
» The National Trust's *Access Guide*, with details of facilities at their more accessible properties in England, Wales and Northern Ireland, is available from The National Trust 'Access for All' office, The National Trust,

Kemble Drive, Swindon, SN2 2NA, UK; tel 01793 817400; accessforall@nationaltrust.org.uk
» For information on travelling with a disability contact National Disability Authority tel 01 6098 0400; www.nda.ie
» There's an online guide to accessible transport in Northern Ireland: www.ni-transportguide.com
» For large-print timetables of any bus or train service in Northern Ireland call Translink (Belfast) on 028 9066 6630.
» For information on accessible accommodation, see Fáilte Ireland's guide Be Our Guest available from tourist information offices. Disability Action (▷ below) produces a guide for accommodation in Northern Ireland.

UK
The Royal Association for Disability and Rehabilitation (RADAR)
12 City Forum, 250 City Road, London, EC1V 8AF tel 020 7250 3222
www.radar.org.uk

Northern Ireland
Disability Action
Portside Business Park, 189 Airport Road West, Belfast, BT3 9ED
tel 028 9029 7882; textphone 028 9029 7880
www.disabilityaction.org

Republic of Ireland
National Disability Authority
25 Clyde Road, Ballsbridge, Dublin 4
tel 01 608 0400
www.nda.ie

US
SATH
347 5th Avenue, Suite 610, New York City, NY 10016
tel +1 212/447-7284
www.sath.org

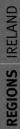

REGIONS

This chapter is divided into six regions of Ireland (▷ 8–9). Places of interest are listed alphabetically in each region.

Ireland's Regions 64–324

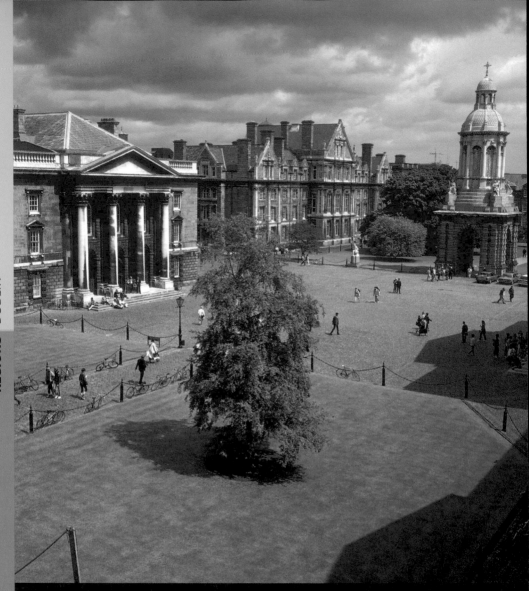

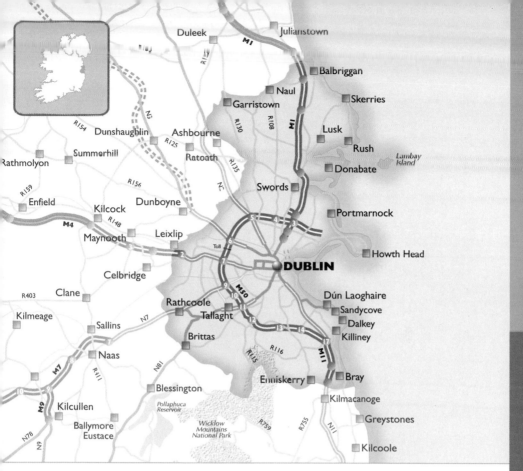

DUBLIN

Situated on the Irish Sea at the mouth of the River Liffey, this compact and easily navigated city takes only a few days of wandering to get to know. In fact, most attractions can be visited on a weekend trip, but rushing around is not the best way to experience Dublin. One of the city's irresistible charms is its welcoming people; it would be a shame not to take time to relax in the pubs and cafés while absorbing the *craic* that is synonymous with the Irish.

When Ireland joined the European Union it initiated an economic boom that flourished in the 1990s—fashion, the arts, food and Irish culture all blossomed turning Dublin into one of the hottest city destinations in Europe. There is something very special about this small city with its split personality—exhilarating and chic on one side but still traditional with an older generation hanging on to pre-EU values, on the other.

Dublin has everything a cosmopolitan capital city should have —excellent shopping, superb museums and galleries, lively nightlife, a thriving arts and cultural scene, fine parks and gardens, and a strong sense of history. Architecture is at its best in the Georgian quarter around Merrion Square and in James Gandon's buildings, such as the Four Courts and Bank of Ireland. Not so long ago, visitors rushed south of the Liffey staying away from the neglected north bank. But a major rejuvenation project has breathed new life into the area around O'Connell Street, and that process still continues apace around the Docks and Grand Canal.

The city centre offers a variety of highlights to visit including the Book of Kells at Trinity College, Christ Church Cathedral and the Guinness Storehouse. To reach several of the main attractions, such as Kilmainham Gaol and the Irish Museum of Modern Art, you will need a taxi or public transport. Or try the open-top bus tours that allow you to jump on and off at significant points en route. Only a few stops away on the DART you can find yourself beside the sea or among spectacular scenery.

DUBLIN

300 m
300 yds

OLD CABRA ROAD
NORTH CIRCULAR ROAD
Ellesmere Avenue
Annamoe Road
Rathdown Road
Grangegorman Road Upper

Glasnevin Cemetery,
National Botanic Gardens

BLACKHORSE AVENUE
Drumalee Road
PRUSSIA STREET
MANOR STREET
AUGHRIM STREET

St Brendan's Hospital

Marlborough Road
North Circular Road
R101
Aberdeen St
Kinahan Street
St Joseph's Road
Aughrim Place
Carnew St
Lower
Ben Edar Road
Niall Street
Arklow St
Ashford St
Finn Street
Swords Street
Oxmantown Road
Halliday Road
Sigurd Road
Aughrim St
Ostman Pl
Murtagh Road
Arran Road
Manor Place
Olaf Road
Sitric Road
Viking Road
Temple Road
Kirwan street
Grangegorman Lower
Morning Star Avenue
Prebend Street
Church Street

Park Gate
O'Devaney Gardens
Moira Road
St Bricin's Hospital (Military)
Brodin Row
Slade Row
Manor Place
Arbour Place
Brunswick Street North
District Court

Peoples' Garden
Infirmary Road
Montpelier Gardens
St Bricin's Park
Arbour Hill Prison
Arbour Hill
NORTH KING STREET
BLACKHALL PLACE
Smithfield & The Chimney
Old Jameson Distillery CEOL

Phoenix Park
Monck Drive
Montpelier Hill
Department of Defence
National Museum of Ireland (Collins Barracks)
Law Society
Blackhall St
HENDRICK STREET
QUEEN STREET
Smithfield
May Lane
St Michan's Church
Four Courts

CONYNGHAM ROAD PARKGATE STREET
Museum
Benburb Street
SEAN HEUSTON BRIDGE
FRANK SHERWIN BRIDGE
Heuston
WOLFE TONE QUAY
VICTORIA QUAY
RORY O'MORE BRIDGE
ELLIS QUAY
JAMES JOYCE BRIDGE
USHER'S ISLAND
MELLOWES BRIDGE
ARRAN QUAY
Stable Lane
Hammond Lane
FATHER MATHEW BRIDGE
INN
MERCHAN

Liffey
HEUSTON STATION
CHEEVERS LANE
USHER'S QUAY
Usher Street
Island Street
Bonham Street
Brazen Head
O'Augustine
P
BRIDGE ST LWR
Cook Stre
St Audoen Chur

ST JOHN'S ROAD WEST
Military Road
St Patrick's Hospital
Guinness Brewery
Watling Street
BRIDGEFOOT STREET
College of Art & Design
John Street
ST UPR

Royal Hospital
Irish Museum of Modern Art
Bow Bridge
Cammock
Bow Lane West
JAMES'S STREET
THOMAS STREET
Oliver Bond Street
CORNMARKET
FRANCIS STREET
Tailo
Ivea Mar

Kilmainham Lane
James's
Ewington Lane
Basin Lane
Echlin Street
Grand Canal place
Portland Street W
Rainsford Street
Crane St
Hanbury Lane
Vicar Street
SREL

Kilmainham Gaol
MOUNT BROWN
Guinness Storehouse
Market St S
Bellevue
School Street
Earl St South
Pimlico
Meath Place
Reginald Street
Gray St
Ash Street
Garden Lane
Carman's Hall
THE COOMBE
DEA

OLD KILMAINHAM
St James's Hospital
Bond St
Newport St
Pim St
Long's Place
Braithwaite Street
Summer Street
MEATH STREET
Ardee St
Weaver's

Donelan Avenue
Fatima
Forbes Lane
MARROWBONE LANE
Allingham St
John Street Sth
Newmarket

Brookfield Road
SOUTH CIRCULAR ROAD
Rialto
St James's Walk
Reuben Street
McCarthy Terrace
Our Lady's Road
Loreto Road
CORK STREET
R110
Brickfield Lane
Ormond St
Chamber Street
Mill Street
Blackpitts

Mountshannon Road
New Ireland Road
Rialto Cottages
Rialto Drive
Reuben Avenue
Lourdes Road
Rosary Rd
Donore Avenue
Cameron St
Fingal Street
Eugene Street
Brown Street South
St Thomas Road
Oscar Square
O'Curry Road
Clarence St
Mangan Road
St Michael's Terr
Hammond St

Uppercross Road
Harold's Cross
Grand Canal
DOLPHIN'S BARN
St Anthony's Road
Haroldville Avenue
DOLPHIN'S BARN STREET
St Teresa's Gardens
Hamilton Terr
Donore Rd
Susan Terr
St Alban's Road
Raymond Street
Greenville Avenue
CLANBRASSIL STR

Dolphin Rd
DOLPHIN ROAD
Rialto Park
Herberton Park
Dolphin House
Drimnagh Castle
Rehoboth Place
Coombe Women's Hospital
Sandford Ave
Merton Avenue
Greenville Avenue

A   B   C

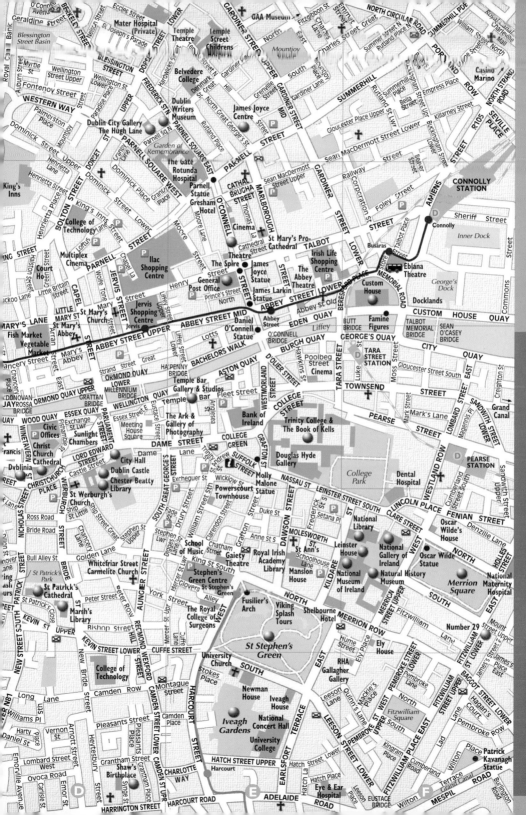

REGIONS DUBLIN • SIGHTS

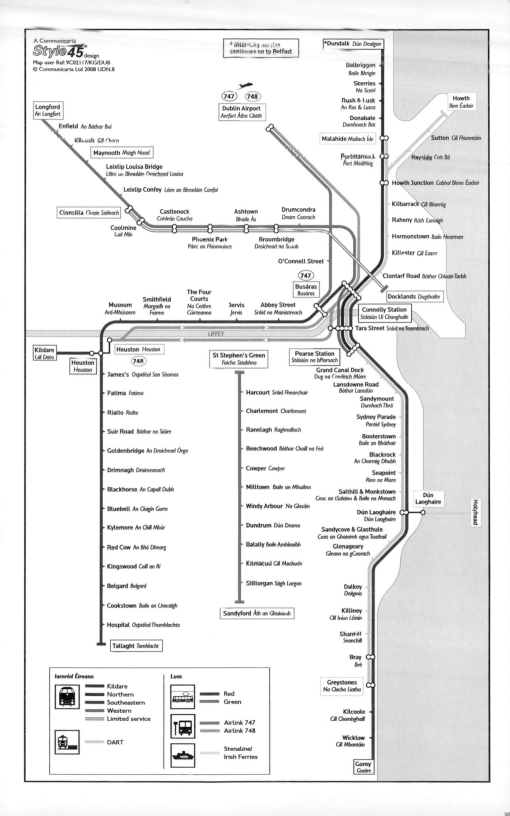

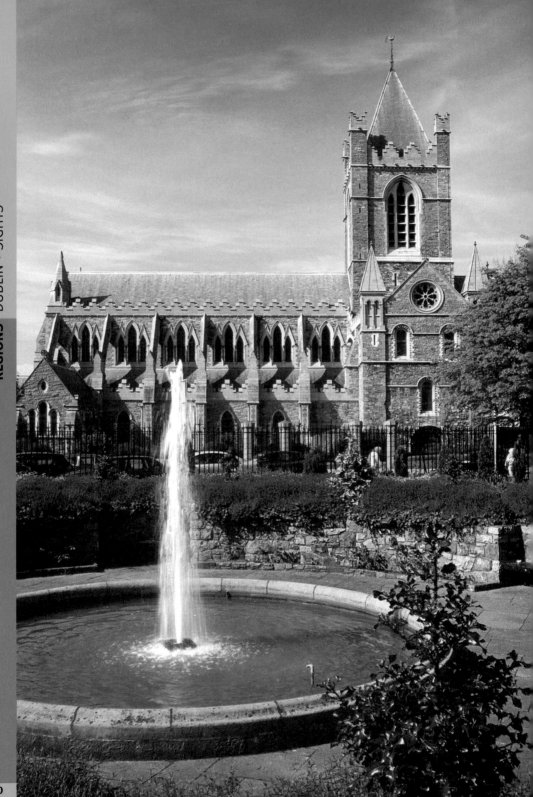

CHRIST CHURCH CATHEDRAL

This Gothic jumble of buttresses and spires has been a Protestant stronghold in Catholic southern Ireland since the Reformation and seat of Irish bishops for 1,000 years. Within its Victorian walls lies a medieval core, and until 1871 it was the main church of the state. Strongbow (▷ 30) was responsible for turning the wooden Viking church to stone in 1172, and his tomb of 1176 is one of Christ Church's oldest remains. The Chapel of St. Laud holds the heart of St. Laurence O'Toole (d1180), archbishop and patron saint of Dublin.

THE BUILDING

Much of the building collapsed in 1562 and had to be rebuilt, but the north wall, now disturbingly out of line with the rest of the building, is original. The transepts and part of the choir retain their Norman features, and there is an impressive eagle lectern dating from the 13th century.

TREASURES OF CHRIST CHURCH

The cathedral's crypt houses the 'Treasures of Christ Church' exhibition (Mon–Fri 9.45–5, Sat 10–4.45, Sun 12.30–3.15). The exhibition, together with the superb video of the cathedral history by Louis Marcus, features manuscripts and artefacts that provide an overview of nearly 1,000 years of worship in the cathedral and nearby churches.

Outstanding among the rare church silver is the stunning royal plate given by King William III in 1697 as a thanksgiving for his victory at the battle of the Boyne. Also on display are the conserved tabernacle and the candlesticks used in 1689 under James II when the Latin rites were restored for a three-month period.

INFORMATION

www.cccdub.ie

🔲 07 J21 🔲 Christchurch Place, Dublin 8 ☎ 01 677 8099 🕐 Jun–end Aug daily 9–6; Sep–end May daily 9.45–5. Check website for times of services 🖐 Adult €6, child free 🚌 50, 51B, 54A, 56A, 65, 77A, 78A from Tara Street DART station; Luas Four Courts 🚉 DART Tara Street, 25-min walk

Opposite *The exterior of Christ Church Cathedral*
Below *Inside the crypt*

CITY HALL

www.dublincity.ie/cityhall

The magnificent Corinthian portico of Thomas Cooley's Royal Exchange of 1779, in front of Dublin Castle on Lord Edward Street, has been the public face of the Dublin Corporation since 1852 and is still the City Hall, their principal meeting place. 'The Story of the Capital' exhibition on the ground floor relates the city's history, while the restored rotunda has statues of various Dublin worthies, and an Arts and Crafts mural depicting Dublin's past. Ireland's first President, Arthur Griffiths, lay in state here, as did Michael Collins after his assassination in 1922.

✚ 67 D3 ✉ Cork Hill, Dame Street, Dublin 2 ☎ 01 222 2204 🕐 Mon–Sat 10–5.15, Sun, public holidays 2–5. Closed Good Fri, 24–26 Dec 🍴 Adult €4, child €1.50 🚌 49, 56A, 77, 77A (from Eden Quay), 123 (from O'Connell Street), 150 🎧 On request

CROKE PARK GAA MUSEUM

www.gaa.ie

That Ireland's capital city should have the fourth largest sports stadium in Europe is no surprise in this sports-mad country. The 85,000 capacity Croke Park will host soccer and rugby internationals while Lansdowne Road is redeveloped. This is the home of the Gaelic Athletic Association (GAA), the governing body of Gaelic games—Gaelic football, hurling, handball and rounders. It fills up every year for the dramatic All-Ireland finals, the excitement of which is portrayed in the film *A Day in September* shown in the stadium's museum. Croke Park plays an iconic part in modern Irish history, not least because of the notorious incident in November 1922, when British troops opened fire on the crowd and players, killing 12 people including Tipperary captain Michael Hogan. The museum explains the different codes (game rules), the political and historic context of the GAA, and you can catch up on missed games through computer-accessed video highlights.

✚ Off map 67 E1 ✉ Croke Park, St. Joseph's Avenue, Dublin 3 ☎ 01 819 2323 🕐 Mon–Sat 9.30–5 (Jul, Aug until 6), Sun, public holidays 12–5 (on match days museum open only to Cusack Stand ticket holders. No stadium tours on match days) 🍴 Museum: adult €5.50 (or €9.50 with stadium tour), child €3.50 (€6) 🚌 11, 11A, 16, 16A, 51A 🚊 DART Connolly, 15-min walk 🎧 Tour of stadium 1 hour

CUSTOM HOUSE

One of the most prominent buildings on Dublin's waterfront, the Custom House was designed by James Gandon and completed in 1791. The classical façade, best seen from the opposite bank of the river downstream from O'Connell Bridge, is 114m (375ft) long, and the huge green copper cupola is 38m (125ft) high. The building of the Custom House marked a high point in the development of the port of Dublin, but it was made virtually redundant only 10 years later when the Act of Union robbed Ireland of her income from duties. Today, the Custom House houses government offices and is closed to the public.

✚ 67 F2 ✉ Custom House Quay, Dublin 1 ☎ 01 888 2538 🚌 Busáras, 5-min walk; Luas Busáras 🚊 DART Tara Street 🍴 Access to staff restaurant

DALKEY

www.dalkeycastle.com

Now a suburb of Dublin, Dalkey (pronounced 'Daw-key') was once an important port in its own right. On its main street the fortified mansions of 15th-century trading families face each other. Of these, Archbold's Castle is little more than a three-floor shell, but Goat Castle contains a Heritage Centre with displays and reconstructions of the town's history, and you can walk around the castle's battlements. Above the harbour stands Bulloch Castle, built in the 12th century by monks from St. Mary's Abbey in Dublin to protect the harbour. Granite quarries on Dalkey Hill are popular with climbers and offer good views.

Boat trips are operated to Dalkey Island, which has, among other things, a Martello tower and monastic oratory. Much of the island is now a bird reserve.

✚ 365 G5 ℹ Dalkey Castle and Heritage Centre, Castle Street, Dalkey, Co. Dublin ☎ 01 285 8366 🕐 Mon–Fri 9.30–5, Sat–Sun, public holidays 11–5 🍴 Heritage Centre: adult €6, child €4, family €16 🚌 59 from Dún Laoghaire 🚊 DART Dalkey 🎧 By arrangement, including visits to Dalkey Island

DOLLYMOUNT STRAND

A tidal lagoon separates this island beach, also called Bull Island, from Dollymount and Clontarf. Stretching 5km (3 miles) and now an important nature reserve, it was created by the construction of the North Bull sea wall, protruding 2.8km (1.75 miles) into Dublin Bay. Before the wall was completed in 1821, the maximum depth in Dublin's harbour at low tide was barely 2m (6ft), but the scouring effect of the River Liffey's waters rushing around the obstacle, has

Below *The Custom House was built on a bed of pine planks to prevent it from sinking*

Above *A visitor examines exhibits in the Dublin Writers Museum*

The house dates from 1762 and the core collection was bequeathed to the nation by Hugh Lane in 1908—2008 marked the centenary of the bequest. A new extension to the building houses some impressive Sean Scully paintings donated by the artist.

🞥 67 D1 ✉ Dublin City Gallery, The Hugh Lane, Charlemont House, Parnell Square North, Dublin 1 ☎ 01 222 5550 🕙 Tue–Thu 10–6, Fri, Sat 10–5, Sun 11–5 💷 Free 🚌 3, 10, 11, 13, 16, 19, 46A 🚈 DART Tara Street; Connolly, 10-min walk 🎧 Guided tours by prior arrangement 🖵 🏛

increased this to 5m (16ft) or more, allowing passage for much larger ships. You can drive onto the sand via a bridge at the west end and a causeway in the middle. There are fine views across the bay to the two Sugar Loaves and the Wicklow Mountains, and an interpretative centre (summer only) illustrates the island's wildlife.

🞥 365 G5 ✉ Bull Island, Causeway Road, off James Larkin Road 🚌 130 (from Finglas); tours run by Dublin Bus 🚈 DART Clontarf Road, 20-min walk 🖵 At Visitor Centre in season

DRIMNAGH CASTLE

Drimnagh Castle hides behind a school complex in the west Dublin industrial estates, but it's worth the search—a medieval, moated castle with a wonderfully restored 17th-century garden. The tower gateway leads into a walled courtyard, a world away from the surroundings. Inhabited for more than 500 years, the castle was abandoned in the 1950s and slid into ruin.

Restoration began in the late 1980s, using traditional craft skills to bring the masonry and woodwork back to their former condition, and 5,500 tiles were specially made for the great hall in 1991. The fireplace is built of English sandstone, a striking effect against the white of the predominant local limestone. Outside, the moat once more flows with

clear water. The castle is said to be haunted by Lady Eleanor Barnewell, who tragically died around 500 years ago on the grave of her lover; he had been killed by Lady Barnewell's father because she was betrothed to someone else.

🞥 Off map 66 B5 ✉ Long Mile Road, Drimnagh, Dublin 12 ☎ 01 450 2530 🕙 Apr–end Sep Wed 12–5, Sun 2–5 or by appointment 💷 Adult €4.50, child (4–18) €3 🚌 18, 77; Luas Drimnagh

DUBLIN CASTLE AND THE CHESTER BEATTY LIBRARY
▷ 74–75.

DUBLIN CITY GALLERY THE HUGH LANE

www.hughlane.ie

This modern art gallery on the north side of Parnell Square may look inauspicious but it conceals some important works by Monet, Degas, Pissarro and Renoir, as well as extensive collections of 20th-century Irish artists such as Jack B. Yeats, Walter Osborne, Sarah Purser, Frank O'Meara and Norman Garstin. The gallery is traditional in its layout, though the Henry Moore figure in the foyer and the bizarre man in a mangle (*The Wringer* by Patrick O'Reilly, 1996) add some three-dimensional interest. Francis Bacon's London studio has been re-created to illustrate the chaotic working lifestyle of this distinctive Irish artist.

DUBLIN WRITERS MUSEUM

www.writersmuseum.com

In a substantial northside Georgian town house, the Dublin Writers Museum reflects the important contribution the city has made to world literature. A portable audio commentary leads you around displays telling the story of Dublin's literary heritage, from the earliest times through to Patrick Kavanagh, Flann O'Brien and Roddy Doyle, taking in along the way Oscar Wilde, W. B. Yeats, Jonathan Swift, George Bernard Shaw and Samuel Beckett. With four Nobel laureates, it's an impressive record.

Notable first editions on display include Joyce's *Ulysses* and *The Dubliners*, and Bram Stoker's *Dracula*. Not so impressive, perhaps, is the collection of memorabilia, which is a little random beyond its literary basis. It includes the phone from Samuel Beckett's Paris apartment, Brendan Behan's typewriter and press pass, and Oliver St. John Gogarty's flying goggles. The annexe has a room devoted to children's literature, a café and a comprehensive bookshop with regular book readings and special exhibitions.

🞥 67 D1 ✉ 18 Parnell Square North, Dublin 1 ☎ 01 872 2077 🕙 Jun–end Aug Mon–Fri 10–6, Sat 10–5, Sun 11–5; Sep–end May Mon–Sat 10–5, Sun, public holidays 11–5 💷 Adult €7.25, child €4.55, family €21 🚌 10, 11, 11A, 11B, 13, 13A, 16, 16A, 19, 19A 🚈 DART Connolly, 20-min walk 🎧 Self-guided audio tour about 30 min 🖵

INFORMATION

www.dublincastle.ie
⊞ 67 D3 ✉ Dame Street, Dublin 2
☎ 01 677 7129 ⏰ Mon–Fri 10–4.45,
Sat–Sun 2–4.45. Closed during state
business ♿ State Apartments,
Undercroft, Chapel Royal: adult €4.50,
child (over 12) €2 🚌 49, 56A, 77, 77A,
77B, 123 ✋ Access by 45-min guided
tour only 🍴 Castle Vaults Bistro in
Lower Yard

INTRODUCTION

Long the symbol of Anglo-Norman power, the Dublin Castle complex is a mix of vice-regal classicism, medieval buildings, modern offices and a world-renowned museum. The Chester Beatty Library and Gallery of Oriental Art contains a collection of early religious manuscripts including fragments of second-century biblical tracts and ninth-century Koranic texts. On view at the castle itself are the fine State Apartments, its Undercroft, showing traces of the Viking fortress that was the earliest incarnation of the city of Dublin, and its Chapel Royal, a neo-Gothic gem of a church built in 1814.

Dublin takes its name from the 'Dubh Linn', the Black Pool at the confluence of the Liffey and Poddle rivers. The castle gardens now occupy that site and their Celtic-design parterre cleverly doubles as a helicopter pad for visiting dignitaries. The castle was built for King John in the 13th century and was renovated for use as a vice-regal palace in the 16th century. The oldest remaining part is the Record Tower, once used as a top-security prison. Red Hugh O'Donnell, son of a Donegal chieftain, was held here in 1592 for rebelling against the Crown. He escaped and, together with Hugh O'Neill, led the Nine Years War. Today the Record Tower houses a simple museum documenting the history of Ireland's police force.

WHAT TO SEE

STATE APARTMENTS

The State Apartments were designed to reflect the extravagant and fashionable lifestyle of the vice-regal court. Following a disastrous fire in 1684, they were remodelled by Sir William Robinson, who also designed the Royal Hospital at Kilmainham. He planned the Upper and Lower courtyards to complement the remaining buildings. From the entrance in the Upper Yard, a guided tour visits the Throne Room dating from 1740, where the throne is said to have been presented to William of Orange to commemorate his victory at the Battle of the Boyne. St. Patrick's Hall is hung with banners of the old order of the Knights of St. Patrick. Its ceiling, painted by Vincenzo Valdré in 1778, depicts links between Ireland and Britain. The apartments, with Killybegs carpets and Waterford crystal chandeliers, are used for presidential inaugurations and other ceremonial occasions.

The Undercroft was revealed when work was done on the Lower Yard in 1990. The city walls join the castle here and a small archway allowed boats to land provisions at the Postern Gate, also visible. In the base of the Norman Powder Tower, the original Viking defensive bank can be made out.

CHAPEL ROYAL

The Chapel Royal (officially the Church of the Most Holy Trinity) was designed by Francis Johnston and is best known for its ornate plaster decorations by George Stapleton and Richard Stewart's woodcarvings.

GARDA MUSEUM

The Garda Museum moved to the Record Tower in 1997. The museum displays uniforms and equipment charting policing in Ireland from the days of the Royal Irish Constabulary to the Civic Guard of 1922 (later renamed Garda Síochána na h'Éireann). The top floor has the best view of the Dubh Linn Garden, and exhibits on the worldwide role of the Garda, working for the United Nations.
✉ The Garda (Police) Museum, Dublin Castle, Dublin 2 ☎ 01 666 9998 🕐 Mon–Fri 9.30–4.30, Sat–Sun by appointment 🖐 Free

CHESTER BEATTY LIBRARY

www.cbl.ie
The Chester Beatty Library and Gallery of Oriental Art houses the collection of Sir Alfred Chester Beatty, a wealthy North American mining magnate of Irish descent, who died in 1968. Chief among the exhibits are the fragments of early religious texts. There are more than 300 Korans, Babylonian tablets over 6,000 years old, Coptic Bibles, Jewish texts, Confucian scrolls and Buddhist literature, with explanations on these religions. The displays and exhibits are supported by touch-screen computers giving more information about the world's religions and the artwork inspired by them. Popular exhibits are the exquisite Burmese and Siamese *parabaiks* describing folk tales and drawn on paper made from mulberry leaves. There are also exhibition spaces here, housing collections of contemporary work. Don't miss the Pauline letters from AD180–200, and the gospels from AD250—the oldest full collections in the world; the delicate papyrus fragment of St. John's Gospel, taken from the Bodmer codex, the oldest New Testament scripture in existence; and the Chinese jade books, engraved then filled with gold.
✉ Chester Beatty Library and Gallery of Oriental Art, Dublin Castle, Dublin 2 ☎ 01 407 0750
🕐 May–end Sep Mon–Fri 10 5, Sat 11–5, Sun 1–5; Oct–end Apr Tue–Fri 10–5, Sat 11–5, Sun 1–5 🖐 Free 🖥

TIPS

» The State Apartments are often closed for security reasons ahead of important events and state occasions so call in advance to make sure you can join a tour.
» The best view of the Dubh Linn Garden is from the roof-top garden of the Chester Beatty Library; if this is closed, try the top floor of the Record Tower (Garda Museum).

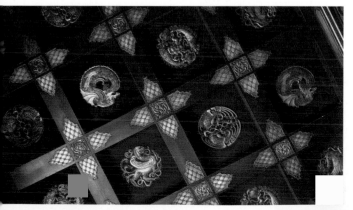

Opposite *Bermingham Hall and the Record Tower, seen from Dublin Castle's Coach House*
Above *An example of Oriental art in the Chester Beatty Library*
Left *Chinese ceiling of the Chester Beatty Library*

DÚN LAOGHAIRE

Part modern port facility and part seaside resort, Dún Laoghaire (pronounced 'Dun Leary'), 13km (8 miles) from central Dublin, is where the Holyhead car ferries have berthed since 1966. The massive stone piers of the harbour were built of Wicklow granite from the quarries on Dalkey Hill in the first half of the 19th century and enclose not only the ferry terminal but also the grand marinas of the Royal Irish Yacht Club. A walk along the piers is a popular seaside stroll of a couple of hours each, and affords splendid views back along the coast to Sandycove, Dalkey island and hill and across Dublin Bay. The spire of the former Mariners' Church dominates the town; it now contains the National Maritime Museum (closed for renovation until early 2009). Among its most popular exhibits are the *Great Eastern* display, the largest ship in the world when built in 1857, and the original optic, worked by clockwork and still functioning, from the Baily lighthouse on the Howth peninsula.

✚ 365 G5 ✉ Dún Laoghaire, Co. Dublin
🚌 7, 7A, 46A, 746 and local buses
🚆 DART Dún Laoghaire

Above left *The Four Courts, seat of the High Court of Justice for Ireland*
Above right *Statue of Cúchulainn in the GPO, O'Connell Street*

DVBLINIA AND THE VIKING WORLD

www.dublinia.ie
Multimedia presentations of medieval Dublin here include the arrival of Strongbow, a merchant's house and the dockside at Wood Quay and a scale model of the city in 1500. There's a wonderful view over the city from St. Michael's Tower.

✚ 67 D3 ✉ St. Michael's Hill, Christchurch, Dublin 8 ☎ 01 679 4611
🕐 Apr–end Sep daily 10–5; Oct–end Mar Mon–Sat 11–4.30, Sun, public holidays 10–4 ♿ Adult €6.25, child (5–18) €3.75, family €17

FOUR COURTS

Designed by Thomas Cooley and James Gandon, the architect of the Custom House farther downriver, the Four Courts was built between 1786 and 1802. A statue of Moses stands on the six-columned portico, flanked by Justice and Mercy in front of the great lantern tower. It takes its name from the old legal divisions: the courts of Common Pleas, Chancery, Exchequer and King's Bench.

This is still Ireland's main criminal court, and public access is allowed when it is in session. What you see now was mostly restored in the 1930s after the building was gutted during the Civil War. It was held by anti-treaty forces and, when the government troops attacked, the resulting fires also destroyed many of Ireland's historic legal records dating back to the 12th century.

✚ 66 C3 ✉ Inns Quay, Dublin 7 ☎ 01 872 5555 🕐 Mon–Fri 10–1, 2–4 when courts are in session 🚌 Cross-city buses; Luas Four Courts

GENERAL POST OFFICE (GPO)

The General Post Office (GPO) building on O'Connell Street would attract little attention in a city of fine Georgian buildings, had it not been seized by Padraig Pearse and his rebel army in Easter 1916. From the steps outside he proclaimed the Irish Republic, then settled down to a week-long siege by the British Army. The building was destroyed, the rebels rounded up and their leaders executed, but the new Irish state adopted their struggle and the GPO became something of a national icon. It was restored in 1929, but traces of bullet marks can still be identified on the outside.

Inside, a bronze sculpture by Oliver Shepherd from 1935 depicts the death of the legendary Irish hero Cúchulainn, and is dedicated to the participants in the Easter Rising.

✚ 67 E2 ✉ O'Connell Street, Dublin 1 ☎ 01 705 7000 🕐 Mon–Sat 8–8 🚌 O'Connell Street buses; Luas Abbey Street 🚆 DART Tara Street, then 10-min walk

GUINNESS STOREHOUSE

For many people a trip to Dublin involves, in some way, a search for the mythical 'best pint of Guinness'. The Dublin brewer's status as a world brand ensures that a ready stream of visiting drinkers arrive to take up the challenge. The Guinness Storehouse off St. James's Gate is a good place to start. Here, an old warehouse next to the vast brewery has been transformed into a cathedral to the creation of this ale.

THE BUILDING

The building was originally constructed in 1904 to house the Guinness fermentation process, in the style of the Chicago school of architecture, with massive steel beams providing the support for the structure. The Storehouse building served the purpose of fermenting this famous beer until 1988, and in 2000, it was transformed into one of Dublin's major attractions. The focus of the building is a giant pint glass, stretching up from reception on the ground floor to the Gravity Bar on the top floor.

THE EXHIBITION

Seven floors of dramatic exhibits take you through the process from the water (it doesn't really come from the Liffey as the legends say), Irish barley, hops and yeast to the finished product. On the way you learn how the beer developed from a dark porter-style ale popular among Irish migrant workers in London to the distinctive global superbrand it is today. Escalators connect the floors in a pleasingly futuristic style redolent of Fritz Lang's classic 1920s film *Metropolis*. The labyrinthine displays include sections dedicated to the transport that has carried Guinness around the world. You get a free pint in the seventh floor Gravity Bar, now reputed to be the best pint in Dublin. The views over the city to the docks and the mountains are impressive. Back on the ground floor is a large, comprehensive Guinness merchandise shop.

INFORMATION

www.guinness-storehouse.com
🔠 66 B4 🗺 St. James's Gate, Dublin 8 ☎ 01 408 4800 🕐 Jul, Aug daily 9.30–7; Sep–end Jun 9.30–5 💷 Adult €15, child (6–12) €5, under 6 free, family €34 🚌 51B, 78A (from Aston Quay), 123 (from O'Connell Street); Luas St James's 🎧 Self-guided 🍴 Three bars and a restaurant 🏛

TIPS

» Use public transport so you can enjoy the free Guinness.
» Visit the excellent Guinness merchandise shop on the ground floor.

Below *A mountain of barrels in this temple to the art of brewing*

Above *Howth has a busy fishing fleet in addition to various boat trips*

GLASNEVIN CEMETERY

www.glasnevin-cemetery.ie

Established in 1832, when Catholics were finally allowed to conduct funerals, the list of occupants of Glasnevin Cemetery reads like a roll call of the key players in Ireland's story from the last 180 years. Daniel O'Connell is commemorated by a round tower standing 49m (160ft) high, Charles Stewart Parnell by a big lump of granite. Here, among the Victorian Gothic memorials, you will also find the last resting place of Eamonn de Valera, a leader in 1916 who went on to be Taoiseach (prime minister) seven times and President of Ireland twice. Michael Collins, Countess Markiewicz, Alfred Chester Beatty and Brendan Behan are among the other names familiar to any visitor to Dublin. There are sad reminders of famine and poverty in the many paupers' graves, and sections devoted to the Irish army and other services. Controversial sites include the grave of Roger Casement (there is some debate as to whether his real remains were returned by the British after his execution for treason), and a plot of more recent Republican activists.

✚ Off map 66 C1 ✉ Finglas Road, Glasnevin, Dublin 11 ☎ 01 830 1133 🕐 Mon–Sat 8.30–4.30, Sun 9–4.30 🚌 40, 40A, 40B, 134 🎦 Wed, Fri 2.30, tel 01 830 1133

GRAND CANAL

www.dublindocklands.ie

An important means of transport during the 18th century, the Grand Canal is now part of an exciting regeneration of the area, which promises to become the new cultural and commercial epicentre of the city. You can take a boat down the canal or walk along the banks stopping to rest alongside the bronze of poet Patrick Kavanagh, who loved this piece of leafy calm. In complete contrast, visit the huge piazza at Grand Canal Dock, which is now a hub of activity surrounded by tinted-glass, shops and restaurants. The centrepiece is a diamond shaped theatre (due to open 2010) fronted by red-glass paving covered with glowing light sticks and green polygon planters.

✚ Off map 67 F3 ✉ Grand Canal Docks, Dublin 2 🚌 2, 3 🚉 DART Grand Canal Dock

HOWTH HEAD

The peninsula of Howth (rhymes with both) Head forms the northern arm of Dublin Bay, and is visible from many parts of the city. It is heavily developed, but the shore itself is mostly cliff and has therefore escaped the middle-class housing that spreads around its central hill. A waymarked path stretches for 8km (5 miles) around the head itself, passing the Baily lighthouse, and makes an invigorating walk (you can catch a bus back).

Howth town is a fishing port, its harbour facing the rocky islet of Ireland's Eye. Boat trips to view its puffin colony, Martello tower and sixth-century monastic ruins are available. The novelist Erskine Childers landed his yacht *Asgard* at Howth in 1914 with a huge consignment of German weapons, destined to be used in the Easter Rising of 1916. Little remains of St. Mary's Abbey except a shell rising above the steep streets of the town, but about 1km (half a mile) to the west, signs to the Deer Park Hotel also lead to the grounds of Howth Castle (not open) and the National Transport Museum. The castle gardens are famous for their azaleas and rhododendrons, and the transport museum contains some lovingly restored trams, buses, fire engines and other vehicles (Heritage Depot, Howth Castle Demesne; tel 01 832 0427; Jun–end Aug Mon–Sat 10–5; Sep–end May Sat, Sun, public holidays 2–5, telephone to confirm; www.nationaltransportmuseum.org).

The best views are from the 155m (510ft) Ben of Howth, near The Summit Inn.

✚ 365 G5 ✉ Howth, Dublin 13 🚌 31, 31B 🚉 DART Howth

IRISH MUSEUM OF MODERN ART

www.imma.ie

Opposite the road to Kilmainham Gaol, a castellated gateway leads to a long drive up to the magnificent buildings of the old Royal Hospital. Based on Les Invalides in Paris this is one of the finest remaining 17th-century buildings in Ireland. A fine formal garden in the French style stretches away on its northern side, while to the west there are smooth lawns extending to the little graveyard of Bully's Acre, where there is a 10th-century cross shaft amid the graves of the hospital's military pensioners. Inside, a small exhibition explains the building's history and the main galleries display current works by leading contemporary artists. The museum's excellent website contains up-to-date information about what is being exhibited when you plan to visit.

✚ 66 A4 ✉ Royal Hospital, Military Road, Kilmainham, Dublin 8 ☎ 01 612 9900 🕐 Tue–Sat 10–5.30, Sun, public holidays 12–5.30 ♿ Free 🚌 51, 51B, 78A, 79, 90, 123; Luas Heuston 🚉 Heuston Station, 5-min walk 🎦 Tours of North Range Tue–Fri 10, 11.45, 2.30, 4, moderate ▢

IVEAGH GARDENS

This lovely park lies hidden behind the huge bulk of the National Concert Hall. To find it, you'll need to locate its only entrance, through a gateway at the end of an inconspicuous looking side street. The gardens were designed by Ninian Niven for the International Exhibition of Arts and Manufactures on Earlsfort Terrace in 1865, and are in three thematic sections. The central parterre, with its lawns, statues and fountains, echoes the Bois de Boulogne in Paris. The southern end has rocky outcrops reflecting North American landscapes. Beside this are a maze and archery lawn.
67 E5 ⊠ Clonmel Street, Dublin 2 ☎ 01 475 7816 🕐 Mar–end Oct Mon–Sat 8–6, Sun 10–6; Nov–end Feb Mon–Sat 8–4, Sun 10–4 🚌 Cross-city buses; Luas Harcourt

THE JAMES JOYCE CENTRE

www.jamesjoyce.ie
Joyce never lived in this restored Georgian terraced house just a few minutes from O'Connell Street but

he did live nearby, in a succession of squalid houses, from 1893 to 1904. You can join a tour of Joyce's Dublin and see the exhibition of memorabilia upstairs, including the furniture from Paul Leon's apartment in Paris, where Joyce and Leon would discuss the progress of *Finnegans Wake* in the 1930s. If you are not familiar with Joyce's work, some of the references will seem obscure, but there is a good introductory video presentation, and a bookshop where you can buy almost everything he ever published.
67 E1 ⊠ 35 North Great George's Street, Dublin 1 ☎ 01 878 8547 🕐 Tue–Sat 10–5 💷 Adult €5, children under 12 free, students €4 🚌 Cross-city buses 🚇 DART Connolly, 10-min walk 🎫 Guided tour, allow 1 hour 30 min 🖥 📖

KILLINEY

This is an affluent suburb of villas and embassies, with exceptional views across the bay to Bray Head and the mountains, and to the north. The pebbly strand is reached through a dark tunnel beneath the DART railway line. From here a bracing seafront stroll stretches 6.4km (4 miles) to Bray, or you can climb for about 30 minutes through trees and gardens to the summit of Killiney Hill.
365 G5 ⊠ Killiney, Co. Dublin 🚌 59 (from Dún Laoghaire) 🚇 DART Killiney

KILMAINHAM GAOL

▷ 80–81.

LEINSTER HOUSE

www.irlgov.ie/oireachtas
Designed by Richard Cassels in 1745, Leinster House is the seat of the Oireachtas, the Irish parliament.

The Dáil (lower house) meets in the former lecture theatre of the Royal Dublin Society. The Seanad (upper house) meets in the North Wing Saloon. Tours are available when parliament is not in session; reserve at least a week advance (tel 01 618 3781).
67 F4 ⊠ Kildare Street, Dublin 2 ☎ 01 618 3781 🕐 Telephone for information 🚌 7, 7A, 8 (from Burgh Quay), 10, 11, 13A (from O'Connell Street) 🚇 DART Pearse 🎫 Admission by tour only, 30 min long

MALAHIDE CASTLE

www.malahidecastle.com
Malahide Castle, in 101ha (249 acres) of grounds, was home to the Talbot family from 1185 to 1976 and incorporates a mixture of styles, from its 12th-century core to the 18th-century embellishments. Family portraits are hung alongside works on loan from the National Gallery. In the stable block is Tara's Palace, a doll's house museum re-creating the 18th-century golden age of Irish great houses at one-twelfth scale (Apr–end Sep, Mon–Fri 10.45–4.45, Sat–Sun, public holidays 11.30–5.30; adult €2, child €1 charity donation). Next door the Fry Model Railway is a reconstruction of a transport system begun by engineer Cyril Fry in the 1930s (tel 01 846 3779, Apr–end Sep Mon–Thu, Sat 10–1, 2–5, Sun 2–6, adult €7, child €4.40).
365 G5 ⊠ Malahide, Co. Dublin ☎ 01 846 2184 🕐 Apr–end Sep Mon–Sat 10–5, Sun, public holidays 10–6; Oct–end Mar Mon–Sat 10–5, Sun 11–5. No tours 12.45–2 💷 Adult €7.25, child (over 12) €4, family €21 🚌 42 🚇 DART Malahide 🎫 Castle by audio tour only, allow 35 min 🍴

KILMAINHAM GAOL

INFORMATION

www.heritageireland.ie

✚ Off map 66 A4 ✉ Inchicore Road, Kilmainham, Dublin 8 ☎ 01 453 5984 🕐 Apr–end Sep daily 9.30–5; Oct–end Mar Mon–Sat 9.30–5, Sun 10–6. Last tour 1hr before closing 🖐 Adult €5.50, child (4–16) €2.10, family €11.50 🚌 51B, 78A, 79; Luas Suir Road 🚉 Heuston Station, 20-min walk ⚐ Access by guided tour only. Allow at least 1 hour plus 30 min to see exhibition ♿ Tours by prior arrangement. Some older parts of the prison are difficult for wheelchair users ◻ Tea room by exhibition

INTRODUCTION

This sinister place is where the leaders of the 1916 rising were executed. Its last prisoner, released in 1924, was Eamonn de Valera, who went on to become Taoiseach, and two-time president. Viewing is by guided tour only. After a video presentation in the basement you are led through the east wing, the chapel, the west wing, then the prison yards. A museum has some grim exhibits illustrating the lives and deaths of former inmates. The tours, accompanied by an enthusiastic and knowledgeable curator, last around 60 minutes and run every half hour. The gaol's history is put in context, not just as a place for political prisoners, but also as a prison for common criminals.

WHAT TO SEE

THE EAST WING

This is a painstakingly restored example of a 19th-century cell block. A three-floor shell, open to skylights in the roof, is ringed by tiny cells opening onto iron lattice landings. From the central ground floor, where the prisoners would eat, every cell door is visible and from the landings observation hatches allow warders to see inside every cell. Unlike older prisons inmates here could not hide in the shadows; their behaviour was monitored 24 hours a day.

THE WEST WING

There's a stark contrast in the West Wing, with its labyrinth of dank, dilapidated corridors and tight, dimly lit cells. Recent graffiti in some corridors enhances the sense of squalor. Connecting the two is the prison chapel, where Joseph Plunkett married Grace Gifford the night before his execution in 1916. They spent 10 minutes together as a married couple before he was led away. Each cell is labelled with the names of the most significant occupants. With risings

Above The main compound of the prison forms the heart of the museum
Opposite top Detail of a sturdy cell door
Opposite bottom The gates are now wide open—for visitors

against British rule in 1798, 1803, 1848, 1867, 1883 and 1916, it is easy to understand the gaol's reputation as the place to hold political prisoners, and graffiti over one doorway threatens the gaolers with the 'vengeance of the risen people'. Charles Stewart Parnell was held here in 1883, in a pleasant suite of rooms that befitted his political standing. Other prisoners were not so lucky and overcrowding was a significant problem. During the famine years, when thousands flocked to Dublin to find food, there were more than 7,000 men and women crammed into the cells.

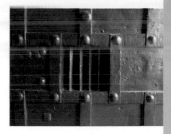

THE YARDS

The exercise yards are where the 14 leaders of the Easter Rising were executed by firing squad and a cross marks the spot where the injured James Connolly was strapped to a chair so he could be upright when he was shot. However, the 1916 rising was not well supported at the time, and its leaders were not portrayed as heroes until much later. In the civil war that followed independence, the Free State government dispatched a further 77 anti-treaty fighters against these grey walls.

THE MUSEUM

Among the grim items in the museum are memento mori of each of the 14 executed. You can also see the block of wood on which Robert Emmet's head was removed following his hanging in 1803. Emmet had hoped to bring Napoleonic firepower to the fight against the British, but it didn't materialize in the way he had planned (▷ 36). On a lighter note, there are many fine banners from the various struggles; a charming home-made selection from the Irish Land League in 1879 declares 'the land for the people'.

TIPS

» Wait for the rest of the tour group to leave before you take photos of the panoptican east wing, the effect is much greater.

» Avoid the busiest times; come early in summer, or later in winter after the school groups have gone.

MARINO CASINO

www.heritageireland.ie

Incongruous amid housing estates, the Casino is all that remains of the 18th-century neoclassical estate of the Earl of Charlemont. Nothing to do with gambling, it was an extravagant summerhouse to complement the now demolished Marino House. Despite its outward appearance, it has 16 rooms on three floors, and a host of architectural tricks retain the exterior integrity, such as drainpipes being hidden in pillars.

✚ Off map 67 F1 ✉ Off Malahide Road, Marino, Dublin 3 ☎ 01 833 1618 🕐 Jun–end Sep daily 10–6; May, Oct daily 10–5; Apr Sat–Sun 12–5; Feb–Mar, Nov, Dec Sat–Sun 12–4 ✋ Adult €2.90, child (3–18) €1.30, family €7.40 🚌 20, 20A, 20B, 27, 27A, 27B, 42, 42C from middle of city; 123 Imp Bus from O'Connell Street 🚊 DART Clontarf Road, 15-min walk 📷 Guided tour only, 45 min

MARSH'S LIBRARY

www.marshlibrary.ie

Behind St. Patrick's Cathedral stands the oldest public library in Ireland. Opened in 1707, and taking its name from Archbishop Narcissus Marsh (1638–1717), the Marsh Library has barely changed. The smell of the 25,000 ancient volumes hits you as you walk in. The farthest room contains the caged reading areas where scholars could view the most valuable of the library's books, but not take them out of the building.

Among the prized volumes on display are Clarendon's *History of the Rebellion*, complete with anti-Scottish scrawlings in the margins by Jonathan Swift, and signed copies of works by Laud, Swift himself, John Donne and Hugh Latimer. The library's guest book includes the signatures of James Joyce and Daniel O'Connell.

✚ 67 D4 ✉ St. Patrick's Close, Dublin 8 ☎ 01 454 3511 🕐 Mon, Wed–Fri 10–1, 2–5, Sat 10.30–1 ✋ Adult €2.50, child free 🚌 49, 49A, 50, 54A, 56A

MERRION SQUARE

From a corner of Merrion Square Park, a reclining statue of Oscar Wilde (▷ below right) gazes across the street to his former home at No. 1 Merrion Square. The gifted writer lived here from 1855 to 1878 in what is now the American College. The house, with its superb Georgian architraves and cornices, has been restored and can be toured only in groups of 25 or more, which must be reserved in advance.

The square itself was laid out by John Ensor in the 1770s, with Leinster House and its attendant galleries on the western side. In the 1930s it passed from the family of the Earls of Pembroke to the Catholic Church, who planned to build a cathedral here. However the cost was prohibitive and the plan was dropped. Many of the fine Georgian buildings around the remaining three sides are still private houses. Daniel O'Connell once resided at No. 58, W. B. Yeats at No. 82, and the Duke of Wellington was born around the corner on Merrion Street Upper. The impressive Georgian museum piece, No. 29 Lower Fitzwilliam Street (▷ 87), is just off the square on the south side.

✚ 67 F4 ✉ Merrion Square, Dublin 2 🕐 Park open daylight hours 🚌 5, 7A, 13A, 45, 48A, 63 🚊 DART Pearse

NATIONAL BOTANIC GARDENS

www.botanicgardens.ie

A few kilometres north of the heart of the city, the National Botanic Gardens line the south bank of the Tolka river. They were founded by the Royal Dublin Society in 1795 and have benefited from extensive restoration work in recent years. The latest project was the Victorian Great Palm House, reopened in 2004. The impressive curvilinear range of glasshouses dates from the middle of the 19th century and was restored in the mid-1990s; they house orchids, ferns, succulents and tropical water plants.

Outside there are 19.5ha (48 acres) of specimen trees, bedding plants and rockeries. The Burren Garden re-creates in miniature the limestone-loving flora of northwest County Clare (▷ 210–211). There is usually something worth seeing here, though spring and summer are the most striking periods.

✚ Off map 66 C1 ✉ Glasnevin, Dublin 9 ☎ 01 804 0300 🕐 Mid-Feb to mid-Nov daily 9–6; mid-Nov to mid-Feb daily 9–4.30 🚌 13, 19 (O'Connell Street), 134 (from middle Abbey street) 📷 Tours by appointment, 1 hour, €2

NATIONAL GALLERY

Forming the western arm of the Leinster House complex, Ireland's National Gallery exhibits an important collection of European art from the 15th century to the present. Established by an Act of Parliament in 1854, it opened to the public 10 years later. With over 2,500 paintings and more than 10,000 works in other media, there is a great deal to see, though obviously not all on display at once. The acquisition of works has been helped by numerous bequests; the legacy of one-third of George Bernard Shaw's residual estate enabled the Gallery to acquire important works by Fragonard and J. L. David, among others.

THE COLLECTION

The interior is confusing, but floor plans help you navigate. Everyone will find their own favourites among the works of Canaletto, Rembrandt, Caravaggio, Rubens and El Greco. There are huge collections of Irish works too, with an entire section devoted to the Yeats family: the work of Jack B. Yeats and his father John Butler Yeats. A popular collection is the portraits of Irish men and women who have made significant contributions to the social, cultural and political life of the country. The Millennium Wing, specializing in 20th-century art and themed exhibitions, opens onto Clare Street and includes a restaurant and shop, contrasting markedly with the quiet Beit, Milltown and Dargan wings of the old Merrion Square side of the building.

INFORMATION

www.nationalgallery.ie
➕ 67 F4 ✉ Merrion Square and Clare Street, Dublin 2 ☎ 01 661 5133
🕐 Mon–Sat 9.30–5.30, Thu 9.30–8.30, Sun 12–5.30 💶 Free, except for special exhibitions in Millennium Wing 🚌 5, 7, 7A, 10, 13A, 44, 48A 🚆 DART Pearse, 5-min walk 🎫 From Shaw Room, Sat 3, Sun at 2, 3, 4; 1 hour 🍴 Two restaurants in Millennium Wing

Above A statue of the founder, William Dargan, proudly fronts the National Gallery
Opposite Oscar Wilde statue on Merrion Square

NATIONAL MUSEUM

INFORMATION
www.museum.ie

NATIONAL MUSEUM OF ARCHAEOLOGY AND HISTORY
✚ 67 F4 ✉ Kildare Street, Dublin 2 ☎ 01 677 7444 ⏱ Tue–Sat 10–5, Sun 2–5 🖐 Free 🚌 7, 7A, 10, 11, 13 🚆 DART Pearse 🎫 Tours last 45 min and depart from main entrance at regular intervals; adult €2, child (under 16) free ☕ Museum café on ground floor 🏛

NATIONAL MUSEUM OF DECORATIVE ARTS AND HISTORY
✚ 66 B2 ✉ Collins Barracks, Benburb Street, Dublin 7 ⏱ Opening times as Kildare Street site 🖐 Free 🚌 25, 25A, 66, 67, 90, 172; Luas Museum 🎫 Tours last 45 min, adult €2, child (under 16) free 🎞 🏛

INTRODUCTION

The National Museum safeguards some of Ireland's most precious and important treasures—gold and silverware found in bogs, caves and burial mounds all across the country and memorabilia from the 20th-century struggle for independence. The Kildare Street site is based around a glorious marble-halled rotunda, and the Benburb Street site is the old Collins Barracks.

The Kildare Street site, opened in 1896, was designed by Thomas Newenham and Thomas Manley Deane, in a style known as Victorian Palladian, with a dome that rises to 19m (62ft). The Collins Barracks, on the other hand, began life as the main barracks for the British garrison in Dublin and were built in 1700. The Irish Free State took them over in 1922 and they remained in military hands until the 1990s, renamed after Michael Collins. In the courtyard-cum-parade ground, you can see 100 marching paces marked against the wall.

WHAT TO SEE
PREHISTORIC IRELAND

The Prehistoric Ireland displays include tools and weaponry from the Stone Age and Bronze Age, with explanations of burial customs and reconstructed graves. One of the most impressive exhibits is the Lurgan Bog Boat, more than 13m (43ft) long, pulled from a Galway bog in 1902 and dated to around 2500BC. There is a huge collection of Sheela na Gigs here too. These weird, often comically sexy, stone carvings of women date from a pre-Christian era. The discovery of Iron Age bodies in the bog at Oldcroghan, County Offaly and Clonacavan, County Meath in 2003 and the subsequent research examining the human remains resulted in a major exhibition. Along with other bog bodies in the collection, the final analysis gives an insight into the lives of the early inhabitants of Ireland. Information on Iron Age burial rituals, along with objects including weapons, textiles and utensils, help to give a picture of life and ritual in Prehistoric Ireland.

ÓR—IRELAND'S GOLD
Bronze Age Ireland produced a wealth of gold jewellery and other items which may come as a surprise to anyone with preconceptions about this 'uncivilized' era. The collection includes gold lunulae dating back to 2000BC, and more sophisticated works made around 700BC.

THE TREASURY
The best known pieces of ancient Irish craftsmanship are preserved in the Treasury. The Tara Brooch, only 5cm (2in) across yet intricately patterned with Celtic motifs is believed to have been made in the eighth century AD of white bronze, silver gilt, amber and glass, and symbolizes the inspirational early Christian design that flourished here while much of the British Isles languished in the Dark Ages. The superb Ardagh Chalice is also from that period—gilded and studded in multi-hued glass and decorated in gold filigree. The exquisite crozier from Clonmacnoise shows the wealth and power of the early church. Be sure to see the rare Tully Lough Cross, the only intact example of a metal-encased cross on a wooden core to be found in Ireland. Located in pieces at the bottom of Tully Lough, County Roscommon, the cross was conserved and reconstructed by conservation staff at the museum. It depicts a human figure between two animals and dates from the eighth or ninth century. The only intact comparison is an eighth-century example at Bischofshofen in Austria.

THE ROAD TO INDEPENDENCE—AR THOIRE NA SOAOIRSE
This part of the museum charts the rise of nationalism in the 19th century then concentrates on the first two decades of the 20th century. The 1916 Easter Rising is heavily represented with a collection of weapons that belonged to notable individuals.

OTHER EXHIBITS
Viking Ireland is explored upstairs, particularly the peaceful trading aspects of the Scandinavians who established their port at Dublin. The Medieval Ireland section feels a bit thin by comparison, perhaps reflecting the decline in indigenous culture during this period. Also on this floor is the Ancient Egypt permanent exhibition. This comprises some 3,000 objects taken mainly from excavations between the 1890s and 1920s, dating from the Stone Age to Middle Ages. A highlight is the beautifully decorated mummy case of Tentdinebu, dating from the 22nd dynasty 945–716BC. There is the rare chance to see some excellent pieces of ceramics and glass from Ancient Cyprus, most of which are from tombs unearthed in the 19th century. There is also a full programme of temporary exhibitions on a range of subjects such as Clothes from Bogs in Ireland.

NATIONAL MUSEUM OF DECORATIVE ARTS AND HISTORY
The striking 18th-century Collins Barracks are the administrative headquarters for all the National Museums of Ireland.

The layout at the Collins Barracks is a little more confusing than at the Kildare Street site, with 13 galleries on four floors around two sides of the central courtyard, but there's a leaflet to help you navigate, available from the reception

TIPS
» Combine a trip out to the Collins Barracks with a visit to Kilmainham or the Museum of Modern Art.
» The Kildare Street museum isn't a large space, and can seem very congested, so try to avoid times when it is most likely to be crowded, for example weekend afternoons in summer.

Opposite *The colonnaded exterior of the Kildare Street site*
Above *The Tara Brooch*
Below *The great hall of the National Museum of Archaeology and History*

Above *Inside the National Museum*
Below *Celtic bronze-work*

desk. The section devoted to Irish Silver takes the silversmith's craft from the early 17th to the 20th century, and another section deals with coinage. It was the Vikings who first brought the concept of currency to Ireland's shores and this exhibition follows its history, from 10th-century hoards to the ATM. 'The Way We Wore' displays 250 years of Irish clothing, and the influence of European trends on local materials. Curator's Choice is an eclectic selection chosen for interesting stories or significance, and includes a wedding gift from Oliver Cromwell to his daughter, and King William's gauntlets from the day of the Battle of the Boyne in 1690. Of particular interest in this gallery is the Fonthill Vase, an early example of Chinese porcelain and highly regarded by the museum. Its well-documented history tracks the vase's travels around Asia and Europe from the 14th century to its final resting place in the museum.

Opened in 2006, in a new three-storey purpose-built space, the exhibition Soldiers and Chiefs: The Irish at War at Home and Abroad, 1550–2001, uses original material including letters, audio accounts and authentic objects to trace the lives of Irish soldiers and the effect of war on the Irish people. The large space enables the display of aeroplanes and armoured vehicles, along with descriptions of the men who have flown or driven them. The social history surrounding the men and women of the armed forces brings to life their time at home as well as in action, from early times right up to date with peacekeeping duty with the United Nations.

On-going improvements and additional building has seen the museum grow rapidly in recent years. The former Riding School now houses temporary exhibitions and a new conservation laboratory has also been added. Further building will accommodate new exhibitions and permanent galleries for the Ethnographical and Earth Science collections.

is suspended from the ceiling, while the giraffe skeleton rises up from the floor below. Also featuring on the top floor are the delightful animal models in glass by Blaschka of Dresden, using refraction in light to re-create the shades of nature. The Natural History Museum, known irreverently as the 'dead zoo', is an excellent example of old-school museum values, showing the preserved bodies of animals with no real attempt at context.

Due to the unavoidable need for renovation, the museum is closed until further notice.

✚ 67 F4 ✉ Merrion Street, Dublin 2 ☎ 01 677 7444 🕙 Check website for latest information 🚌 7, 7A, 8 🚆 DART Pearse

NUMBER TWENTY NINE

www.esb.ie/numbertwentynine
A visit to this well-preserved example of Dublin's elegant Georgian terraced houses gives a clear insight into the lives of the upper middle classes who lived in them. Every room is authentically furnished with items from 1790 to 1820. A short video presentation is followed by the tour, beginning with the kitchen and housekeeper's quarters then going upstairs to the dining room (set for dessert), the drawing room with its Dublin crystal chandeliers and huge windows overlooking the street, and the impressive marble-floored hallway. Upstairs again, you see the boudoir, the master bedroom, and the dressing room, then, on the top floor, the schoolroom and nursery, with toys and educational games.

✚ 67 F4 ✉ 29 Lower Fitzwilliam Street, Dublin 2 ☎ 01 702 6165 🕙 Tue–Sat 10–5, Sun 1–5. Closed 2 weeks before Christmas 💵 Adult €6, child under 16 free 🚌 7, 10, 45 🚆 DART Pearse ♿ Access by guided tour only; 15-min video precedes 30-min tour 🍵 Tea room next to gift shop

NATIONAL LIBRARY

www.nli.ie
In a 19th-century Renaissance-style building on the northern flank of Leinster House, the National Library draws visitors mainly for its genealogical service, helping to trace visitors' Irish origins through the countless records and archives, and giving information about other research facilities across the country. It is the home of the Chief Herald, who can grant arms to those who fulfil the appropriate criteria. The impressive domed reading room counts James Joyce among its historic scholars; viewing is free, a reader's ticket is required for research. Changing exhibitions reflect the library's huge collection. The library also runs the National Photographic Archive in Temple Bar.

✚ 67 F4 ✉ Kildare Street, Dublin 2 ☎ 01 603 0200 🕙 Mon–Wed 10–8.30, Thu, Fri 10–4.30, Sat 10–12.30 🚌 Cross-city buses 🚆 DART Pearse 🎦

NATIONAL MUSEUM

▷ 84–86.

NATURAL HISTORY MUSEUM

www.museum.ie
On the southern flank of Leinster House, the Natural History Museum contrasts markedly with the up-to-date museums that abound in modern Ireland. It is virtually unchanged since its opening in 1857 as the museum of the Royal Dublin Society. The first room you encounter is devoted to Irish animals, starting with the skeletons of huge Irish deer, now extinct. Around the walls, display cases are full of other stuffed Irish creatures, such as martens, otters and bats. There are birds and fish too, and, at the far end, insects and invertebrates. Upstairs, the emphasis is on creatures from the rest of the world. Here on the main floor are monkeys, bears, rhinos and marsupials. There are two gallery floors above this, the first devoted to vertebrates—the dodo is particularly popular—the second covers invertebrates: worms, insects, jellyfish, crabs and so on. A huge skeleton of a humpback whale

Above *Reading room in the National Library*

O'CONNELL STREET

A key thoroughfare in central Dublin, O'Connell Street leads down to the River Liffey and the always-busy O'Connell Bridge. Two of Dublin's most famous department stores are here, Clery's and Easons, and there are busy shopping areas off Henry Street to the west. In the street opposite the GPO rises the Monument of Light, also called The Spire (▷ 20), a 120m (394ft) spike of stainless steel. The site was formerly occupied by Nelson's Pillar (demolished by a rogue IRA man in 1966), and then by a depiction of Anna Livia. The spire was raised in 2002 and, despite problems with its lighting, has become a symbol of modern Dublin. Upper O'Connell Street was originally laid out in the 1740s and was connected to Lower O'Connell Street, then known as Sackville Street, in 1784. O'Connell Bridge, formerly known as Carlisle Bridge, was completed in 1790 and is overlooked by a grand statue of Daniel O'Connell, 'the Liberator', still bearing bullet marks from 1916.

➕ 67 E2 ✉ O'Connell Street, Dublin 1 🚌 Most central city buses 🚆 DART Tara Street, 5-min walk

PHOENIX PARK

www.visitdublin.ie

Often claimed to be the largest city park in the world, Phoenix Park stretches west from Parkgate, near the Collins Barracks, for nearly 5km (3 miles). Within this huge open space, the most visible feature is the 62.5m (205ft) Wellington obelisk, commemorating the Battle of Waterloo in 1815. Nearby is Dublin Zoo, founded in 1830 and one of the oldest in the world (tel 01 474 8900; www.dublinzoo.ie; Mar–end Oct Mon–Sat 9.30–6, Sun 10.30–6; Nov–end Feb Mon–Sat 9.30–dusk, Sun 10.30–dusk; adult €14.50, child €10, family €42). On the northern side of the park, the stately home of the British Viceroys of Ireland became the Áras an Uachtaráin, official residence of the President of Ireland, in 1937. Guided tours are available every Saturday except at Christmas. The park passed into notoriety when the British chief secretary, Lord Frederick Cavendish, and his under secretary, T. H. Burke were assassinated here by a radical republican group known as the Invincibles in 1882.

On the southern side, an area known as the Fifteen Acres is popular for Gaelic sports; Pope John Paul II greeted more than a million people here on his visit in 1979. To get the most from a visit to the park, head for the Visitor Centre, next to Ashtown Castle, which traces the area's history from 3500BC.

➕ 66 A2 ℹ Visitor Centre, Phoenix Park, Dublin 8 ☎ 01 611 0095 ◷ Apr–end Sep daily 10–6; mid- to end Mar, Oct daily 10–5.30; Nov to mid-Mar Wed–Sun 10–5 ✋ Adult €2.75, child €1.25, family €7 **Park** ◷ Daylight hours ✋ Free 🚌 37, 38, 39; Luas Heuston 🚆 Heuston Station ☞ Free tickets for tours (Sat only) of Áras an Uachtaráin from Visitor Centre. No reservations allowed ☕ Coffee shop and restaurant at Visitor Centre

ST. MICHAN'S CHURCH

Unremarkable from the outside, St. Michan's secret lies in its crypt. Here in the dry atmosphere of its vaults, the corpses became mummified rather than decomposing. Guided tours point out ancient remains and bodies of the 18th-century dead, including those of Henry and John Sheares, leaders of the rebellion in 1798. There is also a death mask of Wolfe Tone, and some believe Robert Emmet was buried in the churchyard. The church can trace its origins back to 1095 but the present structure is mostly from 1686.

➕ 66 C3 ✉ Church Street, Dublin 7 ☎ 01 872 4154 ◷ Mar–end Oct Mon–Fri 10–12.45, 2–4.45, Sat 10–12.45; Nov–end Feb Mon–Fri 12.30–3.30 ✋ Tours: adult €4, child €3 🚌 83 ☞ Access to vaults by tour only

ST. PATRICK'S CATHEDRAL

The Victorians restored the largest church in Ireland using money from the Guinness family to reinterpret the Gothic and Romanesque features it had acquired since its founding in 1191. At 91m (298ft) long, with a 43m (141ft) tower at its western end, it is not particularly big by European standards, and until the 1920s it stood amid slum housing, outside the old city walls. Today it overlooks a little park. The church belongs to the Protestant Church of Ireland.

THE INTERIOR

Inside you will find the grave and some memorabilia of its most famous dean, Jonathan Swift. The author of *Gulliver's Travels* became dean of St. Patrick's in 1713. The cathedral organ is the largest in Ireland, and in the south choir aisle are two of Ireland's rare 16th-century monumental brasses. Look for the tomb and effigy of the 17th-century adventurer Richard Boyle, Earl of Cork, and a memorial to the great Irish bard and harpist Turlough O'Carolan (1670–1738).

CHANCING YOUR ARM

One notable curiosity is a wooden door, originally from the chapterhouse but now mounted at the junction of the north transept. Through a hole in this, the Earl of Kildare stretched out his hand to make peace with the Earl of Ormond (▷ 33), the supposed origins of the phrase 'chancing your arm'.

INFORMATION

www.stpatrickscathedral.ie

✚ 67 D4 ✉ Patrick's Street, Dublin 8 ☎ 01 453 9472 ⏰ Mon–Sat 9–5, Sun 9–11, 12.45–3, 4.15–6; Nov–end Feb Mon–Sat 9–5, Sun 10–11, 12.45–3 ✋ Adult €5.50, family €15 🚌 49, 49A, 50, 54A, 56A

Above *The splendidly restored nave of St. Patrick's Cathedral*
Opposite left *Naturally mummified remains in the crypt of St. Michan's Church*
Opposite right *Neon and car lights illuminate wide O'Connell Street*

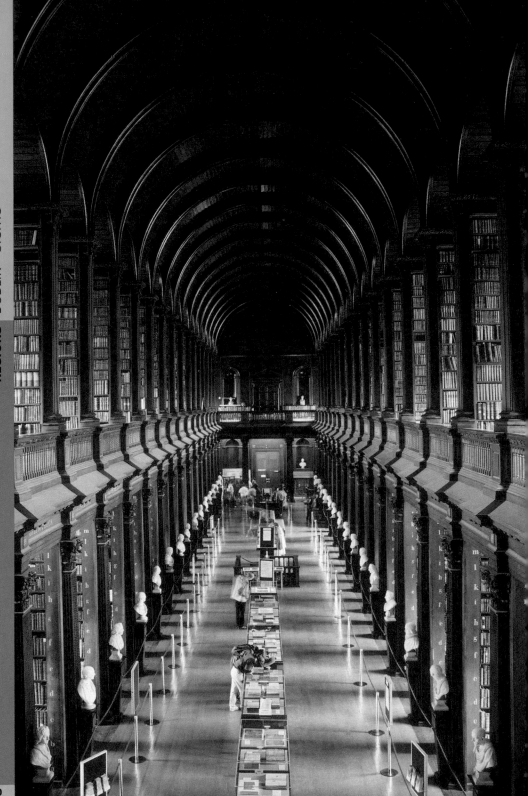

INTRODUCTION

No visit to Dublin is complete without seeing one of the most famous
illuminated manuscripts in the world. The intricate beauty of the Book of
Kells has been imitated countless times, but to see the pages themselves,
and those of the similarly ornate books of Durrow and Armagh, is really
memorable. There is more here than just these revered texts though. The
exhibition 'Turning Darkness into Light' brings a context to the works, and
upstairs the barrell-ceilinged Long Room is filled with the intoxicating musk of
more than 200,000 ancient leather-bound books.

The entrance to the Old Library is through the gap in the square on the right-
hand side. It faces a group of modern buildings including the Berkeley Library,
which was designed by Paul Koralek in 1967. The exhibition is reached through
the shop at street level.

Trinity College is a modern working university and so, unless you visit
on Sunday morning or in high summer, its courtyards are usually teeming
with students and their bicycles. Founded by Queen Elizabeth I in 1592, it is
Ireland's oldest university. Although this Georgian building (1759) is grand in its
own right, its impact is lessened by the proximity of the traffic and the more
overt classicism of James Gandon's east front of the Bank of Ireland across
the road. This dates from 1785 and was added to an older building, which once
housed the Irish parliament.

Past the Porter's Lodge you come out into Parliament Square, with the
chapel, built in 1798, to the left and the Examination Room, of 1791, to the
right. Ahead of you is the Campanile, a bell tower 30m (98ft) high added to
the square in 1853. Beyond it, the red-brick building is known as the Rubrics.
With its origins around 1700, this is the oldest surviving building on the
campus. The playwright Oliver Goldsmith had chambers on the top right-hand
side next to the Old Library. Before the rebuilding work of the 1980s, the
Book of Kells was kept upstairs in the Long Room, and the area known as the
Colonnades below, where the shop, exhibition and Treasury are now, was a
crowded storage area for the library's overflowing book collection. When the
building was originally constructed, this area had been left open to prevent
damp rising into the library. It was filled in to house more books in the 1860s.

WHAT TO SEE

EXHIBITION

'Turning Darkness into Light' is the name of the exhibition in the Old Library
that leads you up to the displayed pages of the Book of Kells. It explains the
context of the book, follows the development of writing and illuminating
manuscripts and has examples of Ogham and Ethiopian scripts. Pages, and
individual illustrations, have been enlarged to the size of a person, so you can
stand back and identify the truly stunning detail of the monastic scribe's art.

THE BOOK OF KELLS

The Book of Kells itself is displayed in a darkened room known as the Treasury.
The book is bound in four volumes, two of which are always on display, so
you are able to see two double page spreads at a time, and these are turned
every three months. It was written, if that is the right word for its spectacularly
ornate pages, in the ninth century AD by monks at St. Columba's monastery
at Iona on the west coast of Scotland. It was transferred to the monastery at
Kells in County Meath for safekeeping during the Viking raids and then its
history is less certain. It arrived in Dublin in 1653, during the Cromwellian
upheavals, and was acquired by Trinity College in 1661. Its brilliantly elaborate

INFORMATION

www.tcd.ie/library/

✚ 67 E3 ✉ College Street, Dublin
2 ☎ 01 896 1661 🕐 May–end Sep
Mon–Sat 9.30–5, Sun 9.30–4.30; Oct–end
Apr Sun 12–4.30. Closed 10 days over
Christmas and New Year 🚾 Adult
€8, family €16 🚌 All cross city buses
🚆 DART Tara Street

Above *Intricate art frames a portrait of
St. John in the Book of Kells*
Opposite *The Long Room is an
atmospheric place with a magnific…
collection of books*

pages reveal both the craft and the wit of its scribes. The text is the four Christian gospels, written in Latin. Each evangelist is portrayed in minute detail and each gospel begins with just a few words on a magnificently decorated page. Some of the pages, known as 'carpet pages', have no words at all, just the swirling abstract ornamentation which has become the hallmark of this incredible era of Celtic art. Also on display in the Treasury are the equally fabulous, but less well-known books of Durrow and Armagh, which may originate from the seventh century AD. They too demonstrate the tremendous scope and vision of the monastic scribes, again displaying an intricacy of penmanship that could scarcely have been visible in that distant age before electric lighting and artificial magnification.

TIPS

» Visit on a Sunday morning in June for the best view of the campus with the fewest students and other visitors.

» You can wander around the main courtyards and admire the historic buildings for free, but remember it's a working university and private property.

» Take your time at the Book of Kells; its intricacy is scarcely credible at first glance.

Above Sphere Within a Sphere *by Arnaldo Pomodoro, outside the Berkeley Library*
Below *Trinity's busy main entrance*

THE LONG ROOM

The Long Room is up the stairs from the Treasury. As in Marsh's Library at St. Patrick's Cathedral, the smell of old books hits you as you walk in. They are piled high to the ceiling, which was extended in 1860 to fit more in. The gallery bookcases were added at this point. The central aisle is lined with busts of scholars and there is also a harp on display, believed to be the oldest in existence, though its 15th-century provenance means it can't be the legendary harp of Brian Boru, the 11th-century High King of Ireland, as one story claims. Another display has a rare copy of the Proclamation of the Irish Republic, as read out by Padraig Pearse from the steps of the GPO in 1916, Robert Emmet's arrest warrant and other papers from the struggle for independence.

ST. STEPHEN'S GREEN

This public park of 9ha (22 acres) was originally a place of public executions and punishments. It was enclosed in 1669, and surrounding land was sold off to property developers. Trees and paths soon followed and Dubliners were charged for access. However, in 1877, Sir Arthur Guinness secured an Act of Parliament to make access free for all, and today it is a popular haven from the din of the surrounding traffic. It includes a sensory garden for the visually impaired. The main entrance is through Fusiliers' Gate on the corner facing Grafton Street.

✚ 67 E4 ✉ Dublin 2 ⊙ Mon–Sat 8–dusk, Sun, public holidays 10–dusk, Christmas Day 10–1 🚌 Inbound buses arrive on the west side of the square, outbound buses leave from the east side; Luas St. Stephen's Green 🚆 DART Pearse

SANDYCOVE

A tiny cove near Dún Laoghaire gives this affluent suburb its name. James Joyce lived briefly in the Martello tower overlooking a rocky peninsula. It features in the opening chapter of *Ulysses* and now houses a museum of Joycean memorabilia: his letters to Nora Barnacle, a 1935 edition of *Ulysses* illustrated by Matisse, a guitar and a waistcoat (vest) (Joyce Tower, Sandycove, tel 01 280 9265, Mar–end Oct Mon–Sat 10–1, 2–5, Sun, public holidays 2–6). Nearby Forty Foot Pool is a sea-bathing facility, popular even in winter, with changing areas cut in the rock. Contrary to the old sign, mixed bathing is allowed.

✚ 365 G5 ✉ 13km (8 miles) south of Dublin 🚌 59 from Dún Laoghaire 🚆 DART Sandycove

SHAW'S BIRTHPLACE

The plaque on 33 Synge Street records George Bernard Shaw as the 'author of many plays', which is how the Nobel Laureate wanted his birthplace to be commemorated. He was born in this terraced house in 1856 and left to go to London in 1876. Inside there isn't a great deal about Shaw himself, but the house has been restored to reflect the life of a middle-class family in Victorian Dublin. Shaw didn't write any of his works (*Pygmalion, Arms and the Man, Man and Superman* to name a few) in Dublin, but like Joyce he drew heavily on his experiences of the city and its characters.

✚ 67 D5 ✉ 33 Synge Street, Dublin 8 ☎ 01 475 0854 ⊙ May–end Sep Mon, Tue, Thu, Fri 10–5, Sat–Sun, public holidays 2–5 ✋ Adult €7.25, child (over 12) €4.55, family €16 🚌 16, 19 🚆 DART Grand Canal Dock, 15-min walk

SMITHFIELD

This corner of Dublin is reinventing itself since its initial redevelopment in the 1990s. You can still find traces of the old Smithfield but modern apartment blocks now dominate and retail spaces are beginning to fill up. The Jameson Distillery is in Bow Street, no longer in production, but tours show how whiskey was made from the sixth century and end with a tasting session (tel 01 807 2355; www.oldjamesondistillery.com; daily 9.30–6; adult €12.50, family €25). The old distillery chimney has a viewing platform on top, 56m (184ft) above the street, via an external glass lift, offering a 360-degree view of the city (tel 01 817 3838, closed for maintenance, telephone for details). Smithfield Square is lit at night by 12 brazier lanterns, each 26m (85ft) high.

✚ 66 C2 ✉ Smithfield Village, Dublin 7 🚌 25, 25A, 67, 67A (from Middle Abbey Street); 68, 69, 79 (from Aston Quay), 90 (from Connolly, Tara and Heuston stations); Luas Smithfield

TEMPLE BAR

www.temple-bar.ie
Promoted as 'Dublin's Cultural Quarter' Temple Bar takes its name from the Anglo-Irish aristocrat Sir William Temple, who owned much of the land in the 17th century. Within this block of narrow streets you'll find countless pubs popular with drinking parties, traditional music, cafés and nightclubs. You'll also find the Gallery of Photography (Meeting House Square; tel 01 671 4654; Tue–Sat 11–6, Sun 1–6), with regular exhibitions; the Irish Film Centre (6 Eustace Street; tel 01 679 5744), showing art-house movies; the Ark (11a Eustace Street; tel 01 670 7788), a cultural facility for four- to 14-year-olds; and Project (39 Eustace Street; tel 01 888 9613), a venerable artist-based venue with a pedigree stretching back to the 1960s when Temple Bar was a rundown wasteland.

By the 1970s the site was earmarked for a bus station, and the bus company began letting out the buildings cheaply to artists and musicians. Temple Bar established a bohemian reputation for its buzzing nightlife, and in doing so won a reprieve from the wrecking ball. The most evocative entrance is over the Ha'penny Bridge (there used to be a toll of a halfpenny to cross the bridge), and through the Merchants Arch. Open-air performances often take place in Meeting House Square.

✚ 67 E3 ℹ Temple Bar Information Centre, 12 East Essex Street, Temple Bar, Dublin 2 ☎ 01 677 2255 🚌 All central-city buses pass Temple Bar

Below *The middle-class home where George Bernard Shaw was born*

GEORGIAN DUBLIN

Stroll back in time passing some of the grandest Georgian buildings in Dublin. You will see many of the best examples of town houses from this period set around the most famous squares in the city.

THE WALK

Distance: 3km (2 miles)
Allow: 1.5 hours
Start at: Bank of Ireland, College Green ✚ 67 E3
End at: Powerscourt Townhouse, William Street South ✚ 67 E3

HOW TO GET THERE

DART Tara Street; Cross-city buses

★ Starting outside the Bank of Ireland (1785) on College Green, a fine example of Georgian architecture, cross the road and walk through the archway into Trinity College.

❶ Trinity College contains some superb Georgian architecture. Within the first square, notice the Chapel (1798), the Dining Hall (1761) and the Examination Room (1791). Other

important Georgian buildings of the college include the magnificent Old Library (1732) in Fellows' Square and the Provost's House (c1760).

Return to College Green and turn left into Grafton Street, a fashionable shopping street lined with Georgian buildings. At the end of the street turn left into St. Stephen's Green.

❷ St. Stephen's Green, originally common land where public executions and punishment beatings took place, is today a haven for visitors and office workers. In the 18th century wealthy Dubliners began to build elegant town houses around the private green. Free entry to all was granted in 1877.

Continue past the splendid Georgian houses with their attractive doors,

balconies and fanlights, passing the 18th-century Shelbourne Hotel into Merrion Row and turn left on Merrion Street Upper. You then pass the Natural History Museum (closed for restoration) and the rear entrance of the imposing Leinster House.

❸ When Leinster House was built in 1745 for the Earl of Kildare, this part of the city was almost open country. Within 20 years it became the most fashionable district of Dublin. In 1814 Leinster House was acquired by the Royal Dublin Society and was finally bought by the Irish Government in 1925 to become the seat of the national parliament. This view of Leinster House resembles a country estate.

Look across to Merrion Square South with its striking Georgian buildings. Continue up the square, past the Victorian National Gallery of Ireland (1859). To your right is Oscar Wilde House, on the corner of Merrion Square North, the first house to be built in the square in 1762. Turn left into Clare Street, then on to Leinster Street South taking the third left into Kildare Street, past the National Library on the left.

4 Seen from this side, Leinster House looks like a large town house and is flanked by the later buildings of the National Library and National Museum.

From here, cross the road to Molesworth Street with some fine Georgian houses including three early ones with huge chimneys known as the Dutch billies. At the end of the street turn left into Dawson Street; St. Anne's Church is on your left.

5 The striking church of St. Anne's was founded in 1707, and ministered to the rapidly growing Georgian

suburbs. The façade was added in 1868.

Continue down Dawson Street to admire the Mansion House on your left, official residence of the Lord Mayor. Turn right into St. Stephen's Green North then left down the west side of the green to the Royal College of Surgeons on your right.

6 A striking building, the Royal College of Surgeons is one of the city's best Georgian houses. Designed by Edward Park in 1806, the college has a neoclassical granite façade and distinctive round-headed windows.

Return to the corner of St. Stephen's Green and turn left into King Street South. Bear right into William Street South and walk up the hill where, on the right, you will find the Powerscourt Townhouse.

7 The attractive 1774 Powerscourt Townhouse is now a shopping mall but still features the original

grand staircase and finely detailed plasterwork.

WHEN TO GO
A pleasant morning stroll or alternatively in the evening when several of the buildings are illuminated.

WHERE TO EAT
There is lots of choice in the Powerscourt Townhouse Shopping Centre, or try one of the many pubs.

Above Oscar Wilde's House near Merrion Square
Opposite Leinster House is now Ireland's parliament building

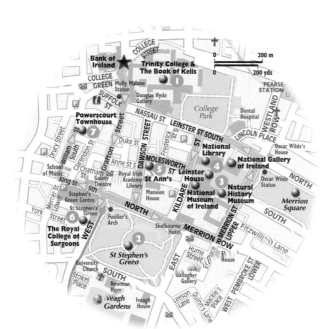

REGIONS DUBLIN • WALK

DUBLIN'S WATERWAYS

A stroll along Dublin's historical quays leads you through the heart of the city, and in contrast, the canals take you away from it all to one of the city's most peaceful spots.

THE WALK
Distance: 5km (3 miles)
Allow: 2 hours
Start at: Bridge Street on Merchant's Quay ✛ 66 C3
End at: Patrick Kavanagh statue, opposite Leeson Street ✛ 67 F6

HOW TO GET THERE
Cross city buses

★ Starting at the bottom of Bridge Street facing Merchant's Quay, to your left you will see the Brazen Head, Dublin's oldest pub. Glance across the water to get a stunning view of the Four Courts building.

❶ The original Four Courts, built between 1786 and 1802, was virtually destroyed in 1922 when Republican rebels seized it in protest against the Anglo-Irish Treaty. Government forces shelled them into submission, events that eventually led to civil war. The current structure houses Ireland's High and Supreme Courts.

Walk right along Merchant's Quay, past the Dublin Council offices. Check out Betty Maquire's bronze *Viking Boat* sculpture; this was the first area settled by Vikings in the ninth century. As you enter Essex Quay, just before Parliament Street are the Sunlight Chambers, built in the early 20th century as the offices of Lever Brothers—look for the unusual terracotta frieze that advertises the company's product. Continue past the Millennium Bridge and cross the river at the next bridge, the Ha'penny Bridge.

❷ Until 1919, there was a halfpenny toll (hence the nickname) to cross this charming pedestrianized structure arching across the Liffey; it is probably the most photographed bridge in Dublin. Drop in at the Winding Stair bookshop near the corner of Liffey Street; there are great views over the river from the top-floor café. Also, don't miss the sculpture known as the 'Hags with the Bags' that stands on the corner.

Drop down onto the riverside boardwalk that takes you away from the traffic. The next bridge is O'Connell, from where there are good views left up sweeping, tree-lined O'Connell Street, with the stainless steel Spire soaring into the sky and the statue of Daniel O'Connell looking up the street that bears his name. Cross O'Connell Street and carry on along the water's edge to Eden Quay and the Custom House.

❸ The Custom House is one of Dublin's architectural masterpieces; the long, white, arcaded and domed building was designed by James Gandon in 1791, and is one of Dublin's most impressive administrative buildings. Opposite

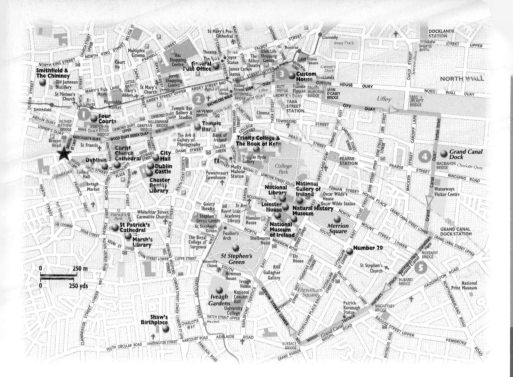

on the waterfront is a series of the scrawny bronze figures that epitomize the awful famine of 1845–49.

Continue to George's Dock, which is undergoing major redevelopment with the addition of the CHQ shopping centre and further restaurants. Take the Sean O'Casey Bridge over the river and glance back for a better view of the Custom House. Turn left on City Quay and keep going until it feeds into the newly restored Sir John Rogerson's Quay. You pass the new Samuel Beckett Bridge (due to open 2009). Just past the old diving bell set into the side of the quay, turn right into Forbes Street, which leads into Grand Canal Quay. You are now in the area known as Grand Canal Dock.

❹ Grand Canal Dock is part of a major revival programme of the docks and canal areas. The impressive piazza, one of the largest paved spaces in Dublin, is destined to be a vibrant cultural hub with a state-of-the-art theatre (due to open

2009), trendy restaurants and cafés, and a five-star hotel. At the far end of the Dock, the eye-catching U2 Tower (due for completion in 2011) will dazzle the skyline—this 183m (600ft) luxury apartment block is predicted to be the tallest building in Ireland, and the band's egg-shaped recording studio will be suspended from the top.

Cross the square and follow Grand Canal Quay alongside the canal basin. Keep going past the Tower Enterprise Centre on the right and the Waterways Visitor Centre on the left (closed for renovation at time of writing). The road then goes under the DART; at the intersection with Grand Canal Street Lower cross over and turn into Clanwilliam Place. From here you can pick up the canal path.

❺ Built to join Dublin with the River Shannon, the Grand Canal forms a 6km (4-mile) route around southern Dublin, but it has not been commercially used since 1960. The regeneration of the Canal has

provided a haven for wildlife, and for walkers and cyclists who want to escape the city hustle and bustle.

Begin your stroll along the nearside of the towpath passing several locks that are still in operation. Ducks and wildfowl splash about on the water, and the area is a favourite retreat for office workers at lunchtime. Continue to Baggot Street Bridge, between here and Leeson Street Bridge you will find a statue of poet Patrick Kavanagh relaxing on a bench—this was one of his favourite spots in the city. Either walk up Leeson Street, which will take you to St. Stephen's Green, or take bus No. 10 or 10A back to the city. Or if you are enjoying the tranquil surroundings, continue your stroll a bit farther along the canal.

WHERE TO EAT

Ocean (▷ 108) at Grand Canal Dock has a lovely waterfront location.

Opposite *People crossing the Ha'penny Bridge*

Above *The lovely central courtyard of Powerscourt Townhouse*

SHOPPING

ARNOTTS
www.arnotts.ie
A huge, long-established department store just off O'Connell Street, Arnotts is popular with Dubliners and visitors alike for fashion, childrenswear, perfume, gifts and home furnishings.
✉ 12 Henry Street, Dublin 1 ☎ 01 805 0400 🕐 Mon–Sat 9–6.30 (Thu until 9), Sun 12–6 🚌 Any O'Connell Street bus; Luas Abbey Street 🚆 DART Connolly

BROWN THOMAS
www.brownthomas.com
This elegant department store on Grafton Street specializes in household furnishings and fashion, gifts and wedding lists. A second store, BT2, is a little farther down Grafton Street and aims at a more youthful market, though the clothes are no less expensive.
✉ 88–95 Grafton Street, Dublin 2 ☎ 01 605 6666 🕐 Mon–Fri 9–8 (Thu until 9), Sat 9–7, Sun 10–7 🚌 Any cross-city bus 🚆 DART Tara Street

CELTIC WHISKEY SHOP
www.celticwhiskeyshop.com
Boasting one of Dublin's best selections of Irish whiskeys, this shop also features a range of handmade chocolates and a rich assortment of wines and liqueurs.
✉ 27–28 Dawson Street, Dublin 2 ☎ 01 675 9744 🕐 Mon–Sat 10.30–8, Sun 12.30–6 🚌 Most cross-city buses 🚆 DART Pearse

CLADDAGH RECORDS
www.claddaghrecords.com
There is a great selection of music to be found in this little treasure trove, in a Temple Bar backstreet. It sells CDs from the countryfied sound of Irish dance bands to the archly traditional and contemporary. The shop is an offshoot of the recording label of the same name, and the staff know their stuff.
✉ Cecelia Street, Temple Bar, Dublin 2 ☎ 01 677 0262 🕐 Mon–Fri 10.30–5.30, Sat 12–5.30 🚌 Most cross-city buses 🚆 DART Tara Street

CLERYS
www.clerys.com
Clerys, one of Dublin's first department stores, has more than 70 departments, including Irish gifts, fashions, home furnishings and sportswear. It faces the Spire.
✉ 18–27 Lower O'Connell Street, Dublin 1 ☎ 01 878 6000 🕐 Mon–Wed, Sat 9–6.30, Thu 9–9, Fri 9–8, Sun 12–6 🚌 Any O'Connell Street bus; Luas Abbey Street 🚆 DART Tara Street/Connolly

DESIGNYARD GALLERY
www.designyard.ie
Created as a platform for modern Irish design, DESIGNyard occupies a Victorian warehouse in Temple Bar. There is custom-made furniture, original jewellery and textiles.
✉ 48–49 Nassau Street, Dublin 2 ☎ 01 474 1011 🕐 Mon–Fri 9–8 (Thu until 9), Sat 9–7, Sun 10–7 🚌 Most cross-city buses 🚆 DART Pearse

DUBLIN WRITERS MUSEUM BOOKSHOP
www.writersmuseum.com
In a city that's world renowned for its extraordinary literary output, it is hardly surprising that the Writers Museum should have an excellent bookshop. It covers all aspects of Irish writing from travel to poetry, including works by many of the writers whose lives and work are featured in the museum.
✉ 18 Parnell Street North, Dublin 1 ☎ 01 872 2077 🕐 Mon–Sat 10–5 (Jun–end Aug Mon–Fri 10–6), Sun 11–5 🚌 10, 11, 11A, 11B, 13, 13A, 16, 16A, 19, 19A 🚆 DART Connolly, 20-min walk

EASON

www.eason.ie

Dublin's largest bookseller has 12 branches around the city, but the O'Connell Street outlet is the flagship. There is a good choice of Irish books, from travel guides to history and literature, as well as the latest blockbusters, fiction and non-fiction.
✉ 40 Lower O'Connell Street, Dublin 1 ☎ 01 858 3800 🕔 Mon–Wed, Sat 8.30–6.45, Thu 8.30–8.45, Fri 8.30–7.45, Sun 12–5.45 🚌 Any O'Connell Street bus; Luas Abbey Street 🚊 DART Tara Street/Connolly

GRAFTON STREET

The premier shopping street in the Irish capital is where you will find the grander designer outlets as well as other stores and Brown Thomas's department store with its funky designer cousin BT2. Buskers (street performers) are an integral part of the whole Grafton Street experience and the side roads are full of interesting little boutiques and smaller independent stores.
✉ Grafton Street, Dublin 2 🚌 Most cross-city buses pass close by 🚊 DART Tara Street/Pearse

HODGES FIGGIS

This famous old bookstore, established in 1768, is revered for its collection of works on Celtic and Irish history, culture, art and literature.
✉ 56–58 Dawson Street, Dublin 2 ☎ 01 677 4754 🕔 Mon–Fri 9–7 (Thu until 8), Sat 9–6, Sun 12–6 🚌 Most cross-city buses 🚊 DART Tara Street/Pearse

HOWTH HARBOUR FARMERS' MARKET

www.irishfarmersmarkets.ie

With more than 35 stalls, the Farmers' Market is the place to find organic vegetables, cheese and fruit, free-range meat, game, fish and poultry, not to mention homemade breads, relishes, chocolates and jam. The farmers in question come from all over Ireland, bringing traditional market products back to the consumer.
✉ The Harbour, Howth, Co. Dublin 🕔 Sun 10–4 🚌 From central Dublin: 31, 31B 🚊 DART Howth

KEVIN AND HOWLIN

www.kevinandhowlin.com

Considered by many to be the best tweed shop in Dublin, Kevin and Howlin is certainly an outstanding place to buy a range of Donegal tweed clothing in both traditional and modern styles.
✉ 31 Nassau Street, Dublin 2 ☎ 01 677 0257 🕔 Mon–Sat 9.30–5.30 🚌 Most cross-city buses 🚊 DART Tara Street

KILKENNY CENTRE

www.christysirishstores.com

This is the Dublin branch of an Ireland-wide chain of stores specializing in Irish branded giftware. You'll find clothing, jewellery, crystal, pottery and ceramics, as well as a café and restaurant on the top floor.
✉ 5–6 Nassau Street, Dublin 2 ☎ 01 677 7066 🕔 Mon–Wed 8.30–6, Thu 8.30–8, Fri 8.30–6, Sat 9–6, Sun 11–6 🚌 Most cross-city buses 🚊 DART Tara Street

MOORE STREET MARKET

A Dublin tradition, Moore Street isn't just for fruit and vegetables. You'll find stalls selling just about anything. You'll need to observe commonsense precautions if you visit, but do go there, not least to hear the banter of the traders.
✉ Moore Street, off Henry Street, Dublin 1 🕔 Mon–Sat 9–5 🚌 Any O'Connell Street bus 🚊 DART Connolly/Tara Street

PATAGONIA

www.patagonia.com

The Patagonia shop is one of only four outlet stores in Europe (and the only one in the British Isles) for this brand of eco-friendly outdoor wear.
✉ 24–26 Exchequer Street, Dublin 2 ☎ 01 670 5748 🕔 Mon–Fri 10–6 (Thu until 8), Sat 9.30–6, Sun 1–5 🚌 Most cross-city buses 🚊 DART Tara Street

POWERSCOURT TOWNHOUSE

www.powerscourtcentre.com

A couple of minutes' walk from Grafton Street, this gracious 18th-century building has been converted to a stylish shopping mall featuring 45 designer outlets, antiques, gift shops, craft galleries, bars and restaurants. Originally built for Lord Powerscourt in 1771, the building retains some fine stucco ceilings.
✉ 59 South William Street, Dublin 2 ☎ 01 671 7000 🕔 Mon–Wed, Fri 10–6, Thu 10–8, Sat 9–6, Sun 12–6 🚌 Most cross-city buses 🚊 DART Tara Street

STEPHEN'S GREEN SHOPPING CENTRE

www.stephensgreen.com

Claiming to be 'where Grafton Street begins', the glittering Stephen's Green Shopping Centre is a spacious, light and airy mall with three floors of international names, gift and fashion outlets as well as several bars and restaurants.
✉ Opposite St. Stephen's Green, at the top of Grafton Street, Dublin 2 ☎ 01 478 0888 🕔 Mon–Wed 9–7, Thu 9–9, Fri, Sat 9–7, Sun 11–6 🚌 Most cross-city buses; Luas St. Stephen's Green 🚊 DART Tara Street/Pearse

TEMPLE BAR MARKETS

www.templebar.ie

The bustling creative quarter has weekly outdoor markets: Cow's Lane Market showcases handmade goods by local designers: fashion bags, jewellery, ceramics, pottery and visual arts. In winter it heads indoors to SS. Michael and John. Temple Bar Food Market fills Meeting House Square and specializes in international foods plus produce from nearby farms.
✉ Temple Bar, Dublin 2 🕔 Cow's Lane: Sat 10–5.30; Temple Bar Food Market: Sat 10–5 🚌 Most cross-city buses 🚊 DART Tara Street

WALTONS WORLD OF MUSIC

www.waltons.ie

Dublin brims over with music and musicians and this outlet supplies everyone from the wannabe rock stars to the stalwarts of the traditional scene with instruments, sheet music and accessories. They also make tin whistles and bodhráns and publish Irish songbooks.
✉ 2–5 North Frederick Street, Dublin 1 (also 69–70 South Great George's Street, Dublin 2) ☎ 01 475 0661 🕔 Mon–Sat 9–6 🚌 Most cross-city buses 🚊 DART Tara Street/Pearse

ENTERTAINMENT AND NIGHTLIFE

ABBEY THEATRE
www.abbeytheatre.ie

This purpose-built home of the National Theatre of Ireland dates from 1966. The main, fan-shaped auditorium seats 628, nearly 100 of which are in a shallow balcony. There are plans to build a new theatre in Docklands to open in 2010.

✉ 26 Lower Abbey Street, Dublin 1 ☎ 01 878 7222 ⏰ All year; box office times: Mon–Sat 10–7 ✋ Varies 🚌 Luas Abbey Street 🚆 DART Tara Street 🍴

ANDREW'S LANE THEATRE
www.andrewslane.com

A small 220-seat theatre staging drama by Irish and international writers. The main theatre has more mainstream productions, while the smaller studio area hosts lesser known touring groups.

✉ 9–17 St. Andrew's Lane, off Trinity Street, Dublin 2 ☎ 01 679 5720 ⏰ Box office: Mon–Sat 10.30–7 ✋ Varies 🚌 Most cross-city buses 🚆 DART Tara Street 🍴

BREAK FOR THE BORDER
www.capitalbars.com

A huge all-round venue on three floors, with gigs giving way to a nightclub after midnight. Many Dublin bands have cut their teeth playing here. There's a busy restaurant.

✉ 2 Johnstons Place, Lower Stephens Street, Dublin 2 ☎ 01 478 0300 ⏰ Mon–Wed 4–11.30, Thu–Sat 4pm–3am, Sun 4–11.30 🚌 Any St. Stephen's Green

CIVIC THEATRE
www.civictheatre.ie

The Civic is a community arts centre in the southwest suburbs of Dublin providing mainstream drama and classical music concerts, as well as some traditional and contemporary music. There is an art gallery upstairs and a small studio space, a popular café that's open during the day and a bar.

✉ Blessington Road, off Belguard Square East, Tallght, Dublin 24 ☎ 01 462 7477 ⏰ All year; box office: Mon–Sat 10–6

✋ Varies 🚌 49, 50, 54A, 56A, 65/B, 77/A/B; Luas Tallaght 🚆 🍴

DOHENY AND NESBITT

A distinguished old pub away from usual tourist drinking spots, Doheny and Nesbitt attracts politicians and media people to its three floors and bars well stocked with whiskeys and stouts. Its mirrored walls, high ceilings and intimate snugs betray its Victorian origins, 130 years ago.

✉ 5 Lower Baggot Street, Dublin 2 ☎ 01 676 2945 ⏰ Daily, late nights Fri, Sat 🚌 10, 15X, 25X, 49X

EAMONN DORAN'S

A sprawling Temple Bar venue with a proper stage and dance floors as well as several bars. Nightly live music includes big names, young bands and traditional music.

✉ 3a Crown Alley, Temple Bar, Dublin 2 ☎ 01 679 9114 ⏰ Daily 12pm–2.30am 🚌 Most cross-city buses

FITZSIMONS
www.fitzsimonshotel .com

A vibrant nightspot, with bars over four floors and a nightclub where DJs play a mix of pop and dance aimed at all-comers. Big, busy and bustling, it has a great atmosphere. There is a roof terrace.

✉ 21–22 Wellington Quay, Temple Bar, Dublin 2 ☎ 01 677 9315 ⏰ Daily 10.30am–late 🚌 Most cross-city buses

GAIETY THEATRE
www.gaietytheatre.com

This is a big old-style theatre in the vicinity of the northwest corner of St. Stephen's Green. It's most famous for its winter pantomimes and also has a lively calendar of events, featuring a mixture of popular drama and music.

✉ South King Street, Dublin 2 ☎ 01 677 1717 ⏰ All year; box office: Mon–Sat 10–6 (or performance start time) ✋ Varies 🚌 Any passing St. Stephen's Green; Luas St. Stephen's Green 🚆 DART Pearse 🍴

GATE THEATRE
www.gate-theatre.ie

One of Ireland's foremost theatres, staging new works and the standards

in a beautiful Georgian-fronted building that has been a theatre since 1928. This was an early showcase for Orson Welles and James Mason.

✉ 1 Cavendish Row, Parnell Square, Dublin 1 ☎ 01 874 4045 ⏰ All year; box office: Mon–Sat 10–7.30 ✋ Varies 🚌 Any O'Connell Street bus 🚆 DART Connolly 🚇 🍴

THE GEORGE
www.capitalbars.com

The George is both a bar and a nightclub and has long been Dublin's main gay and lesbian venue.

✉ South Great George's Street, Dublin 2 ☎ 01 478 2983 ⏰ Mon–Sat 12.30pm–3am, Sun 12.30pm–1am ✋ Charge for nightclub after 10pm 🚌 Most cross-city buses

THE HELIX
www.thehelix.ie

Opened in 2002, this complex at City University has three auditoria—the 1,260 capacity Mahony Hall, the 450-seat Theatre and the 150-seat Space—serving up a flexible mix of classical concerts, drama and mainstream rock and pop music.

✉ Dublin City University, Collins Avenue, Glasnevin, Dublin 9 ☎ 01 700 7000 ⏰ All year; box office: 10–6 (until 8 on performance evenings) 🚌 13, 19, 83, 134 🍴

THE HUB
www.thehubmezz.com

An intimate Temple Bar venue for rock and pop gigs, attached to the Mezz nightclub. Local bands are popular, with Battle of the Bands-style try-outs, DJ competitions and alternative/student nights. Gigs are followed by club sessions.

✉ 23–24 Eustace Street, Temple Bar, Dublin 2 ☎ 01 670 7655 ⏰ All year 🚌 Most cross-city buses 🚆 DART Tara Street 🍴

IRISH FILM CENTRE
www.irishfilm.ie

A state-funded art-house cinema showing retrospectives, foreign language films (with subtitles) and new works that are unlikely to make it to the multiplexes.

✉ 6 Eustace Street, Temple Bar, Dublin 2 ☎ 01 679 5744 🕐 All year, subject to annual or daily membership fee 🖐 Varies 🚌 Most cross-city buses stop nearby 🚆 DART Tara Street 🍴 🍷

McDAID'S

Just off Grafton Street, this is a traditional Dublin pub that has changed little since Brendan Behan and Patrick Kavanagh stood at the bar. It is cramped and noisy most nights of the week.
✉ 3 Harry Street, Dublin 2 ☎ 01 679 4395 🕐 Mon–Thu 10.30am–11.30pm, Fri, Sat 10.30am–12.30am, Sun 12.30pm–11pm 🚌 Most cross-city buses 🚆 DART Tara Street/Pearse

THE MEZZ

www.thehubmezz.com
The Mezz is an eclectic music bar. The sounds cover everything from jazz and easy listening to funk and old fashioned rock 'n' roll.
✉ 23 Eustace Street, Temple Bar, Dublin 2 ☎ 01 670 7655 🕐 Usually 7 midnight but times may vary 🚌 Most cross-city buses

MULLIGANS

www.mulligans.ie
A pub since 1820, Mulligans is a Guinness drinkers' institution.

Retaining its Victorian mahogany furnishings, it has steadfastly resisted change over the decades.
✉ 8 Poolbeg Street, Dublin 2 ☎ 01 677 5582 🕐 Sun–Fri 10.30am–11.30pm, Sat and evenings before a public holiday 10.30am–12.30am 🚆 DART Tara Street

NATIONAL CONCERT HALL

www.nch.ie
Dublin's biggest classical music venue was built for the International Exhibition of Arts and Manufactures in 1865. As well as hosting the greatest visiting musicians of the day, it is home to the RTÉ National Symphony Orchestra.
✉ Earlsfort Terrace, Dublin 2 ☎ 01 417 0000 🕐 All year 🖐 Varies 🚌 14/A, 15A, 44, 74; Luas Harcourt 🚆 DART Pearse 🖥 🍷

O'NEILLS

www.oneillsbar.com
A licensed bar for more than 300 years, this complex of snugs and alcoves is believed to have been built on the site of the Norse parliament or 'thingmote'.
✉ 2 Suffolk Street, Dublin 2 ☎ 01 679 3656 🕐 Mon–Thu 10.30am–11.30pm, Fri–Sat 10.30am–12.30am, Sun 12.30pm–11.30pm 🚌 Most cross-city buses

PEACOCK THEATRE

www.abbeytheatre.ie
Dedicated to brand new works, this place has intimate atmosphere.
✉ 26 Lower Abbey Street, Dublin 1 ☎ 01 878 7222 🕐 All year, see Abbey Theatre 🚌 Most cross-city buses stop nearby; Luas Abbey Street 🚆 DART Tara Street

THE PORTERHOUSE

www.porterhousebrewco.com
One of the few home-brew pubs in Ireland. You can try their own brand of acclaimed stout ale. There is live music most nights of the week with afternoon sessions on Saturday.
✉ 16–18 Parliament Street, Dublin 2 ☎ 01 679 8847 🕐 Mon–Thu 11.30–11.30, Fri 11.30am–2am, Sat 12pm–2am, Sun 12.30–11 🚌 Most cross-city buses

THE TEMPLE BAR

www.templebarpubdublin.ie
With its huge selection of whiskeys, live traditional music sessions and crowds of drinkers, this is perhaps the epitome of tourists' Temple Bar, but the *craic* can be good and the layout means it never overwhelms.
✉ 47–48 Temple Bar, Dublin 2 ☎ 01 672 9286 🕐 Mon–Thu 11am–12.30am, Fri, Sat 11am–1.30am, Sun 11am–12.30am 🚌 Most cross-city buses

Below *Fitzsimons in Temple Bar is buzzing every day of the week*

REGIONS DUBLIN • WHAT TO DO

102

TEMPLE BAR MUSIC CENTRE
www.tbmc.ie
Here you're as likely to see big names in Irish traditional, folk and world music as contemporary rock acts. Popular salsa classes on Tuesday nights are open to beginners.
✉ Curved Street, Temple Bar, Dublin 2 ☎ 01 670 9202 ◷ All year ➊ Most cross-city buses stop nearby ▣ DART Tara Street ◻ ▯

UGC CINEWORLD CINEMAS
www.cineworld.ie
With 17 screens, this huge northside multiplex, only 5 minutes' walk from the Millennium Bridge, shows a full range of current releases.
✉ Parnell Street, Dublin 1 ☎ 1520 880 444 (within Ireland) ◷ Varies ➊ Any O'Connell Street bus ▣ DART Connolly ◻ ▯

SPORTS AND ACTIVITIES

BELFIELD BIKE SHOP
Dublin is perfect for bicycling. You can escape the crowded streets in Phoenix Park, or get out on the coast at Howth or Dalkey, or into the Wicklow Mountains. Main routes into the city have bicycle lanes, but you'll need at least two good locks to keep your wheels safe.
✉ UCD, Belfield, Dublin 4 ☎ 01 716 1697 ◷ Daily 9–6 ✋ €17 per day

BRAM STOKER DRACULA EXPERIENCE
www.thebramstokerdraculaexperience.com
An experience not for the faint-hearted based on Bram Stoker, who was born in the suburb of Clontarf, and his vampire creation, Dracula. The interactive museum uses up-to-the-minute technology to transport you on a spine-chilling adventure to the Count's castle, the Blood Laboratory and Dracula's Lair.
✉ Westwood Club, Clontarf Road, Dublin 3 ◷ Fri 4–10, Sat–Sun 12–10 ✋ Adult €7, child €4 ➊ 20, 20B, 27, 27B, 31, 32 ▣ DART Clontarf Road

DUBLIN CITY TOUR
www.dublinbus.ie
Dublin City Tours are operated by DublinBus and run around the middle of Dublin all day. There is live commentary, and tickets, which you can buy on board, are valid for 24 hours, so you can get on and off to visit the sights. The route takes in Phoenix Park, Collins Barracks, the Dublin Writers Museum, Henry Street/GPO, Trinity College, the National Gallery, Dublin Castle and the Guinness Storehouse.
✉ DublinBus Head Office, 59 Upper O'Connell Street, Dublin 1 ☎ 01 873 4222 ◷ Daily 9.30–5 (every 10 min), 5–6.30 (every 30 min) ✋ Adult €14, child €6

GAELIC ATHLETIC ASSOCIATION
www.gaa.ie
There are dozens of teams in County Dublin playing Gaelic football, hurling, camogie and handball. The easiest place to see football and hurling is the Fifteen Acres area of Phoenix Park, where many local teams in these strictly amateur sports play. The headquarters of the Gaelic Athletic Association (GAA) is Croke Park (▷ 72) in north Dublin. You can get tickets for these games only through local clubs, but semi-final games are also played at Croke Park and tickets are usually available in advance.
✉ Jones's Road, Dublin 3 ☎ 01 836 3222 ◷ Match days are usually Sun ✋ Varies (telephone for information) ➊ 11, 11A, 16, 16A, 51 ▣ DART Connolly, 15-min walk

HISTORICAL WALKING TOURS OF DUBLIN
www.historicalinsights.ie
These historically themed walking tours of the city are led by knowledgeable history graduates from Trinity College. A 2-hour 'seminar on the street' includes Wood Quay in the heart of Viking Dublin, the Four Courts, Trinity College, Christ Church Cathedral and Dublin Castle.
✉ 64 Mary Street, Dublin 1 ☎ 0187 688 9412 ◷ May–end Sep daily 11–3; Oct, Apr daily 11am; Nov–end Mar Fri–Sun 11am ✋ Adult €12

IRISH RUGBY FOOTBALL UNION
www.irfu.ie; www.irishrugby.ie
The best rugby in Ireland is played in the RBS Six Nations tournament (www.rbs6nations.com), in which an all-Ireland side plays against England, Wales, Scotland, France and Italy. Visit the websites above for details of fixtures during the stadium's renovation (due to be completed in 2010), which are played at Croke Park (▷ 72).
✉ 10–12 Lansdowne Road, Ballsbridge, Dublin 4 ☎ 01 647 3800 ◷ Telephone or see press for fixtures ➊ 5, 7/A, 45 ▣ DART Lansdowne Road

JAMES JOYCE CENTRE
From here (▷ 79), walking tours are led around the various Bloomsday (▷ 103) locations and other sites associated with James Joyce.

LEOPARDSTOWN RACECOURSE
www.leopardstown.com
While most of the best racing near Dublin is in Co. Kildare (▷ 126–127), Leopardstown has a modern and popular course. The track is in the southern suburbs and there are one or two meetings a month, mostly National Hunt (steeplechase), but some flat racing too.
✉ Leopardstown Road (off the Stillorgan road), Foxrock, Dublin 18 ☎ 01 289 0500 ◷ Once or twice per month (telephone or see press for details) ✋ From €15 ➊ 86, 118, special buses run from Busáras on race days

PORTMAROCK
www.portmarnock.com
Designed by Bernhard Langer, this is one of Ireland's best links courses, attached to a luxury hotel.
✉ Portmarnock, Co. Dublin ☎ 01 846 0611 ◷ Daily 7.30–dusk ✋ Green fees from €125

ROYAL DUBLIN
www.theroyaldublingolfclub.com
Founded in 1885, this is Ireland's oldest golf club. The championship links course hosts important competitions. Access is from the central causeway across to Bull Island.
✉ Bull Island, Dollymount, Dublin 3 ☎ 01 833 6346 ◷ Daily 8am–dusk; visitors welcome Mon, Tue, Thu, Fri ✋ Green fees from €150

Opposite *St. Patrick's Day Parade*

HEALTH AND BEAUTY
MADISON CLINIC AND DAY SPA
www.madisonclinic.ie

The Madison Clinic is particularly popular with hen (bachelorette) parties. There is a range of facials, manicures, pedicures and massages.

✉ 17 Upper Liffey Street, Dublin 1 ☎ 01 872 5545 🕓 Mon–Wed, Sat 9–6, Thu–Fri 9–0 🚌 O'Connell Street buses; Luas Jervis

FOR CHILDREN
THE ARK
www.ark.ie

This is a cultural venue for 3–14 year olds, located in Temple Bar. It stages varied performances by children and for children in both the indoor theatre and outdoor amphitheatre, and there's a gallery space and workshops concentrating on arts and activities for young people.

✉ 11a Eustace Street, Temple Bar, Dublin 2 ☎ 01 670 7788 🕓 Call for opening times and performances 🚇 DART Tara Street

DUBLIN ZOO
www.dublinzoo.ie

Committed to conservation and education, this modern zoo houses more than 700 animals. The 'African Plains' area allows African animals to roam with greater freedom.

✉ Phoenix Park, Dublin 8 ☎ 01 474 8900 🕓 Mar–end Oct Mon–Sat 9.30–6, Sun 10.30–6; Nov–end Feb Mon–Sat 9.30–dusk, Sun 10.30–dusk ✋ Adult €14.50, child €10, family €42 🚌 10/A, 25, 66, 67; Luas Heuston 🚇 Heuston station 🅿 ☕

MALAHIDE CASTLE
▷ 79.

PHOENIX PARK
▷ 88.

VIKING SPLASH TOUR
www.vikingsplash.ie

This ex-World War II amphibious vehicle tours Viking Dublin before driving into the Grand Canal.

✉ 64–65 Patrick Street, Dublin 8 ☎ 01 707 6000 🕓 Feb to mid-Nov daily from St. Stephen's Green 10, 11.30, 2, 3.30; St. Patrick's Cathedral 10.30, 12, 3.30, 5 ✋ Adult €20, child €10 🚌 49, 49A, 50, 54A, 56A

FESTIVALS AND EVENTS

MARCH
ST. PATRICK'S DAY PARADE
www.stpatricksday.ie

The St. Patrick's Day parade in Dublin usually begins around noon near St. Patrick's Cathedral and threads around the city to O'Connell Street. Merrion Square and Festival Square in Smithfield are full of street entertainers from all over Ireland, and each year it seems to get more ambitious.

✉ St. Stephen's Green House, Earlsfort Terrace, Dublin 2 ☎ 01 676 3205 🕓 17 March

JUNE
BLOOMSDAY
www.jamesjoyce.ie

James Joyce set his masterwork *Ulysses* on 16 June 1904, the day he met Nora Barnacle, his wife and muse. Every year Joycean enthusiasts and academics celebrate the man and his works with tours, readings and seminars.

✉ James Joyce Centre, 35 North Great George's Street, Dublin 1 ☎ 01 878 8547 🕓 16 June

AUGUST
DUBLIN HORSE SHOW
www.rds.ie/horseshow

First held in 1864, the Dublin Horse Show has become Ireland's largest equestrian event, with the third largest prize pool for showjumping in the world. The five-day event takes place at the RDS complex with entrants from all over the world.

✉ Royal Dublin Society, Ballsbridge, Dublin 4 ☎ 818 300 274 🕓 Early August

SEPTEMBER/OCTOBER
DUBLIN FRINGE FESTIVAL
www.fringefest.com

The Dublin Fringe festival features comedy, music, cabaret and alternative theatre, while the mainstream festival concentrates on more highbrow culture.

✉ Sackville House, Sackville Place, Dublin 1 ☎ 01 817 8511 🕓 Early September

DUBLIN THEATRE FESTIVAL
www.dublintheatrefestival.com

Dublin's theatrical tradition makes this one of the most vibrant theatre festivals in Europe. Leading lights of the Dublin drama scene contribute to this celebration of contemporary Irish drama.

✉ 44 East Essex Street, Temple Bar, Dublin 2 ☎ 01 677 8899 🕓 End September–early October

OCTOBER
ADIDAS DUBLIN MARATHON
www.dublincitymarathon.ie

Around 10,000 competitors, over half from other countries, compete in this annual run around Dublin.

✉ Donore Harriers Sports Centre, Chapelizod, Dublin 20 ☎ 01 623 2250 (open 9–5) 🕓 Last week in October

Above *The restaurants in Dublin that flourish tend to be lively, as well as providing tasty and innovative food*

PRICES AND SYMBOLS

The restaurants are listed alphabetically. The prices given are the average for a two-course lunch (L) and a three-course dinner (D) for one person, without drinks. The wine price given is for the least expensive bottle.

For a key to the symbols, ▷ 2.

23

www.gresham-hotels.com
Dinner fare here is French and Irish. Traditional Irish dishes including Wicklow lamb and Irish salmon are created using a modern approach, and there is a good choice of signature dishes and daily specials.
✉ The Gresham Hotel, 23 Upper O'Connell Street, Dublin ☎ 01 874 6881/817 6116 ⊙ Mon–Sat 5.30–10.30 🖐 D €23 (special), €46 (á la carte), Wine €20 🚊 DART Connolly 🚌 Close to the GPO

IL BACCARO

www.ilbaccaro.com
This Italian eatery is located in a 17th-century cellar; you step down into two tiny barrel-shaped rooms with curving ceilings made completely of red brick. It has the rustic informal atmosphere of a traditional Italian *osteria* where young Italian staff serve authentic regional dishes from a weekly changing menu. Il Baccaro faces a pedestrianized square in Temple Bar where outdoor seating is available in summer.
✉ Diceman's Corner, Meeting House Square, Dublin 2 ☎ 01 671 4597 ⊙ Thu–Sat 12–11, Sun–Wed 6–11 🖐 L €20, D €27, Wine €23 🚌 Cross-city buses 🚊 DART Tara Street

BAD ASS CAFÉ

www.badasscafe.com
Bad Ass first opened its doors in 1983 serving affordable burgers, pizza, barbecued chicken wings and coffee. Not a lot has changed at this warehouse-style diner where singer Sinéad O'Connor once worked as a waitress but it hasn't lost its edge as a meeting place for Dublin's youth. The café's heritage is retained in the overhead mechanical pulley that was used to whisk your order to the kitchen and through memorabilia posted on the walls.
✉ 9–11 Crown Alley, Dublin 2 ☎ 01 671 2596 ⊙ Daily 11.30–late 🖐 L €16, D €25 🚌 Cross-city buses 🚊 DART Tara Street

BALZAC

www.lastampa.ie
In a prime spot close to St. Stephen's Green, Balzac combines an intimate atmosphere with superb modern European cooking, which delivers such treats as mussels and clams marinière followed by whole monkfish with pea beurre blanc. Reserve well ahead.
✉ La Stampa Hotel, 35 Dawson Street, Dublin 2 ☎ 01 677 8611 ⊙ Mon–Sat 6–11 (also 12.30–2.30 Thu, Fri) 🖐 L €30, D €44, Wine €25 🚌 Cross-city buses 🚊 DART Pearse

BRAZEN HEAD

www.brazenhead.com
Ireland's oldest pub dates back 800 years and remains the archetypal Irish pub, with a lively atmosphere, good music, food and beer. The Courtyard Restaurant attached to

the pub serves traditional Irish and international cuisine, accompanied by a range of wines. The Brazen Head was frequented by James Joyce, who mentioned it in *Ulysses*.
☎ 20 Lower Bridge Street, Dublin 8
✉ Restaurant: 01 677 9549Bar: 01 679 5186 🕐 Mon–Wed 11–11, Thu–Sat 11am–midnight 🖐 L (carvery) €20, D from €30, Wine €18 🚇 DART Tara Street
🚌 Short walk from the heart of the city on the left-hand side of Bridge Street, just before the bridge

BROWNES RESTAURANT
www.brownesrestaurant.com
In a Georgian town house facing St. Stephen's Green in the heart of Dublin, Brownes provides romantic dining at its best. The spectacular dining room boasts chandeliers and Italian-style friezes and is considered one of the most stylish in the city. Head chef David Willcocks' traditional Irish fare with a modern twist includes dishes like venison served with blue cheese potato gratin, pot-roasted quince and port jus.
✉ 22 St. Stephen's Green North, Dublin 2 ☎ 01 638 3939 🕐 Daily 12.30–2.30, 6.30–10; closed L Sat 🖐 L €25, D €50, Wine €28 🚌 Cross-city buses; Luas St. Stephen's Green 🚇 DART Pearse

CAFÉ MAO
www.cafemao.com
Bold hues and Warhol pictures of Chairman Mao are the themes at this trendy restaurant, which brings a fresh approach to oriental cooking. Asian fusion dishes combine Malaysian, Vietnamese, Indonesian and Thai tastes, cooked to perfection.
✉ 2–3 Chatham Row, Dublin 2
☎ 01 670 4899 🕐 Daily 12–11
🖐 L €26, D €32, Wine €21 🚌 Cross-city buses 🚇 DART Pearse

CANTEEN
www.schoolhouse.ie
This 1892 schoolhouse has been converted into a splendid boutique hotel in a charming spot beside the Grand Canal. The minimalist, award-winning Canteen restaurant has a 12m (40ft) beamed dining room, and offers modern Irish fare;

many people come here specially for the signature dish of seared scallops with black pudding, spiced apple purée and roasting juices. An ideal spot for an early meal on a summer's evening before a stroll along the canal.
✉ 2–8 Northumberland Road, Dublin 4 ☎ 01 614 4733 🕐 Mon–Fri 12.30–3, 6–10, Sat–Sun 6–10 🖐 L €22, D €36, Wine €15 🚌 7, 7A, 45 🚇 DART Grand Canal Dock

THE CHAMELEON
www.chameleonrestaurant.com
Check out this lovely little restaurant in the heart of Temple Bar for a true Indonesian experience. Food is consistently good, and specializes in set meals based on the Dutch-Indonesian *rijsttafel*—a diverse selection of tasty dishes that reflect the cuisine of the area. Dim lights and low ceilings create a romantic atmosphere. If you prefer, you can dine Indonesian style sitting on cushions at low tables. Reservations are recommended as this is one place you won't want to miss out on.
✉ 1 Lower Fownes Street, Dublin 2 ☎ 01 671 0362 🕐 Tue–Sat 5–11, Sun 4–10 🖐 D €30, Wine €20 🚌 Cross-city buses 🚇 DART Tara Street

CHAPTER ONE
www.chapteronerestaurant.com
Chapter One, in the basement of the Dublin Writers Museum, puts a modern twist to consistently excellent classic French cooking, which includes John dory cooked with broccoli purée, mussel and saffron sauce or roast scallop and spiced belly pork with gratinated cauliflower in raisin sauce. For wine lovers, a look at the impressive stocks of the wine cellar is a must.
✉ 18–19 Parnell Square, Dublin 1 ☎ 01 873 2266 🕐 Tue–Fri 12.30–2, Tue–Sat 6–11 🖐 L €25, D €57, Wine €25 🚌 10, 11, 13, 16, 19 🚇 DART Connolly 🚌 To the north of the city hub

THE CHURCH
www.thechurch.ie
Under new ownership since 2007 (formerly John M. Keating), this

unique establishment over four levels has a stunning setting in a converted former church. The elegant galleried area for chic dining features a beautiful church organ. Downstairs, the minimalist bar, overlooked by a spectacular stained-glass window, offers casual dining and there is a café for tea and cakes, an ideal stop-off point during a shopping spree on nearby Henry Street. There is a huge outside terrace, too, where barbecues are held in summer.
✉ Mary Street, Dublin 1 ☎ 01 828 0102 🕐 Restaurant: Mon–Thu 5–10, Fri–Sat 5–11, Sun 5–9; café/bar: Mon–Sat 11–11, Sun 12.30–9 🖐 L €15, D €40, Wine €22 🚌 Luas Jervis

CLARION HOTEL DUBLIN IFSC
www.clarionhotelifsc.com
The Sinergie restaurant at the Clarion Hotel in the International Financial Services Centre serves interesting food flavour combinations based on a modern Italian theme.
✉ North Wall Quay, International Financial Services Centre (IFSC), Dublin 1 ☎ 01 433 8899 🕐 Daily 6–9.45, Mon–Fri 12–2.30 🖐 L €15, D €33, Wine €19 🚇 DART Connolly 🚌 In the city heart, past Custom Quay

CORNUCOPIA
www.cornucopia.ie
A favourite with vegetarians, this cafeteria-style restaurant manages to combine healthy with tasty in a most acceptable way. The intriguing salads are particularly good, as are the wholesome soups and hot dishes such as two cheese cannelloni with sage cream, and the hot breakfast is a must, too. On the menu boards dishes suitable for customers with special dietary requirements are flagged and whether they contain gluten or yeast. The unmistakable bright red frontage conceals a casual atmosphere inside, and as it is always busy you might be asked to to share a table.
✉ 19 Wicklow Street, Dublin 2 ☎ 01 677 7583 🕐 Mon–Sat 8.30–8 (Thu until 9), Sun 12–7 🖐 L €13, D €20, Wine €16 🚌 Cross-city buses 🚇 DART Pearse

DAVY BYRNE'S

This pub was a meeting place for writers including James Joyce, who featured the pub and its owner in *Ulysses*. Today, the pub attracts many visitors for its good food and drink as well as for its literary connections.

✉ 21 Duke Street, Dublin 2 ☎ 01 677 5217 🕐 Mon–Wed 11.30–11.30, Thu, Fri 11am–12.30am, Sat 10.30am–12.30am, Sun 12.30–11 ✋ Hot bar food from €6 🚌 7 🚆 DART Pearse 🚶 A short walk from Grafton Street in the middle of Dublin

DAX

www.dax.ie

Considered by many as the city's best new restaurant, Dax offers sophistication and style in its bright basement dining room. French chef, Olivier Meisonnave excels through his mostly Provençal dishes with a rustic slant, using fresh, seasonal produce. The menu changes regularly and is complemented by an outstanding wine list. The sautéed foie gras is a starter not to be missed and the chestnut risotto is proving to be a favourite main course with clientèle. The early bird and tapas menus offer good value.

✉ 23 Pembroke Street Upper, Dublin 2 ☎ 01 676 1494 🕐 Tue–Fri 12.30–2, 6–10.30, Sat 6–10.30 ✋ L €23, D €48, Wine €25 🚌 11, 11A, 46; Luas Harcourt

L'ECRIVAIN

www.lecrivain.com

Diners can enjoy fine French cuisine and admirable wines at this minimalist, contemporary-style restaurant. Chef Derry Clarke uses fresh local produce to create some outstanding dishes and is known for his fish, which is caught all over Ireland on the same day. A good selection of wines is available.

✉ 109a Lower Baggot Street, Dublin 2 ☎ 01 661 1919 🕐 Mon–Fri 12.30–2, Mon–Sat 7–11 ✋ L €40, D €80, Wine €30 🚌 7, then short walk 🚆 DART Pearse 🚶 From St. Stephen's Green North, go east to Baggot Street, then Lower Baggot Street. Restaurant is on south side of street, which is a divided highway; if driving, telephone for directions

EDEN

www.edenrestaurant.ie

Sleek and chic, Eden is in an ideal spot overlooking a busy square in Temple Bar. Contemporary food with a distinctive Irish taste is served in a relaxed atmosphere. Among the innovative dishes are pan-fried fillet of venison with rosti potato, caramelized pear with Stilton, shaved fennel, rocket and hazelnut salad, or open vegetable tart with butternut squash, feta, caramelized red onion, and fig and almond compote.

✉ Meeting House Square, Dublin 2 ☎ 01 670 5372 🕐 Daily 12.30–3, 6–10.30 ✋ L €22, D €40, Wine €22 🚌 Cross-city buses 🚆 DART Tara Street

FINNSTOWN COUNTRY HOUSE

www.finnstown-hotel.ie

The restaurant in this beautiful old country house hotel offers a surprising choice of international dishes including roast crispy duckling with a fruit stuffing. For dessert lovers, finish with the Finnstown sticky toffee pudding with a caramel sauce. The dishes are beautifully presented. There's also a children's menu.

✉ Newcastle Road, Lucan, Co. Dublin ☎ 01 601 0700 🕐 Mon–Sat 12.30–2.30, 7.30–9.30 ✋ L €31, D €38, Wine €21 🚌 25A from Quays, then a short walk 🚶 From M1 take the first exit onto M50 southbound. First exit after Toll Bridge. At roundabout (traffic circle) take third exit left (N4 W) and continue over next two roundabouts. Hotel with restaurant is on the right

LES FRÈRES JACQUES

www.lesfreresjacques.com

In a great position by the Olympia Theatre, Les Frères Jacques offers French classic cooking with an emphasis on seafood. The home-cured salmon and toasted brioche with an anchovy and lemon mayonnaise is superb. Desserts include red fruit crumble with mango ice cream.

✉ 74 Dame Street, Dublin 2 ☎ 01 679 4555 🕐 Mon–Fri 12.30–2.30, 7.15–10.30, Sat 7.15–11 ✋ L from €18, D from €36, Wine €22 🚌 Cross-city buses 🚆 DART Pearse 🚶 Opposite City Hall

GALLAGHERS BOXTY HOUSE

www.boxtyhouse.ie

A much hyped restaurant in Temple Bar, but it does have the feel of a traditional country kitchen. The menu combines the best Irish cooking with individual touches, based on a unique tradition, the *boxty*—a potato pancake with a range of fillings such as boiled bacon and cabbage, various meats, or fish in a tasty sauce.

✉ 20 Temple Bar, Dublin 2 ☎ 01 677 2762 🕐 Mon–Fri 9am–11pm, Sat–Sun 10am–11.30pm ✋ L €23, D €30, Wine €22 🚌 Cross-city buses 🚆 DART Tara Street

HALÓ RESTAURANT

www.morrisonhotel.ie

This hotel was designed by the renowned John Rocha and Douglas Wallace. The contemporary menu in the dining room offers sophisticated, beautifully presented dishes along the lines of pan-fried sea bass with a barigoule and champagne foam, and organic duck breast, on a bed of celeriac, and apple and potato rosti. A range of equally delicious desserts is also on offer and there is a very good wine list.

✉ The Morrison Hotel, Lower Ormond Quay, Dublin 1 ☎ 01 887 2400 🕐 Daily 6–10.30 ✋ D €45, Wine €23.50 🚌 Cross-city buses 🚆 DART Tara Street 🚶 On the north bank of the River Liffey, opposite Temple Bar

HARBOURMASTER

www.harbourmaster.ie

Housed in the former harbourmaster's office among the thriving financial area, this restaurant's waterside location proves a popular draw for the local workforce at lunchtime. The bar has a warm, traditional pub feel with antique wood and lots of nooks and crannies, while the dining room upstairs is contemporary in style and serves wholesome dishes from the Harbourmaster beefburger to rump of lamb. In summer, a decked patio overlooks the inner harbour.

✉ Custom House Dock, IFSC, Dublin 1

☎ 01 670 1688 ⏰ Mon–Fri 12–9, Sat 12–10, Sun 12–7 ♨ L €20, D €30, Wine €24 🚌 Luas Busáras 🚉 DART Connolly

IL FORNAIO

www.ilfornaio.ie

Serving great authentic Italian food in the up-and-coming docklands area, this place has some of the best pizza and pasta in town, which is served with a friendly Italian smile. The no-frills café style produces a buzzing atmosphere, but inside it is very small so you might not always get a table—in warm weather there are additional tables out on the terrace. Breakfast is available, too.
✉ 1B Valentia House Square, Dublin 1 ☎ 01 672 1853 ⏰ Mon–Fri 9–10, Sat 11–10, Sun 11–9 ♨ L €20 D €26, Wine €20 🚌 Luas Busáras 🚉 DART Connolly,

JACOB'S LADDER

www.jacobsladder.ie

At this light and airy restaurant chef/patron Adrian Roche creates punchy modern food with dishes such as marinated salmon with mange-tout salad. Desserts find inventive uses of fruit such as passion fruit brûlée with coconut and chilli sorbet and citrus tuiles. The wine list has a good selection.
✉ 4 Nassau Street, Dublin 2 ☎ 01 670

3865 ⏰ Tue–Fri 12.30–2.30, 6–10, Sat 12.30–2.30, 7–10 ♨ L €20, D €44, Wine €24 🚌 7 🚉 DART Pearse 🚗 Follow signs for Trinity College and then turn into Nassau Street and park at Satanta Place parking area

JOHNNIE FOX'S PUB

www.jfp.ie

Johnnie Fox's enjoys a lovely position nestled in the Dublin Mountains. Every night you can hear live Irish music, and on the pub's famous hooley nights Irish dancing, traditional music and a four-course meal make the evening special. À la carte meals are served in the restaurant area of the pub and feature a good range of Irish classics using local produce.
✉ Glencullen, The Dublin Mountains, Co. Dublin ☎ 01 295 5647 ⏰ Mon–Sat 10.30am–11.30pm, Sun 12.30–11 ♨ L from €25, D from €30, Wine €21 🚌 44B 🚗 Take N11 south; at Donnybrook turn left on R117 to Kilternan then turn right to Glencullen; about a 30-min drive from Dublin

MERIDIAN RESTAURANT

www.marinehotel.ie

On the road from Dublin to Howth, this stylish hotel restaurant offers Irish- and French-inspired food, specializing in local fish and seafood. Smart dress is preferred.

✉ Marine Hotel, Sutton Cross, Co. Dublin ☎ 01 000 0000 ⏰ Daily 12.30–2.30, 6.30–10.30 ♨ L €25, D €32, Wine €22 🚌 31, 31A 🚉 DART Sutton 🚗 8km (5 miles) from city on Dublin Bay, on the road to Howth

MONTY'S OF KATHMANDU

www.montys.ie

The only Nepalese restaurant in Dublin draws people from far and wide to try the exceptional cooking. Intriguing dishes include deep-fried chicken or prawns with onions, capsicum, tomatoes and green chillies. The dining room is modest and unassuming with white-painted woodwork, paintings of Nepal and dark furniture. Friendly waiters are happy to give advice about the food.
✉ 28 Eustace Street, Dublin 2 ☎ 01 670 4911 ⏰ Mon–Sat 12–2, 6–10.30, Sun 6–10.30 ♨ L €20, D €35, Wine €21 🚌 Cross-city buses 🚉 DART Tara Street

NUDE

At this eco-friendly café its own range of organic products, such as wraps, salads, soup, low-fat desserts, smoothies and juices, are free from additives and contain ingredients like ginseng and bee pollen. These healthy options can be taken away or eaten in.

Below *Finnstown Country House offers innovative international cuisine*

✉ 21 Suffolk Street, Dublin 2 ☎ 01 672 5577 ⊕ Daily 7.30am–9pm (Thu until 10, Sun until 8) 🖐 L €5, D €14 🚌 Cross-city buses 🚊 DART Pearse

OCEAN
www.oceanbar.ie

This spacious, contemporary restaurant/bar, in a waterside setting, has a great atmosphere and is popular with all ages. Ideal for just a drink, where you can lounge on the comfortable couches, or a delicious meal. Windows from floor to ceiling open onto a patio for alfresco dining, with splendid views over the Grand Canal basin. Freshly prepared favourites are served bistro style; seafood dominates the menu. ✉ Ground Floor, Millennium Tower, Charlotte Quay Dock, Dublin 4 ☎ 01 668 8862 ⊕ Mon–Fri noon–10pm, Sat–Sun 12.30–10 🖐 L €15, D €22, Wine €21 🚌 2, 3 🚊 DART Grand Canal Dock

ONE PICO
www.onepico.com

The cooking here makes the most of local produce, with dishes such as roasted skate accompanied by potato with crab and spinach purée or braised beef daube with roasted tomatoes. A carefully selected range of wines complements the food. ✉ 5–6 Molesworth Place, School House Lane, Dublin 2 ☎ 01 676 0300

⊕ Mon–Sat 12.30–2.30, 6–11 🖐 L €30, D €50, Wine €28 🚌 7, 45 🚊 DART Pearse 🚊 Between the Mansion House and the National Museum

OSBORNE
www.portmarnock.com

This chic restaurant allows diners to enjoy sea views while they eat. A comprehensive carte of well-conceived classical dishes is executed with flair and imagination. ✉ Portmarnock Hotel, Strand Road, Portmarnock, Co. Dublin ☎ 01 846 0611 ⊕ Tue–Sat, dinner only 🖐 D €50, Wine €20 🚌 32A, 32B, 32X, 102, 105, 230 🚊 Take M1 north; at intersection with R601 take turn to Malahide. After 3km (2 miles) turn left at intersection, go through Malahide; the hotel is 3.5km (2.2 miles) on the left

THE PAVILION
www.herbertparkhotel.ie

The Pavilion restaurant has fabulous views over parkland. Shuttered glass doors open onto a terrace for fine-weather dining. The carte is essentially Irish but with international influences. In all the dishes fresh Irish produce is to the fore. Jazz buffet lunches and afternoon teas are especially good. ✉ Herbert Park Hotel, Ballsbridge, Dublin 4 ☎ 01 667 2200 ⊕ Daily 12.30–2.30, 5.30–9.30; closed D Sun and public holidays

🖐 L €20, D €45, Wine €23 🚊 DART Pearse 🚌 7 🚊 A 5-min drive from the middle of the city. South over canal into Northumberland Road to Ballsbridge. Turn right and cross the bridge in Ballsbridge then take the first right down Anglesea Road

PEPLOE'S
www.peploes.com

You can eat at any time of the day at this stylish bistro in the restored vaults of a former bank. Vaulted-ceilings, oak floors and leather chairs create a cosy and inviting space, where the tables are laid with sumptuous tableware and the smartly dressed staff provides a professional service. The bistro-type menu offers a wide spectrum of dishes, from staples such as *croque monsieur* and cottage pie to more ambitious dishes like orange-cured sea trout with crushed green beans. ✉ 16 St. Stephen's Green, Dublin 2 ☎ 01 676 3144 ⊕ Daily 12–10.30 🖐 L €20, D €40, Wine €22 🚌 Cross-city buses 🚊 DART Pearse Street

QUEEN OF TARTS
At this tea shop, cake stands and wicker baskets display goodies that the friendly owners bake themselves. Good breakfast options are followed by lunch choices such as hot savoury tarts and sandwiches made from home-baked breads. With your afternoon tea you can indulge in mouthwatering cakes and desserts. Queen of Tarts fans will be pleased to know another branch is to open around the corner in Cow's Lane. ✉ 4 Cork Hill, Dame Street, Dublin 2 ☎ 01 670 7499 ⊕ Mon–Fri 7.30–7, Sat 9–6, Sun 10–6 🖐 B €12, L €14, afternoon tea €10 🚌 Cross-city buses 🚊 DART Tara Street

RESTAURANT PATRICK GUILBAUD
www.restaurantpatrickguilbaud.ie

The contemporary-style dining room is generously sized and flooded with natural light, while a fine collection of modern Irish paintings hangs on the walls. Service is impeccable. 'Modern classic cuisine using Irish produce in season' is the stated philosophy here, and although technique may be firmly rooted in the French tradition, there's plenty of flair and innovation. Particularly impressive signature dishes include a delicate ravioli of lobster served with a coconut scented cream and kari (curry) oil, and a magnificent Challan duck. Desserts are simply superb. The lunch menu is great value.

 Merrion Hotel, 21 Upper Merrion Street, Dublin 2 ☎ 01 676 4192 🕙 Tue–Sat 12.30–2.15, 7–10.15; closed 1st week Jan ✋ L €38, D €90, Wine €30 🚌 7 🚃 DART Pearse 🚌 At the top of Upper Merrion Street on the left, beyond Government Buildings on the right

RHODES D7

www.rhodesd7.com

Since celebrity chef Gary Rhodes set up in Dublin in 2006, his venture has been greeted with much acclaim. Head chef Paul Hargreaves conveys Rhodes' signature dishes to the expected high standard, using the best Irish produce in the unique modern European dishes that have gained Rhodes five Michelin Stars. The spacious, vibrant restaurant, with a mezzanine floor and heated outdoor eating area, makes its mark on this rejuvenated part of the city.

 The Capel Building, Mary's Abbey, Dublin 7 ☎ 01 804 4444 🕙 Tue–Sat 12–10, Mon 12–3.30, Sun 12–4.30 ✋ L €30, D €40, Wine €24 🚌 Luas Jervis

ROLY'S BISTRO

www.rolysbistro.ie

This popular and lively bistro provides robust retro cooking, for example the grilled goat's cheese crostini with raisin salad or breast of chicken stuffed with leeks. Dishes such as vanilla crème brûlée with apple and mincemeat muffins and gingerbread ice cream grace the dessert menu.

 7 Ballsbridge Terrace, Dublin 4 ☎ 01 668 2611 🕙 Daily 12–2.45, 6–9.45 ✋ L €22, D €42, Wine €28 🚌 5, 7, 45 🚃 DART Lansdowne Road 🚌 A 5- to 10-min drive south of the city on Northumberland Road; close to Herbert Park

SADDLE ROOM AND OYSTER BAR

www.marriott.co.uk

Since reopening following major renovations in 2007, the Shelbourne Hotel (▷ 113) launched its Saddle Room and Oyster Bar to great acclaim. It's all about seafood and steak, cooked with simplicity to the high standard that one would expect from the Shelbourne. The restaurant features an oyster bar and an open kitchen. Opulent surroundings enhance your fine-dining experience: discreet lighting in yellow tones, dark wood splashed with gold lamé and leather banquettes. The friendly staff provides a first-class service.

 27 St. Stephen's Green, Dublin 2 ☎ 01 478 2152 🕙 Daily 12–2, 6–10 ✋ L €30, D €50, Wine €30 🚌 Cross-city buses 🚃 DART Pearse

THE TEA ROOM RESTAURANT

www.theclarence.ie

The Tea Room Restaurant can be found in this classic hotel, which has been given a fabulous contemporary look by U2's Bono and the Edge. Flexible menus, offering Irish and French cuisine, include Sunday brunch, a speedy lunch-hour option.

 The Clarence Hotel, 6–8 Wellington Quay, Dublin 2 ☎ 01 407 0813 🕙 Mon–Sat 12.30–2.30, 7–10.30, Sun 12.30–2.30, 7–9.30 ✋ L €28, D €55, Wine €18 🚌 25, 66 🚃 DART Tara Street 🚌 On the south bank of the River Liffey in the Temple Bar area

WINDING STAIR

www.winding-stair.com

A Dublin landmark that is one of the city's hidden gems. After being acquired by the Thomas Read group, this lovely secondhand bookshop has had a makeover, but still retains every bit of its old-world fascination. The top-floor café provides one of the best views over the River Liffey; from here you can tuck into good, simple Irish cooking with an organic influence while watching the world go by.

 40 Lower Ormond Quay, Dublin 1 ☎ 01 872 7320 🕙 Mon–Sat 12.30–3.30, 6–10.30, Sun 12.30–3.30, 6–9.30 ✋ L €16, D €36, Wine €24 🚌 Cross-city buses 🚃 DART Tara Street

WINTER GARDEN RESTAURANT

www.redcowhotel.com

Modern Irish cuisine is a feature of the daily changing menu here. Starters are deliciously light, such as the tian of smoked salmon with a salad of new potato, capers, sun-blushed tomatoes and dill mayonnaise, followed by classics such as grilled fillet of Irish beef set on a rosti potato and served with caramelized parsnip, shallots and Bordelaise sauce. Traditional desserts include crème brûlée and pistachio tart.

 Red Cow Moran's Hotel, Red Cow Complex, Naas Road, Dublin 22 ☎ 01 459 3650 🕙 Mon–Fri 12.30–2.30, 5.30–10, Sat 5.30–10.30, Sun 12.30–10.30 ✋ L €36, D from €42, Wine €20 🚌 51, 69 🚌 At intersection of M50 (ring road) and N7 Naas road, on the city side of the ring road

Below *Chefs preparing dishes*
Opposite *Delicious roast potatoes*

STAYING

Above *Accommodation fills quickly in the capital, so always make reservations*

PRICES AND SYMBOLS

Prices are for a double room for one night. Breakfast is included unless noted otherwise. All the hotels listed accept credit cards unless otherwise stated. Note that rates vary widely throughout the year.

For a key to the symbols, ▷ 2.

ABBERLEY COURT

www.abberley.ie

With the Luas railway on its doorstep, the Abberley Court hotel guarantees a friendly welcome. It is a good option if you prefer to stay away from the city centre's trappings. Located next to a complex of shops, restaurants and a cinema, this establishment boasts stylish surroundings incorporating three public bars, one that serves food all day, and the first-floor Leaf Restaurant, which offers authentic Chinese food.

✉ Belgard Road, Tallaght, Dublin 24 ☎ 01 459 6000 ⊙ Closed 25 Dec–2 Jan ⊌ Double €79–€109 ① 40 ⊟ 49, 65, 65B, 77; Luas Tallaght ☐ Opposite The Square at the intersection of Belgard Road and the N81

ARIEL HOUSE

www.ariel-house.net

This gracious Victorian house is in a southeastern suburb, near Lansdowne Road. Luxurious premier rooms and more contemporary standard rooms are available, and healthy and vegetarian options are on offer at breakfast. Staff are friendly and there is secure parking.

✉ 50–54 Lansdowne Road, Ballsbridge, Dublin 4 ☎ 01 668 5512 ⊙ Closed 23–27 Dec ⊌ Double €99–€190 ① 37 ⊟ 7, 45 ☐ DART Lansdowne Road ☐ From Merrion Square, take Northumberland Road to Ballsbridge. Turn left at Jurys Hotel and Ariel House is on left past the traffic lights

ARLINGTON HOTEL, TEMPLE BAR

www.arlingtonhoteltemplebar.com

An attractive hotel, near to the Temple Bar area and Dublin Castle. Bedrooms are decorated in a modern style, and there's a popular bar and a separate restaurant.

✉ Lord Edward Street, Dublin 2 ☎ 01 670 8777 ⊌ Double €110–€220 ① 63 ⊟ 123 ☐ DART Pearse ☐ Adjacent to Dublin Castle

BEWLEY'S BALLSBRIDGE

www.bewleyshotels.com

This comfortable hotel is near the RDS Showgrounds. It offers good value, and its casual restaurant serves interesting dishes. The spacious lounges on the lower floor are a popular meeting place. Some parking is available (nominal fee); it should be requested on making a reservation.

✉ Merrion Road, Ballsbridge, Dublin 4 ☎ 01 668 1111 ⊙ Closed 24–26 Dec ⊌ Double €199 (breakfast not included) ① 220 ⊟ 7, 7A, 45 ☐ DART Sandymount ☐ Close to the heart of the city, at the intersection of Simmonscourt and Merrion roads. Entrance is on Simmonscourt Road

BLAKES TOWNHOUSE

www.halspinsprivatehotels.com

In this luxurious town house, renovated to a high standard, some of the spacious, air-conditioned bedrooms have four-poster beds. Other rooms have the benefit of a private balcony overlooking the delightful gardens. Parking is available.

50–56 Merrion Road, Ballsbridge, Dublin 4 📞 01 668 8324 📠 Double €129–€189 📶 13 🚇 📶 7, 45 🚉 DART Sandymount 🚌 Take Merrion Road south to Ballsbridge where you will find Blakes opposite the RDS Convention Centre

BROWNES TOWNHOUSE & BRASSERIE
www.brownesdublin.com
A gracious Georgian town house on Dublin's most prestigious square. Bedrooms are luxurious and there is a comfortable sitting room.
✉ 22 St. Stephen's Green, Dublin 2 📞 01 638 3939 📶 Double €220–€375 (breakfast not included) 📶 11 📶 15, 45 🚉 DART Pearse 🚌 On the north side of St. Stephen's Green beside the Shelbourne Hotel

BUSWELLS
www.quinnhotels.com
One of Dublin's 18th-century Georgian town houses, Buswells has well-equipped bedrooms. There's an elegant lobby lounge and restaurant, and a popular bar.
✉ 23–25 Molesworth Street, Dublin 2 📞 01 614 6500 🌐 Closed 25–26 Dec 📶 Double €145–€240 📶 67 📶 10 🚉 DART Pearse 🚌 On the corner of Molesworth Street and Kildare Street, opposite Dáil Éireann (Government Buildings)

CAMDEN COURT
www.camdencourthotel.ie
Just a short walk from St. Stephens Green, this hotel has many fine features. You are greeted by efficient and cheerful staff who do their best to ensure you have a comfortable stay. The bedrooms are tastefully decorated in vibrant, warm colours and are equipped with every modern convenience. Camden Court has just completed a major overhaul and expansion project, which includes the addition of the modern Iveagh restaurant and conference space.
✉ Camden Street, Dublin 2 📞 01 475 9666 📶 Double €145–€185 📶 246 🚌 Indoor 🚌 Cross-city buses, Luas Harcourt 🚌 From College Green take the second left off Dame Street into George's Street. Continue to Aungier Street, then Wexford Street and into Camden Street; the hotel is at the top end on the right

THE CARNEGIE COURT
www.carnegiecourt.com
This modern, tastefully built hotel has comfortable air-conditioned bedrooms. Public areas include a residents' lounge, contemporary Courtyard Restaurant, the dramatic Harp Lounge and conference and banqueting facilities.
✉ North Street, Swords Village, Swords, Co. Dublin 📞 01 840 4384 🌐 Closed 24–26 Dec 📶 Double €130–€155 📶 36 🚇 📶 41 🚉 Malahide Station then bus 230

CASSIDYS HOTEL
www.cassidyshotel.com
This family-run hotel with modern bedrooms is in a redbrick Georgian terrace at the top of O'Connell Street. Groomes Bar is warm and friendly, Cassidy's is decorated in traditional style, and Restaurant 6 is contemporary and stylish. Parking spaces are limited.
✉ 6–8 Cavendish Row, Upper O'Connell Street, Dublin 1 📞 01 878 0555 🌐 Closed 24–26 Dec 📶 Double €99–€185 📶 88 📶 7, 10, 45 🚉 DART Tara Street

CHARLEVILLE LODGE
www.charlevillelodge.ie
This elegant Victorian terrace has been beautifully restored. Lounges are welcoming, and a choice of breakfasts is available in the dining room. Bedrooms are very comfortable, and there's secure parking.
✉ 268–272 North Circular Road, Phibsborough, Dublin 7 📞 01 838 6633 📶 Double €75–€250 📶 30 (4 ground floor) 📶 10 🚌 Near to St. Peter's Church

THE CLARENCE
www.theclarence.ie
The Clarence is at the heart of Dublin City, on the banks of the River Liffey. Contemporary design is tastefully incorporated into the original features of the building, dating from 1850.
✉ 6–8 Wellington Quay, Dublin 2 📞 01 407 0800 📶 Double €350–€400 📶 50 📶 7, 10, 45 🚉 DART Tara Street 🚌 From O'Connell Bridge, go west along quays; the hotel is 500m (550 yards) beyond the first set of lights (at the Ha'Penny Bridge)

COMFORT INN SMITHFIELD
www.comfortinndublincity.com
A chic, modern property, which offers excellent value for money, located in this newly developed historic quarter of Dublin. Some guest rooms boast impressive views over the city from the veranda. The hotel's restaurant, Stir, is open all day. Ideal for both business and pleasure, it is close to the city's principal shopping areas and attractions.
✉ Smithfield Plaza, Dublin 7 📞 01 485 0900 🌐 Closed 29–23 Dec 📶 Double €89–€229 📶 92 🚉 Luas Smithfield

THE FITZWILLIAM HOTEL
www.fitzwilliamhotel.com
This friendly hotel is a pleasing blend of contemporary style and good traditional standards of hotelkeeping. Eating options include the informal Citron, and Thornton's, which offers a truly fine dining experience.
✉ St. Stephen's Green, Dublin 2 📞 01 478 7000 📶 Double €225–€350 📶 140 📶 7, 45 🚉 DART Pearse 🚌 Next to the top of Grafton Street

GRAND CANAL
www.grandcanalhotel.com
The modern Grand Canal hotel is in a peaceful spot on the leafy banks of the Grand Canal, near Ballsbridge. The city centre is a pleasant 15 minutes' walk away but the DART station is close at hand to give easy access. Spacious public areas include a lounge, restaurant and the Gasworks bar, which features live music on Fridays. Bedrooms have been designed with comfort and convenience in mind and are decorated in warm, contemporary shades. There are also conference rooms, and an underground car park on site.
✉ Grand Canal Street, Dublin 📞 01 646 1000 🌐 Closed 23–28 Dec 📶 Double €109–€225 📶 142 📶 5, 7, 7A, 45 🚉 DART Grand Canal Dock 🚌 From the south side of O'Connell Bridge take Aston Quay and cross Father Matthew Bridge, into Church Street. Take the next left to Smithfield Plaza, the hotel is on the left-hand side

THE GRESHAM
www.gresham-hotels.com
Renovation has given a chic look to the popular lounge and brasserie, where there's an emphasis on quality seasonal produce. Bedrooms come in a variety of styles.
✉ 23 Upper O'Connell Street, Dublin 1 ☎ 01 874 6881 👋 Double €100–€650 🛈 288 🆘 🅿 🍴 7, 45 🚊 DART Connolly 🚌 Close to the GPO

HARDING HOTEL
www.hardinghotel.ie
In the lively Temple Bar area, this friendly hotel offers good-value accommodation. Darkey Kelly's Bar & Restaurant serves traditional Irish food and music, and Cooper Alley Bistro provides good value meals.
✉ Cooper Alley, Fishamble Street, Christchurch, Dublin 2 ☎ 01 679 6500 🕔 Closed 23–26 Dec 👋 Double €90–€125 (breakfast not included) 🛈 53 🍴 49, 50, 54A, 56A, 123 🚊 DART Connolly 🚌 Top of Dame Street beside Christ Church Cathedral

JURYS INN CUSTOM HOUSE
www.jurysdoyle.com
A welcome addition to the Jury's chain, this hotel is in the financial district close to the redeveloped docks. Accommodation is of a high standard and offers family rooms.
✉ Custom House Quay, Dublin 1 ☎ 01 854 1500 👋 Double €95–€180 🛈 239 🆘 🍴 1; Luas Busáras 🚊 DART Connolly 🚌 South of city via Merrion Road, at intersection with Northumberland Road

KILRONAN HOUSE
www.dublinn.com
Rose and Terry Masterson welcome guests to this fine period town house. Bedrooms are well appointed and there is a stylish dining room and guest lounge. Breakfasts are wonderful. Parking is at the rear.
✉ 70 Adelaide Road, Dublin 2 ☎ 01 475 5266 👋 Double €110–€180 🛈 12 🍴 7, 45 🚊 DART Pearse 🚌 A 5-min walk from St. Stephen's Green

MARINE HOTEL
www.marinehotel.ie
If you would like a change of scenery, this nicely decorated hotel in attractive gardens on the north shore of Dublin Bay, fits the bill. The Meridian restaurant specializes in Irish cuisine of a high standard. Both the standard and superior bedrooms have all the facilities needed for a comfortable stay, but the superior are larger and many have sea views. There is also a business suite.
✉ Sutton Cross, Dublin 13 ☎ 01 839 0000 🕔 Closed 24–27 Dec 👋 Double €100–€150 🛈 50 🏊 Indoor 🍴 31, 31B 🚊 DART Sutton 🚌 8km (5 miles) from city on the road to Howth

MERRION HALL
www.halpinsprivatehotels.com
This elegant town house in Ballsbridge is convenient for all local amenities. The reception rooms are spacious and the breakfast room overlooks the gardens. The large bedrooms are air-conditioned, and some have balconies.
✉ 54–56 Merrion Road, Ballsbridge, Dublin 4 ☎ 01 668 1426 👋 Double €119–€179 🛈 28 🆘 🍴 45 🚊 DART Sandymount 🚌 Ballsbridge is approximately 1.5km (0.9 miles) along the main route from Dublin to Dún Laoghaire Port. Hotel is between the British and US embassies

THE MERRION HOTEL
www.merrionhotel.com
This terrace of gracious Georgian buildings, reputed to have been the birthplace of the Duke of Wellington, has undergone many changes of use in more than 200 years. Spacious bedrooms offer deep comfort and a wide range of extra facilities, lounges retain the charm and opulence of past times, while the Cellar Bar area is ideal for a relaxing drink. Dining options include Dublin's finest: Restaurant Patrick Guilbaud (▷ 108).
✉ Upper Merrion Street, Dublin 2 ☎ 01 603 0600 👋 Double €470–€2,065 🛈 145 🆘 🏊 Indoor 🍴 7, 10, 45 🚊 DART Pearse 🚌 At the top of Upper Merrion Street on the left, beyond Government Buildings on the right

MOUNT HERBERT HOTEL
www.mountherberthotel.ie
Near to local places of interest, this hotel has comfortable public rooms, well-equipped bedrooms and a friendly atmosphere. There is a spacious lounge, a TV room, a cocktail bar and a lovely, good-value restaurant, which overlooks the floodlit gardens.
✉ Herbert Road, Lansdowne Road, Sandymount, Dublin 4 ☎ 01 668 4321 🕔 Closed 23–28 Dec 👋 Double €100–€350 🛈 168 🍴 10, 45 🚊 DART Lansdowne Road (200m/220 yards)

THE PLAZA HOTEL
www.plazahotel.ie
This contemporary hotel has spacious public areas and secure underground parking. The Vista Café and Olive Tree Restaurant enjoy views of the Wicklow Mountains. There's informal dining in Grumpy McClaffertys bar.
✉ Belgard Road, Tallaght, Dublin 24 ☎ 01 462 4200 🕔 Closed 24–30 Dec 👋 Double €90–€175 (breakfast not included) 🛈 122 🆘 🍴 77; Luas Tallaght 🚌 On the ring road, a 30-min drive southwest of the city on the N81

RADISSON SAS ST. HELEN'S
www.dublin.radissonsas.com
This 18th-century mansion is now a fine hotel, with many original features in the main house. Comfortable bedrooms and suites are in a purpose-built block. Diners can eat in the informal Orangerie bar or the Italian Talavera trattoria.
✉ Stillorgan Road, Dublin 4 ☎ 01 218 6000 👋 Double €155–€200 (breakfast not included) 🛈 151 🆘 🅿 🍴 46A, 46, 700 🚊 DART Booterstown 🚌 On left side of N11, 4km (2.5 miles) south of the city towards Wicklow

Below *Striking design at Stillorgan Park*

Above *The Merrion Hotel*

ST. AIDEN'S
www.staidens.com
The reception rooms here are comfortable and relaxing, and include a hospitality trolley. Bedrooms vary in size from but all have TVs and telephones.
✉ 32 Brighton Road, Rathgar, Dublin 6 ☎ 01 490 2011 👐 Double €80–€100 🛈 8 🚌 15, 15A, 15B 🚗 Off M50 Junction 11 towards city. St. Aiden's is the third premises on the left after the traffic lights in Terenure Village

THE SHELBOURNE
www.marriott.com
A Dublin landmark since 1824, the rare and timeless elegance of this hotel has strong literary and historical links. It has gracious reception rooms, a choice of restaurants, a leisure suite and spa, and popular bars. Bedrooms are stylish and comfortable, many with fine views over St. Stephen's Green. The hotel reopened in 2007 after a magnificent make-over, while keeping its former historic charm.

✉ 27 St. Stephen's Green, Dublin 2 ☎ 01 633 4500 👐 Double €215–€3,000 🛈 265 ▨ Indoor ▤ 🚌 7, 45 🚇 DART Pearse 🚗 Go south across O'Connell Bridge to pass Trinity College, then turn left into Nassau Street and right into Kildare Street; the hotel is on the left

STILLORGAN PARK
www.stillorganpark.com
Bedrooms are stylish and contemporary, and there's a modern restaurant and inviting bar. An air-conditioned banqueting and conference suite is available, and plenty of parking.
✉ Stillorgan Road, Dublin 4 ▨ 01 200 1800 👐 Double €145–€170 🛈 165 ▤ 🚌 46A 🚇 DART Blackrock (15-min walk from hotel) 🚗 Take N11 south, signed Wexford, pass RTE Studios on left, then after the next five traffic lights hotel is on the left

TEMPLE BAR
www.templebarhotel.com
This stylish hotel is in the heart of old Dublin. Well-equipped bedrooms are competitively priced, and good food is served throughout the day.
✉ Fleet Street, Temple Bar, Dublin 2 ☎ 01 621 9200 ⊘ Closed 23–25 Dec 👐 Double €120–€200 🛈 129 🚌 7, 45 🚇 DART Tara Street/Pearse 🚗 From Trinity College, go north towards O'Connell Bridge up Westmorland Street and take first left onto Fleet Street; hotel is on the right

WESTBURY
www.jurys-dublin-hotels.com
Located in the heart of the city just off Grafton Street, this sophisticated hotel is an oasis of calm in Dublin's premier shopping street. Amid chic, sumptuous surroundings, from the relaxing Terrace bar to the Sandbank Bistro and the more formal Russell Room, the service is impeccable. A range of luxury suites and bedrooms is available and all offer unparalleled comfort, many overlooking the roofscape of the city.
✉ Grafton Street, Dublin 2 ☎ 01 679 1122 👐 Double €200–€500 🛈 205 ▤ 🚌 Cross-city buses 🚇 DART Pearse 🚗 Set back on Harry Street, nearer the top end of Grafton Street

THE EAST

Extending from the border with Northern Ireland down to the pretty Wexford coast, with Dublin at the core, Eastern Ireland has many charms: slow-paced towns and villages dotted throughout beautiful remote countryside, clusters of historic sights, glistening lakes, tranquil rivers, beautiful glens and gorges, silent valleys sandwiched between wild, exposed mountains, fine beaches and challenging golf courses.

North of the capital the land is green farming country scattered with relics of an ecclesiastical past, including ancient churches and an astonishing collection of historic Christian monuments packed into the monastic site of Monasterboice. Brú na Bóinne, 11km (7 miles) from Drogheda, is Europe's richest concentration of ancient tombs, which runs 15km (9 miles) alongside the River Boyne. Nearby, the Hill of Tara, the great hill from which the ancient High Kings of Ireland ruled, rises out of the Meath Plain.

Southwest of Dublin, County Kildare is known as prime horse country and is home to the Irish National Stud and The Curragh, one of Ireland's most famous horseracing courses. Farther south, it is worth the detour to visit the richly carved pre-Norman high crosses in the villages of Moone and Castledermot. The town of Kilkenny is a medieval gem, and a great spot to put down roots for a while to soak up the atmosphere created by traditional Irish music heard in the many local pubs.

Venturing south from the capital, cliffs and long sandy beaches fringe the unspoilt coast (despite the presence of Ireland's main ferry port) as it approaches the forest-clad slopes of the Wicklow Mountains—Ireland's most extensive mountain region popular with outdoor enthusiasts. The main attraction here is the monastic site of Glendalough, which stretches along a glorious lake in the heart of the mountains. At the southeastern point, Wexford is a historic Heritage Town with a network of narrow lanes and a huge natural harbour.

BRÚ NA BÓINNE

INTRODUCTION

Brú na Bóinne, the 'palace of the Boyne', is the name given to a large group of neolithic remains in the Boyne Valley 11km (7 miles) west of Drogheda. The huge, white-fronted passage tomb of Newgrange is the best known, but the nearby mounds of Knowth and Dowth were probably of equal importance historically. These great tombs are more than 5,000 years old. We can only guess at the significance of their swirling rock art but the impact of the winter solstice sun, which stunningly lights up the tombs' darkest recesses, was clearly important. You can visit the main site only with an organized tour from the Visitor Centre, but it is worth spending time in the centre itself, learning about the culture that gave rise to these extraordinary monuments.

There are more than 50 lumps and bumps with ritual significance around Brú na Bóinne. Of the three major tombs, you can visit the interiors of Knowth and Newgrange on organized tours, but visitor numbers are restricted. Your ticket buys you a seat on an allotted minibus, which leaves from beneath the Visitor Centre. Some of the stops on these tours are assigned to tour operators coming from Dublin, so if you want to guarantee a visit to the tombs themselves you may be better joining one of those. Otherwise, arrive early and be prepared to wait. Once you have bought your ticket you can explore the surrounding countryside until your tour is due to leave.

The whole Brú na Bóinne area is designated a World Heritage Site by UNESCO, putting it on equal footing with Stonehenge (1,000 years younger) and the pyramids of Giza (100 years younger). The antiquity of the site means it is difficult to know who began the structures and what their cultural significance was. The pre-Celtic founders may have come from the Iberian Peninsula, as some experts have suggested their swirling artwork indicates. But other authorities claim this is a specifically Irish phenomenon. Early Christians also occupied the site, adding their dead to the prehistoric tombs. By the ninth century this was an important stronghold of the Uí Néill clan, but the Middle Ages saw its decline and eventual abandonment. The tombs remained untouched until 1699, when renewed interest in antiquities brought them back into public knowledge.

WHAT TO SEE
KNOWTH

Knowth was certainly already built when the 'beaker people' (named for their characteristic pottery) arrived from mainland Europe and occupied the site around 1800BC. It featured heavily in the lives of the Iron Age Celts from around 500BC, and plays a part in the dazzling array of legends that

INFORMATION

www.meathtourism.ie
⊞ 365 G4 ⓘ Brú na Bóinne Visitor Centre, Donore, Co. Meath ☎ 041 988 0300 ⊙ Jun to mid-Sep daily 9–7; May, mid Sep to end Sep daily 9–6.30; Mar, Apr daily 9.30–5.30; Oct daily 9.30–5; Nov–end Feb daily 9.30–5. Knowth open Easter end Oct only 🖐 Exhibition only: adult €2.90, child (under 16) €1.60, family €7.40; exhibition and Newgrange: adult €5.80, child (under 16) €2.90, family €14.50; exhibition and Knowth: adult €4.50, child (under 16) €1.60, family €11; exhibition, Newgrange and Knowth: adult €10.30, child (under 16) €4.50, family €25.50 🚌 Bus Éireann service 163 to/from Drogheda to Donore village (10-min walk) 🚉 Drogheda Station 8km (5 miles) 🎫 Access by tour only, each lasting 45 min (average length of visit up to 3 hours if visiting all sites) ☕ Café at Visitor Centre

Opposite *Detail on the inscribed stones at Newgrange*
Left *Characteristic whorl motifs in the rocks at Knowth*

was passed down in the Irish language from these people. Knowth is the most westerly of the great tombs, and is accessible only by tour, although it can be seen from the nearby road. The mound is outlined by 127 huge edging stones. Surrounding the main tomb are at least 18 smaller tombs, some of which predate the larger tomb. There has been human activity here from far back in prehistory through to the early Christian period, and understanding the complex story of the site's development has not been easy. Inside the tomb are two passages, both lined with upright stones. Their faces are adorned with swirling patterns and lines. The eastern passage contains a large ditch. This was added in the early Christian era and demonstrates the mound's lasting spiritual importance across the millennia. Knowth tends to attract fewer visitors than Newgrange, so you may well find it easier to get a ticket for this site than for the better known tomb.

NEWGRANGE

Newgrange was supposedly the home of Tuátha dé Danann, troglodytic followers of the goddess Danu. Warrior hero Cúchulainn was conceived here, the kings of Tara were said to have been buried here and Diarmuid, the wounded lover of Finn McCool's wife Gráinne, was carried here to be brought back to life. The mound, fronted by white quartzite, is the most familiar of all the Brú na Bóinne monuments. Actually the frontage is the result of restoration work carried out in the 1960s, but the effect is truly stunning. The nearest source for quartzite is 64km (40 miles) away, beyond Dublin in the Wicklow Mountains, so whoever built this tomb had the ability to transport materials to the site over long distances. The whole mound is 100m (330ft) across and about 10m (33ft) high. There are 97 boulders forming an edging ring and, until the 17th century, there was a large standing stone positioned at the summit. At the entrance, one of these edging stones is adorned with the distinctive spiral and line motifs that characterize the rock art that has been found in the surrounding area. Above it stands the rectangular opening known as the roof box. Studying the site between 1962 and 1975, Professor M. J. O'Kelly made the remarkable discovery that the midwinter sun penetrates a slit in this chamber, sending a narrow shaft of light up the main passageway to illuminate the recess at the back of the north chamber. To be among the lucky few to witness the magic of this moment on the morning of the winter solstice, you must win a lottery draw, which you can enter at the Visitor Centre, but you'll be among more than 20,000 hopefuls who apply each year. For the rest of us, the experience is reconstructed using an accurately positioned electric light. Astronomical calculations reveal that this effect would have been even more dramatic 5,000 years ago. Subtle shifts in the earth's axis and orbits have left the light falling slightly short of illuminating the whole chamber; when it was

Below *Fronted by quarzite, the Newgrange tomb is the most familiar and stunning of the monuments*

constructed the dawn light would have filled the whole of the back wall during the winter solstice. Another particularly remarkable feature of the Newgrange tomb is the construction of its roof. The massive stones above the chambers are interlaced in such a way as to render them watertight, even after 5,000 years. The best examples of rock carving are to be found on the roof and walls of the right-hand chamber as you go in.

DOWTH

Dowth is the least known of the three great tombs, and though it contains some of the finest rock art to be seen anywhere in Ireland, its interior is out of bounds to visitors. However, you are free to roam about its grassy site, a freedom which is not allowed at Newgrange or Knowth. The mound is over 61m (200ft) across and about 14m (46ft) tall; the crater on its summit is the result of enthusiastic Victorian excavations. Some early Christian remains were found within and one of the passages connects to an early Christian *souterrain* (underground chamber). There are two principal neolithic tombs inside and the mound is outlined by 115 edging stones.

THE BRÚ NA BÓINNE VISITOR CENTRE

The Visitor Centre is more than just a conduit to the tomb visits—it deserves at least an hour's attention in its own right. There are detailed touch-screen explanations of how the site evolved, who built it and how it was discovered. Among the life-size reconstructions are a cross-section of an archaeological survey, showing the painstaking methods used by the researchers investigating the site, and a re-creation of the main passage inside the Newgrange tomb, crucially widened so that wheelchairs can fit all the way in (the actual site is not accessible to wheelchair users because the passages are too narrow). A 7-minute audio-visual presentation shows you what the solstice light looks like and there are even hands-on demonstrations of carbon-dating. In addition to viewing the cabinets displaying finds from the sites, you are invited to share your theories on the meanings behind the swirling artforms. The viewing area includes the free use of telescopes and there is a good bookshop, café and tourist information desk.

Above *There is a passage tomb in the nearby Knowth mound*
Below *An insight into past civilizations: This carved mace head was found at Knowth*

AVOCA HANDWEAVERS

www.avoca.ie

It's hard to escape the Avoca brand in Ireland. Whether you're shopping on Grafton Street or browsing in craft outlets, you'll see the name of this little Wicklow Mountains village on high-quality mohair and cashmere garments manufactured in the tiny weaving shed at the Old Mill on the edge of the village. Established in 1723, it is one of the oldest factories in continuous use in Ireland. Visitors can get a feel for the clatter of the weaving shed, with its array of working handlooms and machine looms, before visiting the factory shop. The rest of the village is hardly exciting but is neatly painted, thanks mostly to its starring role in the BBC series *Ballykissangel*.

✚ 365 G6 ✉ Old Mill, Avoca, Co. Wicklow ☎ 0402 35105 🕐 Daily 9–6 (Oct–May daily 9.30–5.30) 🚌 On Bus Éireann service 133 Dublin–Avoca 🚉 Rathdrum Station 9km (5.5 miles) 🚲 Available on request 🖥 🏛

BECTIVE ABBEY

www.meathtourism.ie

Founded in 1147 as a daughter abbey to Mellifont (▷ 131), Bective was an Anglo-Norman, Cistercian foundation, but little survives from that period. What you see today, in a field by the River Boyne, is largely the 15th-century defensive additions. A square tower rises above the remaining walls of the cloister, nave and chapterhouse.

Also discernible are the fireplaces, chimneys and windows of the fortified mansion that the site became after the monastery's dissolution in 1543. A medieval bridge across the river indicates the abbey's former importance.

✚ 365 G4 ✉ Bective, Navan, Co. Meath. ☎ 046 943 7227 🕐 Daily, daylight hours 🖐 Free 🚌 Bus Éireann service 135 Navan to Scurloughstown stops at Bective Cross or 109 Dublin to Navan

BRAY

Bray sits on a long sweep of beach at the south end of Killiney Bay. Once promoted as a resort for wealthy Dubliners, it is now a desirable commuter town, backed by Bray Head and the distinctive cones of the Great and Little Sugar Loaf hills, and home to the National Sea Life Centre (tel 01 286 6939; www.sealifeeurope.com). On the slopes of the Little Sugar Loaf, holding out against the advances of new housing, Killruddery House and Gardens have been in the Brabazon family since 1618. The gardens were designed in French classical style in the 1680s by Bonet. The 17th-century house, redesigned in Elizabethan style in 1820, contains a mantelpiece by Grinling Gibbons and bookcases by Chippendale (tel 040 446024; gardens: Apr Sat–Sun 1–5; May–end Sep daily 1–5; house: May, Jun, Sep daily 1–5).

✚ 365 G5 ℹ Tourist Information Office, The Old Courthouse, Bray, Co. Wicklow,

☎ 01 286 7128 🚌 45, 84 (from Eden Quay, Dublin) 🚉 DART Bray

BRÚ NA BÓINNE

▷ 116–119.

CASTLETOWN HOUSE

www.castletown.ie

An avenue of lime trees 1km (half a mile) long leads up to this grey stone country house, designed for the Irish politician William Conolly in c1722, with a view over meadows to the River Liffey and the mountains. The main hall has stucco work by the Lafrancini brothers and an enormous painting, *The Boar Hunt*, by Paul de Vos (1596–1679). Conolly made his fortune buying and selling forfeited property after the Battle of the Boyne, but never lived to see his great house completed, a task left to Lady Louisa Conolly, the wife of his great nephew, who moved there in 1759. The interiors have been left virtually untouched since her death in 1821. One room, the Print Room, is lined with paper taken from 18th-century magazines. The house was acquired by the Irish state in 1994.

✚ 365 G5 ✉ Celbridge, Co. Kildare ☎ 01 628 8252 🕐 Easter to mid-Nov Tue–Sun 10–6 🖐 Adult €4, child (4–15) €2 🚌 67, 67A from Dublin 🚉 Hazelhatch & Celbridge 🚲 Guided tour only, 45 min 🖥

CARLOW

www.carlowtourism.com

Carlow is a somewhat unremark-able place, although there is good shopping off its wide open square. Away from the heart of town a pleasing tangle of early 19th-century streets suggests future potential, but Carlow's most impressive fea-ture, its castle (open daylight hours), lies stranded in wasteland by the Barrow River amid modern housing schemes. The two remaining round towers and a section of curtain wall date from the 13th century. The rest was bizarrely destroyed in 1814 by a local doctor trying to convert the site into a mental hospital with the aid of high explosives.

The early 19th-century Gothic Cathedral of the Assumption, one of

Left *Looking out from Bray towards the steep slope of Bray Head*

Opposite *The evocative ruins of the Cistercian Bective Abbey stand among peaceful meadows by the Boyne river*

A Martello tower crowns an Anglo-Norman motte from the 12th century. A museum, craft centre and restaurant are in the next door barracks, and there are splendid views (Millmount Museum, tel 041 983 3097; Mon–Sat 9.30–5.30, Sun, public holidays 2–5). There's a Heritage Centre and more medieval defences near Millmount.

✠ 365 G4 ℹ Tourist Information Office, Mayoralty Street, Drogheda, Co. Louth ☎ 041 983 7070 🚍 Bus Éireann from Dublin 🚆 Drogheda

the first Catholic churches built after the Emancipation Act, was designed by Thomas Cobden and is topped by an impressive lantern tower. The courthouse building, somewhat marred by the heavy traffic, is a striking replica of the Parthenon, and was supposedly intended for Cork City until a mix-up of documents gave Carlow one of its grandest buildings. About 3km (2 miles) out of town on the R726 the Browneshill Dolmen (open daylight hours) stands in a field opposite a car showroom. A surfaced track leads from a little parking area to the array of stones which dates from 2500BC, and would originally have been covered in earth. The precarious capstone is believed to be one of the largest in Europe.

✠ 365 F6 ℹ Tullow Street, Carlow, Co. Carlow ☎ 059 913 1544 ⏰ Apr–end Sep Mon–Sat 9.30–5.30, Sun 10–5 🚍 Bus Éireann service from Dublin 🚆 Carlow

CAVAN
www.cavantourism.com

Cavan's narrow main shopping street (Farnham Street) is a pleasant place to linger. The shops are mostly independently owned, their bright frontages harking back to an older Ireland, all but vanished this far east. Of the 14th-century Franciscan friary, to which the town owes its origin, the belfry tower remains in a run-down churchyard near the bus station. The huge green rotunda and neoclassical façade of St. Patrick's Roman Catholic Cathedral, built in 1942, stand out in the north of town. The nearby courthouse is also built in an imposing classical style, but there is little else to detain you here.

✠ 362 F4 ℹ Tourist Information Office, 7 Farnham Street, Cavan Town, Co. Cavan ☎ 049 433 1942 🚍 Bus Éireann service from Dublin

DROGHEDA
www.drogheda.ie

Viking traders established this port town spanning both banks of the River Boyne in AD911. Its name 'Droichead Atha' means 'bridge by the ford', though it was not bridged until the Normans came in the 12th century. The industrial heart of the town is undergoing a renaissance and modern Drogheda has been improved since the M1 toll bridge to the west diverted Dublin–Belfast traffic out of the town.

The north side of the river has the main shopping area and medieval remains such as St. Lawrence's Gate, a four-floor barbican, and Magdalene Tower, a remnant of a once-important Dominican friary from 1224.

On the south side of the river, accessed from the riverside by steep steps, is the Millmount fortification.

DUNMORE CAVE
www.heritageireland.ie

This impressive cave lies on a gentle rise in the limestone hills south of Kilkenny. An interpretative area guards the entrance, and visits to the fantastical arrays of stalactites and stalagmites below ground are by guided tour. A steep series of 706 steps leads into the cave, which has three main chambers and contains traces of occupation stretching back more than 3,500 years. The 7m-high (23ft) Market Cross is just one of the huge stalagmites in chasms known as the 'cathedral' and the 'town hall'.

Back in the interpretative area you can see interactive displays of remains and treasures found in the cave. The most macabre remains are those of the 44 women and children who possibly suffocated during a Viking raid in AD928. In 1999 Viking coins and silver jewellery were discovered here dating from a similar time.

✠ 364 F6 ✉ Ballyfoyle, Kilkenny, Co. Kilkenny ☎ 056 776 7726 ⏰ Mid-Jun to mid-Sep daily 9.30–6.30; mid-Mar to mid-Jun, mid-Sep to end Oct daily 9.30–5; Nov to mid-Mar Sat–Sun, public holidays 10–4.30 ✋ Adult €2.90, child (6–17) €1.20, family €7.40 🚍 Kilkenny 🚆 Kilkenny Station ⓘ Access by guided tour only, 1 hour ☕ Café in Visitor Centre

GLENDALOUGH

INFORMATION

✚ 365 G6 ✉ Glendalough, Bray, Co.
Wicklow ☎ 0404 45325 🄲 Visitor
Centre: mid-Mar to mid-Oct daily
9.30–6; mid-Oct to mid-Mar daily 9.30–5
(last admission 45 min before closing)
✋ Visitor Centre: adult €2.90, child
(6–16) €1.30, family €7.40 🚌 St. Kevin's
Bus Service twice daily from Bray and
Dublin 🚉 Rathdrum 11km (7 miles)
📷 Available on request, allow 40 min

INTRODUCTION

The reclusive St. Kevin first established a monastic presence in this U-shaped glacial valley in AD570. The remote location was ideal for his hermitic tendencies, but he emphasized them still further by spending time in a cave (St. Kevin's Bed), accessible only by boat, on the cliffs above the Upper Lough. St. Kevin came from one of Leinster's ruling families and was abbot here until his death in AD618. He encouraged Glendalough's reputation for learning and its renown spread across Europe.

This was a place of pilgrimage too, seven trips here were equivalent to one trip to Rome even as late as 1862. Though it survived Viking and Norman raids, as well as those of indigenous bandits, the settlement began to decline in importance with the wave of French monastic foundations that followed the Anglo-Norman occupation of Ireland. But there were still monks resident here when the monastery was dissolved in the 16th century. St. Kevin's feast day (3 June) continued to draw visitors to Glendalough into the 19th century, by which time they had acquired a rather bawdy reputation. The middle of that century saw an increased interest in archaeology and the site was taken over by the Commissioners of Public Works in 1869.

The remarkable combination of a well-preserved monastic settlement with a beautiful lake and mountain setting makes Glendalough one of eastern Ireland's premier attractions. The excellent modern Visitor Centre helps you to understand not just what you can see on the ground, but also its place in Irish history. The two lakes and the mountains that surround it are superb walking territory, whether you're looking for a woodland stroll or a more challenging upland circuit. There are clearly waymarked paths between the principal sites, and for the most part these are even, with few steps or gradients. The free Visitor Centre parking area is the best spot to start from if you want to see all the sites on foot.

WHAT TO SEE
MAIN SITE
Glendalough means the 'valley of the two loughs' although the principal site is below the Lower Lough on slightly raised land by the confluence of the Gledasan and Glenalo rivers. Here you'll find the ruins of St. Ciaran's Church, and those of St. Kevin's Church, often called St. Kevin's Kitchen because its tower resembles the chimney stack of a bakehouse. The body of this barrell-vaulted oratory is made from hard mica schist and dates from the 12th century.

A double arch by the Glendalough Hotel leads you into the churchyard where the remains of the cathedral stand, its ninth-century nave and chancel now roofless. The Priest's House contains carvings of St. Kevin and dates from the 12th century. The 33m (110ft) round tower would have served as a belfry, lookout tower and treasury. Although the conical roof has been restored, the rest of the tower is in its original condition, an indication of how well this site has been preserved. There's a high cross here, though its impact is lessened somewhat by the proliferation of wheelhead motifs adorning the surrounding graves—this is still a working cemetery for the residents of the glen and the nearby village of Laragh. On the far side of the churchyard, the 10th-century St. Mary's Church may have housed St. Kevin's tomb.

UPPER LOUGH SITES
Between the Visitor Centre and the bridge stands the Deerstone, which despite its spurious legend of does squirting milk into its hollow to feed Kevin's disciples, is actually a much older grinding stone from the glen's prehistoric inhabitants. Beyond the Lower Lough, another group of important sites includes the 10th-century Reefert Church, with its tombs of local chiefs, and St. Kevin's Cell, the beehive-style hut where the settlement began.

Above here, you can walk up past the tumbling Poulanass Waterfall into the surrounding mountains, or follow the old miners' road up along the northern shore of the Upper Lough to see the remains of the lead and silver mines that were established in the rocky outcrops at the head of the valley. These were part of a larger mining operation in the next glen, and were worked between 1850 and 1875.

On the cliffs on the south side of the lough, the peculiar Teampull na Skellig is a platform cut into the rock, the site of the very early 'Church of the Rock'. Nearby St. Kevin's Bed is a Bronze Age burial site, later associated with Kevin's escape from Kathleen, a temptress whom he eventually threw in the lough to drown.

VISITOR CENTRE
The Visitor Centre also acts as an information outlet for the Wicklow Mountains National Park. It's at the entrance to the glen, just beyond the site of the Trinity Chapel. The main audio-visual presentation lasts 17 minutes and concentrates on Glendalough's Christian heritage. The interactive displays are more balanced, and explain the key features: the high cross, the carvings, the round tower. A scale model shows what the monastic settlement might have looked like in the 12th century.

TIPS
» Access to the site in the valley is free. You pay only if you want to park by the Upper Lake or go to the Visitor Centre.
» A walk on one of the marked trails around the glen will give you a better perspective than just wandering around the ruins and will also get you away from the crowds. Pick up a free leaflet from the Visitor Centre.

Opposite *St. Kevin's Church seen through the headstones of the graves around it*
Above *Glendalough's monastic remains have a beautiful and peaceful lakeside setting*
Below *There are good woodland strolls to enjoy around Glendalough*

GLENDALOUGH
▷ 122–123.

HILL OF TARA

www.meathtourism.ie

Tara has played a central role in early Irish history and has more than 30 visible monuments, part of a ritual landscape with an unbroken history of 4,000 years up to the sixth century AD. Among the more impressive remains is the Mound of the Hostages, a passage grave which contained 40 Bronze Age cremations. Tours and an audio-visual display are available in summer from the Visitor Centre in St. Patrick's Church on the site. If it's closed, a tea and gift shop sells books with explanations of the monuments. Names recall the site's importance as home of the High Kings of Ireland—the Royal Enclosure, Rath of the Synods, Banquet Hall. In a ring feature known as Cormac's House, the Lia Fáil is the stone on which High Kings were crowned.

✚ 365 G5 ✉ Hill of Tara, near Navan, Co. Meath ☎ 046 902 5903 (Nov–end Apr phone 041 988 0300) ⊗ Main site: mid-May to mid-Sep dawn–dusk. Visitor Centre in St. Patrick's Church: mid-May to mid-Sep daily 10–6 ✋ Main site: free. Visitor Centre: adult €2.10, child €1.10, family €5.80 🎧 40 min, available from Visitor Centre in summer 🚌 South of Navan off N3

HOOK HEAD PENINSULA

www.thehook-wexford.com

County Wexford points a finger into the crashing waters of the Atlantic Ocean at Hook Head. The lighthouse at the end of the peninsula is one of the oldest working lighthouses in the world. Records show its origins to be in the fifth century AD and its red sandstone base dates from 1172.

The Head is a strange place. A walk along the water's edge reveals blow holes—best seen on a blustery day as long as you exercise caution—and dangerous rocky ledges. It's no place for a swim: Even on calm days there can be freakishly large waves.

Two abbeys were founded at the base of the peninsula. Dunbrody, dating from 1182 (tel 051 388603, Jul, Aug 10–7; Apr–Jun, Sep daily 10–6), lies in open meadows by a tributary of the Barrow River and its Visitor Centre, in the courtyard of a ruined castle, doubles as a cookery school. Tintern (tel 051 562650, tours daily Jul and Aug), founded in 1200 by Cistercians from the abbey of the same name in South Wales, is more impressive. At the head of a tidal creek on Bannow Bay, it is reached down a gravel road and retains its nave, chancel chapel, cloister and tower.

A tour of Hook Head should also include Duncannon, a seaside resort with a huge sandy beach and an excellent star-shaped fort from the 16th century, and Slade, where the ruins of a 15th-century castle guard a tiny fishing harbour.

✚ 367 F8 ✉ Hook Head, Fethard-on-Sea, Co. Wexford ℹ Hook Lighthouse Centre ☎ 051 397055 ⊗ Guided tours Mar–end Oct daily 9.30–5.30, Nov–end Feb Sun only ✋ Visitor Centre free; lighthouse tour adult €6, child €3.50, family €18 🎧 Access to lighthouse is by tour only (30 min) 🏠 In former keepers' cottages

IRISH NATIONAL HERITAGE PARK

www.inhp.com

On the edge of Wexford, just off the northern bypass, the Irish National Heritage Park is a good place to stop if you have just entered the country from the Rosslare ferry. In 14ha (35 acres) of reclaimed marsh and swamp, 9,000 years of Irish history have been re-created through a series of full-scale models.

There's a mesolithic site with its dolmen and camp, a Bronze Age area showing how a cist burial would have looked, and a ring fort, a common feature of the Irish landscape. You can see how a monastic settlement would have looked, with its high cross, oratory and water mill, visit a *crannóg*, reconstructed on an island in the marsh, and appreciate the craft of the Viking shipbuilders who settled this area.

Against the criticism that this is theme park Ireland (in summer there are actors in costume around the site), the reconstructions can prove invaluable when you are trying to interpret many of the sites you will see in the rest of the country, putting the early Christian era in perspective and helping you to understand other remains such as those at Hill of Tara or Kells.

✝ 365 G7 ▦ Ferrycarrig, Wexford, Co. Wexford ☎ 053 91 20733 ⊙ Daily 9.30–6.30 ✋ Adult €8, child (4–12) €4, child (13–18) €4.50, family €20 ◪ 10-min audio-visual presentation followed by 70- to 90-min tour available on request ⊟ Wexford ◳ Fulacht Fiadh Restaurant

JERPOINT ABBEY

www.heritageireland.ie

The highlights of this 12th-century Cistercian ruin in the Nore Valley are the Romanesque carved figures to be found in the chapels of the north and south transepts. Their surprisingly cartoon-like qualities give a warm, human feel to what would otherwise be another set of cold monastic remains. There are smiling and weeping bishops, monks and knights, and a distinctive woman in a long pleated skirt. The Gothic tower, cloister and roofless nave date from the 14th and 15th centuries. A little Visitor Centre explains the significance of the carvings and traces the history of high crosses in the area.

✝ 367 F7 ▦ Thomastown, Co. Kilkenny ☎ 056 772 4623 ⊙ Jun–13 Sep daily 10–6; Mar–end May, 14 Sep–end Oct daily 10–5; Nov–end Feb daily 10–4 ✋ Adult €2.90, child (6–18) €1.30, family €7.40 ⊟ Bus Éireann service from Kilkenny to Thomastown ⊟ Thomastown ◪ Tour available on request, 45 min

JOHNSTOWN CASTLE

Close to the route from the Rosslare ferry port, Johnstown Castle is well signposted off the N25, just south of the Duncannon intersection. The site is a little confusing, being also the home of an agricultural college and an array of government departments relating to countryside matters, but at its heart lies the fabulously Gothicized castle, and the agricultural and famine museums, established in the castle's stable block. The foyer is as close inside the castle as visitors can get, but you can wander in its 20ha (50 acres) of gardens, see the peacocks, walled garden and ornamental lakes. The agricultural museum re-creates country trades and scenes from the last 200 years. Displays explain transport and farming and show a large collection of furniture and implements. The famine exhibition, within the museum, attempts to put this national tragedy of the 1840s in perspective, explaining the role of the potato and the changes that followed in the wake of the disastrous blight. A fascinating series of farmhouse kitchens in the agricultural museum compares the domestic lifestyles of 1800, 1900 and 1950.

✝ 365 G7 ▦ Johnstown Castle Estate, 6.4km (4 miles) from Wexford, Co. Wexford ☎ 053 91 42888 ⊙ Gardens: daily 9–5 (may alter in winter). Museum: Jun–end Aug Mon–Fri 9–5, Sat–Sun, public holidays 11–5; Apr, May, Sep–early Nov Mon–Fri 9–12.30, 1.30–5, Sat–Sun, public holidays 2–5 ✋ Gardens: May–end Sep, car €5, pedestrian/bicyclist €2, Oct–end Apr free. Museum: adult €5, child (5–16) €3, family €15. Note: May–end Sep museum visitors must also pay garden fee ◳ July, August

KELLS

www.meathtourism.ie

Straddling the lumbering traffic queues of the N3, Kells (Ceanannas Mor) wouldn't get much attention were it not for its connections with the famous book, now in Trinity College, Dublin. St. Colmcille (also known as St. Columba) established a monastic settlement here in AD550. Of this settlement only a well-preserved oratory building (St. Colmcille's House) remains. It's tucked away beyond the church and you'll need to get the keys, as a sign instructs, before you can visit.

The churchyard also contains some good high crosses and an impressive round tower, but the best high cross, the Market Cross, with its graphic depictions of biblical stories, stands under a shelter outside the Old Courthouse. It has moved around a little since its origins in the 10th century: Cromwell's troops used it as a gallows and in the 1990s it was knocked over by a car.

In its present site, the Market Cross draws you into the Heritage Centre, which occupies the delightful Georgian Old Courthouse. Here a 17-minute audio-visual presentation explains how the famous book came to Kells. In AD807 Viking raiders forced the monks on Iona, Scotland (▷ 91) to flee. They came to this older Columban site and brought their beautiful manuscript with them to complete. It is thought that it was stolen for its gold case 200 years later, then buried in a bog before being rediscovered and making its way to Dublin. Touch-screen computers allow you to view pages of a virtual Book of Kells and there are replicas of other valuables to be found in the National Museum. A scale model shows how the monastic town would have looked in its heyday, but it isn't easy to relate this to the trundling lines of cars and trucks you see today. In the nearby village of Crossakeel is a memorial to Jim Connell, the union organizer who wrote the socialist anthem *The Red Flag*.

✝ 365 F4 ℹ Kells Heritage Centre, The Courthouse, Headfort Place, Kells, Co. Meath ☎ 046 924 7840 ⊙ May–end Sep Mon–Sat 10–6, Sun and public holidays 1.30–6; Oct–end Apr Mon–Sat 10–5 ✋ Adult €4, child (4–16) €3, family €12 ⊟ Bus Éireann 109 from Dublin ◳

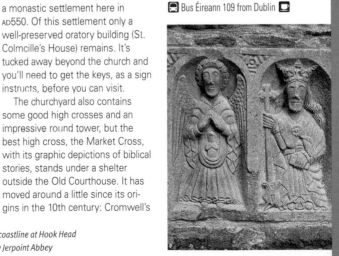

Opposite *Craggy rocks punctuate the low-lying coastline at Hook Head*
Right *Stone tomb decoration at the 12th-century Jerpoint Abbey*

INFORMATION

www.kildare.ie/tourism

✚ 365 F5 ℹ Kildare Tourist Information Office, Market House, Kildare, Co. Kildare
☎ 045 521240 🕐 Mon–Fri 10–1, 2–5
🚌 Bus Éireann service 126 from Dublin
🚉 Kildare

INTRODUCTION

The low-lying county of Kildare is barely half an hour's drive from Dublin on the M7. This is racing territory: More than 140 registered stud farms breed world-class flat-racing horses, and in Punchestown and The Curragh County Kildare has two of the country's leading racecourses. For this reason, Kildare town's principal attractions are related to the National Stud, a state-owned venture breeding some of the most famous horses in the world. Next to the Stud a pair of renowned gardens have been planted. The Japanese Garden reflects the passion of the Edwardian era for Eastern religious design. The more recent St. Fiachra's Garden follows modern concepts, allowing a habitat to develop without heavy-handed interference.

Kildare's central square is pleasantly quiet, with a heritage and information centre in the old Market House. Here you can watch a 12-minute video explaining the area's history and read about the significance of the Curragh for horse racing and the military. In the early Christian period there was a monastic settlement in Kildare, dedicated to St. Brigid. It was badly damaged in a Viking raid in AD835, but its surviving round tower, on the far side of the cathedral, is the second tallest in Ireland. The cathedral itself has had a chequered past. Its Gothic predecessor was destroyed by Cromwell's troops in 1641 and it wasn't until 1896 that its restoration was completed. Today it houses religious artefacts that include a 16th-century vault, religious seals and a medieval water font. The structure reflects the defensive function of the cathedral, with Irish parapets and walkways a distinctive feature of the roof. In the grounds are the foundations of an ancient Fire Temple that was surrounded by a ring of twigs, inside which no man was allowed to enter. The flame was extinguished in the 16th century but plans are underway to rekindle it. Also in the grounds is a fine Celtic stone cross. You can see the last vestiges of Kildare Castle behind the Silken Thomas public house.

For centuries this was a frontier town on the edge of the English Pale. At times its position was so precarious that it almost vanished completely as a settlement. However, with the development of The Curragh, and the construction of the turnpike road from Dublin to southwest Ireland in the middle of the 17th century, the town's fortunes revived.

Although a motorway cuts across its heart, the area known as The Curragh, which begins on the eastern edge of town, is still the largest tract of semi-natural grassland in Europe. The space and grass attracted the attentions of horse breeders in the 13th century and racing enthusiasts from the 18th century. The racecourse is now the headquarters of flat racing in Ireland and stages up to 20 meetings a year. The wide open space of The Curragh has also always appealed to soldiers. The British established military bases here, which are still in use by the modern Irish army; Kildare town's artillery barracks were only recently vacated. The main hub of military life is now at the Curragh Camp 8km (5 miles) or so to the east.

WHAT TO SEE

THE NATIONAL STUD
www.irish-national-stud.ie
The National Stud was founded at Tully on the edge of Kildare town by Colonel William Hall-Walker in 1900. This was once the site of the 12th-century Black Abbey and its scant remains can still be seen. Hall-Walker was the heir to a Scottish brewing family and had theories about the astrological influences on stock breeding. The stable buildings have lantern roofs designed to ensure the correct parts of the night sky would illuminate the stallions. He gave the whole complex to the British government and was rewarded with a title, Lord Wavertree. In the 1940s the complex was transferred to the Irish state. Today there are up to 10 stallions at work per season, with each one able to service more than 70 mares at around €85,000 each.

The best time to visit is between February and July when there will be foals in the stables and paddocks. As well as guided tours of the paddocks and stable blocks, you can visit the Horse Museum, which contains memorabilia and the skeleton of Arkle, one of the stud's most famous racehorses.
✉ Irish National Stud, Tully, Kildare, Co. Kildare ☎ 045 521 617 (visitor centre) ⏰ Mid-Feb to mid-Nov daily 9.30–5 🖐 Both gardens and Irish National Stud: adult €10.50, child (under 5–16) €6, family €27 🚆 Kildare, then shuttle bus (every 20 min) to stud and gardens 🚌 Tours of National Stud every hour, allow 35 min 🍴 Wavertree Restaurant

THE JAPANESE GARDENS
Colonel Hall-Walker established the Japanese Gardens on reclaimed bogland between 1906 and 1910. They were designed by Tassa Eida, a renowned Japanese gardener, and his son Minoru. Their significance is not purely horticultural, they also portray the journey of a man through life, from his birth to the afterlife. The set pieces have names such as the Hill of Ambition, the Marriage Bridge, the Hill of Learning, the Island of Joy and Wonder, and the Tunnel of Ignorance. As you might expect, there are pagodas and little red bridges alongside some important specimen trees and bushes.

ST. FIACHRA'S GARDEN
St. Fiachra's Garden was constructed to commemorate the millennium—the sixth-century Irish cleric St. Fiachra is the patron saint of gardeners. Designed by Martin Hallinan, it uses limestone and water to create an island hermitage. Its woodland, wetland and rock give it a much more natural feel than the otherworldly atmosphere of the Japanese Gardens. An inner subterranean garden is decorated with Waterford crystal, lighting the darkness of the hermit's cave. A statue of St. Fiachra himself, holding a symbolic seed of creation, sits on a rock that juts out into the lake.

TIP
» Visit the National Stud between February and July to see the foals in the paddocks off Tully Walk.

Opposite top *Exercising on The Curragh, the venue for many classic races*
Opposite bottom *A statue in the gardens*
Above *Carving of men on horseback in the National Stud Museum*
Below *Little red bridges lead the way in the Japanese Gardens*

INFORMATION

www.discoverireland.ie/southeast

➕ 364 F7 ℹ️ Shee Alms House, Rose Inn Street, Kilkenny, Co. Kilkenny ☎ 056 77 51500 🕐 Apr–end Oct Mon–Sat 9–6; Nov–end Mar Mon–Fri 9–5 🚌 Bus Éireann services from Dublin 🚆 Kilkenny

INTRODUCTION

Kilkenny rose to prominence in the 13th century with the powerful Anglo-Norman Butler family, the Earls of Ormond. Their castle rises above a bend in the River Nore, looking out over a modern urban core with plenty of historic nooks. The local limestone produces a black stone known as Kilkenny marble, which you can see on many of the city's public buildings.

St. Canice founded the monastic settlement here in the sixth century and by the 13th century the adjacent town had become an important base for Norman rule in Leinster. Parliaments were held here from the 13th to the 15th centuries. In 1366, the notorious Statute of Kilkenny was passed, forbidding English settlers from speaking Irish, wearing Irish clothes or marrying Irish women. The natives were excluded from the city and to this day the area around St. Canice's, which lay beyond the city wall, is known as Irishtown. By the 17th century, however, the city had become a focal point of Catholic resistance. A confederate parliament was established in 1642, with money and arms from the Vatican. It dissolved acrimoniously in 1648, and by 1650 Cromwell arrived at the city gates with a considerable army. The siege lasted five days, but was ended without the bloodletting that characterized his occupation of Wexford or Drogheda. Today the city is best known for its beer—Smithwick's brewery occupies the site of the old Franciscan friary.

WHAT TO SEE

KILKENNY CASTLE

The Anglo-Norman Strongbow (▷ 30) first built a wooden castle on the rocky bend above the river in 1172. His son-in-law William Marshall, Earl of Pembroke, strengthened it with local stone and created the medieval stronghold that remains today. James Butler, Third Earl of Ormond, bought the castle in 1391, and his family stayed until 1935, when the castle was acquired by the Irish state. In the late 17th and early 18th centuries, the Butler family's wealth grew and they improved their castle by adding a classical gateway and removing the war-damaged east wall. In the late 18th century came the gardens and stables (now the Kilkenny Design Centre). The 19th century saw the creation of the Long Gallery to house the family's considerable art collection, and the addition of the south curtain wall created extra bedrooms.

The castle visitors now see displays this Victorian elegance. As well as the impressive Long Gallery, with its portraits and hammer-beam roof, you see the

Below left *Kilkenny is well stocked with good shops and pubs*
Below right *One of the highly decorated ceilings in elegant Kilkenny Castle*
Opposite *The remodelled castle overlooking the Nore*

Chinese bedroom, reflecting the Victorians' Oriental obsession, the Drawing Room, Library and Ante Room, all exquisitely furnished. The parkland extends to 20ha (50 acres) and includes a formal rose garden as well as mature woodland. Off the servants' corridor, by the old kitchen (now a bookshop), is the Butler Gallery of Contemporary Art (free) housing exhibitions by international artists and sculptors.

✉ Kilkenny Castle, The Parade, Kilkenny ☎ 056 77 21450 ⏰ Jun–end Aug daily 9.30–7; Apr, May daily 10.30–5; Sep daily 10–6.30; Oct–end Mar daily 10.30–12.45, 2–5 ✋ Adult €5.50, child €2.10, family €11.50 🎫 Guided tour only, a 15-min audio-visual presentation followed by 45-min tour

ST. CANICE'S CATHEDRAL

The present cathedral was built in the 13th century in the early English Gothic style, but suffered in 1332 when its tower collapsed under the weight of lead on its roof. This over-zealous application was a penance imposed on William Outlaw for consorting with Dame Alice Kyteler, who had been accused of witchcraft. The Kyteler family slab is the oldest memorial in the cathedral. The round tower, to the east of the building, has lost its cone, but still commands impressive views of the town and countryside. It is 30m (100ft) high and dates from AD849, when the cathedral was at the core of a monastic settlement. You can see traces of this Romanesque structure in the arches of the choir's north wall and in the north transept door. Cromwell's troops stabled their horses inside, smashed all the windows and threw out the monuments. When they were put back no one could remember their original places, so they now stand in orderly lines. Just beyond the cathedral, on Kenny's Well Road, you will find a little well house containing St. Canice's Holy Well, dating back to at least the sixth century.

✉ Irishtown, Kilkenny ☎ 056 776 4971 ⏰ Apr, May, Sep Mon–Sat 10–1, 2–5, Sun 2–5; Jun–end Aug Mon–Sat 9–6, Sun 2–6; Oct–end Mar Mon–Sat 10–1, 2–4, Sun 2–4 ✋ Adult €4, child (under 12) free. Round tower: adult €3, child free (minimum age 12); restricted opening in winter

KILKENNY CITY

Kilkenny is a medieval gem. On many occasions war and wild times have swept through the little town, and as well as its impressive castle and cathedral, a walk around Kilkenny reveals so much more. Ask at the tourist office, which is in the Tudor Shee Alms Houses, about the one-hour walking tours that give an amusing introduction to the town. On Parliament Street, the Courthouse has a 19th-century classical frontage on a fortified medieval house, which once served as a prison. Across the road, Rothe House was built in 1594 around a cobbled courtyard and is now home to a small museum (tel 056 77 22893; Mar–end Nov Mon–Sat 10.30–5, Sun 3–5; Dec–end Feb Mon–Sat 1–5, Sun 3–5).

Above *St. Canice's Cathedral*
Opposite left *Impressive carved high cross and round tower at Monasterboice*
Opposite right *The stone circle at Loughcrew*

LOUGHCREW CAIRNS

www.meathtourism.ie

In west County Meath, far from the bustle of Brú na Bóinne, the Loughcrew Hills hold a remarkable series of 5,000-year-old passage graves. On these grassy hilltops, there are no interpretative displays or audio-visual tour. You may even have them to yourself. It's 400m (440 yards) or so from the road up to the eastern summit where Cairn T is the most dramatic feature, 35m (115ft) across, with 37 edging stones. Inside, a cross chamber is lined with inscribed stones. The western summit has more impressive cairns. The Patrickstown cairns are the most easterly group, virtually destroyed by 19th-century enthusiasts, but contain important neolithic artwork. You can get a key to Cairn T from Loughcrew Historic Gardens about 3km (2 miles) away (tel 049 854 1356; mid-Mar to end Sep daily 12.30–5; Oct to mid-Mar Sun and public holidays 1–4).

🕂 365 F4 ✉ Loughcrew Hills, Oldcastle, Co. Meath ☎ 049 854 1060 🕓 Daily all year, daylight hours 🖐 Free (deposit for keys to Cairn T) 🚌 Bus Éireann service to Oldcastle 🍴 At Loughcrew Historic Gardens

MELLIFONT ABBEY

Only a gatehouse and an octagonal lavabo (washhouse) remain above head height at this important medieval abbey in a quiet valley on the banks of the Mattock River. It was founded in 1142 by monks from Clairvaux, France. More than 150 monks fled from here at the time of its suppression in 1536. In the 17th century the abbey became the country mansion of Edward Moore, saw the surrender of Hugh O'Neil in 1607, suffered a Cromwellian siege, and became headquarters for William of Orange during the Battle of the Boyne in 1689. By 1723 it was abandoned, and by the middle of the 19th century its ornate ruins were doubling as a pigsty. Four sides of the Romanesque lavabo remain from 1200 and the 14th-century chapterhouse has been re-roofed and contains a collection of glazed tiles. On a bank above the Visitor Centre stands the roofless shell of a Protestant church dating from 1542.

🕂 365 G4 ✉ Tullyallen, Drogheda, Co. Louth ☎ 041 982 6459 (Oct–end Apr 041 988 0300) 🕓 May–end Sep daily 10–6 🖐 Adult €2.10, child (6–18) €1.10, family €5.80 🚌 Bus Éireann service from Drogheda to Tullyallen Cross (5km/3 miles) 🚆 Drogheda (8km/5 miles) 🎫 40-min tour on request

MONAGHAN

www.monaghantourism.com

Monaghan has a landscape of glacial drumlins, the low 'basket of eggs' topography caused by the passage of great ice sheets. Amid these countless ridges of boulder clay lie dozens of lakes, making this a popular county with anglers, though few other visitors linger. The small county town has a neat shopping street and a good local museum (The County Museum) in a Victorian town house. The nearby Market House is a surprisingly elegant Georgian affair from 1792. Grander in scale is the enormous Gothic Revival Roman Catholic Cathedral of St. Macartan, standing high on the east side of town. Elsewhere, the towns and villages of County Monaghan are largely the creation of 17th-century plantations (▷ 32), with perhaps Clones being the most appealing.

🕂 363 F3 ℹ Castle Meadow Court, Monaghan, Co. Monaghan ☎ 047 81122 🕓 Apr–end Oct Mon–Fri 9–1, 2–5. Closed Nov–end Mar 🚌 Bus Éireann service from Dublin

MONASTERBOICE

This much pictured monastic site is smaller than you might imagine from the coverage it receives. What you'll find, 1.6km (1 mile) from the intersection with the new M1, is a neat, working cemetery, a splendid 34m (110ft) round tower, without its cone, and magnificent high crosses. Little remains of the rest of the monastic settlement first established by St. Buithe in the fifth century. There are some extant walls from a church building, originating in the eighth or ninth century. Also visible are the remains of a smaller 13th-century church. The crosses are among the best in Ireland. The Cross of Muiredach is an elaborate wheel head cross from the 10th century. On its base the inscription translates as 'A prayer for Muiredach by whom was made this cross'. Standing 5m (16ft) tall, its panels are carved with almost cartoonish detail.

🕂 363 G4 ✉ Monasterboice, Drogheda, Co. Louth 🕓 Daily dawn–dusk 🚌 Bus Éireann service from Drogheda to Monasterboice Inn

POWERSCOURT

The most memorable feature of Powerscourt is the view from the terrace, over a broad sweep of wooded garden to the graceful peak of the Great Sugar Loaf on the horizon. This superb vista is the set piece of a house and garden originally designed by Richard Cassels for the First Viscount Powerscourt in 1731. Subsequent additions included the Italian garden, which drops away from the terrace on a grand staircase, lined by winged horses, leading to the circular Triton Lake and a 30m (100ft) fountain. Looking back from here, your eye is carried up to the grey stone Palladian façade with its twin copper domes. This exquisite scene took more than 100 labourers 12 years to create in the middle of the 19th century. On the same level as the house, and dating back to the 1740s, lie the walled gardens. More formal than the rest of the estate but not as severe as some in the French style, they include vivid rose beds and fragrant borders. One entrance is through the Bamberg Gate, an intricate piece of wrought ironwork from Bavaria.

There is an audio-visual presentation to the house and gardens. A map is provided for a self-guided tour of the estate. Efforts have been made to allow for wheelchair access where possible.

POWERSCOURT HOUSE AND WATERFALL

The house itself was gutted by fire in 1974 and stood virtually derelict until 1996, when a clever regeneration was devised. The roof was restored, but most of the interior was left empty. An exhibition space was created and the ballroom carefully restored. Today, a visit to the house exhibition is a peculiar mix of building history and stately home, but the house is greatly overshadowed by the gardens.

Elsewhere the estate has turned its attentions to retail outlets, and these occupy the west wing along with a restaurant, cafés and gift shops. The estate glasshouses now house the Powerscourt Garden Centre, and much of the land to the north front of the house is given over to golf courses.

Also part of the estate, but 5km (3 miles) away is the Powerscourt Waterfall, Ireland's highest at 121m (398ft). This is surrounded by specimen trees and is popular with wedding photographers (summer 9.30–7pm; winter 10.30–dusk; closed 2 weeks prior to Christmas).

INFORMATION

www.powerscourt.ie

⊞ 365 G5 ✉ Powerscourt Estate, Enniskerry, Co. Wicklow ☎ 01 204 6000 🕐 Daily 9.30–5.30 (gardens close at dusk in winter) 👺 House and gardens: adult €8, child (5–16) €5 🚌 44, 44C (from Dublin), 185 from Bray DART 🚆 DART Bray then bus ⏱ 40 min or 1 hour 🍴 Restaurant and café in main house foyer

Opposite *Powerscourt gardens boast superb vistas across to the peak of the Great Sugar Loaf*
Below *A fountain and pool at Powerscourt*

MOUNT USHER GARDENS

www.mount-usher-gardens.com

There is a deliberately natural style to these gardens, which line the banks of the Vartry river on the southern edge of Ashford. They were begun in 1868 by Edward Walpole, a Dublin businessman, who used Mount Usher as a base for walking in the Wicklow Mountains. There are more than 5,000 specimens across the estate's 8ha (19 acres), including azaleas, Chinese conifers, bamboos, Mexican pines and pampas grasses. The maples are particularly fine in autumn and the river acts as a unifying feature.

✚ 365 G6 ✉ Ashford, Co. Wicklow ☎ 0404 40116 🕙 10 Mar–end Oct daily 10.30–6 👣 Adult €7, child (5–16) €3 🚌 Bus Éireann service 133 from Dublin 🚉 Wicklow Station 8km (5 miles) 🍴 In courtyard

NATIONAL 1798 CENTRE

If you are a bit unsure of the details of the 1798 rebellion in the south of Ireland, this superb visitor attraction, built to mark the rising's bicentenary, puts the whole period in perspective. Using a mix of audio-visuals and informative displays you are taken through the economic and political conditions

Below Relive voyages to the New World on the Dunbrody at New Ross

that led up to the conflict. The culmination is a reconstruction of the eventual showdown on Vinegar Hill, where the crown's forces under General Lake stormed the rebels' headquarters, defended by 20,000 pikemen. In the confusion the rebel army was able to slip away with barely 500 dead. The hill rises up on the far side of the Slaney river, while the town itself climbs up the western bank of the river; there is a more traditional museum in the Norman Castle close to the pedestrian-only middle of town.

✚ 364 G7 ℹ National 1798 Visitor Centre, Mill Park Road, Enniscorthy, Co. Wexford ☎ 054 37596 🕙 Mon–Sat 9.30–6.30, Sun 11–6.30 👣 Adult €6, child (4–16) €4, family €16 🚌 Bus Éireann service from Dublin 🚉 Enniscorthy 🔎 Allow at least an hour 🍴 In foyer

NEW ROSS

www.newrosstourism.com

This old inland port on the Barrow river has started to feel the wealth of the euro boom, and its wharfside warehouses are being redeveloped. The narrow streets wind up the steep riverbank to the Three Bullet Gate, a remnant of a once extensive town wall. Cromwellian destruction might have seen the end of the town were it not for the proximity of the Kennedys' ancestral home. Since the 1960s, this has ensured a steady stream of visitors. The John F. Kennedy Memorial Park, opened in 1968, 12km (7.5 miles) south of town, is a 252ha (622-acre) arboretum that's best in spring and autumn (tel 051 388 171; May–end Aug daily 10–8; Apr, Sep daily 10–6.30; Oct–end Mar daily 10–5).

The impressive Dunbrody Heritage Ship, a full-scale reproduction of a New Ross emigrant vessel of the 19th century, has guides in period costume explaining the harsh conditions experienced by the passengers. There's a full database of those who made the journey to the US between 1820 and 1920. The 40-minute tour is preceded by a video about its construction.

✚ 365 F7 ℹ The Quay, New Ross, Co.

Wexford ☎ 051 421857 🕙 May–end Aug daily 9–5; Apr, Sep daily 10–4; Oct–end Mar daily 10–5 👣 Adult €7.50, child (under 16) €4.50, family €20 🚌 Bus Éireann service from Dublin 🍴 At Dunbrody Visitor Centre

POWERSCOURT

▷ 132–133.

SLANE

www.meathtourism.ie

Perhaps better known these days for the huge rock concerts that take place in front of the castle (▷ 14), Slane is a tidy estate village, marred by the major road intersection at its heart. Through the traffic you may discern the four identical Georgian houses that face each other over the crossroads, but it's satisfying to take the winding lane off the N2 in the north of the town, up to the Hill of Slane. From here St. Patrick is said to have lit a Paschal (Easter) fire in AD433, in defiance of the pagan King of Tara, announcing the arrival of Christianity in Ireland. There's a fine view up here, and remains of a friary church and college established in 1512. The castle (tel 041 988 4400; May–end Jul Sun–Thu 12–5), west of the village, is the ancestral home of the Conynghams, offering guided tours.

✚ 365 G4 🚌 Bus Éireann service 177 from Dublin

TRIM

www.meathtourism.ie

This small town on the banks of the River Boyne is home to the largest Anglo-Norman castle in Ireland (tel 046 94 38619; Apr–end Sep daily 10–6; Oct daily 10–5.30; Nov–end Mar Sat–Sun 10–5; access to the keep by 45-min guided tour only). Its curtain wall is more than 400m (quarter of a mile) long and encloses a site of 1.2ha (3 acres). The central keep is 21m (70ft) high and the walls are 3.3m (11ft) thick. Together with the 10 D-shaped towers in the surrounding walls, it has barely been altered since the 13th century, though it does bear the scars one would expect from a fortification so close to the edge of the English Pale

(▷ 38). Many of the castle scenes in *Braveheart* (1995) were filmed here at this castle.

Across the river, the Sheep's Gate and the Yellow Steeple, the belfry tower of an Augustinian abbey, rise from a meadow, left undeveloped on their medieval sites when the town's focus shifted towards the opposite bank in the 18th century.

Downstream of the castle, on the edge of new housing developments, the ruins of the 13th-century cathedral of SS. Peter and Paul is connected to the Hospital of St. John the Baptist by an ancient bridge, on the north side of which is one of Ireland's oldest pubs.

In the Visitor Centre near the castle, 'The Power and the Glory', a multimedia presentation, documents the impact of the arrival of the Normans.

✚ 365 F5 ℹ Town Hall, Castle Street, Trim, Co. Meath ☎ 046 94 37227 ⏰ Mon–Sat 9.30–5.30, Sun, public holidays 12–5.30 🖐 Visitor Centre: adult €3.20, child €1.90 🚌 Bus Éireann service 111 from Dublin

WEXFORD
www.wexfordtourism.com
The Vikings established Wexford as a port and shipbuilding town in the eighth century. In the Middle Ages it was an important English garrison town, but when Oliver Cromwell and his army arrived in 1649 the rebellious spirit of the townspeople cost them dearly and several hundred were executed on the Bullring. Rebelliousness continued, however, and in 1798 a republic was declared here. A statue of a pikeman on the Bullring is a memorial to the town's role in the 1798 rebellion.

The long, narrow main street runs parallel with the quay, only lightly used today. Little obvious remains of the old town, the Westgate tower being the sole survivor of the 14th-century walls. Nearby are the ruins of Selskar Abbey, built by Henry II in penitence for the murder of Thomas Becket. The opera festival every October (▷ 145) attracts performers and

Above *Originally established by the Vikings, the town of Wexford is built on three levels*

devotees from all over the world.
✚ 365 G7 ℹ Tourist Information Office, Crescent Quay, Wexford, Co. Wexford ☎ 053 91 23111 ⏰ Jul–end Aug Mon–Fri 9–7, Sat 10–6, Sun 11–5; May–end Jun, Sep Mon–Sat 9–6; Oct–end Apr Mon–Sat 9.15–5 🚌 Bus Éireann service from Dublin 🚉 Wexford

WEXFORD WILDFOWL RESERVE
Behind the sea wall on the north side of Wexford Harbour lies the North Slobs, 3m (10ft) below high tide level. This wetland area was drained from marshland in the 19th century to form a farming landscape, but its meadows and drainage channels also provided an ideal habitat for birdlife. In winter you might see 29 different species of duck and 42 types of wader. The 10,000 or so Greenland white-fronted geese form as much as one-third of the world's total population and the pale-bellied Brents also arrive on a globally significant scale.

The Reserve's 100ha (247 acres) include a series of accessible hides from which visitors can observe the birds. One is next to the Victorian pumping station—its chimney is a landmark, though its steam pump has long since been replaced by an electric version pumping 4 tonnes of water back into the sea every minute.

✚ 365 G7 ✉ North Slobs, Wexford, Co. Wexford ☎ 053 91 23129 ⏰ Daily 9–5. Closed occasionally: notice on gate 🖐 Free 🚉 Wexford 🕐 1 hour, available on request

WICKLOW MOUNTAINS NATIONAL PARK
www.wicklownationalpark.ie
The Wicklow Mountains National Park rises from the suburbs of south Dublin and covers some 17,000ha (42,000 acres) of high granite moors, wooded valleys and lakes. The highest point is Lugnaquilla, at 925m (3,035ft), a rounded peak rising above Glenmalur. The mountains are traversed by the spectacular military road from Dublin to Laragh, and crossed by the high passes of the Wicklow Gap and the Sally Gap. In the western foothills, several valleys have been flooded to form the beautiful Blessington Lake, sometimes called Pollaphuca Reservoir.

At the core of the park lies Glendalough (▷ 122–123) where, appropriately, the Visitor Centre for the monastic settlement there doubles as a national park information office.

✚ 365 G6 ℹ Upper Lough, Glendalough, Co. Wicklow ☎ 0404 45425 ⏰ May–end Sep daily 10–5.30; Oct–end Apr weekends only 10–dusk 🚌 St. Kevin's bus twice daily from Dublin

WALK

GLENDALOUGH AND THE WICKLOW WAY

Glendalough, the valley of the two lakes, lies at the very heart of the Wicklow Mountains National Park. A walk up this peaceful glen, by the lough sides and into the mountains, reveals the ruins of its monastic past, amid woodlands and waterfalls.

THE WALK
Distance: 8km (5 miles)
Allow: 3 hours
Start/end at: Glendalough Visitor Centre parking area, Glendalough 1:50,000 OSI Discovery Series, map 56 Grid reference 312 196

HOW TO GET THERE
Glendalough is about 40km (25 miles) southeast of Dublin; the R757 leaves the Wicklow Gap road 1.6km (1 mile) or so west of Laragh.

INFORMATION
Pick up the walks leaflets from the Visitor Centre. The colour-coded one is free and there is also a general map of the valley at 1:25,000 scale for €0.50.

★ From the parking area, head left of the buildings across a picnic area to a bridge over the Glenealo

River, following a Wicklow Way marker.

❶ The Wicklow Way is Ireland's oldest long-distance trail. It is well waymarked throughout and it takes about five days to walk its 131km (81 miles) south from the suburbs of Dublin to Clonegall, near Bunclody in County Wexford.

Cross the bridge and turn right, following the sign marked 'Green Road to Upper Lake'. The main monastic site is through the trees across the river on your right. Ignore any turnoffs to the right and follow the broad track past the lower lake, eventually following a sign to the information office, still on the Wicklow Way. At the next intersection bear right, ignoring a path rising to the left. About 50m (55 yards) past the information office,

cross the wooden bridge on your left. Now follow the signs up to Poulanass Waterfall.

❷ The track rises fairly steeply, following the gorge that Poulanass Waterfall leaps, but it is well fenced. There are viewing areas and an interpretative panel.

Continue up the hill, now joining a forest road coming in from the right. When the track forks, bear right, leaving the Wicklow Way, and follow the forest road, which curves around to the right, heading back towards the valley initially and then bending sharply left. Ignore the markers pointing to your right. Instead follow the blue arrow pointing up the glen.

❸ These arrows mark the Spinc Walk and lead you up the glen.

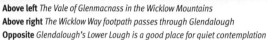

Above left *The Vale of Glenmacnass in the Wicklow Mountains*
Above right *The Wicklow Way footpath passes through Glendalough*
Opposite *Glendalough's Lower Lough is a good place for quiet contemplation*

The walk sometimes goes through plantations, sometimes in clear-felled areas, where the tops of the mountains are visible.

4 Glendalough was naturally wooded until about 1,000 years ago, when climate change and felling timber for charcoal-making began to take its toll. Coppices were managed and much of what you see now is the product of deliberate planting. The oaks, larches and Scots pines on the lower slopes date from the 19th century, when there was a heavy demand for pit props. Higher up you'll see later conifers, initially planted in the early 20th century and still felled commercially.

At the next intersection bear right with the arrow and head up the track for about 100m (110 yards). Now a blue arrow directs you into the forest on your right, up a steep and at times muddy path. A warning sign suggests danger, but the risks are the same as they were lower down. Towards the top, daylight shines through a narrow tunnel of trees and you emerge on a heathered ridge above the Upper Lake.

5 Across the Upper Lake, on the far side of the glen, and to your left, conspicuous mine tailings bleed

down the scree and crags to the road. These are remnants of the Glendalough lead and silver mines that flourished here during the 19th century.

Take a moment to enjoy the view down and up the glen before turning right, along the ridge. You continue on a non-slip boardwalk, which not only protects the vegetation around the path, but also enables you to proceed at a reasonable speed. At the end of the undulating ridge the route drops steeply back to the Poulanass Brook via a long cascade of wooden steps; it is only polite to let those struggling up to pass.

Eventually you come back onto the forest road you walked on earlier. Turn briefly left before following the sweeping bend back down to the right. At the intersection keep left, heading down the hill, and ignore the turnoff back to the waterfall on your right. Follow the forest road down to a bend where a sign indicates a viewpoint. Leave the forest road here and descend steeply, eventually to the remains of the Reefert Church.

6 Reefert Church, an 11th-century Romanesque building, was the burial place of the O'Toole clan.

The ruined nave and chancel can be seen along with many ancient gravestones.

Beyond the church, cross the little bridge, and head for the lakeshore. Walk along the road, with the Upper Lake to your left. Go through the barrier and across the wooden bridge. Now turn right down the road, passing the upper parking area on your right, to a track that drops down from the road on the right. Take it and then turn left, joining the wide boardwalk down the valley below the road. Follow this past the Lower Lough and across the river to rejoin the Green Road. Turn left to return to the Visitor Centre or to view the main monastic site (▷ 122–123).

WHERE TO EAT
THE GLENDALOUGH HOTEL
www.glendaloughhotel.com
The restaurant serves Irish and mainstream world food.
✉ Glendalough ☎ 0404 45135
🕐 Lunch daily 12–2.45; closed 4–6 weeks during winter

CARLINGFORD AND THE TAIN TRAIL

This walk starts from a medieval town hardly touched by development since the 18th century, then ascends Carlingford Mountain. Far-reaching views unfold across Carlingford Lough to the Mountains of Mourne, before you return to the town to explore its ruined Norman castle.

THE WALK

Distance: 8km (5 miles)
Allow: 3 hours
Start/end at: Parking area by Visitor Centre, Carlingford, Co. Louth 1:50,000 OSI Discovery Series, map 36 Grid reference 318 311

HOW TO GET THERE

Carlingford is on the north side of the Cooley Peninsula 17km (10.5 miles) from Dundalk on the R173.

★ From the parking area by the Visitor Centre, walk into town, past Taafe's Castle and the memorial to Thomas D'Arcy Magee (1835–68), a local man who went on to become one of the founders of modern Canada.

❶ Taafe's Castle is a fortified merchant's house dating from the 16th century. The building takes its name from a prominent local family.

Turn left opposite the general store and then bear left down the pedestrianized street when you get to the corner, and go on to the Mint.

❷ The Mint is another fortified 16th-century house, now used as a base for outdoor activities. Look for the fine stone-carved mullions with patterns distinctive of this period of the Celtic Renaissance. The gateway is known as the Tholsel. It once stood higher, being the tollgate through the 15th-century walls, where taxes would be collected. The town's corporation would also meet here, and in the 18th century it served as a prison.

Past the Mint, go through the gatehouse, and turn right into the churchyard to the Church of the Holy Trinity.

❸ The Church of the Holy Trinity can trace its origins to the 13th century,

but most of the building we see today is a result of the renovations of 1804. The crenallated tower was built in the 16th century, but the oldest tombstone is from 1703. Inside, the church is still used for worship. The Heritage Exhibition explains the development of the town, the trading links of its heyday and its subsequent decline.

Leave the churchyard on the far side and turn right. At the intersection turn left and follow the old main road past the remains of the priory on the left and the modern Catholic church on the right.

❹ The Dominican priory was established by Richard de Burgo in 1305 to work with the town's poor. It was similar to most 14th-century monastic foundations, with cloister, refectory, chapterhouse and church, but of these buildings only the church and east range of the domestic quarters remain.

The violence of the late Middle Ages is indicated by the priory's need to fortify itself in 1423. It was dissolved in 1539.

Turn right now, following the Tain Trail signposts. Walk up the road which bears left, past a ruined cottage on the right; a Tain Trail sign lurks on the left-hand side. It directs you right again, up the hill. Follow this winding lane up the hill, with waymarks at the prominent points.

⑤ The Tain Trail is a walking and bicycling route, covering 40km (25 miles), that commemorates one of Ireland's most enduring Iron Age legends, that of the Tain Bo Cuailgne (the Cattle Raid of Cooley). Queen Maeve of Connaught from Rathcroghan in County Roscommon was jealous because her husband was richer than she was. To even the score she set out with a vast army to capture the famous Brown Bull of Cooley. The Ulstermen's defence was led by Cúchulainn, the greatest of all the Irish heroes. He was slain in the battle but, inspired by his bravery, his men repulsed the invaders.

Eventually a waymark points you to the right, off the road through a gap in the gorse. This path leads up, fairly steeply at first, to a gate. Go through this and follow the signs as the Tain Trail bears around to the right, with views of the town and its harbour emerging below you. Follow the well-signposted green track as it traverses the hillside, rising steadily. As it meets an eastern spur of Carlingford Mountain it veers left, back across the face of the slope, gently rising to the col between Carlingford Mountain and Barnavave.

⑥ Walk a few paces over the col to look down into the valley of the Big river on the other side. Slievenalogh rises beyond and the eastern coast stretches away past Dunany Point. Experienced walkers may choose to continue to the rocky summit of Slieve Foye, the mountain's highest point, 587m (1,925ft), though this part of the walk is not signposted and involves some rougher terrain.

Retrace the path back into Carlingford. To visit King John's Castle, carry straight on when you get to Taafe's Castle, passing the Garda station on your left, and the road will take you up a bank to the castle entrance.

⑦ King John's Castle, founded by Hugh de Lacy in the 12th century, has a commanding view of the lough and shows how important Carlingford was to the Anglo-Normans. The castle suffered in the wars of the 17th century and stayed in a ruined state until restoration was started in the 1950s.

To return to the parking area from here, retrace your steps and turn left at Taafe's Castle.

WHERE TO EAT

There are several bistro-style restaurants in Carlingford, among them Ghan House (tel 042 937 3682) and The Oystercatcher (tel 042 937 3989), where Cooley lamb and Carlingford mussels and oysters feature.

Above *Carlingford Harbour has a working fishing fleet*
Below *Ancient buildings line the streets of Carlingford, which is a good base for outdoor activities*
Opposite *Ruined King John's Castle still dominates the loughside village of Carlingford*

PLACE TO VISIT
HOLY TRINITY HERITAGE CENTRE
✉ Carlingford ☎ 042 937 3454
🕐 Mon–Fri 9.30–12.30, 2–4 💶 Adult €3, child €1

DRIVE

WICKLOW MOUNTAINS NATIONAL PARK

From Dublin, escape to the mountains, where rebels and saints once hid away, and where today hydroelectric and water supply schemes have created a new, but still beautiful landscape.

THE DRIVE
Distance: 113km (70 miles)
Allow: 4 hours
Start/end at: Dublin

★ Leave Dublin on the N11, which becomes the M11 briefly on the edge of Bray. As the N11 again it reaches Kilmacanoge under the Great Sugar Loaf, where you turn off on the R755.

❶ Great Sugar Loaf and its companion Little Sugar Loaf look like children's drawings of volcanoes, but they are not volcanic. Their summits are very hard quartzite, left standing when the surrounding rocks were weathered away by water, wind and glacier. You can see the same rocks in the Rocky Valley, which follows a fault line. It's an energetic scramble to the summit of Great Sugar Loaf,

the last part requiring hands as well as feet. Its relatively low elevation of 501m (1,644ft) doesn't qualify it as a proper mountain, but its isolated position means the views on a clear day are unsurpassed from along this coastline.

As you ascend the Rocky Valley, bear right on the R760 through Ballybawn, then turn left on a minor road signposted to Roundwood. Follow this road as it skirts the hillside, ignoring any turnings until you reach a crossroads with the R759. Turn right here and stay with this spectacular mountain road as it ascends to Sally Gap. Lough Tay appears far below you on the left.

❷ Sally Gap breaks the ridge of the Wicklow Mountains. After the failed rising of 1798, many rebels fled to

the hills, and succeeded in evading capture for several years. The British army realized it would have to pacify the Wicklow Mountains so built a road from Rathfarnham on the edge of Dublin, winding for 69km (43 miles) through the mountains to Aghavannagh. It took nine years to complete, with barracks at Glencree, Laragh, Drungoff and Aghavannagh. By the 1830s many of these had been abandoned, but the road became a miners' route. Not surfaced properly until the 1950s, it's now a popular drive.

At Sally Gap, turn left again onto the R115, and follow the winding high-level Military Road across the heather moors and down Glenmacnass into Laragh. Turn right in the village, then right again to enter Glendasan on the R756.

❸ Glendasan, which stretches due west of Laragh, was once an important mining area. Lead was discovered by Thomas Weaver, an engineer working on the Military Road. Mining began in 1809 and was moderately productive throughout the century, extending workings into the next valley of Glendalough. Work ceased after World War I but flourished again briefly in the mid-1950s, only to stop for good in 1963.

Continue on the R756. After 1.6km (1 mile) turn left to visit Glendalough (▷ 122–123).

❹ St. Kevin established a monastic settlement at Glendalough, the valley of the two loughs, in the sixth century. The ruins of his cathedral church, round tower and other buildings lie scattered around this lovely mountain valley. There is a Visitor Centre at the entrance to the main monastic site, explaining the context of the valley, its history and wildlife.

There is no way out of this valley so you will have to return to the R756 to carry on. From the Glendalough road end, turn left and continue up Glendasan. The road takes you high up into the mountains again, to the Wicklow Gap, before dropping down into the remote valley of the King's River.

❺ The Wicklow Gap, a high pass through the Wicklow Mountains, was once used by pilgrims on their way to Glendalough. The mountains stretch high either side of the road, Tonelagee (817m/ 2,680ft) to the north and Camaderry (698m/2,290ft) to the south. Hidden away in the hills here, Lough Nahanagan is supposed to be inhabited by a monster. If it's still there it is very tolerant; the corrie lough has been converted into a reservoir for a pumped-storage hydroelectric scheme deep inside the mountain.

About 9.6km (6 miles) from the Wicklow Gap summit, take the right turn towards Valleymount and Blessington on the R758. Two causeways and bridges carry you over the waters of the Pollaphuca Reservoir.

❻ This three pronged lake (sometimes known as the Blessington Lakes) was created in 1940, by the building of the Pollaphuca Dam across the Liffey Gorge near Ballymore Eustace. It takes its name from a dramatic waterfall, now somewhat reduced, the hiding place of the mischievous water sprite Pooka. Despite its artificial origins, the lake is now an important and beautiful haven for wildlife, and a circuit of its perimeter makes a popular drive. The forest planting began in 1959 and is mostly sitka spruce and Japanese larch for commercial felling. Geologists have shown that there was a large glacial lake here until about 10,000 years ago, which perhaps accounts for the modern lake's natural feel.

Continue north on the R758. At the intersection on the N81, turn right to return to Dublin.

WHERE TO EAT
GLENDASAN RIVER RESTAURANT
www.glendaloughhotel.com
Uses the best Wicklow produce to create both classic and world cuisine.
✉ The Glendalough Hotel, Glendalough
☎ 0404 45135 ⑧ Lunch daily 12–3

Above left Walking in the Wicklow Mountains is rewarded with fine views
Above right The monastic remains at Glendalough are extensive and well preserved
Opposite The wild Wicklow Mountains are reflected in the blue waters of Lough Tay

WHAT TO DO

ASHFORD

TIGLIN – THE NATIONAL MOUNTAIN AND WHITEWATER CENTRE

The foremost body in Ireland for developing outdoor skills, Tiglin provides courses in most outdoor disciplines, including canoeing, climbing, hillwalking and orienteering.
✉ Near the Devil's Glen, Ashford, Co. Wicklow ☎ 0404 40169 ⊕ All activities must be reserved and paid for in advance. Closed last week Jul and first week Aug, and 2 weeks around Christmas ⚡ Prices depend on activity

BRAY

AVOCA WEAVERS

www.avoca.ie
In the grounds of the old Jameson whiskey estate in the foothills of the Wicklow Mountains, the headquarters of Avoca's retail network sells their exclusive lines of knitware, home furnishings, children's clothing, separates and coordinates for men and women. In addition there is a garden shop with a pleasant conservatory and a restaurant.
✉ Kilmacanogue, Bray, Co. Wicklow ☎ 01 286 7466 ⊕ Daily 9–6 🚌 Bus Éireann service from Dublin 🍽

MERMAID ARTS CENTRE

www.mermaidartscentre.ie
Dance, drama and a wide range of musical performances have made the Mermaid a success as County Wicklow's arts centre. A good place to catch the big names in traditional music and professional theatre without paying Dublin prices.
✉ Main Street, Bray, Co. Wicklow ☎ 01 272 4030 ⊕ All year, box office: Mon–Sat 10–6 (to 8 on performance evenings) ⚡ Varies 🚌 45, 84 (from Eden Quay Dublin) 🚇 DART Bray

SEALIFE CENTRE

www.sealife.ie
The feature of this all-weather attraction on the sea front is the 'Lair of the Octopus', a re-creation of the undersea world inhabited by these animals. Look, too, for sea-horses, sharks, moray eels and giant crabs.
✉ Bray, Co. Wicklow ☎ 01 286 6939 ⊕ Mar–end Oct daily 10–5; Nov–end Feb Mon–Fri 11–4, Sat, Sun 10–5 ⚡ Adult €10.50, child €7.90 🚌 45, 84 (from Eden Quay Dublin) 🚇 DART Bray 🍽 🎫

CARLINGFORD

CARLINGFORD ADVENTURE

www.carlingfordadventure.com
Carlingford Adventure arranges courses in sailing, windsurfing, kayaking and canoeing on the nearby lough, as well as climbing, hillwalking and orienteering.
✉ Tholsel Street, Carlingford, Co. Louth ☎ 042 937 3100 ⊕ Closed 2 weeks around Christmas ⚡ Varies according to courses 🚌 Bus Éireann from Newry (NI)

MEMORIES

Cars are banned from the tiny street leading down to the Tholsel gatehouse, within the old town wall. A number of craft and gift outlets trade in the street's medieval buildings, selling Celtic and Irish designs.
✉ Tholsel Street, Carlingford, Co. Louth ☎ 042 937 3093 ⊕ Daily 10–6

CAVAN

ASTRA BOWL

There are few bowling facilities in County Cavan, so these six lanes are very popular and it's a good idea to reserve in advance. There are also pool tables and arcade games.
✉ Storm Cinema Complex, Townspark, Cavan, Co. Cavan ☎ 049 43 72662 ⊕ Mon–Fri 12–10, Sat–Sun 10am–11pm ⚡ From €3.70 per person per hour

FARNHAM STREET

www.cavantourism.com
Despite the growth of out-of-town shopping near the bypass, Cavan still

has much to attract shoppers to its narrow main street, where brightly painted independent shops offer an interesting range of goods.

☎ Tourist Information Centre, Farnham Street, Cavan Town, Cavan, Co Cavan ☎ 049 4377200 ⏰ Individual shop times vary ☐ Bus Éireann service

DROGHEDA
CARBERRY'S

Drogheda's best-known pub for live traditional music has changed very little in the last 30 years and has built its reputation on serving good beer with no frills. There is live music on Tuesday night Sunday afternoons, and singers' night on Wednesday.

✉ 11 North Strand, Drogheda, Co. Louth ☎ 041 983 7409 ⏰ Mon–Thu 8pm–11.30pm, Fri–Sat 8pm–12.30am, Sun 1.30–4, 8.30–11.30 ☐ Bus Éireann services from Dublin ☒ Drogheda

DROGHEDA UNITED FOOTBALL CLUB

www.droghedaunited.ie
The only Leinster soccer team outside Dublin to have any lasting presence in the Eircom League of Ireland, Drogheda United was formed by a merging of two local clubs in 1975. It won the Football Association of Ireland Cup in 2005.

✉ United Park, Windmill Road, Drogheda, Co. Louth ☎ 041 983 0190 ⏰ Mar–end Nov ✋ Telephone or check website for fixtures and ticket prices ☐ Bus Éireann service from Dublin ☒ Drogheda

DUNDALK
THE SPIRIT STORE

www.thespiritstore.ie
This former port merchant's house looks like any other Irish bar but inside it has a unique style all of its own. Upstairs live music, poetry readings, comedy and drama take place four nights a week.

✉ St. George's Quay, Dundalk, Co. Louth ☎ 042 935 3697 ⏰ Daily 4pm until closing (Sun 2pm)

ENNISCORTHY
CARLEY'S BRIDGE POTTERIES

Founded by two Cornish brothers in the 17th century, this pottery is still

in the same family, making it one of Ireland's oldest businesses. Both modern and traditional designs are produced here.

✉ Carley's Bridge, Enniscorthy, Co. Wexford ☎ 054 33512 ⏰ Mon–Fri 9–5, Sat 10–4 (summer only)

ENNISKERRY
POWERSCOURT ESTATE

www.powerscourt.ie
The Powerscourt Garden Centre has made a name for itself with horticulturalists in search of plants and garden equipment. In the entrance to the main house there are gift and furnishing outlets.

✉ Enniskerry, Co. Wicklow ☎ 01 204 6000 ⏰ Daily 9.30–5.30 ☐ 44C from Dublin, 185 from Bray

POWERSCOURT SPRINGS HEALTH FARM

www.powerscourtsprings.ie
Set in a large country estate on the edge of the Wicklow Mountains, this spa runs day sessions of stress release courses which include massages, mud and other skin treatments, hand and foot care, aromatherapy and reflexology.

✉ Coolakay, Enniskerry, Co. Wicklow ☎ 01 276 1000 ⏰ Phone for course details ✋ Day sessions from €150 ☐ 44C from Dublin, 185 from Bray

GOWRAN
GOWRAN PARK RACECOURSE

www.gowranpark.ie
Gowran Park has made a name for itself as the place to see the up-and-coming young jump horses race in January and February. There are also some flat racing meetings.

✉ Gowran Park, Mill Road, Gowran, Co. Kilkenny ☎ 056 772 6225 ⏰ 16 meetings per year, phone for fixtures ✋ From €15 ☐ Bus Éireann service

KILDARE
THE CURRAGH

www.curragh.ie
The word Curragh may even derive from the Gaelic for racecourse, such is the pedigree of this famous flat racing venue. The headquarters for flat racing in Ireland, and its

principal venue since 1741, there are five classic meets here every year and as many as 18 others between March and October.

✉ Co. Kildare ☎ 045 441205 ⏰ Up to 20 meetings per year, phone or check website for fixtures ✋ From €13.50 ☐ Bus Éireann service ☒ Kildare or Newbridge

KILKENNY
ANNA CONDA

Just one of several vividly painted Irish pubs in Kilkenny offering live traditional music and the chance for amateurs to join in the session.

✉ 1 Watergate, Parliament Street, Kilkenny, Co. Kilkenny ☎ 056 777 1657 ⏰ Mon–Thu 11am–11.30pm, Fri–Sat 11am–12.30am, Sun 11am–11pm ☐ Bus Éireann service ☒ Kilkenny

KILKENNY DESIGN CENTRE

www.kilkennydesign.com
Drawing on the skills of more than 200 artisans from all over Ireland, this is a nationally recognized outlet for a wide range of crafts. The emphasis is on natural fibres and materials, be they linen, silk, wool or cashmere for clothing, silver and gold for jewellery, locally made, hand-blown Jerpoint glassware, or traditional and contemporary gifts from wood and porcelain. Upstairs there is an excellent café and restaurant overlooking the courtyard.

✉ Castle Yard, Kilkenny, Co. Kilkenny ☎ 056 772 2118 ⏰ Mon–Sat 10–6, Sun 11–6. Closed Sun Jan–end Mar ☐ Bus Éireann service ☒ Kilkenny

TYNAN WALKING TOURS

The best way to get to know Ireland's medieval capital city is on foot with a knowledgeable guide. Explore its lanes and streets to discover the best shops and pubs.

✉ Depart from Kilkenny tourist office ☎ 087 265 1745/056 65929 ⏰ Mon–Sat 9.15, 10.30, 12.15, 1.30, 3, 4.30, Sun 11, 12.15, 2, 3 ✋ Adult €3, child (under 12) free ☐ Bus Éireann services from Dublin ☒ Kilkenny

Opposite *Stones from the beach at Bray form the pattern on the terraces at Powerscourt*

WATERGATE THEATRE
www.watergatekilkenny.com

With a schedule of professional and amateur drama, contemporary, traditional and classical music, this is one of southeast Ireland's foremost arts complexes.

✉ Parliament Street, Kilkenny, Co. Kilkenny ☎ 056 776 1674 🕐 All year 🖐 Prices vary depending on performance 🚌 Bus Éireann services from Dublin 🚉 Kilkenny

KILMORE QUAY
COUNTRY CRAFTS

With a good selection of paintings by local artists, pottery and crafts from around County Wexford, and some interesting collectables and general bric-à-brac, this is an interesting place on the Hook Peninsula, overlooking the fishing port.

✉ Kilmore Quay, Co. Wexford ☎ 053 91 52618 🕐 May–end Sep daily 10–7; Oct–end Apr Sat–Sun 11–5; Dec–end Feb weekends only

WEXFORD BOAT CHARTERS

Kilmore Quay is one of the best and most organized sea angling bases on the Irish coast. The inshore waters around the Saltee Islands have acquired an international reputation, with a wide range of species to be found.

✉ Kilmore Quay, Co. Wexford ☎ 053 91 29831 🕐 Mid-Mar to mid-Dec 🖐 Varies, telephone for details

MONAGHAN
THE MARKET HOUSE
www.themarkethouse.ie

A mix of classical, traditional and contemporary music is offered in the 18th-century market building, now an arts venue. Performances include folk, jazz and poetry.

✉ Market Street, Monaghan, Co. Monaghan ☎ 047 30500 🕐 All year Mon–Fri from 8.30pm 🖐 Varies depending on performance 🚌 Bus Éireann services from Dublin

NAAS
KILLASHEE HOUSE HOTEL
www.killasheehouse.com

There are extensive spa facilities attached to this hotel in the Kildare countryside. You can choose from a variety of activities here, focusing on health, combating stress or other wellness issues, and the range of leisure facilities includes a gym, pool and children's pool.

✉ Killashee Demesne, Naas, Co. Kildare ☎ 045 895182 🕐 All year round 🖐 Phone for details

NAAS RACECOURSE
www.naasracecourse.com

Naas is one of two horse-racing circuits near this small Kildare town. It's an important course for spotting this year's National Hunt hopefuls in February.

✉ Tipper Road, Naas, Co. Kildare ☎ 045 897 391 🕐 At least 14 meetings per year 🖐 From €15 🚌 Bus Éireann service 🚉 Sallins & Naas station

PUNCHESTOWN RACECOURSE
www.punchestown.com

The Punchestown National Hunt horse-racing festival held in April/May draws racing people from all over Europe, and the course has been redeveloped to reflect this international popularity, with new stands and hospitality facilities.

Above *The Curragh in County Kildare is Ireland's foremost racecourse*

✉ Naas, Co. Kildare ☎ 045 897 704 🕐 At least 19 meetings per year 🖐 From €25 🚌 Bus Éireann service 🚉 Sallins & Naas station

NAVAN
MAGUIRE'S

Next to the parking area on the historic Hill of Tara, Maguire's specializes in gifts and craftwork in the Celtic/New Age tradition. There is also an excellent bookshop, with titles ranging from the academic to the bizarre, all relating to the rich archaeology of the area and beyond. If you're planning to visit the Loughcrew Cairns, you'll find books here explaining their scientific and New Age significance.

✉ Hill of Tara, Tara, Navan, Co. Meath ☎ 046 902 5534 🕐 Daily 9.30–6

NAVAN RACECOURSE
www.navanracecourse.ie

With about 14 meetings a year this is an important course for Irish horse trainers. The earlier ones in the year feature the young hopefuls.

✉ Proudstown, Navan, Co. Meath ☎ 046 902 1350 🕐 14 meetings per year, check website or phone for fixtures 🖐 From €15 🚌 Bus Éireann service

NEWBRIDGE
RIVERBANK ARTS CENTRE
www.riverbank.ie

A modern complex for the arts in one of Kildare's fast-growing towns, the Riverbank promotes all forms of popular, classical and traditional music as well as staging plays and having gallery space.

✉ Newbridge, Co. Kildare ☎ 045 448333
🖐 Varies according to performance 🚌 Bus Éireann services from Dublin 🚉 Newbridge

SLANE

SLANE CASTLE

www.slanecastle.ie

A legendary venue, even though it stages only one big concert a year. Famous acts have included Madonna, the Rolling Stones, Bruce Springsteen, REM, Robbie Williams and, of course, U2.

✉ Slane, Co. Meath ☎ 041 988 4400
🕐 Concerts usually only once per year
🖐 Depends on who is playing 🚌 Bus Éireann services from Dublin with extra services before and after annual concert

STRAFFAN

THE K CLUB

www.kclub.ie

A venue for the European Open and the 2006 Ryder Cup course, the K Club seldom drops out of the top Irish golf courses from the Irish Golf Institute. It was designed by the Arnold Palmer team.

✉ Straffan, Co. Kildare ☎ 01 601 7200
🕐 All year 🖐 Green fees from €132

WEXFORD

GREEN ACRES

www.greenacres.ie

A peculiar delicatessen-cum-art gallery with a good line in locally sourced breads and meats—great for buying picnic supplies. Green Acres has built up a reputation as one of Ireland's leading wine merchants.

✉ 7 Selskar, Co. Wexford ☎ 053 91 22975 🕐 Mon–Sat 9–6, Sun 12–5

WICKLOW

THE EUROPEAN CLUB

www.theeuropeanclub.com

This is one of the most enjoyable golf courses in Ireland, with elevated tees, seaside holes and other links features on its roller-coaster of a round.

✉ Brittas Bay, Co. Wicklow ☎ 0404 47415 🕐 All year 🖐 Green fees: low season from €100, high season from €180

MAY–AUGUST

WICKLOW GARDENS FESTIVAL

www.visitwicklow.ie

County Wicklow is proud of its long-standing reputation as the 'Garden of Ireland', and although some of the 30 venues open for the Gardens Festival are just outside the county, Wicklow still claims the lion's share. Joining the many gardens that are open to the public on a regular basis, the festival sees the temporary opening of such notable private ones as the Bay Garden at Comelin near Enniscorthy—a superb cottage garden—and the Avoca estate garden at Kilmacanogue.

☎ 0404 20070

MAY–JUNE

MURPHY'S CAT LAUGHS COMEDY FESTIVAL

www.thecatlaughs.com

Considered by many to be one of the best comedy festivals in the world, Cat Laughs features five days of stand-up, movies and improv, with a superb line-up. In recent years such home-grown talents as Ed Byrne, Dara O'Briain and Ardal O'Hanlon, British names like Jeff Green, Milton Jones and Boothby Graffoe, and transatlantic stars Dom Irrera, Rich Hall, Louis CK and Mike Wilmott have been on the bill.

✉ Kilkenny, various venues ☎ 056 776 3837 🕐 End May–early June

JUNE–JULY

ENNISCORTHY STRAWBERRY FAIR

What used to be a couple of weeks of funfairs, music and general celebration has distilled into a shorter traditional music festival, focused on the town's pubs and town square.

✉ Enniscorthy, Co. Wexford

JULY–AUGUST

GREYSTONES ARTS FESTIVAL

www.greystonesartsfestival.com

A weekend of recitals, drama, comedy, visual arts and workshops by performers from all over the world. It starts with a Friday evening Mardi Gras parade and ends on Monday evening with a fireworks display.

✉ Greystones, various venues
☎ 01 287 6466 🕐 Early August

AUGUST

KILKENNY ARTS WEEK

www.kilkennyarts.ie

Ten days are given over to a celebration of virtually every branch of the arts. There are visiting orchestras, quartets and bands, theatre workshops and performances, storytelling by children's authors and discussions on adult literature and poetry. The visual arts are represented, as is performance art. Jazz and traditional Irish music also feature in this renowned festival, which has been going for more than 30 years.

✉ 9–10 Abbey Business Centre, Abbey Street, Kilkenny, Co. Kilkenny ☎ 056 776 3663

OCTOBER

WEXFORD OPERA FESTIVAL

www.wexfordopera.com

Held in the town every October since 1951, the opera festival features three new operatic productions every year, plus exerpts from popular operas, classical concerts and lunchtime recitals by soloists. Singers and musicians come from all over the world and the whole town enters into the spirit with decorated shops and pubs and a popular antiques fair running at the same time.

✉ 49 Main Street, Wexford, Co. Wexford
☎ 053 91 22400

EATING

PRICES AND SYMBOLS

The restaurants are listed alphabetically within each town. The prices given are the average for a two-course lunch (L) and a three-course dinner (D) for one person, without drinks. The wine price given is for the least expensive bottle.

For a key to the symbols, ▷ 2.

ARKLOW

HOWARD'S

www.arklowbay.com

Diners can enjoy sweeping panoramic views of Arklow Bay from Howard's restaurant in the Arklow Bay Conference, Leisure and Spa Hotel. The carte emphasizes the commitment to quality and freshness with dishes such as confit of duckling with Clonakilty pudding, and caraway roast halibut steak served with celeriac mash.
✉ Arklow Bay Hotel, Ferrybank, Arklow, Co. Wicklow ☎ 0402 32309 ⊙ Mon–Fri 6–10, Sat–Sun 6–9 ⍟ L €25, D €35, Wine €19 🚍 Come off the N11 at the bypass for Arklow. After 2km (1.25 miles) turn left and the premises can be found 200m (210 yards) on the left

BALLYCONNELL

CONALL CAERNACH RESTAURANT

www.quinnhotels.com

Chef Peter Denny is the inspiration behind this bistro-style restaurant, which leans towards delivering international dishes using Irish ingredients. The fixed-price dinner menu offers such combinations as mango and papaya salad with ginger and coriander and crispy duckling with plum glaze.
✉ Slieve Russell Hotel, Ballyconnell, Co. Cavan ☎ 049 952 6444 ⊙ Daily 12.30–2.15, 7–9.15 ⍟ L €20, D €40, Wine €19.95 🚍 On the left, approximately 9km (6 miles) from Belturbet on N87 west towards Ballyconnell

CARRICKMACROSS

NUREMORE HOTEL

www.nuremore-hotel.ie

The elegant dining room overlooks parkland and a golf course. Head chef Raymond McArdle specializes in classic French and contemporary Irish dishes. The poached and grilled squab pigeon from Bresse served with a blanquette of vegetables is a superb example from the well-conceived menu.
✉ Carrickmacross, Co. Monaghan ☎ 042 966 1438 ⊙ Daily 12.30–2.30, 6.30–9.45; closed L Sat ⍟ L €23, D€52, Wine €26 🚍 3km (2 miles) south of Carrickmacross on N2 Dublin road

ENNISKERRY

GORDON RAMSAY @ POWERSCOURT

www.ritzcarlton.com/en/properties/powerscourt/dining

Gordon Ramsay brought his culinary skills to Ireland in 2007, when he opened at the luxurious Ritz Carlton hotel. Even though the prices are outrageous, you need to book months ahead as Ramsay's reputation always fills the dining room. But the setting is magnificent—looking out onto lush gardens through floor-to-ceiling glass, with sweeping views of the Sugar Loaf Mountain. The stunning dining room occupies a space on the third floor and spills out onto the terrace during warm weather. It is easy to see that Irish chef Paul Carroll is not far away from helping to earn Ramsay another well-deserved Michelin star.

✉ The Ritz Carlton Powerscourt Hotel, Enniskerry, Co. Wicklow ☎ 01 274 8888 🕐 Daily 11.30–2, 6–10 ✋ L €50, D €75, Wine €28 🚗 At Enniskerry, go through village and follow signs to Powerscourt

GOREY
MARLFIELD HOUSE
Dating from around 1830, this mansion has an ornate conservatory restaurant. Fine local produce and trendy ingredients blend in classically based dishes with hints of the Mediterranean. The kitchen garden at Marlfield House supplies most of the vegetables and herbs. Dress restrictions: jacket and tie preferred.
✉ Gorey, Co. Wexford ☎ 053 942 1124 🕐 Mon–Sat 7–9, Sun 12.30–1.45, 7–9 ✋ L €40, D €65, Wine €25 🚗 1.5km (0.9 miles) outside Gorey town on the Courtown Road, R742

KILKENNY
RINUCCINI
www.rinuccini.ie
An acclaimed Italian restaurant that has been family-run since it was established in 1989. Award winning chef Antonio Cavaliere produces classic Italian dishes using fish and seafood direct from the fishing boats in Kilmore Quay and beef and lamb from local suppliers, while other ingredients are imported from Italy. The wine list is sourced from the vineyards of Italy. The intimate dining room, in a basement setting, is always buzzing, so reservations are essential.
✉ 1 The Parade, Kilkenny, Co. Kilkenny ☎ 056 776 1575 🕐 Mon–Sat 12–2.30, 5.30–10, Sun 12–3, 5.30–9.30 ✋ L €18, D €38, Wine €19.95 🚗 In the centre of town, opposite Kilkenny Castle

RIVERSIDE RESTAURANT
www.rivercourthotel.com
This spacious restaurant has huge windows which flood the restaurant with natural light and give lovely views of the River Nore and Kilkenny Castle. The chefs pride themselves on the extensive international dinner menu, with dishes such as

beech-smoked trout layered with spinach and fresh salmon wrapped in filo pastry, a cannon of Slaney Valley lamb, or perhaps, lemon and coriander sea bass.
✉ Kilkenny River Court Hotel, The Bridge, John Street, Kilkenny, Co. Kilkenny ☎ 056 772 3388 🕐 Daily 6–9.30, Sun 12.30–2.30 ✋ L €28, D €35, Wine €21.50 🚗 The hotel is opposite Kilkenny Castle (on the River Nore side of the castle)

LEIGHLINBRIDGE
WATERFRONT RESTAURANT
www.lordbagenal.com
On the banks of the River Barrow, this country restaurant has grounds stretching down to its marina. The restaurant menu is innovative and uses good quality ingredients complemented by a choice of fine wines.
✉ Leighlinbridge, Co. Carlow ☎ 059 972 1668 🕐 Mon–Sat 6–10, Sun 6–9 ✋ L from €15, D €30, Wine €18 🚗 In middle of village

LEIXLIP
THE BRADAUN RESTAURANT
www.leixliphouse.com
The accomplished modern Irish cooking here is given an occasional imaginative twist towards the Mediterranean. Typical dishes include crab-meat profiteroles, cassoulette of rabbit with forestière jus and tarragon, and bread and butter pudding with toffee ice cream and apricot coulis.
✉ Leixlip House Hotel, Captains Hill, Leixlip, Co. Kildare ☎ 01 624 2268 🕐 Tue–Sat 7–10, Sun 12.30–8 ✋ L €25, D from €30, Wine €18.50 🚗 From Dublin follow the N4 and take the Leixlip slip road exit into Leixlip Town. Take a right turn onto Captain's Hill and the hotel is the first on the left

MACREDDIN
THE STRAWBERRY TREE
www.brooklodge.com
Only organic, wild and free range produce is used in this elegant restaurant, and fixed-price menus offer light and fresh summer dishes, and earthy, gamey ones in the winter: pan-fried loin of venison

served with Portobello mushrooms and wild cep cream, followed by ginger and lemon crème with raspberry sorbet.
✉ Brooklodge Hotel, Macreddin, Co. Wicklow ☎ 0402 36444 🕐 Daily 7–9.30 ✋ D €60 (6 courses), Wine €24 🚗 From N11, take R752 to Rathdrum, then R753 to Aughrim and follow signs for Macreddin 3km (2 miles) from Aughrim village

MAYNOOTH
MOYGLARE MANOR
www.moyglaremanor.ie
At this beautiful 18th-century Georgian house food is prepared in true country house style; fruit and vegetables from the gardens and orchards are used, along with quality local meats and fresh fish. Crab claws and prawns on a potato galette might be followed by tender roast breast of duckling, or baked turbot with an aromatic cream and bay leaf sauce.
✉ Moyglare, Maynooth, Co. Kildare ☎ 01 628 6351 🕐 Mon–Sat 12.30–2, 7–9 ✋ L from €34, D €60, Wine €22 🚗 From the main street turn left but keep to the right lane. Turn left at the church and continue for 2km (1.25 miles); go over a humpback bridge and take the first turning on the left

NAAS
TURNERS RESTAURANT
www.killasheehouse.com
The dining room has an air of natural elegance and overlooks the Fountain Garden. A lengthy menu offers plenty of choice and some creative options, such as roasted rack of lamb with pepper and aubergine (eggplant) caviar, pomme fondant, tian of vegetables and a madeira and thyme jus.
✉ Killashee House, Kilcullen Road, Naas, Co. Kildare ☎ 045 879277 🕐 Daily 7–9.30 ✋ D €60, Wine €25 🚗 1.5km (0.9 miles) from Naas on old Kilcullen Road, on the left past the Garda (police station)

Opposite *The East sustains a variety of eating options, from country house hotels to more rustic fare in traditional pubs*

NAVAN
EDEN RESTAURANT
www.edenrestaurant.ie/bellinter
Original period features sit well beside contemporary furniture at this vaulted cellar restaurant, housed in a splendid Palladian mansion on the banks of the River Boyne. Sister to the highly acclaimed Eden in Dublin (▷ 106), the prominently Irish menus are similar but most of the ingredients here are locally sourced. The distinctively modern feel reflects in the innovative food.
✉ Bellinter House, Navan, Co. Meath
☎ 046 903 0900 ◷ Mon–Sun 12.30–3, 6–10.30 ✋ L €30, D €42, Wine €24
🚗 Take the N3 from Dublin through Dunsaughlin and 10 minutes farther on turn left at the pub Tara na Rí. Bellinter House is 3km on the right

NEWBRIDGE
DERBY RESTAURANT
www.keadeenhotel.ie
The finest ingredients go into the various fixed-price menus and bistro carte: From the latter expect several pasta and fish choices, as well as prime Irish beef in various guises.
✉ Keadeen Hotel, Curragh Road, Newbridge, Co. Kildare ☎ 045 431666
◷ Daily 12.30–2, 7–10 ✋ L €22, D €40, Wine €20 🚗 Towards the southwestern outskirts of Newbridge on the Curragh Road

RATHNEW
BRUNEL RESTAURANT
www.tinakilly.ie
The modern cooking at this country-house restaurant blends traditional cuisine with up-to-the-minute culinary ideas. Smart dress is required.
✉ Tinakilly Country House & Restaurant, Rathnew, Co. Wicklow ☎ 0404 69274
◷ Tue–Fri 7.30–9, Sat 7.30–9.30, Sun–Mon 1–8 ✋ D €48, Wine €24.50 🚗 Take R750 towards Wicklow to Rathnew, hotel entrance is approximately 500m (550 yards) from the village on the left

ROSSLARE
BEACHES
www.kellys.ie
The opulent, intimate restaurant features original art from the hotel's renowned collection. There is an emphasis on local produce including vegetables and fresh fish from Kilmore Quay, Wexford beef and the hotel's own lamb. Dishes such as grilled lamb's liver with tossed green salad may be a lunch choice, followed by rhubarb and red fruit crumble and fresh cream, while the grilled Wicklow steak with wild mushroom and Madeira jus or roast Barbary duckling with Grand Marnier sauce features on the dinner menu.
✉ Kelly's Resort Hotel, Rosslare, Co. Wexford ☎ 053 913 2114 ◷ Daily 1–2, 7.30–9; closed mid-Dec to mid-Feb
✋ L €25, D €46, Wine €20 🚗 Turn off the N25 Wexford–Rosslare Harbour road. Hotel is 6km (4 miles) from the ferry harbour

LOBSTER POT
This charming cottage-style pub, in a scenic position near Carnsore Point, is a must for seafood lovers. Inside, low ceilings and interconnecting spaces create a cosy atmosphere. One room is set aside for more formal dining. The speciality here is fresh local seafood—the menu is dictated by the daily catch—carefully prepared to a high standard. For a special treat try lobster from the sea tank or river rush oysters. Tables are set up in the garden in good weather.
✉ Ballyfane Carne, Co.Wexford ☎ 053 913 110 ◷ Tue–Sun 12–9 (Sun until 8.30); closed Jan ✋ L €15, D €22, Wine €18
🚗 On route to Camsore Point, 8km (5 miles) south of Rosslare ferry point

ROUNDWOOD
ROUNDWOOD INN
High in the Wicklow Mountains, this atmospheric 17th-century inn has everything for a perfect break: cosy snugs, blazing log fires, great pub-grub and a formal restaurant (reservations essential). Owned by Jurgen and Aine Schwalm for more than 25 years, their hospitality and excellent food have earned the Roundwood an enviable reputation that stretches far beyond the Wicklow Mountains. The menu is a blend of German and Irish influences, with specialties such as Hungarian goulash, Galway oysters, smoked Wicklow trout and the house version of Irish stew.
✉ Main Street, Roundwood, Co. Wicklow ☎ 01 281 8107 ◷ Bar: daily 12–9.30; restaurant: Fri, Sat 7.30–9, Sun 1–2
✋ L €16, D €30, Wine €18 🚗 On the N11 follow signs for Glendalough

STRAFFAN
BARBERSTOWN CASTLE
www.barberstowncastle.ie
Dining here is a candlelit and atmospheric occasion in the original 13th-century castle keep. In this classic country-house ambience the modern French and Irish cooking comes as a rewarding surprise. From a confident menu that changes seasonally come rosemary prawn kebabs with chilled pipérade and a well-judged saffron dressing, while stylish main dishes might include an imaginatively composed confit and roast Gressingham duck, or baked wild salmon with pan-fried oysters.
✉ Clan Celdridge Road, Straffan, Co. Kildare ☎ 01 628 8157 ◷ Wed–Sat 7.30–9.30 ✋ D €60, Wine €24
🚗 On the Clan Celdridge Road just outside Straffan

BYERLEY TURK
www.kclub.ie
The sumptuous Byerley Turk has lavish furnishings and magnificent garden views. The inspired French cuisine with a unique Irish interpretation uses vegetables, fruit and herbs grown in the hotel's walled garden. Smart dress is required.
✉ The Kildare Hotel, Straffan, Co. Kildare ☎ 01 601 7200 ◷ Tue–Sat 7–9.30
✋ D €75, Wine €28 🚗 From Dublin take N4, at start of M4 turn left on R403. After 11km (7 miles) turn left on R406 for Straffan. The hotel is just outside the village on the right

THOMASTOWN
LADY HELEN DINING ROOM
www.mountjuliet.com
On one of the loveliest estates in Ireland, the Lady Helen Dining Room has an understated elegance

with views of the River Nore beyond. From the extensive choice of main dishes expect sea bass with spinach, scallop, asparagus, potato wafers and beurre blanc or a 'study' of game bass Vegetables and herbs come from the kitchen gardens.

✉ Mount Juliet Conrad Hotel, Thomastown, Co. Kilkenny ☎ 056 777 3000 ◷ Daily 7–9.30 🖐 D €70, Wine €27 🚗 From Thomastown follow signs to Mount Juliet Conrad Hotel

VIRGINIA
THE PARK MANOR HOUSE HOTEL
www.parkhotelvirginia.com

The two elegant dining rooms in this 18th-century hunting lodge look out over Lough Ramoor and the beautiful gardens. The classic European cooking produces delicious starters such as warm goat's cheese tartlet. Main courses to look for include a roast duckling with blackcurrant and beet jus or baked salmon with dill champ. To accompany these delights there's a substantial wine list with many excellent choices.

✉ Virginia, Co. Cavan ☎ 049 854 6100 ◷ Daily 1–2, 6–9; closed Jan 🖐 L €15, D €30, Wine €20 🚗 From the N3 northwest in town, turn down Ballyamesduff Road; the hotel is 480m (500 yards) on the left just past the garden centre

WEXFORD
FORDE'S
www.fordesrestaurantwexford.com

In a great location overlooking the waterfront, stairs lead up to a moodily lit room with candles and mirrors on the walls and oil lamps on the polished tables. The extensive seasonal menu—with a wine list to match—offers classic dishes such as roast fillet of pork wrapped in bacon and garlic, with apples and walnuts or rack of local lamb served with rosemary and raspberry jus. Everything is made fresh on the premises.

✉ Crescent Quay, Wexford, Co. Wexford ☎ 053 912 3832 ◷ Daily 6–10; also Sun 12–6 🖐 L €24, D €36, Wine €20 🚗 Directly on the quay front, opposite the statue

SEASONS RESTAURANT
www.whitford.ie

This long-established hotel has a strong local following, where dinner is served by candlelight in elegant surroundings. The seasonal European menu draws on the best of Wexford produce in dishes such as pan-fired crab claws, flamed with Pernod and garlic; and Irish sirloin steak with stuffed field mushroom and a choice of sauces. To finish, try the hazelnut meringue with butterscotch bananas.

✉ Whitford House Hotel, Wexford, Co. Wexford ☎ 053 914 3444 ◷ Daily 7–9; sometimes closed Mon–Wed out of season 🖐 L €16, D €30, Wine €20 🚗 From Rosslare ferry port follow the N25. At Duncannon Road roundabout turn right onto R733, the hotel is immediately on the left

WOODENBRIDGE
REDMOND RESTAURANT
www.woodenbridgehotel.com

Housed in an elegant property full of character and conveniently situated in the beautiful Vale of Avoca overlooking the Aughrim river. Enjoy fine dining with a refined selection of contemporary Irish dishes on the menu, including lots of fish, as well as duck, lamb, veal and beef. An impressive wine cellar stores a good variety of wines from around the globe.

✉ Woodenbridge Hotel, Woodenbridge, Co. Wicklow ☎ 0402 35146 ◷ Daily 7–9, also Sun 12.30–3 🖐 L €28 (3 courses), D €38 (5 courses), Wine €20 🚗 In the middle of town

Above *Rathnew's Brunel Restaurant in Tinakilly Country House offers stunning sea views*

PRICES AND SYMBOLS

Prices are for a double room for one night. Breakfast is included unless noted otherwise. All the hotels listed accept credit cards unless otherwise stated. Note that rates vary widely throughout the year.

For a key to the symbols, ▷ 2.

ARKLOW

ARKLOW BAY

www.arklowbay.com

This hotel enjoys panoramic views of Arklow Bay. The public areas include a spacious lobby lounge and a comfortable bar with casual dining. Howard's restaurant is more formal.
✉ Sea Road, Arklow, Co. Wicklow
☎ 0402 32309 🛏 Double €90–€160
🛈 92 🏊 Indoor 🅿 🚗 Turn off the N11 at the Arklow by-pass. After 1.5km (0.9 miles) turn left and the hotel is 200m (210 yards) on the left

ASHFORD

BALLYKNOCKEN HOUSE AND COUNTRY COOKERY SCHOOL

www.ballyknocken.com

In the foothills of the Wicklow Mountains, this farmhouse offers great hospitality, very good food and excellent accommodation. The bedrooms have private bathrooms, and are equipped with TV, tea- and coffee-making facilities. Two relaxing sitting rooms overlook beautiful gardens and countryside. Dinner reservations are necessary. The cookery school here uses garden produce and local suppliers.
✉ Glenealy, Ashford, Co. Wicklow
☎ 0404 44627 🛏 Double €119 🛈 7
🚗 From Dublin: turn right after the Texaco garage in Ashford (N11). The house is 5km (3 miles) from Ashford on the right

AUGHRIM

LAWLESS'S

www.lawlesshotel.ie

Located in the picturesque village of Aughrim, Lawless's offers a perfect rural retreat within close proximity of the capital. Established in 1787, the hotel retains its bygone charm but also offers modern facilities. Bedrooms are individually decorated in either Victorian or Country pine style and some boast river views. The public areas are very inviting and include a stylish award-winning restaurant and the popular Thirsty Trout Bar and conservatory where food is served all day.
✉ Aughrim, Co. Wicklow ☎ 0402 36146
🕐 Closed 23–26 Dec 🛏 Double €80–€130
🛈 14 🚗 From Dublin take the N11 heading south; go through Arklow and at the roundabout (traffic circle) at the top of the main street follow signs for Aughrim on the R747. The hotel is between two bridges on the outskirts of the village

BALLYCONNELL

SLIEVE RUSSELL HOTEL GOLF AND COUNTRY CLUB

www.quinnhotels.com

This imposing hotel and country club stands in 120ha (300 acres), with an 18-hole PGA championship golf course and a 9-hole par 3 course. There's a range of lounges, restaurants and extensive leisure and banqueting facilities. Bedrooms are equipped to a high standard. Other amenities include tennis courts, sauna and a hair and beauty salon.
✉ Ballyconnell, Co. Cavan ☎ 049 952 6444 🛏 Double €250–€570 🛈 219
🏊 Indoor 🅿 🚗 On left, about 9km (6 miles) west of Belturbet on the N87 Ballyconnell road

BETTYSTOWN

NEPTUNE BEACH HOTEL AND LEISURE CLUB

www.neptunebeach.ie

Overlooking the sea, with access to a sandy beach, the Neptune also offers a swimming pool, children's pool, sauna and Jacuzzi. Public areas include an inviting lounge and

attractive winter garden, and many rooms enjoy sea views.
✉ Bettystown, Co. Meath ☎ 041 982 7107 ✋ Double from €80 🚪 38 🏊 Indoor 📶 🚌 Just off the N1, Dublin–Belfast road

BRAY
THE ROYAL
www.regencyhotels.com
The Royal Hotel stands near to the seafront and has well-equipped leisure facilities, including sauna, solarium and whirlpool spa, and there's a massage and beauty clinic.
✉ Main Street, Bray, Co. Wicklow ☎ 01 286 2935 ✋ Double €79–€180 🚪 130 🏊 Indoor 📶 🚌 Going south on the N11, take the first exit for Bray. At roundabout (traffic circle) take the second exit and go through two sets of traffic lights. Cross the bridge and the hotel is on the left

RAMADA WOODLAND COURT HOTEL
www.woodlandcourthotel.com
In a beautiful setting opposite Kilruddery House, this attractive hotel has spacious bedrooms, an open-plan lounge with bar and a cosy restaurant.
✉ Southern Cross, Bray, Co. Wicklow ☎ 01 276 0258 🕐 Closed 23–27 Dec ✋ Double €80–€120 🚪 86 🚌 Take the third exit off the N11 after the Loughlinstown turning, then take the turn off for Bray/Greystones

CARLOW
DOLMEN HOTEL
www.dolmenhotel.ie
Surrounded by 8ha (20 acres) of landscaped grounds, the Dolmen enjoys a peaceful setting next to the river. Public rooms include a large bar and restaurant and a luxurious boardroom that doubles as a lounge.
✉ Kilkenny Road, Carlow, Co. Carlow ☎ 059 9142002 ✋ Double €70–€160 🚪 81, 12 lodges 🕐 🚌 1.5km (0.9 miles) south of town on N9

SEVEN OAKS HOTEL
www.sevenoakshotel.com
Staff are friendly and helpful at this hotel, which has undergone extensive refurbishment. The lounge is spacious and there are comfortable

bedrooms and a good leisure club. The popular restaurant has been extended and there is a relaxing bar.
✉ Athy Road, Carlow, Co. Carlow ☎ 059 913 1308 🕐 Closed 25–26 Dec ✋ Double €150–€170 🚪 89 🕐 🏊 Indoor 📶 🚌 From Dublin take the N9 to Carlow; go straight on at the first roundabout (traffic circle), turn right at the second and left at the third. The hotel is on the left

CARRICKMACROSS
NUREMORE HOTEL
www.nuremore.com
Overlooking the golf course and the lakes, this is a quiet retreat with spacious public areas. Chef Ray McFardle's imaginative cooking continues to impress. There's a variety of leisure and sporting facilities.
✉ Carickmacross, Co. Monaghan ☎ 042 966 1438 ✋ Double €140–€200 🚪 72 🕐 🏊 Indoor 📶 🚌 3km (2 miles) south of Carrickmacross on N2 Dublin road

CASTLEDERMOT
KILKEA CASTLE HOTEL
www.kilkeacastle.ie
Said to be Ireland's oldest inhabited castle, dating from 1180, this is a breathtaking setting for this a luxury hotel. Facilities are modern with a comfortable bar and lounge and a fine-dining restaurant on the first floor. The individually decorated bedrooms vary in size and reflect the period charm of the hotel. An 18-hole golf course surrounds the grounds, and there are banqueting facilities in the converted stables.
✉ Castledermot, Co. Kildare ☎ 059 914 5156 🕐 Closed 23–26 Dec ✋ Double €200–€230 🚪 36 🏊 Indoor 📶 🚌 From Dublin take the M9 S and the exit for High Cross Inn. Turn left after the pub and the hotel is 5km (3 miles) on the right

CAVAN
KILMORE
www.hotelkilmore.ie
This comfortable hotel has spacious public areas. Fishing, golf, windsurfing and boating are all available nearby. There is a good restaurant.
✉ Dublin Road, Cavan, Co. Cavan ☎ 049 433 2288 ✋ Double €120–€180 🚪 39 🕐 🚌 3km (2 miles) from Cavan on the N3

DELGANEY
GLENVIEW HOTEL
www.glenviewhotel.com
This hillside hotel has luxurious lounges, a restaurant and delightful conservatory views. The bedrooms are well equipped and there are good leisure facilities.
✉ Glen O' the Downs, Delganey, Co. Wicklow ☎ 01 287 3399 ✋ Double €119–€230 🚪 70 🕐 🏊 Indoor 📶 🚌 Take the N11/M11 south from Dublin for 32km (20 miles) past Bray, turning left to Delganey

DROGHEDA
BOYNE VALLEY HOTEL AND COUNTRY CLUB
www.boyne-valley-hotel.ie
This mid-Victorian mansion stands in 6.5ha (16 acres) of gardens and woodlands. The emphasis is on good food, attentive service and high standards of comfort. There are extensive leisure amenities.
✉ Stameen, Dublin Road, Drogheda, Co. Louth ☎ 041 983 7737 ✋ Double €145–€160 🚪 73 🏊 Indoor 📶 🚌 On the M1 north from Dublin, on right, just before Drogheda

DUNBOYNE
DUNBOYNE CASTLE HOTEL AND SPA
www.dunboynecastlehotel.com
This Georgian house has been expanded into a fine hotel that exudes elegance. It is set in 8.5ha (21 acres) of lush grounds. There is a choice of opulent lounges, including a formal drawing room and an atmospheric bar in the original cellar, and many of the bedrooms and suites have views over the splendid gardens. Pamper yourself at the spa, then unwind before dining in The Ivy, where the food is of high standard.
✉ Dunboyne, Co. Meath ☎ 01 436 6801 ✋ Double €180–€340 🚪 182 📶 🚌 In Dunboyne take the R157 towards Maynooth; the hotel is on the left

Opposite *The Nuremore Hotel at Carrickmacross overlooks its own golf course*

ENFIELD

MARRIOTT JOHNSTOWN HOUSE

www.marriott.co.uk

Built around a Georgian mansion in 32ha (80 acres) of parkland and gardens, this hotel offers conference facilities, comfortable bedrooms and suites, restaurants and bars.

✉ Enfield, Co. Meath ☎ 046 954 0000 🖐 Double €110–€380 ⓘ 126 ⊿ Indoor ▽ 🚌 On the N4, on outskirts of Enfield

ENNISCORTHY

RIVERSIDE PARK HOTEL

www.riversideparkhotel.com

Public areas here all take advantage of the riverside views, including the Mill House pub. The spacious bedrooms have every modern comfort.

✉ The Promenade, Enniscorthy, Co. Wexford ☎ 053 92 37800 🖐 Double €180–€200 ⓘ 60 ⊿ Indoor ▽ 🚌 800m (a half-mile) from New Bridge in Enniscorthy, on the N11 Dublin to Rosslare road

GLENDALOUGH

THE GLENDALOUGH HOTEL

www.glendaloughhotel.com

Forest and mountains provide the setting for this long-established hotel, beside the famous Glendalough monastic site. Guests can enjoy good bar food or eat in the pleasant restaurant overlooking the river and forest.

✉ Glendalough, Co. Wicklow ☎ 0404 45135 ⊕ Closed Dec–end Jan 🖐 Double €120–€190 ⓘ 44 🚌 Take the N11 to Kilmacongue, right onto the R755 and carry straight on at Caragh before turning right onto the R756

GOREY

ASHDOWN PARK HOTEL

www.ashdownparkhotel.com

Overlooking Gorey, this modern hotel has excellent health and leisure facilities, a choice of bars and an attractive first-floor restaurant. Bedrooms match the overall high standards.

✉ The Coach Road, Gorey, Co. Wexford ☎ 053 948 0500 ⊕ Closed 25 Dec 🖐 Double €160–€210 ⓘ 79 ⊿ Indoor ▽ 🚌 Take the N11 south towards Gorey where you take the first left turn before the bridge. The hotel is on the left

KELLS

HEADFORT ARMS HOTEL

www.headfortarms.ie

Family run for more than 35 years, this chic hotel is a prominent landmark in the centre of the heritage town of Kells. Recently renovated throughout, with the addition of a spa, it successfully blends the old with the new. The comfortable lounges have roaring log fires, and other facilities include the Vanilla Pod restaurant, an Irish pub with traditional music sessions, a café/carvery and a nightclub. The bedrooms, in both the newer block and the original building are well decorated and furnished.

✉ Headfort Place, Kells, Co. Meath ☎ 046 924 0063 🖐 Double €130–€160 ⓘ 45 🚌 On N3 between Dublin and Donegal

KILKENNY

KILKENNY INN HOTEL

www.kilkennyinn.com

This hotel is in an ideal central location convenient for the medieval city, yet it is in a very quiet street away from any noise from bars or nightclubs. The hotel has the added advantage of complimentary parking. Rooms are spotless and well finished to incorporate traditional features with modern comforts. Public areas include JB's bar and Grill Room Restaurant.

✉ 15–16 Vicar Street, Kilkenny, Co. Kilkenny ☎ 056 777 2828 ⊕ Closed 24–26 Dec 🖐 Double €110–€170 ⓘ 30 🚌 From Dublin via Castlecomer, as you approach Kilkenny at the first roundabout (traffic circle) take the 3rd exit. Cross the bridge and take the next left. The hotel is 200m (220 yards) on the left

KILKENNY RIVER COURT HOTEL

www.kilrivercourt.com

With its private courtyard, riverside restaurant and bar and views of Kilkenny Castle, this is a great place to stay.

✉ The Bridge, John Street, Kilkenny, Co. Kilkenny ☎ 056 772 3388 ⊕ Closed 23–26 Dec 🖐 Double €110–€400 ⓘ 90 ⊿ Indoor ▽ 🚌 On the River Nore side of the castle

LANGTONS HOTEL

www.langtons.ie

Langtons has long had a reputation as an entertainment venue and bar, which is now complemented by a range of contemporary accommodation, including penthouse and garden suites. Dining is in a stunning art-deco dining room that is popular with both visitors and locals.

✉ 69 John Street, Kilkenny, Co. Kilkenny ☎ 056 776 5133 ⊕ Closed Good Fri and 25 Dec 🖐 Double €80–€250 ⓘ 30 🚌 From Dublin, on the outskirts of Kilkenny turn left; Langtons is 500m (550 yards) in the left

NEWPARK HOTEL

www.newparkhotel.com

This friendly hotel is just a short drive from the city centre, set in 16ha (40 acres) of parkland. There is an impressive foyer lounge, a choice of two dining areas, The Scott Dove Bistro and the more formal Gulliver's, and a leisure club and health spa. A purpose-built bedroom wing offers a variety of rooms decorated and equipped to a very high standard.

✉ Castlecomer Road, Kilkenny, Co. Kilkenny ☎ 056 776 0500 🖐 Double €160–€250 ⓘ 129 ⊿ Indoor ▽ 🚌 1km (0.5 miles) outside the city

LEIXLIP

COURTYARD HOTEL

www.courtyard.ie

Opened in 2005, the stylish Courtyard Hotel was built on the 1756 original birthplace of Guinness. Old stonework combined with contemporary design gives the hotel a unique character. The bedrooms and suites are tastefully furnished and cater for all guests' needs—the Executive Suite has an outdoor hot tub on the verandah. Public areas include a large open courtyard that often features live music during the summer.

✉ Main Street, Leixlip, Co. Kildare ☎ 01 6296 5100 🖐 Double €135–€250 ⓘ 40 🚌 From the M4 follow R148 to Leixlip town centre, then follow Main Street car park signs

MACREDDIN
BROOKLODGE & WELLS SPA
www.brooklodge.com
Comfort predominates among sumptuous bedrooms and luxurious treatments. The Strawberry Tree is Ireland's only certified organic restaurant.

✉ Macreddin Village, Co. Wicklow
☎ 0402 36444 ✋ Double €180–€270
🛏 90 ≋ Indoor 🚗 From N11, take R752 to Rathdrum then R753 to Aughrim and follow the signs to Macreddin, 3km (2 miles)

NEWTOWN-MOUNTKENNEDY
MARRIOTT DRUIDS GLEN HOTEL AND COUNTRY CLUB
www.marriott.co.uk
Best known for its Championship golf course, the hotel is beautifully situated between the Wicklow Mountains and the coast, and offers very smart accommodation equipped to the highest standard. The professional service is faultless and you are always greeted with a smile. Guests can dine in Druid's Brasserie or the more formal Flynn's Restaurant, and to no surprise, the Thirteenth Bar overlooks the course. There are also indoor leisure facilities and treatment rooms.

✉ Newtownmountkennedy, Co. Wicklow

☎ 01 287 0800 ✋ Double €150–€265
🛏 145 ≋ ≋ Indoor 🚗 Take the N11 southbound, and turn off at Newtownmountkennedy; follow signs for the hotel

RATHNEW
TINAKILLY COUNTRY HOUSE & RESTAURANT
www.tinakilly.ie
This hotel has superb views of the Irish Sea and Broadlaugh bird sanctuary. Victorian charm with every modern facility.

✉ Rathnew, Co. Wicklow ☎ 0404 69274
✋ Double €220–€280 🛏 51 🚗 On R750, 500m (550 yards) north of the village

ROSSLARE
KELLY'S RESORT HOTEL AND SPA
www.kellys.ie
The resort stands alongside a stunning sandy beach. The Kelly Family have been offering hospitality here since 1895, where together with a dedicated team, they provide very professional and friendly service. Bedrooms are thoughtfully equipped and furnished with flair—some superior rooms have sea views. Extensive leisure facilities include a spa and swimming pool, and the opulent Beaches restaurant is the focal point of the resort,

recognized for its high standard of cuisine.

✉ Rosslare Strand. Co.Wexford ☎ 053 913 2114 ● Closed mid-Dec to late Feb
✋ Double €165–€198 🛏 118 ≋ Indoor 🚗 20km (12 miles) from Wexford town, turn off the N25 onto the Rosslare/Wexford road, signed Rosslare Strand

WOODENBRIDGE
WOODENBRIDGE HOTEL AND LODGE
www.woodenbridgehotel.com
Established in 1608, this is Ireland's oldest hotel steeped in historic associations—it is said revolutionary Michael Collins stayed here while engaging in secret meetings with the British in 1922. Nestled in the beautiful Vale of Avoca, the hotel is owned and run by the friendly O'Brien family who create a warm atmosphere in the public areas with open fires, and ensure good food in the Italian restaurant. The individual bedrooms are to a high standard, nine of which have balconies. There are more rooms in the Woodenbridge Lodge, which enjoys a peaceful riverside setting.

✉ Woodenbridge, Co. Wicklow ☎ 0402 35146 ✋ Double €90–€150 🛏 63
🚗 Between Avoca and Arklow off N11

Below *Accommodation in the East ranges from manor house hotels, self-catering cottages and B&Bs to resort hotels and coaching inns*

THE SOUTH

This magnificent corner of Ireland, located on the very edge of Europe, draws thousands of people every year with its incomparable beauty. The wild Atlantic coastline, reaching like long tentacles into the sea, and its breathtaking lakes, valleys and mountains make it hard to beat. It is a walker's paradise, but for the less energetic touring by car can take in all the most scenic views.

To the west, the peninsulas of Dingle, Iveagh (better known as the Ring of Kerry), the Beara and down to the beautiful Sheep's Head and Mizen are truly magical. To the south the Cork coastline is less spectacular but there are fine sandy beaches to explore and pretty fishing villages to visit. Watersports enthusiasts can indulge in sailing, diving, seafishing and windsurfing. Inland there are the stunning Shehy and Derrynasaggart mountains and valleys to explore. For good food Kinsale, a picturesque fishing village, is known as the gourmet capital of Ireland, with an annual food festival held in October.

The most popular areas for touring are the Ring of Kerry and the Dingle Peninsula. The striking Muckross House in Killarney National Park makes for a good day out. Away from the sea and countryside there are some interesting towns to visit. Cork, Ireland's second city is a joy to explore with its little lanes and vibrant nightlife. Festivals abound in Cork, from jazz to film, Irish traditional music to circus. A detour can be taken to Blarney Castle to kiss the famous stone. Cobh is a fine Georgian port east of Cork and the final docking place of the *Titanic* before her fateful voyage. To the east, Waterford with its world-renowned glass factory, draws the crowds and to the north of the region is Limerick and Cashel, with its famous rock towering majestically above the town.

ADARE

Adare has a reputation for wealth and prettiness, displayed in its green park, brick houses and thatched cottages that have more the feel of a quaint English commuter village than an Irish one. Much of the town's charm is the result of remodelling carried out by the Earls of Dunraven towards the end of the 19th century.

MEDIEVAL RUINS

Adare's history goes much further back than that, however. Evidence of the settlement's status in medieval times can be seen in the several ruined abbeys within it.

Holy Trinity Abbey was founded in 1230 for monks of the Trinitarian Order, which had been set up to rescue hostages seized during the Crusades. It was known as the White Abbey, for the colour of the monk's habits, and its low square tower, restored and battlemented in 1852, dominates the high street. Tucked behind is the circular dovecot, unusual in Ireland, which would have provided a useful additional food source for the monks.

The Augustinians built a friary on the riverbank opposite the castle around 1314, and the elegant church was restored and reopened as the parish church in 1937.

The extensive ruins of a Franciscan friary, dating to 1464, lie in the parkland of Adare Manor, south of the river. This 19th-century mansion was the seat of the Earls of Dunraven and is now a hotel.

DESMOND CASTLE

The massive remains of the castle lie on the north bank of the River Maigue, a short walk from the middle of the town, and are currently closed for structural work. Known as Desmond Castle, it dates back to 1326 and the Second Earl of Kildare, though there was an earlier O'Donovan structure on the same site. The castle withstood several sieges, but was finally demolished by Cromwell's men in 1657.

INFORMATION

🔢 367 D7 🏠 Heritage Centre, Main Street, Adare, Co. Limerick ☎ 061 396255 🕐 Daily 9.30–5 🚌 Adare
📖 The Heritage Centre on Main Street describes the town's early history, in several languages, and a 20-minute film depicts the town today. You can also take a guided half-hour walk of the town's highlights from here (advance reservations required ☎ 061 396666).

Below and opposite *The neo-Gothic Adare Manor sits in lovely grounds bordering the Maigue river*

AHENNY HIGH CROSSES

There is a dignity and remoteness about this pair of wheel crosses standing 2.5m (8ft) high in a graveyard on a hillside. The pinkish sandstone of these monuments was carved by unknown hands in the eighth century AD. Moss and lichen mellow the effect of the intricate Celtic motifs, spirals and geometric designs carved onto every surface; human figures can be made out on the bases. The crosses are signed off the R697 Kilmaganny road, north of Carrick-on-Suir. From any other direction, signposting is poor.

➕ 364 F7 ℹ️ Heritage Centre, Main Street, Carrick-on-Suir, Co. Tipperaray ☎ 051 640200 🕐 Mon–Fri 10–1, 2–5, Sat 10–1 ✋ Donation box for upkeep of churchyard 🚌 8km (5 miles) north of Carrick-on-Suir

ARDFERT CATHEDRAL

www.heritageireland.ie
In the low-lying coastal landscape north of Tralee, locally born St. Brendan (AD484–577) founded a monastery in the sixth century. Nothing remains, but the importance of this ecclesiastical site can be gauged by the three medieval churches here, and the 13th-century friary to the east. The main structure, just north of Ardfert village, is the roofless cathedral, which dates from the 13th to the 17th centuries. Note

the Romanesque sawtooth carvings around arched doorways, and the blind staircase. There are also remains of two other churches.

➕ 366 B7 ✉️ Ardfert, Co. Kerry ☎ 066 713 4711 🕐 Visitor Centre: Apr–end Sep daily 9.30–6.30. Site: open access at other times ✋ Adult €2.10, child €1.10, family €5.80 🚌 Tralee, 10km (6 miles)

ARDMORE

www.waterfordtourism.org
Golden sands and a stone pencil-tower, 29m (95ft) tall, mark this coastal village at the western end of the scenic South Coast Drive, and the start of St. Declan's Way, stretching for 94km (59 miles) to Cashel on an old pilgrimage route. St. Declan chose Ardmore for a church in the fifth or sixth century, and is believed to have been buried in the small oratory in the churchyard. The round stone tower is a fine example of its kind, built as a retreat for the monks and their treasures in a time of Viking raids. The biggest remains are those of the 12th-century cathedral.

➕ 367 E8 ℹ️ Waterfront car parking area, Ardmore, Co. Waterford ☎ 024 94444 🕐 Seasonal opening

ATHASSEL PRIORY

www.cashel.ie
The broken remains of abbeys are scattered across this rich farmland, and Athassel is a stony ghost of one of the biggest and best. Driving south from Golden (6.4km/4 miles west of Cashel), you get a fine view over the riverside site, accessed

over a stile. Founded in the late 12th century by William FitzAdelm de Burgo (d1205), this was one of the wealthiest monasteries in Ireland until its destruction in 1447. A town grew around it, but was burned down. The walls are high and ruins are not fenced; you go among them at your own risk.

➕ 367 E7 ℹ️ Main Street, Cashel, Co. Tipperary ☎ 062 61333 🕐 Mar–end Oct daily 9.30–5.30; Nov–end Feb Mon–Fri 9.30–5.30

BALTIMORE

This was once a wealthy fishing village, sheltered from the Atlantic by a rocky headland. In 1537 fishermen from rival Waterford burned it down after one of their boats was seized, and in 1631 Algerian pirates pounced, killing dozens and kidnapping hundreds to sell as slaves in North Africa. After the second outrage many inhabitants moved upriver to the relative safety of Skibbereen, which suffered worse than most in the famines. Today, visitors come for the rocky bays and seabirds, for access to the islands of Roaringwater Bay (▷ 175) and to drive to the headland for extensive views.

➕ 366 C9 ℹ️ Tourist Information Office, Town Hall, North Street, Skibbereen, Co. Cork ☎ 028 21766 🕐 Jul, Aug Mon–Sat 9–7, Sun 10–5; May, Jun, Sep Mon–Sat 9–6; Oct–end Mar 9.15–5

BANTRY HOUSE

▷ 159.

BANTRY HOUSE

On the southwestern edge of bustling Bantry town, just off the N71, this pink and white house makes the very best of its views over the wooded islands of Bantry Bay. The mansion dates from 1700, and is still owned by the White family, who acquired it in 1739. In 1945 it became the first great house in Ireland to open its door regularly to the public, who have flocked here ever since to admire the treasures amassed by the Earls of Bantry. Richard White, the second earl, was the chief collector, who brought back much of what is on show today from his wide travels in Europe. Look for the Aubusson tapestries in the Rose Drawing Room, reputedly made for French queen Marie Antoinette, and the portraits of George III and Queen Charlotte by Allan Ramsey in the Blue Dining Room.

THE GARDENS

The house stands on the third of seven terraces, a feature of the extensive formal gardens also created by the second earl. Highlights include the Italian-ate garden, and the glorious Wisteria Circle. Walk up the Stairway to the Sky, 100 restored stone steps, for the best views over the house to Bantry Bay. The house hosts a chamber music festival in late June or early July and a festival of traditional music in mid-August.

ARMADA EXHIBITION

In the courtyard of the house, the Armada Exhibition Centre tells of the attempted French invasion of December 1796, in support of the United Irishmen. The 48 ships made it from Brest, but were prevented from landing in the bay by stormy weather and forced back. It was Richard White (1765–1851) who raised the alarm, and was made an earl for his pains. Nationalist Wolfe Tone (1763–98) was one of those on board the failed fleet, and a statue of him stands in Bantry town's square, which is also named after him.

INFORMATION

www.bantryhouse.ie

➕ 366 C8 ✉ Bantry, Co. Cork ☎ 027 50047 🕐 Mid-Mar to end Oct daily 10–6 💶 Adult €10, child (under 14) free 🎧 Self-guided audio tour of Armada Exhibition available in six languages 🍽 Tea room

Opposite left *Ahenny's crosses still celebrate the art of their ancient carvers*
Opposite right *There are magnificent views from the Beacon at Baltimore*
Below *Bantry House has a superb setting on the bay*

BLARNEY CASTLE

Blarney Castle is a romantic 15th-century ruin beside a pretty village, set in landscaped gardens with 18th century grottoes. In high summer the parking area fills to bursting point, and tour parties from every nation thread their way around the tower and through the park. Out of season, or early in the morning, it has a magical peace about it. A square stone tower, the castle is perched on a rocky hillock framed by trees, with broken battlements and two separate watch-towers. As you enter, above your head is the good-natured banter surrounding the ultimate Irish cliché, the kissing of the Blarney Stone. Entry through the thick stone walls is via a double outer door, complete with murder hole and right-handed spiral staircase to confound attackers. Follow the red arrows and keep to the one-way system, vital with so many narrow winding stairs and awkward doorways. You'll pass chambers described as the great hall, bedrooms, kitchen and so on. They are mostly damp and crumbling, but the countryside views from the windows as you climb somehow make it all worth while.

KISSING THE STONE

'Blarney' means eloquent nonsense, a term said to have been coined by Elizabeth I, who wearied of the successful stalling tactics of owner Cormac McCarthy when she tried to take over his castle. There are many legends surrounding the Blarney Stone: One says that it was the pillow used by Jacob when he had his dream of angels in the desert; the best known is that it is allegedly half of the Stone of Scone, presented to McCarthy by Robert the Bruce after his support at Bannockburn in 1314. Kissing the stone involves lying down and leaning backwards over a parapet. A photograph is taken, and you'll be given a ticket to collect your picture later (it costs about €10; there are no previews and it's not a flattering pose). To avoid the crowds, it is best to arrive early and head straight up the steps to the roof, where you will find the stone.

In the 18th century the castle came into the hands of the Jeffereys, who made the gardens. Follow the path south from the tower, passing through a narrow stone tunnel, to explore the gardens. A network of paths leads through carefully crafted woodland ornamented with lumps of naturally sculpted limestone. A grotto, artfully constructed beneath a giant yew, is named the Witches' Kitchen. Nearby the Wishing Steps lead down to a murky pool (another 'tradition': Walk down and up backwards and your wish will come true). Rock outcrops have such fanciful names as Druids' Circle.

INFORMATION
www.blarneycastle.ie
⊞ 367 D8 ✉ Blarney, Co. Cork ☎ 021 438 5252 🕓 May to mid-Sep daily 9–6.30; mid-Sep to end Apr daily 9–5 💶 Adult €8, child (8–14) €3.50, family €18.50 📖 Guide book, in English, French and German, €5 🏛 Gift shop and bureau de change

Opposite *Blarney Castle is a wonderful old ruin, set amid beautiful gardens*
Below *You have to bend over backwards to kiss the Blarney Stone*

BEARA PENINSULA

www.bearatourism.com

The rugged massif of the Caha Mountains forms the spine of this large peninsula, with Hungry Hill (685m/2247ft) its highest point. It is crossed by the scenic Healy Pass (330m/1082ft), a famine road completed by Bantry-born Timothy Healy and encircled by the Beara Ring Drive. You can walk the Beara Way (197km/123 miles) or follow a 171km (107-mile) bicycle route. Castletown Bearhaven is the main town, a fishing port sheltered by the hills of Bear Island. The Call of the Sea Visitor Centre, north of the town, is good for children. Eyeries, on the northern shore, is the home of Milleen cheese. Allihies is known as an artists' town, and its beach of crushed quartz is the spoil from the old copper mines. Dursey Island lies just off the western tip, linked to the mainland by a cable car.

✠ 366 B8 🛈 St. Peter's Grounds, Castletown Bearhaven, Co. Cork 🕿 027 70054 🕓 Summer Mon–Sat 9.30–5; winter Tue–Fri 9.30–5

BLARNEY CASTLE

▷ 161.

CAHER

This busy little 18th-century town has two main attractions. The first, Caher Castle, stands on a crag beside the River Suir (tel 052 41011; mid-Jun to mid-Sep daily 9–7; mid-Mar to mid-Jun, mid-Sep to mid-Oct daily 9.30–5.30; mid-Oct to mid-Mar daily 9.30–4.30). It is one of the best preserved Norman castles in Ireland, with keep, tower and outer wall largely intact.

The Swiss Cottage is a great contrast—a thatched rustic building with stickwork verandahs, set in parkland. It was built in 1810 to designs by John Nash, and reflects a vogue for the *cottage orné*. Admission is by guided tour (tel 052 41144; Mar–end Nov daily 10–6).

✠ 367 E7 🛈 Castle Car Park, Caher, Co. Tipperaray 🕿 052 41453 🕓 Apr–Oct daily 10–5 🚌 Caher

CLONAKILTY

www.corkkerry.ie

This lively little market town was once known for linen manufacture but is now best remembered for its associations with patriot Michael Collins (1890–1922), whose statue stands on Emmet Square. Collins was born 8km (5 miles) west at Sam's Cross, and you can learn more on the 1921 Trail at the Arigideen Valley Heritage Park, at Castleview (tel 023 46107; www. michaelcollinscentre.com; Jun–end Sep daily, telephone for times).

Lying just to the east of the town are the attractive Lisselan Estate Gardens (tel 023 33249; dawn–dusk). If you prefer a break from sightseeing, there is a sandy beach at Inchydoney Island.

✠ 366 C9 🛈 25 Ashe Street, Clonakilty, Co. Cork 🕿 023 33226 🕓 Jul, Aug daily 9.15–7; Sep–end Jun Mon–Sat 9.15–5 🚌 30km (18 miles) west of Kinsale

CLONMEL

www.visitclonmel.com

Clonmel dates back to the 12th century, and the best way to see its historic buildings is via the Heritage Trail (leaflet from the tourist office). Highlights include the arcaded Main Guard of 1684 and the blue-painted Town Hall on Parnell Street. Hearns Hotel is where Italian Charles Bianconi (1786–1875) established what would become the most famous bus company in Ireland in 1815. Around 20 gleaming antique cars are on display at the Museum of Transport on Emmet Street (tel 052 29727; admission by appointment only). A literary festival in September recalls local authors.

✠ 367 E7 🛈 Sarsfield Street, Clonmel, Co. Tipperaray 🕿 052 22960 🕓 Mon–Fri 9.30–5 🚌 Clonmel

Above *Clonakilty's main street is lined with brightly painted buildings*

COBH

The town of Cobh (pronounced Cove), on the south side of Great Island, east of Cork city, is a naturally sheltered harbour, which made it a significant embarkation point for naval fleets during the Napoleonic Wars of the 18th century, for emigration and prison ships in the 19th, and for the glamorous trans-Atlantic liners of the 20th. Today it is a seaside resort, with brightly painted Regency frontages above little shops and restaurants. Popular with sailors, Cobh is a leading venue for sailing (Cobh Sailing club, tel 021 481 1237 for information). St. Colman's Cathedral, by architects Pugin, Ashlin and Coleman, was completed in 1915 and stands high above the town. The graceful spire, 91.5m (300ft) tall, conceals a carillon of 51 bells, which ring out tunes on summer Sunday afternoons. Inside, note the rose window framed by dummy organ pipes, and the mosaic floors. (Mass: Mon–Fri 8 and 10am, Sat 6pm, Sun 8, 10, 12, 7pm.)

ARRIVALS AND DEPARTURES

Between 1791 and 1853 almost 40,000 convicts passed through Cobh on their way to Australia and other distant penal colonies, banished for crimes that ranged from petty theft to murder. And in the 1820s prison hulks were moored here, dealing with overspill from the crowded land jails. Between 1815 and 1970 more than 3 million people took their last view of Ireland here, as they emigrated to the US, Canada and other places. These stories are well told at the Queenstown Story Heritage Centre at the western end of the seafront (tel 021 4813591; May–end Oct daily 9.30–6; rest of year daily 9.30–5). The town was renamed 'Queenstown' in honour of Queen Victoria who visited in 1849, but reverted to Cobh in 1920.

A statue on the quay by sculptor Jeanne Rynhart depicts three children who left here on the SS *Nevada*. The girl, Annie Moore, was the first to enter the US through Ellis Island, on 1 January 1892. The *Titanic* called into Cobh on 11 April 1912, taking on a final 123 passengers before heading west. The daily Titanic Trail walking tour (▷ 187) highlights the town's links with the notorious liner. Survivors from the *Lusitania*, sunk by a German submarine off the Old Head of Kinsale in May 1915, were brought ashore here, and around 150 bodies lie in the old cemetery, 3km (2 miles) north of town.

INFORMATION

✚ 367 D8 🏠 Old Yacht Club, Westbourne Place, Cobh, Co. Cork ☎ 021 481 3301 🕐 Mon–Fri 9.30–5.30, Sat, Sun 1–5 🚃 Cobh, from Cork 🚢 Vehicle ferry from Glenbrook, Co. Cork, 5-minute crossing, daily 7am–midnight ☎ 021 481 1223

TIP

» Approaching Cobh by road, turn left at ruined Bellvelly Tower and take the shorter route through rolling farmland and over the crest of the ridge to emerge directly behind St. Colman's Cathedral.

Above *Cobh's historic harbourfront*
Below The Navigator, *by M. Gregory*

CORK

INFORMATION

www.cork-guide.ie
www.corkkerry.ie
✚ 367 D8 ℹ Áras Fáilte, Grand Parade,
Cork, Co. Cork ☎ 021 4255100 🕓 Jul,
Aug Mon–Sat 9–6, Sun 10–5; Sep–end
Jun Mon–Fri 9.15–5, Sat 9.30–5 🚆 Cork
🚢 Ferry from Roscoff; ferry port at
Ringaskiddy ☎ 021 437 8401, 16km
(10 miles) southeast

Above *Footbridge over the Lee river*
Opposite top *Well-worn stone of*
Parliament Bridge, over the Lee
Opposite bottom *Cork has a good blend*
of big stores, individual shops and
market traders

INTRODUCTION

Cork's history dates back to the founding of a monastery on marshland here
by St. Finbarr in the mid-seventh century. The Vikings built a town, and walls
were constructed around the core; these were demolished in the 17th century,
after a siege by William of Orange's men. Cork's 19th-century prosperity was
founded on sea trade, notably shipping butter to Australia and South America.
Part of the city was burned in 1921 by the English during the nationalist
uprisings. You can learn more at the Cork Vision Centre on North Main Street
(tel 021 427 9925; Tue–Sat 10–5) and the Public Museum in Fitzgerald Park (tel:
021 427 0679; Jun–end Aug Mon–Fri 11–1, 2.15–6, Sat 11–1, 2.15–4; Sep–end
May Mon–Fri 11–1, 2.15–5, Sat 11–1, 2.15–4; also Apr–end Sep Sun 3–5).

Today Cork is a vibrant, modern industrial and university city. Its status as a
European Capital of Culture for 2005 resulted in major refurbishment, visible in
the improvements along Patrick Street (a main artery of the shopping district)
and increased pedestrianization. The level heart of the city lies between the
North and South Channels of the River Lee, and waterways and bridges have
given it the soubriquet of Ireland's Venice. Three-spired St. Fin Barre's Cathedral
(1870) lies to the south.

WHAT TO SEE
PATRICK STREET

Cork is second only to Dublin for the quality and variety of its shopping, and
exploring is easy in such a compact district. Patrick Street is the hub, curving
south from the North Channel, and you'll find all the big name shops and
department stores here (within Merchant Keys Shopping Centre) including
Roches (which started out in Cork), Dunnes, Penneys and Brown Thomas,
and all the usual high-street chain stores. Step off the main drag, and
pedestrianized lanes branching north to Paul Street and south to Oliver Plunkett

Street (named after a 17th-century martyr) are lined with classy independent retailers and appealing eateries.

ENGLISH MARKET

For the very essence of the city, visit this covered food emporium, in a building designed by Sir John Benson in 1881 and restored after a fire in 1980 (access is from Grand Parade, St. Patrick's Street, Princes Street and Oliver Plunkett Street; Mon–Sat 8.30–6). In the early morning you'll see top local restaurateurs in here, picking out the best of the meat, vegetables and fabulous fresh fish: flatfish, langoustines, conger eels, salt cod, mackerel and smoked salmon.

Buy your black or white puddings from the array of butchers' stalls, or be brave and go for the traditional Cork dish of tripe and drisheen (cow's stomach lining). Iago sells the best Irish cheeses, including delicately smoked Gubbeen (West Cork), Benoskee (Dingle), Cashel Blue and Brie-like Maighen (both from Tipperary)—taste before you buy. Odd corners hold unexpected delights, such as the tiny Good Yarns bookshop, packed from floor to ceiling; and the barber shop (hot towel, shave and massage for about €19). Sit in the upstairs café and watch Cork life passing below.

TIP
» The Visitor Centre is at the eastern end of Grand Parade beside the Grafton multi-level parking; you can buy disks for on-street parking here, and also get tickets for the open-top bus tours which take around 70 minutes.

CRAWFORD ART GALLERY

www.crawfordartgallery.com

This outstanding municipal collection is housed in a redbrick building, erected in 1724 as the custom house, when Emmet Street was the King's Dock. As well as rotating exhibitions from the permanent collection of paintings, and the Sculpture Room, there is a modern space for temporary shows which may include video and photography. Up the big staircase (with brilliant stained glass by James Scanlon, 1993) the displays on the upper floor include depictions of Aran islanders by Charles Lamb RHA (1893–1964), and a portrait of actress Fiona Shaw by Victoria Russell (1964–). There's a historical image of the local sport of road bowls by Daniel MacDonald (1821–53), and James Humbert Craig's Lowryesque figures huddled against the rain in *Going to Mass* (c1935). Séan Keating's icon of Irish nationalism, *Men of the South* (1921) is here.
✉ Emmet Place ☎ 021 490 7857 ⏰ Mon–Sat 10–5

CORK CITY GAOL HERITAGE CENTRE

www.corkcitygaol.com

Whatever time of year you visit, it's always bone-cold inside the walls of this grim, castle-like structure on a steep hillside to the northwest of the city. Inside, the cells and corridors resonate with the unhappiness of the men and women incarcerated here between 1824 and 1928. Cells are furnished in 19th- to early 20th-century style, and the audio tour and audio-visual presentation bring it all to life. In the early days felons were isolated in single cells to avoid further corruption, and left in silence (even the warders' boots were muffled) to contemplate their crimes. In reality, such treatment often led to madness. Dusty dummies portray a sense of waste and decay.

In the 1950s the empty buildings became the unlikely headquarters of the budding Radio Éireann. A separate radio museum is housed upstairs.
✉ Sunday's Well ☎ 021 430 5022 ⏰ Mar–end Oct daily 9.30–6; Nov–end Feb daily 10–4
✋ Adult €7, child €4, family €20

CHURCH OF ST. ANNE SHANDON

The red and white sandstone tower, capped by a gilded weather vane in the shape of a salmon, is one of the city's great landmarks. Built in 1722, the church is most affectionately known for its bells, which were popularized in the 19th-century ballad 'The Bells of Shandon'.
✉ Church Street, Shandon ☎ 021 450 5906 ⏰ Easter–end Oct 9.30–5.30; Nov–Easter Mon–Sat 10–3 ✋ €5

INFORMATION

www.dingle-peninsula.ie

✚ 366 B7 ℹ Strand Street, Dingle, Co. Kerry ☎ 066 915 1188 ⓘ Mid-Jun to mid-Sep daily 9.15–7; mid-Sep to mid-Jun Mon–Sat 9.15–1, 2–5 ⛴ Ferry to Great Blasket (An Blascaod Mór) and a tour around the other islands from Dunquin (Dún Chaoin; Apr–end Sep) ☎ 066 915 6422; from Dingle ☎ 066 915 1344

INTRODUCTION

Seen from anywhere along this coast, it is the mountains which first define the Dingle Peninsula: the Slieve Mish mountains to the east reaching to 851m (2,791ft), and the high peaks of Mount Eagle (Sliabh an Iolair; 516m/1,692ft) and Mount Brandon (Croc Bréanainn; 952m/3,122ft) to the west. In the middle are green valleys becoming steadily more stony towards the western tip and Dunquin.

There are rocky cliffs at Slea Head (Ceann Sléibhe) and Brandon Head (Pointe an Chorra Dhóite), and superb sandy bays on the north shore around Castlegregory, and on the northwest tip around Ballyferriter (Baile an Fheirtéaraigh). One of the best viewpoints is at the top of the Connor Pass (456m/1,496ft), reached by a hair-raising narrow and winding road. The N86 is a more direct route between Tralee and Dingle. The Slea Head Drive is a scenic loop from Dingle; follow it clockwise for the best views. The Dingle Way long-distance path goes from Tralee for 179km (111 miles) around the peninsula. Dingle, on the southern shore, is the only significant town.

The earliest inhabitants of this area left plenty of signs of their habitation, from cup-marked boulders, Iron Age forts and Ogham-inscribed stones to the distinctive drystone cells (beehive huts) of the early Christians who, from the fifth century on, sought refuge here. The nature of the ground makes it hard to tell remains of an ancient dwelling from a pile of stones: Louis Mulcahy's free map is helpful for identifying the best sites (▷ 189). In the sixth century St. Brendan (AD484–577) sailed from Brandon Creek, on the northern coast, at the start of his epic voyage. In 1579 a Spanish army of supporters of the Desmonds built a fort, Dún an Óir, at Ferriter, to be wiped out the following year by the English under Lord Grey.

WHAT TO SEE

BLASKET ISLANDS

The green humps of the Blasket Islands lie off the western end of the Dingle. They have captured a very special place in Irish consciousness for their remarkable literary heritage depicting their world apart. The village on An Blascaod Mór (Great Blasket) was abandoned in 1953, but in summer you can visit by ferry from Dunquin (Dún Chaoin) or Dingle town to see the sandy beach of Trágh Bhán and colonies of seals.

The struggle for, and celebration of, life on these isolated islands is revealed in the modern Blasket Centre, built in 1993. With framed views of the Blaskets, stained glass by Róisín de Buitléar and sculptures, the building itself is a work of art. Exhibitions tell of island life in this remarkable community, focusing on the autobiographies written by three people who lived there: Tomás Ó

Below left *The Slieve Mish Mountains*
Below right *Traditional buildings on Dingle's Dykegate Street*
Opposite *The mystical Blasket Islands (Na Blascaodai) beckon from beyond the tip of the Dingle Peninsula*

TIPS
» Follow the Slea Head Drive clockwise for the best views.
» Dingle is an area where Gaelic is still widely spoken, so road signs are likely to be in Irish.
» The tourist office has a map showing place names in both languages.

Criomhthainn (1855–1937, *The Islandman*), Peig Sayers (1873–1958, *Peig*) and Muiris Ó Súileabháin (1904–50, *Twenty Years A-Growing*).
✉ Blasket Centre, Dunquin ☎ 066 915 6444/3 ⏲ Jul, Aug daily 10–7; Easter–end Jun, Sep, Oct daily 10–6. Closed Nov–Easter 🖐 Adult €3.70, child (under 16) €1.30, family €8.70 ☞ Audio-visual presentation; leaflet in six languages ▢ 🏛 Good bookshop

CELTIC AND PREHISTORIC MUSEUM
Just west of Ventry Strand, this traditional-looking building on the left holds a few surprises. The first is its bright, modern interior and relaxed mood with music playing, and the next is the guidebook that comes on loan with your ticket—a huge spiral-bound affair, mixing *Far Side* cartoon humour with detailed and knowledgeable information about the exhibits. What you go on to see, simply displayed in just six small rooms, is a fabulous collection of antiquities from across the globe. They include a nest of fossilized dinosaur eggs, a genuine mammoth skull with tusks 3m (10ft) long, fished from the North Sea, Stone Age hand-tools of chipped flint and neatly coiled Bronze Age brooches. Through it you get a real sense of the development of human skills in making tools and more decorative items, and an insight into the sort of people who were the early settlers on the Dingle peninsula.
✉ Kilvicadowning, Ventry (Ceann Trá) ☎ 066 915 9191 ⏲ May–end Oct daily 10–5; Nov–end Apr phone for hours 🖐 Adult €5, child (4–12) €3 🏛 Small area for sale of antiques and quirky gifts

GALLARUS ORATORY
Apart from a minor sag in the roofline, this deceptively simple stone church looks much as it did when it was first built, some time between the seventh and 12th centuries, and it is outstanding among the ancient sites of Ireland. The walls are of pinkish sandstone, as thick as your arm and chest together, and constructed entirely without mortar. Its form resembles the keel of an upturned boat and echoes the shapes and hues of the hills around. The Visitor Centre below offers a video interpretation, a restaurant and gift shop and an ugly white path up to the Oratory. Somehow, all this detracts from a serene and beautiful structure which speaks for itself. To avoid these distractions, park by the gate up the side road, and walk the shorter route across.
ℹ Visitor Centre, Gallarus, Ballydavid ☎ 066 915 5333 ⏲ Apr–end Sep daily 9–9 🖐 Adult €3, child (under 16) free

Above left *Gallarus Oratory occupies a lonely hillside*
Above right *The Connor Pass is a spectacular drive*
Below *One of southeast Ireland's most famous pubs*

INCH STRAND

Inch, the most famous beach in Ireland, stretches 5km (3 miles) south of Dingle. To the east, a huge covered with marram grass shelters the marshy shallows of Castlemaine Harbour, beloved of oystercatchers, ringed plovers and other waders. To the west, there seems to be a permanent mist of spray from the waves, softening a view punctuated by people fishing, flying kites and picnicking. A lifeguard is on duty in summer. For some, the golden sands are synonymous with the 1972 movie *Ryan's Daughter*. Credited with putting Dingle on the world map, the movie has its own memorial stone at a windswept picnic spot above a tiny harbour west of Slea Head.

ANASCAUL (ABHAINN AN SCÁIL)

This little village is set amid green hills, halfway between Inch and Dingle. Among several pubs on the broad main street, you might recognize the traditional pink-painted Dan Foley's from many a postcard. A more surprising find is the South Pole pub, by the bridge. It was bought and named by sailor Tom Crean (1877–1938), a remarkable and modest man who took part in three of the most famous voyages of Antarctic discovery with Robert Falcon Scott and Ernest Shackleton. In the early 1920s he retired here and opened the pub, with his wife, Nell. Today it is full of photographs and memorabilia, a popular haunt of modern explorers for whom the ice presents the ultimate challenge—and the Guinness is good, too. A statue of Crean with two husky pups stands in the little park opposite, and a 13km (8-mile) walk in the area is named after him.

DINGLE (AN DAINGEAN)

Dingle started out as the site of a fort and trading port, developed into a fishing town, and is now the main tourist hub for visitors to the peninsula. Its narrow streets clog up quickly with traffic in summer, but there are good pubs, craft and antiques shops, and diving, sea-angling, sailing and dolphin watching.

Separated from Dingle Bay (bá na daingin) by a long, hilly spit of land, the town has a sheltered harbour. Waterborne tours leave from the western quay, near the tourist office. The most popular are those that include a visit with Fungi, a wild Atlantic bottlenose dolphin who has made the area his home since 1983, and who seems to love the company of visitors. Also along the waterfront here, the Dingle Oceanworld Aquarium (tel 066 915 2111; Jul, Aug daily 10–7.30; Apr–end Jun daily 10–6; Sep–end Mar daily 10–5) celebrates local marine life; it features a tunnel that goes 9m (29.5ft) through the middle of the ocean tank.

Below left *Drombeg Fort sits on a high promontory on the coast*
Below right *Dingle clusters around its busy harbour*

DROMBEG STONE CIRCLE

At this Bronze Age site east of the coastal village of Glandore, 17 stones form one of the best prehistoric circles in the country. During excavations in the 1950s the cremated remains of a body were found in an urn in the middle of the circle. The remnants of two round huts stand to the west of the circle, with a lined pit from around AD368.

✚ 366 C9 🏛 Town Hall, North Street, Skibereen, Co. Cork ☎ 028 21766 🕔 Jul, Aug Mon–Sat 9–7, Sun 10–5; Sep–end Jun Mon–Sat 9.15–5

FOTA WILDLIFE PARK

www.fotawildlife.ie

More than 90 species of exotic animals live in this wildlife park, 10km (6 miles) east of Cork city. It was established in 1983 to breed endangered species, and the cheetahs are a particular success story, with more than 150 cubs born here. Ostriches, giraffes, zebras, kangaroos and ring-tailed lemurs are some of the animals in the 28ha (70 acres) of lush countryside.

Opulent Fota House, with famous gardens and arboretum (Mon–Sat 10–5, Sun 11–6), is a neoclassical mansion dating from 1825. Stories of its residents are brought to life with videos.

✚ 367 D8 ✉ Carrigtohill, Co. Cork ☎ 021 481 2678 🕔 Mid-Mar to end Oct Mon–Sat 10–6, Sun 11–6; Nov to mid-Mar Sat 10–4.30, Sun 11–4.30. 👋 Adult €13, child (2–16) €8.50, family €54 🚉 Fota Wildlife Park station on Cork–Cobh route 🖥 🎫

GARINISH ISLAND/ILNACULLIN

Of all the islands in Bantry Bay, Garinish, or Ilnacullin, is the most intriguing, for it is the site of a wondrous Italianate garden. The island covers just 15ha (37 acres) and was a barren rock until 1910, when Annan Bryce bought it from the British War Office and engaged the services of garden designer and architect Harold Peto. Bryce's planned house was never started, but his semi-tropical gardens survive, and were gifted to the nation in 1953. Camellias, magnolias and rhododendrons thrive in the mild climate.

Ferries leave from Glengariff, a small leafy town with a nature reserve to the north, sheltering ancient woodland. The Glengarriff Bamboo Park (tel 027 63570; www.bamboo-park.com; daily 9–7) on the eastern edge has 30 species of bamboo.

✚ 366 C8 ✉ Garinish Island, Bantry Bay, Co. Cork ☎ 027 63040 🕔 Jul–end Aug Mon–Sat 9.30–6.30, Sun 11–6.30; Apr–end Jun, Sep Mon–Sat 10–6.30, Sun 12–6.30; Mar, Oct Mon–Sat 10–4.30, Sun 1–5 👋 Adult €3.70, child €1.30, family €8.70 ⛴ Ferry from opposite Eccles Hotel, Glengariff ☎ 027 63116 🖥

HOLY CROSS ABBEY

In a landscape dotted with ruined abbeys, Holy Cross is a surprise—restored and very much alive. It was founded as a Cistercian house in 1180 by Donal Mór O'Brien, and extensively rebuilt in the mid-15-th century by the wealthy James Butler, fourth Earl of Ormond. Its fragment of the True Cross made it Ireland's top pilgrimage site, until the effects of the Dissolution took their toll in the 16th century and it was abandoned. An Act of Parliament in 1969 enabled its reconstruction, and it reopened in 1975.

Functional buildings form two sides of the cloister, with the mighty limestone church on the north side. Inside, the church feels cool and modern, with its whitewashed walls, vaulted roof of grey stone, plain glass windows, modern altar and raked floor. Look for the faint traces of a medieval mural which can still be seen on the west wall, and the Gothic stone sedilia (canopied seats) in the chancel.

The modern Padre Pio gardens have bronze Stations of the Cross by Enrico Manfrini.

✚ 364 E6 ✉ Holy Cross, Co. Tipperary ☎ 0504 43241 🕔 Abbey church: daily all year; visitor centre May–end Sep daily 10.30–5, Oct–end Apr Sun afternoon. Services daily 👋 Donations welcomed 🚩 Guided tours, summer only 🎫

JAMESON'S OLD MIDLETON DISTILLERY

www.whiskeytours.ie

Midleton is a small town dominated by the silver-grey spire of its cathedral and the massive bulk of its distillery, which took over whiskey production in 1975. The original 1825 distillery has been restored.

A gleaming copper still stands before the Visitor Centre and a 10-minute film, followed by a 50-minute guided tour (largely out of doors), give an insight into the history and skills of whiskey manufacture. You see the progress of the grain through malting, fermenting and blending, and the world's biggest pot still (capacity 144,000 litres/32,000 gallons). The tour ends with a whiskey tasting.

✚ 367 D8 ✉ Midleton, Co. Cork ☎ 021 461 3594 🕔 Mar–end Oct frequent tours daily 10–6, last tour 5; Nov–end Feb tours daily at 11.30, 1.15, 2.30 and 4 👋 Adult €11, child €6, family €25 🚩 Tours and leaflet available in seven languages, also Braille 🍴 🖥 🎫

Below *Excavations at Drombeg revealed a ceremonial burial*

Above *Romantic Lismore castle sits on a wooded hilltop*

KINSALE

www.kinsale.ie

The elegant little town of Kinsale, south of Cork, has become known as a culinary oasis, bolstered by the prestigious annual Gourmet Festival. It has a mixture of interesting little shops and chic small hotels, including the famous Blue Haven on the site of the old fish market of 1784. The back streets are stuffed with restaurants to suit all tastes and budgets.

A huge rusted iron buoy and anchors outside Kinsale Regional Museum in Market Square (Wed–Sat 10.30–5.30, Sun 2–5.15; times reduced hours in winter) reflect the town's fishing heritage. In fact, many streets are on land reclaimed from the sea during the 13th century. The modern harbour, bristling with sailing masts, is popular for diving and fishing, including deep-sea angling and blue shark fishing. Wading birds occupy the mudflats, and swans complete the idyllic scene. Desmond Castle, on Cork Street, dates from 1500 and served as a prison in times of war; it now houses the International Museum of Wine (tel 021 477 4855; Easter–end Oct daily 10–6).

Charles Fort, a 17th-century fortress, lies on the east side of the bay in Summer Cove (mid-Mar to end Oct daily 10–6; Nov to mid-Mar 10–5).

🗝 367 D8 🛈 Pier Road, Kinsale, Co. Cork ☎ 021 477 2234 🕐 Jul, Aug Mon–Sat 9–7, Sun 10–5; Sep–end Jun Mon–Sat 9–5

LISMORE

www.discoverlismore.com

Dancer Fred Astaire (1899–1987) was just one celebrity who succumbed to the charms of this pretty Georgian town, as a blue plaque on Maddens Bar on Main Street testifies. He came initially to visit his sister Adèle, who lived in the splendid Lismore Castle, its square towers visible from the north bank of the River Blackwater. It had previously passed through the hands of Sir Walter Raleigh and Richard Boyle (▷ 34), father of the famous physicist Robert (1627–91), whose story is depicted at the Heritage Centre. The castle is now the Irish home of the Dukes of Devonshire and not open, but visitors can explore the magnificent gardens (17 Mar–30 Sep daily 11–4.45). Edmund Spenser, a friend of Raleigh, composed his epic poem *The Faerie Queen* (1590) while staying here.

North Mall, bedecked with hanging baskets, leads to the cathedral, named in honour of St. Carthagh, who founded a monastic school of international importance here in AD633. The present building mostly dates from the 17th and 18th centuries. Highlights include a window in the south transept by English Pre-Raphaelite artist Edward Burne-Jones (1833–98), the splendidly carved 16th-century McGrath tomb, and the carved stones from earlier churches on the site, dating back to the ninth century, now set into the end wall. An unmarked spot in the northeast corner of the churchyard is the site of a famine grave.

A 40-minute circular walk through the woods to the 19th-century folly towers of Ballysaggartmore is sign-posted from the road about 1.6km (1 mile) west of the town.

🗝 367 E8 🛈 Lismore Heritage Centre, Lismore, Co. Waterford ☎ 058 54975 🕐 Easter–end Nov Mon–Fri 9.30–5.30, Sat 10–5.30, Sun 12–5.30; Jan–Easter Mon–Fri 9.30–5.30. Closed Nov, Dec

LISTOWEL

Listowel has two main claims to its place on the visitors' map: an imaginative literary museum and an antique monorail. Seanchaí (pronounced Shanakey), meaning storyteller, is the name of the former, in a fine Georgian house on the town square (tel 068 22212; www.kerrywritersmuseum.com; Jun–end Sep Mon–Sat 10–5; Oct–end May Mon–Fri 10–4.30). It celebrates the works of John B. Keane, Bryan MacMahon, Brendan Kennelly, Maurice Walsh and others. In contrast, there is the Lartigue Monorail of 1888, which runs on the coast between Listowel and Ballybunion (tel 068 22212).

🗝 366 C7 🛈 St. John's, The Square, Listowel, Co. Kerry ☎ 068 22590 🕐 Jun to mid-Sep Mon–Sat 10–6

LOUGH GUR STONE AGE CENTRE

www.shannonheritage.com

Some 3,000 years ago neolithic farmers picked out the prettiest spot in County Limerick for their settlement: crescent-shaped Lough Gur. The site has been excavated, and its story is told in the replica longhouse and roundhouse above the lake. The ruined castle visible from the parking area dates from 1500, and is private, but adds to the picture, with cattle across the water and swans. Nearby are a wedge tomb and the Grange stone circle. More antique sites can be seen from the lakeside.

🗝 367 D7 ✉ Ballyneety, Co. Limerick ☎ 061 385186 🕐 Site: open access. Visitor Centre May–end Sep daily 10–6 ✋ Adult €5.25, child (4–12) €3.15, family €13.50–15.75 🖶 🎫

KILLARNEY AND KILLARNEY NATIONAL PARK

INFORMATION

www.killarney.ie

➕ 366 C8 ℹ️ Beech Road, Killarney,
Co. Kerry ☎ 064 31633 🕐 Jul, Aug
Mon–Sat 9–8, Sun 10–5.45; Jun, Sep
Mon–Sat 9–6, Sun 10–4; Oct–end May
Mon–Sat 9.15–5 🚉 Killarney

INTRODUCTION

Killarney has catered for large numbers of tourists since the Victorian era. For the national park, we have to thank Californian William Bowers Bourn, who bought the Muckross estate in 1911 and, with his son-in-law Arthur Rose Vincent, presented it to the nation in 1932. It was Ireland's first national park.

The park encompasses three island-spotted lakes: Lough Leane, or Lower Lake, Muckross or Middle Lake, and Upper Lake. For a breathtaking overview, visit Ladies' View to the south. Macgillycuddy's Reeks, rising to 1,039m (3,408ft), loom to the west. Killarney on the eastern edge of the park, is the main hub for accommodation, shopping, pubs and restaurants.

There are lots of ways to explore, including bicycle routes and signposted nature trails. Make the classic round trip from Kate Kearney's Cottage by horse-drawn jaunting car, on horseback or by bicycle, cross over the high pass called the Gap of Dunloe, and return to Killarney by cruise boat. The tourist office in Killarney has maps, information and more to help you decide, and there is information about the park itself at Muckross House.

WHAT TO SEE

KILLARNEY

Killarney is a seasoned vacation town that fills to bursting point in summer, and has done so since the Victorians started flocking here to admire the romantic scenery. A poorly signed one-way system makes driving through the middle of the town bewildering, but once you have parked your car, you'll find it's quite compact. The stately Catholic cathedral, St. Mary's, is on the western edge. It was designed by A. W. N. Pugin and dates from 1842, but underwent restoration in the 1970s, and again in recent years.

Scenic walks lead from the western end of New Street to Lough Leane and the lakeside tower of Ross Castle (tel 064 35851; Jun–end Aug daily 9–6; mid-Mar to end May, Sep to mid-Oct daily 9.30–5.30; mid-Oct to mid-Nov daily 9.30–4.30; adult €5.30, child €2.10, family €11.50). A square stone keep, surrounded by the remains of curtain walls, the castle dates from the late 15th century and was a residence of the O'Donoghues. It is famed as the last castle to stand out against Cromwell's English armies, falling at last in 1652, and

Above *Killarney National Park's lakes and hills, from Ladies' View*
Opposite *Enjoying the scenery and the banter on a jaunting-car trip through the gap of Dunloe*

guided tours show it furnished to reflect that period. Nearby, you can rent a boat and row to Inisfallen Island, with its monastic remains.

GAP OF DUNLOE

The Gap is a deep cleft in the mountains to the west of the park, splitting Purple Mountain (832m/2,729ft) from the long range of Macgillycuddy's Reeks. A rough road winds through the ravine and over the pass between the mountains, through the park's most wild and romantic scenery, and it's not hard to believe that the last wolf in Ireland was killed up here in 1700. You can drive only as far as Kate Kearney's Cottage (pub, restaurant and souvenirs); after that, it's a walk of 11km (7 miles) to the other side, but in summer most people go by jaunting car or on the back of the somewhat jaded horses, who know the route only too well. On the way there are stone bridges dwarfed by sweeping mountains, thrilling dark pools (including the Black Lough, where St. Patrick is said to have drowned the last Irish serpent), and magnificent views to the north and south. The road brings you down to the shores of the Upper Lake and Lord Brandon's Cottage café, from where you can catch a boat (not during winter months) through the lakes to Ross Castle.

MUCKROSS ESTATE

www.muckross-house.ie
The Muckross estate, properly called Bourn-Vincent Memorial Park, lies within the national park 6.5km (4 miles) south of Killarney. At its heart is the Victorian mansion of Muckross House, with its extensive gardens, a crafts centre and the Traditional Farms—three working farms, dating from the 1930s, complete with animals. The house was designed in 1843 by Edinburgh architect William Burns, and its interior is comfortably and richly furnished. Highlights include the room where Queen Victoria stayed in 1861, items of Killarney inlaid furniture in the library, and watercolours of local views by Mary Herbert, wife of Henry Herbert, who built the house.
☎ 064 31440 ⓒ House, gardens and craft centre: Jul, Aug daily 9–7; Mar–end Jun, Sep, Oct daily 9–6; Nov–end Feb daily 9–5.30; Farms: Jun–end Sep daily 10–6; Mar–end May, Oct 1–6 ✋ Estate: free. House or farms: adult €5.75, child (under 18) €2.35, family €15; joint ticket adult €10, child €5, family €27.50 ☕ Garden Restaurant

TIP
» Horse-drawn jaunting cars are a great way to travel between Killarney town and Muckross, and the jarvies (drivers) have a fund of local knowledge and stories.

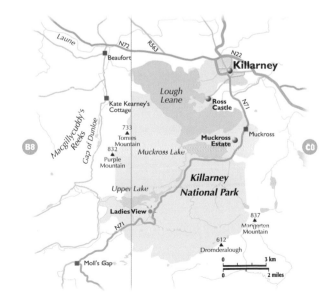

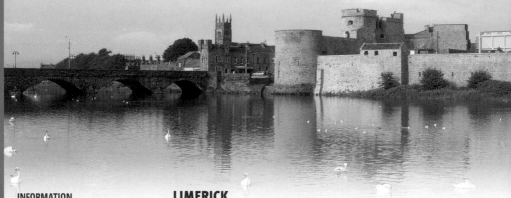

INFORMATION
www.limerick.com
✚ 367 D6 🔲 Arthur's Quay, Limerick,
Co. Limerick ☎ 061 317522 🌐 Jul,
Aug Mon–Fri 9–6, Sat, Sun 9.30–5.30;
may, Jun, Sep, Oct Mon–Sat 9.30–5.30;
Nov–end Apr Mon–Sat 9.30–5.30
(Sat closed 1pm); closes 1–2 for lunch
🚆 Limerick

LIMERICK

You won't go far in Limerick today without seeing references to *Angela's Ashes*, Frank McCourt's grim 20th-century memoir of childhood poverty. You can take a tour based on the book (▷ 190), but there's a great deal more to discover in this intriguing city.

Limerick was founded by Vikings around AD922 as a trading port and the town prospered. In the 12th century the settlement on King John's Island (between the Shannon and Abbey rivers) was fortified by a wall, and became known as English Town, with Irish Town on the opposite bank. In Georgian times it spread south, with the best developments around the People's Park. Today the two areas are linked by ruler-straight O'Connell Street, parallel to the river and the main shopping street of the city, usually choked by traffic.

MAIN ATTRACTIONS

There are two medieval highlights to explore. The first is King John's Castle, dating from 1200, whose great drum towers loom above the river (tel 061 360788; Apr–end Oct daily 10–5.30; Nov–end Mar 10.30–4.30). Inside, animated and interactive exhibits bring the story of the castle to life. Adjacent to King John's Castle, is the restored palace that once housed the Protestant Bishops of Limerick, which is related to the English Palladian style with a classical façade. The house is currently occupied by Limerick Civic Trust who look after the fine architecture seen all around the city.

The second medieval treasure is square-towered St. Mary's Cathedral, parts of which date back to 1168. It was founded by King Donal Mór O'Brien (also responsible for Cashel and Holy Cross), and restoration in the 1990s removed the interior plaster for greater authenticity. A new place has yet to be found for the oak misericords of 1480–1500, superbly carved with griffons, swans, other beasts and angels, that lie propped up in a side chapel. A single limestone slab, more than 4m (13ft) long, forms the altar, and the cannon balls date from 1691, when William of Orange's troops besieged the city.

The Hunt Museum, in a modest grey-fronted Georgian customs house of 1765, has an eclectic collection spanning 9,000 years, amassed by John and Gertrude Hunt (tel 061 312 833; www.huntsmuseum.com; Mon–Sat 10–5, Sun 2–5). They include a virtually intact disk shield of *c*750BC, found in County Antrim; a Roman pierced bronze cooking strainer from the second century; a small bronze horse believed to be by Leonardo da Vinci; an emerald seal that belonged to Charles I; a delicate 17th-century German dish made of lapis lazuli; sketches by Henry Moore and paintings by Jack B. Yeats; and a menu card by Picasso. Exhibits are beautifully displayed.

Above *The towers and ramparts of King John's Castle dominate the town*

MITCHELSTOWN CAVE

The entrance to this spectacular natural wonder is about as low key as you can get. If it weren't for the flagstaff outside the farmhouse, it would be easy to miss. An unpromising grey metal door in the rock leads to the 88 concrete steps that descend into a wonderland of limestone, created over millions of years by dripping water depositing limestone to form the translucent stone curtains, stalactites, stalagmites and even sideways-growing halectites. The temperature is a steady 12°C (54°F), and the air feels dry and fresh. For 1km (half a mile), successive caverns open out, revealing ever more fantastic formations, and culminating in the Tower of Babel. The rich hues are natural, not a trick of artificial light.

🔢 367 E7 ✉ Burncourt, Caher, Co. Tipperary ☎ 052 67246 🕐 Easter–end Oct daily 10–5.30; Nov–Easter daily 11–4.30 ✋ Adult €7, child €2, family €16 ➡ 45-min tour, according to demand 🚌 12km (7.5 miles) east of Mitchelstown signed on country roads from the N8

MIZEN PENINSULA

This rugged peninsula stretches southwest between Dunmanus and Roaringwater bays, with the

Below A boat moored in Dunmanus Bay on the Sheep's Head Peninsula

high point of 407m (1,334ft) Mount Gabriel at its landward end, and 23m (75ft) high cliffs at its seaward end. Ballydehob has a statue of local wrestling hero Dan O'Mahony on the main street and a disused 12-arch tramway viaduct. Skull is an amiable fishing village, with Eire's only planetarium (tel 028 28315; May–end Aug; phone for times). At the tip of the peninsula, beyond Goleen and the beaches of Barley Cove, lies Cloghane Island, linked to the mainland by a bridge, and site of the Mizen Head Visitor Centre (tel 028 35115, www.mizenhead.net; Jun–end Sep daily 10–6; mid-Mar to end May, Oct daily 10.30–5; Nov to mid-Mar Sat, Sun 11–4).

🔢 366 B9 ℹ Town Hall, North Street, Skibbereen, Co. Cork ☎ 028 21766 🕐 Jul, Aug Mon–Sat 9–7, Sun 10–5; Jun, Sep Mon–Sat 9–6; Oct–end Mar Mon–Fri 9.15–1, 2–5.15; Apr, May Mon–Sat 9.15–1, 2–5.15 ⛴ Summer sailings to Baltimore and Clear Island (Oileán Cléire)

ROARINGWATER BAY

www.oilean-chleire.ie (Clear Island)
In the far southwest corner of Ireland, Roaringwater Bay is around 12km (7.5 miles) long and up to 8km (5 miles) wide. Of the 15 islands within the bay, Sherkin and Cape Clear are the largest. Sherkin, a 10-minute boat ride from Baltimore, has a 15th-century abbey, a ruined castle, good beaches and rare plants. Cape Clear is a stop-off point for migratory birds, and its observatory is well established.

Distinctive modern features of the bay are the buoys and snaking black lines of the mussel- and oyster-culture industries. Both species thrive here in the plankton-rich, clear waters.

🔢 366 C9 ℹ Town Hall, North Street, Skibbereen, Co. Cork ☎ 028 39153 🕐 Jul, Aug Mon–Sat 9–7, Sun 10–5; Jun, Sep Mon–Sat 9–6; Oct–end Mar Mon–Fri 9.15–1, 2–5.15; Apr, May Mon–Sat 9.15–1, 2–5.15 ⛴ To Sherkin Island from Baltimore (☎ 028 20218) and Skull (☎ 028 28138), May–end Sep. To Clear Island from Baltimore (☎ 028 39126), and Skull in summer only (☎ 028 28278)

ROSCREA

Noted for its medieval architecture, Roscrea is dubbed Ely O'Carroll Country, after the two ancient Irish families who dominated its history until their lands were seized by the English in the 17th century. In the middle of town stands a huge 13th-century golden-towered castle, with a Queen Anne mansion and formal walled garden within the high curtain wall. The Roscrea Castle Complex Heritage Centre and Damer House (Mar–end Oct daily 10–6) has exhibitions about the town's history and there's a heritage walk taking in the weathered 12th-century wheel cross and round tower of St. Cronin's, and the tower of a 15th-century Franciscan friary.

An incongruous fountain in the town square features four cherubs pouring water.

🔢 364 E6 ℹ Roscrea Castle Complex Heritage Centre, Roscrea, Co. Tipperary ☎ 0505 21850 🕐 Mar–end Oct daily 10–6 ✋ Adult €3.70, child €2.30, family €8.70 🚆 Roscrea

SHEEP'S HEAD PENINSULA

This fertile peninsula lies between Dunmanus and Bantry bays and its main town, Durrus, gives its name to a distinctive local cheese. Low rocky hills in the east give way to a rugged shoreline, and there are great views to the north and south from the Seefin pass above Kilcrohane (346m/1,136ft). The climate is mild, encouraging exotic growth at Kilravock Garden (tel 027 61111; 1 May–end Sep, telephone for opening days and times).

Yachts moor in Ahakista Bay, and it feels like a prosperous, tranquil backwater. A memorial garden on the shore just east of the bay, however, shows that it is also sadly touched by tragedy: The garden honours the 329 people who were killed on 23 June 1985, when Air India flight 182 from Montréal to Bombay exploded off the coast here.

🔢 366 B9 ℹ The Courthouse, The Square, Bantry, Co. Cork ☎ 021 438 1624 🕐 Seasonal opening

INFORMATION

⊞ 367 E7 ✉ Cashel, Co. Tipperary
☎ 062 61437 ⓘ Apr–end Sep daily
9.30–5.30; Oct–end Mar daily 9.30–3.30
✋ Adult €5.30, child (6–18) €2, family
€12 🚌 On Dublin–Cork route 📹 20-min
video, in restored choir buildings, sets
the scene

TIP

» There are no toilet facilities on the
Rock itself but there are some in the
parking area.

Below *Majestic ruins atop the Rock of
Cashel stand out in romantic silhouette
against the surrounding flat land*
Opposite top *Blackball Head, Youghal*
Opposite bottom *The clock tower in
Youghal*

ROCK OF CASHEL

In an area of rich farmland scattered with ruined monastic sites, this is the best
of all, visible for miles, and a microcosm of an age when archbishops behaved
like kings. The rock was actually the seat of Munster kings from the fourth
century, including Brian Boru, who later became king of all Ireland. In 1101 King
Muircheartach Ua Briain presented the site to the Church, and it remained in
use until the mid-18th century, when its decaying buildings, costly to maintain,
were abandoned in favour of St. John's Church in the town below.

EXPLORING THE ROCK

The steep climb to the main door gives a sense of the majesty and impreg-
nability of the site, and leaves you breathless in all respects. Above is the
outer wall of the Hall of the Vicars Choral, constructed for the medieval choir
and restored inside. Beyond the stairs of the gatehouse is a replica of the
12th-century St. Patrick's Cross, then the first building you see is the cathedral,
a vast cruciform dating from 1230, and roofless since 1848. Look up at the
gargoyles around the Gothic windows. The squat, brooding tower was added in
the 15th century, when the archbishops were at the height of their power, and
this end of the church was rebuilt as a fortified tower house. Its appearance
today is grim and forbidding. In contrast, the older Cormac's Chapel, wedged
uncomfortably between the choir and the south transept of the cathedral,
seems positively light-hearted, with its twin square towers and Romanesque
arches. It was built by Bishop Cormac MacCarthy in 1127, and traces of wall
paintings in blue, red and gold can be seen in the chancel. The carving around
the doorways is particularly good. The deeply carved tomb is probably Viking,
and was moved here from the cathedral for shelter. The oldest building of the
Rock is a round tower of 1101, 28m (92ft) high.

CASHEL TOWN

In the town, seek out one of Ireland's most prized cheeses, creamy Cashel
Blue. The Heritage Centre (tel 062 62511; www.casheltouristoffice.com; mid-
Mar to end Oct daily 9.30–5.30; Nov to end Feb Mon–Fri 9.30–5.30) portrays
the history of the town. At the Bolton Library on John Street you can see a
monk's encyclopaedia of 1168 and the smallest book in the world (Mon–Fri
10–4.30). The Folk Village, in a row of thatched cottages on Dominic Street,
re-creates 18th-century rural life and has displays on Republican history (tel 062
62525; daily 9.30–7.30; winter daily 9.30–6). The handsome Cashel Palace Hotel
was originally the archbishops' palace of 1732.

TIMOLEAGUE ABBEY
The monks who selected this site for their abbey in the sixth century chose well. It's on a bend of the Argideen, renowned for its fish and birdlife, where it runs into Courtmacsherry Bay. For the best views, approach from the south. The substantial ruin dates from 1312, when Franciscans moved in at the behest of Donal Glas MacCarthy. Forced out at the Reformation, they returned in 1604, but were burned out again in 1642 by Cromwell's men, who discovered thousands of barrels of wine in the vaults.

Of the two later churches in the village, the Church of the Ascension reflects in miniature the square tower of the abbey; the Catholic church has a window dating from 1929 by artist Harry Clarke, whose work is prominently displayed in Cork's Crawford Art Gallery (▷ 165). The formal castle gardens, with terraces and herbaceous borders date from the 1820s (Jun–end Aug Mon–Sat 11–5.30, Sun 2–5).

✚ 367 D9 ✉ Timoleague, Co. Cork
🕐 Open access

TRALEE
www.discoverkerry.com
This is the county town of Kerry, the northeast gateway to the Dingle Peninsula (▷ 166–169) and known for its Rose of Tralee International Festival—a week-long party and beauty pageant that brings more than 200,000 visitors into town in August (▷ 191). The town sprawls on the flatlands east of Tralee Bay

and has plenty of accommodation and sandy beaches nearby at Banna and Derrymore. The town was founded in the 13th century by the Earls of Desmond. Its chequered history is told in time-journey style at the Kerry County Museum located in the Ashe Memorial Hall at the head of Denny Street (tel 066 712 7777; www.kerrymuseum.ie; Jun–end Aug daily 9.30–5, Apr, May, Sep–end Dec Tue–Sat 9.30–5; Jan–end Mar Tue–Fri 10–4.30).

✚ 366 B7 ℹ Ashe Memorial Hall, Tralee, Co. Kerry ☎ 066 712 1288 🕐 Jul, Aug Mon–Sat 9–7, Sun 10–6; May, Jun, Sep Mon–Sat 9–6; Mar, Apr, Oct–end Feb Mon–Sat 9.15–5 🚊 Tralee

VALENCIA ISLAND AND SKELLIGS
Valencia, just off the northwest tip of the Iveragh Peninsula, makes an interesting detour from the Ring of Kerry (▷ 184–185). It is 11km (7 miles) long and boasts its own signposted Ring drive and a coastal walk, both of which offer great views. Shortly after the bridge crossing from Portmagee, look for the cliff-top memorial marking the spot where the first transatlantic telegraph message was sent in 1866.

The slate slabs used in the walls of some field boundaries came from the old quarry, signposted north of Knightstown, which has a grotto to Our Lady and St. Bernadette. On the eastern end of the island is the Georgian village of Knightstown. Glanleam Sub-Tropical Gardens, west of here were created in the mid-19th century.

The jagged islands off the end of the peninsula are Great Skellig, or Skellig Michael (An Sceilg Mhicíl), and Little Skellig (An Sceilg Bheag), making it the second largest gannetry in the world. Skellig Michael is the more distant of the pair, 13km (8 miles) offshore and up to 217m (712ft) high, and has a lighthouse from 1820. Christian monks sought refuge here in the sixth century, surviving on trade with passing ships before abandoning it in the 11th century. Hundreds of

precipitous steps lead up to their beehive huts. Visit on a cruise from the Skellig Experience Visitor Centre on Valencia Island, over the bridge from Portmagee (tel 066 947 6306; www.skelligexperience.com; Jun–end Aug daily 10–7; Apr, May, Sep–end Oct daily 10–6).

✚ 366 A8 ℹ Beech Road, Killarney, Co. Kerry ☎ 064 31633 🕐 Mon–Sat 9.15–5 🚋

WATERFORD
▷ 178–179.

YOUGHAL
www.youghal.ie
This venerable harbour and market town (pronounced Yawl) is at the mouth of the Blackwater river on a broad, sandy bay. In the 16th century it was plagued by pirates, and the rebel Earl of Desmond landed here in 1579. For helping to suppress the Desmond rebellion, English adventurer Sir Walter Raleigh was rewarded with lands in the area. One of the most notable buildings in town is the Clock Gate of 1777, straddling the narrow Main Street. In 1954 the old harbour area became a film set for John Houston's *Moby Dick*. Guided walks start from the Heritage Centre. Fox's Lane Folk Museum is dedicated to 1850–1950 domestic gadgets (summer Tue–Sat 10–1, 2–6).

✚ 367 E8 ℹ Heritage Centre, Market Square, Youghal, Co. Cork ☎ 024 20170 🕐 Apr–end Sep Mon–Fri 9–5.30, Sat–Sun 9.30–5; Oct–end Mar Mon–Fri 10–3 🚊 Youghal

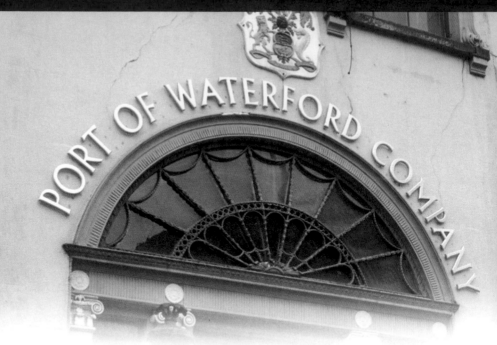

INFORMATION

www.waterfordtourism.org
www.waterfordvisitorcentre.com
➕ 364 F7 ℹ️ The Quay, Waterford, Co.
Waterford ☎ 051 875 788 🕐 May–end
Oct Mon–Fri 9–5, Sat 10–5. Also at
Waterford Crystal ☎ 051 358 398
🕐 Mar–end Oct daily 8.30–6; Nov daily
9–5 🚆 Waterford

INTRODUCTION

Waterford dates back to 7000BC, when Stone Age hunter-gatherers congregated on the banks of the Suir. By 2000BC settlers were mining copper all along this coast. Viking raids in AD795 turned to settlement after 914, with a fort called Dundory built on the triangle of high ground between two rivers, and the establishment of a town they called Vadrafjordr. The Anglo-Normans gained power here in the 12th century, and largely held on to it until the upheavals of the mid-17th century, when the city walls failed to repel Cromwell's army. Despite this, the town has the largest collection of medieval walls and towers still standing in Ireland. In the 18th and 19th centuries Waterford prospered, and much of the town dates from this era.

The city today spreads along the south bank of the River Suir. Broad Merchant's Quay runs beside the river, with a variety of shops, hotels and other buildings facing the water. These include the handsome old Granary of 1872 housing the tourist office and Treasures Exhibition at the western end, and the circular medieval Reginald's Tower at the eastern end.

The main shopping area lies in the rabbit warren of small streets behind Merchant's Quay. The Georgian elegance of the city is epitomized by the Port of Waterford Company building, at the top of Gladstone Street, with its imposing blue door topped by the city crest and a magnificent fanlight. Architect John Roberts' Catholic Cathedral of the Most Holy Trinity of 1793, lit inside by 10 exquisite crystal chandeliers, is equally elegant.

WHAT TO SEE

TREASURES EXHIBITION

www.waterfordtreasures.com
Waterford's Heritage Centre tells the story of the city's development in the context of the history of Ireland. A glass lift rises to the third floor for a tour of the Viking, Anglo-Norman and medieval city, then you proceed to the 18th

century on the second floor, where a 12-minute audio-visual show takes you to the 19th century and beyond.

LOOK for a curved Viking flute of c1150, made from a swan or goose bone; a gold kite-shaped brooch of the same era; the medieval Great Charter Roll, depicting all the lord mayors of Waterford; and a red velvet hat given by Henry VIII to the mayor in 1536. There's also the tale of local boy Thomas Francis Meagher, convicted of treason after the Young Ireland Rebellion of 1848. He escaped being sent to Australia and fled to New York, where he became a Civil War hero and founded the *Irish News*; he is also credited with introducing the Irish flag. Other famous sons of Waterford featured include Shakespearean actor Charles Kean (1811–68) and opera composer William Vincent Wallace (1812–65).

✉ The Granary, Merchants Quay, Waterford ☎ 051 304 500 ⊙ Apr–end Sep Mon–Sat 9.30–6, Sun 11–6; Oct–end Mar Mon–Fri 10–5, Sun 11–5 ✋ Adult €7, child (9–18) €3.20, family €15 ▣ ▦

WATERFORD CRYSTAL

It is easy to take for granted the sparkling chandeliers made of hand-cut crystal that adorn the public and private buildings of Waterford and, indeed, the rest of the world. But visit the factory where that crystal is made, and you realize how much skill and time goes into every piece of glass. The skills required to blow, cut and polish the glassware, from a tumbler to a trophy, are a revelation.

Glassmaking became an industry here in 1783 and thrived until 1851, when heavy taxation and a lack of funds stopped production. Waterford Crystal was revived in 1947, and now dominates the top end of the market in much of Europe and America. It has an excellent Visitor Centre, one of the most popular attractions in Ireland.

The factory is modern, covers 16ha (40 acres) and employs around 1,600 workers. Though working conditions have upgraded since the early days, the skills are much the same, and an apprenticeship still takes about eight years. During the factory tour, with the roaring furnace ever present, you'll see the whole process, from blowing molten glass at 932°C (1,710°F) to wedge-cutting the finished piece on a diamond wheel. Waterford crystal is distinctive for its clarity, sparkle and weight—the thicker glass allows for deeper facets. Afterwards, visit the gallery and shop with new appreciation.

✉ Off N25 Dungarvan road ☎ 051 332 500 ⊙ Gallery: Mar–end Oct daily 8.30–6; Nov–end Feb daily 9–5; factory tours: Mar–end Oct daily 9–4.15; Nov–Feb Mon–Fri 9–3.15 ✋ Gallery: free. Tours: adult €10, child under 12 free ⏱ 45 min, Mar–end Oct daily 9–4.15; Nov–end Feb Mon–Fri 9–3.15 ▣ ▦

Above *Reginald's Tower—one of many medieval relics in Waterford*
Below left *Sculpture in Broad Street*
Below right *A stained-glass window in the Cathedral of the Most Holy Trinity*
Opposite *Port of Waterford Company building*

THE SHEEP'S HEAD PENINSULA

This walk through farmland around Kilcrohane takes in part of the Sheep's Head Way, a spectacular long-distance footpath of 88km (55 miles) that encircles the peninsula and is one of the great walks of Ireland.

THE WALK

Distance: 5km (3 miles)
Allow: 2 hours. Good boots required: lots of stiles, two small streams to ford, and some muddy fields to cross
Start/end at: Kilcrohane village
1:50,000 OSI Discovery Series, map 88 Grid reference 081 037
Parking: Kilcrohane main street

HOW TO GET THERE

Take the R591 from Bantry.

★ Kilcrohane is on the minor road which runs down the south side of the Sheep's Head peninsula in the far west of County Cork. Bantry Bay spreads on the northern shores of the peninsula, and to the west, the next land is North America.

Walk west from the main street of Kilcrohane beside the main road, past a children's playground on the left. Ignore a turning to the left, signed Kilcrohane Pier, and keep straight on. Pass a pink cottage on the right; a stream gushes under the road. Soon after this turn left, following the yellow waymarker painted on a stone. Immediately cross a cattle grid, and follow the rough gravel road towards the sea.

❶ As you walk down here, behind and to the left is the summit of Seefin, 345m (1,132ft), with Rossk-errig Mountain in front of it. The high pointy peak on the Mizen Peninsula opposite is Knocknamaddry.

Follow the gravel track as it curls away from the village. Go through a gateway into a farmyard. Just before the farm buildings, turn left through a field gate and bear right, down to a gap in the wall at the bottom of

the field. Follow a path around to the left, ford a small stream, and bear right towards the shingle beach. Cross a high wooden stile over a fence, waymarked, and bear right along the fence.

❷ Stay alongside this fence. Black fingers of rock poke into the next little bay along; look for black and white oystercatchers on the shingle.

Cross the next high stile. Ford a small stream on the other side, and continue ahead across the grass. Towards the other side of this bay, look for another waymarker. Bear left along the edge of the field. In the corner of the field, cross a low wooden stile. Continue straight ahead towards a metal field gate. Cross the stone stile beside the field gate, and continue ahead, following a rough track. Go through a field gate and keep straight on, with the stream broadening to your right.

❸ From here, look right to see waves crashing on the reef to the west of Carbery Island.

The track becomes stony just before a field gate. Climb the stone stile, cross the stream, and walk straight ahead on the minor road through a hamlet. Go between two white houses, and keep straight ahead over a stone stile. Bear left up an overgrown path. Turn sharp left over a stone stile by a gate, and right, following the arrow, up the edge of a field. Continue straight ahead, up a short lane. Cross a stone stile and continue up the lane between stone walls. The stone stile at the end takes you into a private garden. Cross the grass and bear left around

Above *Distinctive signs mark the path of the Sheep's Head Way*

a building. Pass through a gap in the wall, descend stone steps, cross a slab bridge to a road and turn right.

❹ The road leads past the village graveyard, and down to the quay.

Return to the slab bridge and turn right through a private gateway. Cross in front of a garage and climb stone steps. Go through a field gate, bear left through a gateway, waymarked, and bear right through a field gate. Turn right before farm buildings over a stile into a field. Keep left and at the far corner cross the stone stile and continue straight ahead over the next field. Cross a stone stile and bear left up the tarmac road back to Kilcrohane.

WHERE TO EAT

There's no café, but the village store sells supplies, or try Fitzpatrick's pub or the Bay View pub.

A CIRCUIT OF MUCKROSS LAKE

The beautiful woods and mountain scenery in the heart of Killarney National Park make a wonderful backdrop for a walk.

THE WALK
Distance: 11km (8 miles)
Allow: 3–4 hours
Start/end at: At the lower parking area at Muckross House 1:50,000 OSI Discovery Series, map 78 Grid reference 096 085

HOW TO GET THERE
Muckross is signed from the N71, 5.5km (3.5 miles) south of Killarney.

★ Leave the parking area by the path signed Lake Shore and Nature Trails. Bear right to 'Jaunting Cars for Hire', with Muckross House to your left. You could catch a jaunting car (pony and trap) from Killarney.

❶ Muckross House (▷ 173), a Tudor-style 19th-century mansion, houses the Kerry Folklife Museum. Within the Muckross Estate lie the ruins of 15th-century Muckross Abbey.

Keep left across the yard where the jaunting cars wait, and walk straight on down the road to the lake, passing Muckross House to your left. The road bends sharp left, signed to the Torc Waterfall. Continue along the road with the lake on your right. Pass Dundag Bay. Torc Mountain 535m (1,755ft) is ahead. The route runs through woodland. Ignore a turning

marked Boathouse Trail and keep on the road. This section is part of the Kerry Way long-distance footpath. Walk through an iron gate, and stay on the road across open ground. This is the bottom end of Lough Leane. Ahead are the wooded slopes of Torc Mountain, and to the left, beyond a fence, is the footpath which leads to the Torc Waterfall.

❷ Torc Waterfall drops 18m (60ft) and a path climbs up beside it. From the top there's a good view over Macgillycuddy's Reeks to the west.

Where the road meets the trees, veer right onto a footpath and over a stone bridge. This gravel path bears right and climbs uphill. For some distance the path runs parallel to the road above, with good views to the lower end of the lake. The path ends at the N71 road. Turn right and walk along the side of the road. After about 1.5km (1 mile) bear right onto an unsigned road, across a parking space. The narrow road is signed to Meeting of the Waters and Dinis Cottage, and leads down to the lake.

❸ At Meeting of the Waters, a beauty spot, Lough Leane, Middle Muckross Lake and a river meet.

The undulating road runs through woodland, with views to the left of Purple Mountain 832m (2,728ft), Tomies Mountain 735m (2,411ft) and Shehy Mountain 571m (1,873ft), to Bog Bay. Cross a wooden bridge, then pass Dinis Cottage (no public access) on the left. After a reed bed on your left, you will see Lough Leaner. Continue over the arched Brickeen Bridge, where the waters of the two lakes flow.

❹ The views of Lough Leane get better as you go along, framed by trees and with a series of coves.

After about 1.5km (1 mile), take a rough track off to your left, by a signpost for Dinis Cottage. (If you prefer to avoid this path, which is muddy after rain and includes a short scramble up a bank, stay on the tarmac.) This leads through beech and oak woods. The path turns inland and rises sharply to meet a metal field gate. Turn right before the gate, and follow the grassy path around the edge of the field, keeping the fence to your left. The track descends, and there are views through the trees to water on your right—Doo Lough.

❺ Doo Lough is hidden among trees and is a tranquil place to rest.

Continue beside a stream, and scramble up a short bank. At a metal field gate on the left, turn right down the track to the road. Turn left through an ancient gateway, then through an open pole-gate. At the intersection ahead, keep to the right, past a pink cottage. A sign points to Muckross House (400m/436 yards). At a crossing of tracks, turn right and walk towards the house. Bear left through the jaunting-car parking area to where you started.

WHERE TO EAT
MUCKROSS VISITOR CENTRE
The bright, modern Garden Restaurant serves coffee, teas and lunches.
☎ 064 31440 ⊘ Open all year

Left *Riding a pony and trap in Muckross*

THE BLACKWATER VALLEY

This loop drive starts inland up the Blackwater River valley, goes through the little town of Lismore and up, over moorland, to the high point of the Vee. You descend via Clonmel to Dungarvan and back along the coast.

THE DRIVE

Distance: 156km (97 miles)
Allow: 1 day
Start/end at: Tourist Office, Market Square, Youghal

★ Youghal is a thriving port and resort. Its historical significance is shown by the massive town walls, still standing in places.

From the tourist office in Youghal, head north through the town along North Main Street. At a roundabout (traffic circle) as you leave the town go straight on, signed N25 and Rosslare. The Blackwater Estuary is to the right.

❶ The Blackwater Estuary provides feeding grounds for waders, wildfowl and marsh birds. Look for little egrets, widgeon and reed buntings in the marshy reserve of Foxhole.

At the next roundabout turn right onto the N25 for Rosslare. After about 1.5km (1 mile) take the next turning left onto a minor road, by the sign for the River Blackwater. Follow this narrow road through woodland, with the river on your right. After 3km (2 miles), you pass the gateway to Ballynatray House and Demesne.

❷ The grounds of Ballynatray House shelter the ruins of the 13th-century Molana Abbey.

Continue on this road, and at an unsigned fork bear right uphill between houses and through trees. At another unsigned intersection keep right. Where the road turns back on itself keep left, signed Scenic Route. The road climbs, with open farmland on the left, the Knockmealdown Mountains ahead. At Knockanore continue ahead

downhill. After 0.75km (0.5 miles) and turn right at the intersection, again signed as a Scenic Route. Continue downhill, through two sharp bends, and after 2.5km (1.5 miles) turn right at an intersection. In another 0.75km (0.5 miles) turn right, signed Lismore and Cappoquin, at a three-way intersection. Cross a bridge over the river. After a sharp left bend, the road runs beside the river again, with a view of mountains. At the next intersection keep straight on for Lismore, and at then turn left into town.

❸ Lismore Castle on its bluff above the river is an imposing 19th-century mock Tudor edifice, built around the remains of the 12th-century original. In the town turn right downhill, passing the castle. Cross a bridge and take the R668, the second turning left, signed Clogheen. Follow this road as it ascends through

Above Sailing boats moored in the sheltered waters of Dungarvan Harbour
Opposite The lush foothills of the Comeragh Mountains

woods and onto moorland. At an intersection keep ahead, signed to the Vee. The parking area is 3km (2 miles) farther on.

❹ The Vee is a natural cleft between two hills, with views north over the patchwork plains of the Galtee Valley to the Galtee Mountains.

Follow the road downhill around two hairpin bends. Descend through woods, and after 7km (4.5 miles), on the edge of Clogheen, take the turning right, signed Newcastle. Drive east across farmland and go through Goaten Bridge village. Continue ahead beside the River Tar. After 4km (2.5 miles) keep left, signed Clonmel, and pass through Newcastle village. Keep ahead, signed Dungarvan. Cross the Tar and at a crossroads turn left, signed Clonmel. Soon afterwards you reach a major intersection and turn left onto the R671. Go through Kilmanahan and at the intersection turn right. After half a mile you will reach a roundabout. Turn left here to explore Clonmel.

❺ On the northern bank of the River Suir, Clonmel was a stronghold of the important Butler family, the Earls and Dukes of Ormond.

Leaving Clonmel turn right down an unsigned road. At an intersection follow the road keeping the River Suir on your left. At a roundabout turn right onto an unsigned road and go past a sports club, then a golf

club. Pass a waterfall at a left bend, and 0.75km (0.5 miles) later turn sharp right onto a minor road, signed Hanora's Cottage, that turns back on itself uphill. After a hairpin bend look for a viewpoint on the left. Cross a cattle grid and go over the high moorland tops. Descend through conifers, and at an intersection keep straight on. Continue down, cross a bridge and keep right on the main road through the Nire Valley. At the intersection in Ballymacarbry turn left onto the R671. Keep straight ahead for Dungarvan on the R672, passing through horse country. Descend towards Dungarvan, to the bypass. Turn left onto the N72, and almost immediately keep straight on, on the R672, signed Dungarvan. After 3km (2 miles), at a roundabout intersection with the N25, go straight over for Dungarvan.

❻ Dungarvan is a market town, with a big central square and a sandy beach. The bay's mudflats attract a variety of wading birds in winter.

Leave Dungarvan on the N25, following signs to Cork. As you approach the top of the ridge pull

in to the viewpoint on the left for a great view along the coast. Still on the N25, you can see Knockadoon Head, with Capel Island off the end. After about 26.5km (16.5 miles) cross Old Youghal Bridge, and stay on the N25. At the roundabout (traffic circle) turn left to Youghal.

WHERE TO EAT
Lismore has several options for lunch, including Eamonn's Place, a traditional bar serving good food, and Castle Lodge, both on Main Street. There are good pubs in Clonmel and Dungarvan, and Ormonde's Café and Restaurant in the main square at Dungarvan also sells cakes.

PLACES TO VISIT
MOLANA ABBEY
🕐 Easter–end Oct Tue–Thu 9.30–4.30, gates lock automatically at 4.30

LISMORE HERITAGE CENTRE
✉ Lismore ☎ 058 54975

TOURIST INFORMATION
✉ Heritage Centre, Market Square, Youghal
☎ 024 20170

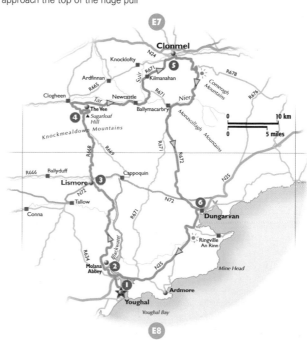

DRIVE

THE RING OF KERRY

The most famous scenic drive in Ireland begins at Killarney and encircles the Iveragh Peninsula. Spectacular mountain scenery on one side contrasts with the unspoiled coastline on the other.

THE DRIVE

Distance: 214km (134 miles) plus diversions
Allow: 1–2 days
Start/end at: Killarney

★ Killarney (▷ 172–173) is the foremost tourist town in western Ireland, mainly because it is a superb starting point for excursions to some famous landscapes.

Leave Killarney on the N72, signed Ring of Kerry, passing the cathedral on the right. As you leave the town, turn left at a roundabout (traffic circle), signed Dingle (An Daingean) and Killorglin. Continue through Fossa, with the peaks of Macgillycuddy's Reeks rising to your left. Pass the turning to Kate Kearney's Cottage, from where the Gap of Dunloe is clearly visible to the south. Continue ahead across farmland, beside the River Laune, to Killorglin. Turn left into the town and veer right at the bottom of the high street.

❶ Killorglin is famous for its August Puck Fair (▷ 191). Before you cross the bridge to the town, look left for a bronze statue of King Puck—a goat.

Leaving Killorglin, at the roundabout follow signs to Glenbeigh, on the N70. After 3km (2 miles), look for a sign right to Cromane beach—a sandspit that runs inland of Inch (▷ 168–169). Continue past a peat bog, with stacks of drying turfs. A haze of blue peat smoke heralds Kerry Bog Village on the right.

❷ Kerry Bog Village preserves a long-gone scene, a township of thatched 18th-century cottages.

Return to the N70 and after 3km (2 miles) enter Glenbeigh, perhaps diverting right to the glorious sands of Ross Behy beach. Continue on the N70, crossing narrow stone bridges, and after 8km (5 miles) there are viewing points with telescopes trained on the Dingle.

❸ The Dingle Peninsula (Corca Dhuibhne, ▷ 166–167) is a dramatic sight. On its northern edge stands Mount Brandon, the second highest peak in Ireland. The large number of ancient stones on the Dingle, some from the early Christian period, indicate its importance in Ireland's early history.

Stay on the N70, go over a pass, then along the inlet to Cahersiveen.

❹ Cahersiveen is superbly set on the estuary of the Valencia river. The Heritage Centre is a square keep with odd baronial towers, looking towards the harbour.

Leave Cahersiveen on the N70, and after 3km (2 miles) turn to Valencia Island R565, an excellent diversion from the Ring.

❺ The bridge to Valencia Island (▷ 177) goes from Portmagee, 10.5km (6.5 miles) west of N70.

The Skellig Experience Visitor Centre is just over the bridge on Valencia.

Return to the N70 and continue across the broad tip of the Iveragh peninsula. After 10.5km (6.5 miles) enter Waterville (An Coireán).

6 Waterville, a seaside town, stands on Ballinskelligs Bay (Bá na Scealg), with Lough Currane (Loch Luíoch) behind. Movie actor Charlie Chaplin (1889–1977) holidayed here for many years, and a memorial to him stands in the green park by the waterfront.

Continue on the N70 over the high Commakesta Pass, with views to Deenish (Dúinis) and Scariff (An Scairbh) islands, and the Beara Peninsula. Below are the sands of Derrynane Bay. The road winds down to Caherdaniel (Cathair Dónall). Make a detour here to Derrynane.

7 Follow signs to Derrynane House, passing an Ogham stone (▷ 29), to enter Derrynane National Historic Park. A small Georgian house with a castellated, slate-covered square tower is the focus of 120ha (296 acres) of beautiful woodland gardens on the shore. It was the home of Daniel O'Connell (1775–1847), the great political reformist.

Return to the main road and continue around the rugged point, passing prehistoric Staigue Fort, and through Castle Cove to Sneem.

8 The houses in Sneem are painted in rainbow shades. Look for the odd stone sculptures by the churchyard, and a memorial on the triangular village green to former French president, Charles de Gaulle.

Keep on the N70, signed Ring of Kerry. The road follows the bank of the Kenmare River. After 17.5km

Opposite Inch Strand is one of Ireland's most famous beaches

(11 miles) a sign points to Blackwater Pier for a diversion onto the shore. Continue on a narrow bridge over the Blackwater River, and pass through Templenoe. On the outskirts of Kenmare, turn right on the N71 to visit the town.

9 A compact and handsome old town, Kenmare is famous for lacemaking. Learn more at the Heritage Centre.

Leave Kenmare on the N71, signed to Killarney. This is a spectacular stretch of mountain road, passing over Moll's Gap, with views to the south side of the Gap of Dunloe. Ladies View is just one of the viewpoints in the Killarney National Park. Pass the turning to Muckross Estate and return to Killarney.

WHERE TO STAY
Cahersiveen, Waterville and Caherdaniel have plenty of accommodation. Cahersiveen Ocean View bed and breakfast has spectacular views of the Kerry coastline and Valencia Harbour.

BUTLER ARMS HOTEL
✉ Waterville ☎ 066 94 74144
🕔 Apr–end Oct

WHERE TO EAT
Red Fox Inn by Kerry Bog Village promises snacks and Irish coffee; for chargrilled seafood, try QC's restaurant at 3 Main Street, Cahersiveen; the Bridge Bar in Portmagee serves crab; Sneem has several cafés, including the Riverside Coffee Shop.

PLACES TO VISIT
DERRYNANE HOUSE
✉ Caherdaniel (Cathair Dónall) ☎ 066 94 75113 🕔 House: May–end Sep Mon–Sat 9–6, Sun 11–7; Nov–end Mar Sat, Sun 1–5; Apr, Oct Tue–Sun, 1–5. Gardens: all year

HERITAGE CENTRE
✉ The Square, Kenmare ☎ 064 41233
🕔 Easter–end Sep

TOURIST INFORMATION
KILLARNEY
✉ Beech Road, Killarney ☎ 064 31633

KENMARE
✉ The Square, Kenmare ☎ 064 41233

WHAT TO DO

ADARE

BLACK ABBEY CRAFTS

A friendly shop, housed in the Heritage Centre specializing in fine Irish crafts, including, ceramics, slate, iron and glass items. There are many items not found in other shops.
✉ Adare, Co. Limerick ☎ 061 396021
🕐 Daily 9–6

CURRANS HERALDRY

www.curransheraldry.com
For an unusual souvenir, check out your family coat of arms at this booth in the Heritage Centre, from their database of 120,000 worldwide. You can then buy or commission it as a mounted parchment, embroidery, a hand-painted plaque or perhaps a special piece of jewellery. Or buy a poster map featuring crests of American and European names.
✉ Adare Heritage Centre, Adare, Co. Limerick ☎ 061 362460 🕐 Mar–end Oct daily 9–6 ✋ €20

BANTRY

THE CRAFT SHOP

In a yellow-painted house in the north of town, this craft shop has a wide range of works by local artists—unusual pottery (including Nick Mosse's spongeware), willow baskets, driftwood mirrors and turned wood, silk scarves by Anne O'Leary, leatherwork, greetings cards and many items that you won't see elsewhere.
✉ Glangarriff Road, Bantry, Co. Cork ☎ 027 50003 🕐 Mon, Tue, Thu–Sat 10–6 (also Wed in summer)

McCARTHY SPORTS SHOP

'For all your sporting needs', announces the bright yellow shop front, and it's true. You can rent fishing tackle, get your live bait, and obtain salmon fishing and other permits. There's excellent brown- and sea-trout fishing in the area, as well as shore and sea fishing, and the owners are a mine of local information.
✉ Round Tower, Main Street, Bantry, Co. Cork ☎ 027 51133 🕐 Daily 9.30–6

BLARNEY

BLARNEY WOOLLEN MILLS

www.blarneywoollenmills.ie
After the castle, Blarney's second biggest attraction is this shop and visitor complex. The mill dates to 1824, and was originally Mahony's Mills. You'll find leather jackets and haute couture suits for ladies and men, high-quality goods in wool and silk, a gift shop with souvenirs, CDs and music, and household goods including crystal, china and linen. There's also an Irish food section. There are branches of Blarney Woollen Mills throughout the Republic of Ireland.
✉ Blarney, Co. Cork ☎ 021 451 6111
🕐 Mon–Sat 9.30–6, Sun 10–6 🍴

CAHER

CRAFT GRANARY

www.craftgranary.com
For quality crafts, or just a cup of coffee, try this big shop in a converted granary, off the main square. You'll find turned and polished wood, Gallùnic soap, beaded jewellery, textiles and basketry, and edibles including fudge, and rhubarb and orange marmalade. There are temporary exhibitions on the first floor.
✉ Church Street, Caher, Co. Tipperary
☎ 052 41473 🕐 Mon–Fri 10.30–6, Sat 9–5

CAHIR
CAHIR PARK GOLF CLUB
www.cahirparkgolfclub.com
Delightful 18-hole course situated in what was once the heart of Lord Cahir's estate. The River Suir divides this parkland course with its mature trees, streams and lakes. Facilties include a pro shop.
✉ 1km (0.5 miles) from Cahir on the Clogheen road, Co. Tipperary ☎ 052 41474 🕐 Daily ✋ Green fees: Mon–Fri €30, Sat, Sun €35 ♿ 🍴

CASHEL
BRÚ BORÚ
www.comhaltas.com
A sculpted trio of dancing figures announces this heritage and performance venue, in the shadow of the imposing and romantic Rock of Cashel. It serves as a base for Celtic and genealogical studies, as well as staging music, song, dance, storytelling and theatre. Evening banquets are held in the restaurant.
✉ Cashel, Co. Tipperary ☎ 062 61122 🕐 Mid-Jun to mid-Sep Tue–Sat 9am–11.30pm, Sun–Mon 10–5; mid-Sep to mid-Jun Mon–Fri 9–5 ✋ Adult €18, child (over 12) €10

CASTLEISLAND
CRAG CAVE
www.cragcave.com
Discovered in 1938 this cave, thought to be a million years old, is a popular destination for all ages. Guides show visitors the stalagmites and stalactites with a dramatic sound and lighting backdrop. For families with children up to 12 years there is the adjoining Crazy Cave Indoor and Outdoor Adventure Centre will all manner of activities and fun come rain or shine.
✉ Castleisland, Co Kerry ☎ 066 714 1362 🕐 Mar–end Dec daily 10–6; Jan–end Feb Wed–Sun 10–6

CLONAKILTY
O'DONOVAN'S HOTEL
www.odonovanshotel.com
O'Donovan's is a family-run, central hotel that's full of character. There are three bars, two restaurants and a beer garden. In summer, traditional musicians play every night for set-dancing in the little An Teach Beag pub, in a 200-year-old cottage behind the hotel.
✉ Pearse Street, Clonakilty, Co. Cork ☎ 023 33250

TIGH DE BARRA
www.debarra.ie
There's live music of some sort nearly every night at this lively pub; it might be folk or funk—check the website for upcoming gigs.
✉ 55 Pearse Street, Clonakilty, Co. Cork ☎ 023 33381

CLONMEL
CLONMEL RACE TRACK
www.clonmelraces.ie
Horse racing took place here for at least a century before the racecourse was properly enclosed in 1913. Around 120 horses will race at any meeting, and these take place most months (not July or August).
✉ Powerstown Park, Clonmel, Co. Tipperary ☎ 052 22611 ✋ From €15, on the gate or online in advance, child (12–18) €10 🍴 📷 🎫 🏧

OMNIPLEX CINEMA
www.filiminfo.net
Mainstream films are the fare at this five-screen cinema on the edge of the Market Place shopping mall.
✉ Kickham Street, Clonmel, Co. Tipperary ☎ 052 27722 🕐 Daily 11–9 ✋ Adult €6.50, child €4, family €16

WHITE MEMORIAL THEATRE
This theatre, housed in a former Wesleyan chapel of 1843, seats an audience of just 225. It is named after James White, founder of the St. Mary's Choral Society, which performs here along with the Clonmel Theatre Group.
✉ Wolfe Tone Street, Clonmel, Co. Tipperary ☎ 052 23333 🕐 Mostly evening performances; times vary ✋ Varies according to production

COBH
SAIL CORK
www.sailcork.com
In these sheltered waters you'll see little sailboats and sailboards out at

Above The Titanic Bar in Cobh recalls the town's link with that vessel
Opposite Celtic maidens dancing at the Rock of Cashel visitor centre

all times of the year—instructors come here in winter to train. Lessons and charters are available from this well-established, family-run company, including dinghy sailing, canoes and powerboats. All abilities—from novice to expert—are welcome, and there's a multi-activity course for children.
✉ East Beach, Cobh, Co. Cork ☎ 021 481 1237 🕐 Main sailing season May–end Sep ✋ Varies depending on activity

TITANIC TRAIL
www.titanic-trail.com
You've seen the movie, hummed the tunes—now see some of the real sites associated with the *Titanic* and her first and last fateful voyage. This 90-minute walking tour of the town provides lots of information about Cobh's rich maritime and emigrant heritage, and there's a spooky Ghost Trail on offer too for groups of eight or more.
✉ Departs from Commodore Hotel, Cobh, Co. Cork ☎ 021 481 5211 🕐 Daily at 11; also 2pm Jun–end Sep. Reservations essential in winter ✋ Adult €9.50, child (4–12) €4.75

CORK
AN SPAILPÍN FANAC
The name of this pub, which has been serving since 1799, means The Wandering Labourer. You can enjoy hearty Irish pub food in a cosy old-world atmosphere and listen to Irish music seven nights a week, and bluegrass on Sundays.
✉ 28 South Main Street, Cork, Co. Cork ☎ 021 427 7947 🕐 Daily from 11am, normal pub opening times

BUCKLEY BROTHERS

Behind an old-fashioned and unusual green art-deco front, this tiny confectioner's shop specializes in handmade chocolate and other sweets from all over Ireland. There's a small café squeezed in at the back, too. A little treasure.

✉ 30 Oliver Plunkett Street, Cork, Co. Cork ☎ 021 427 2126 ⊘ Daily 10–4

LE CHATEAU

Established in 1793, this bright yellow pub is the perfect place to relax for a while when you're dropping from your shopping. Food is served all day, and you can also get hot drinks, including Irish coffee, hot whiskey and the traditional hot port.

✉ 93 Patrick Street, Cork, Co. Cork ☎ 021 427 0370 ⊘ Mon–Thu 10.30am–11.30pm, Fri–Sat 10.30am–12.30am, Sun noon–11pm

CORK OPERA HOUSE

www.corkoperahouse.ie

Musical drama and family entertainment, from jazz concerts and pantomime (vaudeville-style fairy tales) to international touring ballet, set the scene at this modern, glass-fronted venue. The back stage door gives access to the Half Moon Theatre, with more experimental drama, live music and a nightclub.

✉ Emmet Place, Cork, Co. Cork ☎ 021 427 4308 ⊘ Box office: daily 9–7 ✋ Varies depending on performance

CURRAHEEN PARK GREYHOUND STADIUM

Cork's state-of-the-art stadium includes not only the excitement of 10 races a night, but also live music afterwards, not to mention the comforts of tote betting from your restaurant table. Curraheen Park offers a memorable and very Irish complete night out.

✉ Curraheen, Cork, Co. Cork ☎ 021 454 3095/1850 525575 ⊘ Racing Wed, Thu and Sat from 7.50, doors open 6.45 ✋ Adult from €7, child (4–16) from 50c 🚌 Bus 8 from city; also free courtesy bus to city every 20 min between 10.30pm–12.30am 🍴 Laurels Restaurant, advance reservations essential ☎ 021 493 3154 ⊡ ⊞

EVERYMAN PALACE THEATRE

www.everymanpalace.com

A lively mixture of comedy, touring theatre and opera productions, with pantomime (vaudeville-style fairy tales) over the Christmas period, are staged in this Victorian building. Irish plays dominate the summer season.

✉ 15 MacCurtain Street, Cork, Co. Cork ☎ 021 450 1673 ⊘ Box office: Mon–Sat 10–6, 7.30 on performance nights ✋ Varies depending on performance

LA GALERIE

Original modern landscapes and seascape paintings of Ireland are on sale at this classy art gallery on Grand Parade.

✉ 32 Grand Parade, Cork, Co. Cork ☎ 021 427 7376 ⊘ Mon–Sat 9–1.30, 2.30–5

IMB DESIGN

www.imbdesign.com

Exquisite jewellery handcrafted in silver and gold is the pride of this tiny shop by the entrance to Paul Street Mall, off the west side of Patrick Street. One of the young owners is usually to be seen in the corner workshop. The results are beautiful, and understandably expensive.

✉ 10a Paul Street, Cork, Co. Cork ☎ 021 425 1800/427 4912 ⊘ Mon–Sat 10–1.30, 2.30–5.30

MARTIN FAHERTY

Martin Faherty is a craftsman and instrument maker, and you'll see the bones of lutes, cellos, fiddles, guitars, mandolins and bouzoukis in every state of creation. The craft outlet is in the old butter market.

✉ Unit 3, Shandon Craft Centre, Shandon, Cork, Co. Cork ☎ 021 430 2368 ⊘ Mon–Fri 9–5; Sat 9–1

SCOTTS OF CAROLINE STREET

www.scotts.ie

This is an elegant and streamlined bar, where glasses and bottles gleam in the soft lighting and tall bucket seats are gathered around the tables. There's a nightclub upstairs, open Friday and Saturday; patrons under 21 must produce some form of photo-ID.

✉ Caroline Street, Cork, Co. Cork ☎ 021 422 2779 ⊘ Lunch 12–3.30, Dinner 4–9.30; Bar Sun–Wed to 12.30am, Thu–Sat to 2am

DINGLE PENINSULA (CORCA DHUIBHNE)

COMMODUM ART AND DESIGN

www.commodum.ie

An eye-catching display of knitted sheep, in natural undyed wools, sets the scene at this craft shop. Within, there are superb etchings capturing the essence of the Dingle as well as mohair rugs, Avoca throws, woolly hats and ceramic Celtic brooches.

✉ Main Street, Dingle, Co. Kerry ☎ 066 915 1380 ⊘ Jun–end Aug daily 9–7; Sep–end May daily 9–6 (Sat until 5)

DICK MACK'S

The pavement outside this blue pub, opposite St. Mary's Church, is set Hollywood-style with the names of the famous who have stopped by for a drink here. They include the Antarctic explorer Tom Crean, actors John Mills and Robert Mitchum, former taoiseach Charles Haughey and singer Christy Moore.

✉ Green Street, Dingle, Co. Kerry ☎ 066 915 1583 ⊘ Opening times vary

DINGLE MARINE ECO TOURS

Enjoy the magnificent landscape and abundant sealife around the Dingle Peninsula from the sea, on an informative 2-hour cruise from Dingle harbour. Advance reservations are essential.

✉ The Pier, Dingle, Co. Kerry ☎ 086 285 8802 ⊘ Apr–end Oct daily ✋ Telephone for times and prices 🍴 Refreshments available on board

JAMIE KNOX WATERSPORTS

www.jamieknox.com

Towards the tip of the sandy spit to the north of Castlegregory, Jamie Knox Watersports offers tuition in all kinds of watersports, including activities such as surfing, boardsailing and kite-surfing.

✉ The Maharees, Castlegregory, Co. Kerry ☎ 066 713 9411 ⊘ Apr–end Oct daily 9–5, Nov–end Mar five days a week 9–5 (telephone to confirm) ✋ Prices vary, depending on activity

LISBETH MULCAHY
www.lisbethmulcahy.com
Lisbeth Mulcahy is a weaver of great renown (as well as being the wife of the famous ceramic artist, Louis, featured below). Here she sells her beautiful wall hangings, scarves of the softest, silkiest lambswool, and the luxury throws made of wool mixed with alpaca, in natural greys and browns, or warm red and blue.

✉ Green Street, Dingle, Co. Kerry ☎ 066 915 1688 🕐 Summer Mon–Fri 9–9, Sat 10–6, Sun 11–6; winter Mon–Fri 9.30–6, Sat 10–6

LONGS HORSE RIDING AND TREKKING CENTRE
www.longsriding.com
If the idea of a canter along the sands has always appealed, this friendly riding centre to the west of Dingle (An Daingean) town is the place to go. The emphasis here is on safety and fun, and activities on offer range from a short hack to a full day's trekking.

✉ Kilcolman, Ventry, Co. Kerry ☎ 066 915 9034/087 225 0286 🕐 Mid-May to mid-Oct daily 10–6 👋 From €30, reductions available

LOUIS MULCAHY: POTADÓIREACHT NA CAOLÓIGE
www.louismulcahy.com
The large, bright pots that are displayed on the grass beside a cluster of white buildings announce the workshop of Louis Mulcahy, one of Ireland's foremost ceramic artists. His imaginative decoration of such practical items as dishes, lampstands, jugs and other vessels uses a variety of shades and glazes that reflect the wonderful light and hues of the Dingle.

✉ Clogher, Dingle, Co. Kerry ☎ 066 915 6229 🕐 May–end Aug daily 9–7; Sep–end Apr daily 9–6

KILLARNEY
GRAND HOTEL
There's plenty of music in the front bar of this hotel, with rock bands taking over when the folk musicians stop. There's a nightclub, too, and on Wednesday a set dancing night.

✉ Main Street, Killarney, Co. Kerry ☎ 064 31159 🕐 Traditional music nightly 9–11, rock music 11.30pm–1.30am

KILLARNEY BOOKSHOP
www.killarneybookshop.ie
In the upstairs section of this great bookshop they have maps and guides, while downstairs is an excellent selection of Irish biographies, including all the best Blasket books—perfect holiday reading—as well as a good range of modern fiction.

✉ 32 Main Street, Killarney, Co. Kerry ☎ 064 34108 🕐 May–end Sep Mon–Sat 9am–10pm, Sun 11–10; Oct–end Apr Mon–Sat 9–6, Sun 11–6

KILLARNEY RIDING STABLES
www.killarney-reeks-trail.com
This large equestrian establishment is located on the northwestern edge of town, on the N72 Killorglin road. It offers a wide range of trekking, hacking and trail riding, with excursions lasting from one hour to five days.

✉ Ballydowney, Killarney, Co. Kerry ☎ 064 31686 🕐 Daily from 8am 👋 From €35 for a 1-hour ride, to €85 for 3 hours

KINSALE
BOLAND
www.bolandkinsale.com
In this pretty seaside town, Boland is a busy shop that stocks lots of unusual, high-quality craft items, including leather belts, ceramic birds and mirrors, traditional spongeware crockery by Nick Mosse, fine knitwear and jewellery, fun children's clothing in fleece and wool, and hand-painted silk ties. There's a range of good quality outdoor clothing, too.

✉ Corner Pearse and Emmet streets, Kinsale, Co. Cork ☎ 021 477 2161 🕐 Apr–end Sep Mon–Sat 9–8, Sun 10–6; Oct–end Mar Mon–Sat 9.30–6, Sun 10–6

CRUISE OF KINSALE HARBOUR
www.kinsaleharbourcruises.com
Enjoy a cruise of the harbour area aboard the *Spirit of Kinsale*. The boat takes you to the outer harbour, and up the River Bandon, with full commentary. There's also music, a bar and snacks on board.

✉ Summercove, Kinsale, Co. Cork ☎ 021 477 8946 🕐 Mon–Sat 2, 3, 4pm, Sun 12, 1, 2, 3, 4pm 👋 Adult €12.50, child (7–12) €6, family €32

HEATHER MOUNTAIN
The modest exterior of this shop belies its spacious interior, which extends behind the building next door. It's piled high with Irish craftwork, from felt handbags, traditional shirts and designer knitwear to wooden mobiles and therapeutic soap products.

✉ Market Street, Kinsale, Co. Cork ☎ 021 477 3384 🕐 May–end Oct daily 9–9; Nov–end Apr daily 10–6

Left *Picturesque Kinsale rises above its harbour on Compass Hill*

LIMERICK

ANGELA'S ASHES WALKING TOURS

www.freewebs.com/walkingtours
Explore the locations associated with Frank McCourt's moving memoir of poverty and childhood in the city, in the company of an expert guide and friend of the author.
✉ Tours leave from Tourist Office, Arthur's Quay, Limerick, Co. Limerick ☎ 061 327108/087 6353648 🕙 Daily at 2.30; tours take around 2 hours ✋ Adult €10, child (4–16) €5

BELLTABLE ARTS CENTRE

www.belltable.ie
The city's premier theatre shows a wide selection of Irish and mainstream touring productions, and also hosts temporary art exhibitions and music events. The arts cinema offers movies from around the world. The coffee shop is also a gallery.
✉ 69 O'Connell Street, Limerick, Co. Limerick ☎ 061 319866/315871 🕙 Box office: Mon–Fri 9.30–5.30 ✋ From €10

THURLES

LÁR NA PAIRCE

www.tipperary.gaa.ie
Thurles was the birthplace, in 1884, of the Gaelic Athletic Association, and here you can find out all about hurling, football, camogie and handball. Displays include a lively 18-minute audio-visual show, and a Hall of Fame.
✉ Slievenamon Road, Thurles, Co. Tipperary ☎ 0504 22702 🕙 Mon–Sat 10–1.30, 2.30–5.30 ✋ Adult €5, child €2.50

TIPPERARY

TIPPERARY EXCEL HERITAGE CENTRE

www.tipperary-excel.com
This community-driven development incorporates the intimate Simon Ryan Theatre, plus cinemas that screen the latest releases. There's also an internet café, art gallery and gift shop. The Visitor Centre here has interactive media to illustrate the town's past.
✉ Mitchel Street, Tipperary, Co. Tipperary ☎ 062 80520 🕙 Mon–Sat 10–10. Theatre and cinema nightly; Sunday cinema 2pm

TRALEE

AQUA DOME

www.aquadome.ie
You can enjoy water-based fun in all weathers here. There's a wave pool, water slides, rapids and geysers and a sauna for adults. Children under 8 must be accompanied, and wear inflatable armbands. Outside, there's a miniature golf course, and remote-control toys.
✉ Dingle Road, Tralee, Co. Kerry ☎ 066 712 8899 🕙 Mon, Wed, Fri 10–10, Tue, Thu 12–10, Sat, Sun 11–8 ☎ 066 712 9150 ✋ Adult €12, child (3–16) €10 ▯ ▤

BLENNERVILLE WINDMILL

This white-painted windmill with red sails was built in 1780 by Roland Blennerhasset, and has been restored to working order. It's the focus of a Craft and Visitor Centre, which tells of Blennerville's role as an emigration port in the 19th century. The windmill is 1.6km (1 mile) from Tralee beside the N86, and a fun way to get there is by vintage steam train from the town.
✉ Blennerville, Tralee, Co. Kerry ☎ 066 712 1064 🕙 Jun–end Aug daily 9–6; Apr, May, Sep, Oct daily 9–6 ✋ Adult €5, children (5–14) €3, family €15

SIAMSA TÍRE THEATRE

www.siamsatire.com
This striking modern building is home to the National Folk Theatre of Ireland. The company was set up in 1974, and maintains an accessible, entertaining schedule of drama, mime, dance and music.
✉ Townpark, Tralee, Co. Kerry ☎ 066 712 3055 🕙 Box office: Mon–Sat 9–6 ✋ Free art exhibition; prices for shows vary

WATERFORD

T&H DOOLANS

A traditional pub with a wood-lined interior, open fires, old-fashioned booths, and live music every night. Food is served at lunchtime and on summer evenings.

✉ 31–32 George's Street, Waterford, Co. Waterford ☎ 051 841504 🕙 Mon–Thu 10am–11.30pm, Fri, Sat 10am–12.30am, Sun 10am–11.30pm

THEATRE ROYAL

The most prestigious of Waterford's three theatres, located in the City Hall behind a modern glass front, hosts Irish and international drama productions and opera.
✉ The Mall, Waterford, Co. Waterford ☎ 051 874402 🕙 Box office: Mon–Fri 10–6 ✋ Prices vary

WALKING TOURS OF HISTORIC WATERFORD

There are many layers of history to explore in Waterford, and lots of unusual and fascinating facts to discover. It's all revealed on a one-hour guided walking tour.
✉ Granville Hotel, Waterford, Co. Waterford ☎ 051 873711/851043 🕙 Mar–end Oct daily 11.45 and 1.45 ✋ €7

WATERFORD BOOK CENTRE

Three floors of books, magazines, stationery and music are inside this gem of a bookshop. International newspapers are available here, and there's an outlet for Leonidas handmade chocolate bars.
✉ Roberts Square, Waterford, Co. Waterford ☎ 051 873823 🕙 Mon–Thu 9–6, Fri 9–9, Sat 9–6, Sun 2–6

JUNE/JULY

KILLARNEY SUMMERFEST

www.killarneysummerfest.com

This 10-day event started only in 2002 but looks set to become very popular, with indoor and outdoor activities for all ages—street performers, top bands, a fun run and a big parade.

✉ Killarney, Co. Kerry ☎ 064 71560
🕓 Late June to early July

JULY

CORK YACHT WEEK

One of the largest sailing events in Europe, this prestigious regatta takes place every two years (even dates). Events focus on the famous Yacht Club at Crosshaven.

✉ Royal Cork Yacht Club, Crosshaven, Co. Cork ☎ 021 4831179 🕓 Mid-July

KINSALE ARTS WEEK

www.kinsaleartsweek.com

Local and international acclaimed artists and performers take part in more than 50 events over eight days. The carnival atmosphere embraces the very best in music, art, drama, and lots more.

✉ Kinsale, Co. Cork ☎ 021 470 0010
🕓 Mid-July

AUGUST

PUCK FAIR

www.puckfair.ie

This is one of the biggest events in Kerry, and it has been going strong for some 400 years; it's believed to have its origins in a pre-Christian celebration. Today's festivities include open-air music concerts, lively parades, drinking, story-telling and lots of family events—and the highlight of it all is the crowning of King Puck, a billy goat.

✉ Killorglin, Co. Kerry ☎ 066 976 2366
🕓 10–12 August

WATERFORD SPRAOI STREET FESTIVAL

www.spraoi.com

Events are free at this weekend fiesta of street theatre and world music. With more than 300 shows by international performers, it's the biggest event of its kind in Ireland.

✉ Waterford, Co. Waterford ☎ 051 841808 🕓 August Bank Holiday

LIMERICK SHOW

www.limerickshow.com

Munster's biggest agricultural show takes place over a weekend and features show-jumping, carriage driving, sheep and cattle judging, dog show and agility classes, horticulture, craft and trade stands and classic cars.

✉ Limerick Racecourse, Patrickswell, Co. Limerick ☎ 061 355298 🕓 End August
🖐 Adult €10, child (under 12) free

ROSE OF TRALEE INTERNATIONAL FESTIVAL

www.roseoftralee.ie

One of Ireland's best-loved festivals has 200,000 visitors, five days of partying and huge TV coverage. The event began in 1959 and now has entries from across the world. The Rose, picked for character and personality, recalls a sentimental song by William Mulchinock.

✉ Rose of Tralee Festival Office, Ashe Memorial Hall, Denny Street, Tralee
☎ 066 712 1322 🕓 End August

SEPTEMBER

CORK FOLK FESTIVAL

www.corkfolkfestival.com

Six days of folk music in bars and other venues all over the city, with top musicians from across Ireland, and traditional music from elsewhere in Europe.

✉ Cork, Co. Cork ☎ 087 275 9311
🕓 Early September

OCTOBER

CORK JAZZ FESTIVAL

www.corkjazzfestival.com

Ireland's premier jazzfest, taking over some 75 venues around the city for four days. Up to 1,000 musicians from 25 countries take part, and 40,000 visitors are expected. And it's not all pricey concerts—many pub events are free.

✉ Event office: 20 South Mall, Cork, Co. Cork ☎ 021 427 8979 🕓 End October

EATING

PRICES AND SYMBOLS

The restaurants are listed alphabetically within each town. The prices given are the average for a two-course lunch (L) and a three-course dinner (D) for one person, without drinks. The wine price given is for the least expensive bottle.

For a key to the symbols, ▷ 2.

ADARE
MAIGUE RESTAURANT
www.dunravenhotel.com
Antiques and open fireplaces give charm to this friendly country inn that dates back to 1792. The Maigue Restaurant serves modern cuisine. A well-balanced menu has some tempting options: You might start with a coarse country terrine, and then try sea bass with pak choi, beetroot and coriander salsa.
✉ Dunraven Arms, Main Street, Adare,Co. Limerick ☎ 061 396633 ◉ Daily 7–9.30, also Sun 12.30–1.30 ✋ L €30, D €52, Wine €22 🚗 In the middle of town

BALLYLICKEY
SEA VIEW HOUSE HOTEL
www.seaviewhousehotel.com
The food lives up to the promise of the stylish surroundings, with some classical ideas sharing menu space with more modern interpretations. Fresh Bantry Bay crab salad twinned with scallop mousse with vermouth sauce, and warm goat's cheese salad with blackberry compote make interesting starters before roast rack of lamb, or brill in a light wine sauce.
✉ Ballylickey, Co. Cork ☎ 027 50073 ◉ Daily 7–9.30; also Sun 12.30–1.45; closed Nov–end Mar ✋ L €25, D €30, Wine €20 🚗 5km (3 miles) north of Bantry towards Glengariff, 70m (75 yards) off the main road

BALTIMORE
THE BALTIMORE ROOM
www.caseysofbaltimore.com
Beloved of locals, this simply decorated restaurant boasts stunning sea views. Not surprisingly, the accent is on seafood, especially mussel and lobster dishes. The seafood comes from the catches of the Baltimore fishing fleet and the restaurant has a mussel farm to provide fresh mussels. All dishes are simply cooked to accentuate the tastes and make the best use of fresh local farm produce.
✉ Casey's of Baltimore, Baltimore, Co. Cork ☎ 028 20197 ◉ Daily 12–2.30, 6.30–9 ✋ L €25, D €40, Wine €18 🚗 Overlooking the harbour

ROLF'S COUNTRY HOUSE RESTAURANT
www.rolfesholidays.eu
Rolf's is a complex of old stone buildings that have been converted into holiday cottages with a restaurant, café and wine bar. The surrounding area is one of outstanding beauty and the effects of the gulf stream add balmy weather to complete the picture, which can be enjoyed on the pleasant terraces. Chef Johannes Haffner uses organic and local ingredients in his eclectic range of dishes and all breads and pastries are home-made. Start your meal with the likes of smoked Irish salmon or West Cork black pudding and follow with a fish dish of lemon sole or meats such as beef fillet steak stroganoff cooked in vodka.
✉ Baltimore Hill, Baltimore, Co. Cork ☎ 028 20289 ◉ Daily 8am–9.30pm ✋ L €28, D €35, Wine €23 🚗 Take the R595 to Baltimore. Follow the road towards the harbour (through the one-way system). Before the harbour you will see a sign for Rolf's on the left. Turn sharp left up the hill and continue up the lane until you see Rolf's on your left

6–9.30, Sun 6–9.30 (also Mon Jul and Aug) 👋 L €15, D €35, Wine €19 🚗 In the centre of Cahersiveen

BANTRY

O'CONNOR'S SEAFOOD RESTAURANT

www.oconnorseafood.com

All things maritime at this lovely restaurant in the heart of Bantry. From the model sailing ships in the window, to the live lobster and oyster tank inside, and the delectable local seafood on the menu, O'Connor's is a triumph. Renovated in 2006 the interior is light and airy but certainly comfortable. Start with fresh oysters or the house speciality mussels and move on to pan-seared local scallops or chunky cod fillets. If you prefer meat try the local lamb or Irish chicken fillet stuffed with spinach and mushrooms served in a white wine cream sauce. There is always a vegetarian 'dish of the day', on the menu too. For a lighter bite at lunch O'Coonor's does delicious open sandwiches.

✉ The Square, Bantry, Co. Cork ☎ 027 50221 🕐 Daily 12.15–3, 6–10 (closed Sun and Mon in winter) 👋 L €15, D €35, Wine €19 🚗 In Bantry town centre on the central square

CAHERSIVEEN

QC'S SEAFOOD BAR & RESTAURANT

www.qcbar.com

Owners Kate and Andrew Cooke have a love affair with the sea, which is reflected in their charming restaurant with its nautical ambience in the centre of Cahersiveen. Kate's family business is Quinlan's Kerry Fish at Renard Point where all the fresh fish and seafood comes from to be served up in the superb dishes so lovingly prepared. There is a strong Spanish influence evident in the preparation with the resulting chargrills a speciality. The use of olive oil and garlic also predominates. The menu does not consist of seafood alone and the chargrilled steaks are superb. A restaurant not to be missed.

✉ 3 Main Street, Cahersiveen, Co. Kerry ☎ 066 947 2244 🕐 Tue–Sat 12–2.30,

CASHEL

THE BISHOPS' BUTTERY

www.cashel-palace.ie

This Queen Anne property has beautiful views of the surrounding countryside. Superb modern Irish cooking uses locally sourced produce as well as organically grown vegetables and herbs from the hotel's garden. To complement the neatly presented food there is a wide choice of wines from around the world. Service is friendly and professional.

✉ Cashel Palace Hotel, Main Street, Cashel, Co. Tipperary ☎ 062 62707 🕐 Mon–Sat 12.30–2.30, 6–9.30 👋 L €25, D €60, Wine €20 🚗 On the N8, near the traffic lights in Main Street in the heart of town

CHEEKPOINT

McALPIN'S SUIR INN

www.mcalpins.com

McAlpin's is a 16th-century inn beside the river in a pretty village, 11km (7 miles) to the east of Waterford. It has been owned and run by the McAlpin family for more than 30 years and is well known for its excellent seafood and dining in general. The food is hearty fare, the atmosphere is friendly and the location is superb.

✉ Cheekpoint, Co. Waterford ☎ 051 382220 🕐 Mon–Sat 6–9.45 (closed Mon in winter) 👋 D €26, Wine €9 🚗 In Cheekpoint village

CLONAKILTY

GLEESON'S RESTAURANT

www.gleesons.ie

Behind the pretty blue-painted façade in the quaint town of Clonakilty, Gleesons is a temple of fine dining run by Robert and Alex Gleeson. Top chef Robert brings his expertise and produces some incredible international and French-influenced dishes using the best of local produce. His special Food and Wine nights give you the chance to experience the best of

food complemented by the perfect wine. The à la carte menu features highlights such as seared south coast scallops, cauliflower purée and raisin viaigrette, followed by baked breast of Irish chicken filled with pumpkin and buffalo mozzarella, Niçoise vegetables and tarragon café au lait sauce—foodie heaven.

✉ 3–4 Connolly Street, Clonakilty, Co. Cork ☎ 023 21834 🕐 Tue–Sat 6–9.30 👋 D €50, Wine €24 🚗 In Clonakilty town centre. Connolly Street is the first street on the left after the statue on the triangle of land known as Astna Square (the first block of Connolly Street is known as Rossa Street)

CLONMEL

SLIEVNA MON

www.hotelminella.ie

Friendly staff welcome diners into the comfortable dining room, with an open fire to complete the setting. The menu offers traditional choices based on accomplished cooking of fresh produce; warm smoked chicken salad, oven-baked fillet of cod Provençale, and apple pie with crème anglaise.

✉ Minella Hotel, Coleville Road, Minella, Clonmel, Co. Tipperary ☎ 052 22388 🕐 Daily 12.30–2.30, 6.30–9.30 👋 L €28, D €40, Wine €22 🚗 Just outside town beside the river

COBH

JACOB'S LADDER RESTAURANT

www.watersedgehotel.ie

The brightly painted exterior of this waterfront hotel hides a chic modern restaurant with tall windows and wooden floors. Irish continental cuisine dominates the menu with dishes such as chargrilled salmon fillet with a mango and lime salsa for lunch or Atlantic hot seafood platter for dinner.

✉ Waters Edge Hotel, Yacht Club Quay, Cobh, Co. Cork ☎ 021 481 5566 🕐 Daily 12–4.30, 6.30–10 👋 L €24, D €35, Wine €19.95 🚗 On the waterfront, follow signs for Cobh Heritage Centre & Fota Golf Club

CORK

CAFÉ PARADISO

www.cafeparadiso.ie

A lively vegetarian restaurant not

far from University College Cork. The imaginative lunch menu offers choices such as feta, pinenut and couscous cake with lemon and cumin wilted spinach, while the dinner menu may list sage-grilled portobello mushrooms with tomato and glazed walnut dressing with red onion jam, smoked gubeen mash and braised cannellini beans.

✉ 16 Lancaster Quay, Western Road, Cork, Co. Cork ☎ 021 427 7939 ◷ Tue–Sat 12–3, 6.30–10.30 ✋ L €25, D €28, Wine €22 🚌 Follow Washington Street in the direction of Universtiy College Cork, opposite the entrance to Jurys Hotel

GALLERY RESTAURANT
www.rochestownpark.com
The Gallery Restaurant offers a wide choice ranging from simple fish dishes (pan-fried sole with lemon and parsley butter) to more complex carnivorous fare (sautéed pheasant, braised cabbage, lardons and red wine jus). Or for something more down to earth plump for tender steak with onions, mushrooms and french fries.

✉ Rochestown Park Hotel, Rochestown Road, Douglas, Co. Cork ☎ 021 489 0800 ◷ Daily 12.30–2.30, 6.30–10 ✋ L €18, D €38, Wine €16.50 🚌 From central Cork take south link road. Take the third exit at the roundabout (traffic circle) for Rochestown. At

the small roundabout take the third exit into Rochestown Road

ISAACS RESTAURANT
www.isaacsrestaurant.ie
Vibrant Isaacs Restaurant is located on MacCurtain Street, one of the trendiest streets in Cork. The building is an 18th-century warehouse and it has been sympathetically restored and modernized. Canice Sharkey's kitchen produces first-class modern Irish dishes, always aware of seasonal produce and using the freshest of local fare. The menus are constantly changing, with new specials twice a day. A typical dinner could consist of a sea-food chowder starter, roast breast of chicken wrapped in pancetta with baked stuffed flat mushrooms and cream sauce for the main course, and a delicious spiced pear tart with warm butterscotch sauce and cream for dessert.

✉ 48 MacCurtain Street, Cork, Co. Cork ☎ 021 450 3805 ◷ Mon–Sat 12.30–2.30, 6–10, Sun 6–9 ✋ L €21, D €37, Wine €20 🚌 Opposite the Everyman Palace Theatre on MacCurtain Street, near Patricks Quay

JACOBS
www.jacobsonthemall.com
Jacobs has a light, airy feel, a modern oasis in the bustling

financial district of the city. Add to that the skilful, creative menus using top-notch ingredients, it is no wonder that this restaurant is ever popular.

✉ 30a South Mall, Cork, Co. Cork ☎ 021 425 1530 ◷ Mon–Sat 12.30–2.30, 6.30–10 ✋ L from €19, D from €50, Wine €22 🚌 In the heart of the city

ORCHIDS RESTAURANT
www.hayfieldmanor.ie
This house with classically styled rooms is set in secluded grounds just 2km (1 mile) from Cork city centre. The period features include original fireplaces, pillars, and high ceilings alongside contemporary additions. The elegant Orchids Restaurant serves French and European dishes with a cosmopolitan feel in a room overlooking a classical garden. Using the freshest Irish produce, a meal could include crispy langoustine, pancetta and basil parcels with a red capsicum purée, followed by fillet of Irish beef and rounded off with warm *crêpes* smothered in Jameson whiskey sauce and vanilla ice cream. There is also a less formal restaurant, Perrotts, in the conservatory.

✉ Hayfield Manor, Perrott Avenue, College Road, Cork, Co. Cork ☎ 021 484 5900 ◷ Mon–Sat 7–10 ✋ D €60, Wine €32

Opposite *Dine by a floodlit waterfall at Kenmare's La Cascade*
Above *Ballyrafter House in Lismore specializes in local salmon*

From Cork take the N22 to Killarney. On Western Road at the university gates turn left into Donovan's Road, then right into College Road and immediately left into Perrott Avenue

DINGLE
HALF DOOR
This popular restaurant serves excellent fresh fish dishes and traditional Irish fare. You can choose a dish of the day, or select from the interesting menu. Starters may include baked crab au gratin and the main menu has dishes such as crispy monkfish fillets with tomato and basil sauce pasta gratin.
✉ 3 John Street, Dingle, Co. Kerry ☎ 066 915 1600 🕐 Mon–Sat 6–10; closed mid-Dec to mid-Feb 🍴 L €22, D €40, Wine €20 🚌 In the heart of the village

DURRUS
THE GOOD THINGS CAFÉ
www.thegoodthingscafe.com
Chef Carmel Somers serves up dishes using the best of West Cork produce is her little café-cum-restaurant just outside the village of Durrus. The dining room and menu alike have an elegant simplicity. The menus are full of local organic ingredients—West Cork fish soup, grilled Ahakista lobster, Kilcrohane new potoates Mount Callan cheese. For dessert you could might find warm chocolate and banana cake served with cookies-and-cream ice cream. Ms Somers also sells Irish and international produce and she runs cookery courses. Home-made truffles are served with your coffee.
✉ Ahakista Road, Durrus, Co. Cork ☎ 027 61426 🕐 Daily 12.30–3, 6.30–8.30 🍴 L €20, D €40, Wine from €18 🚌 From Durrus village take the Ahakista/Kilcrohane Road, the restaurant is about 2km (1 mile) out of the village on the right

KENMARE
LA CASCADE
www.sheenfallslodge.ie
Dramatic views of the floodlit Sheen waterfalls are the backdrop to your meal while the resident pianist plays softly in the background. The food isn't outdone by the views—fresh local produce and home-grown herbs contribute to dishes full of taste and panache. The sommelier knows his wines, and the choice is extensive. The Lodge catches and smokes its own salmon. Smart dress is required.
✉ Sheen Falls Lodge, Kenmare, Co. Kerry ☎ 064 41600 🕐 Daily 7–9.30 🍴 D €65, Wine €41.50 🚌 From Kenmare take N71 towards Glengariff. Take first left after suspension bridge

LIME TREE
www.limetreerestaurant.com
The Lime Tree is a bustling, seasonally inspired restaurant. The food is impeccably served and the Kenmare Bay seafood pot pourri, made of four types of fish cooked in parchment, is popular.
✉ Shelbourne Street, Kenmare, Co. Kerry ☎ 064 41225 🕐 Daily 6.30–10; closed Nov–end Mar 🍴 D €40, Wine €22 🚌 At the top of the town

PARK HOTEL KENMARE
www.parkkenmare.com
The period dining room of this renowned hotel looks out on gardens that sweep down to the water's edge. The finest produce from the neighbouring sea and the Kerry hills is used in an enticing carte of traditional dishes with a strong streak of creativity; perhaps pan-fried foie gras on Sneem black pudding, with rhubarb chutney, Granny Smith sorbet and truffle jus. Lunch is served in the lounge. Smart dress is required in the restaurant.
✉ Kenmare, Co. Kerry ☎ 064 41200 🕐 Daily 11–6, 7–9; closed Nov–end Apr (open Christmas and New Year) 🍴 L €30, D €60, Wine €39.50 🚌 In Kenmare, take R569 past the golf club and continue on through the town where the hotel is on the left, at the top of the main street

KILLARNEY
THE BLUE POOL RESTAURANT
www.muckrosspark.com
The elegant dining room overlooks the delightful gardens at this traditional country house. The serious approach to food is evident from a carte devoted to seasonal Kerry produce: stuffed crab's toes with salmon mousse, hot-smoked salmon smokies, and pan-fried black sole caught in the nearby sea, plus moist roast duck breast and tender rack of lamb. Try the dark chocolate Grand Marnier parfait for a delicious conclusion to your meal.
✉ Muckross Park, Muckross Village, Killarney, Co. Kerry ☎ 064 31938 🕐 Daily 7–9.30 🍴 D €60, Wine €20 🚌 4km (2.5 miles) from Killarney within the Killarney National Park

THE GARDEN ROOM RESTAURANT

www.themalton.com

Diners can feast on the magnificent setting as well as the cuisine at this elegant restaurant. Leek and crabmeat roulade with lime and herb cream, and scallops with turmeric sauce are typical of the carte. Warm plum pudding makes a lovely end to a meal. Breakfast is also available.

✉ The Malton Hotel, Killarney,Co. Kerry ☎ 064 38000 🕐 Daily 6.30–9 🖐 D €46, Wine €26 🚌 In the heart of the town

THE HERBERT ROOM

Expect the odd international influence to the cuisine. Local produce is skilfully used by the master chef to give a good range of Irish traditional and international dishes including a selection of vegetarian ones. There is an extensive wine list.

✉ Cahernane House Hotel, Muckross Road, Killarney, Co. Kerry ☎ 064 31895 🕐 Daily 7–9.30; closed Dec, Jan 🖐 D €60, Wine €25 🚌 From Killarney follow signs for Kenmare, then from Muckross Road go over the bridge and the hotel is signposted on the right

THE LAKE ROOM

www.aghadoeheights.com

A stylish, modern restaurant where every table has magnificent views of Killarney's lakes and national park. Long acknowledged as one of Ireland's finest restaurants, The Lake Room draws inspiration from the surrounding natural environment (loin of Kerry lamb, mélange of local seafood) and the cuisine is modern Irish and European. A varied wine list complements the balance of the food. Reservations are required.

✉ Aghadoe Heights Hotel, Lakes of Killarney, Co. Kerry ☎ 064 31766 🕐 Daily 6.30–9.30, also Sun 12.30–2 🖐 L €50, D €72, Wine €30 🚌 5km (3 miles) north of Killarney, signed off the N22 Tralee road

KINSALE

FISHY FISHY CAFÉ

www.fishyfishy.ie

This is a treasure trove of great seafood served any number of ways by helpful, friendly staff. All

Above *Sheep roam outside The Presidents' Restaurant in Mallow*
Opposite *The South of Ireland is the country's food capital*

the food provided here is good, but a popular choice is the warm salad of chilli seafood which comprises a mixture of fish including monkfish, salmon and prawns with a sweet chilli sauce on a bed of mixed leaves. Lunch only.

✉ Crowley's Quay, Kinsale, Co. Cork ☎ 021 470 0415 🕐 Apr–end Oct Tue, Wed, Thu, Fri 12–8, Sat, Sun, Mon 10–4.30; Nov–end Mar daily 12–4.30 🖐 L €30, Wine €25 🚌 Opposite St. Multose Church

JIM EDWARDS

www.jimedwardskinsale.com

This nautically themed restaurant serves a varied menu based on local produce such as fish and seafood. The lobster could not be any fresher, taken from a tank inside the restaurant, and there's a variety of lamb, beef and duck dishes to choose from.

✉ Market Quay, Kinsale, Co. Cork ☎ 021 477 2541 🕐 Daily 12.30–3, 6–10 🖐 L €18, D €50, Wine €21 🚌 Market Quay

SAVANNAH WATERFRONT RESTAURANT

www.tridenthotel.com

An attractive harbourside restaurant in one wing of a 17th-century corn store. As well as friendly service, diners can enjoy superb views across to Scilly and Summercove. The best of local produce from land and sea is used to create dishes

with a modern edge. There is a wide range of desserts.

✉ Trident Hotel, Worlds End, Kinsale, Co. Cork ☎ 021 477 9300 🕐 Mon–Sat 7–9, Sun 1–2.30, 7–9 🖐 L €30, D €40, Wine €21 🚌 At end of Pier Road, along the waterfront

THE SPANIARD INN

www.thespaniard.com

The Spaniard Inn is a welcoming traditional Irish inn where good food, beer and the *craic* can be found in abundance. Meals tend to be in the Irish tradition: bacon and cabbage, and oysters and smoked Bandon salmon. The Spaniard is also renowned for its traditional Irish music evenings.

✉ Scilly, Kinsale, Co. Cork ☎ 021 477 2436 🕐 Mon–Thu 10.30am–11pm, Fri–Sat 10.30am–12.30am, Sun 12.30–11.30 🖐 Bar lunch from €10, D €35, Wine €20 🚌 In Scilly, 1km (0.6 miles) out of town

THE VINTAGE RESTAURANT

Friendly staff welcome you to this traditional restaurant where the food reflects the wealth of the local sea and land harvests. Interesting starters and main courses include oysters, sea bass and other locally caught fish as well as Irish red deer and wild duck. A good selection of wines complements the food and the desserts maintain the very high standard.

✉ Main Street, Kinsale, Co. Cork ☎ 021 477 2502 🕐 Mar–end Oct daily from 6.30pm, Nov–end Feb telephone for opening hours 🍴 D €45, Wine €23 🚗 In the middle of town

LIMERICK
McLAUGHLIN'S RESTAURANT
www.castletroy-park.ie

Probably the only restaurant in the world named after the inventor of hydroelectric power, McLaughlin's offers a contemporary menu that incorporates both international and local influences. Light snacks are available from the hotel pub.

✉ Castletroy Park, Dublin Road, Limerick, Co. Limerick ☎ 061 335566 🕐 Daily 12.30–2, 6–9.30 🍴 L €24, D €45, Wine €23 🚗 5-min east from Limerick on the N7

LISMORE
BALLYRAFTER HOUSE
www.waterfordhotel.com

At this delightful country house expect modern Irish food along the lines of tasty crab claws served with a kirsch and fresh orange juice sauce, a symphony of white fish including cod, brill, turbot and lemon sole with dill butter, followed by fresh cherries with a brandy chocolate sauce. Much is made of the local fresh and smoked Blackwater salmon, and home-produced honey and local cheeses are also served.

✉ Lismore, Co. Waterford ☎ 058 54002 🕐 Easter–end Oct daily 7.30–9; closed Nov–Easter 🍴 L €28, D €44 (4 courses), Wine €18 🚗 1km (0.6 miles) out of town, opposite Lismore Castle

MACROOM
CASTLE HOTEL
www.castlehotel.ie

This establishment has been run by the Buckley family for more than 50 years. The dining room is an attractive mix of modern and traditional with dark wood tables and high-backed chairs. Steps lead up from the main dining to a snug of extra tables. The menu combines international and more traditional dishes, all made from the freshest of local ingredients.

✉ Main Street, Macroom, Co. Cork ☎ 026 41074 🕐 Daily 12–2.30, 6.30–8.30 🍴 L €26, D €46 (4 courses), Wine €19.50 🚗 On N22, 37km (23 miles) west of Cork

MALLOW
THE PRESIDENTS' RESTAURANT
www.longuevillehouse.ie

Dinner is served in various places in the house throughout the year, including the restored Turner conservatory, with candlelight, white drapes and delicate flowers. A talented team, led by chef William O'Callaghan, offers a blend of modern and classical French cuisine, based largely on produce from the hotel's own farm, river and gardens. The carefully selected wine list encompasses European and New World wines. Smart dress is preferred.

✉ Longueville House, Mallow, Co. Cork ☎ 022 47156 🕐 Daily 6.30–9; closed Jan to mid-Mar 🍴 L €35, D €65, Wine €30 🚗 5km (3 miles) west of Mallow via N72 towards Killarney, turn right at the Ballyclough intersection, the hotel is 200m (220 yards) on the left

WATERFORD
THE MUNSTER DINING ROOM
www.waterfordcastle.com

The Munster Dining Room in the castle on its river island is inviting, wood-panelled and furnished with antiques. A pianist often plays through dinner. The seasonal menus, created by chef Michael Quinn, place an emphasis on Irish specials as well as international cuisine, so Dublin Bay prawns may come as kebabs with roast garlic, basil and cherry tomatoes, while skate au poivre has a sauce lie de vin. Dress code: no denim or trainers (sneakers).

✉ Waterford Castle, The Island, Ballinakill, Co. Waterford ☎ 051 878203 🕐 Daily 7–8.45, also Sun 12.30–1.45 🍴 L €25, D €65, Wine €29 🚗 5km (3 miles) east of the city, then ferry. Telephone for directions

THE NEW SHIP RESTAURANT
www.dooleys-hotel.ie

A friendly, family-run bright restaurant with an inviting ambience. The menu has an international appeal, with dishes such as chicken liver paté on a bed of fresh leaves, and perhaps a traditional apple pie with cinnamon cream to finish. There is also a good value 'early-bird' menu. Every Wednesday night there is traditional Irish music and on Friday and Saturday nights diners are entertained by live music.

✉ Dooley's Hotel, 30 The Quay, Waterford, Co. Waterford ☎ 051 873531 🕐 Mon–Sat 6–9.30, Sun 1–3, 6–9 🍴 L €19, D €25, Wine €18.95 🚗 Along the quay, a 5-min walk from the heart of the town

WATERVILLE
FISHERMAN'S RESTAURANT
www.butlerarms.com

The Huggard family and their staff extend a warm welcome to guests at this traditional hotel restaurant. Locally caught fish prevails on the menu, including salmon cooked simply with lemon parsley butter, and fresh Ballinskelligs Bay lobster. There is an excellent wine list.

✉ Butler Arms Hotel, Waterville, Co. Kerry ☎ 066 947 4144 🕐 Daily 7.30–9; closed 31 Oct to mid-Mar 🍴 D €35, Wine €20 🚗 On the waterfront in the middle of Waterville

STAYING

PRICES AND SYMBOLS

Prices are for a double room for one night. Breakfast is included unless noted otherwise. All the hotels listed accept credit cards unless otherwise stated. Note that rates vary widely throughout the year.

For a key to the symbols, ▷ 2.

ADARE

DUNRAVEN ARMS

www.dunravenhotel.com
This traditional country inn was established in 1792. It has comfortable lounges and bedrooms, attractive gardens, leisure and beauty facilities and good food.
✉ Ferrybank, Adare, Co. Limerick ☎ 061 396633 🖐 Double from €190 ① 86 🏊 Indoor 🅿 🚘 In the middle of town

ARDMORE

ROUND TOWER

Round Tower is a large, friendly country house set in grounds in a pretty fishing village. There's a comfortable lounge, bar and a conservatory, and the menu features local seafood.
✉ Ardmore, Co. Waterford ☎ 024 94494 🖐 Double €80–€120 ① 12 🚘 In the middle of the village

BALTIMORE

ROLF'S

www.rolfsholidays.eu
The converted stone farmhouse and buildings have been carefully restored in original style and character offering luxury guest rooms. Outside is the courtyard and pretty gardens with sunny terraces and sea views. Other facilities at Rolf's are a café and restaurant. There is also a kitchen and wine shop, and a wine bar with regularly changing exhibitions of contemporary art.
✉ Baltimore Hill, Baltimore, Co. Cork ☎ 028 20289 🌐 Closed 17–26 Dec 🖐 Double €90–€100 ① 14 🚘 On Baltimore Hill, outside the village

BANDON

GLEBE COUNTRY HOUSE

This lovely old guesthouse stands in well-tended gardens and is run with great attention to detail. The breakfast menu offers a range of unusual options, and a country-house style dinner is available by prior arrangement.
✉ Ballinadee, Bandon, Co. Cork ☎ 021 477 8294 🌐 Closed 21 Dec–3 Jan 🖐 Double from €90 ① 4 🚘 Turn south off N71 at Innishannon Bridge, signed Ballinadee, for 8km (5 miles) along the river bank, turn left after village sign

BANTRY

WESTLODGE HOTEL

www.westlodgehotel.ie
Superb leisure facilities are provided at the Westlodge, and the wants and needs of children are catered for, making this hotel popular with families. The bedrooms and public rooms are decorated to an impressively high standard.

Bantry, Co. Cork ☎ 027 50360
⊙ Closed 23–27 Dec 👋 Double €130–
€170 ⚙ 90 🛏 ⚲ Indoor 🚗 🚌 N71 to
west Cork

CAHER

CAHIR HOUSE HOTEL
www.cahirhousehotel.ie
This hotel has been extending
hospitality to visitors since the days
of the famous Bianconi horse-drawn
coaches. It offers modern comforts
in well-equipped and tastefully
furnished rooms.
✉ The Square, Caher, Co. Tipperary
☎ 052 43000 ⊙ Closed 25 Dec
👋 Double from €110 ⚙ 42 🚌 and Spa
🚌 On the town square, with parking at
the rear

CASHEL

CASHEL PALACE
www.cashel-palace.ie
The Rock of Cashel, is a dramatic
backdrop to this 18th-century
former bishop's palace. An elegant
drawing room has garden access,
and bedrooms in the main house are
luxurious. Those bedrooms in the
adjacent mews are ideal for families
or groups.
✉ Main Street, Cashel, Co. Tipperary
☎ 062 62707 ⊙ Closed 23–27 Dec
👋 Double from €225 ⚙ 33 🚌 Near
traffic lights in the middle of the town

CLONAKILTY

DUVANE HOUSE
www.duvanehouse.com
This comfortable guesthouse
includes one room with a four-poster
bed, and two on the ground floor,
sharing a bathroom—ideal for

family groups. There's a guest sitting
room, and a wide choice available
at breakfast.
✉ Ballyduvane, Clonakilty, Co. Cork
☎ /fax 023 33129 ⊙ Closed Nov to mid-
Mar 👋 Double from €80 ⚙ 4 🚌 1.5km
(0.9 miles) southwest on N71

THE LODGE AND SPA AT
INCHYDONEY ISLAND
www.inchydoneyisland.com
Steps from this modern coastal
hotel lead down to two long sandy
beaches. Guests can eat in the
third-floor Gulfstream restaurant
or the more casual Dunesbar and
bistro. There is also a sauna and
thalassotherapy spa.
✉ Clonakilty, Co. Cork ☎ 023 33143
⊙ Closed 24–26 Dec 👋 Double
€135–€365 ⚙ 67 ⚲ Indoor 🚗 🚌 From
the N71, at the entry roundabout (traffic circle)
in Clonakilty, take the second exit and follow
the signs

COBH

WATERS EDGE HOTEL
www.watersedgehotel.ie
This hotel has spectacular views
of the harbour, notably from the
restaurant. Most bedrooms overlook
the waterfront and the ground-floor
rooms have the benefit of private balconies. Secure parking is available.
✉ Yacht Club Quay, Cobh, Co. Cork ☎ 021
481 5566 ⊙ Closed 23–28 Dec and 1–4
Jan 👋 Double €110–€160 ⚙ 19 🚌 On
the waterfront. Follow the signs for Cobh
Heritage Centre

CORK

GARNISH HOUSE
www.garnish.ie
Rooms here are tasteful, and some
have a private Jacuzzi. The breakfast
menu provides a huge choice. It's
convenient for the ferry and airport,
and has 24-hour reception.
✉ 1 Aldergrove, Western Road,
Co. Cork ☎ 021 427 5111 👋 Double
€80–€140 ⚙ 13 🚌 Opposite Cork
University College

GRESHAM METROPOLE
www.gresham-hotels.com
Bedrooms at this city hotel are well
equipped. There is a leisure suite,

waterside restaurant and a café. Ask
reception for car parking information
✉ MacCurtain Street, Cork, Co. Cork
☎ 021 450 8122 👋 Double from
€99 (breakfast not included) ⚙ 113
🚗 ⚲ Indoor 🚗 🚌 In the middle of
the city

HAYFIELD MANOR
www.hayfieldmanor.ie
Part of a grand estate with lovely
gardens, this fine secluded hotel has
every modern amenity and a tranquil
atmosphere. Bedrooms offer high
levels of comfort, and public rooms
have fine furnishings and real fires in
the winter.
✉ Perrott Avenue, College Road, Cork, Co.
Cork ☎ 021 484 5900 👋 Double from
€220 ⚙ 88 ⚲ ⚲ Indoor 🚗 and Spa
🚌 Take N22 towards Killarney, in 2km
(1.25 miles) turn left at University Gates off
Western Road. Turn right into College Road,
then left into Perrott Avenue

DINGLE

HEATON'S GUEST HOUSE
www.heatonsdingle.com
This is a great place to stay down by
the water's edge in Dingle but with
the town close by to explore. The
rooms are stylish, with cream-and-
white furnishings and with natural
wood fittings. The Junior Suite has
a sitting area overlooking Dingle
Harbour. All have flat-screen TV, WiFi
internet access and complimentary
tea and coffee. Breakfast in the
dining room is a treat with fabulous
views of the bay. The buffet has all
manner of fruits and cereals and the
cooked dishes include a traditional
Irish breakfast or a fresh fish of
the day plate as well as choices
of kippers of smoked salmon with
scrambled egg.
✉ The Wood, Dingle, Co. Kerry ☎ 066
915 2288 ⊙ Closed Dec 👋 Double €140
⚙ 16 🚌 Just past the marina overlooking
the bay

Opposite *Cork is one of Ireland's most*
visited counties
Left *Cork's Garnish House is a short walk*
from the city centre

PAX GUEST HOUSE
www.pax-house.com
This guest house must have one of the best views ever of Dingle Harbour. Perfectly placed for touring the Dingle Peninsula, it is also only a 10-minute walk from the town with its craft and antiques shops, pubs and traditional music. The atmosphere is homely and the rooms pleasantly furnished; each has its own bathroom and has good facilities. Free-range eggs, organic porridge, Dingle kippers and freshly baked bread are just some of the tasty offerings for the scrumptious breakfast included in the price.
✉ Upper John Street, Dingle, Co. Kerry ☎ 066 915 1518 🕐 Closed Nov–end Apr ✋ Double €120–€160 🛈 12 🚪 Take the N86 into Dingle town and at the intersection with Strand Street turn right and follow the Pax House sign turning right into John Street

FERMOY
ABBEYVILLE HOUSE.
www.abbeyvillehouse.com
Abbeyville House is conveniently situated in the heart of Fermoy overlooking the town park and is only 100m (110 yards) away from the renowned fishing river, the Blackwater. This large, 19th-century three-storey house combines old-world charm with modern comfort and is also only a stone's throw away from local pubs, shops and restaurants. All bedrooms are well appointed with TV and tea- and coffee-making facilities and have private bathrooms. Guests can also enjoy the residents' lounge and library with open fire. The hotel has private parking.
✉ Abercromby Place, Fermoy, Co. Cork ☎ 025 32767 🕐 Closed late Nov–end Apr ✋ Double €90–€150 🛈 6 🚪 On the N8 Dublin to Cork road opposite town park

BALLYVOLANE HOUSE
www.ballyvolanehouse.ie
An Italianate country house, built in 1728, in a magnificent setting of parkland and gardens (open to the public in May). Comfortable bedrooms overlook the park, where one of the three lakes is stocked with brown trout. Dinner is served around one fine table.
✉ Castlelyons, Fermoy, Co. Cork ☎ 025 36349 🕐 Closed 23 Dec–3 Jan ✋ Double €130–€170 🛈 6 🚪 From N8, take R628 and follow signs to Ballyvolane House

GOUGANE BARRA
GOUGANE BARRA
www.gouganebarrahotel.com
Its lakeside location makes this hotel very popular. The restaurant, bedrooms and bathrooms all have lovely views.
✉ Gougane Barra, Macroom, Co. Cork ☎ 026 47069 🕐 Closed 13 Oct–13 Apr ✋ Double from €140 🛈 27 🚪 Turn off N22 onto R584 and continue west for 32km (20 miles)

INNISHANNON
INNISHANNON HOUSE
www.innishannon-hotel.ie
This attractive 1720 house has gardens running down to the River Bandon. Public areas are comfortable and the atmosphere is relaxed.
✉ Innishannon, Co. Cork ☎ 021 4775121 🕐 Closed 2 weeks in late Jan ✋ Double from €150 🛈 12 🚪 Off N71 Kinsale road, at the eastern end of the village

KENMARE
LANSDOWNE ARMS
www.lansdownearms.com
Kenmare's first hotel dates back to the 1760s, and is now owned by the Quill family. Blending modern facilities with a traditional Victorian building creates an elegant and efficiently run hotel, perfect for touring the Ring of Kerry. Fine formal dining is available in the Quill Room restaurant or there is the more relaxed ambience of the Poet Bar and Restaurant.
✉ Kenmare, Co. Kerry ☎ 064 41368 🕐 Closed 25 Dec ✋ Double €95–€160 🛈 26 🚪 Kenmare is on the R569 off the N22 from Cork. The hotel is at the intersection of Main Street and Shelbourne Street

SHEEN FALLS LODGE
www.sheenfallslodge.ie
This former fishing lodge has been developed into a beautiful hotel on the banks of the Sheen river. Outstanding cuisine is available in the La Cascade restaurant. Bedrooms are comfortably appointed, and there's a leisure suite and beauty therapy facilities.
✉ Kenmare, Co. Kerry ☎ 064 41600 🕐 Closed 2 Jan–1 Feb ✋ Double €240–€430 🛈 66, two 2-bedroom cottages ▥ Indoor 🚪 From Kenmare take the N71 Glengariff road, then first left after suspension bridge

Below *Sheen Falls Lodge overlooks the eponymous waterfalls*

SHELBURNE LODGE

www.shelburnelodge.com

Despite its proximity to the town, Shelburne Lodge is a delightful hide-away set in its lovely gardens well back from the road. It is the oldest house in Kenmare and a pleasure to stay in. The rooms are located in the 1740s lodge and the coach house, and are all maintained to a very high standard, the furniture is in keeping with the period features. A full Irish breakfast is served in the lovely dining room overlooking the garden and comes with fresh-baked bread and home-made preserves.

✉ Cork Road, Kenmare, Co. Kerry ☎ 064 4103 ⊕ Closed Dec–end Feb ✋ Double €100–€160 🛏 9 🚗 The hotel is located 250m (270 yards) outside Kenmare on the main Cork Road (R569)

KILLARNEY

AGHADOE HEIGHTS

www.aghadoeheights.com

Superbly located overlooking Loch Lein, this hotel has a first-floor restaurant that enjoys the same mountain and lake views as the stylish bedrooms. There is a spacious lounge, cocktail bar and conference suite.

✉ Lakes of Killarney, Co. Kerry ☎ 064 31766 ⊕ Closed 30 Dec–14 Feb ✋ Double from €200 🛏 75 🏊 Indoor 💆 and Spa 🚗 5km (3 miles) north of Killarney, signed off the N22 Tralee road

ARBUTUS

www.arbutuskillarney.com

This chic hotel, located in the centre of the town, has been run by the friendly Buckley family since 1926. Everything is on hand yet you can be out in the surrounding countryside in a matter of minutes. There is a comfortable drawing room, guest sitting room, traditional bar and restaurant. Some of the rooms retain the features of the Celtic deco-style of the 1920s. Traditional music can be heard in Buckley's Bar on selected nights.

✉ College Street, Killarney, Co. Kerry ☎ 064 31037 ⊕ Closed 12 Dec–20 Jan ✋ Double from €140 🛏 35 🚗 In the middle of town

Above *The coastal villages of the South have lovely country house hotels*

GLENEAGLE HOTEL

www.gleneaglehotel.com

Excellent facilities for both leisure and corporate guests are provided in this large family-run hotel. Comfortable bedrooms, many for families, are well equipped and some have splendid views over the National Park. There are three restaurants within the hotel, The Flask Restaurant for fine dining, the Argyll Bistro for a more relaxed casual meal and O' D's Chestnut Tree Restaurant with an extensive menu highlighting Irish cuisine. This restaurant holds regular music sessions and features live bands. The hotel particularly caters for families, providing activities for young children and sports for older children.

✉ Muckross Road, Killarney, Co. Kerry ☎ 064 36000 ✋ Double from €140 🛏 250 🏊 Indoor 💆 🚗 1.5km (1 mile) from Killarney on the N71 Kenmare Road

KINSALE

ACTONS HOTEL

www.actonshotelkinsale.com

In waterfront gardens, this hotel has a bar and bistro and the Captain's Table restaurant. Bedrooms are all of a good standard, and staff are friendly.

✉ Pier Road, Kinsale, Co. Cork ☎ 021 477 9900 ⊕ Closed 24–27 Dec ✋ Double from €179 (breakfast not included) 🛏 73 🏊 Indoor 💆 🚗 Overlooking Kinsale harbour, close to the Yacht Club Marina

PORTMAGEE

THE MOORINGS GUEST HOUSE

www.moorings.ie

Portmagee is a small village right at the end of one of the fingers of coastline reaching down to the sea just off the Ring of Kerry. It is opposite Valentia Island and you can make a trip there or to the Skellig Islands, the jagged islands off the end of the peninsula to the south. The Moorings Guest House is a delightful place to stay: the rooms are beautifully presented and each has a luxury marble bathroom. The Moorings Restaurant offers first-class Irish food and the Bridge Bar is the place to be for an evening of *craic* and traditional music.

✉ Portmagee, Co. Kerry ☎ 066 947 7108 ✋ Double €100 🛏 16 🚗 Into the village of Portmagee on the R565, drive past the church and the Moorings is 45m (50 yards) farther on the left

ROSSCARBERY

CELTIC ROSS HOTEL

www.celticrosshotel.com

Overlooking a lagoon on the edge of the village, this is a luxurious and striking hotel. There is a cocktail bar and a pub with a lunch carvery.

✉ Rosscarbery, Co. Cork ☎ 023 48722 ⊕ Closed mid-Jan to mid-Feb ✋ Double €110–€190 🛏 66 🏊 Indoor 💆 🚗 From the N71 Bandon–Clonakilty road, follow signs for Skibbereen and you'll find the hotel on main road

THE WEST

The west of Ireland is surely one of the most striking regions of the country. The landscapes are ever changing, from the towering sea cliffs to the stark bogland of the interior, to the limestone plateau of the Burren with its unique ecosystem and wildlife. This is where true Irishness has its roots, where the Irish language is spoken and the most traditional of Irish music played in some of the most authentic pubs in the country. Irish dancing, too, is popular.

At its centre is the city of Galway, the Republic of Ireland's third largest and fastest growing metropolis. It is often referred to as the 'bilingual capital of Ireland' with its strong Gaeltacht (Irish speaking area) associations and Irish culture, kept alive through theatre and television productions. Lively festivals throughout the year add to this cultural awareness.

The region encompasses the counties of Galway and Mayo, and to the northwest, Sligo and Donegal, divided by the small county of Leitrim. The region also runs down to Clare in the south, home of the Burren. The westernmost part of County Galway is Connemara, with an area of bog in its midst. Within Connemara is some of the finest scenery in Ireland, with a rugged Atlantic coastline, impressive mountain ranges and moorland famous for its sturdy ponies. The roads are narrow and winding, more suited to cyclists or walkers. The west of Ireland has a fantastic selection of outdoor pursuits, ranging from popular walking and cycling trails, to specialist activities such as horse-riding, angling, golf and adventure sports.

To round off a trip to the west it is possible to explore the islands off the rugged coast. The three stunning Aran Islands or Oileáin Árann, as they are known in Irish, can be reached by ferry or plane, while Achill Island is connected to the mainland by a bridge.

ACHILL ISLAND

Achill is Ireland's largest island, an irregular chunk of mountainous land some 22km (14 miles) wide and 19km (12 miles) from north to south. The mountains of Knockmore (340m/1,115ft) and Minaun (403m/1,322ft) dominate the southern half, while the peaks of Croaghaun (668m/2,191ft) and Slievemore (672m/2,204ft) rise in the north. Around 2,500 people live here.

ATLANTIC DRIVE

Achill Island is connected to the mainland by Michael Davitt Bridge. The narrow coast road signposted 'Atlantic Drive', which runs south along the sound, is the best introduction to the island. It passes austere 15th-century Carrickildavnet Castle, one of the strongholds of County Mayo's famed and feared pirate queen Grace O'Malley (c1530–1600), also known as Granuaile, whose family motto was 'Invincible on land and sea'. Granuaile harassed the English by land and sea in Tudor times, and few, if any, got the better of her. Fearing that enemies would steal her ships by night, she slept with one end of a silk thread tied to her toe and the other running through the window out to hawsers of her fleet. Next to the castle stands the ruin of Kildownet church. A location map of the graveyard on the wall of the church locates several poignant sites that reflect hard times on Achill.

The 'Atlantic Drive' turns north for a beautiful run up the wild west coast. Towards the top of the island you reach the village of Keel, with its long beach and spectacular view of the lofty Cliffs of Minaun. Just beyond lies Dooagh, where on 4 September 1987 Don Allum, the first man to row the Atlantic both ways, came ashore after 77 days at sea. The village pub has photographs of the event. The road ends 5km (3 miles) beyond Dooagh at Keem Strand, a lovely unspoiled beach in a deep bay with a memorable cliff walk (▷ 226).

DESERTED VILLAGE

Another of Achill Island's remarkable sites is the deserted village of 74 roofless houses on the southern slope of Slievemore. The village was abandoned during the Great Famine, but was used as a 'booley' village—a summer grazing and milking settlement—until the 1940s.

INFORMATION

www.achilltourism.com

⊞ 368 B4 ℹ Achill Tourism, Cashel, Achill Island ☎ 098 47353 🕓 Jul, Aug daily 9–5.30; Sep–end Jun Mon–Sat 9–5.30

Opposite *Keem Beach*
Below *A sandy beach, dominated by the rugged cliffs of Achill Island*

www.visitaranislands.com
www.iol.ie/~discover/islands.htm
✚ 368 C5 ❓ Tourist Information:
Inishmore ☎ 099 61263; Inishmaan,
☎ 099 73010; Inisheer ☎ 099 75008
🛥 Island Ferries ☎ 091 561767.
Departs from Rossaveal several times
a day ✖ Aer Arann ☎ 091 593034;
www.aerarannislands.ie
Flights depart from Connemara Regional
Airport, hourly during peak season

✉ Aran Heritage Centre, Kilronan,
Inishmore ☎ 099 61355 🕓 Summer
season, telephone for times

ARAN ISLANDS (OILEÁIN ÁRANN)

The three Aran Islands lie in line across the mouth of Galway Bay. The largest
and most seaward of the group is Inishmore (Inis Móir), 14.5km (9 miles) long.
In the middle lies Inishmaan (Inis Meáin; 5km/3 miles long), while the smallest
and roundest island, Inisheer (Inis Óirr; 3km/2 miles wide) is the most easterly.
All three islands share the same distinctive landscape of bleak grey limestone,
void of grass in most parts but supporting sheets of wild flowers. Narrow
boreens, or lanes, thread through the islands, and like the small rocky fields,
are bounded by stone walls that are sturdy, but so loosely constructed that you
can see blue sky or green sea between each individual stone. Life on these
windswept, barren islands has always been hard, and still is. The houses are
built low with small windows to give maximum protection from bad weather.
Traditional hide-covered boats *(currachs)* are still used for fishing, and transport
is mostly on foot or bicycle. The pace of life is determined by the tides and
winds, and by tasks completed, rather than the clock.

Irish is spoken throughout the islands, but principally on Inishmaan, the
most isolated of the three. Here you'll find plenty to photograph.

INISHMORE

Inishmore has the most striking archaeological remains, the largest village,
Kilronan (Cill Rónáin), and more visitors than the other two islands put together.
There's an excellent Heritage Centre and island museum in Kilronan, and you
can buy genuine hand-knitted Aran sweaters in An Púcán Craft Shop before
taking a pony-and-trap or minibus tour of the island. The main attraction is Dún
Aengus, a large Iron Age stone fort perched on the edge of a 90m (295ft) cliff.
Its sister stronghold of Dún Dúchathair, the Black Fort, is on its own lonely
cliff top.

INISHMAAN (INIS MEÁIN) AND INISHEER (INIS ÓIRR)

Of the three islands Inishmaan is farthest from a mainland harbour, and is the
least affected by tourism. The playwright J. M. Synge stayed here each year
between 1898 and 1902, researching his definitive book *The Aran Islanders*;
you can visit Teach Synge (tel 099 73034; May–end Sep Mon–Sat 10–6,
other times by appointment), the cottage where he lodged and which is now
restored. The island co-operative works hard to maintain employment and to
encourage a sympathetic understanding of Inishmaan among visitors.

Inisheer, easily reached from Doolin, is small enough to walk in a morning,
and there's a cheerful pub with frequent music sessions.

Below *The remains of Dún Aengus
fort blend with the rocky landscape of
Inishmore*

Above *Prehistoric burial stones at Carrowmore Megalithic Cemetery*
Right *Arranmore has a rugged coastline with tiny islets offshore*

ARRANMORE (ÁRAINN MHÓR)

Arranmore is also called Aran Island, but is generally referred to as Arranmore to prevent confusion with the Aran Islands in Galway Bay (▷ 206). The Arranmore ferry from Burtonport (Ailt an Chorráin) takes just 20 minutes. Most visitors come for the day, but it's best to stay overnight—especially in August, during Arranmore's annual festival, which is centred on the cultivated eastern side, in the bars and shops of Leabgarrow. From here you can wander narrow lanes towards the rugged west coast, or turn aside to climb one of the three modest peaks for the view from 227m (745ft).

✚ 362 D1 ℹ Donegal Tourist Information Office, The Quay, Donegal, Co. Donegal ☎ 074 972 1148 🔵 Jul, Aug Mon–Sat 9–6, Sun 10–4; Sep–end Jun Mon–Fri 9–6 🚢 From Burtonport (Ailt an Chorráin) Ferry Office, Sat 11–3, ☎ 074 952 0532

BLOODY FORELAND (CNOC FOLA)

The best time to be at Bloody Foreland is an hour before sunset, when the sun tips the red cliffs around Altawinny Bay and makes them glow blood-red to dramatic effect. With the cone of Bloody Foreland rising 314m (1,030ft) behind, you look out over sloping fields of heather and gorse, across 11km (7 miles) of sea towards the long, low bar of Tory Island (Toraigh; ▷ 225) on the northern horizon. The headland is signposted off R257

between Bunbeg (An Bun Beag) and Gortahork (Gort an Choirce).
✚ 362 E1 ℹ Dungloe Tourist Information Office, The Quay, Dungloe, Co. Donegal ☎ 074 952 1297 🔵 Jun–end Sep, or Donegal Tourist Information Office (▷ Arranmore)

CARRICK-ON-SHANNON

www.irelandnorthwest.ie
Carrick-on-Shannon, a pleasant, town on a fine fishing and boating river, has thrived since the reopening of the Ballyconnell and Ballinamore Canal as the Shannon–Erne Waterway in 1994. It provides the missing link between Upper Lough Erne and the Shannon, opening up a boating route from Belleek though the heart of Ireland to Limerick and the Shannon Estuary, a distance of 380km (236 miles).

The town's situation on the River Shannon has resulted in it becoming one of the most popular destinations for leisure cruising in Ireland. You can rent boats for the day or a longer trip from various companies at the Carrick marina. Anglers also find the river very rewarding for its variety of fish; contact the Carrick-on-Shannon Angling Club (tel 071 962 0313) for information on fishing permits, tackle and advice.

There is a golf course on the outskirts of the town.
✚ 362 E4 ℹ The Marina, Carrick-on-Shannon, Co. Leitrim ☎ 071 962 0170 🔵 Apr–end Oct, Tue–Sat 9.30–1, 2–5.30 🚉 Carrick-on-Shannon

CARROWMORE MEGALITHIC CEMETERY

www.irelandnorthwest.ie
Out in low-lying country west of Sligo town, off the Strandhill road (look for brown 'heritage' road signs), are scattered burial sites known as the Carrowmore Megalithic Cemetery. The oldest of these tombs may date back more than 7,000 years to early Stone Age times, making this the oldest and largest prehistoric burial site in Ireland.

Over centuries many of the tombs have been robbed of their stone; others were dug into out of curiosity or in hopes of unearthing buried treasure, but around 30 are still easily identifiable. Some are not much more than a pile of stones, but others retain their doorways and side walling, and are complete enough to crawl inside.

The dates of burial items recovered from the graves span 3,000 years and include the remains of human bones that were burned in cremation.

A little way to the north Creevykeel court tomb is signposted off the N15 at Cliffony, 22km (14 miles) north of Sligo. In contrast to the older and cruder Carrowmore tombs, this structure of 3000 2000BC is a sophisticated mound with several chambers.
✚ 362 D3 ℹ Tourist Information Office, Aras Reddan, Temple Street, Sligo, Co. Sligo ☎ 071 916 1201 🔵 Open access

INFORMATION

www.shannonheritage.com

⊕ 367 D6 ⊠ Bunratty Castle and Folk
Park, Bunratty, Co. Clare ☎ 061 360788
⊘ Daily 9.30–5.30. Last admission to
castle 4pm all year ♿ Adult €15, child
(under 12) €9

BUNRATTY CASTLE AND FOLK PARK

Visitors landing at Shannon Airport don't have far to go for a taste of 'Ould
Ireland', because Bunratty Castle and Folk Park are set up to present an agree-
ably nostalgic version of Irish history. The Folk Park re-creates a corner of 19th-
century Ireland with a large number of carefully reconstructed buildings and
workplaces, some incorporated into a 'village street'. These include cottages
and farmhouses into which visitors are welcomed by guides in period costume;
and, at the other end of the social scale, the fine Georgian country residence of
Bunratty House into which the last resident owners of Bunratty Castle moved
in 1804. The Folk Park has a working watermill producing flour for sale, and a
forge at which the blacksmith makes the sparks fly. There's a church, a pub for
relaxing over a Guinness or two, and a teashop/bakery where you can buy or
eat scones and bread. Garden-lovers will be delighted by the restored walled
garden of Bunratty House, and also by the other gardens which have been
laid out in the authentic vernacular style appropriate to their parent dwelling:
cottage garden, farmhouse garden and so on. There are plenty of domestic
and farm animals in the 10ha (25 acres) of the Folk Park, along with working
thatchers, weavers, churners of fresh butter, and other costumed guides. All
this makes the Folk Park a very child-friendly attraction, and you may be competing for space and the guides' attention with some of the school parties that
frequent Bunratty. Coach parties are another common cause of congestion.

BUNRATTY CASTLE

A tall tower house, Bunratty Castle was built around 1425 on the site of a
former castle by the MacNamara clan, before passing into the hands of the
O'Briens, who later became Earls of Thomond. The castle has been very
thoroughly and expertly restored, and fitted out with rare and appropriate
furniture, paintings and tapestries from the 15th and 16th centuries. The Main
Guard, a splendid vaulted feasting hall with a minstrels' gallery, nowadays
hosts 'medieval banquets' twice an evening (reservations required). Guests
eat with their fingers, drink copious quantities of mead poured by serving
wenches in low-cut gowns, and sing along with the robed and caped Bunratty
Singers. This is not for everyone; your enjoyment will depend on your mood
and companions—the bigger and jollier your party, the better.

Above Bunratty's restored 15th-century
tower house

Opposite The Cliffs of Moher rise sheer
out of the water on Ireland's rocky west
coast, with nothing but ocean between
them and America

CÉIDE FIELDS

Céide Fields Visitor Centre has been designed in a pleasing pyramid shape to blend with the landscape. A display explains how climate change and forest clearance around 3000–2000BC allowed blanket bog to creep in and smother a Stone Age agricultural landscape. A guided tour across the bog shows the excavations, which have revealed walls of massive stones built in straight lines.
✛ 368 C3 🛈 Visitor Centre, off R314 east of Ballycastle, Co. Mayo ☎ 096 43325 ☀ Jun–end Sep daily 10–6; mid-Mar to end May daily 10–5 ✋ €3.70

CLARE ISLAND

www.anu.ie/clareisland/welcome
Clare Island's humped green shape lies at the mouth of Clew Bay. The gaunt castle at the harbour was the chief stronghold of the 16th-century pirate queen Grace O'Malley or Granuaile—who probably lies buried in the ruined abbey on the island's south coast road. The climb to the Knockmore summit (461m/1,512ft) is rewarded by the view over Clew Bay. If you stay overnight in summer, be warned that the pub often doesn't open until midnight.
✛ 368 B4 🛈 James Street, Westport, Co. Mayo ☎ 098 25711 ☀ Mar–end Oct Mon–Sat 9–5.45, Sun 10–5.45; Nov–end Feb Mon–Fri 9–4.45, Sat 10–1 ⛴ Ferry (☎ 098 26307 or 25045) from Roonagh Pier, 11km (7 miles) west of Westport, Co. Mayo

CLIFFS OF MOHER

www.cliffsofmoher.ie
Shale, sandstone and silt form a rampart 208m (682ft) high, facing Galway Bay. In summer this is generally crowded with visitors, taking in superb views of the Aran Islands and along the Clare coastline for 48km (30 miles) southwest to Loop Head. The cliff edge is unguarded, so take care, especially in windy weather.

In 1835 Sir Cornelius O'Brien, the local member of parliament, built the tower that stands on the cliffs. On a clear day, you may see the mountains of County Kerry to the southwest and Connemara's Twelve Bens to the northeast from the roof.
✛ 368 C6 🛈 Cliffs of Moher Visitor Centre, near Liscannor, Co. Clare ☎ 065 708 6141 ☀ Visitor Centre: Jul, Aug daily 9–9; Mar–end Jun, Sep daily 9–6; Oct–end Feb daily 9–5 ✋ Exhibition adult €4, child €2.50 🚌 Bus from Lahinch

CLONFERT CATHEDRAL

Clonfert Cathedral is an architectural gem with masterful stonework. The site was originally occupied by a monastery founded in AD563 by St. Brendan the Navigator, the putative discoverer of America. The Cathedral of St. Brendan was built around 1160 with a 13th-century chancel, and a 15th-century tower added. St. Brendan's monastery was burned by Vikings three times during the 12th century and rebuilt by the monks, but was finally destroyed in 1541. A 1900s restoration accounts for its excellent state of repair and continued use for worship.
✛ 364 E5 ✉ Clonfert, Co. Galway 🛈 Keller Travel, Bridge Street, Ballinasloe, Co. Galway ☎ 0909 642604 ☀ End May–end Sep Mon–Fri 10–5, but telephone to confirm 🚗 Signposted off R356 Banagher–Eyrecourt road

CONG

Most visitors come to Cong to see the abbey, but the village is where John Ford shot most of his celebrated 1952 film *The Quiet Man*. The thatched Quiet Man Heritage Cottage on Circular Road (tel 092 46089; Easter–end Oct daily) has a display on the archaeology and history of the area. You can follow a dry canal dug as a relief project during the Great Famine of 1845–49. It was intended to connect the two lakes, but the limestone is so porous that it never held water.

Cong Abbey (open daily) consists of a range of 12th-century limestone buildings with elaborately carved pillars. Beside the river is the monks' fishing house—when a fish entered the net a bell rang in the kitchen.
✛ 368 C4 🛈 Tourist Information Office, Abbey Street, Cong, Co. Mayo ☎ 0949 546542 ☀ Jul, Aug daily 9.30–6.45; Mar to end Jun, Sep, Oct daily 10–5.45; closed Nov–end Feb 🚗 On R345 Clonbur–Headford road

THE BURREN

INFORMATION

www.theburrencentre.ie
✚ 368 C6 ⓘ Burren Centre, Kilfenora,
Co. Clare ☎ 065 708 8030 ⊘ Jun–end
Aug daily 9.30–6; Mar–end May daily
10–5.30; Sep, Oct daily 10–5; Nov–end
Apr by appointment

INTRODUCTION

The Burren rises as a cluster of grey domed hills in the northwest corner of
County Clare with terraced sides whose western feet slope to the sea at
Galway Bay. Villages are scattered around the fringes: Ballyvaughan on the
north coast, Doolin and Lisdoonvarna to the west, Kilfenora with its Burren
Visitor Centre in the south, connected by the R477 coast road and the R476
and R480. One main road, the N67, crosses the interior from Ballyvaughan to
Lisdoonvarna. There are no settlements here, but this is where many of the
most interesting historical sites are to be found. The 'Folding Landscape' (Tim
Robinson's) map of The Burren, available locally, is invaluable.

The porous, almost waterless limestone of The Burren, scraped smooth
by glaciers, has never provided easy living conditions for humans, although it
makes an ideal bedrock for plant life. By the mid-17th century General Ludlow
was reporting to Oliver Cromwell that The Burren possessed 'not any tree to
hang a man, nor enough water to drown him, nor enough earth to bury him.'
Cattle herding still takes place, though, keeping the scrub down and aiding
growth of wild flowers. Tourism is an ever stronger factor in the growth of the
local economy.

WHAT TO SEE

WILD FLOWERS

The Burren supports Ireland's richest flora. In spring you'll find the royal blue
trumpets of spring gentians and the sulphur-yellow of primroses; in summer
the hills flush crimson with bloody cranesbill and are spotted white with

eyebright. Orchids of many kinds grow here: spotted, early purple, marsh, bee, butterfly and frog orchids. Plants that wouldn't normally be found within a thousand miles of each other grow contentedly in neighbouring cracks and hollows in the limestone pavements and on the hill slopes: northern species such as mountain avens, southern species such as the bright yellow hoary rockrose; alpine saxifrages flourish down at sea level; woodland ivies and violets thrive in this exposed and treeless place.

VILLAGES AND MUSIC

The Burren villages are great places for traditional music, for which County Clare is famous. Ballyvaughan on Galway Bay is the 'capital' of the north Burren, and Monk's Bar (tel 065 707 7059) is the place for music here (traditional Thursday, pop Saturday) and Greene's Bar (tel 065 707 7147) is a classic Clare pub with traditional music. South across the hills lies Kilfenora where you can get an overview of the region in the Burren Centre, and find great music in Linnane's (tel 065 708 8157) and Vaughan's (tel 065 708 8004). On the coast to the west, Doolin is the best known village for music in Ireland; you'll find tunes in McDermott's (tel 065 707 4328) and lively songs in O'Connor's (tel 065 707 4168). Near Doolin, Lisdoonvarna is Ireland's only spa whose waters are still drunk for medicinal purposes. The village is known for its Matchmaking Festival in September (tel 065 707 4005 or 065 707 40442), when lonely and not so lonely hearts get together. Try the Roadside Tavern (tel 065 707 4084) for live music.

ARCHAEOLOGICAL AND HISTORICAL SITES

The middle of The Burren is deserted today, but evidence of former human settlement is plentiful. Two impressive Stone Age tombs stand beside the R480 Ballyvaughan to Corofin road: Poulnabrone portal dolmen (*c*4000BC), a square stone chamber topped by a huge capstone, and the nearby Gleninsheen wedge tomb (*c*2500BC). Later Burren settlers built stone ring forts: Two excellent examples are Caherballykinvarga just east of Kilfenora, still standing up to 4.5m (15ft) high in places, and the poignant ruin of Cahermacnaghten, beside the Ballyvaughan to Kilfenora road.

There is fine stonework at Corcomroe Abbey to the east of Ballyvaughan; four heavily carved 12th-century High Crosses stand outside the roofless Kilfenora Cathedral; and there is another farther south near Dysert O'Dea church. Towers and fortified houses of note include Newtown Castle, home to the Burren Collage of Art (just southwest of Ballyvaughan; tel 065 707 7200; daily 9.30–5.30), and Leamaneh Castle east of Kilfenora (closed to public, but visible from the road).

AILLWEE CAVE

www.aillweecave.ie

This show cave leads you into the subterranean world of The Burren, a honeycomb of caverns and passages eaten out of the rock by the chemical action and the friction of rainwater on limestone. You'll see stalactites and stalagmites, sheets of glittering calcite, open caverns of church-like size, and a rushing underground waterfall.

✉ South of Ballyvaughan off R480 ☎ 065 707 7036 🕐 Jul, Aug daily 9.30–6.30, Jan–end Jun, Sep–end Nov daily 9.30–5.30; Dec by appointment 💷 Adult €12, child €5.50, family €29

THE BURREN WAY

This is one of Ireland's official 'Waymarked Ways', a walk that runs for 45km (28 miles) from Ballyvaughan southwest through the heart of The Burren to Liscannor. Old country roads, tracks and walled *boreens* take you across the hills and valleys to Doolin. From here a delightful coastal path leads to the Cliffs of Moher (▷ 209).

TIPS

» A flower book and a small hand lens will increase your enjoyment of the wild flowers.

» Wear walking shoes and watch your step when exploring The Burren's limestone pavement—loose chunks can be ankle-breakingly wobbly underfoot.

» Traditional music sessions tend to start around 9.30pm. In summer get to the pub at least an hour beforehand if you want a seat anywhere near the musicians. If you want to join in, just ask—but be sure you can play to a high enough standard not to spoil the tune.

Above *The seemingly bleak Burren is extremely rich in plant life*
Opposite top *The sun rises over the Burren at Glen Inagh*
Opposite bottom *Spring gentian*

CONNEMARA

INFORMATION

www.connemara-tourism.org
✚ 368 B5/C5 ℹ Connemara Tourism,
The Square, Clifden, Co. Galway ☎ 095
22622 ⏰ Mon, Wed, Fri 9.30–4

INTRODUCTION

Connemara is the westernmost part of County Galway, between the great Lough Corrib in the east and the ragged, wild Atlantic on the west. In the north, it slopes to the narrow fiord of Killary Harbour, while the southern border is formed by Galway Bay. The heart of Connemara is a vast stretch of lonely bog, broken by the dramatic rise of twin mountain ranges—the Maumturks (Sléibhte Mhán Toirc) to the east, and the Twelve Pins (Na Beanna Beola) farther west. The N59 runs west from Galway City through the Connemara heartland, bordering the wild, lonely and beautiful area known as Iar-Connacht, the 'back of Connacht' on its way to Clifden, the region's 'capital' and sole town of any size. Then it bends back through northern Connemara. Buses are few, trains non-existent. The narrow winding roads are good for slow drivers, excellent for bicyclists, and best of all for walkers.

The most romantic place-name in Ireland, Connemara evokes images of steep mountains, ragged coasts, turf cutters, horse and donkey carts, fishermen in black curragh canoes—a landscape for poets, artists and dreamers that's wildly, extravagantly beautiful. But the poor soil, stony bogs, harsh mountains and rocky coasts reveal that this has always been a poor region. Many of the long, straight bog roads, the lonely jetties and causeways were built as famine relief works in the 19th and early 20th centuries. As a result of geographical and cultural isolation in the past, much of Connemara is a Gaeltacht or Irish-speaking region. People still struggle to make a living, and tourism (of a more or less 'green' variety) is a cornerstone of the economy.

WHAT TO SEE

CLIFDEN

www.irelandwest.ie

The only town in Connemara, Clifden has everything you could want from banks, supermarkets and music pubs to the excellent Connemara Walking Centre (Island House, Market Street, Clifden; tel 095 21492) which will help

Above *Ballyconneely beach*
Opposite *A typical Connemara scene, near Roundstone, with Mount Errisbeg as a distant backdrop*

with guided and solo walks. Its focus is the town square and Main and Market streets, teeming with visitors in summer. The town comes fully alive in mid-August when it hosts the Connemara Pony Show (▷ Tips).

🔼 368 B4 🛈 Clifden Tourist Information Office, Galway Road, Clifden, Co. Galway ☎ 095 21163 🌐 Mar–end Sep Mon–Fri 9–5, telephone for weekend hours

KYLEMORE ABBEY
www.kylemoreabbey.com

Kylemore Abbey, grey and impressive, dominates Pollacappul Lough just east of Letterfrack. The house was built as a grand Gothic country seat in the 1860s by Manchester businessman Mitchell Henry, and in the late 19th century was the heart of a 5,600ha (13,850-acre) estate. After World War I it became a convent of Belgian nuns. They run a school here now, so it's not open to the public, but the beautiful Walled Garden is a major attraction.

🛈 Kylemore Abbey Visitor Centre and Walled Garden, Kylemore, Connemara, Co. Galway ☎ 095 41146 🌐 Visitor centre: daily 9–6; gardens: mid-Mar to mid-Nov daily 9.30–5.30 ✋ Adult €12, child (12–16) €7

ROUNDSTONE (CLOCHNARÓN)
www.irelandwest.ie

On the shores of Bertraghboy Bay, Roundstone has a diminutive harbour and a scatter of pubs and small shops. Beside O'Dowd's bar a track leads to the summit of Errisbeg, the hill that rises 300m (985ft) behind the village. Roundstone Musical Instruments (IDA Craft Centre, Roundstone, tel 095 35808; Jul, Aug daily 9–7, May, Jun, Sep, Oct daily 9.30–6, Nov–end Apr Mon–Sat 9.30–6) is based on the workshop of Malachy Kearns, Ireland's master maker of *bodhrán*, drums that power Irish traditional music.

🔼 360 D5 🛈 Clifden Tourist Information Office (▷ 212)

TWELVE PINS (NA BEANNA BEOLA), THE MAUMTURKS (SLÉIBHTE MHÁM TOIRC) AND THE INAGH VALLEY
Much of the drama and beauty of Connemara derives from the mountain ranges that rise from the central bogs of the region: the amorphous mass of the Maumturks, and on their western flank the more shapely peaks of the Twelve Pins. Guided walks in the mountains, including the ascent of Benbaun (Binn Bhán; at 729m/2,392ft the highest of the Twelve Pins), are offered by Connemara Walking Centre (▷ 212, Clifden) and the Connemara National Park Visitor Centre (▷ 214); you can also climb 438m (1,437ft) Diamond Hill by a waymarked track. Bisecting the Twelve Pins/Maumturks massif is the outstandingly beautiful Inagh Valley with its long lake. The N59 road encircles the mountains, while the R344 runs through the Inagh Valley.

CAUSEWAY ISLANDS
www.irelandwest.ie

At Costelloe (Casla) on the R336 Galway City–Maam Cross (An Teach Dóite) road, a left turn goes west across the islands of Lettermore (Leitir Moir), Gorumna (Garumna) and Lettermullan (Leitir Mealláin). They are linked by causeways that were built as part of a famine relief scheme. Well off the beaten tourist track, these Irish-speaking islands have thatched cottages, sprawling villages and tiny stone-walled fields in a windswept landscape.

🛈 Galway Tourist Information Office, Aras Failte, Forster Street, Galway, Co. Galway ☎ 091 537700 🌐 Daily 9–5.45; closed Sun in winter

NORTHERN CONNEMARA
The N59 runs from Clifden to Leenane through northern Connemara, with side roads leading north to a beautiful coast of deeply indented bays. Letterfrack, a neat little 19th-century village built by Quakers, is home to the Connemara

TIPS
» Book early if you want to stay in Clifden when the Connemara Pony Show takes place (mid-Aug), as the event attracts big crowds.
» The south coast route from Galway to Clifden is slower but far more scenic than the fast N59.

National Park Visitor Centre (▷ 214). North of Letterfrack there are some superb white sand beaches, Rusheenduff and Glassillaun being especially striking. Out at Renvyle Point, the Renvyle House Hotel was formerly the country retreat of Dublin surgeon and man of letters Oliver St. John Gogarty ('Buck Mulligan' in James Joyce's *Ulysses*) who entertained W. B. Yeats, George Bernard Shaw and other Irish literary luminaries.

✚ 368 B4/B5 ℹ Clifden Tourist Information Office (▷ 212)

INISHBOFIN

www.inishbofin.com

Inishbofin lies some 5km (3 miles) north of Aughrus Point, some 45 minutes by ferry from the fishing village of Cleggan, and has a population of just 200. The islanders are very welcoming, and the pace of life here is easy. Inishbofin is ideal for exploring on foot, and is particularly attractive to birdwatchers for its huge population of seabirds. The best guidebook is *Inis Bó Finne/Inishbofin, A Guide to the National History and Archaeology* by David Hogan and Michael Gibbons (available on the island or from Connemara Walking Centre at Clifden, ▷ 138). Sites include a Heritage Centre at the pier, a star-shaped Cromwellian fort built in 1656 to house Catholic gentry condemned to transportation, and the ruins of a 14th-century church on the site of the seventh-century monastery of the hermit St. Colman.

✚ 368 B4 ℹ Clifden Tourist Information Office (▷ 213) ⛴ Inishbofin Ferry Service from Cleggan, ☎ 095 45903 ✋ Adult €20 return, child (5–8) €5, student €10

CONNEMARA NATIONAL PARK

www.connemaranationalpark.ie

Around 3,000ha (7,400 acres) of blanket bog and four of the Twelve Ben peaks are protected as the Connemara National Park. Birdlife and flora are rich and varied, red deer have been reintroduced and a herd of wild Connemara ponies was presented to park by the late President Childers. The herd is currently managed under agreement with the Connemara Pony Breeders' Society. Common songbirds include meadow pipits, skylarks, stonechats, chaffinches, robins and wrens, and birds of prey such as kestrel, sparrowhawk, merlin and peregrine falcon are sometimes spotted. In recent years both pine marten and non-native mink have been seen, the latter is a threat to some of the native wildlife species. The Visitor Centre in Letterfrack offers an audio-visual display 'Man and the Landscape' introducing the Connemara National Park, and gives information about guided walks, self-guided nature trails and pony trekking.

✚ 368 B4 ℹ Connemara National Park Visitor Centre, Letterfrack, Co. Galway ☎ 095 41054 🕐 Jul, Aug daily 9.30–6; Jun daily 10–6; Apr, May, Sep to mid-Oct daily 10–5.30; grounds open all year 🅿

Above left *Alcock and Brown Monument, south of Clifden*
Above right *Padraig Pearse's Cottage*

ALCOCK AND BROWN MONUMENT

Two signposted routes lead from the crossroads on the R341. A right turn brings you to the Alcock and Brown monument, a tall splinter of dark stone silhouetted on a hillside between Mannin Bay and Ardbear Bay, with wonderful views over west Connemara. The memorial commemorates Sir John Alcock and Sir Arthur Whitten Brown, who accomplished the first non-stop transatlantic flight in June 1919. The rough road on the left from the crossroads (better walked than driven) leads in 1.5km (1 mile) to the site where they landed their Vickers Vimy bomber plane nose-down in Derrygimlagh bog.

✉ Ballinaboy, signposted from R341, 3.5km (2 miles) south of Clifden
🕐 Open access

MORE TO SEE

PADRAIG PEARSE'S COTTAGE

On the shores of Lough Oiriúlach near Gortmore (Angort Mór) stands the thatched, whitewashed cottage built by poet, teacher and ardent nationalist Padraig Pearse in 1903–04, now a national monument. In these small, simply furnished rooms, and out in the rocky countryside round about, Pearse perfected his Gaelic, taught students from Dublin, and formulated his ideas for Irish national independence. It was he who proclaimed the infant Irish Republic from the steps of Dublin's GPO (▷ 76) on Easter Monday 1916. A few days later Pearse was shot as a traitor in Kilmainham Gaol (▷ 80–81).

✉ Turlough, Gortmore, Rosmuck, Co. Galway, signposted from R340 ☎ 091 574 4292
🕐 May–end Aug daily 10–6; Easter week daily 10–5 ✋ Adult €1.60, child €1, family €4.50

ROMANTIC ROADS

The beautiful switchback road that runs west out of Clifden to encircle the Kingstown Peninsula is called the Sky Road, while the drunkenly twisting and bumping road between Ballyconneely and Roundstone is known as the Brandy and Soda Road. Another, built between Cashel and Rosmuck as a famine relief measure using turf and grass, is *Bóthar na Scrathóg*, the road of the top-sods.

Above *Robust little Connemara ponies*
Below *Clifden, the capital of Connemara, with the Twelve Pins beyond*

COOLE PARK

www.coolepark.ie

Lady Augusta Gregory (1852–1932), patron of the Irish literary revival of the late 19th and early 20th centuries, entertained writers and artists at Coole. The house was demolished in 1941, but the wooded grounds and 'glittering reaches of the flooded lake'—as W. B. Yeats wrote in 1931—now form a forest park.

The Autograph Tree is a lovely copper beech which bears the signatures of many literary and artistic lions of the past.

✚ 364 D5 ✉ Co. Galway ☎ 091 631804 ◉ Visitor Centre: Jun–end Aug daily 10–6; Apr, May, Sep daily 10–5 🚍 Signposted off N18, 2km (1.2 miles) northeast of Gort

CRAGGAUNOWEN PROJECT

Craggaunowen is one of the best 'step-into-the-past' open-air sites in Ireland. It's all too easy to gain a mistily romantic notion of life in pre-Christian Celtic Ireland, but at Craggaunowen, costumed guides interpret the realities of the fifth and sixth centuries in the re-created buildings here.

Exhibits include a fenced dwelling built on a *crannóg* or artificial island in a lake, a ringfort with a round, solid rampart of earth protecting a huddle of cylindrical thatched huts, a *fulacht fiadh* or cooking pit used for boiling meat over fire-heated stones, and a length of planking road that crossed the bog some 2,000 years ago.

You can also see the leather-hulled currach *Brendan*, which explorer Tim Severin built and sailed to Newfoundland in 1976–77 to substantiate the claim that St. Brendan once made the journey. Look for the

Above *Croagh Patrick is topped by a statue of St. Patrick*
Below left *The simple gravestone of W. B. Yeats in Drumcliff churchyard*

patched-up hole that an iceberg tore in her side.

✚ 364 D6 ✉ Quin, Co. Clare ☎ 061 360788 ◉ Mid-Apr to mid-Oct daily 10–6 ✋ Adult €8.95, child (under 12) €5.85 🚍 6km (4 miles) southeast of Quin

CROAGH PATRICK

In AD432 St. Patrick preached at the summit of Croagh Patrick and banished all the snakes from Ireland. The cone-shaped peak that overlooks Clew Bay is Ireland's holy mountain (▷ 353), with a steepish path up from Campbell's Bar in Murrisk to a saddle at 450m (1,475ft), then a knee-cracking scramble up a very steep boulder slide to the summit chapel at 762m (2,500ft). The reward is a superb view.

✚ 368 C4 ℹ James Street, Westport, Co. Mayo ☎ 098 25711 ◉ Jul, Aug Mon–Sat 9–5.45, Sun 10–5.45; Mar–end Jun, Sep, Oct Mon–Fri 9–5.45, Sat 10–5.45; Nov–end Feb Mon–Fri 9–4.45, Sat 10–1 🚍 Off the R335 at Murrisk, 8km (5 miles) west of Westport

DRUMCLIFF

It was near Drumcliff in AD561 that St. Columba's kinsmen killed around 3,000 followers of St. Finian in the notorious 'Battle of the Book'. The grey stone Protestant church of Drumcliff is dedicated to

St. Columba, who founded a monastery here.

The main attraction at Drumcliff, though, is the grave of poet W. B. Yeats in the churchyard, marked by a plain limestone headstone bearing his self-penned epitaph:

Cast a cold Eye
On Life, on Death.
Horseman, pass by!

✚ 362 D3 ℹ Aras Reddan, Temple Street, Sligo, Co. Sligo ☎ 071 916 1201 ◉ Apr–end Sep Mon–Sat 9–5.30; Oct–end Mar Mon–Fri 9–5

ENNIS

www.shannonregiontourism.ie

Ennis, county town of Clare, is the bustling heart of commercial and social life for a wide rural region, where old-fashioned shop-fronts are lining the streets. In the town, a column commemorates Daniel O'Connell (1775–1847), who swept to Parliament in 1828 after holding a mass meeting in Ennis.

Ennis Friary on Abbey Street (tel 065 682 9100; Mar–end Oct) contains the beautifully carved McMahon tomb.

✚ 367 E6 ℹ Arthur's Row, Ennis, Co. Clare ☎ 065 682 8366 ◉ Jul, Aug daily 9.30–5.30; mid-Mar to end Jun, Sep Mon–Sat 9.30–5.30; Oct to mid-Mar Mon–Fri 9.30–1, 2–5.30 🚆 Ennis

DONEGAL

Although it's the county town, Donegal is a modest little place with attractively small-scale streets overshadowed by the gabled walls and turrets of Donegal Castle. The town in its present form was laid out in the early 17th century around a central square known, as in many of the northerly Irish towns, as 'The Diamond'. Looming up on its rocky knoll behind The Diamond is Donegal Castle, a great Jacobean mansion. It was built in 1623 on what remained of a 15th-century fortress of the O'Donnell clan, who demolished it late in the 16th century rather than let it fall into the hands of the English. In 1601 'Red Hugh' O'Donnell also caused the ruin of Donegal Friary while besieging his cousin Niall Garbh, who was holed up inside with some English allies. The bombardment ignited barrels of English gunpowder.

A STROLL THROUGH TOWN

You can tour the castle (Tirchonaill Street; tel 074 972 2405; Mar–end Oct daily 10–6; Nov–end Feb daily 9.30–4.30), which is furnished in mid-17th-century style. Wandering through the ruins of the friary, 1.5km (1 mile) south by the River Eske, try to picture the learned Michael O'Clery and his assistants Peregrine O'Clery, Peregrine O'Duignean and Fearfeasa O'Maolconry laboriously compiling their 'Annals of the Four Masters'. This wonderful document (copies can be seen in the National Library in Dublin) is a vivid history of the island from 2958BC (40 years before Noah's Flood) until AD1616. The Donegal Railway Heritage Centre (Tirchonaill Street; tel 074 972 2655; Mon–Fri 10–5, also weekends 2–5 in Jul and Aug) recalls a now defunct scenic local line, with a simulator and rail exhibits.

INFORMATION

www.irelandnorthwest.ie

362 F2   Donegal Tourist Information Office, The Quay, Donegal, Co. Donegal   074 972 1148   Jul, Aug Mon–Sat 9–6, Sun 11–4; Sep–end Jun Mon–Fri 9–5 (times may vary)

Below *The Diamond, the central square of Donegal*

INFORMATION

www.irelandwest.ie

✚ 368 C5 🛈 Aras Fáilte, Forster Street, Galway, Co. Galway ☎ 091 537700 🕐 Jun–end Oct daily 9–5.45; Nov–end May Mon–Sat 9–5.45 🚉 Galway

TIPS

» If you're going to be in the city in the last two weeks of July (Arts Festival) or the first week in August (Galway Races), reserve accommodation well in advance.

» For traditional music, try Taaffes in Shop Street, Roisin Dubh in Upper Dominick Street or The Crane, across the river in Sea Road, where they often have Irish set dancing in the upstairs room (visitors are welcome to join in).

GALWAY

Galway is the liveliest city in the west of Ireland largely thanks to its university and the number of job providing industries that have come to the town. July is particularly atmospheric when the Galway Arts Festival takes place. Galway is a great city to explore on foot. The centre is undergoing a makeover, with its heart Eyre Square being spruced up. From here, Galway's chief thoroughfare runs south through the city.

Medieval Galway enjoyed great prosperity through trade, not only with the rest of Ireland, but also with Spain and with other continental countries. It all came to an end after the city was attacked by Oliver Cromwell in 1652, and again by King William III in 1691, but you can see evidence of this former wealth in embellishments to ancient doorways, window frames and walls. Rich merchants would employ the best stone-carvers to adorn their town houses with their coats of arms, and with grotesque sculptures and heraldic beasts. Lynch's Castle, an impressive 15th-century tower house (now a bank; ground-level display open during business hours) at the intersection known as the Four Corners where William Street becomes Shop Street, is especially well provided with sculptures, as is the Collegiate Church of St. Nicholas in Church Lane (always open) with its grave slabs adorned with bas-reliefs showing the tools of the trade followed by the departed. Overlooking the River Corrib, the grand 1965 Roman Catholic cathedral is dubbed the 'Taj Michael' by locals after the then Bishop of Galway, Michael Brown—topped by a huge copper dome.

MEMORIALS AND MUSEUMS

Behind Lynch's Castle on Market Street, a 17th-century window is preserved to mark the spot where in 1493 Mayor James Lynch Fitzstephen personally hanged his own son Walter for murdering a visiting Spaniard. Across the street you'll find No. 8 Bowling Green, the home of Nora Barnacle before she eloped with James Joyce in 1904. It is now the Nora Barnacle House Museum (tel 091 564743; mid-May to mid-Sep Tue–Sat 10–5).

On Quay Street nearer the River Corrib you'll find Thomas Dillon's Claddagh Gold jewellery shop (tel 091 566365) where you can browse through a small museum and learn the story of the Claddagh Ring, Galway's world-famous love token. Just around the corner behind the Tudor-era Spanish Arch is the brand new Galway City Museum (tel 091 536 4000; Mon–Fri 10–5), a fascinatingly unfocused collection of mementoes from ancient fishing tools and traps for badgers to the orations of heroes and the pikestaffs of rebels. A highlight is the Claddagh Exhibition.

Below Galway's streets are lined with bright frontages

GLENCOLUMBKILLE (GLEANN CHOLM CILLE) AND SLIEVE LEAGUE (SLIABH LIAG)

Seen from the little parking bay high on a windy ledge at Bunglass, the Slieve League cliffs are hugely impressive—a great wall of multihued rock that plunges 595m (1,952ft) into the sea below, claiming the title of 'highest sea cliffs in Europe'. Walkers with a good head for heights can teeter along the very narrow 'One Man's Path' to the summit of Slieve League, but not in windy conditions or when the ground is slippery.

There's something special about the atmosphere in Glencolumbkille, tucked away in a hidden cleft among these remote seaward mountains 10km (6 miles) along the R263 from Carrick. This peaceful green valley is where St. Columba (born in Donegal in AD521) established a monastery. There's a Folk Village Museum with traditionally built and furnished thatched homes (tel 074 973 0017; Easter–end Sep Mon–Sat 10–6, Sun 12–6). Walkers can follow *An Turas Cholmcille*, Columba's Journey, for 5km (3 miles) around 15 stations or sacred sites, to reach St. Columba's Chapel, Bed and Well.

Above *Rocky Malin Head is the most northerly point in Ireland*

✚ 362 D2 🛈 Donegal Tourist Information Office (▷ 217) 🚌 On R263, west of Killybegs. Slieve League signposted 'Teelin Pier' from Carrick (An Charraiga), then 'Bunglass: The Cliffs'

GLENVEAGH NATIONAL PARK

Queen Victoria had popularized 'Scottish Baronial' style when John George Adair built Glenveagh Castle in 1870–73. Adair, a harsh, evicting landlord, bought a vast area of Donegal and chose the most scenic spot for his granite castle and its gardens and grounds, looking across Lough Beagh to the rugged backbone of the Derryveagh Mountains (Sléibhte Dhoire Bheatha). Adair's American wife Cornelia introduced the rhododendrons that now flower so vividly here in early summer. Later owner Henry McIlhenny improved and landscaped the gardens, so that today's visitor, after a tour of the chic but comfortable rooms of the castle, can stroll through a judicious blend of native and exotic plants and trees. Out in the wider National Park there are walks which range from family-friendly to more demanding.

✚ 362 E1 ✉ Glenveagh National Park Visitor Centre, Co. Donegal ☎ 074 913 7090 🕐 Mar–end Sep daily 10–6; Oct–end Feb daily 9–5; shuttle bus to castle.

Glenveagh Castle and Gardens

☎ 074 913 7262 🕐 Mar–end Sep daily 10–6; Oct–end Feb daily 9–5; castle interior by tour only, last tour 1 hour before closing 💷 Adult €3, child (6–18) €1 🚌 Signposted on the R251 Gweedore (Gaoth Dobhair)–Letterkenny road, 16km (10 miles) east of Dunlewy (Dun Lúiche)

INISHOWEN

The diamond-shaped Inishowen Peninsula stretches north from Derry city, flanked on the east by Lough Foyle and on the west by Lough Swilly. Many visitors make the long journey up through Inishowen for the sake of standing on Malin Head, with its prevailing view of mountain, moor and rugged coastline. Inishowen is a remote and underpopulated region of Donegal, and once you get down to west facing beaches such as White Strand Bay (Malin Head), Pollan Bay (Doagh Isle), Tullagh Bay (Clonmany) and Crummie's Bay (Dunree Head) you're likely to have them to yourself. The tremendous White Strand, which runs for 5km (3 miles) south from Buncrana, is better known and more frequented. Doagh Island, in reality a peninsula to the south of Malin Head, is rich in sand dunes covered in wild flowers in summer, and has the ruin of 16th-century Carnickabraghy Castle at its edge. Birdwatchers may spot waders at Trawbreaga Bay and on the mudflats around Inch Island. The 3,700-year-old circular stone fort of Grianan of Aileach (off N13, 5km/3 miles west of Derry) was a stronghold of the O'Neill Kings of Ulster. Stone steps climb to the top of the 5.5m (18ft) walls for a fabulous view over loughs Swilly and Foyle.

✚ 362/363 F1 🛈 Letterkenny Tourist Information, Blaney Road, Letterkenny, Co. Donegal ☎ 074 912 1160 🕐 Jun–end Aug Mon–Fri 9.15–5.30, Sat 10–4 (also Sun 11–2 in Jul and Aug); Sep–end May Mon–Fri 9.15–1, 2–5

KILLARY HARBOUR

www.irelandwest.ie

Killary Harbour, lying between counties Galway and Mayo, is the northern boundary of Connemara. The fiord-like inlet is 45m (150ft) deep; mountains rise dramatically on both sides—south the 550m (1,800ft) bulk of the Maumturks (Sléibhte Mhám Toirc); north the flanks of Mweelrea (819m/ 2,687ft) and Ben Gorm (750m/2,460ft). At the eastern end lies Leenane, huddled under the mountains; here the Leenane Sheep and Wool Museum (tel 095 2323/42231; Apr–end Oct daily 9.30–6) displays spinning and dyeing techniques, and information on rare breeds.

✚ 368 B4 🛈 Tourist Information Office, Galway (▷ 218)

KILMACDUAGH MONASTIC SITE
www.irelandwest.ie

Kilmacduagh monastic site, founded around AD610 by St. Colman MacDuagh, stands against a backdrop of the domed limestone hills of The Burren in County Clare. The impression is of a close-knit community, which reflects a thousand years of Christian occupation of Kilmacduagh, despite Viking attacks in the ninth and tenth centuries. The most striking feature today is the 11th-century round tower, 34m (111ft) tall, which leans noticeably. The roofless cathedral nearby predates the coming of the Normans to Ireland, though it was rebuilt in graceful Gothic style in the 14th century. Nearby is the Abbot's House or Bishop's Castle, a two-floor, square block of a fortified tower house. Also on the site are O'Hyne's Abbey, founded in the 10th century, and St. John's Oratory, a lovely little building that might date back to St. Colman's time.

✚ 364 D6 ✉ Co. Clare ℹ Tourist Information Office, Galway (▷ 218) 🚗 On the R460 Gort–Corofin road, 5km (3 miles) southwest of Gort

KILRUSH
www.shannonregiontourism.ie

There's an attractive Georgian air to Kilrush, a laid-back town near the mouth of the Shannon. Kilrush looks seaward for its livelihood and entertainment: The marina contains 120 berths. On Merchant's Quay you'll find the Scattery Island Centre (tel 065 905 2114; mid-Jun to mid-Sep daily 10–6) with an exhibition about the monastic site on Scattery Island 1.5km (1 mile) from Kilrush. At the centre you can reserve a 2/3-hour boat ride to the island, where a fine round tower stands 33m (108ft) high and the remains of several medieval churches mark the site of St. Senan's monastery. Other attractions of Kilrush are its horse fair in June, October and November, and the beautiful Vandeleur Walled Garden (tel 065 905 1760/1047; Apr–end Sep daily 9–6; Oct–end Mar Mon–Fri 9–5).

Above *The conical outline of Mount Errigal, east of Gweedore, is not snow-capped as it may appear, but topped with pale rock*

Dolphin-watching trips run regularly from the town, and there's a lively Dolphin Festival in July to view and celebrate these creatures.

✚ 366 C6 ✉ Kilrush Tourist Information Office, Francis Street, The Square, Kilrush, Co. Clare ☎ 065 905 1577 🕐 Jun–end Aug daily 9.30–5.30; Sep–end May Mon–Fri 9.30–1, 2–5.30

LISSADELL HOUSE
www.lissadellhouse.com

Lissadell House, though somewhat grim and grey from the outside, is one of the most romantic Great Houses in Ireland, thanks to its associations with Ireland's 'national poet' W. B. Yeats and with the celebrated nationalist leader Constance Gore-Booth, Countess Markievicz. The Gore-Booth family had lived at Lissadell on the northern shore of Drumcliff Bay since 1604, and Sir Robert Gore-Booth built the present neoclassical house there in 1832. Yeats first visited in 1894 at the height of his romantic nationalist 'Gaelic Revival' phase, and became firm friends—and maybe fell in love with—the two Gore-Booth sisters, Constance and Eva:

'Two girls in silk kimonos, both Beautiful, one a gazelle.'

Constance, who married Count Casimir Markievicz, became an ardent nationalist, and took a leading part in the Irish independence movement. She was condemned to death (later commuted) for her part in the Easter Rising of 1916.

The house and grounds saw decades of neglect during the 20th century, but have now been restored. On a tour of the rooms of the house you can see caricatures of the Gore-Booth family, servants and pets painted on the dining room walls by Count Markievicz. Photographs and portraits of the Gore-Booth sisters help to bring their story to life, while the billiard room is devoted to an exhibition of the 19th-century Arctic explorations of Sir Henry Gore-Booth, father of Constance and Eva.

✚ 362 D3 ✉ Drumcliff, Co. Sligo ☎ 071 916 3150 🕐 Mid-May to end Sep daily 10.30–6 🏠 House: adult €6, child (under 16) €3; house, gardens and exhibition: adult €12, child €6; gardens only €5 🚗 13km (8 miles) northwest of Sligo; signed off N15 Sligo–Bundoran road

LOUGH GILL
www.irelandnorthwest.ie

Lough Gill straddles the Sligo–Leitrim border. There are plenty of W. B. Yeats-related sites around the western or Sligo end of this beautiful lake, which both the Yeats brothers—poet William and painter Jack—knew and loved from early boyhood. The R286, 287 and 288 roads form a circuit of Lough Gill, a lovely half-day excursion. On the southern shore the R287 leads past the signposted Dooney Rock beauty spot, a cliff-top viewpoint over the lake, and Slish Wood where young William once camped out alone overnight.

On the north shore the R286 makes a delightful lakeside run east over the Leitrim border to Parke's Castle (near Dromahair; tel 071 64149; Mar–end Oct daily 10–6), a strikingly impressive and complete-looking fortified house with a turreted *bawn* or enclosed courtyard. It was built on the site of an O'Rourke tower in 1609 by Captain Robert Parke, and after centuries of dereliction has been restored with Irish oak roofs pegged in traditional style. From the shore there's a good view of tiny, thickly wooded Innisfree, subject of Yeats's best-known poem, *The Lake Isle of Innisfree*. You can rent a boat at the jetty and row out to where he dreamed of living:

'I will arise and go now, and go to Innisfree,
And a small cabin build there, of clay and wattles made.'

+ 362 D3 **i** Tourist Information Office, Aras Reddan, Temple Street, Sligo, Co. Sligo ☎ 071 916 1201; Apr–end Sep Mon–Fri 9–5.30; Oct–end Mar Mon–Fri 9.30–5

MOUNT ERRIGAL (AN EARAGAIL)

The quartzite cone of Mount Errigal is a landmark in northwest County Donegal. At 752m (2,468ft) Errigal is the highest of Donegal's many mountains, and its peak of naked quartzite gleams like snow. Approaching along the R251 from Bunbeg you see the rugged screes, corries and cliffs of the mountain's west face at their most formidable. But once you have passed the bulk of Errigal it seems less daunting.

Errigal is in fact an easy mountain to climb if you are sensibly shod, reasonably fit and prepared for a sudden change in the weather. The path up the eastern ridge leaves a pull-off on the R251 at a 'walking man' waymark and makes a steady ascent of around 530m (1738ft), following a clear track over heather and then broken quartzite.

There's a surprise at the top—the mountain has a twin summit, with the two peaks linked by a very narrow ridge. Wonderful views over the lakes and mountains of Donegal reward the effort of the climb; it is

said that a person with exceptionally good eyesight on an exceptionally clear day can see Scotland, 320km (200 miles) away.

+ 362 E1 **i** Dunlewy Lakeside Centre, Dunlewy, Co. Donegal ☎ 074 953 1699 ⊕ Easter–end Oct Mon–Sat 10.30–6, Sun 11–7 **i** The Quay, Dungloe (An Clochán Liath), Co. Donegal ☎ 074 952 1297 ⊕ Seasonal opening **i** Blaney Street, Letterkenny, Co. Donegal ☎ 074 912 1160

MULLET PENINSULA AND NEPHIN BEG MOUNTAINS

The Mullet Peninsula hangs like a ragged arm from the rounded shoulder of northwest County Mayo, one of the wildest and least-populated corners of Ireland. The low-lying, isolated Mullet, composed mostly of mountain and bog, is a Gaeltacht area, so you will hear only Irish spoken in the peninsula's sole village of Binghamstown (An Geata Mór). The eastern or landward side of the Mullet cradles Blacksod Bay (Cuan An Fhóid Dhuibh) and is sandy in parts, but also with mud flats.

Birdwatching is sensational here, as it is by Termoncarragh Lake (Loch Tearmainn) at the head of the peninsula, where you may with luck spot the rare red-necked phalarope. The western or Atlantic coast of the peninsula has a succession of beautiful sandy (and seaweedy) strands. From the beaches of Belderra and Cross there are good views of the tiny island of Inisglora 1.5km (1 mile) out to sea, where—according to legend—the four children of Lir spent 300 years in exile in the shape of swans, thanks to the evil magic of their jealous stepmother.

Inland of the Mullet, the Nephin Beg Mountains are the loneliest in Mayo if not in the whole of Ireland. In these 130sq km (50sq miles) of unpopulated, roadless mountains you can feel truly alone. The waymarked Bangor Trail, a long-distance path that runs for 45km (28 miles) from Bangor Erris south to Newport through the heart of the range is a true challenge for strong and determined walkers.

+ 368 B3/C3 **i** Tourist Information Office, James Street, Westport, Co. Mayo ☎ 098 25711; ▷ 225

SKREEN CHURCHYARD

www.irelandnorthwest.ie
At first glance there's nothing very special about the tombs scattered in the tangle of undergrowth in Skreen churchyard. But take your time here and you'll discover some fine pieces of stone carving. Many of the stone grave slabs and tomb chests are heavily carved with cherubim, seraphim, skulls, crossbones and other *memento mori*. Most are the work of the Diamond family, a dynasty of stonemasons that has been living and working locally for more than 200 years. Pride of the place is the tomb-chest that Andrew Black commissioned in 1825 in memory of his father Alexander (*d*1810), a prosperous farmer. The carving shows Mr Black Senior dressed dapperly in tall hat, waistcoat and buckled shoes, ploughing a field with a prancing pair of what appear to be racehorses.

+ 362 D3 ✉ Skreen, Co. Sligo **i** Tourist Information Office, Aras Reddan, Temple Street, Sligo, Co. Sligo ☎ 071 916 1201; ▷ 223 🚌 On N59 Sligo–Ballina road, between Dromard and Templeboy

Below *The round tower of Kilmacduagh*

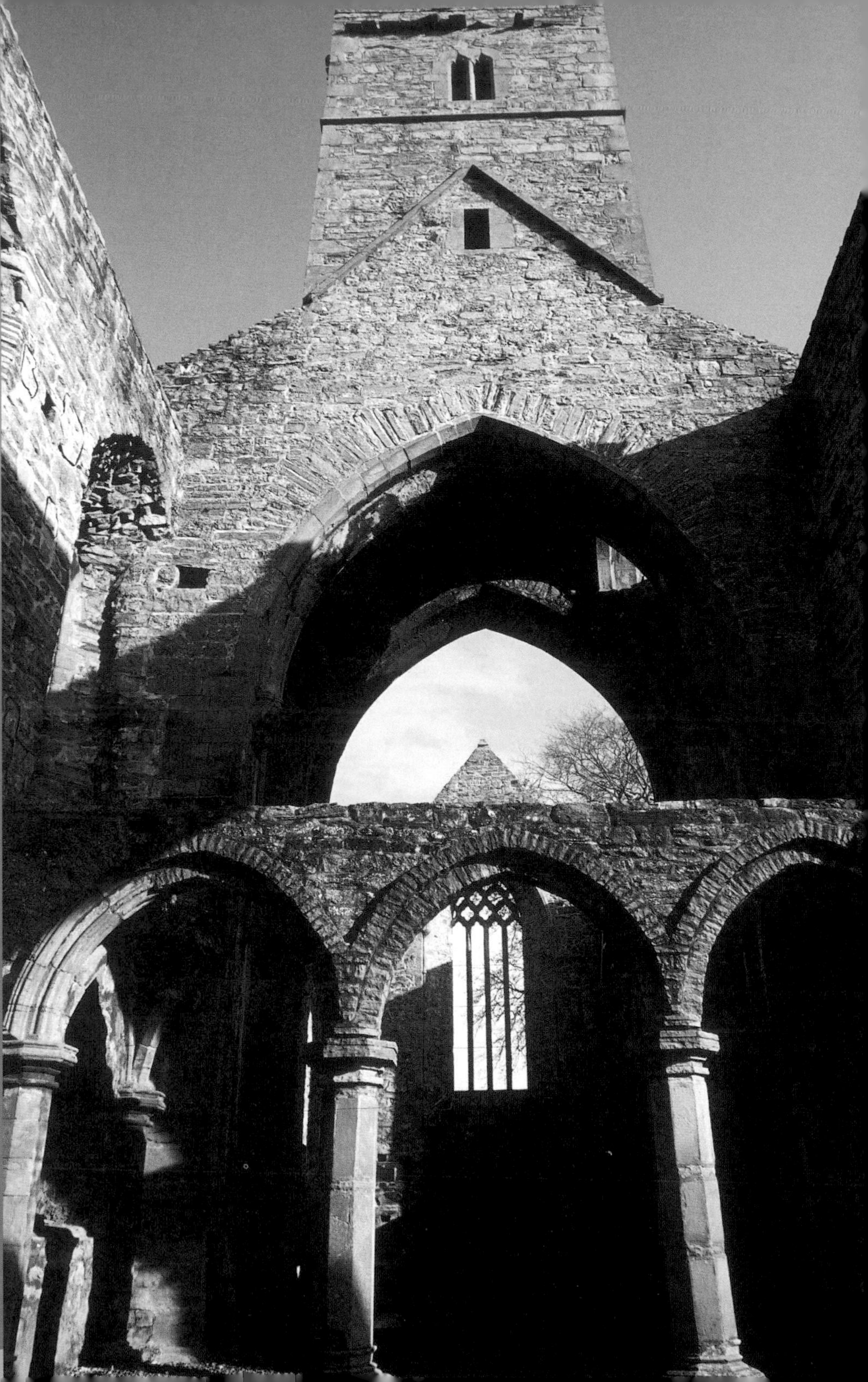

SLIGO

INTRODUCTION

Sligo is the heart of 'Yeats Country', where Ireland's national poet William B. and his painter brother Jack are commemorated and celebrated. Victorian shopfronts line the narrow streets yet it has all the amenities of a modern town. It is extremely walkable, with a tight grid of central streets containing most of the attractions. The Garravogue river bisecting the town is spanned by Hyde Bridge and New Bridge and one block to the south, running parallel to the river, is the main shopping thoroughfare of Castle Street.

On the main route between the ancient provinces of Ulster and Connacht, Sligo was always an important town. Georgian and Victorian houses, churches and commercial premises survive in large numbers, giving it an appealingly settled and old-fashioned air. It's the Yeats connection, however, that fixes Sligo on the tourist map. The long holidays that William and Jack spent here with their Pollexfen cousins in the 1870s and 1880s installed Sligo deep in the affections of both brothers, and Yeats' aficionados come from all over the world to see the place that inspired so many memorable poems and paintings.

INFORMATION

www.irelandnorthwest.ie

✛ 362 D3 ℹ Tourist Information Office, Aras Reddan, Temple Street, Sligo, Co. Sligo ☎ 071 91 61201 ◷ Apr–end Sep daily 9–6; Oct–end Mar Mon–Fri 9–5, Sat 10–2 (times may vary) 🚉 Sligo

WHAT TO SEE

YEATS MEMORIAL BUILDING

www.yeats-sligo.com

The handsome redbrick building at the west end of Hyde Bridge is the headquarters of the Yeats Society. Dedicated to promoting the work and reputation of Ireland's national poet, William Butler Yeats (1865–1939), the Society hosts an annual Yeats Summer School in the first two weeks of August, with talks, readings and excursions to Yeats' sites attracting thousands. Whatever your question about W. B. Yeats, you'll find your answer here, and there's also a permanent photographic exhibition. Sligo Art Gallery (tel 071 914 5847), on the upper floors, mounts 15–20 exhibitions a year.

✉ Hyde Bridge ☎ 071 914 2693

YEATS STATUE

Rowan Gillespie's bronze sculpture of W. B. Yeats was erected on Stephen Street, at the east end of Hyde Bridge, by the people of Sligo in 1989 to commemorate the 50th anniversary of the poet's death. Yeats is shown in archetypal poetic stance, luxuriant locks streaming, one hand artistically poised, staring into space with an absent expression on his bespectacled face. His billowing cloak is overprinted with a jumbled mass of lines from his poems.

SLIGO COUNTY MUSEUM AND YEATS MEMORIAL ROOM

A former presbytery is home to Sligo County Museum which gives an enjoyable run-through of local history via photographs and objects, including a fiddle that belonged to Michael Coleman, one of the brightest stars in Ireland's traditional music firmament. The main attraction is the Yeats Memorial Room, a small room with formal and informal photographs (including images of his funeral), as well as letters and his 1923 Nobel Prize for literature.

✉ Stephen Street ☎ 071 914 1623 ◷ Jun–end Sep Tue–Sat 10–12, 2–4.30; Oct–end May Tue–Sat 2–4.30 🎟 Free

MODEL ARTS AND NILAND GALLERY

Model Arts puts on concerts of jazz, contemporary and classical music, and runs literary and music festivals. The Niland Gallery, based on a collection started by Sligo's late county librarian Nora Niland, has a dazzling range of art, with Irish artists predominating. Pride of the gallery is its definitive collection

Above The dramatic monument to W. B. Yeats in Sligo town
Opposite Sligo Abbey

TIP

» Extra-special music sessions can take place at Furey's/Sheela-na-gig (▷ 224). Brian McDonagh, a member of the band Dervish, is the licensee, and when not away touring he'll often sit down to trade tunes with any musicians there. Other members of Dervish are often around, too, for the *craic* and a few tunes. Tuesday is the best regular traditional Irish music night.

Above *Strolling across a bridge in Sligo town*
Opposite *A whole spectrum of colours accompanies the sunset over Clew Bay, less peaceful by far when pirates ruled the waves here*

of paintings, watercolours and drawings by Jack B. Yeats (1871–1957), brother of poet William. Yeats's mystic and elliptical Sligo landscapes-with-figures such as *The Sea and The Lighthouse* and especially the haunting, ghostly late work *Leaving The Far Point* are wonderful to linger over. Among the other works you'll find landscapes by Paul Henry and Sean Keating, and the subtle portraits of Estella Solomons.

✉ The Mall, Sligo, Co. Sligo ☎ 071 914 1405 🕔 Tue–Sat 10–5.30, Sun 11–4 ✋ Free

SLIGO ABBEY

The 13th-century Dominican friary, under an arched tower, is in a remarkably good state of preservation, considering its history of fires and vandalism. It has a beautiful medieval rood screen, elaborate carving on the high altar and the tomb of Cormac O'Crean (*d*1506), a graceful east window and retains cloister arches and a chapter house.

✉ Abbey Street ☎ 071 914 6406 🕔 Mar–end Sep daily 10–6; Oct, Nov weekends only

FUREY'S/SHEELA-NA-GIG

Furey's (Bridge Street; tel 071 914 3825), is owned by the well-known Sligo traditional band Dervish, and a tremendous session may burst out at any moment. In fact, Furey's is so good they named it twice: It's also known as the Sheela-na-gig, after a fertility symbol. Irish music is played on Mon, Tue and Sat, other nights there is music ranging from jazz to bluegrass and country. Sligo county is a hot spot for traditional music.

THOOR BALLYLEE

I the poet William Yeats
Restored this tower for my wife
George.

William Butler Yeats characteristically celebrated in verse his restoration of the 16th-century tower house that became his country retreat and preferred writing spot. You can wander through the four floors, viewing Yeats's first editions and memorabilia, while listening to recordings of the man reading his own works, including extracts from his 1928 collection *The Tower*, inspired by Thoor Ballylee.

➕ 364 D5 ✉ Gort, Co. Galway ☎ 091 631436, off season 091 537700 🕐 May– end Sep Mon–Sat 9.30–5 💷 Adult €6, child (under 12) €1.50 🚌 Signposted off N66, 5km (3 miles) northeast of Gort

TORY ISLAND (TORAIGH)

www.irelandnorthwest.ie

The crossing to Tory Island can be a corkscrew affair. All the more pleasant, then, to be welcomed with a handshake or a kiss by the King of Tory, a post first created by St. Columba in the sixth century AD, and still filled by a resident Tory islander. The 'walls' of Tory are formidable cliffs, topped by a flat, treeless and windswept plateau. Around 150 Irish-speaking people live on Tory Island, and they are often cut off for weeks at a time in winter; they are correspondingly hospitable and pleased to see visitors.If the weather allows, birdwatching and walking are superb here, and there is a tremendous atmosphere in the pubs when musicians are on the island, especially during the Tory Island Festival in July. Some members of the community have created a 'naïve' school of art, and you can enjoy these spirited landscapes and portraits at the Dixon Gallery (West Town; tel 074 913 5011; May–end Sep daily 11–4.30), which occupies the former cottage of James Dixon, the island's pioneer fisherman-painter.

➕ 362 E1 ✉ 11km (7 miles) north of Bloody Foreland ⛴ For ferries contact tourist information office for details;

for cruises to Tory Island contact Donegal Coastal Cruises ☎ 074 953 1320

ℹ Donegal Tourist Information Office (▷ 217)

WESTPORT AND CLEW BAY

Westport is a delightful town. Before good roads were built into western Mayo during the 19th century, it was an isolated place, and still retains that sense of self-sufficiency. Westport was laid out for the Marquess of Sligo in the 1780s by James Wyatt, one of the supreme architects of the Georgian era. His grid pattern, with the parallel thoroughfares of Bridge Street and James Street running uphill from The Mall beside the Carrowbeg River, still survives, and gives the town an orderly, manageable air. At the top of Bridge Street there's a tall clock tower; on the Octagon, at the top of James Street, a column supports a statue of St. Patrick, whose holy mountain of Croagh Patrick (▷ 216) is visible from the outskirts of town.

The Westport Arts Festival in the second half of September brings music, plays, painting, poetry, street theatre and other events to the town. Westport is also one of the best towns in Ireland for traditional music session pubs. The best known of these is the bar on Bridge Street that's named after its owner, Matt Molloy, who plays flute with Ireland's most famous traditional music band, The Chieftains. When world tours and other commitments allow, he joins in the sessions. Other venues include Hoban's at the Octagon, and McHale's on Lower Peter Street.

Westport House (signposted on the road to Westport Quay; tel 098 27766/25430; Mar–end Oct daily) was completed in 1779 by Wyatt, and contains beautiful ceilings and a collection of furniture, silver, glass and pictures that reflects the taste of the Browne family, Marquesses of Sligo, through the centuries. The grounds are great for children, with a log flume, miniature train and pedal-yourself boats on the lake.

Westport Quay is lined with restored stone warehouses converted to restaurants, a hotel and shops. Here you'll find the Clew Bay Heritage Centre (The Quay; tel 098 26852; Apr, May, Oct Mon–Fri 10–2; Jun–end Sep Mon–Fri 10–5, also Sun 3–5 in Jul and Aug), with a small museum of local interest and an introduction to Clew Bay, which opens from Westport Bay to the west of the town.

There may not be 365 islands in Clew Bay, as locals claim, but there are certainly a lot of them. Clew Bay is a beautiful wide bay some 13km (8 miles) wide and 21km (13 miles) long, lined with sandy beaches at Mulrany on the north and between Louisburgh and Murrisk on the south. If you want to get active, contact Mayo Sailing Club at Rosmoney Quay. The tourist information office has details of various sporting activities.

➕ 368 C4 ℹ Tourist Information Office, James Street, Westport, Co. Mayo ☎ 098 25711 🕐 Jul, Aug Mon–Sat 9–5.45, Sun 10–5.45; Mar–end Jun, Sep, Oct Mon–Fri 9–5.45, Sat 10–5.45; Nov–end Feb Mon–Fri 9–4.45, Sat 10–1 🚆 Westport

AROUND KEEM BAY, ACHILL ISLAND

County Mayo is rugged, mountainous and breathtakingly beautiful. This walk, set around Keem Bay at the western end of Achill Island, starts with a short, stiff climb, negotiable by anyone reasonably fit and wearing shoes with grip in the soles. The climb gets you high up on the cliffs, with spectacular views. The return passes an abandoned village, the ruin of a house once owned by Ireland's most notorious landlord, and the poignant Mass Rock.

THE WALK
Distance: 8km (5 miles)
Allow: 3 hours
Total ascent: 374m (1,227ft)
Start/end at: Keem Bay
1:50,000 OSI Discovery Series,
map 30 Grid reference 056 304
Parking: Keem Bay parking area

HOW TO GET THERE
Keem Bay is at the western end of the R319 from Achill Sound.

★ Keem Strand lies in a deep green-sided bay overlooked by Croaghaun (664m/2,178ft), a mountain of quartzite. Amethysts have been found in this southern flank of Croaghaun, and if you're exceptionally sharp-eyed (and lucky) you may spot one on the beach.

The walk starts from the south side of the beach. From the beach, follow the ridge of an old boundary wall as it rises steeply 200m (655ft) up to the ruined watchtower on the summit of Moyteoge Head. After this climb, the worst is already behind you!

❶ The watchtower on the summit of Moyteoge Head, now in ruins, was constructed during World World II to give observers a bird's-eye view of shipping off the Mayo coast. The views more than justify the climb from Keem Strand. Northeast stands the bulk of Croaghaun, with huge cliffs falling from its seaward shoulder, and the cap of Slievemore (672m/2,204ft) to the east. Turning southward the view opens out along the mighty Minaun Cliffs, with the Nephin Beg Mountains on the skyline beyond, round to Clew Bay, the cone of Croagh Patrick, the hump of Clare Island, and the islands of Inishturk, Inishbofin and Inishshark.

Bear right (northwest) along the cliff-top track which rises and falls for 1.5km (1 mile) until it climbs to the top of Benmore (332m/1,090ft), the summit of the cliff ridge and the highest point of this walk. Continue until you are nearly level with the landward end of Achill Head.

❷ There is a view to your left over Achill Head, a narrow promontory which projects at a right-angle into the sea from the cliffs of Benmore.

Now turn right and make a steep descent from the cliff tops, to the ruins of Bunowna booley village, 150m (490ft) in the valley below.

❸ Bunowna was a 'booley village' used for summer milking and making butter and cheese. The name is derived from the Irish word for milk. Along the banks of the stream in the valley below are the shapes

of 17 roughly built, circular stone houses and cattle pens of the long-abandoned booley village.

Cross the stream and turn right along its east bank towards Keem Bay. After 1.5km (1 mile) you reach the ruin of Captain Boycott's house.

❹ Captain Charles Boycott gained notoriety at Ballinrobe in the 1870s, when his overcharging of rents led to the withholding of his tenants' labour and rent—the famous 'boycott' that immortalized his name (▷ 39).

Just beyond the house is an altar, built on the site of a Mass Rock.

❺ During the 18th century, when the Penal Laws outlawed Catholic practices, Mass was celebrated at isolated open-air sites such as this.

Walk down from the altar to Keem Bay parking area.

WHERE TO EAT
Buy picnic materials from Gieltys Foodstore (tel 098 43107) in Dooagh, 5km (3 miles) from Keem; or eat at Dooagh's pub, which is called simply 'The Pub' (tel 098 43109).

PLACES TO VISIT
BUNOWNA BOOLEY VILLAGE
🕐 Open access 🖐 Free

CAPTAIN BOYCOTT'S HOUSE (RUIN)
🕐 Open access 🖐 Free

Above *Achill Island*
Opposite *The Miner's Bar*

ARIGNA AND THE MINER'S WAY

Few people associate the gritty, grimy business of coal mining with rural Ireland but Arigna on the shores of Lough Allen was until recently the hub of the small Irish coal industry. This walk, much of it waymarked as 'The Miner's Way', passes through some of the now greened-over pit sites, but there's nothing grimly industrial about it, as you cross moorland, and pass ancient sauna houses and a prehistoric cairn. But there is a proper mine to explore!

THE WALK

Distance: 8km (5 miles)
Allow: 3 hours
Total ascent: 150m (490ft)
Start/end at: The Miner's Bar, Derreenavoggy Bridge, Arigna
1:50,000 OSI Discovery Series, map 26 Grid reference 193 314
Parking: By the Miner's Bar

HOW TO GET THERE

Arigna is signposted from the R280 Drumshanbo–Drumkeeran road just north of the junction with the R285 Keadew road, 4km (2.5 miles) from Drumshanbo.

★ The Miner's Bar is adorned with murals and photographs depicting the coal and iron-mining industries, the lifeblood of Arigna until the last coal mine closed in 1990.

From the Miner's Bar bear right up the hill. On your left is the factory of Arigna Fuels Ltd.

❶ Arigna Fuels produces coal briquettes, Arigna's sole connection with the mining trade these days.

Just past the factory a brown 'Arigna Mining Experience' sign points left up the road, but keep straight ahead along a narrow lane which in 275m (300 yards) leads to a crossroads. Keep ahead up the hill for 0.75km (0.5 miles) passing a lane on your right. In another 92m (100 yards) look over the hedge on the right to see a pair of sweathouses.

❷ Until modern medicine made them redundant, sweathouses were used to treat many ailments from insanity to rheumatism. The door of these tiny preheated subterranean chambers was sealed and the sufferers left to sweat it out, before being plunged into an ice-cold stream.

In 184m (200 yards) a 'Miner's Way' fingerpost points you to the right up stone steps, over a stile and on up a steep, narrow sunken path. At the top a right turn (arrow) leads past another sweathouse. Follow marker posts and yellow blobs on rocks; then turn left over a stile onto a green path over stony moorland. In 0.5 km (0.25 miles) a rough sign 'Mega Tomb' points to a big cairn on the skyline of Kilronan Mountain.

❸ From the cairn you have stunning views, east over Lough Allen to the humpback shape of Slieve Anierin (585m/1,920ft), highest point on the Iron Mountains, and west over the twin loughs of Meelagh and Skean.

Turn left along the main track. In 0.5km (0.25 miles) a yellow arrow points right (northeast) along a path making for Lough Allen. On the edge of the escarpment the path swings left, marked by yellow arrows, and over stiles and through gates. In 0.75km (0.5 miles) you reach a 3-finger 'Miner's Way' post. 'Arigna' points downhill; don't follow this, but continue ahead for 1km (0.6 miles) through old colliery sites. Past a cast-iron bracket, cross the stile, and in 18m (20 yards) turn right downhill to the road. Turn right Arigna. In 1.25km (0.75 miles) turn right to the Mining Experience.

❹ An ex-miner will take you on an underground tour of the damp, cramped workings.

Back on the lane turn right and bear left down a lane to the Miner's Bar.

WHERE TO EAT

The Miner's Bar has hot food; there's a café at the Mining Experience.

PLACES TO VISIT
THE MINER'S BAR, ARIGNA
☎ 071 964 6007 / 🕓 Daily 9.30am–11.30pm

SWEATHOUSES AT CROSSHILL
🕓 Open access 🖐 Free

KILRONAN MOUNTAIN CAIRN
🕓 Open access 🖐 Free

ARIGNA MINING EXPERIENCE
☎ 071 964 6466 🕓 Apr–Sep daily 10–6; Oct–Mar 10–5; closed 23 Dec–5 Jan
🖐 Adult €8, child €6

LOUGH CORRIB AND LOUGH MASK

This leisurely circuit of two of Ireland's most attractive large lakes is a beautiful expedition from Galway city on surprisingly unfrequented roads, up the eastern side of Lough Corrib (Loch Coirib) by way of Ross Errilly Abbey to Cong, a handsome small town with another striking medieval abbey. Moving north, you circle Lough Mask (Loch Measca). The return runs beside the untamed bogs of Iar-Connacht, down side roads close to the west shore of Lough Corrib, and back to Galway.

THE DRIVE
Distance: 200km (125 miles)
Allow: 5 hours
Start/end at: Galway city

★ Leave Galway city north along the N84 Headford and Ballinrobe road. Three kilometres (2 miles) north of the city you'll see the tower of Ballindooley Castle on your right.

❶ Ballindooley Castle, a fine, if grim, medieval castle, was a stronghold of the Burke clan. In a ruinous condition not so long ago, it has been restored and is now a private residence once more (no public access).

Continue north on the N84 to Cloonboo (Cluáin Bú), where you turn left at Cloonboo Cross with a sign reading Annagadow Pier (and also Cé Annach Dhúinn) winding down to Annaghdown. At the intersection turn left following a

further sign to the pier, and the graveyard is off to the right on a minor road for 8km (5 miles) to the ruin of Annaghdown Priory.

❷ The ruins of medieval Annaghdown Priory are blunt, weathered and massive, contrasting the fine architecture you'll see later in the tour. The shell of 15th-century Annaghdown Cathedral is adjacent; one of its windows is richly carved with animal heads, monsters, trees, flowers and shamrocks.

Return to the N84, where you turn left for 8km (5 miles) to Headford. Signs here point left along a minor road to Ross Errilly Abbey.

❸ Ross Errilly Abbey, a well-preserved Franciscan friary, consists of a tight cluster of plain, dignified 14th- and 15th-century buildings. Though the buildings stand in a lonely position among the fields

beside the Black River, the domestic details—bread ovens, vast fireplaces, water spouts, fuel chutes—summon up shades of the bustling monastic community that lived here.

Turn left on the R334 for 6.5km (4 miles), crossing the county boundary from Galway into Mayo. At Cross bear left on the R346 for 5km (3 miles) to Cong.

❹ Cong's great abbey (▷ 209) tells of the past importance of the town and is the main reason to stop here, but the town itself is a delightful place.

From Cong take the R345 Ballinrobe road for 4km (2.5 miles) to Neale, where you turn left on the R334 to Ballinrobe for 6.5km (4 miles).

❺ The parish church in Ballinrobe has wonderful stained-glass windows by master-craftsman Harry

Clarke (1889–1931). In late July you'll see the town at its moment of annual glory during Ballinrobe Races, the archetype of all Irish country race meetings in their energy and good humour.

Follow the N84 Castlebar road north out of Ballinrobe, passing the racecourse on your left and continue for 10km (6 miles) to Partry. Turn left here on the R330 Westport road, then in 1km (0.5 miles) bear left to Srah (An Sraith), where you turn left onto a minor road.

6 This scenic road skirts the west bank of Lough Mask (Loch Measca). It's worth stopping every now and then to enjoy the wonderful views.

Follow the road for 21km (13 miles) by way of Toormakeady (Tuar Mhic Éadaigh) before you turn sharp left on the north shore of Lough Nafooey (Loch na Fuaiche) along the Clonbur (An Fhairche) road. Another 13km (8 miles), through Finny (Fionnaithe) and across the spectacular narrows at Ferry Bridge, bring you back across the border into Galway and onto Clonbur between Lough Mask and Lough Corrib. Follow the R345 Maum (An Mám) road from Clonbur for 14km (9 miles), and on the outskirts of Maum turn left on the R336 to Maam Cross (An Teach Dóite). Here you bear left on the N59 for 16km (10 miles) through magnificent bogland scenery to Oughterard. Continue on the N59 for 2.5km (1.5 miles) beyond the town, then turn left on a signposted road to Aughnanure Castle.

7 Built in the 16th century, Aughnanure Castle is the best preserved medieval castle on the lakes. The O'Flaherties built it six floors high within strong walls, gave it a lookout tower and filled it with secret chambers and murder holes in true fairy-tale castle tradition.

From Aughnanure weave your way via Carrowmoreknock through a maze of lanes beside Lough Corrib,

to meet the N59 again at Moycullen (Maigh Cuilinn). Or you can return from the castle directly to the N59, and turn left for 24km (15 miles) back to Galway city.

WHERE TO EAT
Burke's pub in Clonbur (tel 094 954 6175) serves good food, sometimes spiced with live music. In Ballinrobe, Flannery's Restaurant in the Cornmarket (tel 094 9541055) is popular.

PLACES TO VISIT
ANNAGHDOWN PRIORY
✉ Off N84, 8km (5 miles) south of Headford
🕐 Open access 🖐 Free

ROSS ERRILLY FRIARY
✉ Signed from R334 at Headford
🕐 Open access 🖐 Free

AUGHNANURE CASTLE
✉ Oughterard ☎ 091 552214
🕐 13 Mar–end Oct daily 9.30–6 🖐 Adult €2.90, child (under 12) €1.30, family €7.40

TOURIST INFORMATION
GALWAY TOURIST OFFICE
✉ Forster Street, Galway 🕐 Daily 9–5.45; closed Sun Nov–end May

Above *Aughnanure Castle window*
Opposite *Lough Corrib (Loch Coirib), an angler's paradise, is Ireland's second-largest lake*

CONG TOURIST OFFICE
✉ Abbey Street, Cong ☎ 094 954 6542
🕐 Jul, Aug daily 9.30–6.45; Sep–end Oct, mid-Mar to end Jun daily 10–5.45

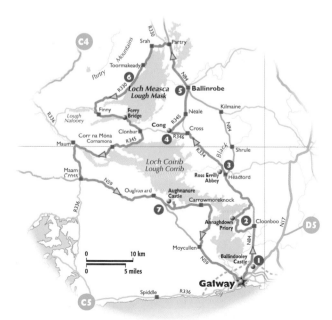

NORTHWEST MAYO

You'll see some of Ireland's most bleakly beautiful landscapes on this drive into the heartland of County Mayo's western bogs and mountains. It's not all melancholy moodiness, however: There are stunning golden beaches on the Mullet peninsula, abbey ruins and gaunt old castles to stimulate the imagination, and some hidden villages that are as friendly as they are remote.

THE DRIVE
Distance: 257km (160 miles)
Allow: 5 hours
Start/end at: Newport

★ Newport is a Georgian town with elegant old houses. If you fancy stretching your legs before spending the day in the car, stroll over the former railway viaduct.

Set off westward from Newport on the N59 towards Mulrany. In 2.5km (1.5 miles) turn left down a signposted road to Burrishoole Abbey.

❶ Burrishoole Abbey stands on the Shromore estuary. The tower and ruined walls remain. It was here that 'Iron Dick' Burke, the unfortunate second husband of Grace O'Malley (see Rockfleet Castle, below), spent the last years of his life.

Return to the N59 and turn left for 4km (2.5 miles); bear left on a signposted minor road to Rockfleet (formerly Carrigahowley) Castle.

❷ Rockfleet Castle, a Tudor-era fortified tower, was once occupied by Clare Island's famous pirate queen Grace O'Malley, otherwise known as Granuaile. In 1567 she divorced her second husband of only one year, 'Iron Dick' Burke, by slamming the door of Rockfleet Castle against him. He was left without houses or land.

Return to the N59 and turn left. Continue for 11km (7 miles), with the mountains of Achill Island ahead, to Mulrany (An Mhala Raithní, 'the ferny hilltop'). From here the N59 runs north for 32km (20 miles) past the Mayo bogs to Bangor Erris.

❸ The moody landscape of the Mayo bogs rises to the Nephin Beg Mountains (▷ 221) on your right, making a striking contrast with the green of the Achill Island mountains and mainland shores to the left.

At Bangor Erris (Baingear Iorrais, 'the pointed hill of Erris') turn left on the R313 for 19km (12 miles) to Belmullet (Béal an Mhuirthead, 'mouth of the Mullet peninsula'). From here continue along the R313 to the end of the peninsula, enjoying the coast and sea views, and back again to Belmullet (43km/27 miles). Return along the R313 towards Bangor Erris for 4km (2.5 miles), then bear left onto the R314. Follow this road for 45km (28 miles) through more wild bogland to Ballycastle, with two detours north to the coast. For the first detour turn left by Barnatra (Barr na Trá) post office, 6km (4 miles) after joining the R314. The road loops for 16km (10 miles) around a peninsula.

❹ Halfway around the peninsula you pass the Bronze Age stone circle at Dooncarton. Return through Pollatomish village.

Turn left on the R314 for 1.5km (1 mile), then make a second detour by taking the first left to Portacloy (Port a'Chlóidh) and Porturlin (Port Durlainne).

❺ Portacloy and Porturlin, two remote villages, both have tiny harbours; the one at Portacloy is almost shut in by high cliffs. Off shore are the 97m-high (318ft) rock stacks the Stags of Broad Haven (NáStracaí).

Return to the R314 and turn left for 27km (17 miles) passing through wild bog country. After Belderg (Béal Deirg) pass the archaeological site of Céide Fields (▷ 209) before reaching Ballycastle, a charming village with a slanting main street. Bear left just beyond Ballycastle on a signposted road through Gortmore to the parking area at Downpatrick Head.

❻ Downpatrick Head itself can be reached by a footpath from this parking area. The high cliff promontory of the Head has Doonbristy ('the broken fort'), a sea stack 46m (150ft) high, standing majestically offshore. Just inland of the cliff edge you'll pass a wide gash in the ground. This is Poll na Seantainne, a blowing hole which connects via a cave with the sea. You can generally hear the sound of waves rising from the chasm, and on stormy days the gash sends up a fine spout of water—so beware! In 1798 a force of Frenchmen landed at nearby Killala Bay to assist an Irish uprising against the English; the locals who supported them, and who were subsequently massacred while hiding in the Poll na Seantainne caves, are commemorated on a monument nearby.

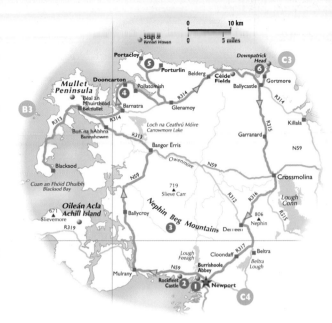

Return to Ballycastle and follow the R315 south for 19km (12 miles) through Crossmolina. Continue for 4.5km (3 miles) beyond Crossmolina then turn right on the R316 to Derreen. Turn left on the R312 Castlebar road for 6.5km (4 miles). Just before Beltra turn right on the R317 for 14km (9 miles) back to Newport.

WHERE TO EAT
MARY'S BAKERY AND TEA ROOMS
Excellent home-baking and teas.
✉ Main Street, Ballycastle ☎ 096 43361 🕐 Mar–end Sep daily 10–6; Oct–end Feb Mon–Sat 10–4. Closed Jan 1–22

PLACES TO VISIT
BURRISHOOLE ABBEY
✉ Off N59, 1.5km (1 mile) west of Newport 🕐 Open access ✋ Free

ROCKFLEET CASTLE
✉ Off N59, 6.5km (4 miles) west of Newport 🕐 Open access ✋ Free

DOONCARTON STONE CIRCLE
✉ 3km (2 miles) northwest of Pollatomish 🕐 Open access ✋ Free

DOWNPATRICK HEAD SEA STACK AND BLOWING HOLE
✉ Off R314 at Ballycastle 🕐 Open access ✋ Free

INFORMATION
TOURIST OFFICE
✉ James Street, Westport ☎ 098 25711

Opposite Carrigahowley Castle at Newport
Below The amazing sea stack at Downpatrick Head

ARAN ISLANDS
AN PÚCÁN
A delightful thatched cottage that houses a small family business established in 1977. Here you will find beautiful Aran sweaters, which are hand-knitted by women in their own homes to their own distinctive patterns, using only the best 100 per cent pure wool. Items on sale include pullovers, cardigans, waistcoats, scarves, gloves, socks and a range of children's wear.
✉ Kilronan, Aran Islands, Co. Galway ☎ 091 757 677 ⊕ Daily, hours vary

BALLYCONNEELY
AN TRÁ MHÓIR, THE GREAT BEACH
There is great swimming to be enjoyed in the sea all along the Connemara coast, provided you have sufficient knowledge of which beaches have gently shelving sand and are free of clogging seaweed. *An Trá Mhóir*, the Great Beach, below the Connemara Golf Club, is one that fits this bill exactly.
✉ Creggoduff, Bunowen, Ballyconneely, Co. Galway 🚌 From Clifden, turn right off

the R341 in Ballyconneely, and follow the road for 5 km (3 miles); turn right just before reaching Bunowen Pier at a Connemara Golf Club sign and follow the lane across the golf course to the club house 🚗 At Connemara Golf Club ☎ 095 23502 ⊕ Daily

CONNEMARA SMOKEHOUSE
www.smokehouse.ie
The Connemara Smokehouse beside Bunowen Pier is superbly sited on Bunowen Bay and the smoked salmon and trout that are produced and sold here make wonderful gifts (the Smokehouse also has a postal service). The marinated gravadlax is highly recommended, and you can buy some of their special marinades to enjoy at home.
✉ Bunowen Pier, Ballyconneely, Co. Galway ☎ 095 23739 ⊕ Mon–Fri 9–1, 2–5 🚌 From Clifden, turn right off the R341 in Ballyconneely, and follow the road for 5 km (3 miles) to Bunowen Pier

BALLYSHANNON
DONEGAL PARIAN CHINA
www.donegalchina.ie
The showroom offers examples of fine Donegal Parian ware. This

delicate, glossy china is available as vases, tea-sets such as the Irish Rose service, clocks, wildlife sculptures and figurines. Most coveted of all are the exquisite latticework baskets.
✉ Ballyshannon, Co. Donegal ☎ 072 51826 ⊕ Jun–end Sep Mon–Sat 9–5.30, Sun 2–6; May Mon–Sat 9–5.30; Oct–end Apr Mon–Fri 9–5.30 👋 Free guided tours 🚌 On N15 Sligo road just outside Ballyshannon 🚗

BRUCKLESS
DEANE'S EQUESTRIAN CENTRE
www.deanesequestrian.ie
The Deane family have farmed in this lovely location since 1790 and now operate an all-year-round equestrian centre, with wide ranging facilites that include lessons, indoor and outdoor arena and showjumping grounds. Cross-country trekking, pony rides and a livery/schooling service are also available, and there is a tack shop.
✉ Darney, Bruckless, Co. Donegal ☎ 074 973 7160 ⊕ Equestrian centre: Tue–Sat, riding by appointment 👋 Adult from €22, child from €19, pony rides €5 for 5 minutes

BUNRATTY

MEDIEVAL FEASTS AT BUNRATTY CASTLE

Feasting with your fingers while buxom maidens and courtly squires in medieval costume ply you with wine and song can seem like a wonderful way to have a bit of fun—if you are with like-minded friends and in the mood.

✉ Bunratty, Co. Clare ☎ 061 360788 ⏰ At 5.30 and 8.45 (subject to demand); reservations essential ✋ Adult €57.50, child (10–12) €43.25 (6–9) €28.75

CARRICK-ON-SHANNON

GENE ANDERSON'S THATCH PUB

If you are shy about joining in a pub music session, you will be greatly reassured by spending an evening in this old thatched pub. The place is full of character, and local musicians and singers on Wednesday and Saturday gently ease you into participation in an easy-going atmosphere.

✉ Elphin Road, Carrick-on-Shannon, Co. Leitrim ☎ 087 228 3288 ⏰ Music 8.30pm until late; pub hours Mon–Wed 10am–11.30pm, Thu–Sat 10am–12.30am, Sun 10am–11.30pm

LEITRIM DESIGN HOUSE

www.leitrimdesignhouse.ie
More than 40 Irish design studios and craft workshops supply Leitrim Design House with an eclectic range of original products: sculptures fashioned from recycled plastic and bog oak, modern and rustic furniture crafted in Irish wood, wrought-iron pieces, lamps made of recycled glass, fabric crafts such as cushions and wall hangings, jewellery and glasswork.

✉ Market Yard, Carrick-on-Shannon, Co. Leitrim ☎ 071 965 0550 ⏰ Mon–Sat 10–6

MOON RIVER CRUISE

www.moon-river.net
Float gently from Carrick Quay along the starlit Shannon with a drink in your hand, serenaded by the cream of local singers and bands.

✉ Main Street, Carrick-on-Shannon, Co. Leitrim ☎ 071 962 1777 ⏰ Summer day trips 12, 2, 3.15, 4.30; night trips board

at 11.30, return 1.30 3am as requested. Telephone for reservations from Carrick Quay ✋ Adult from €12, child from €6

CASTLEBAR

MAYO LEISURE CYCLING

www.mayocycling.ie
Peadar Leonard is a passionate and knowledgeable bicyclist, and will rent you a bike for the day (with the appropriate maps) or take you on a guided tour. Reservations are essential.

✉ New Antrim Street, Castlebar, Co. Mayo ☎ 094 902 5220 ⏰ Mon–Sat 9–6 ✋ Bicycle rental from €12 a day 🍴 Packed lunch available on request

TWEED CENTRE

www.tweedcentre.com
A one-stop shop if you're looking for a keepsake or souvenir. The Tweed Centre stocks the Guinness range of clothes, toys and trinkets, as well as Aran sweaters and other Irish merchandise, with a Mayo bias.

✉ Main Street, Castlebar, Co. Mayo ☎ 094 902 1183 ⏰ Mon–Sat 9.30–6

Opposite and below Mountain-biking and horseback riding are great ways to enjoy the Irish countryside

CROLLY

LEO'S TAVERN

Leo's Tavern is the 'home pub' of famous singing group Clannad and their sister, Enya. Singers and musicians are drawn to Leo's, and you never know who may turn up for a sing-song.

✉ Meenaleck, Crolly, Co. Donegal ☎ 074 954 8143 ⏰ From 11am; music summer Thu–Sun; winter Sat from 9pm

DONEGAL

DONEGAL BAY WATERBUS

www.donegalwaterbus.com
A purpose built, luxury passenger boat with an open-top deck that operates a sightseeing cruise. This 80-minute cruise explores the the wildlife, history and environment around Donegal Bay. There is a bar onboard and the boat is fully wheelchair accessible. The boat is moored at Donegal Pier, 3 minutes' walk from the town centre.

✉ The Pier, Donegal, Co. Donegal ☎ 074 972 3666 ⏰ Call for sailing times ✋ Varies

MAGEE OF DONEGAL

www.mageeclothing.com

Donegal tweed is famous the world over, and Magee's is the best known and best-stocked shop in County Donegal for hand-woven tweeds and wool-mohair-cashmere. You can order a bolt of cloth, or buy jackets, skirts, caps, hats, scarves, ties and a whole range of other goods, all made from Magee's own cloth.

✉ The Diamond, Donegal, Co. Donegal
☎ 073 22660 🕐 Mon–Sat 9.30–6

DOOLIN

DOOLIN CRAFTS GALLERY

www.doolincrafts.com

Husband-and-wife team Mary Gray and Matt O'Connell created the Doolin Crafts Gallery and the split-level garden that surrounds it. Here you can browse carefully chosen items, some exclusive to the gallery, that include knitwear, leather bags and belts, pottery, jewellery, ornaments and *objets*.

✉ Doolin, Co. Clare ☎ 065 707 4309
🕐 Easter–end Sep daily 9–7; Oct–Easter Tue–Sat 10–6

McGANN'S

McGann's pub by the bridge can be just as jolly as O'Connor's, but you'll find a more serious and quiet atmosphere here, as listeners concentrate on the wonderful music that locals and visitors create.

✉ Doolin, Co. Clare ☎ 065 707 4133
🕐 From 11am

O'CONNOR'S

www.oconnorspubdoolin.com

O'Connor's pub is an institution among singers and players of Irish traditional music; most of the great names have probably played here. These days it's a jolly, singalong sort of place, great for a night's music and chatter with some friends.

✉ Doolin, Co. Clare ☎ 065 707 4168
🕐 From 11am

ENNIS

GLÓR IRISH MUSIC CENTRE

www.glor.ie

A superb purpose-built concert venue, Glór has a mission to present the cream of Ireland's artists and performers and their work, especially in the field of traditional music. Performances feature the best Irish bands, individual musicians and singers, plus a variety of theatre, children's plays, film and dance. Exhibitions held at the Centre include paintings and photography.

✉ Friar's Walk, Ennis, Co. Clare ☎ 065 684 3103 🕐 Box office: Mon–Sat 10–5
✋ Varies depending on performance; adult from €12 🎫 Mon–Sat 10–5

ENNISCRONE

KILCULLEN'S SEAWEED BATHS

A traditional Irish west coast remedy is offered in this fine Edwardian bathhouse with its original fittings. Relax in an iodine-rich, silky-smooth seaweed bath, and emerge feeling a million dollars. Private rooms; no need to reserve.

✉ Enniscrone, Co. Sligo ☎ 096 36238
🕐 May–end Oct daily 10–10; Nov–end Apr daily 12–8 ✋ Adult from €20; room with 2 baths, double occupancy €35

FOXFORD

FOXFORD WOOLLEN MILLS

www.foxfordwoollenmills.ie

Foxford Woollen Mills were established in 1892 to bring employment to a poverty-stricken area. Learn all about it on a Mill Tour before visiting the Mill Shop. Goods for sale are of excellent quality and include mohair and merino rugs, tweed caps and vibrant rugs and throws, baby blankets, scarves and other clothing and furnishings.

✉ Foxford, Co. Mayo ☎ 094 925 6104
🕐 Mon–Sat 10–6, Sun 12–6

GALWAY

CLADDAGH GOLD

www.claddaghring.ie

Thomas Dillon's Claddagh Gold shop is Ireland's longest-established jeweller's, and the oldest makers of the Claddagh Ring, the lovers' token with the two hands clasping a heart. Buy one and take a tour of the shop's little museum.

✉ 1 Quay Street, Galway, Co. Galway

☎ 091 566365 🕐 Mon–Sat, 10–5.30, Sun 12–4 (summer only)

COBWEBS

www.cobwebs.ie

Overlooking the Spanish arch in Galway, Cobwebs has developed from a derelict building to one of the prettiest in Galway—the shop is constantly being photographed by visitors. Established in 1972 by Phyllis MacNamara, the cute two-storey building boasts a magical display of antique and contemporary jewellery, all with a distinct style.

✉ 7 Quay Lane, Galway, Co. Galway
☎ 091 564 388 🕐 Mon–Sat 9.30–5.30

THE CRANE

www.thecranebar.com

The Crane hosts Galway's best traditional music sessions, and staff and musicians are friendly and knowledgeable. There are two bars, one featuring Irish music every night. There is also an upstairs concert venue featuring national and international acts, three or four nights a week.

✉ 2 Sea Road, Galway, Co. Galway
☎ 091 587419 🕐 From 11am; music from 9.30pm

DRUID THEATRE

www.druidtheatre.com

One of Ireland's best modern theatre companies, Druid is based in a refurbished former warehouse. This dynamic company puts on Irish classics, and also premières up-and-coming young playwrights.

✉ Chapel Lane, off Quay Street, Galway, Co. Galway ☎ 091 568617 🕐 Box office: daily 9–5.30 ✋ Varies depending on performance 🎫

GALWAY MARKET

This is one of the liveliest street markets in the west of Ireland, a must for visitors to the city who want to see local life. Here you'll find everything from paintings and pottery to fruit and flowers, from local meat and cheeses to olives, toys, herbs and crafts—and a great helping of chat, too.

✉ Market Street, Galway, Co. Galway

Above *The west is the heartland of traditional Irish music*
Left *Lace-making*

sessions get going. Some well-known names have performed here.
✉ 19–20 Shop Street, Galway, Co. Galway
☎ 091 564 066 ⏲ Music every night 5.30–7pm, 9.30 until closing

LETTERKENNY
AN GRIANÁN THEATRE
www.angrianan.com
County Donegal's biggest and most versatile theatre offers a varied schedule that includes new and classic plays, stand-up comedy, modern dance, children's plays and shows, musicals, and a wide range of music, from rock to jazz and from cabaret to crooners.
✉ Port Road, Letterkenny, Co. Donegal
☎ 074 912 0777; information 074 912 3288
⏲ Box office: Mon–Fri 9.30–6, Sat 10–6
✋ Adult from €12, child €8 🖥 🎭 Before and after performances

LISDOONVARNA
BURREN SMOKEHOUSE
www.burrensmokehouse.ie
All kinds of smoked foods are on sale here, but it's primarily fish. Delicious offerings include organic salmon, hot-smoked salmon, eels, trout and mackerel, and there are also smoked cheeses. There are also Irish chocolates and preserves, sheep and goat cheeses, Burren honey, wines, gourmet foods and specialty teas.

Visitor information: ☎ 091 537700 ⏲ Sat, early morning until mid-afternoon (some stands on Sun in summer)

GPO
www.gpo.ie
A really enjoyable club with a good mix of techno and hip-hop nights, R&B, established bands, local hopefuls and up-and-coming groups.
✉ 21 Eglinton Street, Galway, Co. Galway
☎ 091 563073 ⏲ From around 9pm
✋ From €8

JUDY GREENE POTTERY
www.judygreenepottery.com
Judy Greene has been making her exquisite pottery for more than 20 years, and her range of earthenware—hand-painted in the shop—is collectable. You can browse the goods and visit the workshop upstairs to see how items are made.
✉ Kirwan's Lane, off Cross Street, Galway, Co. Galway ☎ 091 561753 ⏲ Mon–Sat 9.30–6

KENNY'S BOOKSHOP AND ART GALLERIES
www.kennys.ie
Kenny's is an art gallery, an antiquarian's dream, and heaven for those who love 'interestingly' organized bookshops. Stock is stored on shelves or heaped in baskets.
✉ Liosbán Business Park, Tuam Road, Galway, Co. Galway ☎ 091 709350
⏲ Mon–Fri 9–5

TAAFFES BAR
This friendly pub is popular with both visitors and locals. It's particularly crowded in the evening when the traditional Irish music

✉ Lisdoonvarna, Co. Clare ☎ 065 707 4432 ⊕ Visitor Centre: Jun–end Aug daily 9–6; Apr, May, Sep–end Dec daily 9–5; Mar Sat–Sun 10–4

ROUNDSTONE

ROUNDSTONE MUSICAL INSTRUMENTS

www.bodhran.com

Malachy Kearns, known as 'Malachy Bodhrán' to one and all, is Ireland's Master Maker of *bodhráns*, or traditional goatskin drums. Since he established his workshop here in the old monastery buildings at Roundstone his fame has spread worldwide. You can buy a beautifully made *bodhrán* (Malachy's wife adds the lovely Celtic designs) or other musical instruments, and browse in the well-stocked gift and craft shop.

✉ IDA Craft Centre, Roundstone, Co. Galway ☎ 095 35808/35875 ⊕ Jul, Aug daily 9–7; May, Jun, Sep, Oct daily 9.30–6; Nov–end Apr Mon–Sat 9.30–6

SHANNON AIRPORT

BALLYCASEY CRAFT AND DESIGN CENTRE

The workshops of Ballycasey Craft and Design Centre are in the courtyard of the Georgian mansion, Ballycaseymore House. Before you buy you can watch the craftspeople at work producing jewellery, knitwear and clothing, forged ironwork, pottery and a range of delicious oatables.

✉ Ballycaseymore House, Airport Road (N19), Shannon Airport, Co. Clare ☎ 061 364115 ⊕ Daily 10–5

SLIGO

FUREY'S, A.K.A. THE SHEELA-NA-GIG

www.fureys.ie

This is Sligo's Number One venue for traditional music. The pub is owned by well-known, world-travelling Sligo band Dervish; they frequently play here.

✉ Bridge Street, Sligo, Co. Sligo ☎ 071 914 3825 ⊕ Mon–Sat noon–11.30pm, Sun noon–11. Traditional music Mon, Tue, Thu from 9.30pm, often at other times. Jazz on Wed

HAWK'S WELL THEATRE

www.hawkswell.com

The Hawk's Well is a good quality provincial theatre that stages a big variety of events. They include classical concerts and gigs by well-known Irish bands; musicals; plays with local settings and international pieces; dance; singers and traditional musicians; comic plays and stand-up comedians.

✉ Temple Street, Sligo, Co. Sligo ☎ 071 916 1518 ⊕ Box office: Mon–Sat 10–5.30

(open until 10 on performance nights) ✋ Adult from €18, child €12 ⌘

STRANDHILL GOLF COURSE

www.strandhillgc.com

Strandhill is one of the prettiest golf courses in Ireland; an 18-hole seaside links with a wonderful panorama over Ballysadare Bay and superb views of the mountain of Knocknarea.

✉ Strandhill, Sligo, Co. Sligo ☎ 071 916 8188 ⊕ From 9.30 ✋ Adult green fees Mon–Fri €40, Sat–Sun €50; child €20 ⊠ ⌘

WESTPORT

MATT MOLLOY'S

Matt Molloy plays flute with Ireland's best known traditional band, The Chieftains. When he's at home he's usually found joining in the session in the bar of his own pub. Molloy's is generally jumping and crowded; if too busy, try Hoban's on The Octagon (tel 098 27249) or McHale's on Lower Peter Street (tel 098 25121) for excellent music.

✉ Bridge Street, Westport, Co. Mayo ☎ 098 26655 ⊕ Mon–Fri 2–11.30pm, Sat, Sun 12.30–11. Traditional music from 9.30pm

Below *Riverside Westport House has lots of attractions for children*

FESTIVALS AND EVENTS

JANUARY
CONNEMARA FOUR SEASONS WALKING FESTIVAL
http://indigo.ie/~walkwest/cwc.html
Walk all day in and around the Twelve Pins (Na beanna beola) and Maumturk mountains (Sléibhte Mhám Toirc), then party at night in and around Clifden.
✉ Clifden, Co. Galway ☎ 095 21379
🕐 Four times a year; phone to confirm

FEBRUARY
FESTIVAL OF WORDS AND MUSIC
www.glor.ie
Irish writers and musicians, both local and national, are celebrated at Ennis's Glór Arts Centre.
✉ Glór, Ennis, Co. Clare ☎ 065 684 3103
🕐 Late February

APRIL
CÚIRT INTERNATIONAL FESTIVAL OF LITERATURE
www.galwayartscentre.ie
The most prestigious literary festival in Ireland, with local, national and international writers and events.
✉ Galway, Co. Galway ☎ 091 565886
🕐 Late April

MAY
FLEADH NUA
www.fleadhnua.com
The county town plays host to the very best in Irish traditional music, song and dance.
✉ Ennis, Co. Clare ☎ 065 684 0406
🕐 Late May

JUNE
WESTPORT INTERNATIONAL SEA ANGLING FESTIVAL
One of the best of its kind in Ireland, taking place in the sheltered and well-stocked waters of Clew Bay.
✉ Clew Bay, Co. Mayo ☎ 098 27297/27344 🕐 Late June

JULY
GALWAY FILM FLEADH
www.galwayfilmfleadh.com
Directors, actors and movie-goers descend for six days of talking, seeing and being seen.
✉ Galway, Co. Galway ☎ 091 751655
🕐 Mid-July

GALWAY INTERNATIONAL ARTS FESTIVAL
www.galwayartsfestival.com
Music, plays, films, exhibitions, street parades and theatre are all part of this two-week festival.
✉ Galway, Co. Galway ☎ 091 566577
🕐 Mid- to late July

CROAGH PATRICK PILGRIMAGE
Join 60,000 pilgrims on a climb to the top of the holy mountain.
✉ Croagh Patrick mountain, near Westport, Co. Mayo 🕐 Last Sunday in July

JULY–AUGUST
MARY FROM DUNGLOE (AN CLOCHÁN LIATH) FESTIVAL
www.maryfromdungloe.info
Ten days of music, singing and informal fun, leading up to the crowning of this year's 'Mary'.
✉ Dungloe, Co. Donegal ☎ 074 952 1254
🕐 Late July to early August

YEATS INTERNATIONAL SUMMER SCHOOL
www.yeats-sligo.com
All a Yeats fan could crave, with talks, readings and excursions on the life of Ireland's 'national poet'.
✉ Sligo, Co. Sligo ☎ 071 914 2693
🕐 Late July to early August

AUGUST
CRUINNIÚ NA MBÁD
www.kinvara.com
Restored traditional sailing boats, gather, including Galway hookers, Donegal Drontheims, Cork mackerel boats, Wexford cots and more.
✉ Kinvara, Co. Galway ☎ 091 850687
🕐 Early August

CONNEMARA PONY SHOW
www.cpbs.ie
Where the adorable semi-wild Connemara ponies meet their public; festival-style fun, shows and sales.
✉ Clifden, Co. Galway ☎ 095 21863
🕐 Third Thursday in August

AUGUST–OCTOBER
LISDOONVARNA MATCHMAKING
www.matchmakerireland.com
A not-too-serious (if you don't want it to be) get-together, with dancing, singing, flirting and meeting up with lonely and not-so-lonely hearts from all over the world.
✉ Lisdoonvarna, Co. Clare ☎ 065 707 4005 🕐 Late August to early October

SEPTEMBER
GALWAY INTERNATIONAL OYSTER FESTIVAL
www.galwayoysterfest.com
World Oyster-Opening Championship, selection of the 'Festival Pearl', Mardi Gras party, sailing, oyster eating and Guinness drinking.
✉ Galway, Co. Galway ☎ 091 522066
🕐 Late September

OCTOBER
BALLINASLOE HORSE FAIR
Ireland's greatest horse fair has music, fireworks, entertainment, parades and thousands of horses to ride and buy.
✉ Ballinasloe, Co. Galway ☎ 0909 644763 🕐 First half of October

OCTOBER/NOVEMBER
SLIGO INTERNATIONAL CHORAL FESTIVAL
www.sligochoralfest.org
Choirs from across the world compete and perform.
✉ Sligo, Co. Sligo ☎ 071 917 0733
🕐 Late October/early November

PRICES AND SYMBOLS

The restaurants are listed alphabetically within each town. The prices given are the average for a two-course lunch (L) and a three-course dinner (D) for one person, without drinks. The wine price given is for the least expensive bottle.

For a key to the symbols, ▷ 2.

BALLINROBE

FLANNERY'S TAVERN

This is fishing country with abundant fish stocks, especially brown trout. Flannery's Tavern is a haven for anyone looking to try the local fish in wholesome Irish food, as well as international cuisine. Customers are looked after by the friendly, courteous staff, and on fine days there are picnic tables set outside for patrons.

✉ Cornmarket, Ballinrobe, Co. Mayo ☎ 094 954 1724 ☺ Mon–Sat 10.30am–11pm, Sun 12.30–11 ✋ L €13, D €26, Wine €18 🚌 In the middle of town

BALLYBOFEY

LOOKING GLASS RESTAURANT

www.keeshotel.ie

Dinner in the Looking Glass Restaurant is a relaxed but elegant affair at this hotel run by the Kee family for four generations. The traditional cooking has been touched by European influences. Lighter snacks are also available in the Gallery Bistro.

✉ Kee's Hotel, Stranorlar, Ballybofey, Co. Donegal ☎ 074 913 1018 ☺ Daily 12.30–3, 5–9.30 ✋ L €16, D €34, Wine €18 🚌 2km (1.25 miles) northeast on the N15, in Stranorlar village

BALLYVAUGHAN

GREGAN'S CASTLE

www.gregans.ie

The modern French cooking here takes some beating. You could try a starter of warm salmon mousse stuffed with a wild mushroom velouté, or the salad of smoked chicken and pistachio. To follow there may be pan-seared medallions of local beef with a creamy whiskey sauce, or baked cod wrapped in organic smoked salmon.

✉ Ballyvaughan, Co. Clare ☎ 065 707 7005 ☺ Daily 7–8.30; closed Nov–early Feb ✋ D €55, Wine €25 🚌 6km (4 miles) south of Ballyvaughan on N67

BUNRATTY

DURTY NELLYS

www.durtynellys.ie

This fine old pub has the benefit of two restaurants, and traditional Irish songs ring out to add to the atmosphere. Upstairs is the Loft Restaurant, which offers international cuisine in an informal setting. The Oyster Restaurant on the lower ground floor serves traditional Irish fare such as bacon, cabbage and potatoes.

✉ Bunratty, Co. Clare ☎ 061 364861 ☺ Mon–Sat 10.30–11.30, Sun 12–11 ✋ L from €15, D €30, Wine €15 🚌 Right next to the castle

PJ'S

This friendly, bistro-style restaurant is decorated with striking contemporary artwork. The comprehensive menu shows a selection of modern dishes, and may feature chowder, wantons, pan-fried chicken breast or salmon with sweetcorn and rice cakes. The chef's choice of the day is always a sure bet.

✉ Fitzpatrick Bunratty Hotel, Bunratty, Co. Clare ☎ 061 361177 ⏰ Daily 6.30–9 (Sun also 12–2.30) 🍴 D €30, Wine €19 🚗 Next to Bunratty Castle

CASHEL
CASHEL HOUSE

www.cashel-house-hotel.com
A large conservatory overlooking the garden houses the semi-formal restaurant at this country-house hotel by the sea. Excellent ingredients such as Connemara lamb and fresh fish bless the area, and with them the chef produces an array of well-balanced dishes with clear tastes and good textures. Smart casual dress.

✉ Cashel, Co. Galway ☎ 095 31001 ⏰ Daily 12.30–2.30, 7–8.30; closed 1 Jan–1 Feb 🍴 L €17, D €60, Wine €28 🚗 Turn south off N59 on to R340 1.5km (0.9 miles) west of Recess and the hotel is well signposted

ZETLAND COUNTRY HOUSE

www.zetland.com
The kitchen at this peaceful country house overlooking Cashel Bay makes good use of local produce, including herbs and vegetables grown in the hotel gardens.

✉ Cashel Bay, Co. Galway ☎ 095 31111 ⏰ Daily 7–9 🍴 D €60, Wine €28 🚗 Turn south off N59 after Recess on to R340; after approximately 6.5km (4 miles) turn left onto R341, and the hotel is on the right

CLIFDEN
ROCK GLEN COUNTRY HOUSE

www.rockglenhotel.com
Comfort abounds at this 19th-century former shooting lodge set in lovely gardens beside the Atlantic. The well-constructed modern Irish cooking, with hints of the Pacific Rim and classical French, uses freshly caught seafood and free-range meat. Old-fashioned desserts like bread and butter pudding are offered alongside white and dark chocolate mousse. The wine list has some fine examples. Smart casual dress (no shorts).

✉ Clifden, Co. Galway ☎ 095 21035 ⏰ Daily 7–9; closed Jan, Feb 🍴 D €48 (5 courses), Wine €22 🚗 From Clifden take the Ballyconneely road for 3km (1.5 miles); hotel is signposted on right

DONEGAL
HARVEY'S POINT COUNTRY HOTEL

www.harveyspoint.com
Enjoy an aperitif in front of the peat fire as the pianist plays, before being seated in the dining room. A menu of accomplished French cuisine presents some interesting taste combinations. The lunch menu may have poached salmon fillet with mashed potato and fennel chips while the dinner menu might include tournedos of beef fillet on pommes dauphines, with shallot cream and bordelaise sauce. To end your meal there are desserts such as a tulip of marinated fruit with lemon sorbet on raspberry coulis or a selection of Irish and French cheese. Not surprisingly, the wine list includes some very good wines.

✉ Lough Eske, Co. Donegal ☎ 074 972 2208 ⏰ Daily 12.30–2.30, 6.30–9.30; closed D Sun Nov–end Feb, also Mon–Tue Nov–Easter 🍴 L €35, D €62, Wine €25 🚗 From Donegal take the N56 west, then take the first right signed Lough Eske/ Harveys Point. The hotel is about a 10-minute drive from Donegal

ENNIS
JM'S BISTRO

www.templegatehotel.com
In this Gothic-themed former convent, the dining room has painted wood panels, luxurious drapes and chandeliers all of which contribute to its elegant charm. An international menu is served by friendly, helpful staff. Shrimps might be followed by oriental stir-fry. Reservations are strongly recommended.

Opposite Dromoland Castle restaurant
Below Galway's Park Room Restaurant offers inspired fusion cuisine

✉ Temple Gate Hotel, The Square, Ennis, Co. Clare ☎ 065 682 3300 ⏰ Mon–Sat 7–9.45, Sun 12.30–3 🍴 L €22, D €37, Wine €18.50 🚗 Follow signs for the Tourist Office; the hotel is on the same square

ENNISCRONE
JASPER'S RESTAURANT

www.oceansandshotel.net
You can enjoy Atlantic sea views from the terrace while dining in this restaurant in the coastal village of Enniscrone. The menu caters for all tastes and includes an interesting variety of tasty meat and fish dishes, while also providing for a choice for vegetarians. Jasper's is family friendly and a children's menu is available.

✉ Ocean Sands Hotel, Main Street, Enniscrone, Co. Sligo ☎ 096 26700 ⏰ Mon–Sat 7.30am–9pm 🍴 D €25, L €16, Wine €18.50

GALWAY
COUCH POTATAS

You can fill up for very little money here at Couch Potatas—hence its popularity with students—as long as you like baked potatoes! There is a wide selection of fillings to choose from and the servings are generous. The cheerful interior reflects the attitude of the staff and the relaxed mood makes this a great place to take a break.

✉ 40 Upper Abbeygate Street, Galway, Co. Galway ☎ 091 561664 ⏰ Daily 12–10 🍴 From €7 🚗 In the middle of Galway city centre

PARK ROOM RESTAURANT
www.parkhousehotel.ie

An original 19th-century grain store houses this celebrated restaurant, where paintings of old Galway help to keep the past alive. Classical French cuisine with Italian and Chinese additions inspires dishes such as honey-glazed breast of duckling with an orange jus, grilled veal sirloin with Madeira, and ostrich fillet with garlic potato and shallot.

✉ Park House Hotel, Forster Street, Eyre Square, Galway, Co. Galway ☎ 091 564924 🕐 Mon–Sat 6–10, Sun 6–9 🖐 L €30, D €44.50, Wine €19.50 🚌 In the heart of the city, off Eyre Square

PIERRES RESTAURANT
www.pierresrestaurant.com

Pierre's is a popular French bistro in the middle of town that serves traditional French cooking using fresh Galway ingredients. The atmosphere is informal and fun, and the staff are friendly and helpful. The fixed-price menu may include steamed mussels with garlic and white wine or brochette of salmon, monkfish and tiger prawns with saffron pilaf rice. An early bird menu is available between 6 and 7.

✉ 8 Quay Street, Galway, Co. Galway ☎ 091 566066 🕐 Daily 5.30–10.30 🖐 D €22, Wine €19.90 🚌 In the middle of the city

KILCOLGAN
MORAN'S OYSTER COTTAGE
www.moransoystercottage.com

A must for all seafood lovers, this dreamy thatched pub on Galway Bay even has its own oyster beds. Moran's reputation has spread far and wide and you couldn't want for anything more than sitting outside with a glass of wine, eating succulent oysters watching the swans float by. Apart from oysters, other wonderful specialities include chowder, smoked salmon and delicious crab sandwiches and salads. The pub dates back almost 300 years and is still family owned.

✉ The Wier, Kilcolgan, Co. Galway ☎ 091 796 113 🕐 Mon–Sat 10.30am–11.30pm, Sun noon–11.30 🖐 D €21–€35, Wine €18

🚌 South of Galway city on the N6 (the Limerick road) signed between Clarenbridge and Kilcolgan

KINVARA
KEOGH'S BAR AND RESTAURANT
www.kinvara.com/keoghs

Keogh's is a traditional bar, well worth the half-hour drive around Galway Bay from Galway city. A menu of simple, Irish fare made using fresh local produce is served, featuring popular dishes such as seafood chowder and mussels—pub food at its best.

✉ The Square, Kinvara, Co. Galway ☎ 091 637145 🕐 Daily 10–10 🖐 L €14, D €22, Wine €15 🚌 30-min drive south of Galway

LETTERKENNY
CASTLEGROVE COUNTRY HOUSE
www.castlegrove.com

The restaurant at this hotel offers accomplished cooking on a wide-ranging menu. Local produce is very much to the fore, using fresh fish caught nearby and vegetables grown in the hotel's own kitchen garden. The dining room itself is a picture of sophistication and elegance; tables laid with crisp white linen topped by sparkling glasses and vases of fresh flowers, drenched in natural sunlight from the long windows which look out onto beautifully landscaped gardens. Staff are friendly and helpful and there is an extensive wine list.

✉ Ballymaleel, Letterkenny, Co. Donegal ☎ 074 915 1118 🕐 Mon–Sat 6.30–9, Sun 12.30–1.30, 6–10 🖐 L €30, D €56, Wine €20 🚌 7km (4.5 miles) northeast of Letterkenny off R245, Ramelton road

NEWMARKET-ON-FERGUS
DROMOLAND CASTLE
www.dromoland.ie

Dinner is served in the very grand Earl of Thomond room with its Venetian silk wall hangings, Irish linen and crystal chandeliers. The superior, yet relaxed, setting is reflected in the food served and is world renowned. A sizeable carte is complemented by a four-course fixed-price menu, both designed by chef McCann with simplicity

and freshness in mind. The comprehensive wine list is also first class. Dress code: jacket and tie.

✉ Newmarket-on-Fergus, Co. Clare ☎ 061 368144 🕐 Daily 7–9.30 (Sun also 12–1.30) 🖐 L €40, D €68, Wine €28 🚌 2.5km (1.6 miles) northeast of Newmarket-on-Fergus; signed off N18; 13km (8 miles) from Shannon Airport, 27km (17 miles) from Limerick City

PONTOON
HEALY'S RESTAURANT & COUNTRY HOUSE
www.healyspontoon.com

Traditional fare is served in the Lough Cullin dining room which has large picture windows affording beautiful lake views. Succulent breast of chicken kiev or grilled fillet of Atlantic salmon hollandaise may feature on the *table d'hôte*, followed by tropical fresh fruit salad or Healy's House gateau. The Sunday lunch choices may include roast stuffed leg of lamb with rosemary jus or prime rib of beef accompanied by fresh seasonal vegetables. Smart dress is required.

✉ Pontoon, Co. Mayo ☎ 094 925 6443 🕐 Daily 6–10, also Sun 12.30–4.30 🖐 L €29, D €45, Wine €25 🚌 From Ballina go south on N26 for 1.5km (0.9 miles), then bear right on R310 to Pontoon between loughs Conn and Collin

RATHMULLAN
FORT ROYAL
www.fortroyalhotel.com

The hotel enjoys a fine and deserved reputation for good food. The short menus pay tribute to Ireland's outstanding natural larder. Fish is well represented on the four-course dinner menu: Expect Donegal salmon mayonnaise, followed by grilled monkfish, and whole Dover sole, along with roast rack of Donegal lamb, sirloin steak with Bordelaise sauce, and roast loin of pork with roast apples and a port and thyme jus. Desserts might include lemon and lime cheesecake, or a robust banana split.

✉ Fort Royal, Rathmullan, Co. Donegal ☎ 074 915 8100 🕐 Daily 7.30–8.45; closed Nov–end Mar 🖐 D €50, Wine €20

Take N247 through Rathmullan and continue north for 1.5km (0.9 miles); hotel signposted

RECESS
LOUGH INAGH LODGE HOTEL
www.loughinaghlodgehotel.ie
The Turk Mountains form a dramatic backdrop to this intimate restaurant which overlooks Lake Inagh. Seafood and wild game dishes are specialties here, and the freshly baked breads are a treat. From the fixed-price dinner menu come terrine of chicken with blue cheese and peppernut sauce; succulent fresh prawns tossed in butter with a hint of garlic and cinnamon parfait with apple sauce. Inspired wine choices complement the food perfectly.
⊠ Inagh Valley, Recess, Co. Galway
☎ 095 34706 ◷ Daily 7–9 ✋ D €40, Wine €22 🚌 Turn right off N59 after Recess on R344 towards Kylemore Abbey and go up the Inagh Valley

ROSSNOWLAGH
SEASHELL RESTAURANT
www.sandhouse.ie
Cooking at this elegant restaurant incorporates the finest produce, including locally landed seafood, prime beef and lamb, and Irish cheeses. Special dishes include sea trout, Donegal Bay salmon and Fresh Bay oysters.
⊠ Sand House Hotel, Donegal Bay, Rossnowlagh, Co. Donegal ☎ 071 985 1777 ◷ Daily 7–8.30, also Sun 1–2; closed Nov–end Feb ✋ L €27, D €50, Wine €20 🚌 From the coast road, N15, south of Donegal, turn off on R231 to Rossnowlagh

WESTPORT
ARDMORE COUNTRY HOUSE
www.ardmorecountryhouse.com
A luxurious little family-run hotel with wonderful views over Clew Bay, with breathtaking sunsets. The menu offers soup, warm or cold starters and a good selection of main courses. Chef, and patron, Pat Hoban has introduced a comprehensive menu. Fish comes fresh from Clew Bay, the vegetables are grown nearby and are organic for the most part, while meats include local lamb and Irish beef. There is a good range of wines to choose from, and the locally made cheese should not be missed.
⊠ The Quay, Westport, Co. Mayo ☎ 098 25994 ◷ Daily 7–9; closed Jan to mid-Mar ✋ D €50, Wine from €22.50 🚌 1.5 km (0.9 miles) west from Westport on coast road, R335

BLUE WAVE RESTAURANT
www.atlanticcoasthotel.com
Take your seat in the top-floor Blue Wave Restaurant and enjoy the stunning west coast views across the shores of Clew Bay. The food's as modern as the setting. Main courses might include duck on Thai noodles in a zesty teriyaki marinade, or celeriac and garlic risotto. To finish you may be offered a light and dark chocolate tower with spiced apricot compote. Classic wines are stocked alongside New World wines.
⊠ The Atlantic Coast Hotel, The Quay, Westport, Co. Mayo ☎ 098 29000 ◷ Daily 6.30–9.15 ✋ D €39, Wine €17.50 🚌 1 km (0.75 miles) west from Westport on coast road, R335

ISLANDS RESTAURANT
www.hotelwestport.ie
Located in the heart of Westport, this restaurant is popular with both locals and visitors. The menu is carefully designed each day and offers dishes such as Clewbay seafood hors d'oeuvres, warm chicken and pepper kebabs, or pan-fried breast of pheasant with wild mushroom sauce. There is an extensive wine list.
⊠ Hotel Westport, Newport Road, Westport, Co. Mayo ☎ 098 25122 ◷ Daily breakfast 7.30–11, dinner 6–9, lunch Sun only 1–2.30 ✋ L €24, D €41, Wine €17.50

THE LEMON PEEL
www.lemonpeel.ie
In the middle of Westport, this buzzy bistro-style restaurant is just the place for a good night out. The menu reflects influences from around the world with delights such as Cajun blackened shrimp, paillard of chicken breast and home-made seafood ravioli. The staff are helpful and the food is beautifully presented. The wine list includes New World wines alongside classic French and Italian labels. There is also a good early bird menu.
⊠ The Octagon, Westport, Co. Mayo ☎ 098 26929 ◷ Tue–Sat 6–late ✋ D from €30 (2 courses), Wine €18 🚌 In the middle of town, at the end of Shop Street

Left *Castlegrove Country House sits in beautiful gardens*

STAYING

PRICES AND SYMBOLS

Prices are for a double room for one night. Breakfast is included unless noted otherwise. All the hotels listed accept credit cards unless otherwise stated. Note that rates vary widely throughout the year.

For a key to the symbols, ▷ 2.

ACHILL ISLAND
ACHILL CLIFF HOUSE
www.achillcliff.com
This whitewashed family-run hotel has spacious bedrooms with large bathrooms. The restaurant specializes in local seafood. No children under 10 years.
✉ Keel, Achill Island, Co. Mayo ☎ 098 43400 ◎ Closed 23–26 Dec 🖐 Double €90–€140 🛈 10 🚗 In Keel village

BALLYBOFEY
KEE'S HOTEL
www.keeshotel.ie
The fourth generation of the Kee family run their hotel with warm hospitality. The restaurant is open daily and has both a bistro menu and a fine dining menu.
✉ Stranorlar, Ballybofey, Co. Donegal ☎ 074 913 1018 🖐 Double €140–€166 🛈 53 ☒ Indoor 🚗 1.5km (0.9 miles) northeast on the N15

BALLYVAUGHAN
GREGANS CASTLE
www.gregans.ie
Gregans Castle has splendid views towards Galway Bay. Bedrooms are sumptuous and individually decorated (but do not have TVs), and superior rooms and suites offer the ultimate in comfort.
✉ Ballyvaughan, Co. Clare ☎ 065 707 7005 ◎ Closed end Nov to mid-Feb 🖐 Double €196–€235 🛈 21
🚗 6km (4 miles) south of Ballyvaughan on N67

HYLANDS BURREN
www.hylandsburren.com
This tranquil village hotel, dating from the 18th century, is set in the quaint village of Ballyvaughan. In the heart of the dramatic natural landscape of the Burren, it is ideally located for touring in the area. Open fires burn in the traditional bar and lounges, and local seafood is a specialty in the restaurant. The individually decorated bedrooms are tastefully modernized yet still have a warm, homely feel.
✉ Ballyvaughan, Co. Clare ☎ 065 707 7037 ◎ Closed 22–25 Dec, 3–31 Jan 🖐 Double €110–€140 🛈 30 🚗 South of Galway on the N67, in the centre of the village

BUNRATTY
BUNRATTY SHANNON SHAMROCK
www.shamrockhotelbunratty.com
Nestled in a pretty village overshadowed by Bunratty's famous medieval castle, the hotel is surrounded by well-maintained lawns and mature trees. The spacious public areas include a bar and piano lounge, where guests can relax beside the fire and enjoy

afternoon tea. The fully equipped
bedrooms vary in size but all are
elegantly furnished and are designed
with comfort in mind. There is a
leisure centre plus impressive
conference and banqueting facilities.

✉ Bunatty, Co. Clare ☎ 061 471 252
🕐 Closed 24–26 Dec ✋ Double €89–€189
🛏 115 ❄ Indoor ✦ 🚗 Take the
Bunratty by-pass and exit at the Limerick/
Shannon turn off. Proceed to Bunratty village
and the hotel is on the left

CASHEL

CASHEL HOUSE HOTEL

www.cashel-house-hotel.com
Cashel House is set in superb
gardens with woodland walks. The
attentive service is balanced by
friendliness and professionalism
from the McEvily family and their
staff. The comfortable lounges
have turf fires and antiques. The
restaurant serves local produce,
including Connemara lamb and fish
straight from the sea.

✉ Cashel, Co. Galway ☎ 095 31001
🕐 Closed 4 Jan–4 Feb ✋ Double €190
🛏 32 🚗 Turn south off N59, onto R340
1.5km (0.9 mile) west of Recess and the
hotel is well signposted

CLIFDEN

ABBEYGLEN CASTLE

www.abbeyglen.ie
The beautiful romantic setting
overlooking Clifden, and the
dedication of the Hughes' father-
and-son team and their helpful staff,
combine to guarantee that you
will have an unforgettable stay at
Abbeyglen. Each of the attractive
bedrooms takes on a character of
its own through the stylish interior
designs and furnishings; some of
the superior rooms or suites have
four-poster beds, open fires and
Jacuzzis. The restaurant is widely
complimented on the exquisite
food served, particularly the
delicious dishes using freshly
caught seafood.

✉ Sky Road, Clifden, Co. Galway ☎ 095
21201 🕐 Closed 4–29 Jan ✋ Double
€120–€300 🛏 45 🚗 Take the N59 from
Galway towards Clifden; the hotel is 1km
(0.5 miles) before Clifden

ARDAGH HOTEL

www.ardaghhotel.com
At the head of the Ardbear Bay, this
family-run hotel makes full use of the
spectacular views. The restaurant
is renowned for its cuisine. Rooms
are individually decorated, with great
attention to detail.

✉ Ballyconneely Road, Clifden, Co. Galway
☎ 095 21172 🕐 Closed Easter
✋ Double €150–€175 🛏 21 🚗 Take the
N59 to Clifden and then follow the signs for
Ballyconneely

ROCK GLEN COUNTRY HOUSE

www.rockglenhotel.com
The pretty façade of this house is
but an introduction to the comfort
that lies inside. The hospitality of the
owners Peadar Nevin and Fabrice
Galand and their staff makes a visit
to this hotel relaxing and extremely
pleasant. Many of the bedrooms
have great views of the gardens and
the bay.

✉ Clifden, Co. Galway ☎ 095 21035/
21393 🕐 Closed Jan, Feb ✋ Double
€177–€214 🛏 26 🚗 Take the
Ballyconneely road from Clifden for 3km
(1.5 miles); hotel is signposted on right

DONEGAL

HARVEY'S POINT COUNTRY HOTEL

www.harveyspoint.com
In a clearing beside Lough Eske is
this distinctive hotel where ensuring
that guests benefit from comfort,
quality, good cuisine and attentive service is the top priority. At
Harvey's Point Country Hotel only
the wildlife disturbs the tranquillity.
Comfortable bedrooms are in the
adjacent Swiss-style building. Junior
suites are available.

✉ Lough Eske, Co. Donegal ☎ 074 972
2208 ✋ Double from €198 🛏 60
🚗 From Donegal take the N56 west, then
first right signed Lough Eske/Harvey's Point.
The hotel is about a 10-minute drive from
Donegal

MILL PARK

www.millparkhotel.com
Expect a warm Irish welcome at this
hotel overlooking Donegal Bay. High
wooden ceilings and stonework are

Above *Atlantic Heights overlooks Galway Bay*
Opposite *Lough Corrib, Connemara*

incorporated with flair in the design
of the open-plan lobby, which is
centred round a towering fireplace.
The first-floor Granary and the less
formal café bar provide a wide
range of food; the café opens onto
the terrace where you can listen to
the tranquil flow of the millpond.
There is a range of well-presented,
spacious bedrooms with relaxing
mood lighting and an array of
modern amenities. The leisure and
banqueting facilities are extensive.

✉ The Mullins, Donegal Town, Co. Donegal
☎ 074 972 2880 🕐 Closed 24–26 Dec
✋ Double €110–€180 🛏 115 ❄ Indoor
✦ 🚗 Take the N15 signed Lifford; at
the roundabout take the 2nd exit signed
Killybegs. The hotel is on the right after
about 1.5km (1 mile)

DOOLIN

ARAN VIEW HOUSE

www.aranview.com
Surrounded by 40ha (100 acres)
of rolling farmland and panoramic
views of the Aran Islands, this
Georgian house offers attractive and
comfortable accommodation. Staff
are welcoming, the atmosphere
is convivial, and there's traditional
music in the nearby pubs.

✉ Coast Road, Doolin, Co. Clare ☎ 065
707 4061/707 4420 🕐 Closed Nov to mid-
Mar ✋ Double €110–€140 🛏 19 🚗 On
the R453 north of Doolin

ENNIS

WOODSTOCK

www.dghotels.com

This secluded modern hotel overlooks an 18-hole golf course. Public areas include comfortable lounges with welcoming log fires. Modern Irish cuisine is served in Spikes Brasserie. Spacious bedrooms offer comfort and individuality. The hotel has extensive health and leisure facilities.

✉ Shanaway Road, Ennis, Co. Clare ☎ 065 684 6600 ✋ Double €200–€230 ⓘ 67 ⛵ Indoor 🛇 🚗 From Ennis take N18 and at roundabout (traffic circle) take N85 Lahinch road. After 800m (875 yards) turn left for Woodstock; hotel is 800m (875 yards) farther on

Above *Castle Grove Country House overlooks Lough Swilly*

GALWAY

ATLANTIC HEIGHTS

www.galway.net/pages/atlantic-heights

Enthusiastic hosts, Robbie and Madeleine Mitchell take great pride in their home, a fine balconied house overlooking Galway Bay. Bedrooms have TV, tea- and coffee-making facilities, telephone, and many thoughtful extras. The breakfast menu, features home baking. There is a laundry service.

✉ 2 Cashelmara, Knocknacarra Cross, Salthill, Co. Galway ☎ 091 529466/528830 🕐 Closed Nov–end Mar ✋ Double €80–€100 ⓘ 6 🚗 1km (0.6 miles) from Salthill Promenade in Upper Salthill on R336. Turn right after Spinnaker House Hotel, just before the junction

DAYS HOTEL GALWAY

www.dayshotelgalway.com

This modern hotel on the southeastern outskirts of the city provides good leisure facilities including tennis and a sports hall. The bedrooms are well equipped and decorated in tasteful, contemporary shades. Food is served all day in Bar Solo and Rueben's restaurant offers good Irish fare in an elegant setting. The hotel has been awarded the Ireland's Best Award for service excellence by Failte Ireland.

✉ Dublin Road, Galway, Co. Galway ☎ 091 753181 ✋ Double €88–€140

ⓘ 360 ⛵ Indoor 🛇 🚗 Follow signs to Galway City East off the N6, N18, N17, past Galway Crystal factory on the left and the hotel is 2km (1 mile) on the right

GALWAY BAY HOTEL

www.galwaybayhotel.net

The Galway Bay Hotel is in a spectacular location overlooking Galway Bay and most bedrooms, lounges and the restaurant enjoy excellent sea views. There is fine dining in the Lobster Pot restaurant and more casual meals in the Café Lido. The conference and leisure facilities are impressive.

✉ The Promenade, Salthill, Galway, Co. Galway ☎ 091 520520 ✋ Double from €150 ⓘ 153 ⛵ Indoor 🛇 🚗 On the promenade in Salthill on the coast road to Connemara

THE HARBOUR

www.harbour.ie

This contemporary hotel is situated beside the redeveloped harbour in the heart of Galway city. Krusoes café bar and restaurant offers modern cuisine. Bedrooms are well furnished and well equipped with all the usual facilities.

✉ The Harbour, Galway City, Co. Galway ☎ 091 569466 ✋ Double €99–€189 ⓘ 96 🚗 Follow signs for Galway City East, at roundabout (traffic circle) take the first exit to Galway City. Follow signs to the

docks and the hotel is 1km (0.6 miles) from the roundabout, on the left

KILKEE

HALPIN'S TOWNHOUSE

www.halpinsprivatehotels.com

The finest tradition of hotel service is offered at this hotel that has a commanding view over the old Victorian town. The hotel has been owned and run by the Halpin family for more than 20 years and they have always maintained a hospitable atmosphere. Flagstone floors and an open fire in the bar give an old-world charm, while the bedrooms offer every modern facility.

✉ 2 Erin Street, Kilkee, Co. Clare ☎ 065 905 6032 🕐 Closed 16 Nov–14 Mar ✋ Double €89–€129 ⓘ 12 🚗 In the middle of town

KNOCK

KNOCK HOUSE HOTEL

www.knockhousehotel.ie

Next to the Marian Shrine and Basilica, this creatively designed building is set in landscaped gardens. Facilities include lounges, conference rooms and a restaurant. Six bedrooms are adapted for wheelchairs.

✉ Ballyhaunis Road, Knock, Co. Mayo ☎ 094 938 8088 ✋ Double €119–€160 ⓘ 68 🚗 Just outside Knock on Ballyhaunis Road

LETTERKENNY
CASTLE GROVE COUNTRY HOUSE
www.castlegrove.com
This elegant Georgian house enjoys spectacular views of Lough Swilly. The dining room serves dishes using local produce. Bedrooms are spacious, equipped with modern necessities and furnished with some fine antiques.

✉ Castlegrove, Ballymaleel, Letterkenny, Co. Donegal ☎ 074 915 1118 ✋ Double from €150 ⓘ 15 🚗 7km (4.5 miles) northeast of Letterkenny off R245, Ramelton road

NEWMARKET-ON-FERGUS
DROMOLAND CASTLE
www.dromoland.ie
Dating from the early 18th century and standing majestically in its 166ha (410-acre) estate, Dromoland Castle offers extensive indoor leisure activities and outdoor pursuits. The distinguished bedrooms and suites vary in style and size but all provide the impressive levels comfort and are thoughtfully equipped. The public rooms are warmed by log fires and have spectacular views over the lake. There are two restaurants, the elegant Earl of Thomond, and the less formal Fig Tree in the golf clubhouse. A team of efficient staff is committed to caring for guests.

✉ Newmarket-on-Fergus, Co. Clare ☎ 061 368 144 🕐 Closed 25–26 Dec ✋ Double €238–€607 ⓘ 99 ♒ Indoor 🛁 🚗 Take the N18 to Ennis/Galway from Shannon for 8km (5 miles) to the Dromoland interchange signed Quin. Take the slip road left, then fourth exit at the 1st roundabout (traffic circle), 2nd exit at the 2nd roundabout, and the hotel is 500m (550 yards) on the left

RECESS
BALLYNAHINCH CASTLE
www.ballynahinch-castle.com
Open log fires and friendly professional service are just some of the delights of staying at this 16th-century castle, set among 142ha (350 acres) of woodland, rivers and lakes. The restaurant and many suites and rooms have stunning views.

✉ Recess, Co. Galway ☎ 095 31006 🕐 Closed 17–27 Dec, 30 Jan–end Feb ✋ Double €190–€240 ⓘ 40 🚗 From Recess take the Roundstone left turn, then turn off in 4.5km (3 miles)

LOUGH INAGH LODGE
www.loughinaghlodgehotel.ie
Amid the stunning scenery of the Connemara Mountains on the shores of Lough Inagh, it would be hard to find a more idyllic setting for this 19th-century, former fishing lodge. It is akin to staying in a family home where you can totally relax and unwind, while enjoying some of what the surrounding country-side has to offer. The lounges have turf fires in winter and there is an oak-panelled bar. Each comfortable bedroom has a separate dressing room. The delightful restaurant specializes in dishes of wild game and lake caught fish.

✉ Recess, Connemara, Co. Galway ☎ 095 34706 🕐 Closed mid-Dec to mid-Mar ✋ Double €176–€256 ⓘ 13 🚗 From Recess take the R344 towards Kylemore

ROSSNOWLAGH
SAND HOUSE HOTEL
www.sandhouse.ie
Beside a crescent of golden sand, 8km (5 miles) north of Ballyshannon, this hotel is well known for its hospitality, food and service. Many rooms have sea views and a there's a relaxing conservatory lounge.

✉ Rossnowlagh, Co. Donegal ☎ 071 985 1777 🕐 Closed Dec, Jan ✋ Double €180–€280 ⓘ 60 🚗 From the N15 south of Donegal turn off on R231 to Rossnowlagh

SHANNON
SHANNON COURT
www.irishcourthotels.com
This friendly hotel is conveniently close to Shannon Airport and near Bunratty Castle. There's a comfortable bar, themed restaurant and meeting rooms, as well as contemporary style bedrooms.

✉ Ballycasey, Shannon, Co. Clare ☎ 061 364588 🕐 Closed 24–26 Dec ✋ Double €79–€89 (breakfast not included) ⓘ 54

🚗 On the western edge of Shannon village, 5km (3 miles) from the airport

SPANISH POINT
ARMADA HOTEL
www.armadahotel.com
On the coast overlooking the breaking waves and golden sands, this hotel has stunning views, especially the restaurant and patio. Bedrooms, most facing the sea, are spacious.

✉ Spanish Point, Co. Clare ☎ 065 708 4110 ✋ Double €150–€300 ⓘ 61 🚗 From N18 in Ennis take N85 to Inagh, then R460 to Miltown Malbay. Follow signs for Spanish Point

WESTPORT
ARDMORE COUNTRY HOUSE
www.ardmorecountryhouse.com
A pretty country-house hotel. The restaurant and lounges overlook Clew Bay, with Croagh Patrick in the background. Individually styled bedrooms are spacious and most have spectacular views. No children under 12 years.

✉ The Quay, Westport, Co. Mayo ☎ 098 25994 ✋ Double €170–€250 ⓘ 13 🚗 1.5km (1 mile) west from Westport on coast road, R335

HOTEL WESTPORT
www.hotelwestport.ie
Set in private woodland and just a short walk into town, this hotel is a perfect place to truely relax and be pampered. Facilities include Ocean Spirit spa and leisure complex, Islands Restaurant (▷ 241), and the Maple bar with musical entertainment. Outside there are attractive patio gardens and an outdoor children's play area. The hotel is fully wheelchair accessible.

✉ Newport Road, Westport, Co. Mayo ☎ 098 25122 🕐 All year ✋ Double €200 ⓘ 129 ♒ Indoor 🛁 and spa 🚗 In heart of Westport

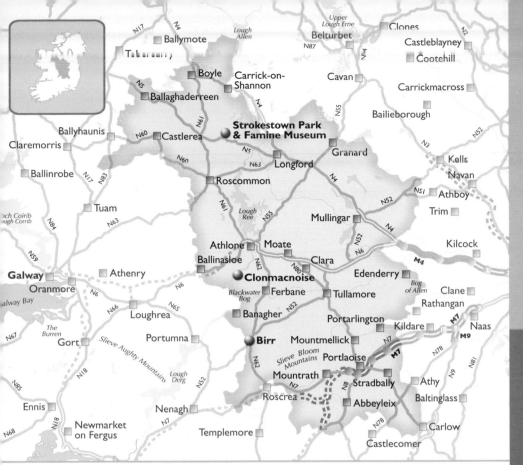

THE MIDLANDS

This overlooked part of Ireland may attract fewer visitors than other parts of the Emerald Isle, but it has a charm of its own and fascinating places to visit. Ireland's heartland is still predominantly rural and mostly flat with vast empty areas of bogland, which give way to a network of lakes beneath gentle mountains with the River Shannon cutting through the middle.

Stretching across much of County Laois is the Bog of Allen, which is harvested for its valuable source of peat fuel. To the northwest of the county, along the border with County Offaly, are the Slieve Bloom Mountains, a small rocky range of peaks that form a perfect ring. County Offaly is also covered extensively by inland bog, and bordered by the River Shannon to the west. Its county town is Tullamore, a picturesque market town where Tullamore whiskey has been distilled since the 16th century. On the western borders, overlooking the River Shannon, is the ancient monastic town of Clonmacnoise, one of the most atmospheric places in Ireland. Another of Offaly's attractions is the town of Birr, famous for its castle with stunning gardens and jousting displays held each May.

Roscommon is a county of quiet country lanes, fertile farmland, undulating hillsides and sparkling lakes, and home to one of Ireland's best lakeside attractions, Lough Key Forest Park. On the eastern edge of the historic town of Boyle stands Boyle Abbey, an impressive and well-preserved Cistercian Monastery. Westmeath is a county of rich pastureland and lakes, with Athlone the largest town set in a strategic location at an important intersection of the River Shannon.

Longford is one of Ireland's smallest counties, mainly flat with fertile agricultural land and peat bogs, and a network of criss-crossing waterways and lakes. The main reason people visit Longford is Lough Ree, renowned for its trout fishing and sailing. The county's extensive waterways of the Shannon basin and the upper River Erne make Longford a popular stopover for boat cruises.

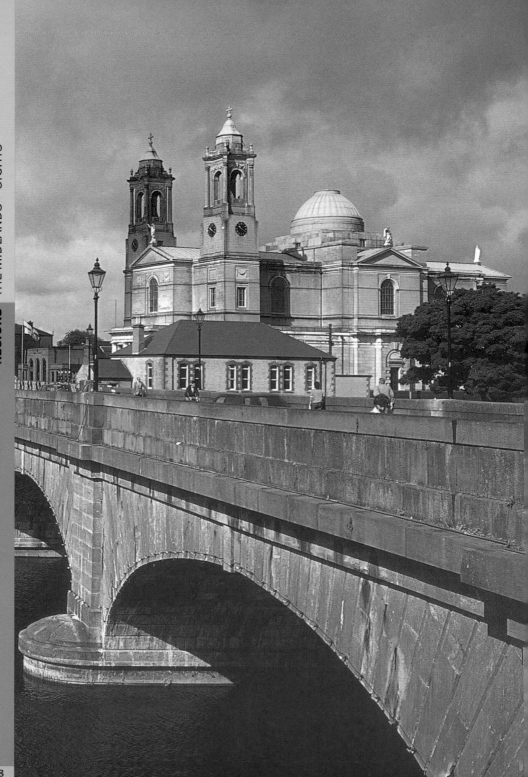

ABBEYLEIX

www.eastcoastmidlands.ie

Abbeyleix is a handsome Georgian town that was laid out at the gates of his park by Viscount de Vesci, the 18th-century Lord of Abbeyleix House. At Abbeyleix Heritage House (tel 0502 31653, May–end Sep Mon–Fri 9–5, Sat, Sun 1–5; rest of year Mon–Fri 9–5), in the former boy's school, you can learn about the town's development from its origins as a huddle of houses around a 12th-century Cistercian monastery. There's also a display on the town's long-defunct carpet industry; when the ill-fated *Titanic* set sail on her disastrous maiden voyage in 1912, her stateroom floors were covered with Abbeyleix carpets.

In the old walled garden of Abbeyleix's former convent is the Abbey Sense Garden (tel 0502 31325/31636; Mon–Thu 9–5, Fri 9–4), designed for touching, seeing, hearing, smelling and tasting.

🚑 364 F6 🛈 Tourist Information Office, Lawlor Avenue, Portlaoise, Co. Laois ☎ 0502 21178 🕓 Jun to mid-Sep Mon–Fri 9.30–5.30

ATHLONE

www.eastcoastmidlands.ie

As the county town and the commercial and social hub for a wide rural area, Athlone is a lively base for boating and fishing on the River Shannon. The best place for a pint, a tune and all the local information, is Sean's Bar on Main Street (tel 0906 492358), an establishment of great character that has been a pub for at least 400 years.

The world-renowned tenor John McCormack (1884–1945) was born in The Bawn at the heart of Athlone. From the battlements there's a good view of the town and the River Shannon towards Lough Ree.

🚑 364 E5 🛈 Civic Offices, Church Street, Co. Westmeath ☎ 0906 494630 🕓 Apr–end Oct daily 9.30–5.30 🚉 Athlone

BELVEDERE HOUSE

www.belvedere-house.ie

With its fine plasterwork ceilings and decoratively carved woodwork, this 18th-century fishing and hunting lodge and gardens make an enjoyable excursion. Pride of place among the many follies in the grounds goes to the Jealous Wall, a large sham castle frontage, complete with turrets, Gothic arches and 'shattered' windows. It was built in 1760 on the orders of the 'Wicked Earl', Robert Rochfort, First Earl of Belvedere, to block his view of Tudenham Park, the home of his younger brother, with whom he had quarrelled. The Wicked Earl also suspected his other brother, Arthur, of having an affair with his young wife, Mary, in 1743. Lord Belvedere sued Arthur for £20,000, and at length had him imprisoned, where he eventually died. Mary, was shut away in another of the earl's houses, where she remained under lock and key for more than 30 years. After the earl's death in 1774, one of her sons released her, still clad in a dress she had worn before her incarceration and still protesting her innocence.

🚑 364 F5 ✉ Mullingar, Co. Westmeath ☎ 044 49060 🕓 May–end Aug daily 9.30–9; Mar, Apr, Sep, Oct daily 10.30–6; Nov–end Feb daily 10.30–4.30 💷 Adult €8.75, child €4.75, family €24 🚗 On N52, 5.5km (3.5 miles) south of Mullingar

BLACKWATER BOG

www.bnm.ie

The Blackwater Bog covers some 8,000ha (19,770 acres) of counties Offaly, Westmeath, Roscommon and Galway, some untouched, other parts exploited for fuel and fertilizer. Destruction of the bogs over the past 50 years has been on such a massive scale that an international outcry by conservationists ensued, and exploitation is due to cease by 2030. In the meantime, the 'Clonmacnoise & West Offaly Railway' will take you for 8km (5 miles) round the bog and you can see how it has been turned into a desolate quagmire and how it will be developed for eco-recreation in the future.

🚑 364 E5 ☎ 0909 674114 🕓 Tours every hour, Jun–end Aug daily 10–5; Apr, May, Sep Mon–Fri 10–5 💷 Train ride adult €7, child (12–16) €5, family €23.50 🚗 Signed off R357 Cloghan road, 1.5km (1 mile) southeast of Shannonbridge

Opposite *Athlone on the River Shannon*
Below *Athlone Castle is still an imposing place*

364 E6 Birr Tourist Information Office, Castle Street, Birr, Co. Offaly ☎ 057 91 20110 Jun–end Aug Mon–Sat 9–6; Sep–end May Mon–Sat 9.30–5.30

TIPS

To avoid disappointment, telephone Birr Castle Demesne in advance for telescope demonstration times.

» Children might enjoy searching for Sweeney, a legendary Irish king driven mad and forced to live as a bird after being cursed by St. Ronan. They'll find his gradually dissolving wickerwork figure perched in a holly tree, hidden in the undergrowth near Lover's Walk.

BIRR

Birr has wide streets of Georgian houses but its greatest attraction is the Birr Castle Demesne, its Science Centre and the Giant Leviathan telescope.

The Parsons family settled at Birr in 1620, and as the Earls of Rosse they directed the fortunes of the area from then on. During the 18th century they laid out a model Georgian town with a central square and wide tree-lined streets or 'malls' flanked with well-built houses and neat gardens. The Birr Town Trail, set out in a little leaflet obtainable from the Tourist Information Office, takes you around the best parts. Notice the carved surrounds of the shop-fronts here.

BIRR CASTLE DEMESNE

The chief attraction of the town is undoubtedly Birr Castle Demesne (tel 0509 20340/20336; www.birrcastle.com, mid-Mar to end Oct daily 9–6, Nov to mid-Mar 10–4). The castle itself, founded in 1170 and altered in the succeeding centuries, is still the private residence of the Earl and Countess of Rosse, and is not open to the public. But the family have tastefully developed the demesne (grounds) as a public attraction, with woodland walks, formal and informal gardens and water features. There are rose gardens and a very fine collection of magnolias, and a path between gigantic hedges of box that date back to the 17th century. The demesne is also home to the National Birds of Prey Centre.

Plenty of experimental plant work has been carried out at Birr Castle Demesne, and the Birds of Prey Centre is actively involved with schemes to reintroduce birds into the wild. The earls and countesses of Rosse seem always to have had enquiring, scientific minds. The Science Centre in the castle stables gives a very accessible account of the family's various achievements in science, including the development by the Third Earl, William Parsons (1800–67), of the huge telescope named Leviathan which is still kept in the grounds and is demonstrated three times a day. This telescope, 21m (70ft) long, contains the largest cast metal mirror ever made. Gazing through it in April 1845, the Third Earl was the first man to see a whirlpool nebula. The photographs taken of the newly installed telescope by the earl's wife, Mary, a noted pioneer of photography, are remarkable.

Above *Intriguing face sculptures in the castle grounds*

BOG OF ALLEN

www.loughbooraparklands.com

The great Bog of Allen stretches some 100km (62 miles) from County Kildare through County Offaly to the River Shannon. This is a 'raised bog', formed when water trickles down from higher ground and collects on an impermeable base which, in this case, is a thick sheet of clay spread by the retreating glaciers of the last Ice Age. The bog holds up to 20 times its own weight of water and the peat can be 10m (32ft) or more in depth. At first glance it appears lifeless, but closer inspection reveals abundant plant life, including many kinds of sedges, sundews and the brilliant orange stars of bog asphodel.

The practice of cutting peat (turf) for domestic fuel makes little impression on the bog, but commercial exploitation for industrial fuel and gardening since World War II by the Irish Peat Board has seen destruction on a vast scale. Learn all about the conversion of the bog into wildlife and amenity parks at Lough Boora Parklands near Kilcormac.

🕂 365 F5 🚹 Lough Boora Parklands on the R357 near Kilcormac, off N52 between Birr and Tullamore, Co. Offaly; Bog of Allen Nature Centre, Lullymore, Rathangan, Co. Kildare ☎ 045 860133 🕓 Mon–Fri 10–4 ✋ Adult €5

BOYLE

Boyle is a handsome town with a pleasing mixture of Georgian and Victorian architecture. By far the most important and striking building

is Boyle Abbey (tel 071 966 2604; Apr to mid-Nov daily 10–6), standing magnificently beside the River Boyle on the eastern edge of town. Founded in 1148 by the Cistercian community, the remains of the old monastery cloister garden, kitchens and refectory are in a very good state of preservation, as is the abbey church itself. The humorous carvings, floral capitals and decorative pillars are rare for the austere Cistercian order.

There's an exhibition in the gatehouse, where jambs are scored with sword cuts and ancient graffiti from the garrison that occupied the abbey from 1603 until 1788. In that year the Connaught Rangers, or 'The Devil's Own' as the roughneck militia were called, moved to King House at the east end of Main Street (tel 071 966 3242; daily 10–6). This lovely early Georgian mansion had just been vacated by the King family in favour of their grand Rockingham estate (now Lough Key Forest Park, ▷ 257). King House is a wonderful place for children, with storytelling, activities and dressing-up to help bring history to life; adults can watch audio-visual displays on the history of the King family and the area, and also on the Great Famine. Frybrook House (tel 071 966 3515; Jul, Aug by appointment only), a well-preserved Quaker house, dates from the mid-18th century.

🕂 362 D4 🚹 Boyle Tourist Information Office, The Courthouse, Market Street, Boyle, Co. Roscommon ☎ 071 966 2145 🕓 Mon–Sat 9–5.45

CHARLEVILLE FOREST CASTLE

www.charlevillecastle.com

Five beautiful avenues of Irish yew trees radiate from the castle, an imposing neo-Gothic country house built with grand spires, turrets and pinnacles in 1798, and walled as if to shut out the world. There is elaborate stucco in the gallery which runs the whole width of the house; here the Bury family could promenade and admire the gardens in inclement weather. Thickly tangled oak woods add to the eerie atmosphere

surround 'the most haunted house in Ireland'.

🕂 364 E5 ✉ Tullamore, Co. Offaly ☎ 057 93 21279 🕓 Daily 10–6 ✋ Adult €16 (min 2 people, thereafter €6 per person) 🚗 On N52 Birr road south of Tullamore

CLONALIS HOUSE

www.clonalis.com

Clonalis House is a late Victorian Italianate country house. Its interest lies in the antiquity of its owners, the O'Conors, once the Kings of Connacht. One Ruaidri Ua Conchobair (Rory O'Conor) reigned from 1166–86 as the last High King of Ireland. The O'Conors preserve an enormous archive of family papers and historical documents. You can also see the great Stone on which the O'Conor chiefs have been inaugurated since pre-Christian times, and the harp that belonged to Turlough O'Carolan (1670–1738), the blind harpist, composer and poet known as the last of the traditional court bards. The O'Conor Don (clan chief) of the day was a keen patron of O'Carolan.

🕂 362 D4 ✉ Castlerea, Co. Roscommon ☎ 094 962 0 014 🕓 Jun–end Aug Mon–Sat 11–4 ✋ Adult €7, child €5 🚆 Castlerea 🚌 On N60, just west of Castlerea

Above *Charleville Forest Castle is richly ornamented*

Left *Extensive remains of the 12th-century Boyle Abbey*

CLONMACNOISE

INTRODUCTION

Clonmacnoise lies on a great bend of the River Shannon, some 11km (7 miles) downstream of Athlone, near the meeting point of three counties: Offaly, Westmeath and Roscommon. The site, one of Ireland's most popular tourist destinations, is well signposted from all roads in the region. It also has its own jetties on the river bank for foot-passengers arriving by water.

Whether you arrive by road or by boat, you'll enter through the Visitor Centre, essential to your appreciation of Clonmacnoise. The monastic site lies immediately east of the Visitor Centre, with the Round Tower and churches huddled compactly together inside their surrounding wall. As you enter the site, O'Rourke's Tower lies to the left beyond the copy of the Cross of the Scriptures. Ahead is the copy of the South Cross, with the cathedral just beyond it. At the far side of the site you can follow a marked path for 450m (490 yards) to the Nuns' Church.

When he founded the monastery of Clonmacnoise around AD548, St. Ciarán chose the site extremely well. The monastery stood not only on Ireland's largest navigable river, but also on the glacial ridge called Esker Riada, the King's Highway, the main east–west high road of the kingdoms of Connacht and Leinster. Clonmacnoise enjoyed more than six centuries of prosperity and pre-eminence as Ireland's chief religious and educational centre. Monks from all over Europe came and Kings of Ireland were buried here. Yet those were tough times. The Vikings attacked at least eight times; the locals outdid them, attacking on nearly 30 occasions and setting the monastery on fire a dozen times. After the arrival of the Normans in 1180, Clonmacnoise began to decline, and in 1552 English soldiers stole every treasure, and smashed what they could not carry away.

WHAT TO SEE

CLONMACNOISE FROM THE RIVER SHANNON

By far the most enjoyable way to arrive is to rent a boat at Athlone and cruise here. The view is of towers, churches and a snowdrift of gravestones, enclosed within a protective wall on a green bank and reflected in the river. Altogether this aspect of Clonmacnoise forms an unforgettable ensemble and a perfect subject to photograph.

CROSS OF THE SCRIPTURES

The High Crosses facing wind and weather on the monastic site are copies; the originals, too precious to be exposed to the elements, are on display in the Visitor Centre. The best-preserved, the Cross of the Scriptures, stands 4.5m (15ft) high. It is sometimes called Flann's Cross—an inscription on the base attributes it to King Flann, High King of Ireland at the turn of the 10th century when the cross was carved. Abbot Colman Conailleach probably erected the cross AD910. It is richly carved with biblical scenes: St. Anthony besting the Devil, the Saved called to eternal life, and Christ in his tomb being awoken by a peck on the lips from a bird that might be the Holy Dove.

The Cross of the Scriptures may be the most striking of the Clonmacnoise high crosses, but don't ignore the other two great crosses on display. The ninth-century South Cross, badly weathered, shows a Crucifixion with the identifiable figures of Longinus the lance-bearer and Stephaton the sponge-bearer; while the North Cross, perhaps dating back as far as AD800, has stiffly posed lions and a motif of spiralling foliage. The cross-legged figure here might be Cernunnos, the horned god of the woods and of virility, revered in Celtic pagan mythology.

INFORMATION

➕ 364 E5 ✉ Co. Offaly 🛈 Visitor Centre ☎ 090 967 4195 ◷ Mid-May to early Sep daily 9–7; mid-Mar to mid-May, early Sep–end Oct daily 10–6, Nov to mid-Mar daily 10–5.30 💶 Adult €5.30, child (under 18) €2.10, family €11.50 🚗 Signposted from N62, 21km (13 miles) south of Athlone, or from Shannonbridge on R357, 13km (8 miles) southeast of Ballinasloe

Above *Detail of a Celtic cross at Clonmacnoise*
Opposite *The Round Tower and Celtic crosses*

» If you visit in the summer, try to be there by 9am. The site gets very crowded, especially at weekends.

» Purely for fun: why not join a cruise to Clonmacnoise from Athlone aboard a replica Viking ship? The crew of the *Viking* (tel 0906 473383/473392 for reservations) will be dressed as Vikings, and you can borrow a costume to make your arrival at the monastery exciting for all concerned!

GRAVE SLABS

Also in the Visitor Centre exhibition is a unique collection of grave slabs. Dating from the eighth century to the twelfth, they represent Europe's largest collection of early Christian burial markers. Some are decorated with interlace carving and incised crosses of various shapes. One of the slabs is clearly marked 'Colman', another implores, '*Ior do thuathal saer*, a prayer for Thuathal the Craftsman'.

O'ROURKE'S TOWER (ROUND TOWER)

Once out of the Visitor Centre and into the roughly circular walled site of the monastery, most visitors turn left past the copy of the Cross of the Scriptures and head for the most obvious landmark, O'Rourke's Tower. The O'Rourke in question was probably Fergal O'Rourke, King of Connacht, who died in AD964, roughly the same time the tower was built for protection against the frequent attacks of the Danes. The tower, 20m (65ft) high, is built of beautifully shaped, slightly curved stones. But the top is incomplete; the cap was blasted off by a lightning strike in 1135, as meticulously recorded by the monks.

THE CATHEDRAL OR MACDERMOT'S CHURCH

East of O'Rourke's Tower is Clonmacnoise Cathedral, a neat incorporation of the original church built in AD904 by Abbot Colman and High King Flann Sinna (▷ 253, Cross of the Scriptures) within a 12th-century rebuilding. Many ancient fragments of carved stones lie in a side chapel. The Gothic arch of the north door is made up of a whole nest of recessed courses carved with barley-sugar fluting and foliage, in which the sculptor has set the dragons of sin to writhe helplessly. This door has a special property—if you bring your mouth close to the stonework on one side and whisper, the sound will be carried around the top of the arch and down to a listener's ear pressed against the opposite jamb. In medieval times, priests could thus hear the confession of a leper without risk of contamination. Nowadays children rejoice in the secret of the Whispering Door.

ST. CIARÁN'S CHURCH (TEMPLE CIARÁN)

Immediately east of the Cathedral lies the diminutive St. Ciarán's Church, cAD800. The founder of Clonmacnoise is said to be buried at the far end. For centuries farmers would anoint the corners of their fields with earth

Right *MacCarthy's Church and its round tower*
Below *Among the ruins of the Nun's Church*

scraped from the floor of St. Ciarán's Church to protect their corn and cattle. Eventually the floor became so hollowed that stone slabs were laid. But old beliefs die hard, and you may still see pilgrims furtively collecting a handkerchief full of earth from just outside the church. Sufferers from warts anoint them with rainwater from the hollow of the *bullaun* or ancient quernstone inside St. Ciarán's Church, a practice that persists in rural Ireland.

Above *Looking out over the river at Clonmacnoise as the sun sets*
Below *Detail of the ancient carvings on a Celtic cross*

MACCARTHY'S CHURCH (TEMPLE FINGHIN)
Against the monastery's surrounding wall due north of St. Ciarán's Church stands the 12th-century MacCarthy's Church, unmistakable because of the miniature round tower with its herringbone cap of stone tiles that rises from the south wall of the church. The tower, probably a belfry rather than a defensive stronghold as its door is vulnerably placed at ground level, was built in 1124, some say by Big Finian MacCarthy. The Romanesque chancel arch is decorated with weathered but still beautiful chevron carving.

THE NUNS' CHURCH
Many visitors miss this exquisite little church because it lies a short walk east of the main site. The carvings are superb, far richer than in any of the other Clonmacnoise churches, with Romanesque chevrons, faces, beaked beasts and other grotesques. The church was built in 1167 as an act of penance by Dervorgilla O'Rourke, whose act of folly led indirectly to the end of the Golden Age of Celtic Ireland.

Among the carvings around the west door and the chancel arch of the Nuns' Church is another pagan symbol; you can pick out a couple of Green Men. These enigmatic figures are always shown with foliage emerging from one or more of their facial orifices. They seem pagan in character, yet are found in medieval church decoration all over Europe and beyond.

255

EMO COURT

Architect James Gandon, who is best known for great public building works such as Dublin's Custom House, the Four Courts and O'Connell Bridge, designed the Earl of Portarlington's grand neoclassical mansion of Emo Court in 1792. The family was in residence here until 1920, when it became a Jesuit seminary. The house was restored during the 1970s, and it was acquired by the Irish nation in 1996.

The focal points as you approach the mansion are the great green dome that tops the building and the imposing colonnaded portico through which you enter. The inside is full of fine plasterwork and *trompe l'oeil* decoration.

The gardens are divided into two principal parts—the Grapery, which has a path leading through the shrubberies down to the lakeshore, and the Clucker—so called because it was laid out on the site of a former nunnery—where rhododendrons and azaleas bring a riot of early summer hues among the cedars, pines and maples.

➕ 364 F6 ✉ Emo village, Co. Laois ☎ 057 86 26573 🕐 Easter–end Oct daily 10–6 💰 Adult €3, child (5–18) €1.50, family €7.30 🚗 Signposted from N7 Kildare–Portlaoise road

FORE

The village of Fore is famous for the legendary Seven Wonders of Fore, evidence of which lies in the fields on the outskirts. Pilgrims visit regularly, and though the Wonders may look rather unremarkable to sceptics, local belief is strong.

The first of them is 'the monastery in the quaking scraw', a fine range of monastic buildings, complete with gatehouse and dovecot, which were built on a rock that's surrounded by a quaking bog. Then comes the 'water that flows uphill' and the 'mill without a race'—the ruin of a mill that is said to have been founded here by St. Fechin in a then waterless place; the stream, apparently defying gravity by flowing uphill, appeared with a stroke of his staff. 'The tree that won't burn' is next—a stump that has been poisoned by the thousands of copper coins pushed into its trunk as offerings by miracle-seekers. Then there's the 'water that won't boil'—but who's going to try, when legend has it that the water of the muddy remnants of St. Fechin's holy well brings bad luck to anyone even attempting to boil it.

On the other side of the road you'll find 'the stone raised by St. Fechin's prayers'. The massive lintel of a 12th-century church, carved with a Greek cross in a circle, reputedly rose into place on the saint's prayers. Lastly, there's the 'anchorite in a stone', which is actually the cell of 17th-century hermit Patrick Begley, within what looks like a church but is in fact the mausoleum of the Greville Nugent family. Should the mausoleum be locked when you arrive, collect the key for it from the Seven Wonders pub in the village.

➕ 365 F4 ℹ Mullingar Tourist Information Office, Market House, Mullingar ☎ 044 93 48650 🕐 Seasonal hours, telephone for information 🚗 Signposted off the R195 near Castlepollard (on R394, 21km/13 miles north of Mullingar)

HEYWOOD HOUSE GARDENS

Nothing remains of Heywood House—the 18th-century mansion was burned to the ground in 1950—but the gardens are remarkable. They were designed in 1909 by celebrated architect Sir Edwin Lutyens and planted in the subsequent three years by his frequent collaborater, garden designer and plantswoman supreme, Gertrude Jekyll. The well-tended landscape includes fine terraces and garden 'rooms'—themed areas enclosed within 'walls' of neatly clipped hedges—and there's a lovely lime walk and a scatter of pavilions.

➕ 364 F6 ✉ Ballinakill, Co. Laois ☎ 057 87 33334 🕐 May–end Aug daily, dawn to dusk 💰 Free 🚗 Off R432 outside Ballinakill, 7km (4 miles) from Abbeyleix

KILBEGGAN

Kilbeggan is a good example of the kind of wayside settlement that grew into a flourishing town by virtue of its position on the Grand Canal. Locke's Distillery on Main Street (tel 057 93 32134; www.lockesdistillery.com; Apr–end Oct daily 9–6; Nov–end Mar 10–4) was in production for a full 200 years, until 1957, and is now a fine museum of whiskey. Exhibits include an old steam engine and a working millwheel. You can still buy Locke's whiskey—among the range sold here, are bottles of Locke's single malt, which nowadays is made at Cooley's Distillery in Co. Louth. Devotees say it's one of the smoothest whiskeys in Ireland.

➕ 364 E5 ℹ Mullingar Tourist Information Office, Market House, Mullingar, Co. Westmeath ☎ 044 93 48650 🕐 Mon–Fri 9.30–5.30

LOUGH KEY FOREST PARK

www.loughkey.ie

Lough Key Forest Park comprises 350ha (870 acres) of woodlands with footpaths and the Island-dotted Lough Key. It forms part of the once grand Rockingham Estate. Activities on offer are The Lough Key Experience: with an audio-trail describing of the park's history, flora and fauna. Walk through underground tunnels to the top of the five-storey Moylurg viewing tower and the unique tree canopy walk. Boda Borg is an adventure house (for visitors aged over 10 years) and a minimum of three people is needed to solve puzzles while moving from room to room. The Adventure Play Kingdom is a safe outdoor play area.

✚ 362 E4 ✉ Boyle, Co. Roscommon ☎ 071 967 3122 ⏰ Estate all year. Lough Key Centre and Activities: Jul, Aug Mon–Thu 10–6, Fri–Sun 10–9; Mar–end Jun, Sep, Oct daily 10–6; Nov–end Feb Fri–Sun 10–4. (Last admission to Boda Borg 2 hours before closing, Lough Key Experience 1.5 hours before closing, Adventure Play 1 hour before closing) 💰 Adult from €7.50, child from €5, family from €20 🚌 Boyle 🚗 Signposted on N4 Carrick-on-Shannon road, 3.2km (2 miles) east of Boyle 🖥 ♿

LOUGH REE

www.athlone.ie

Lough Ree is a ragged, fishtail-shaped lake 25.5km (16 miles) long. Islands dot this mighty stretch of water, superb for both boating and fishing. You can rent boats and fishing tackle at various places around the lake. Athlone has several tackle shops, such as Strand Fishing Tackle (The Strand, tel 0906 479277), and day-boat and cruiser rental companies include Waveline Cruisers of Quigley's Marina (tel 0906 485711), both at Killinure near Glasson, 6.5km (4 miles) north of Athlone; and Athlone Cruisers at Jolly Mariner

Right *A misty, distant view of the Slieve Bloom Mountains*
Opposite *Clonalis House, ancestral seat of the O'Conor family*

Marina, Coosan (tel 0906 472892). Check at the marina which islands you can land on (your craft will need an anchor, and a rowing dinghy). The most rewarding island is Inchcleraun or Quaker's Island towards the north end of Lough Ree (anchor near red lake navigation marker No. 7). You can explore the ancient churches of Teampull Diarmuid and Teampull Mor, the tiny 12th-century Chancel Church and the Church of the Dead near the shore, and near the middle of Inchcleraun the 12th-century Clogás Oratory with its bell tower.

✚ 364 E5 ✉ North of Athlone ℹ Tourist Information Office, Athlone Castle, Athlone, Co. Westmeath ☎ 0906 494630; ▷ 249

ROCK OF DUNAMASE

www.eastcoastmidlands.ie

Rising dramatically from the countryside is the Rock of Dunamase with its ruined castle, built during the mid-12th century by Dermot MacMurrough, King of Leinster, who eloped with Dervorgilla, wife of Tiernan O'Rourke (▷ 255) and later invited the Normans to Ireland. The alliance was cemented when his daughter Aoife married their leader Richard de Clare ('Strongbow'), who turned the fort into a stronghold. It lasted nearly 500 years, until Cromwell's men blew it up in 1650. You can climb the steeply sloping wards to reach the sturdy keep, from where there are views from the Slieve Bloom Mountains to the Wicklow Hills.

✚ 364 F6 ℹ Tourist Information Office, Lawlor Avenue, Portlaoise, Co. Laois ☎ 057 86 21178; ▷ 249

SLIEVE BLOOM MOUNTAINS

www.eastcoastmidlands.ie

Journeying across the waist of Ireland, the gently domed ridges of the Slieve Bloom Mountains will be in view for much of the way. They are a shapely range of hills that assumes mountainous proportions amid the low landscape. They are surprisingly wild, given their small compass, with swathes of upland moor, hidden waterfalls and deep forested valleys. The Slieve Bloom Way loops around their heights.

✚ 364 E6 ℹ Tourist Information Office, Lawlor Avenue, Portlaoise, Co. Laois ☎ 057 86 21178; ▷ 249

STROKESTOWN PARK AND FAMINE MUSEUM

▷ 258–259.

TULLYNALLY CASTLE AND GARDENS

www.tullynallycastle.com

Tullynally Castle has been the seat of the Pakenham family (now Earls of Longford) since 1655, and they still live in the house that was rebuilt during the 19th century into a full-scale Gothic castle. The tour takes in the Great Hall, library, dining room and domestic rooms such as the Victorian kitchen, laundry and drying room. Outside are lovely gardens.

✚ 364 F4 ✉ Castlepollard, Co. Westmeath ☎ 044 96 61159 ⏰ Gardens: Jul–17 Aug daily 2–6; Jun, May, weekends and public holidays only; castle: groups only by appointment 💰 Gardens: adult €6, child (6–16) €3, family €16 🚗 Signposted off R394, 21km (13 miles) north of Mullingar

INFORMATION

www.strokestownpark.ie

✚ 362 E4 ✉ Strokestown, Co. Longford
☎ 071 963 3013 ⊙ Mid-Mar to end
Oct daily 9.30–5.30 ✋ House, Famine
Museum and Gardens individually: adult
€9.50, child (under 13) €4; combined
ticket for all three: adult €14, child (under
13) €7, family €29.50 🚌 Signposted in
Strokestown on N5 between Scramoge
and Tulsk, 23km (14 miles) west of
Longford 🍴 Restaurant

Above *In spite of its size, Strokestown
Park House retains a very personal air*
Below *A photographic exhibit in the
Famine Museum*

INTRODUCTION

Strokestown Park is a fine, predominantly 18th-century Palladian building,
where a conducted tour starts in the entrance hall and continues by way of
the Drawing Room and Library. On the upper floor you view the Lady's and
Gentleman's Bedrooms, the Schoolroom and Nursery, before descending
to the Dining Room and discovering the world of the family's servants in
the Kitchen.

The story of the Mahons is that of many other Anglo-Irish families: a huge
17th-century grant of land by the English crown, the laying out and working of a
vast estate, the building and improvement of the fine mansion, three centuries
of ease and prosperity as bastions of the Ascendancy, followed by a gradual
decline during the 20th century and the eventual sale of house and lands.
The difference here is that the family's attitudes to its tenants are explored
with insight and honesty in the remarkable museum dedicated to the
Great Famine.

The Famine Museum that occupies the old stable block is arranged in a
series of rooms. Room 1 sets the Ascendancy scene, Room 2 shows the
growth of destitution among the Irish poor. Room 3 examines the role of the
potato in 19th-century Ireland and the beginning of the catastrophic potato
blight, while Rooms 4 and 5 look at the relief efforts that were employed during
the Great Famine. There's also a display on eviction and emigration, and some
images and discussion of famines across the world today.

The Walled Garden provides a quiet place to process the stark, terrible
images of famine.

WHAT TO SEE

STROKESTOWN PARK HOUSE: THE PERSONAL TOUCH

What distinguishes Strokestown Park from most of the other mansions open
to the public is the very strong image of successive generations of its owners
that visitors receive. This highly personal atmosphere springs from the fact
that everything you see was chosen and used by the owners over their three
centuries of incumbency, right up until the sale of the property in 1979 by
Olive Pakenham-Mahon, the last of the family to live here, in a poignant
genteel poverty.

Upstairs, the Schoolroom (1930s copybooks 'Please rule your margins all the
same width' neatly laid out on tiny desks) and Playroom (miniature Baby Austin
car, doll's house, rocking horse, dressing-up clothes) mirror the privileged yet
highly regulated life of an Ascendancy child.

FAMINE MUSEUM

As with the house, the impact of the Famine Museum comes from the interplay between the intimate details of the Mahon family's attitudes and behaviour during the Famine, and the wider picture in Ireland and in mainland Britain (▷ 38–39).

The exhibition describes how incoming 17th-century Anglo-Protestants took over most of Ireland. In the 1620s Irish Catholics owned two-thirds of the land, but after the Cromwellian suppressions of the 1650s, only 30 years later, they held less than one-tenth. In those decades one in three of the Catholic population died of famine, disease or massacre, a far higher proportion than died during the Great Famine, and the system of land tenure kept the poor in abject poverty. British political cartoons depicted the Irish tenantry as 'indolent, idle, inclined to do evil, and beyond the pale of civilization', and the Anglo-Irish landlords as feckless drunkards. Such contemptuous attitudes contributed to the disaster of the Great Famine of 1845–49, when the *Phytophthora infestans* fungus wiped out the potato crops on which the people were utterly dependent. The British Government fumbled its relief efforts with clumsiness and callousness; mass evictions and emigration added to the misery.

Against this background moves the story of the Mahons on their estate that stretched for 2,400ha (5,930 acres), and of the evictions carried out by Major Denis Mahon during the Famine. Family papers exhibited include a letter of 7 November 1847 from Mahon's agent proposing the eviction and enforced emigration to America of two-thirds of the local population, and a pathetic letter to the Major from his tenants which asks, 'What must we do?—our families really and truly suffering at present, and we cannot much longer withstand their cries for food.' The letter makes veiled threats of action unless relief is forthcoming; and such action did follow, later that year, when the Major was shot dead. This picture of seigneurial hard-heartedness is balanced by a thoughtful coda by the Major's great-great-grandson, pointing out that landlords like Denis Mahon had insufficient resources and no government grants to help their tenants, and that paying for them to emigrate was preferable to letting them starve.

WALLED GARDENS

In 1997 the refurbished Walled Gardens were opened to the public after years of neglect. You can enjoy roses, wild flowers and the longest herbaceous border in the British Isles, as well as the neat green swards of the lawn tennis court and the croquet lawn, a magnificent lily pond and shady walkways under the trees.

Below left *The intricately worked wrought-iron gates of Strokestown Park*
Below right *The Famine Museum displays many poignant exhibits*

GRAND CANAL, TULLAMORE

The Grand Canal was a typically ambitious Georgian idea—a great water highway across the waist of Ireland, connecting the Irish Sea and the Atlantic Ocean. Adapted for pleasure cruising, the canal now has a new lease of life and its towpath gives mile after mile of level walking through the green farming country and the great bogs of the Midlands. This stroll into the countryside west of Tullamore shows you a couple of fine old castles, some handsome canal architecture, and waterside wildlife in peaceful rural surroundings.

THE WALK
Distance: 8km (5 miles)
Allow: 2 hours
Start/end at: Tullamore Dew Heritage Centre 1:50,000 OSI Discovery Series, map 48 Grid reference 233 225
Parking: Tullamore Dew Heritage Centre

HOW TO GET THERE
Signposted from William Street, Tullamore's main street, just south of Kilbeggan Bridge.

★ The Tullamore Dew Heritage Centre (▷ 266) is housed in the distillery's handsome Victorian bonded warehouse. Here you can shovel barley and fill bottles before a tasting session, and also learn about the town. From the early 19th century onwards, Tullamore was famous for producing fine whiskey, notably Tullamore Dew, and also for Irish Mist, a smooth liqueur blend of whiskey, honey and herbs. These days, however, both Dew and Mist are made elsewhere. The Heritage Centre also contains an exhibition on how Tullamore flourished when the Grand Canal reached the town from Dublin in 1798. Eastwards, Tullamore was linked to the capital, and via the Irish Sea to the ports and markets of the British mainland; westwards to the River Shannon and the Atlantic trade.

Leave the Tullamore Dew Heritage Centre and turn west along the quay and follow the Grand Canal towpath as it heads out of town. You pass Lock 27 and cross the next bridge, Cox's Bridge, to the north bank of the canal. A brown 'Grand Canal Way' fingerpost points you to the left down Rahan Way. Soon the canal passes under a road bridge and then a rail bridge, before emerging around a right bend into open countryside. On your right rises the gaunt ruin of Srah Castle (not open to the public).

① Srah Castle was built in 1588 by John Briscoe, 'an officer of rank and merit who served the Crown in the wars of Queen Elizabeth'. Local stories say that the garrison was armed with a blunderbuss so heavy that one man could hardly lift it. That didn't deter the Irish chief O'Neill from arriving in force at Srah to challenge the aged Briscoe. The English officer recognized O'Neill, which caused the Irishman to spare him. When O'Neill's band rode away, they took with them Briscoe's daughter Eleanor, tied on horseback to one of the men, and she was subsequently forcibly married to O'Neill's nephew Hugh McManus.

Continue along the towpath for 2km (1.25 miles), passing Srah Bridge, until you meet a road which you follow for 0.5km (0.25 miles) to reach the ruin of St. Brigid's Church on the right.

② All that is left of St. Brigid's Church, founded in the late eighth or early ninth century, are two ivy-hung gables and a mass of higgledy-piggledy gravestones. It was destroyed in the late 17th or early 18th century at the start of the Penal era, when Catholics could no longer use their churches but had to celebrate the outlawed Mass at secret locations. During the Great Famine of 1845–49 the churchyard was still in use to bury the dead.

Continue past Lock 29 to Ballycowan Bridge, beyond which stands the ruin of Ballycowan Castle (not open to the public).

③ Tall chimneys and mullioned windows are the most notable features of Ballycowan Castle, a four-floor fortified house built in 1626 by Sir Jasper Herbert on the site of a former stronghold of the O'Melaghlin clan.

Cross Ballycowan Bridge and turn left along the south bank of the Grand Canal for the 4km (2.5 mile) walk back to Tullamore.

WHERE TO EAT
BRIDGE HOUSE INN
Excellent hot lunches.
✉ Bridge Street, Tullamore
☎ 057 93 21704

TULLAMORE DEW HERITAGE CENTRE
(▷ 266) has a coffee shop, restaurant and pub.

PLACE TO VISIT
ST. BRIGID'S CHURCH
✉ Kilbride, north bank of canal 0.75km (0.5 miles) east of Ballycowan Bridge
🕐 Open access 🖐 Free

TOURIST INFORMATION
TULLAMORE
✉ Bury Quay, Tullamore ☎ 057 93 52617

Left to right *A lock gate on the Grand Canal; a boat moored at Tullamore*

FROM ATHLONE TO CLONMACNOISE

This drive takes a wide swing through the contrasting landscapes of the Irish Midlands: green dairying country, and vast expanses of bogland. It includes two very different monastic sites—the little ancient church and holy well at Lemanaghan, and the world-famous monastery at Clonmacnoise with its round tower and many churches overlooking the River Shannon.

THE DRIVE

Distance: 96km (60 miles)
Allow: 2 hours
Start/end at: Athlone

★ Leave Athlone (▷ 249) on the N6 Dublin road, and just outside the town bear right onto the N62, running south for 26km (16 miles) through Ballynahown to Ferbane. Turn left here on the R436 Clara road, and in 5.5km (3.5 miles) you'll reach the signposted site of St. Manchan's Church and Holy Well in Lemanaghan.

❶ Lemanaghan graveyard and the well-restored 12th-century church have yielded many ancient crosses and other carved stones, displayed in an exhibition in the old school across the road. Just east of the church is St. Manchan's Well, set in a keyhole-shaped surround with steps leading down to the water. Religious statuettes, a *bullaun* stone (pre-historic quern), and a guardian ash

tree festooned with prayer rags demonstrates that this holy well is still in use. St. Manchan (dAD664) founded his monastery at Lemanaghan, and is still venerated in these parts. One legend tells how St. Manchan's cow was stolen by rival monks, butchered, put in a pot and boiled. But St. Manchan managed miraculously to restore her to full health (all but one of her thigh bones), and she continued to be an excellent milker.

Opposite the church turn left off the R436 beside the old school, down a winding lane that loops round the back of Lemanaghan. In 457m (500 yards), where the lane bends back on itself, bear left over a hump and turn right along a long, straight bog road. In 1.25km (0.75 miles) turn left on another rough road running north-west out into the heart of the bog.

❷ This is classic machine-cut bog, a wide dark wasteland of raw peat harvested for commercial purposes

by Bord na Móna, the Irish Peat Board (▷ 251). It is interspersed with vast tracts of uncut bog, an expanse of heather and ragged stands of pine trees and scrub, full of glinting pools and wild flowers.

After 1.5km (1 mile) you meet the track of an old industrial railway with a farm beyond. Turn around here and return to the bog road crossroads, where you keep ahead to turn left on the R436 for 3km (2 miles). On the outskirts of Ballycumber turn left by Flynn's Bar along a minor road (signed 'Athlone'). In 0.75km (0.5 miles) you pass a Church of Ireland church with its tall tower on your right; in another 1.25km (0.75 miles) you reach the Catholic church of Boher on the right.

❸ Boher Church displays the 12th-century Shrine of St. Manchan. The box of yew wood contains the bones of the founder of Lemanaghan monastery, and is decorated with gold, bronze and enamelling. Continue along the road for 2km (1.25 miles) to a crossroads. Turn left (signed 'Ferbane') for 5.5km (3.5 miles). At a 'Yield' sign bear left, then right along the N62. At the crossroads turn left (signed 'Endrim'); in 1.25km (0.75 miles) cross the crossroads, and in 1.25km (0.75 miles) bear right and the lane circles Endrim Hill for 3km (2 miles).

❹ The landscape here is also typical of the Irish Midlands: flattish, green fields of dairy cows with plenty of hedges and patches of woodland.

Continue over the crossroads, and in another 2.5km (1.5 miles) bear left to an intersection on the western outskirts of Ferbane. Turn right, and in 1.5km (1 mile) right again (signed 'Glebe Church' and 'Clonmacnoise 14'). Follow the Clonmacnoise signs along this road for 10km (6 miles) to the R444. Turn left and then right to reach the historic monastic site.

❺ Clonmacnoise (▷ 252–255) was one of the most important monasteries in Europe in the sixth century, but it suffered from Viking raids. The ruins show its size.

Return to the R444, where you bear left; in 0.75km (0.5 miles) turn left again onto the 'Pilgrim's Road' and follow this minor road for 11km (7 miles) to Ballynahown. Turn left on the N62 to return to Athlone.

WHERE TO EAT
LEFT BANK BISTRO
Left Bank Bistro is one of the best

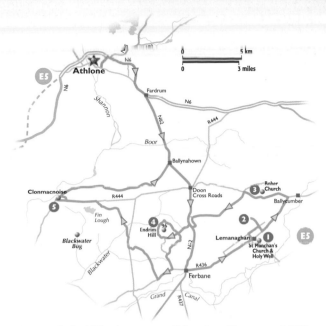

restaurants in the Midlands.
✉ Fry Place, Athlone ☎ 090 649 4446

HINEY'S
A cheerful family-run eating pub.
✉ Main Street, Ferbane ☎ 090 645 4344

CLONMACNOISE
Coffee shop.
✉ On R444, signposted from N62, 13km (8 miles) south of Athlone ☎ 090 96 74195

PLACES TO VISIT
ST. MANCHAN'S CHURCH AND HOLY WELL
✉ Lemanaghan on the R436, 5.5km (3.5 miles) east of Ferbane ⊙ Open access ✋ Free

ST. MANCHAN'S SHRINE IN BOHER CHURCH
✉ On the country road between

Ballycumber and Doon crossroads (N62), 3km (2 miles) west of Ballycumber
⊙ During daylight hours ✋ Free

TOURIST INFORMATION
ATHLONE
✉ Civic offices, Church Street ☎ 090 649 4630 ⊙ Apr–end Oct daily 9.30–5.30

CLONMACNOISE
✉ Shannonbridge ☎ 090 967 4159
⊙ For hours ▷ 253

Opposite *Athlone Castle*
Below left *Blackwater Bog*
Below *St. Finghin's church and round tower*

ATHLONE

ADVENTURE VIKING CRUISE

www.vikingtoursireland.com

Dress up in full Viking gear and cruise the waters of the Shannon in a Viking longship, from The Strand in Athlone upriver into Lough Ree, or downstream to Clonmacnoise.
✉ 7 St. Mary's Place, Athlone, Co. Westmeath ☎ 086 262 1136 🕐 Apr–end Oct daily, telephone for times 💰 Lough Ree cruise: adult €12, child €10, family €40; Clonmacnoise cruise: adult €20, child €15, family €60

ATHLONE CRYSTAL AND GIFT GALLERY

Master craftsman Eddie Halligan established Athlone Crystal in 1988 in the heart of Athlone town. He is available to work with the customer on specially commissioned pieces according to their wishes. The Gallery stocks a wide range of crystal and other giftware.
✉ St. Mary's Square, Athlone, Co. Westmeath ☎ 090 647 7774 🕐 Mon–Sat 10–6

ATHLONE LITTLE THEATRE CO. LTD

www.athlonelittletheatre.ie

This popular theatre was founded in 1936 and started staging productions in St. Mary's Little Hall in 1965. It is an intimate space seating an audience of only 100. The company produces around six performances a year and past productions have included Mike Leigh's *Abigail's Party* and *Rumours* by Neil Simon. Check the website for details of current productions.
✉ St. Mary's Place, Athlone, Co. Westmeath ☎ 090 647 4324 🕐 Tickets available from 7pm from three nights in advance of any production

ATHLONE SPORTS CENTRE

www.athlonesportscentre.ie

The best-equipped sports complex in the region, with a big swimming pool, children's pool, state-of-the-art gym, Jacuzzi and sauna. There are Over-50s and Adults-Only sessions, an activity club for children and a childcare facility.

✉ Ballymahon Road, Athlone, Co. Westmeath ☎ 090 647 0975 🕐 Daily, Athlone Sports Academy (supervised indoor and outdoor sports and games): Sat 3–5 💰 Swim: adult €6.50, child €3.50. Gym €7.50; gym-and-swim: €9. Over 50s sessions telephone for details

DEAN CROWE THEATRE & ARTS CENTRE

www.deancrowetheatre.com

There's plenty of different entertainment for all ages staged at the Dean Crowe Theatre, one of Ireland's largest provincial theatres. The All-Ireland Drama Festival is held here annually for nine days in May, which also includes poetry, puppetry, exhibitions and dance. The theatre has been a favourite venue for dancing and entertainment since its days as the church hall in the 1950s. Classes, workshops and exhibitions relating to the arts are also held at the theatre.
✉ Chapel Street, Athlone, Co. Westmeath ☎ 090 649 2129 🕐 Box office: Mon–Fri 11–3 💰 Tickets various prices

HODSON BAY WATER SPORTS CENTRE

Fishing, powerboat driving, boat handling, boardsailing and other water sports are available at the marina here. There's a golf club too.

✉ Hodson Bay, Lough Ree, Co. Westmeath ☎ 1890 704090 ◷ Daily ✋ Varies 🚌 Dublin–Galway route 🚗 8km (5 miles) north of Athlone via N6 Galway road and N61

PASSIONFRUIT THEATRE

www.passionfruittheatre.com
This company was founded in 2005 by Irish playwright and novelist Joe Ducke, Old Vic graduate Emily Campbell and lighting designer Emma Lohan. Their first productions were on tour but in March 2008 their theatre in Northgate Street finally opened. It is a small, intimate space with seating for just 60 people. Playwright Eugene O'Brien performed on the opening night. Music will be a prominent feature at the theatre with Irish performers including Ciaran Flynn, Eleanor McEvoy and Nicole Maguire. Check the website for different musical styles and performers, and for future productions.

✉ 9 Northgate Street, Athlone, Co. Westmeath ☎ 087 410 5901 ◷ Telephone for times and prices

TICKETY BOO!

Parents can relax for a couple of hours with a cup of coffee while the kids go wild with slides, climbing frames, a bouncy castle and a ball-pool.

✉ Unit 6, Monksland Business Park, Tuam Road, Athlone, Co. Westmeath ☎ 090 644 4612 ◷ Mon–Thu 10–6, Fri, Sat 10–7, Sun 12–6 ✋ €8 (family rates available) ⛺

BALLYNAHOWN
CELTIC ROOTS STUDIO

www.celticroots.ie
A unique gallery and shop devoted to the local bogwood, which has lain hidden in the Irish bogs for more than 4,000 years. The studio produces superb sculptured items from the bogwood—oak, yew and pine— in a multitude of forms. Choose

from birds, human forms, nature and the sea and Celtic designs. Also for sale are gifts such as lamps, clocks, bottle openers and much more, all incorporating bogwood. This is a special place to buy that unique gift.

✉ The Old School House, Ballinahown, Athlone, Co. Westmeath ☎ 090 643 0404 ◷ Mon–Fri 10–6, Sat 11–6

BANAGHER
SHANNON ADVENTURE CANOEING HOLIDAYS

www.iol.ie/~advcanoe/index.html
Being the master of your own craft is by far the best way to explore the Shannon and its lakes. Renting a two-person canoe gives you that freedom.

✉ The Marina, Banagher, Co. Offaly ☎ 057 91 51411 ◷ Mar–end Oct daily 9–5 ✋ From €15 hourly, €60 day, €140 weekend, €120 week (€170 with camping equipment)

COOLRAIN
LAOIS ANGLING CENTRE

www.laoisanglingcentre.ie
For all your angling needs, the Laois Angling Centre is based at Clonoghil House in the heart of the countryside. The four tranquil lakes are surrounded by woodland and are regularly stocked with fish—brown and rainbow trout, bream and carp. The centre caters for all abilities, both the beginner and the expert are welcome, and you can enjoy a half-day or full-day's fishing.

Other facilities at the Centre include a nature trail, a picnic area and barbecue, refreshments and equipment rental.

✉ Clonoghil House, Coolrain, Portaloise, Co. Laois ☎ 057 873 5091/087 996 2864 ◷ Call for details

DRUM
GLENDEER OPEN FARM

www.glendeer.com
This family farm has cows, sheep, chickens, ostriches, emus, deer, peacocks and rabbits. Some of these can be stroked and cuddled. There is a special Christmas re-creation of 'Lapland'.

✉ Drum, Co. Westmeath ☎ 090 643 7147

◷ Easter–end Sep Mon–Sat 11–6, Sun 12–6; Ireland Lapland: Dec Mon–Fri 5–8pm, Sat, Sun 3–8pm ✋ Farm: adult €7; Lapland (Dec) including gift from Santa, child €15, adult €7 🚗 Off N6, 6.5km (4 miles) west of Athlone ▣

EDENDERRY
IRISH PARACHUTE CLUB

www.skydive.ie
Experience the ultimate adrenalin thrill, if you have the nerve. An hour's instruction is followed by the jump from a plane attached to an instructor.

✉ Clonbullogue Airfield, near Edenderry, Co. Offaly ☎ 046 973 0103 ◷ Sat, Sun and Bank Holidays dawn–dusk; also midweek in summer ✋ Tandem or solo jump €320 🚗 On R401, 11km (7 miles) south of Edenderry

KILBEGGAN
KILBEGGAN RACE COURSE

Irish National Hunt meetings are held on this nine-furlong track. The punters of Offaly and Westmeath turn out in force, and it's a great occasion.

✉ Kilbeggan, Co. Westmeath ☎ 057 93 32176 ✋ Adult from €15, child (under 14) free ▣

LOUGH ENNELL
LILLIPUT ADVENTURE CENTRE

www.lilliputadventure.com
Children and young adults get their thrills under careful supervision at this activity centre. Day activities might include kayaking, abseiling, rock climbing, canoeing, pier jumping, gorge walking, orienteering, archery, hill walking and even a manhunt! There are residential courses, too.

✉ Lilliput House, Lough Ennell, Mullingar, Co. Westmeath ☎ 044 92 26789 ◷ Day and residential courses ✋ Daily fee: adult €50 (with lunch), under 18 €37.50 (with lunch) 🚗 Follow signs from R390 and R391, 8km (5 miles) southwest of Mullingar ▣

Opposite *Children having a canoe lessson*

LILLIPUT BOAT HIRE

Lough Ennell is one of the Midlands' best fishing lakes, with plentiful trout, pike and perch as well as many other species. Rent a boat, either with an engine or with oars, and set out to see what luck you'll have. Fishing gear can be rented. ✉ Lilliput House, Lough Ennell, Mullingar Co. Westmeath ☎ 087 649 2866 ⏰ Mar–Oct, daily—telephone in advance for times ✋ Boat rental: €50 per day for boat with engine; €30 per day for boat without engine 🚗 8km (5 miles) southwest of Mullingar off N52 💻

MULLINGAR

GENESIS GIFT GALLERY

Here you can buy the collectable range of hand-crafted copper figurines produced by Genesis Fine Arts. The Gift Gallery is a great place to buy other quality Irish products such as Waterford crystal, Belleek china, Galway crystal, and Newbridge Silverware's jewellery and cutlery. Between Mullingar and Kinnegad. ✉ The Downs, Mullingar, Co. Westmeath ☎ 044 44948 ⏰ Mon–Fri 9.30–6, Sat 10–6 🚗 5km (3.5 miles) from Mullingar on N4 Dublin road

IRISH FARM-SAFARI PARK

www.farmsafari.com
An all-weather fun and educational facility, where enthusiastic owner Greg takes visitors on a safari tour in his bus. Animals include: red deer, donkies, emus, llamas, pot belly pigs and more. There are also discovery walking trails, a visitor centre, souvenirs and farmers' market shop. ✉ Churchtown, Mullingar, Co. Westmeath ☎ 044 935 5104 ⏰ By arrangement, call in advance; closed Feb, Oct, Nov ✋ Adult €12.50, child €7.50

MULLINGAR ARTS CENTRE

www.mullingarartscentre.ie
Mullingar Arts Centre presents a wide variety of entertainment. There are regular exhibitions in its Art Gallery, art workshops, and a whole range of performance events that include clubbing dance nights, early music, plays, comedy, party nights and films. ✉ Mount Street, Mullingar, Co. Westmeath ☎ 044 93 47777 ⏰ Box office: Mon–Fri 9.30–9.30, Sat 10–6 ✋ Varies depending on performance 💻

MULLINGAR GOLF CLUB

www.mullingargolfclub.com
The golf club is located at Belvedere just to the south of Mullingar town and was designed in 1935 by Scotsman James Braid. The course is 6,458 yards and a classic par 72, a pleasurable testing course set among undulating parkland and woodland. The second hole is considered one of the toughest in Irish golf and the club hosts important amateur events. Visitors are welcome. ✉ Belvedere, Mullingar, Co. Westmeath ☎ 093 41499 ⏰ Green fees: Mon–Fri €40, Sat–Sun and public holidays €45

MULLINGAR GREYHOUND STADIUM

www.mullingargreyhoundstadium.ie
The people of the Midlands adore their greyhound racing, and the Mullingar stadium makes a great night out. The emphasis here is on family fun and it's packed with humorous, knowledgeable punters. ✉ Ballinderry, Mullingar, Co. Westmeath ☎ 044 93 48348 ⏰ Racing on Thu and Sat, doors open 6.30pm, racing starts at 8 ✋ Adult €10, child €5 💻 Restaurant, food stands, bars

THE STABLES

www.stableslive.com
Great evenings happen out of the blue at this club. There's a very eclectic bill—everything from rock and local cover bands to indie outfits, cheesy old handbag nights and more cutting-edge hip-hop. ✉ Yukon Bar, Dominic Street, Mullingar, Co. Westmeath ☎ 044 93 40251 ⏰ Daily from around 9 pm ✋ From €10

PORTLAOISE

KAVANAGH'S COMEDY CLUB

www.kavanaghscomedyclub.com
It's surprising to find one of the most established comedy clubs in Ireland, in fact the third longest running club in Ireland, in this small town in the Midlands, but it features some high-profile acts—Ardal O'Hanlon has performed here—and is planning to expand in 2008. The pub also plays host to some good

traditional Irish bands and soloists. Check the website or telephone to find out what's on.

✉ 28 Main Street, Portlaoise, Co. Laois ☎ 057 862 1744 🕓 Usual pub opening times, comedy club times vary

SHANNONBRIDGE
CLONMACNOISE & WEST OFFALY RAILWAY

Take a 9km (5.5-mile) train ride with a difference through the bogs of Offaly. You will be guided through this unusual landscape and learn about the flora and fauna and its 6,000-year-old bog oaks. Check in advance for individual times, special trains and prices.

✉ Bord na Móna Blackwater Works, Shannonbridge, Co. Offaly ☎ 090 967 4450 🕓 Apr–early Oct

TULLAMORE
TULLAMORE DEW HERITAGE CENTRE

www.tullamoredew.com

Take a tour in the original 1897 warehouse and learn all about the story of Tullamore Dew Whiskey and the various stages of production from malting to the finished whiskey in the oak barrel. Carry on through the interesting section devoted to the Tullamore Irish Mist Liqueur where there is a community of 70,000 live bees busily collecting nectar for the queen of the hive. There is also a section devoted to the growth of Tullamore town. Don't forget your complimentary glass at the end of the tour.

✉ Bury Quay, Tullamore, Co. Offaly ☎ 057 932 5015 🕓 May–end Sep Mon–Sat 9–6, Sun 12–5; Oct–end Apr Mon–Sat 10–5, Sun 12–5 💷 Tour: €6 for self-guided, €7 guided plus complimentary glass of whiskey

Opposite Hire a boat from somewhere like Lilliput Boat Hire and explore the lakes
Above Traditional Irish music can be heard at festivals and in pubs

FESTIVALS AND EVENTS

APRIL/MAY
FAIR OF BALLYCUMBER

A weekend festival of music and fun and an agricultural show.

✉ Ballycumber, Co. Offaly ☎ 057 93 52617 🕓 Late April/early May

MAY–JUNE
GOLDSMITH SUMMER SCHOOL

Talks, tours and song to commemorate poet Oliver Goldsmith.

✉ Ballymahon, Co. Longford ☎ 086 829 4093 🕓 Late May–early June

JULY
BOYLE ARTS FESTIVAL

www.boylearts.com

Features jazz, world music, art and storytelling.

✉ Boyle, Co. Roscommon ☎ 071 966 3085 🕓 Late July

JULY–AUGUST
O'CAROLAN INTERNATIONAL HARP AND TRADITIONAL MUSIC FESTIVAL

www.ocarolanharpfestival.ie

Song, music, concerts and *ceilidhs*, and a harping competition to honour harper Turlough O'Carolan.

✉ Keadue, Co. Roscommon ☎ 071 964 7204 🕓 End July–early August

AUGUST
NATIONAL TRACTION ENGINE STEAM RALLY

www.irishsteam.ie

The behemoths of steam go through their paces in exhibitions of stone crushing, log hauling and threshing. Also tractors, fairground organs and sheepdog trials.

✉ Stradbally, Co. Laois ☎ 0502 41795 🕓 Early August

SEPTEMBER
JOHNNY KEENAN BANJO BLUEGRASS FESTIVAL

www.johnnykeenan.com

Over four days, this celebration of traditional Irish and Bluegrass music features jamming sessions, busking and concerts on the streets, in pubs and at other venues.

✉ Longford, Co. Longford ☎ 087 281 7825 🕓 Mid-Sep

OCTOBER
AISLING CHILDREN'S FESTIVAL

A week-long event introducing children to music, dance and drama through workshops and theatre performances at various venues throughout the town.

✉ Longford, Co. Longford ☎ 043 47455 🕓 Mid-October

NOVEMBER
BOYLE CHRISTMAS CRAFT FAIR

www.kinghouse.ie

Crafts of all kinds are sold in the striking surroundings of Kings House, with seasonal refreshments.

✉ Boyle, Co. Roscommon ☎ 071 966 3242 🕓 Late November

EATING

PRICES AND SYMBOLS

The restaurants are listed alphabetically within each town. The prices given are the average for a two-course lunch (L) and a three-course dinner (D) for one person, without drinks. The wine price given is for the least expensive bottle.

For a key to the symbols, ▷ 2

ATHLONE

L'ESCALE RESTAURANT

www.hodsonbayhotel.com
Dishes in the hotel's L'Escale restaurant use the finest produce, with fresh fish delivered daily. Head chef Kevin Ward runs a tight ship. The standard and presentation of the food, especially the fresh lobster, available each day, is impressive.
✉ Hodson Bay Hotel, Hodson Bay, Athlone, Co. Westmeath ☎ 090 644 2000 ⏰ Daily 12.30–2.30, 7–9.15
🖐 L €29, D €42, Wine €18.75
🚘 From Athlone take the N61 8km

(5 miles) towards Roscommon and turn right to Lough Rea

THE LEFTBANK BISTRO

www.leftbankbistro.com
Close to Athlone Lock on the River Shannon, this is a stylish restaurant within an old building. The Irish chef, Michael Durr, provides an eclectic choice of imaginative dishes originating from around the world, such as Thai spiced chicken and baked salmon on smoked bacon mash with basil oil.
✉ Fry Place, Athlone, Co. Westmeath
☎ 090 649 4446 ⏰ Tue–Sat 10.30–9.30
🖐 L €15, D €25, Wine €20

BIRR

SPINNER'S TOWNHOUSE

www.spinnerstownhouse.com
Situated near Birr Castle in a house that maintains many of its Georgian features, Spinner's Townhouse has a good varied menu that uses local,

seasonal ingredients. Food is served in the dining room and also in the lobby, drawing room or the courtyard in fine weather. An early bird menu is available.
✉ Castle Street, Birr, Co. Offaly ☎ 057 912 1673 ⏰ Mon, Wed, Thu 6.30–9, Fri, Sat 6.30–10, Sun 12.30–2.30, 6.30–9
🖐 L €18, D €30, Wine €18

GLASSAN

GROGAN'S PUB

Just 10km (6 miles) north of Athlone on the N55, Glassan is in the heart of Oliver Goldsmith country. This ancient pub, established in 1750, serves excellent bar food year-round, including succulent steaks and delicious seafood. There's also traditional Irish music performed at Grogan's every Wednesday and Sunday evening.
✉ Glassan, Co. Westmeath ☎ 090 648 5158 ⏰ Mon–Sat 12–9, Sun 1–8
🖐 L €15, D €30, Wine €14.95

WINEPORT LODGE

www.wineport.ie

Customers can arrive by land or water and dine on the deck overlooking Lough Rea or in the attractive dining room. Chef Feargal O'Donnell serves innovative food, made with the best local produce. The menu changes regularly and there is a daily special. A good selection of desserts and a comprehensive wine list complement the excellent main meals. Service is friendly and the setting is superb, making this a very relaxing place to dine. Light snacks only are available at lunchtime.

✉ Glassan, Co. Westmeath ☎ 090 6439010 ⏰ Daily 6–10, Sun lunch 3–4 ✋ L €45, D €50, Wine €30 🚌 Take N55 north of Athlone for 9km (6 miles); turn left at the Dog and Duck pub. Wineport Lodge is about 2km (1.25 miles) on the left-hand side

LONGFORD

EDWARD J. VALENTINE

www.edwardjvalentine.com

This distinctive building on Main Street houses a great pub. Though it's only been open since 1990, it has the furnishings and the ambience of a traditional town pub. It serves standard pub fare for lunch, such as steak burgers, cajun chicken wraps, and fish and chips, which are well cooked and in generous portions.

✉ 65–66 Main Street, Longford, Co. Longford ☎ 043 45509 or 043 48704 ⏰ Mon–Thu 10.30am–11.30pm, Fri–Sat 10.30am–12.30am, Sun 12.30pm–11pm ✋ L €10, Wine €4.75 (only quarter bottles available)

MULLINGAR

BELFRY RESTAURANT

www.belfryrestaurant.com

Housed in a magnificently converted church, the Belfry has a stylish new mezzanine bar. Top-quality local produce, including Mullingar beef and lamb and organic vegetables, are crafted into imaginatively presented traditional and modern dishes. Reservations are advised.

✉ Ballynegall, Mullingar, Co. Westmeath ☎ 044 93 42488 ⏰ Wed–Sat 12.30–2, 6–10, Sun 1–4 ✋ L €15, D €30, Wine €20

🚌 6km (4 miles) north of Mullingar on the R384 Castlepollard road

PORTLAOISE

TREACY'S PUB

Dating from 1780, this pub offers renowned hospitality. In the shadow of the Rock of Dunamaise, it's about as authentic as you will find—a lovely setting in which to enjoy the traditional Irish cooking. At weekends, you can also join in the occasional singalong sessions in the bar.

✉ The Heath, Portlaoise, Co. Laois ☎ 057 86 46539 ⏰ Mon–Fri 7am–9.45pm, Sat 7am–8.45pm, Sun 12–8.45 ✋ L €15, D €25, Wine €15.75 🚌 4.5km (3 miles) east of Portlaoise on the N80 Stradbally road

ROSCOMMON

DURKINS

www.durkins.org

Durkin's is a large pub with two bars, each with a traditional counter and wooden bar stools and warmed by an open fire. The restaurant serves a selection of Irish and international cuisine.

✉ The Square, Ballaghaderreen, Co. Roscommon ☎ 094 986 0305 ⏰ Mon–Sat 10–9 (Durkins Bar also 9.30pm–2am), Sun 12.30–2 ✋ L€19, D €26, Wine €15 🚌 In the middle of town

THE MANSE RESTAURANT

www.gleesonstownhouse.com

Gleeson's Townhouse Hotel is on Roscommon's historic town square, right next to the museum, and is a convenient place to drop in for a snack in the café, or alternatively a full meal in the formal restaurant. The owners are committed to sourcing quality-assured meats, poultry, fish and farm vegetables. With Irish and European influences, the menu includes seafood chowder, duck leg confit, Roscommon rack of lamb or After Eight cheesecake and pistachio ice cream for desert.

✉ Gleeson's Townhouse, Market Square, Roscommon, Co. Roscommon ☎ 090 662 6954 ⏰ Daily 12.30–2.30, 6.30–9.30 ✋ L €20, D €35, Wine €18

TARMONBARRY

KEENAN'S

www.keenans.ie

In the heart of the village, on the banks of the River Shannon, Keenan's is a lovely family-run traditional pub. You can get just a sandwich here, or choose from the varied menu (available in the bar or the restaurant). Seafood chowder is a signature dish. For dessert, try the brown bread, Guinness and honeycomb ice cream.

✉ Tarmonbarry, Co. Roscommon ☎ 043 26052 ⏰ Mon–Sat 12.30–8.30 ✋ L €25, D €30, Wine €19

Opposite *Athlone's colourful Leftbank Bistro, on the River Shannon*
Below *Dining alfresco at Glasson's Wineport Lodge*

STAYING

PRICES AND SYMBOLS

Prices are for a double room for one night. Breakfast is included unless noted otherwise. All the hotels listed accept credit cards unless otherwise stated. Note that rates vary widely throughout the year.

For a key to the symbols, ▷ 2.

ABBEYLEIX

ABBEYLEIX MANOR HOTEL

www.abbeyleixmanorhotel.com
The Abbeyleix Manor Hotel is to the south of the Georgian town of Abbeyleix. Bedrooms at this modern establishment are spacious and stylishly furnished to the high standard that is evident throughout the hotel. Food is served all day in the bar.

✉ Cork Road, Abbeyleix, Co. Laois ☎ 057 87 3011 ⊗ Closed 25 Dec ✋ Double from €110 ⓘ 46 🚘 On the N8 just south of Abbeyleix

ATHLONE

HODSON BAY HOTEL

www.hodsonbayhotel.com
This modern hotel is near the River Shannon and on the shore of Lough Rea. With a golf course to the rear and a marina to the front, most of the bedrooms have excellent views. Public areas include a sun lounge, two restaurants and a bar.

✉ Hodson Bay, Athlone, Co. Westmeath ☎ 090 648 0500 ✋ Double from €198 ⓘ 182 🏊 Indoor 🍴 🚘 From Athlone take the N61 8km (5 miles) towards Roscommon and then turn right to Lough Rea

RIVERVIEW HOUSE

www.riverviewhousebandb.com
Modern accommodation is provided here in attractively decorated bedrooms. There's a comfortable lounge and a breakfast room that opens on to the garden. Nearby Lough Ree attracts anglers.

✉ Galway Road, Summerhill, Athlone, Co. Westmeath ☎ 090 649 4532 ⊗ Closed 18 Dec–1 Mar ✋ Double €70 ⓘ 4 🚘 On N6, 1.5km (0.9 miles) west of town

SHAMROCK LODGE COUNTRY HOUSE HOTEL

www.shamrocklodgehotel.ie
Located in the historic town of Athlone, this hotel offers tasteful surroundings and good hospitality. The hotel provides every modern facility, while retaining a country-house atmosphere. There are spacious, well-equipped bedrooms, some with balconies. The Iona bar overlooks the gardens, while the An Luain Restaurant uses the best of local produce.

✉ Clonown Road, Athlone, Co. Westmeath ☎ 0906 492601 ✋ Double from €150 ⓘ 40, 12 family suites 🚘 Close to the town centre on the west side of the River Shannon

BALLINLOUGH
WHITEHOUSE HOTEL
www.white-house-hotel.com

A comfortable and appealing hotel with spacious bedrooms. Facilities include a restaurant, bars and a well-equipped conference/ banqueting suite. The hotel is convenient for Lough O'Flynn and Knock Airport.

✉ Ballinlough, Co. Roscommon ☎ 094 96 40112 ⊙ Closed 25 Dec ✋ Double €99–€125 ① 19 ⚅ 🚍 Between Castlerea and Ballyhaunis

BIRR
COUNTY ARMS HOTEL
www.countyarmshotel.com

This fine Georgian house has comfortable bedrooms overlooking the walled Victorian gardens, which supply fruit, vegetables and herbs to the hotel kitchens. There is a choice of two restaurants, a bar and a lounge.

✉ Birr, Co. Offaly ☎ 057 91 20791 ✋ Double from €140 ① 80 ⚅ ⛲ 🚍 Take N62 north to Birr, the hotel is on the right, just before the church

DRUMLISH
LONGFORD COUNTRY HOUSE
www.longfordcountryhouse.com

An hospitable, Tudor-style house where the parlour has a wrought-iron stairway to the library loft, as well as a sitting room with turf fire. Other facilities include a games room and pitch-and-putt course. Self-catering cottages are also available.

✉ Drumlish, Co. Longford ☎ 043 23320 ✋ Double €70–€150 ① 6 🚍 From the second roundabout (traffic circle) of the N4 Longford bypass, take the R194 north for 5km (3 miles). After the Old Forge pub, turn left at the crossroads and it's the second house on the right

HORSELEAP
WOODLANDS FARM
In this delightful farmhouse set in rolling countryside, the sitting and dining rooms are relaxing, and tea and coffee are available at all times.

Right *The Hodson Bay Hotel provides up-to-date accommodation*
Opposite *Birr Castle*

✉ Streamstown, Horseleap, Co. Westmeath ☎ 044 92 26414 ✋ Double from €70 ① 0 ✋ Take the N6 through Kilbegan to Horseleap, turn right at the filling station, and the farm is 4km (2.5 miles) farther on

MULLINGAR
HILLTOP COUNTRY HOUSE
www.hilltopcountryhouse.com

This is a lovely country house in glorious gardens. Public areas and bedrooms are well furnished and the breakfast menu is extensive. No children under 15 years.

✉ Delvin Road, Rathconnell, Mullingar, Co. Westmeath ☎ 044 93 48958 ⊙ Closed Dec–end Feb ✋ Double €80 ① 5 🚍 From the Mullingar bypass (N4) take the N52 towards Delvin. Hilltop sign is a short drive from the exit roundabout (traffic circle)

PORTLAOISE
IVYLEIGH HOUSE
www.ivyleigh.com

This Georgian town house, just off the main street and close to the railway station, is an oasis of calm and luxury. The elegant drawing rooms are complemented by a fine dining room where breakfast is served. No children under 8 years.

✉ Bank Place, Church Street, Portlaoise, Co. Laois ☎ 057 86 22081 ⊙ Closed 20 Dec–4 Jan ✋ Double from €125 ① 6 🚍 Opposite the multi-level parking in the middle of town

O'SULLIVAN
This period semi-detached house on the outskirts of town is family run, and has a nice home-from-home atmosphere. Bedrooms are comfortable and all have private bathrooms. Secure parking is provided.

✉ 8 Kelly Ville Park, Portlaoise, Co. Laois ☎ 057 86 22774 ✋ Double €90–€96 ① 6 🚍 Opposite the County Hall parking

ROSCOMMON
ABBEY HOTEL
www.abbeyhotel.ie

Set in its own grounds just outside Roscommon, this manor house has bedrooms individually decorated, with a choice of period style rooms in the original part of the house. Contemporary rooms are in the newer wing.

✉ Galway Road, Roscommon, Co. Roscommon ☎ 090 662 6240 ✋ Double €110–€280 ① 50 ⚅ Indoor 🏊 🚍 In Roscommon town, take the Galway Road and the hotel is the first left after the library

STRADBALLY
TULLAMOY HOUSE
This pleasant limestone farmhouse was built in 1871, and is just south of Stradbally on the Carlow Road. Caroline and Pat Farrell and their children welcome guests and offer tea and home baking, served beside the fire in the sitting room. Attractively decorated bedrooms are comfortably furnished. Credit cards are not accepted.

✉ Stradbally, Co. Laois ☎ 059 862 7111 ⊙ Closed Nov–end Feb ✋ Double from €80 ① 3 🚍 Just off N80, 5km (3 miles) south of Stradbally

NORTHERN IRELAND

Despite the troubles of its recent past, Northern Ireland, with its regenerated capital Belfast, has much to offer the visitor. Northern Ireland consists of six of the nine counties of the province of Ulster. From capital to coast, from scenic mountains to pretty market towns, this accessible and compact country is a region of contrasts.

The best way to start a visit to Belfast is to take a sightseeing bus tour of the city. There are still grim reminders of its troublesome past, especially seen through the walls, gates and political murals of north and west Belfast, but rejuvenation is seeing the city develop its unique character with good shopping, excellent bars and restaurants, award-winning cultural venues and spruced-up impressive 19th-century architecture. As part of the city's major renovation plan Donegall Square, at the heart of the city, has undergone a facelift. The world's most famous ocean liner, the *Titanic*, was built in Belfast and the shipyards and redeveloped waterfront are now being transformed as the Titanic Quarter.

Beyond Belfast other towns in the province include Londonderry (known locally as Derry) where you can walk around the splendid city walls; Georgian Armagh with its two cathedrals; Lisburn, Its wealth built on the linen industry and Ballycastle, a pleasant old-fashioned seaside resort. For a unique experience visit the Ulster American Folk Park just outside Omagh with its original buildings and story of immigration across the Atlantic.

Leaving the towns and cities behind most visitors head north to the World Heritage Site of the Giant's Causeway with its fascinating 40,000 interlocking stones. For spectacular scenery without the crowds, the Antrim coast offers beautiful unspoiled beaches. The Fermanagh Lakelands and Northern Ireland's loughs are well worth visiting; Strangford, with some of the best birdwatching in the British Isles, and Erne, with its ancient buildings and fascinating cruises. Away from the water the majestic mountains of Mourne and Sperrin provide excellent walking and touring opportunities.

ARDBOE OLD CROSS

www.cookstown.gov.uk

On the flat western shore of Lough Neagh (▷ 296), the magnificent Ardboe Old Cross, carved in the ninth or tenth century, stands 5.5m (18.5ft) tall. The shaft and head are heavily carved with biblical scenes, but weathering has blurred the finer details. The cross suffered at the hands of pilgrims, too, especially those making their final prayers before emigrating, who would take a fragment for good luck.

The carvings on the east and south faces are of Old Testament scenes, while the west face deals with New Testament themes. Look on the east side for Adam and Eve under a spreading Tree of Knowledge, Abraham about to sacrifice Isaac and Shadrach, Meshach and Abednego in the Fiery Furnace. On the south is Cain dealing brother Abel a thump with a flail, Samson and his lion and a cramped David and Goliath. The west has the Adoration, the miracles of the wine and water at Cana and the loaves and fishes at Galilee, and Christ's entry into Jerusalem on a smartly stepping donkey. The Passion occupies the west face of the cross head, while the east depicts the Last Judgement.

Behind the cross stands a beech tree, pierced by thousands of coins pushed into its trunk by supplicants hoping to leave their troubles behind—or transfer them to anyone who would steal the coin. Sadly, the metal of the coins has gradually poisoned the tree. Beyond the tree is the ruin of a 17th-century church, on the site of a monastery established in the sixth century by St. Colman Muchaidhe. Legend has it that when the workers building it became faint from lack of food, the saint sent his cow to walk across the lake and bring them milk. It is also said, somewhat at odds with chronology, that the left-over milk was mixed

with the mortar used to build the High Cross, ensuring its survival over the centuries and naming it: *Ard Bo* means 'the hill of the cow'.

🕂 363 G2 🔟 Open access 🔟 Free
🛈 Tourist Information Office, The Burnavon, Burn Road, Cookstown, Co. Tyrone, BT80 8DN ☎ 028 8676 9949 🕔 Jul–end Sep Mon–Sat 9–5, Sun 2–4; Oct–end Jun Mon–Sat 9–5 🚌 Signposted from Newport Trench on B73, 16km (10 miles) east of Cookstown

ARDRESS HOUSE

www.ntni.org.uk

Dublin architect George Ensor acquired Ardress by marriage in 1760 and embarked on a project to transform the 17th-century farmhouse into a neoclassical country house. Ensor added a new wing, a matching mock wing (with false windows) on the other side, and an imposing frontage entered through a pedimented porch. Yet you can still see the original farmhouse roof, peeping over the curly gables and urns of the Georgian extension. Inside, there's stucco work in the drawing room, and fine Chippendale furniture and Waterford crystal. Outside, it's all geared towards family fun. The cobbled 18th-century farmyard attached to the house has a collection of agricultural tools and a variety of farm animals—goats, ducks, hens, pigs and ponies—and there's a children's play area. The walled garden has old Irish roses, and the orchard has old Irish apple varieties. Farther afield, footpaths lead through the woods and along the Tall river.

🕂 363 G3 ✉ 64 Ardress Road, Portadown, Co. Armagh, BT62 1SQ ☎ 028 8778 4753 🕔 Mid-Mar to end Sep Sat–Sun 2–6 🔟 Adult £4.40, child (under 18) £2.20 (NT members free) 🚌 Signposted on B28 between Portadown and Charlemont

ARDS PENINSULA

▷ 276–277.

THE ARGORY

www.ntni.org.uk

Time at The Argory is frozen in the year 1906. This handsome country house in its 130ha (320 acres) by the River Blackwater presents a picture of a well-to-do Anglo-Irish home immediately before Independence. Built in 1824 by Walter McGeogh, it is entered through a fine wide portico, into the hall with its massive cast-iron stove, and visitors are plunged into the Edwardian era. Photographs and portraits hang on the walls of the study, dining room and billiard room. The Steinway grand piano stands in the drawing room. Up the curved staircase is a barrel organ that was an original fixture of the house. It is played once a month (telephone for dates). There is no electricity, and lamps diffuse the soft yellow light of acetylene gas from the plant installed in the stables in 1906. Inspect the gas plant and the horse carriages in the stable yard, and then go on through the formal gardens and along the riverbank footpaths.

🕂 363 G3 ✉ 144 Derrycaw Road, Moy, Dungannon, Co. Armagh, BT71 6NA ☎ 028 8778 4753 🕔 House: Jul, Aug daily 2–5.30; May, Jun, Sep Sat, Sun 2–5.30. Grounds: May–end Sep daily 10–6; Oct–end Apr daily 10–4 🔟 Adult £5, child (4–18) £2.80 (NT members free) 🚌 Signposted off M1 at Junction 14

Opposite *The Argory, topped by a weather vane, and its sundial garden*
Right *Ardress House overlooks its beautiful rose garden*

INFORMATION

✚ 363 H3 🚹 Bangor Tourist Information Office, 34 Quay Street, Bangor, Co. Down, BT20 5ED ☎ 028 9127 0069 🌐 Jul, Aug Mon–Fri 9–6 (opens 10am on Wed), Sat 10–5, Sun 1–5; Jun Mon–Fri 9–5 (opens 10am on Wed), Sat 10–4, Sun 1–5; Jan–end May, Sep–end Dec Mon–Fri 9–5 (opens 10am on Tue), Sat 10–4

🚹 Downpatrick Tourist Information Office, St. Patrick's Centre, 53a Market Street, Downpatrick, Co. Down, BT30 6LZ ☎ 028 4461 2233 🌐 Jul, Aug Mon–Fri 9–6, Sat 9.30–6

INTRODUCTION

The Ards Peninsula has always been a place apart from the mainstream, full of small farms and fishing villages, and Strangford Lough shares its feeling of isolation. The scatter of islands in the lough, some accessible by causeways known only to locals, made ideal defensive positions for early settlers, and the pioneer Christians also found them safe havens. The Ards was a busy place, and Donaghadee served as Ulster's main entry port from mainland Britain, but now the area is one of the most peaceful spots in Northern Ireland.

Strangford Lough and the Ards Peninsula are just to the east of Belfast, and are easily reached from the city. The A2 road runs east from Belfast through Bangor before turning south along the outer Ards coast through a string of east-facing seaside villages, down to Portaferry at the southern tip. Here it meets the A20, which has come from Belfast through Newtownards, and then goes south along the inner, or Strangford Lough, shore of the Ards Peninsula by way of Mount Stewart and Grey Abbey.

The A22 Downpatrick–Belfast road follows the landward or western shore of Strangford Lough. The A25 from Downpatrick links to the A2/A20 at the southern tip of the Ards Peninsula by way of the Portaferry–Strangford ferry.

WHAT TO SEE

COAST AND VILLAGES OF THE ARDS PENINSULA

East of Belfast, the Ards Peninsula hangs off the shoulder of County Down like a long, outward-crooked arm. The peninsula stretches south for some 40km (25 miles) and is edged with a fine sweep of coastline. From the seaside resort of Bangor you follow the A2 to Donaghadee, Ulster's chief passenger port from the 16th to the 19th centuries. Boats ran from Portpatrick in Scotland, and the big harbour with its lighthouse and Georgian houses speaks of its past importance. But competition with the Stranraer–Larne ferry route overcame the Portpatrick–Donaghadee service, and it stopped in 1849.

Above *A brightly painted fishing boat in Strangford Harbour*

The switchback coast road runs beside a shoreline of wonderful sandy beaches, passing through Ballywalter and Ballyhalbert and the fishing village of Portavogie. Stop here to sample some Portavogie prawns, straight out of the sea, before continuing to Cloughey, where you turn off to Kearney, a former fishing village that has been restored to an unlikely but beautiful neatness by the National Trust.

GREY ABBEY

Grey Abbey was founded in 1193 by Affreca, wife of the Norman Lord of Ards, Sir John de Courcy. Then, only 20 years after the Norman invasion, Irish-born monks were thought to be too sympathetic to local warlords, so Grey Abbey's first monks were imported from Cumbria in northwest England. The imposing ruins by the shore incorporate a re-created herb garden.

✚ 363 H3 ✉ Church Street, Greyabbey, Co. Down ☎ 028 9181 1491 ✪ Apr–end Sep Tue–Sat 9–6, Sun 2–6; Oct–end Mar Sat 10–4 ✋ Free

STRANGFORD LOUGH

Strangford Lough is a giant tidal inlet, 30km (19 miles) long, between the Ards Peninsula and the mainland. A twice-daily flush of tides pours through a tiny gap only 458m (500 yards) wide at Portaferry. Strangford Lough contains 70 islands and vast mudflats and sandbanks, exposed at low tide. Birdwatching is first class. A haven for wildlife, it is protected by designations that include Site of Special Scientific Interest, Marine Nature Reserve and National Nature Reserve. The lough is managed by the National Trust (Wildlife Centre at Castle Ward, tel 028 4488 1411, ▷ 288). At Portaferry, visit Exploris aquarium in the Rope Walk, Castle Street, with its 'Touch Tank', and the seal sanctuary (Apr–end Aug Mon–Fri 10–6, Sat 11–6, Sun 12–6; Sep–end Mar Mon–Fri 10–5, Sat 11–5, Sun 1–5). From Portaferry you can catch the ferry across the mouth of the lough to Strangford, entering what is known as 'St. Patrick's Country'. Here Ireland's patron saint is said to have landed in AD432 on his great mission to convert the heathen Irish; and here at the monastery of Saul he died in AD461.

✚ 363 H3

SCRABO TOWER

For a memorable view, climb the 122 steps to the top of Scrabo Tower at the summit of Scrabo Hill Country Park, off the A21 southeast of Newtownards (tel 028 9181 1491; Apr–end Sep Sat–Thu 10.30–6). The tower was erected in 1857 by the tenants of Charles Stewart, third Marquis of Londonderry (▷ 297, Mount Stewart), to commemorate his charity during the Great Famine. From the viewing platform 41m (135ft) high, you enjoy a fabulous view over the Ards Peninsula and Strangford Lough, south to the Mountains of Mourne and east across the sea to the Scottish hills.

Above *A lifebelt by the harbour of Strangford*
Below *Scrabo Tower*

BIRDWATCHING

The birdwatching on Strangford Lough is among the best in the British Isles. The varied habitats of the lough give food and shelter to birds all year round. Especially spectacular are the winter gatherings of up to 40,000 waders (oystercatcher, lapwing, curlew, knot, redshank) and 20,000 waterfowl (gadwall, pintail, wigeon, goldeneye, red breasted merganser, Slavonian grebe), as well as up to 15,000 pale-bellied Brent geese. In spring/summer breeding species include heron, cormorant, great crested grebe, eider and black guillemot, gulls and terns. There's birdwatching at Castle Espie Wildfowl and Wetlands Centre, signposted off the A22, 5km (3 miles) south of Comber (tel 028 9187 4146; Mar–end Oct Mon–Fri 10.30–5, Sat–Sun 11–5.30; Nov–end Feb Mon–Fri 11.30–4, Sat–Sun 11–4.30) and Quoile Pondage Countryside Centre, signposted off the A25 at Downpatrick (tel 028 4461 5520; Apr–end Aug daily 11–5, Sep–end Mar Sat–Sun 1–5). Visit www.birdwatchireland.ie for details.

INFORMATION

www.visitarmagh.com

✠ 363 G3 🛈 Tourist Information Office, Old Bank Building, 40 English Street, Armagh, Co. Armagh, BT61 7BA ☎ 028 3752 1800 🕔 Jun–end Aug Mon–Sat 9–5, Sun 12–5; Sep–end May Mon–Sat 9–5, Sun 2–5

TIPS

» If you happen to be in Armagh on or around 12 July, the day of Orange Order parades all across Northern Ireland, don't be surprised if you find all public attractions have been closed for the day. Best to telephone and check.

» There are several saucy medieval carvings, including a donkey-eared Sheela-na-gig, in the Chapter House of the Anglican Cathedral.

Below The Catholic Cathedral of St. Patrick sits at the top of a long flight of steps

ARMAGH

Two splendid cathedrals and handsome Georgian buildings greet visitors to Armagh. One of the oldest cities in Ireland, this little grey-roofed city was the capital of Ulster, and the seat of both Catholic and Anglican Bishops of Ireland.

THE CATHEDRALS

Exploring Armagh, you can hardly help but start with its two great cathedrals—they are by far the most eye-catching and significant buildings in town. The Anglican Cathedral of St. Patrick (Apr–end Oct daily 10–5; Nov–end Mar daily 10–4) is the smaller and by far the older of the two. Its largely 19th-century exterior of pink sandstone conceals parts of a mid-13th-century cathedral, which itself was preceded by other churches going back in time to AD444 when St. Patrick himself built the first church on this site. Enjoyable highlights of the present cathedral include the various gargoyles and stone-carved grotesques high on the walls both inside and out. The Chapter House contains the grinning Iron Age effigy called the Tandragee Idol. Brian Boru, the High King of Ireland, killed in 1014 as his army defeated the Vikings at the Battle of Clontarf, lies buried somewhere inside the hill.

Across the valley on Cathedral Road are the two huge rocket-like towers of the Roman Catholic Cathedral of St. Patrick (Mon–Sat 10–5). The interior is an unrestrained Gothic burst of mosaic, marble and golden angels on the wing. Construction of the cathedral, funded chiefly through public subscription, bazaars and raffles, started in 1838, but was halted during the Great Famine of the 1840s. It was finally completed in 1873. The long-case clock in the cathedral was first prize in one of the raffles held to raise money for building works, and is still waiting to be claimed by the person who won it—in 1865.

AROUND THE CITY

There are several other enjoyable attractions in Armagh. On English Street near the neat Georgian Mall, St. Patrick's Trian (tel 028 3752 1801; Mon–Sat 10–5, Sun 2–5) has displays covering the city's links with the saint, the story of the city itself and *Gulliver's Travels* (the author Johathan Swift spent a lot of time in Armagh). Life in Armagh in the 18th century is entertainingly re-created at the Palace Demesne (tel 028 3752 9629; Jun–end Aug Mon–Sat 10–5, Sun 12–5; Apr, May, Sep Sat 10–5, Sun 12–5). Armagh's old-fashioned Robinson's Library (Abbey Street; tel 028 3752 3142; Mon–Fri 10–1, 2–4) has, among its ancient leather-bound tomes, a first-edition *Gulliver's Travels* marked up by Swift himself. The Planetarium on College Hill (tel 028 3752 3689; shows Tue–Sat, telephone for information) is a popular attraction.

BALLYCASTLE

Retaining the appearance of an old-fashioned, Georgian seaside resort, Ballycastle makes a very convenient base for exploring the beautiful Antrim coast and glens. To get the most out of your explorations, you can learn all about the area's history and culture in the well-kept Ballycastle Museum (59 Castle Street; tel 0208 2076 2942; Jul, Aug Mon–Sat 12–6). Lammastide (the last Monday and Tuesday of August) is the best time to be here, for the Auld Lammas Fair. Held in the town since 1606, it is Ballycastle's great social event, with music, dancing, street entertainment, food markets and more. You're guaranteed ritual tastings of two local delicacies: yellowman (a kind of toffee) and dulse, an edible seaweed.

➕ 363 G1 ℹ️ Sheskburn House, 7 Mary Street, Ballycastle, Co. Antrim, BT54 6QH ☎ 028 2076 2024 🕐 Jul, Aug Mon–Fri 9.30–7, Sat 10–6, Sun 2–6; Sep–end Jun Mon–Fri 9.30–5

BELFAST

▷ 280–287.

BELLEEK POTTERY

www.belleek.ie

Since Belleek Pottery began production in the late 1850s, the business has concentrated on high-quality products, especially white Parian ware, famous for its hard shiny surface and delicate shape. On the factory tour you see a fascinating process: beating the air out of a dough-like mixture of glass and clay with wooden paddles, teasing the material out and moulding it into plates, cups, vases and statuettes. You also get the chance to talk to the workers about what they are doing. These are very skilled people, working with tools they make themselves and hand down through the generations. The basket ware, a lattice of finely meshed clay strings, is probably the best-known of Belleek products. Hand-painting is another remarkable skill you can watch.

A Visitor Centre explains the history and technicalities, and there is a showroom where you can admire beautifully lit pieces before parting with your money. Belleek ware is expensive, and there are no 'seconds' for sale.

One story about the pottery's early days concerns a workman who slipped while helping to build the roof and tumbled about 10m (33ft) to the ground. Somehow he contrived to land on his feet. After a reviving tot of whiskey he went back up to the roof and carried on with his work. They're cool customers in Belleek.

➕ 362 E3 ✉ Belleek, Co. Fermanagh, BT93 3FY ☎ 028 6865 9300 🕐 Mar–end Oct Mon–Fri 9–6, Sat 10–6, Sun 12–6; Nov, Dec Mon–Fri 9–5.30, Sat 10–5.30; Jan, Feb Mon–Fri 9–5.30 🎟 Visitor Centre free; tours: adult £4, child (under 12) free

BUSHMILLS DISTILLERY

www.bushmills.com

Bushmills is the oldest distillery in the world; it started production after gaining a licence in 1608, and has been distilling superb malt whiskeys ever since. The buildings, with their pagoda-style roofs, are a pleasure to look at. The tour takes you past the huge round mash tuns where the wash bubbles and ferments, and the great stills shaped like gleaming copper onions. In the cool gloom of the warehouse you inhale the faint, sweet smell of whiskey evaporating from the seams of the wooden barrels in which Bushmills matures. The guide tells you that this unreclaimable whiskey vapour is known as the 'angels' share'.

At the end of the tour you can sip a complimentary dram, buy a bottle of whiskey and reflect on the Bushmills mantra: 'Here's to health and prosperity, To you and all your posterity, And them that doesn't drink with sincerity, May they be damned for all eternity!'

➕ 363 G1 ✉ Distillery Road, Bushmills, Co. Antrim, BT57 8XH ☎ 028 2073 3218 🕐 Apr–end Oct Mon–Sat 9.30–5, Sun 12–5; Nov–end Mar Mon–Fri, telephone for times 🎟 Adult £5, child (8–17) £2.50 🚌 Signposted off A2

Above *People and horses throng the streets of Ballycastle at the Auld Lammas Fair in August*

BELFAST

INFORMATION

www.gotobelfast.com

✚ 363 H2 ℹ️ Belfast Welcome Centre, 47 Donegall Place, Belfast, BT1 5AD ☎ 028 9024 6609 🕐 Jun–end Sep Mon–Sat 9–7, Sun 11–4; Oct–end May Mon–Sat 9–5.30 🚃 Belfast

INTRODUCTION

Belfast is a solid Victorian city built largely on the sea trading, shipbuilding and textile trades, with large public buildings that sit grandly amid fading red-brick terraces and commercial premises. Parts of Belfast are a bit shabby, but down along the River Lagan and around the heart of the city the old place is smartening and modernizing itself at a great rate. It is a city packed with attractions, most of them uncrowded. And, contrary to many first-time visitors' expectations, it is a friendly city. Belfast people are generous with their time and help; they may speak with black humour; and they enjoy conversation.

The River Lagan flows north through Belfast into Belfast Lough, cutting the city in two; just about everything that a visitor would want to see or do is west of the river. Most of the grand public buildings, such as St. Anne's Cathedral and the Town Hall, are in the middle of the city, while along the river are Sinclair Seamen's Church, Waterfront Hall and the other riverside attractions. Just to the west are the Falls and Shankill roads with their vivid murals—black taxi tour territory (▷ 284). About 1.5km (1 mile) to the south of the city lies Belfast's university quarter with Queen's University, the Botanic Gardens, the Ulster Museum and some fine parks.

Belfast is very easy to negotiate—most of the main attractions are within a few minutes' walk of each other—and there are a number of green and pleasant ways to get around: on foot or by bicycle, on one of the frequent city buses or cruising along the River Lagan by boat (or walking along its towpath).

WHAT TO SEE

DONEGALL SQUARE

The heart of Belfast is Donegall Square, whose broad pavements and flowerbeds surround the giant City Hall (▷ below). Buildings to admire around Donegall Square include the Italianate sandstone Marks & Spencer, the Scottish Provident Building with its cavorting dolphins and guardian lions, and the Linen Hall Library (tel 028 9032 1707; Mon–Fri 9.30–5.30, Sat 9.30–1), a wonderful, hushed, old-fashioned library (with a tea room that's a Belfast institution) whose Political Collection offers an overview of the recent Troubles.
✚ 286 B3

CITY HALL

The great green dome of the City Hall (opened in 1906) rises 53m (173ft) into the sky and is a prime Belfast landmark. Patterned Italian marble and elaborate stucco greet you in the hall, from where tours of the building ascend beneath the dome to the oak-panelled Council Chamber. This splendid civic apartment contains two tellingly contrasted items. One is the Lord Mayor's handsomely carved throne. The other is an icon for all Orangemen: the plain and simple round wooden table at which the Unionist leader, Sir Edward Carson, signed the Solemn League and Covenant of Resistance against Home Rule on 28 September 1912. More than 400,000 Ulster Protestants were to follow him as signatories, some in their own blood.
✚ 286 B3 ✉️ Donegall Square, Belfast, BT1 5GS ☎ 028 9027 0456 🕐 Temporarily closed until 2009; grounds remain open to visitors 🎫 Free

GRAND OPERA HOUSE

www.goh.co.uk

The Grand Opera House is a splendid example of a late Victorian music hall. Ornate outside and all overblown opulence within, it has suffered various vicissitudes down the years, from relegation to a second-class cinema in the

Above *A Shankill Road mural*
Opposite Big Fish *at Lagenside*

Above *The Crown Liquor Saloon's interior is pure Victoriana*
Below *Carving on the façade of the Grand Opera House*

1950s to a brace of IRA bombs in 1991 and 1993, which damaged but failed to destroy it. Yet one look at the giant gilt elephants, the cherubs and swags of golden fruit and flowers tells you of its aspirations when it was opened in 1895. Nowadays restored and refurbished, the Grand Opera House puts on a wide variety of entertainment that include, of course, opera productions.

✚ 286 A4 ✉ 2–4 Great Victoria Street, Belfast, BT2 7BA ☎ 028 9024 1919
☛ By arrangement

CROWN LIQUOR SALOON

www.crownbar.com

This Victorian 'temple of intemperance' is, as its owners the National Trust proudly claim, 'the most famous pub in Belfast'. The Trust bought the pub in 1978 and spent £400,000 restoring it because they recognized it for what it was: a supreme example of the Golden Age of public house design. From the colonnaded gilt and marble frontage to the interior with its curved bar, embossed ceiling and ornate wood snugs, with frosted glass and service bells, the Crown Liquor Saloon is gloriously, frothily over the top. Note the inlaid crown on the floor at the entrance. It was installed there in 1895 by the nationalist owner Patrick Flanagan, so that all his customers could tread it underfoot.

✚ 286 A4 ✉ 48 Great Victoria Street, Belfast, BT2 7BA ☎ 028 9027 9901 ⊕ Mon–Sat 11.30am–midnight, Sun 12.30–11pm

PUBS

A good way to sample the best of Belfast pubs is to join the Historical Pub Tour of Belfast (tel 028 9268 3665; May–end Oct Thu 7, Sat 4) that starts at the Crown Dining rooms (upstairs at the Crown Liquor Saloon, ▷ above). Belfast's most characterful pubs include White's (tel 028 9024 3080)—Belfast's oldest pub (so it claims)—in Winecellar Entry, and the Morning Star (tel 028 9032 3976) in Pottinger's Entry, an old coaching stop for the Belfast to Dublin mail with a superb semi-elliptical bar and a menu of dishes using local ingredients. Bittles Bar (tel 028 9031 1088) in Victoria Street is a wedge-shaped corner pub with some splendid paintings of Irish literary figures; the Kitchen Bar (tel 028 9032 4901) on Victoria Square offers local real ales and traditional music; Kelly's Cellars (tel 028 9032 4835) in Bank Street is a dark, delightful old place.

SINCLAIR SEAMEN'S CHURCH

This is an L-shaped Presbyterian church of 1857, furnished in a nautical style to attract visiting sailors. The font is a ship's binnacle; the pulpit resembles the prow of a ship; nautical themes feature in the stained-glass windows; the mast of a Guinness barge and ships' riding lights decorate the walls Services commence with the ringing of HMS *Hood's* brass ship's bell. Even the welcome sign by the door conveys its message by semaphore flags. Seafaring worshippers will never be turned away—50 seats are reserved for them.

✚ 286 C1 ✉ Corporation Square, Belfast, BT1 3AJ ☎ 028 9071 5997 🕐 Wed 2–5, Sun for services at 11.30 and 7 ✋ Free

BOTANIC GARDENS

These classic 19th-century gardens beside the river contain two pieces of High Victorian glass-and-cast-iron architecture: the great Glasshouse of 1839–40 with its Cool Wing full of bright plants, and its steamy Stove Wing and mighty central dome. There's more steam in the nearby Tropical Ravine, where you stroll around a gallery looking down through the canopy of a miniature tropical rain forest. The wide lawns of the Botanic Gardens provide a place to relax for students from nearby Queen's University.

✚ Off map 286 A5 ✉ Stranmillis Road, Belfast, BT9 5JH ☎ 028 9031 4762 🕐 Gardens: daily until dusk; Greenhouse and Tropical Ravine: Apr–end Sep daily 1–5; Oct–end Mar daily 1–4) ✋ Free 🚌 Metro 8A, 8B

ULSTER MUSEUM

www.ulstermuseum.org.uk

A massive £12 million redevelopment of the museum is due for completion in spring 2009, bringing one of Northern Ireland's most impressive institutions into the 21st century. In the interim objects from the museum will be displayed in exhibitions around the city and the rest of Northern Ireland.

✚ Off map 286 A5 ✉ Botanic Gardens, Stranmillis Road, Belfast, BT9 5AB ☎ 028 9038 3000 🕐 Telephone for latest information

ST. ANNE'S CATHEDRAL

www.belfastcathedral.org

Consecrated in 1904, St. Anne's Cathedral is an impressive church built of stone from all 32 counties of Ireland. Highlights include the 'Occupations of Mankind' carvings on the capitals of the nave pillars, the modern stained glass of the east window, and the maple and marble of the nave floor, the 1920s mosaics by the Martin sisters, and the prayer book written out by hand on cigarette paper by a World War II captive in a Japanese prisoner-of-war camp.

✚ 286 B2 ✉ Donegall Street, Belfast, BT1 2HB ☎ 028 9032 8332 🕐 Mon–Sat 10–4 ✋ Free

HOME FRONT EXHIBITION

www.niwarmemorial.org

The Northern Ireland Memorial has a new home in Talbot Street, close to St. Anne's Cathedral. The exhibition inside relates to the involvement of the people of Belfast and Northern Ireland in World War II. Footage of the time can be seen, and displays include the 1941 Belfast Blitz when nearly 1,000 people lost their lives and some 100,000 were made homeless. Other exhibits include a striking memorial window and books of remembrance.

✚ 286 B2 ✉ NI War Memorial, 21 Talbot Street, BT1 2LD ☎ 028 9032 0392 🕐 Mon–Fri 10–4 ✋ Free

RIVER LAGAN EXPLORATIONS

The Lagan Boat Company (tel 028 9033 0844) runs trips from Donegall Quay: upriver past the fine new developments in the area now known as the Titanic Quarter and out into green countryside; downriver to view the shipyards of Harland & Wolff where *Titanic* was built and where the twin giant yellow cranes called Samson and Goliath are familiar Belfast landmarks. You can

Above *The Botanic Gardens*
Below *A maritime theme pervades the Sinclair Seamen's Church*

TIPS

» Getting around the city without a car is easy. Guided bicycling tours are offered by City Cycle Tours and Lifecycles (Smithfield Market; tel 028 9043 9959; www.lifecycles.co.uk). For guided walking tours of historic Belfast, and for a Titanic Trail telephone 028 9024 6609 (Belfast Welcome Centre). Independent city walkers will find the 'On the Hoof' map and guide useful, available from the Belfast Welcome Centre (▷ 280, Basics).

» If you want to appreciate the architecture of St. George's Market as a building, try to arrive there after 4pm when the stallholders are packing up and the crowds have thinned out.

take the Thompson Titanic Trail at the Northern Ireland Science Park (tel 028 9073 7813, Mon–Sat 11–6, Sun 12–6) around the Thompson Dry Dock and Pump House. You can also walk or bicycle along the Lagan's towpath south to Lisburn. Leaflet guides are available from the Belfast Welcome Centre (▷ 280).

BLACK TAXI TOURS

Black Taxi tours let you see West Belfast, the area where the Troubles were focused, from an insider's viewpoint, thanks to the local knowledge of the drivers. They will show you the loyalist Shankill Road and nationalist Falls Road, the battered, graffiti'd Peace Line that separates the two opposed communities, and the sectarian gable-end murals for which Belfast is famous. ☎ 028 9064 2264 or 0800 052 3914 Ⓘ Depart Belfast City Centre daily, 10, 12, 2, 4, 6, also 8 in summer 🖐 £25 for up to 3 people, £8 per person for 4 or more people

NORTH BELFAST

To the north, the city rises up to Cave Hill, 367m (1,204ft). Metro 1A, 1B, 1C, 1D, 1E, 1F, 1G and 1H from Donegall Square will take you up to Belfast Castle on its lower slopes. This splendid Victorian 'Scottish Baronial' edifice, built for the third Marquess of Donegall in 1870, contains a small Heritage Centre on its top floor. Close by is Belfast Zoological Gardens (tel 028 9077 6277; Apr–end Sep daily 10–5; Oct–end Mar daily 10–2.30), where animals of Africa, Asia and South America live in the relative freedom of large, grassy enclosures.

Try the Cave Hill walk if you need a breath of air outside the city. You can get a free trail map, literature and information from Cave Hill Heritage Centre (Belfast Castle, Antrim Road, Belfast, BT15 5GR, tel 028 9077 6925). The waymarked trail leads up through woods, then by the neolithic caves in the great basalt cliff of Napoleon's Nose, to a mountain path leading to the old earthwork called McArt's Fort at the summit of Cave Hill. From here the view over Belfast, the Ards Peninsula and Belfast Lough is superb.

Above *The dome of Belfast's City Hall is a historic landmark*
Below *Waterfront Hall, the city's principal concert and conference centre*

MORE TO SEE
STORMONT CASTLE

Seat of the on–off Northern Ireland Assembly, Stormont Castle lies 8km (5 miles) east of the city, easily accessible by Metro bus 4A and 23. The imposing castle at the end of its mile-long drive is open to the public only by appointment, but there are walks in the woods and across the open parkland. ✚ Off map 286 C3

THE PEOPLE'S MUSEUM

A re-created 1930s working-class house telling the story of life in the Shankill area and also of Unionism in Northern Ireland.

✚ Off map 286 A2 ✉ Fernhill House, Glencairn Road, Belfast, BT13 3PU ☎ 028 9071 5599 🕓 Daily 10–4

AN McADAM CULTÚRLANN ÓFIAICH

Here exhibitions, music concerts and a bookshop promote the Irish language and culture.

✚ Off map 286 A3 ✉ 216 Falls Road, Belfast, BT12 6AH ☎ 028 9096 4180 🕓 Mon–Fri 9.30–5.30

ST. MALACHY'S CHURCH

The church may look unprepossessing from the outside with its dingy red brick and lurid pink paintwork, but inside you'll find an early Victorian extravaganza of stucco, fan-vaulting, a fine altarpiece carved by the Piccioni family (from the Tirol), and later window glass with art nouveau lilies.

✚ 286 B4 ✉ Alfred Street, Belfast, BT2 8EN ☎ 028 9032 1713 🕓 Daily 8–5.45

ST. GEORGE'S MARKET

This handsome 1896 red-brick and stone building at the intersection of May and Oxford streets is Belfast's only surviving Victorian market hall. Organic produce, flowers and a lively fish market, under a restored roof of glass and cast iron, are the focus for shoppers (Fridays and Saturdays).

✚ 286 C4

THE HARBOUR COMMISSIONER'S OFFICE

The city has few grander buildings than this one, built in 1854. The interior has floors of mosaic and inlaid marble, heavy plaster mouldings and stained-glass windows. Upstairs in the barrel-roofed Barnet Room the stained-glass windows depict the arms of old colonial partners in trade such as the United States.

✚ 286 C1 ✉ Corporation Square, Belfast, BT1 3AL, off Donegall Quay ☎ 028 9055 4422 ◄ Tours for reserved parties only

ORMEAU BATHS GALLERY

Frequently changing exhibitions of contemporary art from Ireland and elsewhere are displayed on two floors of a converted old public baths.

✚ 286 B4 ✉ 18a Ormeau Road, Belfast, BT2 8HS ☎ 028 9032 1402 🕓 Tue–Sat 10–5.30 by appointment 💲 Free

Below *A Japanese exhibit in the Ulster Museum*

BELFAST TALES

LIGHT THAT LASTED

In Sinclair Seamen's Church, look for the silver torch displayed next to the brass bell of HMS *Hood*. Survivors of a shipwreck were left clinging to a rock with only this torch. Its light lasted just long enough for them to be rescued.

BELLS AFORE YE GO

Messrs Dunville's, whiskey distillers, conducted their craft next to St. Malachy's Church on Alfred Street. Judging that the vibrations caused by the tolling of the bell were spoiling their product, they complained—and the bell was removed.

LEANING TOWER OF BELFAST

Some will tell you that W. J. Barre was drunk when he designed the Albert Memorial Clock Tower in 1865, and it certainly inclines perceptibly—1.25m (4ft) out of true, in fact. The truth is more prosaic. The wooden foundations have warped and shifted over the years. Still, it's given the locals the opportunity to joke: 'Albert's got the time, and he's got the inclination too.'

BELFAST

200 m
200 yds

A12

Belfast Castle, Cave Hill

GREAT GEORGE'S STREET

CLIFTON STREET

Lancaster Street

NORTH QUEEN STREET

FREDERICK STREET

GREAT GEORGE'S ST

YORK STREET

Little Patrick Street

NELSON STREET

CORPORATION STREET

Clarendon Road

Sinclair Seamen's Church

Harbour Commissioner's Office

Clarendon Dock

CORPORATION SQUARE

St Patrick's Church

Regent Street

Stanhope Drive

Wall Street

CARRICK HILL

Little Donegall Street

Library

DONEGALL STREET

Curtis St

Academy Street

DUNBAR LINK

Great Patrick Street

Tomb Street

CORPORATION STREET

QUAY

M3

LAGAN BRIDGE

Dargan Bridge

Isle of Man Seacat Terminal

Queen's Quay

Donegall Quay

The People's Museum, Shankill Road

B39 PETERS HILL

WEST

Brown Square

Gardiner Street

NORTH STREET

Samuel Street

Brown Street

MILLFIELD

Smithfield Sq N

Gresham Street

Wilson Street

A12

Royal Avenue

ROYAL AVE

St Anne's Cathedral

Talbot Street

Gordon Street

Hill Street

Dunbar St

Home Front Exhibition (NI War Memorial)

ALBERT SQ

Albert Memorial Clock Tower

Custom House

QUEEN'S SQUARE

DONEGALL QUAY

Dargan Bridge

QUEEN'S QUAY

QUEEN ELIZABETH II BRIDGE

Stormont Castle

BRIDGE END

Laganside Walkway

Castle Court Centre

Presbyterian Oval Church

NORTH STREET

Rosemary Street

BRIDGE ST

HIGH STREET

WARING STREET

St George's

OXFORD STREET

QUEEN'S BRIDGE

DIVIS STREET

St Mary's

A501 COLLEGE SQ

CASTLE STREET

CASTLE PLACE

High Park Centre

Cornmarket

Ann Street

ANN STREET

VICTORIA STREET

Police Station

Belfast Waterfront Hall, Conference & Concert Centre

Falls Road, An Culturlann Macadam O'Fiaich

Hamill Street

Old Museum Arts Centre

Belfast Welcome Centre

College St

Donegall Place

Castle Lane

Callender Street

Arthur Street

Victoria Square Centre

Victoria Square

Old Town Hall

Place

Lan-Yon

COLLEGE SQUARE NORTH

Christ Church

Linen Hall Library

WELLINGTON PLACE

DONEGALL SQUARE NTH

CHICHESTER STREET

Gloucester Street

Montgomery Street

Royal Courts of Justice

DURHAM STREET

Royal Belfast Academic Institute

EAST FISHERWICK

Queen Street

DONEGALL SQUARE WEST

Donegall Square

City Hall

DONEGALL SQUARE EAST

DONEGALL SQUARE STH

Upper Arthur Street

MAY STREET

Joy Street

St George's Market

Police Station

GROSVENOR ROAD

Spires Centre

HOWARD STREET

Linen Hall

Joy Street

St George's Market

CROMAC SQUARE

BELFAST CENTRAL STATION

Grand Opera House

Crown Liquor Saloon

Brunswick St

Franklin Street

Alfred Street

Russell St

CROMAC STREET

Friendly Street

Glengall Street

Europa Bus Centre

Amelia Street

Ulster Hall

Clarence Street

St Malachy's Church

Eliza Street

Lower Stanfield St

GREAT VICTORIA STREET STATION

BEDFORD STREET

ADELAIDE STREET

Welsh Street

Mcauley Street

Raphael Street

Stewart Street

GREAT VICTORIA STREET

Hope St

Bruce St

BRUCE ST

DUBLIN ROAD

ORMEAU AVENUE

Joy Street

Bankmore Street

Ormeau Baths Gallery

Cromac Place

Laganside Walkway

SANDY ROW

Rowland Way

Wellwood Street

Ventry St

Salisbury Street

Lindsay Street

Charlotte St

Howard Street Sth

ORMEAU ROAD

Cromac Street

Lagan

Majestic Drive

Blyth Road

SANDY ROW

Albion Street

SHAFTESBURY SQUARE

Maryville Street

DONEGALL PASS

Elm Street

Oak Way

Pine Way

Walnut Street

A24

ORMEAU EMBANKMENT

Ormeau Park

DONEGALL ROAD

CITY HOSPITAL STATION

Botanic Gardens, Ulster Museum

BOTANIC STATION

BOTANIC AVENUE

Posnett Street

Vernon Street

A   B   C

BELFAST STREET INDEX

Above *The ancient castle at Carrickfergus, a backdrop for the National Mirra Championships*

CARRICKFERGUS CASTLE

Carrickfergus, with its grey Norman stronghold, is the southern gateway to the Antrim coast. Carrickfergus Castle was built on its shore promontory in 1180 by Sir John de Courcy to guard Belfast Lough. Its strategic position has always made it liable to attack and siege, but it has survived remarkably intact. Tableaux, effigies and explanatory plaques tell its story to visitors, and there are sometimes visiting displays.

✠ 363 H2 ✉ Marine Highway, Carrickfergus, Co. Antrim, BT38 7VG ☎ 028 9335 1273 ◷ Jun–end Aug Mon–Sat 10–6, Sun 12–6; Apr, May, Sep Mon–Sat 10–6, Sun 2–6; Oct–end Mar Mon–Sat 10–4, Sun 2–4 ♿ Adult £3, child (under 16) £1.50, family £8 ◻ Carrickfergus

CASTLE COOLE

www.ntni.org.uk
Legend says that if the resident flock of greylag geese ever leaves the Castle Coole estate, so will the Earls of Belmore. The geese still live there, however, and so does the family who built the great Palladian mansion. One of Ireland's finest country houses, with its huge portico and long arcaded wings, Castle Coole was designed by James Wyatt and finished in 1798, the year after Armar Lowry-Corry was created first Earl of Belmore. The first earl never really enjoyed Castle Coole. Apart from his money worries (he died penniless in 1802), he was devastated when his wife—a dark-haired beauty—left him. Her portrait is one of the attractions of a tour around the interior.

One other poignant fact: The gorgeously appointed State Bedroom, with its red and gold canopied bed, was created for a state visit by King George IV in 1821 that never actually took place.

✠ 362 E3 ✉ Co. Fermanagh, BT71 6JY ☎ 028 6632 2690 ◷ House: Jul, Aug daily 12–6; Jun Fri–Wed 1–6; Sep, Apr, May Sat–Sun 1–6. Grounds: Apr–end Sep daily 10–8; Oct–end Mar daily 10–4 ♿ Adult £5.50, child (under 17) £2.50, family £13.50 (NT members free) ◻ Signposted on A4, 2.5km (1.5 miles) southeast of Enniskillen

CASTLE WARD

www.ntni.org.uk
Castle Ward is an intriguing monument to an ill-matched couple. Bernard Ward, first Viscount Bangor, and his wife Anne could not agree on the architectural style of the new house they were building in the 1760s on the southern shores of Strangford Lough. So Lord Bangor designed a restrained Classical frontage and set of front rooms, while his wife ordered a feast of exuberant Strawberry Hill Gothic to the back of the house. The result is both eccentric and delightful, from the austere symmetry of Bernard's music room to the frothy fan vaulting dripping down the walls of Anne's boudoir. Only in the entrance hall do whimsicality and classicism meet— for among the stucco ornamentation are a genuine hat, basket and fiddle, dipped in plaster and stuck up amid all the artifice.

In the grounds you'll find a farmyard with a sawmill, the original 16th-century fortified tower, the

Strangford Lough Wildlife Centre (▷ 276–277), and a high-tech adventure playground. There are lovely walks through bluebell woods and along the lake.

✠ 363 H3 ✉ Co. Down, BT30 7LS ☎ 028 4488 1204 ◷ House and Wildlife Centre: Jul, Aug daily 1–6; Apr–end Jun, Sep Sat, Sun 1–6. Grounds: May–end Sep daily 10–8; Oct–end Apr daily 10–4 ♿ House tour adult £2.70, child £1.80. Grounds and Wildlife centre only: adult £4.80, child £2.40 (NT members free) ◻ Signposted on A25 between Downpatrick and Strangford

CASTLEWELLAN FOREST PARK

This beautiful forest park occupies the estate of the Annesley family in the northern foothills of the Mountains of Mourne. Special features are the National Arboretum of rare trees, which surrounds an 18th-century garden; a long lake in which you can fish (you will need a permit and canoeing permission: telephone the Park Ranger); the Grange Yard, an early 18th-century farmstead; and many miles of interesting footpaths.

✠ 363 H3 ✉ Castlewellan, Co. Down, BT31 9BU ☎ 028 4377 8664 ◷ Daily 10–sunset ♿ £2 pedestrian, £4 car ◻ Entrance off the main street, on A25, 19km (12 miles) southwest of Downpatrick

CROM ESTATE

www.ntni.org.uk
A great variety of woodland and the presence of Upper Lough Erne in so many of the views make Crom Estate an ideal spot for walking, especially in late autumn when the changing leaves reflected in the lake are at their most spectacular. Paths lead to Crom Old Church, and the ruin of Crom Old Castle of 1611. With luck you'll see some of the resident herd of deer, and the huge variety of birdlife gives endless opportunities for birdwatching.

✠ 362 F3 ✉ Co. Fermanagh, BT92 8AP ☎ 028 6773 8118 ◷ Jun–end Aug daily 10–7; mid-Mar to end May, Sep, Oct daily 10–6 ♿ £6 car (pedestrians and NT members free) ◻ 5km (3 miles) west of Newtownbutler, signposted from A25 in the town

DERRY/LONDONDERRY

Northern Ireland's lively, friendly second city has the finest city walls walk in Ireland. Its monuments to hope in adversity, and the city's proudest Loyalist relics in St. Columb's Cathedral, reflect it's turbulent history.

It's easy to find your way around Derry, which is still referred to by its Loyalist population as Londonderry—the name given to the city in 1613 when James I and the livery companies of London established English and Scottish settlers here. To add further confusion for visitors, the official county name remains Londonderry. The wide River Foyle shapes the east boundary, while 'old Derry', the walled city, forms a neat rectangle whose four radiating streets—Shipquay Street, Butcher Street, Ferryquay Street and Bishop Street Within converge on The Diamond or central market square. There's a good Craft Village within the angle of Butcher Street and Shipquay Street, where small workshops rub shoulders with cafés, wine bars and trendy eateries. The 'street of pubs' is Waterloo Street outside the western wall between Butcher's Gate and Waterloo Square; here you'll find great traditional and modern music in the bars.

WALKING THE WALLS

Derry's chief visitor attraction is undoubtedly the splendid city walls, built for defence between 1613 and 1618 by the trade guilds that had come from London to commercialize the old Celtic settlement. You can climb to the top and make the circuit of 1.6km (1 mile), with views over the old city and away to the hills. A town walls walk starting at Shipquay Gate should begin with a visit to the eye-catchingly florid Guildhall (tel 028 7137 7335; Mon–Fri 9–5, Sat–Sun by appointment). Inside, fine stained-glass windows depict the city's history.

Numerous cannon stand on the walls, reminders of the great historic defence of Derry in 1688–89 when the Catholic army of King James II laid siege to the city. Before the siege was lifted, in April 1689, 7,000 of the 30,000 citizens had died. At Bishop's Gate you can descend from the walls to see St. Columb's Cathedral (tel 028 7126 7313; Apr–end Sep Mon–Sat 9–5; Oct–end Mar 9–1, 2–4) and its treasured relics of the Great Siege. In the Tower Museum (tel 028 7137 2411; Tue–Sat 10–5) the history of Derry, including the dark, desperate days of the Troubles, is laid out in exemplary fashion. The museum's tower, a replica of a medieval round tower, was built by Paddy O'Doherty, as an article of faith and a pointer to better times to come.

INFORMATION

www.derryvisitor.com

362 F1 ℹ Derry Visitor and Convention Bureau, 44 Foyle Street, Derry, Co. Londonderry, BT48 6AT ☎ 028 7126 7284 🕐 Jul–end Sep Mon–Fri 9–7, Sat 10–6, Sun 10–5; mid-Mar to end Jun, Oct Mon–Fri 9–5, Sat 10–5 🚉 Derry (Londonderry Waterside)

TIPS

» St. Columb's has the First Air Mail Letter—an iron mortar bomb fired into the city in 1689, with a note of the Jacobite surrender demands.
» St. Columb's has some fine Victorian stained glass.

Below *The uplifting* Peace Statue *on the city walls*

DOWNHILL ESTATE

www.ntni.orq.uk

The collection of buildings and ruins on the cliffs near Castlerock is all that remains of the 18th-century glories of the Downhill estate, laid out in 1783–85 by the red-blooded Protestant Bishop of Londonderry, Frederick Hervey, the fourth Earl of Bristol. He lived life to the full, with a string of mistresses, one of whom was reputedly installed in the cylindrical Mussenden Temple. The ruin of the Bishop's Palace of Downhill, its walled garden and icehouse lie near the Lion Gate (topped with leopard sculptures).

✚ 363 F1 ✉ Co. Londonderry, BT51 4RP ☎ 028 2073 1582 ◉ Grounds: daily dawn–dusk. Mussenden Temple mid-Mar to end Sep daily 11–5 ✋ Adult £2.30, child £1.60, family £6.20 (per site) (NT members free) 🚌 Just east of Downhill, on A2 Coleraine–Limavady coast road

DOWNPATRICK

Built on two hills, Downpatrick is a market and cathedral town. Down Cathedral (English Street; tel 028 4461 4922) stands on a site occupied by a cathedral since the sixth century, but the present building is mostly of the 18th and 19th centuries. Outside a massive stone slab, inscribed 'Patric', is usually bright with floral offerings; but whether Ireland's patron saint really does rest here is open to conjecture. Down County Museum (English Street; tel 028 4461 5218), housed in the old jail, features county history and an illuminating view of St. Patrick's story. Families and railway buffs will enjoy the Downpatrick Railway Museum (Railway Station, Market Street; tel 028 4461 5779; mid-Jun to end Sep Sat–Sun 2–5, guided tours available each operating day; walking tours mid-Jun to mid-Dec Wed–Sat 11–2).

✚ 363 H3 ℹ️ St. Patrick's Centre, 53a Market Street, Downpatrick, Co. Down, BT30 6LZ ☎ 028 4461 2233 ◉ Jul, Aug Mon–Fri 9–6, Sat 9.30–6, Sun 2–6; Sep–end Jun Mon–Fri 9–5, Sat 9.30–5

DUNGIVEN PRIORY

The chancel of the 12th-century Augustinian Dungiven Priory holds one of the finest medieval tombs in Ireland, that of Cooey-na-Gal (d1385), a chieftain of the O'Catháin clan. His effigy lies under a canopy of carved foliage. In niches under the tomb stand six guardians in the act of drawing their swords. Their pleated tunics may well be kilts, and they may be 'gallowglasses' or mercenaries from Scotland. It was unwise to come upon their master without an introduction—his nickname means 'The Stranger's Bane'.

✚ 363 F2 ✉ Dungiven, Co. Londonderry ☎ 028 7776 0307 ◉ Open access ✋ Free 🚌 Signed off A6 Maghera road, south of Dungiven

ENNISKILLEN

www.fermanagh.gov.uk

Enniskillen is the bustling capital town of County Formanagh Attractions include Castle Barracks (tel 028 6632 5000; Mon 2–5, Tue–Fri 10–5, also May–end Sep Sat 2–5 and Jul, Aug Sun 2–5) with its regimental and county museums; the Cole Monument in Forthill Park (tel 028 6632 3110; Apr–end Sep daily 1.30–3) from the top of which there's a splendid view over the town; and Blakes of the Hollow (tel 028 6632 2143), a pub with traditional music.

✚ 362 E3 ℹ️ Enniskillen Tourist Information Office, Wellington Road, Enniskillen, Co. Fermanagh, BT74 7EF ☎ 028 6632 3110 ◉ Jul, Aug Mon–Fri 9–7, Sat 10–6, Sun 11–5; Easter–end Jun, Sep Sat 10–6, Sun 11–5; Oct Sat–Sun 10–2, public holidays 10–5

FLORENCE COURT

www.ntni.org.uk

The Cole family, later Earls of Enniskillen, built Florence Court early in the 18th century within sight of rugged 665m (2,180ft) Cuilcagh Mountain. The beauty of its wooded parkland is still it's greatest asset. Inside you can admire the plasterwork, antique Irish furniture, portraits of generations of red-haired Coles, and a Belleek chamberpot with a portrait of Victorian British Prime Minister William Gladstone painted provocatively at the bottom. Gladstone supported Home Rule: the Coles family did not.

✚ 362 E3 ✉ Co. Fermanagh, BT92 1DB ☎ 028 6634 8249 ◉ House: Jul, Aug daily 12–6; Jun Wed–Mon 1–6; mid-Mar to end May, Sep Sat–Sun 1–6. Grounds: Apr–end Oct daily 10–8; Nov–end Mar daily 10–4 ✋ Adult £5.50, child (under 12) £2.50, family £13.50 (NT members free); Grounds: car £3.50 🚌 Signposted off A32 Swanlinbar road, 13km (8 miles) southwest of Enniskillen via A4 Sligo road

Left *This stone at Downpatrick may mark St. Patrick's burial place*

GLENS OF ANTRIM

Only a short drive away from the crowded Antrim coast you'll find peace and quiet amid beautiful scenery of basalt cliffs, green valleys and dense woodland. Waymarked walks for all tastes and abilities in Glenariff Forest Park take you past water in motion: fast mountain rivers, streams, rapids and waterfalls.

The nine Glens of Antrim form one of Ireland's most beautiful landscapes. But because they are close to the spectacular basalt extravaganza of the Antrim coast, Northern Ireland's most popular (and most advertised) tourist attraction, the glens see less tourist activity than they might. That is good news for walkers, birdwatchers, photographers and other lovers of peace and quiet in the wide open spaces. Not that the glens are particularly wide. Great water-cut clefts in Antrim's coastal shelf, they tend to be U-shaped and high-sided, in some cases (notably Glenariff) with imposing cliffs forming their upper flanks. Iron ore was mined in the glens until the early 20th century, but now all is peaceful and green. Narrow roads wind up one glen and down the next, so that you can spend a very enjoyable day cruising the glens in low gear.

FROM SOUTH TO NORTH

The most southerly pair of glens are Glenarm, running down to Glenarm village, and Glencloy, the Glen of the Stony Dykes, which runs through its rocky defile to reach the harbour of Carnlough. North of these is Glenariff (see below), and then come four close together: wide Glenballyemon descending to Cushendall, and the threesome of Glendun, Glenaan and Glencorp. Glendun, the Glen of the Brown River, is spanned by a viaduct designed by the great architect Charles Lanyon; while at the foot of the Little Blue Glen, Glenaan, you'll find the signposted track to Ossian's Grave, a fine 'horned cairn' burial mound perhaps 5,000 years old. Legend says this is the resting place of bold Ossian, the warrior-poet son of the giant hero Fionn MacCumhaill. North again, Glenshesk and Glentaisie run down to Ballycastle.

Glenariff, sited between Glencloy and Glenballyemon, is the most spectacular glen, and the one most geared to tourism. Waymarked trails run from the Glenariff Forest Park Visitor Centre signposted on the A43 Cushendall–Ballymena road (tel 028 2955 6000; open all year 10–dusk). The Viewpoint Trail (1km/0.5 miles) enables you to look down the glen to the sea. Following this walk takes you back to the car park via the ornamental gardens. The popular Waterfall Walk Trail (4.5km/3 miles) passes the lovely waterfalls of the Glenariff River, while the slightly more demanding Scenic Trail of 9km (5.5 miles) goes by way of forest, moorland and river. The Rainbow Trail (0.6km/0.4 miles) is an optional detour on the Waterfall Walk Trail. Many of these paths and footbridges were laid out in Victorian times, giving the walks a period charm.

INFORMATION

www.northantrim.com

363 G1 Narrow Gauge Road, Larne, Co. Antrim, BT40 3AL 028 2826 0088 Easter–Sep Mon–Fri 9–5, Sat 10–4; Oct–Easter Mon–Fri 9–5

 Sheskburn House, 7 Mary Street, Ballycastle, Co. Antrim, BT54 6QH 028 2076 2024 Jul, Aug Mon–Fri 9–7, Sat 10–6, Sun 2–6; Sep–end Jun Mon–Fri 9–5

TIPS

» Don't ignore the glens on a wet day, especially Glenariff, where rain-swollen streams are spectacular.

» The narrow lane that climbs to Ossian's Grave is really too steep for a car, and there's nowhere sensible to park at the top. Walk up instead.

Above *Wild flowers cloak the slopes of Glenballyemon*

INTRODUCTION

The complex geology of the Antrim Coast includes rocks laid down more than 500 million years ago on an ancient ocean floor, pudding-stone that was a later desert floor, a belt of coal formed out of a swampy delta, salt trapped in the stone 200 million years ago, and mudstones and limestones from the time of the dinosaurs. The basalt that formed the Giant's Causeway comes from a volcano that dates from around 60 million years ago.

The Antrim Coast is well served by its spectacular coast road, the A2, running north from Larne to hug the coast for the 40km (25 miles) to Cushendall. From here it bypasses Cushendun to take a 50km (30-mile) inland route over the moors to Ballycastle, then 2–3km (about 1.5 miles) inland of the basalt coast around Carrick-a-Rede and the Giant's Causeway. There's an enjoyable, if slow and bumpy, 'Scenic Route' detour on the coast road, starting in Cushendun and winding for 19km (12 miles) around Torr Head, to rejoin the A2 at Ballyvoy.

WHAT TO SEE

CLIFFS AND VILLAGES OF THE COAST

The Antrim Coast is especially striking for its cliffs, bluffs, headlands and glen mouths. Driving north you encounter white limestone cliffs around Carnlough Bay, beyond which dark red sandstone rises dramatically to 250m (820ft). Garron Point curves into Red Bay, where three of the Glens of Antrim (▷ 291) meet the sea around the great flat-topped promontory of Lurigethan, 350m (1,148ft). Farther north comes paler pudding-stone around Cushendun, before you swing west towards the basalt of the Giant's Causeway. Each of the villages has a particular charm: Glenarm, beautifully set at the foot of its glen; Carnlough, with sandy beach and harbour, and white limestone houses; Waterfoot or Glenariff, below the rampart of Lurigethan; Cushendall, the 'Capital of the Glens', with bright houses, sandstone Curfew Tower jail and a huddle of houses designed by Clough Williams Ellis.

CARRICK-A-REDE ROPE BRIDGE

www.ntni.org.uk

The Carrick-a-Rede rope bridge is the only means of crossing the 25m (80ft) gap between the cliff and the Carrick-a-Rede basalt stack offshore. It was originally a scary fly walk with a single guide rope slung in the air by salmon fishermen to reach their offshore fishing station. The National Trust has made it more stable, but it still sways enough to raise the hairs on the back of your neck. There are no recorded instances of anyone being injured falling off the old bridge, although there have been times when visitors were unable to face the return walk and needed to be taken back by boat. Outlandish stunts, including riding a bicycle across and doing handstands on a chair in the middle, have been performed on the bridge.

✉ 800m (875 yards), including 161 steps, from parking area signposted on B15 between Ballycastle and Ballintoy ☎ 028 2076 9838 ⏰ Jun–end Aug daily 10–7; Sep, Oct, Mar–end May daily 10–6 (weather permitting) 🎫 Adult £2.75, child £1.50

GIANT'S CAUSEWAY

www.northantrim.com

A UNESCO World Heritage Site, the Causeway is a hump-backed promontory, formed of the wave-eroded stubs of 37,000 mostly hexagonal basalt columns created some 60 million years ago when lava from an undersea volcano cooled rapidly on contact with the cold sea water. Taller columns can be seen in the

INFORMATION

www.northantrim.com

✚ 363 G1 🅸 Narrow Gauge Road, Larne, Co. Antrim, BT40 3AL ☎ 028 2826 0088 ⏰ Easter–Sep Mon–Fri 9–5, Sat 10–4; Oct–Easter Mon–Fri 9–5

🅸 Sheskburn House, 7 Mary Street, Ballycastle, Co. Antrim, BT54 6QH ☎ 028 2076 2024 ⏰ Jul, Aug Mon–Fri 9–7, Sat 10–6, Sun 2–6; Sep–end Jun Mon–Fri 9–5

Opposite *The remarkable hexagonal columns of the Giant's Causeway*
Below *The slipway at Ballintoy harbour on the Antrim coast*

TIPS

» Though a new design of Carrick-a-Rede rope bridge makes it easier to cross, you still need both hands.

» To see the Giant's Causeway from above, walk until you are under the 'Organ Pipes'; here a path turns back towards the Visitor Centre, rising to the cliff tops for a fabulous kittiwake's-eye view of the Causeway.

cliffs behind. Legend says that the hero-giant Fionn MacCumhaill laid down the Causeway as a stepping stone, so he could stride across the Sea of Moyle to his giantess girlfriend's cave in the Hebridean island of Staffa, where there are similar columns. But whatever created the Causeway, it is a magnificent sight, especially when approached on foot from above. A coastal path can be joined at Blackrock or from the Causeway Visitor Centre on the cliff top. The Visitor Centre is a good introduction to the site, and tells the story of the formation of the Causeway through a 12-minute audio-visual show. There is also an exhibition area with displays on the legend of Finn McCool and the local birdlife. The area is a haven for sea birds such as fulmar, petrel, cormorant, shag, redshank, guillemot and razorbill. Rock pippits and wagtails explore the shoreline and eider duck are found in sheltered water. Guided tours are available from the centre, and you can catch a minibus (adult £2 return, child £1), or walk down to the Causeway from the parking area in 10 minutes. Beside the centre is the Causeway School Museum, a reconstructed 1920s schoolroom complete with learning aids and toys of the era.

Many ships have foundered below these towering cliffs but none so tragic as that of the Spanish Armada galleon *Girona*. On that fateful day in 1588, the ship was sunk during severe weather conditions in view of the Giant's Causeway. Only five of the crew are believed to have survived out of 1,300 men. Treasure of gold, silver and jewels that went down with the ship was salvaged in 1968 and is now on display in Belfast's Ulster Museum.

A narrow gauge steam train runs between the town of Bushmills (where you can drop in for a nip of whiskey at the Old Bushmills Distillery) and the Giant's Causeway World Heritage Site. It travels along a magnificent coastal stretch following the track bed of the former Giant's Causeway Tram (tel 028 2073 2844; www.freewebs.com/giantcausewayrailway; open Jul–Aug daily; Easter–end Jun, Sep, Oct Sat–Sun).

✉ 44 Causeway Road, Bushmills, Co. Antrim, BT57 8SU ⊙ Open access ♿ Free ℹ Visitor Centre: on B66 near Bushmills ☎ 028 2073 1855 ⊙ Daily ♿ £5 car, £1 audio-visual display

DUNLUCE CASTLE

The poignant ruin of Dunluce Castle stands on the edge of the cliffs—so close that during a 1639 storm the kitchens fell into the sea and the kitchen workers were killed. Surrounded by myth and legend and inhabited by giants, ghosts and banshees wailing through the sea mist, Dunluce is associated with many stories—the most romantic concerns its recapture from the English in 1584 by the owner, Sorley Boy MacDonnell, whose men had been hauled 60m (200ft) up the cliffs in baskets. Look for the pretty blue flower of Dunluce and drifts of seapinks that cluster around the castle's ruined shell.

✉ 87 Dunluce Road, Bushmills, Co Antrim, BT57 8UY ☎ 028 2073 1938 ⊙ Apr–end Sep daily 10–6; Oct–end Mar daily 10–5 ♿ Adult £2, child (4–16) £1 🚗 Off A2 just west of Portballintrae

Above left *Dunluce Castle on the Antrim coastline*

Above right *People climbing the rocks of the Giant's Causeway*

Opposite *The precarious, swaying Carrick-a-Rede rope bridge*

GOSFORD CASTLE AND FOREST PARK

The Gosford estate, former seat of the Acheson family, has strong literary connections. Dean Swift used to visit the family here, as he acknowledged in his poem 'Lady Acheson Weary of the Dean'. The grand mock-Norman castle, built of granite in the 1820s–50s now stands empty. It features as 'Castlemallock' in The Valley Of Bones, Volume 7 of Anthony Powell's saga A Dance to the Music of Time. Today the estate forms the Gosford Forest Park with an arboretum and walled garden, and four waymarked trails.

✚ 363 G3 ✉ Co. Armagh, BT60 1GD ☎ 028 3755 1277 ◷ Daily 10–sunset ✋ Car £4; pedestrians: adult £1.50, child (under 12) £0.50 🚍 Signposted on A28 just west of Markethill

HEZLETT HOUSE

www.ntni.org.uk

The National Trust look after this picturesque thatched cottage, one of the oldest domestic buildings in Northern Ireland. The simple, cosy interior is furnished in mid-Victorian style. The house is home to the Downhill Marble collection.

✉ 107 Sea Road, Castlerock, Colraine, Co Londonerry, BT51 4TW ☎ 028 2073 1582 ◷ Telephone for opening times ◷ Guided tour only adult £3, child £2

INCH ABBEY

Sir John de Courcy, whose wife, Affreca, founded Grey Abbey (▷ 277), was a warrior—he led the Norman invasion of East Ulster in 1177—and also a spiritual man. He founded Inch Abbey in 1180 on its marshland site by the River Quoile, and until the Dissolution in the 1540s the monks proved their Anglo-Irish loyalties by rejecting all Irish applicants.

✚ 363 H3 ✉ Downpatrick, Co. Down, BT30 6LZ ◷ Open access ✋ Free 🚍 Signed off A7, 1.5km (1 mile) north of town 🛈 Tourist Information Office, St. Patrick's Centre, 53a Market Street, Downpatrick, Co. Down ☎ 028 4461 2233 ◷ Jul, Aug Mon–Fri 9–6, Sat 9.30–6, Sun 2–6; Sep–end Jun Mon–Fri 9–5, Sat 9.30–5

IRISH LINEN CENTRE AND LISBURN MUSEUM

Linen-making was once the Lagan Valley's biggest industry, and the Irish Linen Centre offers a window into the mystique and craftsmanship of the trade. You can try your hand at parts of the manufacturing process, learn about scutching, hackling and retting, look at the lives of Victorian linen workers, chat to a weaver working on a restored 19th-century hand loom, and visit the museum shop (tel 028 9266 0074). Local history is detailed in the Lisburn Museum alongside.

✚ 363 G3 ✉ Market Square, Lisburn, Co. Antrim, BT28 1AG ☎ 028 9266 3377 ◷ Mon–Sat 9.30–5 ✋ Free 🚍 Lisburn

KNOCKMANY CHAMBERED CAIRN

At the end of your uphill walk from the parking area a modern structure protects the Bronze Age passage tomb of Knockmany, its stones incised with whorls, spirals and cup-marks. It's also adorned with graffiti cut over the centuries, hence the locked gate through which you are obliged to stare at them, but you can climb to the roof for a better view.

The vista from the hilltop is quite wonderful; it's said you can see seven counties from here.

✚ 363 F3 ✉ Co. Tyrone ◷ Kept locked: arrange access with Peatlands Country Park ☎ 028 6632 3110 ✋ Free 🚍 Signed off B83, 2.5km (1.5 miles) north of Clogher on A4 Dungannon–Enniskillen road 🛈 Killymaddy Tourist Information Office, Ballygawley Road, Dungannon, Co. Tyrone, BT70 1TF ☎ 028 8776 7259 ◷ Jul, Aug Mon–Fri 9–6, Sat 9–5; Easter–end Jun Mon–Fri 9–5, Sat–Sun 10–4; Sep–Easter Mon–Fri 9–5

LECALE PENINSULA

Drive around the Lecale penin-sula and you'll find a quiet corner of countryside and coast that sees few tourists. From Downpatrick you go across country on the B176 to Killough, the port for the farm produce of Castle Ward (▷ 288) in the 18th century. Turning east on the A2 you'll run through Ardglass, with its ancient fortifications around the

harbour, to Kilclief. The 15th-century tower house here was the scene of a medieval scandal when the Bishop of Down was caught with a married woman and was defrocked.

✚ 363 H3 🛈 Tourist Information Office, St. Patrick's Centre, 53a Market Street, Downpatrick, Co. Down, BT30 6LZ ☎ 028 4461 2233 ◷ Jul, Aug Mon–Fri 9–6, Sat 9.30–6, Sun 2–6; Sep–end Jun Mon–Fri 9–5, Sat 9.30–5

LONDONDERRY

▷ 289.

LOUGH ERNE

▷ 298–299.

LOUGH NEAGH

This huge inland sea is the biggest lake in the British Isles, measuring 29km (18 miles) long and 18km (11 miles) wide. For birdwatching and an exhibition on Lough Neagh's natural history, visit Oxford Island Discovery Centre on the south shore (off Junction 10 of M1; tel 028 3832 2205; Jul, Aug Mon–Fri 9–6, Sat–Sun 10–6; Sep–end Jun Mon–Fri 9–5, Sat–Sun 10–5, also Sun until 6 Easter–end Aug).

✚ 363 G2

Below The lighthouse at St. John's Point, on the Lecale peninsula

MOUNT STEWART

Mount Stewart, on the eastern shore of Strangford Lough, is the home of the Stewart family, Marquesses of Londonderry. The Stewarts were major players in British and Irish politics, and the atmosphere in their 18th-century mansion is a nice mixture of the grand and the homely.

THE HOUSE

A tour of the house starts in the pink and white galleried central hall. Look for the tail of the racehorse Hermit, which hangs beside his portrait here. Hermit won the Derby in 1867, causing the Marquis of Hastings, a deadly enemy of Hermit's owner Henry Chaplin, to lose £120,000. From here, you move through the richly appointed dining room, the study, the drawing room with its Aubusson carpets and huge pier glasses, the Rome Bedroom looking out over the terrace and Italian garden, a room full of copper pans and knife machines, the library with its signed volumes by Sean O'Casey, the sitting room lit by a ship-shaped crystal chandelier, and a wonderful music room with a floor whose inlay is mirrored by the pattern of the plaster ceiling. Between the sitting room and music room you'll find a charming feature—the door jamb against which the growing Stewart children measured their respective heights in the 1920s; you can see their progress, neatly ruled in pencil.

THE GARDENS

The estate is especially well known for its gardens, laid out between the 1920s and the 1950s with verve, imagination and more than a dash of eccentricity by Edith, Lady Londonderry, an early 20th-century Tory hostess with daringly tattooed legs and a circle of friends both great and raffish. Rare and beautiful plants thrive on all sides.

In a pond in Lady Mairi's Garden there's a 'Mary, Mary, Quite Contrary' statue, surrounded, as in the nursery rhyme, by silver bells and cockle shells. The Dodo Terrace is decorated with freakish animal sculptures, and the Red Hand of Ulster is planted in red daisies and begonias. Water gardens, formal gardens, woods and dells lead on to the 'Land of the Fairies', and also to the Temple of the Winds, a Georgian banqueting-hall on a hillock looking out over Strangford Lough.

INFORMATION

www.ntni.org.uk

✚ 363 H2 ✉ Portaferry Road, Newtonards, BT22 2AD ☎ 028 4278 8387 🕐 House: Jul, Aug daily 12–6; Jun Mon–Fri 1–6, Sat–Sun 12–6; May, Sep Mon, Wed–Fri 1–6, Sat–Sun 12–6; Oct Sat–Sun 12–6. Lakeside gardens: daily 10–dusk. Formal garden: May–end Sep daily 10–8; Apr, Oct daily 10–6; Mar Sat–Sun 10–4. Temple of the Winds: Apr–end Oct Sat–Sun 2–5 👍 Adult £7, child (5–18) £3.50 (NT members free). Grounds only adult £5.35, child £2.70 🚌 On A20 Newtownards–Portaferry road, 8km (5 miles) south of Newtownards

TIPS

» If you have children with you, ask for the Children's Quiz/Trail.

» If your eyesight is impaired, ask to be shown the areas of scented plants.

Above The stately house overlooks spectacular gardens

LOUGH ERNE

Above *Ruins of the 12th-century round tower on Devenish Island*

INFORMATION

www.fermanagh.gov.uk
www.fermanaghlakelands.com
✚ 362 E3 ℹ Fermanagh Tourist Information Centre, Wellington Road, Enniskillen, Co. Fermanagh, BT74 7EF
☎ 028 6632 3110 🕐 Jul, Aug Mon–Fri 9–7, Sat 10–6, Sun 11–5; Easter–end Jun, Sep Mon–Fri 9–5.30, Sat 10–6, Sun 11–5; Oct Mon–Fri 9–5.30, Sat–Sun 10–4, public holidays 10–5

TIP

» Bring binoculars with you to Devenish to see what many visitors miss: the four little carved heads under the conical cap of the round tower.

INTRODUCTION

Lough Erne's shape has been likened to a leaping dolphin scattering a shower of broken water drops behind it. It measures some 80km (50 miles) in total. The surrounding soil is mostly clay and peat, poor land that has resisted agriculture and remained a beautiful mixture of moorland, forest and marsh.

From Enniskillen, the hub of the Lough Erne system, you can circle Lower Lough Erne clockwise taking the A46 along the western shore to Belleek, returning down the east side of the lake on the A47 over Boa Island to Kesh, then on the A35 and B72 to Lisnarrick and B82/A32 back to Enniskillen. Upper Lough Erne, a maze of islets and small stretches of water, is flanked on the west by the A509, which becomes the N3 as it crosses the border into the Republic and reaches Belturbet. On the east, the A4 leaves Enniskillen; a turning to the B514 runs southeast to Lisnaskea and the A34 goes on to Newtownbutler, from where you steer south by minor roads for the border. Boating is a wonderful way to get to know the lakes.

WHAT TO SEE

ISLANDS OF LOUGH ERNE

The monastery established by St. Molaise in the sixth century stands on Devenish Island just north of Enniskillen (ferry from Trory jetty, tel 028 6862 1588; or Erne Tours from Enniskillen, tel 028 6632 2882). Here you'll find a tall round tower, built by monks around 1120, the ruins of the beautiful little 15th-century abbey church and a fine High Cross. There's an explanatory exhibition, and you can climb the ladders inside the tower for a wonderful view over Lough Erne. On White Island (boat from Castle Archdale Marina, tel 028 6862 1892) seven extraordinary stone carvings have been built into a wall: a grinning sheela-na-gig, a seated man with a book, another holding two gryphons, a warrior and a bishop, a King David figure and a morose face. In Caldragh cemetery on Boa Island, reached by causeways on the A47, stands the 'Janus Man', a stumpy figure, thought to be 2,000 years old, with two back-to-back faces, both with bulging eyes and pointed beards. Near him is his swollen-headed brother the 'Lusty Man'. It is uncertain what these figures represent.

On the causeway islands and shores of Upper Lough Erne are fine carvings of definite Christian tradition. Aghalurcher Old Church (signposted off the A43 just south of Lisnaskea), abandoned in 1484 after a murder at the altar, has elaborately carved skull-and-crossbones gravestones; so does the graveyard on Galloon Island (5km/3.5 miles southwest of Newtownbutler).

BOATING AND FISHING

Boating is the classic activity here, with boat rental on Lower Lough Erne from Manor House Marine Day Boats at Killadeas (tel 028 6862 8100), or Belleek Angling Centre (tel 028 6865 8181). Or you can take a trip on the *Lady of the Lake* (Inishclare Restaurant, Killadeas; tel 028 6862 2200) or MV *Kestrel* (Erne Tours Ltd., Enniskillen; tel 028 6632 2882). On Upper Lough Erne, try *Inish-cruiser* (Share Holiday Village, Lisnaskea; tel 028 6772 2122) or Belleek Charter Cruising (tel 028 6865 8027). For fly fishing on a lovely small lake, contact Rob Henshall at Coolyermer Lough Fishery (tel 028 663 41676).

COUNTRY PARKS AND COUNTRYSIDE ACTIVITIES

Lough Erne is wonderful for wildlife, with a good overview from ExplorErne's displays (Erne Gateway Centre, Belleek; tel 028 6865 8866; Jul–end Sep daily 11–5). Three Country Parks around Lower Lough Erne provide lakeside and woodland walks. Castle Caldwell Forest Park (A47 near Kesh; all year) has good birdwatching, and at the entrance is the Fiddler's Stone, a violin-shaped memorial to drunken fiddler Denis McCabe who drowned in 1779. Castle Archdale Forest Park (A32 near Kesh; all year) has a boating marina, fine gardens, and an exhibition about the World War II flying boats based here (Jul, Aug Tue–Sun 11–7, Easter–end Jun Sat, Sun 11–6). At Lough Navar Forest (near Derrygonnelly; all year) an 11km (7-mile) scenic drive ends at the spectacular Cliffs of Magho viewpoint (▷ 304).

SHEELIN LACE MUSEUM

Ireland's best collection of antique lace is displayed here; some was made locally at Inishmacsaint, other pieces, from babies' caps to wedding dresses, have been collected from all over the country.

✉ Bellanaleck, Enniskillen, Co. Fermanagh, BT92 2BA ☎ 028 663 48052 🕒 Mar–end Oct Mon–Sat 10–6 (closed 1–2 for lunch); Nov–end Feb by appointment 💷 Adult £3, child (4–16) £1

Above *The 'Lusty Man' stands on Boa Island*
Below *Lough Erne is popular with pleasure cruisers*

Above *Rocky debris from above litters the coastline of Murlough Bay below Fair Head*

MARBLE ARCH CAVES

www.marblearchcaves.net

Tours here start with the caving and mineral display in the Visitor Centre, then a spectacular underground route takes you by boat and on foot through the caverns, including the 'Moses Walk' through a subterranean river. Stalagmites, stalactites, glistening sheets of calcite and rock minerals are all revealed by lamplight. Telephone in advance and reserve a tour.

✚ 362 E3 ✉ Visitor Centre, Marlbank, Florencecourt, Co. Fermanagh, BT92 1EW ☎ 028 6634 8855 🕐 Jul, Aug daily 10–5; mid-Mar–end Jun, Sep daily 10–4.30 ♿ Adult £8, child (5–18) £5 🚌 5km (3 miles) west of Florence Court (▷ 290), signed from Drumlaghy crossroads on A32

MOUNTAINS OF MOURNE

www.mournelive.com

'...I'll wait for the wild rose that's waiting for me
Where the Mountains of Mourne sweep down to the sea.'
With these words the Victorian songwriter Percy French launched the Mountains of Mourne into the consciousness of the world's romantics. The Mournes are beautiful, a tight huddle of granite peaks that rises more than 650m (2,100ft) from the southern coast of County Down. Most people have heard of these mountains, and many come to see them, but few bother to penetrate

the narrow roads that lead up to the Silent Valley reservoir and through the spectacularly steep-sided Spelga Pass. Fewer still pull on walking boots for the walker-friendly paths. Those who do get up to the peaks are rewarded with some breathtaking views. Up here, too, is the Mourne Wall, a granite drystone wall some 35km (22 miles) long, linking all the main summits. It is a memorial to the hungry, jobless men who built it early in the 20th century.

✚ 363 G3 🛈 Mourne Heritage Trust's Countryside Centre, 87 Central Promenade, Newcastle, Co. Down, BT33 0HH ☎ 028 4372 4059 🕐 Mon–Fri 9–5 🛈 Newcastle Tourist Office, 10–14 Central Promenade, Newcastle, Co. Down, BT33 0AA ☎ 028 4372 2222 🕐 Jul, Aug Mon–Sat 9.30–7, Sun 1–7; Apr–end Jun, Sep Mon–Sat 10–5, Sun 2–6; Oct–end Mar Mon–Sat 10–5, Sun 2–5

MURLOUGH BAY

You have to walk a section of the Ulster Way cliff path to reach the extremely beautiful and peaceful Murlough Bay, so it's rarely crowded. The curved bay is book-ended by Torr Head and Fair Head, with a mostly rocky shore beneath green slopes and woods. Sheltered by craggy cliffs, it has rich plant life, from orchids to sea thrift, and birds such as peregrines and buzzards. There are remains of old lime kilns and of Drumnakill Church, where

Independence activist Sir Roger Casement, executed in 1916 for his part in the Easter Rising (▷ 38–39), had asked to be buried (though he is actually buried in Dublin).

✚ 363 G1 ✉ Signposted from Torr Head, on Cushendun–Ballyvoy scenic route off A2 (▷ 293); follow footpaths from first car park 🛈 Ballycastle Tourist Information Office, Sheskburn House, 7 Mary Street, Ballycastle, Co. Antrim ☎ 028 2076 2024 🕐 Jul, Aug Mon–Fri 9.30–7, Sat 10–6, Sun 2–6; Sep–end Jun Mon–Fri 9.30–5

NESS WOOD COUNTRY PARK

A beautiful wooded area with deep ravines thick with ferns, Ness Country Park has a spectacular walk from the parking area to where the River Burntollet makes a fine double leap of 9m (30ft) into a pool. Above, is the viewpoint of Shaun's Leap. Whether or not the famed 18th-century highwayman Shaun Crossan really escaped justice by leaping across this narrow gap, it's not a feat to try to emulate.

✚ 363 F2 ✉ Signposted off A6 Derry–Claudy road, 13km (8 miles) southeast of Derry, Co. Londonderry 🕐 Open access ♿ Free

PORTSTEWART

www.colerainebc.gov.uk

This trim little Victorian seaside resort sits on a gracefully curving waterfront. Its chief attraction is the sandy beach, stretching for 3km (2 miles) west of the town and cared for by the National Trust, who make a good job of keeping it clean, though, unfortunately, not car free. You can walk, fish, surf, swim or just make sandcastles and sunbathe on Portstewart Strand.

✚ 363 G1 🛈 Town Hall, The Crescent, Portstewart, Co. Londonderry ☎ 028 7034 4723 🕐 Jul, Aug 🛈 Railway Road, Coleraine, Co. Londonderry, BT52 1PE ☎ 028 7034 4723 🕐 Mon–Sat 9–5

PRESIDENT WILSON ANCESTRAL HOME

James Wilson was 20 years old when he emigrated to America from this little whitewashed cottage in 1807; his grandson, Woodrow

Wilson, served as the 28th President of the United States from 1913–21. You can see the family's box beds, and furniture typical of the period, and you get the chance to chat to members of the Wilson family, who still live next door.

✚ 362 F2 ✉ 28 Spout Road, Dergalt, Strabane, Co. Tyrone, BT82 8NB ☎ 028 7138 2204 ⏱ Jul, Aug Tue–Sun 2–5 ✋ Free 🚌 Signposted off B72 Strabane–Newtownstewart road, just east of Strabane

RATHLIN ISLAND

www.calmac.co.uk

Rathlin Island has a distinctive L-shape, and a reputation as one of the friendliest of Ireland's islands. It's a good idea to rent a bicycle (reserve in advance in peak season, tel 028 2076 3954) to explore the island, which measures 8km (5 miles) by 5km (3 miles). Out at the west end, the Kebble Cliffs National Nature Reserve is the largest and most remarkable cliff-nesting site in Northern Ireland. The cliffs are home to some quarter of a million seabirds during the nesting season (Apr–end Aug), and you don't need to be an expert to appreciate the numbers, the sights and the noise. For these months the hugely spectacular viewing point is open under the Warden's supervision (telephone 028 2076 3948 to make sure he/she is there). Rathlin also has an excellent small museum right on the harbour, the Boathouse Centre (tel 028 2076 2024; telephone for opening times), run by the islanders.

✚ 363 G1 ✉ Off Ballycastle (A2 Antrim coast road) 🚢 Caledonian MacBrayne ☎ 028 2076 9299; from Ballycastle, 45 min ✋ Adult £10 return, child (5–16) £5 ℹ Ballycastle Tourist Information Office, Sheskburn House, 7 Mary Street, Ballycastle, Co. Antrim, BT54 6QH ☎ 028 2076 2024 ⏱ Jul, Aug Mon–Fri 9.30–7, Sat 10–6, Sun 2–6; Sep–end Jun Mon–Fri 9.30–5

ROE VALLEY COUNTRY PARK

The River Roe runs red, hence its name, through the Roe Valley Country Park, a succession of gorges and rapids interspersed with tranquil stretches running for 5km (3 miles). There are tree-lined paths by the river, remnants of old flax mills, and a stone shed that housed the plant of a Victorian hydroelectric scheme.

✚ 363 F1 ✉ Dogleap Road, Limavady, Co. Londonderry, BT49 9NN ☎ 028 7772 2074 ⏱ Park: daily. Visitor Centre: Easter–end Sep daily 9–6; Oct–Easter daily 9–5 ✋ Free 🚌 Signposted on B192 Limavady–Dungiven road, just west of Limavady

ROWALLANE GARDEN

Rowallane Garden is testimony to the energy and imagination of one man, Hugh Armytage Moore, who during the first half of the 20th century laid out the walled garden's azalea display, the long sloping rhododendron walk (brilliant in late spring/summer) and the rock garden of various heathers, alpine plants and primulas. Nowadays, there are wild-flower meadows, too.

✚ 363 H3 ✉ Co. Down, BT24 7LH ☎ 028 9751 0131 ⏱ Mid-Apr to mid-Sep daily 10–8; mid-Sep to mid-Apr daily 10–4 ✋ Adult £4.50, child (5–16) £2 (NT members free) 🚌 Signposted off A7 Belfast–Downpatrick road, 18km (11 miles) from Belfast at Saintfield

SAUL

St. Patrick is said to have landed at Saul on his return to Ireland in AD432, and it is here he died in AD461. In 1932, to commemorate the 1,500th anniversary of St. Patrick's arrival, a church and round tower were built here. You can learn of the saint's life in the church's exhibition, and climb the nearby hill of Slieve Patrick, up a path lined with Stations of the Cross, for a wonderful view.

✚ 363 H3 ✉ Off A25 just east of Downpatrick, Co. Down ℹ Downpatrick Tourist Information Office, St. Patrick's Centre, 53a Market Street, Downpatrick, Co. Down, BT30 6LZ ☎ 028 4461 2233 ⏱ Jul, Aug Mon–Fri 9–6, Sat 9.30–6, Sun 2–6; Sep–end Jun Mon–Fri 9–5, Sat 9.30–5

SLIEVE GULLION FOREST PARK

This lovely, partly wooded volcanic mountain has a scenic drive that runs for 13km (8 miles). A waymarked track leads on up to the summit at 573m (1,879ft), with views over South Armagh, a Bronze Age cairn and a dark little lake of enchanted waters—even Fionn MacCumhaill was transformed into a withered old man by their magic.

✚ 363 G3 ✉ Co. Armagh ☎ 028 3755 1277 ⏱ Daily 10–dusk ✋ Free 🚌 Signposted off B113 between Meigh and Forkhill

Below *A rural scene within Slieve Gullion Forest Park*

SOMME HERITAGE CENTRE

www.irishsoldier.org

Set in the Whitespots Country Park, the Somme Heritage Centre commemorates Ireland's role in World War I. Guided tours take you back to the Home Rule crisis of 1910 and you can experience life in the front line in a recreation of the trenches of the Battle of the Somme.

363 H2 ✉ 233 Bangor Road, Newtonards, Co. Down ☎ 028 8164 8188 ◉ Jul, Aug Mon–Fri 10–5, Sat–Sun 12–5; Apr–end Jun, Sep Mon–Thu 10–4, Sat 12–4; Oct–end Mar Mon–Thu 10–4 ♿ Adult £3.75, child £2.75

SPRINGHILL

The Conynghams, 'planters' who came from Scotland, built Springhill around 1690 and created a comfortable home. The ladderback chairs, tables and cabinets were made by estate workers from the Conynghams' own timber, and the Georgian library and gunroom, with historic weaponry displayed, retains its 18th-century wallpaper. In the former laundry is a collection of costumes, and there are walks through the wooded grounds.

363 G2 ✉ 20 Springhill Road, Moneymore, Magherafelt, Co. Londonderry, BT45 7NQ ☎ 028 8674 8210 ◉ Easter, Jul, Aug daily 1–6; Apr to end Jun, Sep Sat–Sun 1–6 ♿ Adult £6, child (under 12) £3, family £15 (NT members free) 🚌 Signposted on the B18 Moneymore–Coagh road, 8km (5 miles) northeast of Cookstown

STRUELL WELLS

Each of the many springs in this green valley has a reputation for healing. During the 18th century Struell Wells became a major place of healing and of pilgrimage. Enthusiasm was spurred by the story that St. Patrick had spent a night in the freezing water of the drinking well known as The Tub. From The Tub, with its domed roof, the water flows through the Eye Well (said to cure eye diseases) to reach a pair of 19th-century bathhouses: a small, now roofless, one for women, and a larger house under a vaulted roof with male and female changing rooms. There's also a men's pool fed by a fall of water.

363 H3 ✉ Downpatrick, Co. Down ◉ Open access ♿ Free 🚌 Signed off the B1 Ardglass road, 3km (2 miles) east of town ℹ Downpatrick Tourist Information Office, St. Patrick's Centre, 53a Market Street, Downpatrick, Co. Down, BT30 6LZ ☎ 028 4461 2233 ◉ Jul, Aug Mon–Fri 9–6, Sat 9.30–6, Sun 2–6; Sep–end Jun Mon–Fri 9–5, Sat 9.30–5

TULLY CASTLE

On the shore of Lower Lough Erne, the fortified house of Tully Castle was built around 1610 by Sir John Hume. The defensive enclosure that surrounds the gaunt ruin of the house has been planted in the style of a 17th-century herb garden.

Tully Castle has a tragic and bloody history. During the 1641 rebellion, Roderick Maguire, whose family had lost all their land, besieged the castle. Lady Hume, trying to protect the 16 men and 69 women and children in the castle with her, negotiated safe conduct to Enniskillen in return for surrender. But as soon as he had possession, Maguire and his men stripped the women and shut them in the cellars, then tied up the male retainers and left them outside overnight. In the morning every man, woman and child was murdered; the castle was looted and burned.

362 E3 ✉ Co. Fermanagh ☎ 028 6862 1588 ◉ Easter–end Sep daily 10–6 ♿ Free 🚌 Signposted off A46 Enniskillen–Belleek road, 5km (3 miles) north of Derrygonnelly

ULSTER AMERICAN FOLK PARK

▷ 303.

ULSTER FOLK AND TRANSPORT MUSEUM

www.uftm.org.uk

The Folk Museum explores Ulster history and life through reconstructed buildings, which include thatched cottages and farmhouses, a flax mill, a school and a rural Orange Hall. The Transport Museum consists of a number of galleries of beautifully maintained exhibits—gleaming steam locomotives, horse-drawn carriages, penny-farthings and racing bicycles and a horse-drawn tram. Ulster-built cars on show here include the stylish De Lorean (of *Back To The Future* fame), with its impractical gull-winged doors.

363 H2 ✉ 153 Bangor Road, Cultra, Holywood, Co. Down, BT18 0EU ☎ 028 9042 8428 ◉ Jul–end Sep Mon–Sat 10–6, Sun 11–6; Mar–end Jun Mon–Fri 10–5, Sat 10–6, Sun 11–6; Oct–end Feb Mon–Fri 10–4, Sat 10–5, Sun 11–5 ♿ For each museum: adult £5.50, child (5–18) £3.50; joint ticket £7, child £4 🚌 11km (7 miles) east of Belfast on A2

WELLBROOK BEETLING MILL

Beetling (beating linen cloth smooth) played a vital part in Ulster's linen industry, and at the 18th-century Wellbrook Mill you can see the waterwheel and original machinery, learn about the industry in an enjoyable exhibition, and wince as the guide sets the beetles (wooden hammers) clattering.

363 F2 ✉ Wellbrook Road, Corkhill, Co. Tyrone, BT80 9RY ☎ 028 8675 1735 ◉ Jul, Aug Sat–Thu 2–6; mid-Mar to end Jun, Sep Sat–Sun 1–6 ♿ Adult £3.80, child (under 12) £2.20 (NT members free) 🚌 Signed off A505 Omagh road at Kildress, 5km (3 miles) west of Cookstown

ULSTER AMERICAN FOLK PARK

Just north of Omagh, the Ulster American Folk Park offers a multi-faceted experience. The site is divided into Irish and American areas, linked by a reconstruction of one of the ships in which Irish emigrants journeyed to the New World. Costumed guides work as their ancestors would have worked, and are always ready to explain and to answer questions. The Park came into being thanks to the generosity of the Mellon family of the United States, whose ancestor Thomas emigrated from the Omagh area with his family in 1818 when he was just five years old. Like so many Irish emigrants he prospered, becoming a judge; his son Andrew founded Pittsburgh's steel industry. The park's large collection of original buildings has been assembled from locations all over Northern Ireland and also from America.

IRISH AREA

In the Irish area you'll find the Mellon house, with its dark interior smelling of turf smoke, its cosy kitchen, and the ducks and hens in the yard outside. The family houses of other eminent Americans are here, too: The Hughes house, birthplace of John Joseph Hughes, the first Catholic Archbishop of New York, and the McKinley house, ancestral home of William McKinley, US president from 1897 until his assassination in 1901. There's a simpler peasant cabin, too, with just a single room and a total lack of privacy, the state in which most Irish people were living back then. You'll also find a weaver's cottage complete with costumed spinner working at her wheel, and a blacksmith's forge where the fire often glows red and the sparks fly; also a Mass House from the era of the Penal Laws, and a splendid schoolhouse where visiting schoolchildren experience Victorian-style lessons.

ACROSS TO THE AMERICAN AREA

A replica of a 19th-century Ulster street leads to the dockside and the cramped, dark, frightening hold of a ship, similar to that in which emigrants made their dangerous and miserable three-month crossings of the Atlantic. On the far side is the American area with another replica of a street, this one in an American port. Beyond are the buildings encountered or built by the Irish in America: log cabins and barns, a smoke-house for preserving food, and the 18th-century house built by Samuel Fulton of Donegal Springs, Pennsylvania, with stones from his fields, exactly as he would have built it in Ireland.

INFORMATION

www.folkpark.com

✚ 362 F2 ✉ Co. Tyrone, BT78 5QY
☎ 028 8224 3292 ◷ Apr–end Sep
Mon–Sat 10.30–4.30, Sun 11–5; Oct–end
Mar Mon–Fri 10.30–3.30 💷 Adult £5,
child £3 🚌 273 Belfast–Derry route
🚌 On A5 Omagh–Newtownstewart
road, 8km (5 miles) north of Omagh

TIPS

» Follow your nose as you enter the Mellon house: Fresh bread is often baked in the kitchen, and you may even be offered a share.

» The Park is extremely busy in school time, so it's worth arriving late in the day to avoid the school party crowds.

» The Centre for Migration Studies based at the park has a specialist reference library available to any member of the general public wishing to research any aspect of emigration and genealogy.

Above *History is enthusiastically re-created at the Ulster American Folk Park*
Opposite *A steam locomotive forms the backdrop for a talk at the Ulster Folk and Transport Museum*

CLIFFS OF MAGHO AND LOUGH ERNE

An opportunity to enjoy one of the best views in Ireland, and to earn your enjoyment too! There's a stiff climb to start with, helped by handily placed flights of steps, from the south shore of Lower Lough Erne to the rim of the Cliffs of Magho and that amazing view. Then you make a damp detour (wear strong shoes or boots) over heather moorland and through pine woods to a secret lake, before returning by way of forest roads and the cliffs.

THE WALK
Distance: 4.5km (2.5 miles)
Allow: 2 hours
Total ascent: 250m (820ft)
Start/end at: Car parking area on the A46 Enniskillen–Belleek road, 13km (8 miles) east of Belleek.1:50,000 OSNI Discoverer Series, map 17 Grid reference 206 358

★ From the parking area follow the 'viewpoint' sign into the wood on a path that soon steepens and zigzags up through trees by flights of steps.

❶ In the damp woods grow hart's tongue and broad buckler ferns, bracken, horsetails, mosses and pale green lichens that only flourish where the air is unpolluted.

It's a short, steep climb. Near the top pass a little well, and emerge at a parking place where you can stop and admire the view.

❷ Ireland is a country packed full of good views, but this is among the best. The waters of Lower Lough Erne stretch to the north, with green country beyond. In the distance rise the Blue Stack Mountains of County Donegal, and beyond those, some 65km (40 miles) away, the pale cone of Mount Errigal (▷ 221). To the northeast roll the round-backed Sperrin Hills of County Tyrone, while to the west lie the waters of Donegal Bay. Some 55km (34 miles) away the cliffs of Slieve League rise above the bay to the north, and to the southeast in County Sligo the unmistakable ship's-prow shape of Benbulbin, W. B. Yeats's favourite mountain, stands out 526m (1,726ft)

tall. After gazing your fill, turn right (west) along the cliff-edge path for 0.5km (0.25 miles) until you reach a wooden fence guarding the drop on your right. Beside the sixth upright of this fence, bear inland (south) on a faint path to a double post waymarked with yellow arrows, and follow the arrows in the same direction across moorland and up through a gap between blocks of coniferous woodland.

❸ You are now in Lough Navar Forest, with conifers interspersed with heather moorland and patches of sphagnum moss. The moors support a variety of wildlife, including red deer, feral goats, hares, peregrines, hen harriers and owls; crossbills and woodcock are among less common woodland birds.

Reaching little Finnauan Lough, bear right along its bank; then turn left at a post with a yellow arrow at the west end of the lake, walking south towards the trees.

4 Try jumping up and down here, and you can feel the earth move! You are walking on a bog of spagnum moss which holds many times its own weight of water. Its floating surface is knitted together by marsh cinquefoil roots.

Enter the trees beside a post whose yellow arrow points left. Follow it to the left inside the fringe of the trees on a path that soon bears right and emerges from the trees. Head south on this narrow path between more blocks of trees to a forest road and turn left for 92m (100 yards), then left again on another forest road which leads you back to the viewpoint parking area on the Cliffs of Magho.

5 Two war memorial stones stand at the side of the car parking place:

One remembers the crew of a Sunderland flying boat that sank in Lough Erne in November 1943 with the loss of three lives; the other is dedicated to the eight crewmen who died when their Catalina crashed at Lough Anlaban in the following year.

Follow the steep path back down to the lower parking area.

WHERE TO EAT

There are no facilities on the walk itself. In Enniskillen, stock up for a picnic at Forthill Fine Foods delicatessen in Forthill Street. After the walk, enjoy tea and cakes in Johnson's Jolly Sandwich Bar at 3 Darling Street, or Leslie's Home Bakery and Coffee Shop on Church Road.

PLACE TO VISIT
CLIFFS OF MAGHO VIEWPOINT

✉ 229m (750ft) above and due south of parking area on the A46
🕐 Open access ✋ Free

Above *Boats on Lower Lough Erne*
Below *Fishing from a jetty on Lower Lough Erne*
Opposite *Sunrise at Lough Erne*

HILLS AND GLENS OF TYRONE

The wild uplands and valleys of the Sperrin Mountains of County Tyrone make a superb half-day car tour. Starting to the south of the Sperrins you travel through boglands rich in archaeological remains, cross through the scenic Barnes Gap into the lovely Glenelly Valley, then over the highest part of the range, before winding your way back to Omagh.

THE DRIVE

Distance: 130km (80 miles)
Allow: 3 hours
Start/end at: Omagh

★ Omagh, a quiet market town, blazed into the headlines on 15 August 1998 when a huge bomb, planted by a dissident group calling itself the Real IRA, exploded killing 29 people and injuring 200 more. The horror was such that rather than derail the peace process, as it was most likely intended to do, it probably helped it on its way.

Leave Omagh on the A505 Cookstown road. After 7km (4 miles) bear right on the Drumnakilly–Carrickmore road, and in 137m (150 yards) turn left along the bog road to Milltown. In 1km (0.7 miles) you'll pass Fernagh Ceilidh House. Continue for another 2km (1.5 miles),

then bear right at an intersection for 3km (2 miles) to Milltown. Turn left here, and keep on for 1.5km (1 mile) to Loughmacrory Wedge Tomb.

❶ Loughmacrory Wedge Tomb is said to be guarded by a fairy tree, so no one has disturbed its great capstones that still stand supported by their massive edging stones as they have done for 4,000 years.

Return to Milltown and turn left on the Carrickmore road, bearing left in 1.5km (1 mile) towards Kildress and Drumshanbo Glebe. Cross the B46 Carrickmore–Creggan road, and in another 2.5km (1.5 miles) turn left at a crossroads for 3km (2 miles) to the A505, where you turn right for the An Creagán Visitor Centre.

❷ An Creagán Visitor Centre's exhibition tells how the great blanket

bogs grew, and of the rich archaeological treasures they contain.

Return 3km (2 miles) to the crossroads and continue straight over on the Pomeroy road for 1.5km (1 mile) to find the signposted path to Creggandevesky Court Tomb on your right.

❸ Lying in a beautiful position overlooking Lough Mallon, Creggandevesky (c3,500BC) is one of Ireland's best examples of a court tomb. Its huge hillock of stones contains three burial chambers, with the curved wings of the ceremonial court facing the lake.

Back at the crossroads turn right and continue for 7km (4.5 miles) to the A505. Turn right for 3km (2 miles) if you want to visit Wellbrook Beetling Mill.

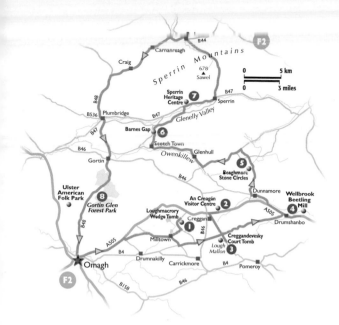

Forest Park lies just off the B48 5km (3 miles) south of Gortin.

8 A drive runs for 8km (5 miles) through the forest, and footpaths wind through the coniferous woods of Gortin Glen Forest Park.

Continue for 11km (7 miles) back to Omagh.

WHERE TO EAT
AN CREAGÁN VISITOR CENTRE
✉ Creggan ☎ 028 8076 1112

LEO MCCULLAGH'S PUB
✉ Plumbridge ☎ 028 8164 8417

BADONEY TAVERN
✉ Gortin ☎ 028 8164 8157

PLACES TO VISIT
LOUGHMACRORY WEDGE TOMB
✉ 1.5km (1 mile) north of Milltown
🕐 Open access 👆 Free

AN CREAGÁN VISITOR CENTRE
✉ Creggan ☎ 028 8076 1112
🕐 Mon–Fri 11–5.30, Sat–Sun 11–5
👆 Free

CREGGANDEVESKY COURT TOMB
✉ 4.5km (2.75 miles) south of Creggan
🕐 Open access 👆 Free

BEAGHMORE STONE CIRCLES
✉ 3km (2 miles) north of Dunnamore
🕐 Open access 👆 Free

SPERRIN HERITAGE CENTRE
✉ On B47, 14km (9 miles) east of Plumbridge ☎ 028 8164 8142 🕐 Apr–end Oct Mon–Fri 11.30–5.30, Sat 11.30–6
👆 Adult £2.60, child £1.60

GORTIN GLEN FOREST PARK
✉ 10km (6 miles) north of Omagh ☎ 028 8164 8217 🕐 Daily 10–dusk 👆 Car: £3

INFORMATION
TOURIST INFORMATION
✉ Strule Arts Centre, Townhall Square, Omagh ☎ 028 8167 0666 🕐 Mon–Sat 10–6

Opposite *The Gortin Glen Forest Park cloaks the rolling hills north of Omagh*

4 The Wellbrook Beetling Mill (▷ 302), still powered by water, shows the last stage in the production of linen. You can watch a beetling machine at work.

Continue by turning left along the A505. In 2.75km (1.75 miles) turn right to cross the Ballinderry River and pass through Dunnamore. Cross a stream and take the next right across the bogland north for 3km (2 miles) to the signposted Beaghmore Stone Circles.

5 Beaghmore Stone Circles consist of dozens of stone alignments, dating from 2000–1200BC. Stone circles stand in pairs and solo, along with many round cairns, and several stone rows or avenues.

Continue north for 4km (2.5 miles), over a crossroads, towards the Sperrin Mountains. At an intersection turn left for 6.5km (4 miles) to another intersection, where you turn right for 8km (5 miles) along the Gortin road, through Glenhull to Scotch Town. Turn right here into the hills, crossing the Barnes Gap pass.

6 A narrow crack in the hills, Barnes Gap has stunning views over the valleys of the two rivers, the Faughan and the Glenelly, that run on either side of Sawel Mountain.

Descend into the Glenelly Valley. Turn right here on the narrow road along the south side of the valley, and in 5.5km (3.5 miles) bear left to reach the B47 beyond Oughtboy Bridge. Turn right and drive for 1.5 km (1 mile) to reach the Sperrin Heritage Centre.

7 You are now deep into the beautiful Sperrin Mountains, and the Sperrin Heritage Centre will give you an insight into the life and history of this range of moorland hills, indented with deep fertile valleys.

Continue for 2.5km (1.5 miles) to Sperrin village. Turn left up the mountain road through the heart of the northern Sperrins for 11km (7 miles) to Park village. Turn left through Park village and on via Carnanreagh and Craig for 16km (10 miles) to the B48, where you turn left for Omagh by way of Plumbridge and Gortin. Gortin Glen

BELFAST REGENERATED

This walk takes you from the heart of Victorian Belfast, through the up-and-coming Cathedral Quarter and down to the regenerated riverside development, demonstrating how new life and hope is being brought to a city, more often remembered for its troubled past.

THE WALK

Distance: 5km (3 miles)
Allow: 2 hours plus stops
Start at: The Crown Liquor Saloon, Great Victoria Street ✚ 286 A4
End at: Donegall Square South ✚ 286 A4

HOW TO GET THERE

Metro Bus 8

★ Start at the Crown Liquor Saloon in Great Victoria Street, a superb example of Victorian splendour, but beware, there are said to be six ghosts in this historic pub.

❶ Just ahead on your left is the Europa Hotel, at the height of the Troubles said to be the most bombed hotel in Europe. Next to it is the splendid Grand Opera House.

Just after the Opera House turn right into Howard Street. On your left

is the former Presbyterian Church House and Assembly Rooms of 1902, now the Spires Mall Shopping Centre. Continue down Howard Street into Donegall Square. Take the first left along the square, Donegall Square West.

❷ This impressive square is dominated by the magnificent City Hall, built of Portland stone and completed in 1906. Turn right in front of City Hall into Donegall Square North. Across the road you will see the small Linen Hall Library, the city's oldest library (1788), with its fine collection of Irish manuscripts.

Take the next left into Donegall Place and shortly on the left you come to the Belfast Welcome Centre. Continuing up the street take the second right, crossing the busy road into Castle Place. Take the second

left into Bridge Street, then the first right into Waring Street and then turn immediately left into Donegall Street.

❸ You are now entering the Cathedral Quarter, fast becoming Belfast's new cultural area. As you walk down Donegall Street, the Belfast Contemporary Gallery of Photography is on the right and just beyond is the John Hewitt pub, once popular with the literary set following a tradition set by political poet Hewitt (1902–87). Ahead in the distance you will see the spire of St. Patrick's Catholic Church.

At the intersection with Talbot Street is the Protestant St. Anne's Cathedral (1904). Take a detour to visit the church with its beautiful mosaics. Note the stainless steel Spire of Hope added in 2006, which goes right down inside the church and is illuminated at night. Continue right along Talbot Street.

4 Talbot Street is the new home of the Northern Ireland War Memorial—Home Front Exhibition, and is also becoming popular for its trendy restaurants. Turn right into cobbled Hill Street, where you will find warehouses converted into galleries and restaurants. Attractive narrow alleys radiate off Hill Street, adding a degree of quaint charm to the area.

Continue along Hill Street and cross over into Skipper Street. To the left is the grand façade of the Merchant Hotel, formerly the headquarters of the Ulster Bank. At the bottom of Skipper Street turn left into High Street and continue to the end of the street; ahead is the striking, if slightly leaning, Albert Memorial Clock Tower.

5 The Clock Tower was erected in honour of Prince Albert, consort of Queen Victoria, in 1865. Note the rather small statue of the prince: It is said Queen Victoria was 'not amused' when she saw her beloved in miniature. On the right just beyond the clock in Queen's Square is McHughs Bar, the oldest building in Belfast (1711) and an excellent place for a lunch.

Continue across the square to admire the Custom House on the left, a fine building designed by Charles Lanyon in 1857. Ahead is Donegall Quay where the ceramic statue, *The Salmon of Knowledge* (1999) by John Kindness, also known as the 'Big Fish', was installed to celebrate fish returning to the cleaned-up River Lagan. Look out over the water and you will see the giant cranes of H & W (Harland & Wolff), the company who built the *Titanic*—from the jetty here you can take a Titanic boat tour. Turn right to walk along the waterfront.

6 Along this section of the riverside you cross two bridges and eventually arrive in Thanksgiving Square, where the female figure *Beacon of Hope* towers over the decorative Queen's Bridge. A little farther on is the Belfast Waterfront Hall, the city's landmark concert and conference centre. Look back for a fine view of the hills above the city.

Cross the main road in front of the hall and turn left with the Law Courts on your right. Then take the next turning right into May Street. On the corner of May Street is St. George's Market (open Friday 6am–2pm and there is a Saturday Farmers' Market). Carry on along May Street to return to the south side of Donegall Square.

WHERE TO EAT

There are plenty of opportunities for coffee or lunch along the way. A popular spot is McHughs Restaurant (▷ 318) and Bar.

Opposite *Belfast City Hall*
Below left *The Victorian Crown Liquor Saloon marks the start of the walk*
Below *Lord Dufferin statue in Donegall Square*

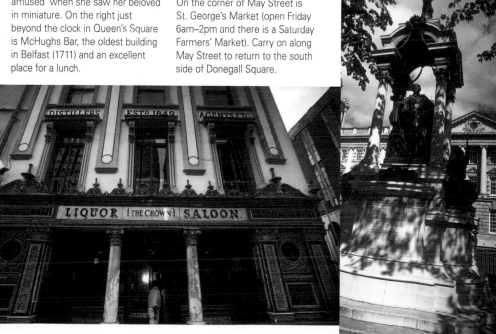

WHAT TO DO

ANTRIM

ANTRIM FORUM LEISURE COMPLEX

This is one of Northern Ireland's most important leisure complexes, regularly hosting international tournaments. Facilities include pools, gym, tennis courts and the health suite with full spa facilities.

✉ Lough Road, Antrim, Co. Antrim, BT41 4DQ ☎ 028 9446 4131 ⊛ Mon–Fri 8.15am–10pm, Sat 9.30–6, Sun 2–6 ✋ Adult swim £2.90

JUNCTION ONE

www.junctionone.co.uk
Northern Ireland's biggest outlet mall has top-flight names like Estée Lauder and Ralph Lauren, plus chain-store brands like Next.

✉ M2 Junction Ballymena Road, Antrim, Co. Antrim ☎ 028 9442 9111 ⊛ Mon–Wed 10–6, Thu, Fri 10–9, Sat 9–6, Sun 1–6 🚌 1km (0.5 miles) from J1 of M22

ARMAGH

MARKET PLACE THEATRE AND ARTS CENTRE

www.marketplacearmagh.com
This state-of-the-art facility for visual and performing arts has everything from set dancing to children's shows and serious theatre. Jazz features prominently and there's late-night bar entertainment on Fridays and Saturdays.

✉ Market Street, Armagh, Co. Armagh BT61 7BW ☎ 028 3752 1821 ⊛ Box office: Mon–Sat 9.30–4.30; performance 7pm ✋ £5–£18.50

PALACE STABLES

www.visit-armagh.com
A perfect place for family outings, the old stable block of the Bishop's Palace has been converted to provide first-rate children's activities, some with historical themes. There are games for special occasions and an adventure playground. The stables also contain living history exhibits and an imaginative display on servant life. You can also visit the Bishop's Palace at weekends.

✉ Palace Demesne, Armagh, Co. Armagh, BT60 4EL ☎ 028 3752 1801 ⊛ Jun–end Aug Mon–Sat 10–5, Sun 12–5; Apr–end May, Sep Sat 10–5, Sun 12–5 ✋ Adult £5, child (4–18) £3.25, family £15

THE SHAMBLES MARKET

Everything from radishes to ribbons are sold at this traditional variety market, all day Tuesdays and Fridays.
Try the car boot (trunk) sales on alternate Saturday mornings if you like to rummage for hidden treasure.

✉ Cathedral Road, Armagh, Co. Armagh, BT61 7AT ☎ 028 3752 8192

BALLYCASTLE

WATERTOP OPEN FARM

www.watertopfarm.co.uk
At this large cattle and sheep farm in the Glens of Antrim, you can go pony trekking or boating and there are scenic walks in the surrounding area. There are also shearing demonstrations and an interesting farm museum.

✉ 188 Cushendall Road, Ballypatrick, Ballycastle, Co. Antrim ☎ 028 2076 2576 ⊛ Daily July, Aug 11–5.30 ✋ Adult £2, child £1.50 entry fee

BANGOR

BANGOR CASTLE LEISURE CENTRE

www.northdown.gov.uk
Four pools, a fully equipped health suite, a great range of the latest exercise classes and everything

Above *Fireworks over Belfast*

from trampolining to indoor bowling make this excellent as a wet-weather option.

✉ Castle Park Avenue, Bangor, Co. Down, BT20 4BN ☎ 028 9127 0271 ◷ Mon, Fri 7.30am–10pm, Sat 7.45–6, Sun 2–6 ♿ Swim: adult £2.05, child (3–18) £1.55

CAFÉ CEOL AND BOOM BOOM ROOM

Upstairs is for hedonists, downstairs is funky at this top spot for young partygoers. Japanese themes portray 'a delightful weirdness' and it's a heady blend of zest and Zen.

✉ 17–21 High Street, Bangor, Co. Down ☎ 028 9146 8830 ◷ Daily 7pm to late ♿ Downstairs usually free, upstairs, £5–£7

PICKIE FUN PARK

Family fun on the seashore, within a safe environment. Activities include rides on giant floating swans, the Pickie Puffer, mini karts and an adventure playground.

✉ Marine Gardens, The Promenade, Bangor, Co. Down ☎ 028 9127 4430 ◷ Easter–end Oct, daily 10–10; Nov–Easter Sat–Sun 10–dusk ♿ Free; charges for rides.

BELFAST

APARTMENT

www.apartmentbelfast.com

A funky, stylish bar/restaurant with hip décor, resident and guest DJs, attracting a sophisticated and stylish crowd. It's right in the middle of Belfast, and window tables give great views over the City Hall.

✉ 2 Donegall Square, Belfast, BT1 6JA ☎ 028 9050 9777 ◷ Daily 8am–1am ♿ Usually free

BAMBU BEACH CLUB

This huge, beach-themed club is popular with students. Clubbers may have to wait in line, but at least they can do so under cover in the Odyssey Arena. Music is mainstream, and the five bars on two floors offer a choice of exotic cocktails.

✉ Odyssey, Queen's Quay, Belfast, BT3 9QQ ☎ 028 9046 0011 ◷ Tue, Thu–Sun 8pm–1am ♿ Free–£15

BELFAST ZOO

www.belfastzoo.co.uk

This excellent zoo provides good facilities for its animals. It is set under the dramatic headland of Cave Hill, and has become a top visitor attraction, with plenty of activities especially designed for families.

✉ Antrim Road, Belfast, BT36 7PN ☎ 028 9077 6277 ◷ Apr–end Sep daily 10–7, Oct–end Mar daily 10–4 ♿ Mid-Mar to end Sep: adult £8.10, child £4.30, family £22; Oct to mid-Mar: adult £6.70, child £3.40, family £18 🚌 Metro 1A/B/C/D/E/F, 2A

THE BOOKSHOP AT QUEEN'S

One of the few remaining independent bookshops, with helpful staff and a good selection, including Irish books.

✉ 91 University Road, Belfast, BT7 1NL ☎ 028 9066 6302 ◷ Mon–Sat 9.30–5.30 🚌 Metro 8

CASEMENT PARK

In the west Belfast heartland, Casement Park is the top stadium for Gaelic games in Ulster.

✉ Andersonstown Road, Belfast, BT11 9AS ☎ 028 9038 3815 ◷ Telephone for information about games and prices 🚌 Metro 10A/B/C/D/H

DUNDONALD INTERNATIONAL ICE BOWL

www.theicebowl.com

Dundonald's Olympic-size ice rink is part of a very popular leisure complex that includes an indoor adventure playground and a 30-lane bowling alley.

✉ Old Dundonald Road, Belfast, BT16 1XT ☎ 028 9080 9123 ◷ Telephone for times of individual activities ♿ Telephone for prices of activities 🚌 Metro 18, 19

EMPIRE

www.thebelfastempire.com

Anything from salsa classes to stand-up comedy is staged at the Empire, distinctively set in a con-verted church in the university area.

✉ 42 Botanic Avenue, Belfast, BT7 1JD ☎ 028 9024 9276 ◷ Mon–Tue 11.30–11, Wed–Sat 11.30am–1am, Sun 7–12 ♿ £2–£19

GRAND OPERA HOUSE

▷ 280–282

☎ Ticketline: 028 9024 1919 ◷ Box office: Mon–Fri 8.30am–9pm, Sat 8.30–6. Performance: usually 7.30pm ♿ £5–£40

THE LYRIC THEATRE

www.lyrictheatre.co.uk

The Lyric began as a small company specializing in performing the plays of W. B. Yeats. These days it has diversified putting on a varied calendar, still with an emphasis on Irish plays.

✉ Ridgeway Street, Belfast, BT9 5FB ☎ 028 9038 5685 ◷ Box office: Mon–Fri, 10–7, Sat 4–7 Performance: 8pm ♿ £7–£18

NINE

An independent boutique featuring designers including Nicole Farhi, Vivienne Westwood, Emilio Pucci and many more. Lovely surroundings to showcase the styles.

✉ 9 Chichester Street, Belfast, BT1 4JA ☎ 028 9023 3303 ◷ Mon–Sat 9.30–5.30 (Thu until 7pm)

ODYSSEY

www.odysseyarena.com

Dozens of international eateries, bars, clubs, multiplex cinemas, ten-pin bowling and games rooms fill this riverside complex, Belfast's most popular nightspot for all ages. There's also a sports and music performance arena.

✉ Queen's Quay, Belfast, BT3 9QQ ☎ 028 9073 9074 ◷ Box office: Mon–Sat, 10–7 ♿ £14–£60

ODYSSEY ARENA

www.odysseyarena.com

The Belfast Giant's Ice Hockey team competes here in the National League. The matches are great family occasions and worth going for the full USA-style razzmatazz. Odyssey Arena is also home to occasional indoor sports events and motorcycle shows.

✉ Queen's Quay, Belfast, BT3 9QQ ☎ 028 9073 9074 ◷ Box office: Mon–Sat 10–7 ♿ Adult £14, child (4–16) £8, family £37

OLD MUSEUM ARTS CENTRE
www.oldmuseumartscentre.org
Belfast's most adventurous contemporary arts organization is housed in one of its finest buildings. The Old Museum Arts Centre presents creative fringe and cutting-edge events.
✉ 7 College Square North, Belfast, BT1 6AR ☎ 028 9023 3332 🌐 Box office: Mon–Sat 9.30–5.30 👆 Adult £9.50, child £7

OZONE TENNIS CENTRE
www.belfastcity.gov.uk
This indoor tennis arena provides the only public tennis courts in the city. It is in a park by the river, offers classes and lessons, and there's a climbing wall too.
✉ Ormeau Embankment, Belfast, BT6 8LT ☎ 028 9045 8024 🌐 Mon–Sat 9am–10pm, Sun 10–5 👆 Tennis from £2.50 🚌 Metro 7A/D

ROSS'S AUCTIONS
Thursday is auction day in this long-established auction house, which handles the best country-house furniture, silver, glass, porcelain and paintings, and items of local interest.
✉ 37 Montgomery Street, Belfast, BT1 4NX ☎ 028 9032 5448 🌐 Auctions: Wed 9–5 (viewing for Thu sale), Thu 10am

ROTTERDAM BAR
www.rotterdambar.com
Tucked between Belfast's old dock area and a prestigious office and residential development, the tiny Rotterdam is well known as a great place for live music. There are different styles on different nights—jazz, folk, reggae, rock, disco.
✉ 54 Pilot Place, Belfast, BT1 3AH ☎ 028 9074 6021 🌐 Daily 11am–1am, Thu sessions begin 9pm 👆 £5

ST. GEORGE'S MARKET
▷ 285.

SMYTH'S IRISH LINENS
In the heart of the city, Smyth's offers a wide selection of Irish linens and souvenirs. Cloth of any size or shape can be made and shipped back to your home. A VAT-free export scheme is offered.
✉ 65 Royal Avenue, Belfast BT1 1FF ☎ 028 9024 2232 🌐 Mon–Sat 9–5.30

SURF MOUNTAIN
Outdoor sports fans head to this specialist in water sports, mountain sports and adventure travel for expert advice and the latest gear. Leading the field in Northern Ireland, the shop also has cool sunglasses, caps and more.
✉ 12 Brunswick Street, Belfast, BT2 7GE ☎ 028 9024 8877 🌐 Mon–Sat 9.30–5.30

ULSTER HALL
www.ulsterhall.co.uk
Stately Victorian architecture and great acoustics make this the preferred home of the Ulster Orchestra. The hall is closed for renovation until late 2008 as part of a £7.43 million restoration project.
✉ Bedford Street, Belfast, BT2 2FF ☎ 028 9032 3900

W5
www.w5online.co.uk
The five Ws are who? what? when? where? why? Enquiring young minds find learning lots of fun here, and experts are always on hand to help out.
✉ Odyssey, Queen's Quay, Belfast, BT3 9QQ ☎ 028 9046 7700 🌐 Mon–Thu 10–5 (school holidays until 6), Fri–Sat 10–6, Sun 12–6 👆 Adult £6.50, child (3–16) £4.50, family £19

WATERFRONT HALL
www.waterfront.co.uk
Even without its full calendar of cultural events and pop concerts, it's worth going to this stunning 3,000-seat auditorium just to enjoy the views from the bars overlooking the River Lagan and Belfast Lough.
✉ 2 Lanyon Place, Belfast, BT1 3WH ☎ 028 9033 4400 🌐 Box office: Mon–Sat 9–5 👆 £7–£60

WINDSOR PARK
Home of the Northern Ireland international football team, Windsor Park welcomes top European teams in the build-up to the World Cup.
✉ Donegall Avenue, Belfast, BT12 6LW ☎ 028 9024 4198 🚌 Metro 93

BELLEEK
BELLEEK POTTERY SHOP
▷ 279.

CASTLEWELLAN
MOUNT PLEASANT TREKKING & HORSE RIDING CENTRE
www.mountpleasantcentre.com
Safe experienced horses, expert guides and beautiful scenery combine to make a memorable visit. All levels of expertise are catered for, but reserve in advance to make sure.
✉ 15 Bannanstown Road, Castlewellan, Co. Down, BT31 9BG ☎ 028 4377 8651 👆 1-hour trek £15

COMBER
PURE DAY SPA
www.puredayspa.com
Pure is a rural day retreat that offers a comprehensive range of relaxing treatments. The service is highly personalized.
✉ 48a Ballybunden Road, Killinchy, Co. Down, BT23 6RF ☎ 028 9754 3000 🌐 Mon–Fri 9–6, Sat–Sun by appointment 👆 Treatments from £25

CROSSGAR
JAMES NICHOLSON, WINE MERCHANT
www.jnwine.com
Connoisseurs travel a long way to sample James Nicholson's latest wine discoveries. His shop in a small village holds treasures from France, the rest of Europe and the new world.
✉ 27a Killyleagh Street, Crossgar, Co. Down, BT30 9DQ ☎ 028 4483 0091 🌐 Mon–Sat 10–7

CUSHENDALL
ARDCLINIS OUTDOOR ADVENTURE CENTRE
www.ardclinis.com
A thoroughly professional provider, offering everything from corporate team-building and solo challenges to family fun. Activities on offer include power-boating, windsurfing and abseiling.
✉ High Street, Cushendall, Co. Antrim, BT44 0NB ☎ 028 2177 1340 🌐 Daily from 9am 👆 Telephone for prices

MCMULLANS CENTRAL BAR

Traditional and contemporary music nights cater for all tastes at this well-known County Antrim pub. Children and parties are warmly welcomed. Check first to see what music is on. A good value menu is available while you listen.

✉ 7 Bridge Street, Cushendall, Co. Antrim ☎ 028 2177 1730 🕐 Daily (extended to 1am some nights)

DERRY

BOOKWORM

A bibliophile's delight, this well-established bookshop stocks a wide selection of local and Irish titles, and has an out-of-print search facility and a coffee shop.

✉ 18–20 Bishop Street, Derry, Co. Londonderry, BT48 6PW ☎ 028 7128 2727 🕐 Mon–Sat 9.30–5.30

CAFÉ ROC

Derry's top club attracts national DJs. Clubbers like to dress up here.

✉ 125–139 Strand Road, Derry, Co. Londonderry, BT48 7PA ☎ 028 7136 0556 🕐 Bar daily from 12; club 10.30pm–late 🖐 Tue £5, Sat £6

THE CRAFT VILLAGE

Craftspeople work in this imaginative historic project right in the heart of Derry. Visitors quickly sense the great atmosphere of creative activity. The Craft Village provides a welcome alternative to the multinational chains.

✉ Shipquay Street, Derry, Co. Londonderry ☎ 028 7126 0329 🕐 Individual shop times vary

FISHING

www.loughs-agency.org
The Foyle system is one of the best salmon rivers in the world. Contact the Loughs Agency for permits and licences.

☎ 028 7134 2100

FOYLE CRUISE LINE

www.foylecruiseline.com
Enjoy views of Derry's walls and Lough Foyle's shores from the water, and learn its eventful history. Evening cruises have entertainment.

✉ Harbour Museum, Harbour Square, Derry, Co. Londonderry, BT48 6AF ☎ 028 7136 2857 🕐 Daily cruises 2pm, evening sailings 8pm; telephone to confirm 🖐 Adult £8, child £5, family £22

THE GUILDHALL

Taking its name from historic ties with the Guilds of the City of London, Derry's neo-Gothic civic and cultural complex hosts a varied calendar of performances.

✉ Guildhall Square, Derry, Co. Londonderry, BT48 6DQ ☎ 028 7137 7335 🕐 Tickets (and prices) for performances are advertised locally

LISNAGELVIN LEISURE CENTRE

A wave pool and water-based adventure play area make this more than just a swimming pool. There are spa facilities and a fitness room.

✉ Richill Park, Derry, Co. Londonderry, BT47 5QZ ☎ 028 7134 7695 🕐 Mon 2–9.40, Tue–Fri 10–9.40, Sat 10–5.40, Sun 12–4.40 🖐 Swim: adult £2.50, child (5–17) £1.90

MILLENNIUM FORUM

www.millenniumforum.co.uk
This large theatre stages a variety of shows. The brand new performance arena attracts top international stars as well as local talent.

✉ Newmarket Street, Derry, Co. Londonderry, BT48 6EB ☎ 028 7126 4455 🕐 Box office: Mon–Sat 10–5, evenings of performance 7–9 🖐 £7.50

THE NERVE CENTRE

www.nerve-centre.org.uk
Cutting-edge music and film are major elements of this adventurous arts venue.

✉ Magazine Street, Derry, Co. Londonderry, BT48 6HJ ☎ 028 7126 0562 🕐 Box office Mon–Fri 9.30–5.30, Sat 2–5 🖐 Price varies 🖥

OGMIOS

This specialist shop has an extensive range of Irish language books, cards, crafts and music items, including musical instruments.

✉ 34 Great James Street, Derry, Co. Londonderry, BT48 7DB ☎ 028 7126 4132 🕐 Mon–Thu 9.30–5, Fri 9.30–4

DONAGHADEE

GRACE NEILL'S BAR

www.graceneills.com
A mix of music including acoustic traditional folk and country can be heard at this pub, one of many claiming to be the oldest in Ireland. The food is good, and some famous musicians have been known to join in a session.

✉ 33 High Street, Donaghadee, Co. Down, BT21 0AH ☎ 028 9188 4595 🕐 Mon–Thu 11.30–11, Fri, Sat 11.30am–1am, Sun 12.30pm–10

DUNAMANAGH

RASPBERRY HILL HEALTH FARM

www.raspberry-hill.co.uk
With treatments designed to ease stress and reduce weight, Raspberry Hill offers a full range of beauty products and spa facilities, plus indoor bowls, tennis and a gym. Guests are encouraged to participate for a whole day here, and can choose whether to follow the active programme or the relaxation programme.

✉ 29 Bonds Glen Road, Killaroo, Co. Londonderry, BT47 3ST ☎ 028 7139 8000 🖐 Full day 9.30–7.30, £65 including meals; treatments extra

DUNGANNON

DUNGANNON GOLF CLUB

www.dungannongolfclub.com
The home of international golf star Darren Clarke, this is a mature 18-hole par 72 parkland course. The best days for visitors are Monday, Thursday and Friday.

✉ 34 Springfield Lane, Dungannon, Co. Tyrone, BT70 1QX ☎ 028 8772 7338 🖐 £20–£25, 24-hour advance reservations required

THE LINEN GREEN

www.thelinengreen.com
Well designed and small in scale, the Linen Green has excellent designer shopping at discount prices. People come here for the Irish linens, fine Moygashel fabrics, and the factory shop of international designer Paul Costelloe.

✉ Moygashel, Co. Tyrone, BT71 7HB ☎ 028 8775 3761 🕐 Mon–Sat 10–5

TYRONE CRYSTAL
The shop at the home of Tyrone Crystal stocks a wide range of products, together with a few 'seconds'. For a small charge, visitors can get a guided tour of the factory.
✉ Coalisland Road, Dungannon, Co. Tyrone, BT71 6TT ☎ 028 8772 5335 🕐 Mon–Sat 9–5, tours vary, telephone for details ✋ Adult £5, child (under 12) £2.50 🚍

ENNISKILLEN
ARDHOWEN THEATRE
www.ardhowentheatre.com
This lakeside theatre has a lovely setting and presents events of broad appeal, from local artists to drama festivals.
✉ Dublin Road, Enniskillen, Co. Fermanagh, BT74 6HN ☎ 028 6632 3233/5440 🕐 Box office: Mon–Fri, 10–4.30, 7–8.30, Sat 11–1, 2–5, also 6–7 on performance evenings ✋ £8–£15

BLAKES OF THE HOLLOW
Catch traditional music sessions on Friday or Saturdays in this lovely old pub, owned by the same family since the 1880s.
✉ 6 Church Street, Enniskillen, Co. Fermanagh, BT74 7EJ ☎ 028 6632 2143 🕐 Mon–Sat 11.30am–1am, Sun 11.30am–midnight

THE BUTTERMARKET
www.thebuttermarket.com
The restored Buttermarket makes an ideal focus for local craftworkers, who present a fascinating range of items. Among the many lovely pieces for sale here are Frankie McPhillips' classic salmon fly collection, pottery, textile designs, jewellery and art.
✉ Down Street, Enniskillen, Co. Fermanagh, BT74 7DU ☎ 028 6632 3837 🕐 Mon–Sat 10–5

FISHING AND CRUISING
Fermanagh has a huge selection of cruising opportunities on the Erne–Shannon waterway or loughs. Fishing is good, too, alone or with a ghillie for local expertise. The Tourist Office has full details.

MANOR HOUSE MARINE BOAT HIRE
www.manormarine.com
Spend half or a whole day soaking up the breathtaking scenery of Lough Erne from a boat. No experience or licence is required for rental. Full tuition is given to first-timers.
✉ Killadeas, Co. Fermanagh ☎ 028 6862 8100 🕐 Daily 10–2 or 2–6 ✋ Half-day £50, full day £70

HOLYWOOD
THE BAY TREE
In an attractive courtyard, this pottery shop and gallery also has a restaurant and garden.
✉ 118 High Street, Holywood, Co. Down, BT18 9HW ☎ 028 9042 1419 🕐 Mon–Sat 8–4.30, dinner Fri only 7–9.30

LARNE
CARNFUNNOCK COUNTRY PARK
www.larne.gov.uk/carnfunnock
A family-friendly park with a maze in the shape of Northern Ireland, a miniature railway and other activities, all overlooking the Irish Sea.
✉ Coast Road, Larne, Co. Antrim, BT40 2QG ☎ 028 2827 0541/2826 0088 🕐 Telephone for times ✋ Maze free. Laser clay shooting £2.50. Table tennis £1.50. Miniature train £1.60

LISBURN
DOWN ROYAL RACECOURSE
www.downroyal.com
Home of the Ulster Derby, held in summer, this attractive course aims to become one of the best in the whole of Ireland.
✉ Maze, Lisburn, Co. Down, BT27 5RW ☎ 028 9262 1256 ✋ £10–£15

NEWCASTLE
ROYAL COUNTY DOWN GOLF CLUB
www.royalcountydown.org
Marvellously scenic, this championship course borders the Irish Sea, beneath the Mourne Mountains. It is one of the world's toughest golf challenges.
✉ Golf Links Road, Newcastle, Co. Down, BT33 0AN ☎ 028 4372 3314 ✋ £25–£175 (telephone in advance)

TOLLYMORE MOUNTAIN CENTRE
www.tollymore.com
A full range of mountain-based activities, including climbing and white-water kayaking. Fortuitously, they offer first-aid courses, too!
✉ Bryansford, Newcastle, Co. Down, BT33 0PT ☎ 028 4372 2158 ✋ Introduction to kayaking £62

PORTADOWN
CRAIGAVON WATERSPORTS CENTRE
www.craigavon.gov.uk
Waterskiing, sailing, banana boating or windsurfing. Tuition and equipment are provided.
✉ Lake Road, Craigavon, Co. Armagh, BT64 1AF ☎ 028 3834 2669 🕐 Telephone in advance ✋ Windsurfing hire £15 per hour

PORTAFERRY
EXPLORIS
www.exploris.org.uk
This aquarium is popular with families. Expert guides tell of the enormous marine riches of Strangford Lough in an easy-to-understand way.
✉ The Ropewalk, Portaferry, Co. Down, BT22 1NZ ☎ 028 4272 8062 🕐 Apr–4 Sep Mon–Fri 10–6, Sat 11–6, Sun 12–6 ✋ Adult £6.90, child (4–16) £4

PORTRUSH
DUNLUCE CENTRE
www.dunlucecentre.co.uk
Interactive games, turbo rides and a treasure hunt make the Dunluce Centre a perfect refuge if the weather's bad.
✉ Sandhill Drive, Portrush, Co. Antrim, BT56 8BF ☎ 028 7082 4444 🕐 Jul, Aug 10–6; mid-Mar to end Jun, Sep, Oct Sat–Sun 12–5 ✋ Adult £8.50, family £27

TOOME
CROSSKEYS INN
One of Ireland's most famous traditional music pubs, with sessions on Saturdays, and impromptu music other nights.
✉ 40 Grange Road, Ardnaglass, Toome, Co. Antrim, BT41 3QB ☎ 028 7965 0694 🕐 Daily 11.30am–2am

FESTIVALS AND EVENTS

MARCH

ST. PATRICK'S DAY

www.discovernorthernireland.com
Throughout the province, events mark the day dedicated to Ireland's patron saint. Carnivals, concerts and parades in Belfast, Derry and Downpatrick, and religious services at Armagh and Saul.

📋 Tourist information: Belfast ☎ 9024 6609; Derry ☎ 028 7126 7284; Down, ☎ 028 4461 2233 🕔 17 March

MAY

BELFAST CITY MARATHON

www.belfastcitymarathon.com
Belfast's marathon takes competitors on an undulating course through the city. It attracts serious athletes and fun-runners.

✉ Belfast ☎ 028 9060 5944 🕔 First weekend in May

BALLYCLARE HORSE SHOW

www.discovernorthernireland.com
Today this traditional horse fair has lots of street activities, music and carnival fun.

☎ 028 9334 1110

MAY/JUNE

BELFAST CHILDREN'S FESTIVAL

www.belfastchildrensfestival.com
An annual international festival for children up to 12 years and accompanying adults. The festival lasts for about a week and includes performances, workshops and exhibitions in the city centre, many of which are free.

✉ Venues around the city ☎ 028 9031 2264 🕔 End May/early June

JUNE

THE LORD MAYOR'S CARNIVAL

www.gotobelfast.com
The streets of Belfast are full of floats, bands and carnival fun in this traditional civic parade.

✉ Belfast ☎ 028 9050 0579 🕔 End June

GALWAY HOOKERS REGATTA AND FESTIVAL

www.ards-council.gov.uk
Portaferry is one of Ireland's most beautifully positioned coastal villages, and the annual visit of the traditional red-sailed hookers from Galway is celebrated with bands, *ceilidhs*, traditional music and yacht racing.

✉ Portaferry, Co. Down ☎ 028 9182 6846 🕔 End June

JULY

GLENARM CASTLE HIGHLAND GAMES

www.glenarmcastle.com
A world-class event featuring international competitors ensures a great day out for all the family. There are all manner of Highland sports, plus bagpipes, a funfair, rare breeds and traditional entertainment. There is even a sheep-shearing competition.

✉ 2 Castle Lane, Glenarm, Ballymena, Co Antrim, BT44 0BQ ☎ 028 2884 1203 🕔 Mid July

JULY–AUGUST

ORANGEMEN'S CELEBRATIONS

www.discovernorthernireland.com
Marches (sometimes controversial) celebrating the Loyalist tradition take place throughout the summer. They range from the marches to commemorate the World War I Battle of the Somme to those remembering the Battle of the Boyne.

☎ 028 9024 6609

AUGUST

AULD LAMMAS FAIR

www.moyle-council.org
Claiming to be Ireland's oldest traditional market fair, 'the Auld Lammas' fills the narrow streets of Ballycastle with horse traders, market stalls and street entertainment. Iry local delicacies 'dulse' (edible seaweed) and 'yellow man' (honeycomb).

✉ Ballycastle, Co. Antrim ☎ 028 2076 2024 🕔 Last weekend in August

AUGUST/SEPTEMBER

HILLSBOROUGH INTERNATIONAL OYSTER FESTIVAL

www.hillsboroughoysterfestival.com
Sample the traditional combination of Guinness and oysters in the pretty Georgian village of Hillsborough at this established festival of quality food and great entertainment.

✉ Hillsborough ☎ 028 9268 9717 🕔 Late August/early September

OCTOBER/NOVEMBER

BELFAST FESTIVAL AT QUEENS

www.belfastfestival.com
One of the biggest events of its kind in Europe, this arts festival (inaugurated by Queens University) attracts big names from all branches of the performing and visual arts. The schedule includes an eclectic range of events.

✉ Belfast ☎ 028 9097 1197

Below *Belfast's marathon takes place in May*

PRICES AND SYMBOLS

The restaurants are listed alphabetically within each town. The prices given are the average for a two-course lunch (L) and a three-course dinner (D) for one person, without drinks. The wine price given is for the least expensive bottle.

For a key to the symbols, ▷ 2.

ARMAGH
THE STAGE BAR & BISTRO

www.thestagearmagh.com
This bar and bistro is located in Armagh city centre and is part of the local arts and conference complex. The style is cool and retro and the menu a blend of European and Irish. It is a popular meeting place for coffee, drinks or pre-theatre meals. Highlights include the 'trio' of sausages—wild boar/venison/pork and honey—and you can choose from delights such as fried duck breasts with pickled red cabbage and gooseberry compote. There is live music every Saturday night.
✉ The Market Place Theatre & Arts Centre, Market Square, Armagh, Co. Armagh, BT61 7AT ☎ 028 3752 1828 ◉ Mon–Wed

9.30–5, Thu–Sat 9–9, Sun 12–6 👋 L £15, D £20, Wine £11.50 🚌 Market Square is in the centre of Armagh

BALLYCASTLE
WYSNER'S

This is an elegant little French-style café serving delicious food throughout the day, with a more sophisticated upstairs restaurant open in the evenings. It serves an interesting range of modern Irish cuisine, using local seafood and produce. Head chef Jackie Wysner's Bushmills malt cheesecake is legendary.
✉ 16 Ann Street, Ballycastle, Co. Antrim, BT54 6AD ☎ 028 2076 2372 ◉ Mon–Sat 9–5, 7–9.30 👋 L £10, D £25, Wine £11.50 🚌 Ballycastle is on the A2, on the north Antrim coast

BANGOR
THE AVA RESTAURANT

www.theava.co.uk
Located on the first floor, the Ava Restaurant opened in 1998 and has been serving good honest food with an innovative twist ever since. The bright dining room with its colourful chairs and modern décor

is conducive to a pleasant lunch or dinner served by friendly staff. Locally sourced Ulster produce is a mainstay of the menu prepared and presented with flair. The Ulster beefburgers are a popular choice, served plain or with spicy sauces. There are some great steak dishes but fish lovers and vegetarians are well catered for, and there is a good range of speciality coffees. Ava also has a lively bar and an off-sales enterprise selling all manner of drinks, cheeses and chocolates.
✉ 132 Main Street, Bangor, Co. Down, BT20 4AG ☎ 028 9146 5490 ◉ Mon–Fri 12–2.30, 5–9, Sat 12–2.30, 5–9.50, Sun 12.30–8 👋 L £7.45, D £20, Wine £8.95 🚌 Main Street lies on the A2 in central Bangor

JEFFERS BY THE MARINA

www.stephenjeffers.com
Stephen Jeffers, one of the most respected chefs in Northern Ireland, produces beautifully balanced seasonal food in lovely surroundings overlooking the marina at Bangor. Tangy starters include the likes of goat's cheese and chive fritters and

zesty houmous. Mains tempt the taste buds with dishes such as crisp fillet of sea trout or slow cooked Strangford lamb. You might also like to try Jeffers' new restaurant The Boat House on Seacliff Road on the other side of the marina.

✉ / Gray's Hill, Bangor, Co. Down, BT20 3BB ☎ 028 9185 9555 ⏰ Mon 10–4, Tue–Sat 10–10, Sun 10–8 ✋ L £12, D £20, Wine £9.50 🚌 Take Main Street A2 towards the marina, turn left into Queen's Parade which leads into Gray's Hill, Jeffers is at the bottom of the hill overlooking the marina

OLD INN
www.theoldinn.com

Choose from the 1614 restaurant, the Churn Bistro or the Parlour Bar for a range of eating experiences. The restaurant produces classic dishes with a modern slant using the best of local produce. The cosy Parlour Bar is a popular venue for good pub food.

✉ 15 Main Street, Crawfordsburn, Co. Down, BT19 1JH ☎ 028 9185 3255 ⏰ Mon–Sat 7–9.30, Sun 12.30–2.30, 5–10 ✋ L £18.95, D £35, Wine £13.75 🚌 5km (3 miles) past Holywood on the A2 there is a sign for the Old Inn and 100m (110 yards) past this sign, turn left at the traffic lights; the hotel is on the left in the village

BELFAST
ALDENS
www.aldensrestaurant.com

The purple-canopied, frosted glass frontage gives a striking first impression of this sophisticated restaurant. Cooking is crisp, clear and technically advanced, providing a wide-ranging menu with many luxury ingredients. Lunch specials may include pork and leek sausages with mash and onion gravy, or goat's cheese, pear and caper pie. The home-made ciabatta and rolls are excellent.

✉ 229 Upper Newtownards Road, Belfast, BT4 3JF ☎ 028 9065 0079 ⏰ Mon–Sat 12–2.30, 6–10.30 (Sat until 11) ✋ L £34, D £44, Wine £13.95 🚌 Metro 19, 19A 🚌 3km (2 miles) east of city on A20 towards Newtownards

ARC BRASSERIE
www.waterfront.co.uk

In the splendid Waterfront Hall overlooking the River Lagan, you can have coffee, lunch or afternoon tea in this restaurant with views. For lunch there are tasty starters such as shredded duck spring roll with chilli and coriander dipping sauce followed by main courses including seafood, pasta or vegetarian options. Take advantage of the special pre-theatre menu served between 5 and 8pm with dishes ranging from steaks to risotto of butternut squash. Good value.

✉ Waterfront Hall, 2 Lanyon Place, Belfast BT1 3WH ☎ 028 9024 4966 ⏰ Mon–Fri 10–4.30, event evenings 5–8pm ✋ L £10, D £19.95, Wine £12 🚌 Any Metro bus to Laganside Buscentre 🚌 Lanyon Place is just off Oxford Street, follow signs for city centre and Belfast Waterfront Hall via East Bridge or Oxford Street. Parking at multi-storey Lanyon Place

BEATRICE KENNEDY
www.beatricekennedy.co.uk

Rich hues and lazy colonial ceiling fans give an intimate Victorian period atmosphere. Expect familiar themes and ingredients, enhanced by some big bold tastes and an occasional whiff of the Orient. Chef/owner Jim McCarthy has created dishes with influences from around the world. A good value express menu is served from 5pm to 7pm.

✉ 44 University Road, Belfast, BT7 1NJ ☎ 028 9020 2290 ⏰ Tue–Sat 5–10.15, Sun 12.30–2.30, 5–8.15 ✋ L £17.50, D £30, Wine £12.50 🚌 Metro 8A, 8B 🚌 Adjacent to Queen's University on the main University road, A55

BOURBON
www.bourbonrestaurant.com

The quirky interior combines Victorian Gothic with a feel of the American Deep South, and touches of Spanish colonial architecture. Food influences come from America, the Far East and Britain. The chef focuses on freshness and taste in dishes such as Aberdeen Angus fillet steak or king prawn, smoked haddock, salmon, mussels, tomato

and red pepper stew. Luscious desserts include apple strudel with custard and whipped cream.

✉ 60 Great Victoria Street, Belfast, BT2 7BB ☎ 028 9033 2121 ⏰ Mon–Fri 12–3, 5–11, Sat 5–11, Sun 5–10 ✋ L £18, D £30, Wine £15.95 🚌 Opposite Great Victoria Street Bus Station

CAYENNE
www.rankingroup.co.uk

The Rankins' lively, minimalist restaurant is still the place to see and be seen. The food is predominantly modern international with Pacific, Indian and Mediterranean touches, using well-sourced Irish ingredients. The cooking is imaginative but not over-embellished. Dishes may include such delights as crispy pork belly and chargrilled squid, followed by Indian spiced lamb shank with curried cous cous.

✉ 7 Ascot House, Shaftesbury Square, Belfast, BT2 7DB ☎ 028 9033 1532 ⏰ Daily 5–late (opens 6 on Sat), Mon–Fri 12–2.15 ✋ L £12, D £35, Wine £17 🚌 Metro 7 🚌 South, down Great Victoria Street from the city centre towards University Road

DEANE'S DELI
www.michaeldeane.co.uk

With a deli store next door this stylish, casual branch of Michael Deane's restaurant empire serves innovative and traditional food all day. Try the breads, oils and tapenades to share, or treat yourself to slow roast rump of lamb or braised sausages, colcannon and pickled onions. There is a good wine list to choose from. You can always buy something from the deli to try at home.

✉ 44 Bedford Street, Belfast, BT2 7FF ☎ 028 9024 8800 ⏰ Mon–Fri 12–3, Mon–Tue 5–9, Wed–Fri 5–10, Sat 12–10 ✋ L £17, D £25, Wine £15 🚌 Metro 7 🚌 City centre just south of Donegall Square

Opposite *A tasty sandwich*

DEANE'S RESTAURANT AND BAR

www.michaeldeane.co.uk

All change for Michael Deane with his radically altered restaurant. No longer the upstairs, downstairs set up, this is an open-plan restaurant with a new bar area. Here sophistication meets modernism, and the food still shines. Prepare to be smitten by the perfection of dishes such as Lough Neagh eel with pressed roast beetroot, watercress and apple, or a main course of slow braised beef Bourguignon with truffled mash.

✉ 34–40 Howard Street, Belfast, BT1 6PF ☎ 028 9033 1134 🕐 Mon–Sat 12–3, 6–10 🍴 L £17.50, D £40, Wine £20 🚍 In the middle of the city, just west of City Hall

THE EDGE BANK GALLERY RESTAURANT

www.at-the-edge.co.uk

A hidden gem overlooking the River Lagan, the Edge has built up a reputation for consistent quality. Head chef Donal Keane insists on using freshly prepared local produce inspiring a varied and mouthwatering menu, where the portions are generous and the food good value. He is particularly noted for his fish cooking. The panoramic views over the Lagan and the city centre make for an unforgettable dining experience.

✉ Mays Meadow, Laganbank Road, Belfast BT1 3PH ☎ 028 9032 2000 🕐 Mon–Sat 12–2.30, 5.30–10 🍴 L £12, D £25, Wine £11.95 🚍 Laganside, close to Waterfront Hall 🚍 Five minutes' walk from Central Railway Station and Laganside Bus Centre

HARBOUR VIEW TEPPANYAKI & ORIENTAL RESTAURANT

www.harbourviewbelfast.co.uk

In a great location near Waterfront Hall and overlooking the River Lagan you have the opportunity to experience a teppanyaki meal cooked for you at your table. You can also opt for sushi dishes or try the excellent fresh seafood dishes comprising oysters, squid or lobster. A Japanese extravaganza and something special for the taste buds.

✉ 1 Lanyon Quay, Belfast, BT1 3WH ☎ 028 9023 8823 🕐 Daily 12–11 🍴 L £9.95, D £30, Wine £12 🚍 Any Metro bus to Laganside Buscentre 🚍 Lanyon Place is just off Oxford Street; follow signs for city centre and Belfast Waterfront Hall via East Bridge or Oxford Street. Parking at multi-storey Lanyon Place

HILL STREET BRASSERIE

www.hillstbrasserie.com

Located in the delightfully renovated Cathedral Quarter, the Hill Street Brasserie is quietly situated along the cobbled street. The remit is to use only the best local fresh ingredients and head chef Stephen Taylor Winter produces some great dishes with an eclectic menu of Mediterranean and modern plates. Get the taste buds going with a starter such as grilled beef satay with a spicy peanut sauce, following with baked halibut fillet or roast breast of duck with blueberry compote. Try the excellent early bird menu for great value.

✉ 38 Hill Street, Belfast, BT1 2LB ☎ 028 9058 6868 🕐 Tue–Sat 12–2.30, 5–10 🍴 L £14, D £30, Wine £15 🚍 Metro 3 to High Street and walk 🚍 In the Cathedral Quarter, nearest parking is in Laganside

JAMES STREET SOUTH

www.jamesstreetsouth.co.uk

An elegant restaurant, James Street South occupies the ground floor of a refurbished linen mill. Owner and head chef Niall McKenna chooses dishes using only the best of local seasonal ingredients. A special pre-theatre set dinner is good value. You might start your meal with white onion soup and follow it with Dover sole with braised fennel and crab cream. Round off with white chocolate brûlée with mixed berry compote or apple tarte tatin with vanilla bean ice cream. The wine list is extensive.

✉ 21 James Street South, Belfast, BT2 7GA ☎ 028 9043 4310 🕐 Mon–Sat 12–2.45, 5.45–10.45, Sun 5.30–9 🍴 L £13.50, D £35, Wine £18 🚍 Metro 7 🚍 Off Bedford Street, just south of Donegall Square in the city centre

LA BOCA

www.labocabeflast.com

It may not be Argentina but this restaurant, named after the dockside district of Buenos Aires, brings a taste of South America to Belfast. Decked out in solid beech furniture it makes a great place to taste your sirloin or rib-eye steak served with papas fritas (chips), chimichurri (Argentinian sauce for grilled meat) and vegetables. There are plenty of other choices such as tapas, vegetarian options, steak sandwiches and an array of salads—from seared beef salad to grilled mushroom, bacon and blue cheese salad.

✉ 6 Fountain Street, Belfast, BT1 5ED ☎ 028 9032 3087 🕐 Mon–Wed 9–7, Thu 9–9, Fri–Sat 9am–10pm 🍴 L from £6.50, D from £14.95, Wine £12.95 🚍 Metro 3, 4, 5 to City Hall 🚍 Fountain Street runs north from the corner of Donegall Square North

McHUGHS BAR AND RESTAURANT

www.mchughsbar.com

The traditional exterior of McHughs belies its contemporary interior, where you can relax and just have a drink or go through to the restaurant and have a meal. The lunch menu incorporates anything from Irish stew and wheaten bread to a sizzling selection from the wok station. Reservations are essential.

✉ 29–31 Queen's Square, Belfast, BT1 3FG ☎ 028 9050 9999 🕐 Restaurant: Mon–Sat 12–10.30, Sun 12–9 🍴 L from £10, D from £16, Wine £12.95 🚍 On the corner of Queen's Square and Princes Street

THE METRO BRASSERIE

www.crescenttownhouse.com

The Metro Brasserie displays a trendiness not normally associated with hotel restaurants. Some flashes of brilliance are detectable together with a commitment to simplicity. The early bird menu is a good option.

✉ The Crescent Townhouse, 13 Lower Crescent, Belfast, BT7 1NR ☎ 028 9032 3349 🕐 Mon–Thu 5.45–9.30, Fri 5.45–10, Sat 5.30–10, Sun 5–9 🍴 D from £30, Wine £14 🚍 Metro 8A, 8B 🚍 South towards Queen's University; the hotel is on corner of Botanic Avenue and Lower Crescent, opposite Botanic Train Station

THE MORNING STAR

www.themorningstarbar.com

This listed building, a pub since 1854, serves excellent Irish food such as Ulster beef steaks and Irish stew alongside some innovative dishes featuring the exotic—from kangaroo, crocodile and shark to ostrich, bison or emu. All ingredients for the less adventurous dishes are sourced locally.

✉ 17–19 Pottinger's Entry, Belfast, BT1 4DT ☎ 028 9023 5986 🕙 Mon–Sat 11–11, Sun 12–7 🍽 Bar buffet £5, Main £13, Dessert £3.50 🚌 Metro 3 🅿 In a narrow alley between High Street and Ann Street in the city centre

NICK'S WAREHOUSE

www.nickswarehouse.co.uk

One of the first restaurants to open in the renovated Cathedral Quarter, Nick's has been in business since 1989. Popular with local business people and tourists alike, the menu features modern Irish cuisine innovatively produced by chef Nick Price and his staff. Kick off with a tasty seafood chowder, followed by the likes of Cajun spiced swordfish or pan fried chicken strips with basmati rice and a Thai red curry.

✉ 35 Hill Street, Belfast, BT1 2LB ☎ 028 9043 9690 🕙 Mon 10–5, Tue–Fri 10–10, Sat 6–10 🍽 L £16.50, D £30, Wine £14.10 🚌 Metro 3 to High Street then walk 🅿 In the Cathedral Quarter, nearest parking Laganside

NO 27

www.no27.co.uk

A new, sleek, modern establishment close to St. Anne's Cathedral in Talbot Street. You could try the likes of rare beef with blue cheese, walnut and cos leaf salad to start, followed by roast rump of lamb with chorizo, chickpea, basil and rocket cassoulet, rounded off with

Right *At Shu, inventive dishes complement the cool ambience*

lemongrass crème brûlée or a classic tiramisu. It also boasts a cocktail bar.

✉ 27 Talbot Street, Belfast BT1 2LD ☎ 028 9031 2884 🕙 Mon–Fri 12–3, Tue–Sat 6–10 🍽 L £14, D £27, Wine £15 🚌 Metro 3 to High Street then walk 🅿 In the Cathedral Quarter, nearest parking Laganside

ROSCOFF BRASSERIE

www.rankingroup.co.uk

Returning to their roots with a new venue for their originally named restaurant, Paul and Jeanne Rankin have chosen a location directly behind Belfast's City Hall. The brasserie, serving classic French food, is perfect for business lunches, a welcome recharging point for tired sightseers and the perfect place for pre- or post-theatre dinners. On sale are artworks by local-born artist Peter Anderson.

✉ 7–11 Linehall Street, Belfast, BT2 8AA ☎ 028 9031 1150 🕙 Mon–Fri 12–2.15, 6–10.15 (Fri, Sat until 11.15), Sun 1–5 🍽 L £19.50 (3 courses), D £35, Wine £16.50 🚌 Metro 7 🅿 Linenhall Street leads south off Donegall Square South in the city centre

SHU

www.shu.killercontent.net

Were the ancient Egyptian god of the atmosphere to pay a visit, he'd be pleased with his namesake. Shu's minimalist ambience provides the perfect background for the

discreet, lazy jazz soundtrack. The eclectic menu takes a loose fusion line, but all is executed with a light touch. Freshness and seasoning in seared salmon, bacon and crab risotto with shellfish vinaigrette are beyond reproach. Desserts include sticky toffee pudding and spiced rice pudding with apples.

✉ 253 Lisburn Road, Belfast, BT9 7EN ☎ 028 9038 1655 🕙 Mon–Sat 12–2.30, 6–10 🍽 L £20, D £25, Wine £15 🚌 Metro 9A, 9B 🅿 From the middle of the city take Lisburn road, A1, for 1.5km (0.9 miles) southwest

TEDFORDS

www.tedfordsrestaurant.com

In a former ship chandler's building, the theme of the sea continues in this excellent seafood restaurant. There is a choice of dining areas, with a more informal restaurant on the ground floor and a more sophisticated eatery upstairs. Fish and seafood are certainly a speciality—Dundrum mussels, crispy fried squid, pan roast turbot—but there are some good steak and poultry dishes too. There is a pleasant lounge bar in the basement for a before- or after-dinner drink.

✉ 5 Donegall Quay, Belfast, BT1 3EA ☎ 028 9043 4000 🕙 Tue–Fri 12–2.30, Tue–Sat 5–late 🍽 L £20, £, D £26, Wine £14.95 🚌 Any Metro bus to Laganside Buscentre 🅿 On Donegall Quay, opposite Queen Elizabeth Bridge

VILLA ITALIA

www.villaitaliarestaurant.co.uk

This lovely rustic Italian restaurant is in a listed Georgian building. Popular with students, locals and visitors it never fails to please with its endearing Italian ambience and first-rate food. Choose from an array of pizzas, pastas and grills surrounded by memorabilia of the Italian countryside. Delicious desserts complete the picture.

✉ 37–41 University Road, Belfast, BT7 1ND ☎ 028 9032 8356 🕐 Mon–Fri 5–11.30, Sat 4–11.30, Sun 4–10.30 ✋ D £20, Wine £12 🚇 Metro 8 🚗 On the main A55 University Road south of the city centre

BUSHMILLS

BUSHMILLS INN

www.bushmillsinn.com

The restaurant of this famous inn is a beautiful conversion of the former stables and wine cellar. Prime Ulster meat, fish and vegetables are used in creative dishes such as salmon with a chestnut mushroom cream sauce or mature Ulster fillet steak cooked with peppercorns and flambéed in Bushmills whiskey and finished with cream. Try the Bushmills tart tatin for dessert, served with cinnamon ice cream.

✉ Bushmills, Co. Antrim, BT57 8QG ☎ 028 2073 3000 🕐 Mon–Sat 12–6.45, 7–9.30, Sun 12–6, 7–9 ✋ L £15, D £26, Wine £14 🚗 On the A2, east of Portrush, just south of the Giant's Causeway

THE DISTILLERS ARMS

www.distillersarms.com

Convenient for both the Giant's Causeway and the Old Bushmills Whiskey Distillery, this attractive pub/restaurant is worth a visit in its own right, with its cosy log fire in winter and friendly atmosphere. Food is served in a pleasant stone dining room on two levels. The menu changes seasonally and features Ulster produce such as free-range chicken and delights such as Old Bushmills whiskey cured salmon served with wheaten bread. Wild boar, venison and Irish mussels also feature.

✉ 140 Main Street, Bushmills, Co. Antrim, BT57 8QE ☎ 028 2073 1044 🕐 Tue–Thu 5.30–9, Fri–Sun 12–3, 5.30–9 (also Mon in summer) ✋ L £15, D £28, Wine £12.95 🚗 Off the A2 in centre of the village

COOKSTOWN

OTTER LODGE WINE BAR AND RESTAURANT

www.otterlodge.co.uk

This is a lovely riverside wine bar and restaurant. With an interior as warm as the welcome, it offers good-value meals, including such dishes as pork fillet with roast apples, beef with peppercorn sauce and chicken kiev.

✉ 26 Dungannon Road, Cookstown, Co. Tyrone, BT80 8TL ☎ 028 8676 5427 🕐 Mon–Thu 12–2, 5.30–9.30, Fri–Sat 12–2, 5.30–10, Sun 12–2.30, 5–9.30 ✋ L £13, D £16, Wine £7 🚗 On the A29 17km (11 miles) north of Dungannon

CREGGAN

AN CREAGÁN VISITOR CENTRE

www.an-creagan.com

In the very south of Northern Ireland, this visitor complex (▷ 307) includes this lovely bar-restaurant. The sizeable menu has seafood, steak and grills, chicken and duck, and vegetarian options, and some evenings there's music, singing and storytelling.

✉ Omagh, Co. Tyrone, BT79 9AF ☎ 028 8076 1112 🕐 Mon–Tue 11–3, Wed–Sat 12–2.30, 6–9, Sun 12.30–3, 6–9 ✋ L £16, D £20, Wine £8.95 🚗 20km (12.5 miles) east of Omagh on A505

DERRY

BEECH HILL COUNTRY HOUSE

www.beech-hill.com

Just 3km (2 miles) from Derry, this rural retreat displays the finest tradition of country house elegance and sophistication. The restaurant has creative menus and friendly service. Try pan-fried dry-aged Fermanagh fillet of beef with woodland mushrooms, red onion marmalade and Madeira cream, or summer lamb with creamy black beans and rosemary jus. The wine list offers good value for money.

✉ 32 Ardmore Road, Derry, Co.

Londonderry, BT47 3QP ☎ 028 7134 9279 🕐 Daily 12–2, 6.30–9 ✋ L £17.95, D £30, Wine £13.50 🚗 Take the A6 Derry–Belfast road and turn off at Faughan Bridge and continue for 1.5km (0.9 miles). The hotel is opposite Ardmore Chapel

DUNDRUM

THE BUCK'S HEAD

The Buck's Head serves up a wonderful traditional roast at a bargain price every weekend. The rest of the week, this 100-year-old pub offers a good variety of dishes, including seafood straight from Dundrum Bay.

✉ 77–79 Main Street, Dundrum, Co. Down, BT33 0LU ☎ 028 4375 1868 🕐 Daily 12–2.30, 5–9.30 (Sun until 8.30) ✋ L £15, D £25, Wine £11 🚗 9.5km (6 miles) north of Newcastle on the A2, on an inlet of Dundrum Bay

ENNISKILLEN

FRANCO'S RESTAURANT

www.francosrestaurant.co.uk

This pretty restaurant covered in creepers and surrounded by plants is attractively illuminated at night. There is a great choice of pizzas—usually as many as 14 ranging from a seafood special to Franco's Special, a pizza of your own choice. The Specials Menu brings in more sophisticated and pricier dishes such as grilled black sole in a lemon butter and chargrilled rack of lamb marinated in honey and rosemary served with spinach and drizzled with a rich jus.

✉ Queen Elizabeth Road, Enniskillen, Co. Fermanagh, BT74 7DY ☎ 028 6632 4424 🕐 Mon–Sat 12–11, Sun 12–10.30 ✋ L £12, D £18–£30, Wine £12.95 🚗 In central Enniskillen: Queen Elizabeth Road runs parallel to the High Street

GLENAVY

McGEOWN'S

www.mcgeowns.co.uk

The restaurant here serves high-quality food, with choices such as lobster or medallions of fillet steak with courgettes (zucchini) and aubergines (eggplant). Desserts are of the same high quality and there is an excellent wine list.

22 Main Street, Glenavy, Co. Antrim, DT20 7LW ☎ 020 0442 2467 ◷ Mon–Thu 12–9, Fri–Sat 12–9.30, Sun 11.30–4, 5–9 ✋ L £20, D £30, Wine £10 🚗 In the middle of Glenavy

KILLYLEAGH
DUFFERIN ARMS
www.dufferinarms.com
This lively pub is well known for its good food and music. It has been in operation for more than 200 years and has a traditional pub atmosphere. The Kitchen Restaurant is in country style, and the regularly changing menu features such appetizers as seafood chowder and local Finnebrogue venison paté served with an apricot and brandy jelly. Main courses might include grilled sea bass on roast leeks or pan-fried venison on garlic champ. There's also an extensive menu of meals in the bar.

35 High Street, Killyleagh, Co. Down, BT30 9QF ☎ 028 4482 1182 ◷ Mon–Wed 12–3, 5.30–9, Thu–Sat 12–9 ✋ L £17, D £24, Wine £9.35 🚗 Killyleagh is on the western shore of Strangford Lough, 8.4km (5.5 miles) north of Downpatrick on the A22

LIMAVADY
THE LIME TREE
www.limetreerest.com
A small, owner-run restaurant where Stanley Matthews cooks and Maria Matthews manages. Simple cooking is used to great effect and the meals are complemented by a good selection of wine. Choose from delights such as home-made crab cakes followed by seafood thermidor, the restaurant's most popular fish dish. Desserts could include steamed banana and ginger sponge with custard. There is an early bird menu for budget dining which can be either a two- or a three-course option.

60 Catherine Street, Limavady, Co. Londonderry, BT49 9DB ☎ 028 7776 4300 ◷ Tue–Sat 6–9; closed 1 week Nov, 1 week Feb/Mar, 1 week Jul ✋ L £22, D £27, Wine £12.50 🚗 Entering Limavady from the Derry side, the restaurant is on the right on a small slip road

LISBURN
SABAI THAI
www.sabaithai.co.uk
This restaurant produces authentic Thai food to a high standard. The ambience is enhanced with Thai statues and pictures, and the friendly and attentive staff make your meal a memorable one. Choose from the extensive menus specialities such as drunken noodles with prawns or meat and the beef panang—beef cooked in curry paste, peanuts, coconut milk and lime leaves. Takeaway is also available.

71–73 Bachelors Walk, Lisburn, Co. Antrim, BT28 1XN ☎ 028 9264 0202 ◷ Mon–Thu, Sun 5–10, Fri–Sat 5–midnight ✋ D £13, Wine £12 🚗 From the M1 motorway take the Hillsborough Road into Market Place, turn right into Bow Street and left into Antrim Street, Bachelors Walk is on the right

PORTRUSH
RAMORE WINE BAR
www.ramorerestaurant.com
This hugely popular restaurant thrives on providing cosmopolitan dishes with flair and creativity. The quayside location blends with a modern, funky interior and busy lunchtimes swing to a smooth jazz soundtrack. The large menu has something for all tastes including British and spicy Thai dishes.

The Harbour, Portrush, Co. Antrrm, BT56 8BN ☎ 028 7082 4313 ◷ Wine bar: Mon–Sat 12–2, 5.30–9; restaurant: Tue–Sat 6.30–10.30 ✋ L £15, D £20, Wine £9.95 🚗 On the harbour in Portrush

STRANGFORD
THE CUAN
www.thecuan.com
The perfect place for a lunch or dinner stop after a visit to Strangford Lough and situated close to the shore in the pretty conservation village of Strangford. Seafood is the specliality here and with Ardglass harbour only 10 minutes away you can be assured of the freshest of local ingredients. One of the signature dishes is chef Peter McErlean's delectable seafood chowder made with locally caught seafood and served with the delicious home-baked wheaten bread. Leave room for the scrumptious home-made desserts. Traditional music is played on the last weekend in the month.

The Square, Strangford, Downpatrick, Co. Down, BT30 7ND ☎ 028 4488 1222 ◷ Mon–Thu 12–9, Fri–Sat 12–9.30, Sun 12–8.30 ✋ L £12, D £20, Wine £13 🚗 Take the A2 Shore Road down towards the Strangford ferry and The Square is close to the shore

Above *Many restaurants have great service*

PRICES AND SYMBOLS

Prices are for a double room for one night. Breakfast is included unless noted otherwise. All the hotels listed accept credit cards unless otherwise stated. Note that rates vary widely throughout the year.

For a key to the symbols, ▷ 2.

AGHADOWEY

BROWN TROUT

www.browntroutinn.com
Set in an attractive spot alongside the Agivey river and featuring its own 9-hole golf course, this welcoming inn offers a choice of accommodation. Attractively furnished bedrooms are situated around a courtyard while the cottage suites have comfortable lounge areas. Home-cooked meals are served in the restaurant; lighter fare is offered in the character lounge bar. Game fishing is available for guests.
✉ 209 Agivey Road, Aghadowey, Co. Londonderry, BT51 4AD ☎ 028 7086 8209 🖑 Double £80–£110 ① 15 🛐 🚗 At the intersection of the A54/B66 on the road to Coleraine

ARMAGH

CHARLEMONT ARMS

www.charlemontarms.com
Centrally placed, the Charlemont Arms has been under the same family ownership for almost 70 years and offers a choice of dining styles and bars. The mostly spacious bedrooms have been decorated in a contemporary style.
✉ 57–65 English Street, Armagh, Co. Armagh, BT61 7LB ☎ 028 3752 2028 🕔 Closed 25 Dec 🖑 Double from £75 ① 30 🚗 In the heart of the city, a 5-min walk from the cathedrals

BALLYGALLEY

BALLYGALLY CASTLE

www.hastingshotels.com
This is a stylish, welcoming hotel, occupying a converted fine 17th-century castle. A large part of the attraction for guests is the panoramic sea view from the lounge and many of the bedrooms. Most of the bedrooms are to be found in a modern wing, but all are comfortable. The lounges are spacious and roaring log fires are lit in cooler months. Diners in the Garden Restaurant can select from the varied creative menus.
✉ Coast Road, Ballygally, Co. Antrim, BT40 2QZ ☎ 028 2858 1066 🖑 Double £155 ① 44 🚗 Some 6.5km (4 miles) north of Larne on the Antrim coast road

BALLYMENA

GALGORM RESORT AND SPA

www.galgorm.com
Standing in 34ha (84 acres) of private woodland and sweeping lawns beside the River Maine, this 19th-century mansion offers guests spacious and comfortable bedrooms. Public areas include a welcoming cocktail bar and an elegant restaurant, as well as Gillies, a lively and atmospheric locals' bar. The Spa and Wellness Centre provides a range of relaxing and rejuvenating treatments and therapies. For guests who prefer the outdoors, horse-riding is available for guests from the estate's stables.
✉ Ballymena, Co. Antrim, BT42 1EA ☎ 028 2588 1001 🖑 Double £145 ① 75 🛐 🚗 2km (1.25 miles) outside Ballymena on the A42, between Galgorm and Cullybackey

BANGOR
MARINE COURT HOTEL
www.marinecourthotel.net

Overlooking the marina, Marine Court offers a good range of leisure facilities. There are extensive public areas, including the first-floor restaurant and cocktail bar. Alternatively, the popular Nelson's restaurant/bar is more relaxed and there is also the lively Bar Mocha.

✉ 18–20 Quay Street, The Marina, Bangor, Co. Down, BT20 5ED ☎ 028 9145 1100 🕐 Closed 25 Dec ⛭ Double from £100 ⓘ 51 ⚓ Indoor 🔲 🚗 Take A2 through Holywood to Bangor, follow the main street and then go left for the seafront

OLD INN
www.theoldinn.com

This delightful hotel, dating from 1614, enjoys a peaceful, rural setting just a short drive from Belfast. The bar and restaurant offer a variety of creative menus and staff throughout are keen to please. Individually styled bedrooms, many with feature beds, offer plenty of comfort and modern facilities.

✉ 15 Main Street, Crawfordsburn, Co. Down, BT19 1JH ☎ 028 9185 3255 ⛭ Double from £105 ⓘ 31 🚗 5km (3 miles) past Holywood on the A2 there is a sign for the Old Inn and 100m (110 yards) past this sign, turn left at the traffic lights; the hotel is on the left in the village

BELFAST
THE CRESCENT TOWNHOUSE
www.crescenttownhouse.com

This stylish, smartly presented Regency town house is close to the Botanic Gardens and railway station. The popular Bar Twelve and Metro Brasserie are to be found on the ground floor; the reception office and the well-equipped and comfortable bedrooms are all located on the upper floors.

✉ 13 Lower Crescent, Belfast, BT7 1NR ☎ 028 9032 3349 🕐 Closed 25–27 Dec and part of Jul ⛭ Double £110–£150 ⓘ 17 🔲 🚗 Metro 8A, 8B 🚗 South of the city centre towards Queen's University; the hotel is on corner of Botanic Avenue and Lower Crescent, opposite Botanic Train Station

EXPRESS BY HOLIDAY INN
www.exhi-belfast.com

This modern hotel is ideal for families. The comfortable bedrooms include satellite TV, power shower and tea- and coffee-making facilities.

✉ 106a University Street, Belfast, BT7 1HP ☎ 028 9031 1909 ⛭ Double from £65 ⓘ 114 🚗 Behind Queen's University in the south of the city. Turn left at the lights on Botanic Avenue onto University Street where the hotel is 500m (550 yards) farther on left

JURYS BELFAST INN
www.jurysdoyle.com

Central for most sights and shops, this hotel makes a good base for seeing Belfast. The public areas include a lounge, a bar and a stylish restaurant. The spacious bedrooms are stylishly decorated, with good facilities, including satellite TV.

✉ Fisherwick Place, Great Victoria Street, Belfast, BT2 7AP ☎ 028 9053 3500 🕐 Closed 24–26 Dec ⛭ Double from £69 ⓘ 190 🚗 Grosvenor Road and Great Victoria Street, by Opera House

MALONE LODGE HOTEL
www.malonelodgehotel.com

In the leafy suburbs of the university area of south Belfast, this stylish hotel forms the focal point of an attractive Victorian terrace. The unassuming exterior belies a pleasant interior with a lounge, popular bar and elegant restaurant.

✉ 60 Eglantine Avenue, Belfast, BT9 6DY ☎ 028 9038 8000 ⛭ Double £89–£129 ⓘ 51 🔲 🚗 Metro 8B, 8C (to Malone Road) 🚗 South of the city, turn right onto Lisburn Road, then left onto Eglantine Avenue, where the hotel is on the left

CARNLOUGH
LONDONDERRY ARMS
www.glensofantrim.com

Originally built in the mid-19th century as a coaching inn, the building was owned at one time by war-time British Prime Minister Winston Churchill. The hotel has a prime location in this pretty fishing village.

✉ 20 Harbour Road, Carnlough, Co. Antrim, BT44 0EU ☎ 028 2888 5255 ⛭ Double from £85 ⓘ 35 🚗 Go north from Larne on the coast road, A2, for 22km (14 miles)

CARRICKFERGUS
DOBBINS INN HOTEL
www.dobbinsinnhotel.co.uk

Bright window boxes adorn the front of this popular inn, near the ancient castle and the waterfront. The public areas are furnished to modern standards without compromising the historic character. Bedrooms vary in size and style but all provide modern comforts. The staff are helpful.

✉ 6–8 High Street, Carrickfergus, Co. Antrim, BT38 7AP ☎ 028 9335 1905 🕐 Closed 25–26 Dec, 1 Jan ⛭ Double from £68 ⓘ 15 🚗 From Belfast take the M2, keep right at the roundabout (traffic circle) and follow the A2 to Carrickfergus; turn left opposite castle

DERRY
BEECH HILL COUNTRY HOUSE
www.beech-hill.com

Beech Hill is an impressive 1729 mansion, standing in 13ha (32 acres) of woodlands and gardens. Day rooms are traditionally styled and ambitious cooking is served in the dining room. Bedrooms are spacious,and classically decorated. There is a tennis court, a 9-hole golf course, and holistic therapies.

✉ Ardmore Road, Derry, Co. Londonderry, BT47 3QP ☎ 028 7134 9279 🕐 Closed 24–25 Dec ⛭ Double £100–£130 ⓘ 27 🔲 🚗 Turn off the A6 Derry–Belfast road at Faughan Bridge; after 1.5km (0.9 miles), the hotel is opposite Ardmore Chapel

CITY HOTEL
www.cityhotelderry.com

This busy, contemporary hotel over looks the River Foyle. The executive rooms are spacious and have good facilities, including internet access. The restaurant provides traditional Irish cooking with a modern twist.

✉ Queens Quay, Derry, Co. Londonderry, BT48 7AS ☎ 028 7136 5800 🕐 Closed 25 Dec ⛭ Double from £100 ⓘ 145 ⚓ Indoor 🔲 🚗 On the waterfront adjacent to the Guildhall

Opposite *Derry's accommodation ranges from B&Bs to fine country-house hotels outside the city*

DA VINCI'S

www.davincishotel.com

This hotel is convenient, yet far from the hustle and bustle. The well-designed bedrooms are spacious and all have two double beds and satellite TV. The public areas include the main bar for pub food and the Grillroom for creative cooking.

✉ 15 Culmore Road, Derry, Co. Londonderry, BT48 8JB ☎ 028 7127 9111 🕙 Closed 25 Dec 🛏 Double £55–£100 🛎 67 🚗 From the city take Strand Road for 1.5km (0.9 miles) north and turn onto Culmore Road; hotel is on the right

HASTINGS EVERGLADES

www.hastingshotels.com

This purpose-built hotel situated on the edge of the city, offers comfortable bedrooms, with family and interconnecting rooms also available. There are 20 bedrooms on the ground floor. Stylish open-plan day rooms include a relaxing lounge and Library bar leading into the bright Satchmo restaurant. Outside, guests can put in some golf practice on the putting green.

✉ Prehen Road, Derry, Co. Londonderry, BT47 2NH ☎ 028 7132 1066 🛏 Double from £140 🛎 64 ♿ 🚗 On the A5, Omagh to Derry road, 2km (1.25 miles) from the city

TOWER HOTEL DERRY

www.towerhotelderry.com

A chic hotel that's proving to be a big hit with tourists and corporate guests alike. Modern bedrooms are furnished with flair and style and those on the upper floors enjoy fine views of the city. The minimalist day rooms include a popular bistro and the staff in the contemporary bar provide friendly Irish hospitality.

✉ 7–17A Butcher Street, Derry, Co. Londonderry, BT48 6HL ☎ 028 7137 1000 🕙 Closed 24–27 Dec 🛏 Double from £75 🛎 90 ♿ 🚗 From the Craigavon Bridge drive into the middle of the city, to Carlisle Road, where the hotel is straight ahead

DUNGANNON
GRANGE LODGE

Grange Lodge dates back to 1698 and sets the highest of standards. Award-winning cooking is served in the airy dining room, and guests can enjoy home-baked afternoon teas in the sumptuous drawing room.

✉ 7 Grange Road, Dungannon, Co. Tyrone, BT71 7EJ ☎ 028 8778 4212 🕙 Closed 21 Dec–9 Jan 🛏 Double £65–£85 🛎 5 🚗 Turn off M1 at junction 15 on A29 Armagh road for 1.5km (0.9 miles). Follow sign for 'Grange' then take the first right; Grange Lodge is first on the right

ENNISKILLEN
WILLOWBANK HOUSE

www.willowbankhouse.com

Willowbank House has some bedrooms suitable for families. Breakfasts are served in the conservatory dining room.

✉ 60 Bellevue Road, Enniskillen, Co. Fermanagh, BT74 4JH ☎ 028 6632 8582 🕙 Closed 21 Dec–9 Jan 🛏 Double £50–£60 🛎 5 🚗 From Enniskillen take the A4 Belfast road. Turn right 500m (550 yards) after Killy Hevlin Hotel and follow signs for Upper Lough Erne and Willowbank House; hotel is 3km (2 miles) on left

LIMAVADY
RADISSON SAS ROE PARK RESORT

www.radissonroepark.com

This impressive hotel has its own golf resort. The spacious, modern bedrooms are well equipped. There is Greens Restaurant or the Coach House brasserie. The Fairways Leisure Club, offers golf tuition and a floodlit driving range.

✉ Limavady, Co. Londonderry, BT49 9LB ☎ 028 7772 2222 🛏 Double £70–£135 🛎 118 🏊 Indoor 🚗 Take the A2 Derry to Limavady road. The hotel is 2km (1.25 miles) outside Limavady along this road

MAGHERA
ARDTARA COUNTRY HOUSE

www.ardtara.com

Ardtara is a Victorian country house with extensive grounds. The public rooms include a choice of lounges and a conservatory. Bedrooms vary in style and size but all are tastefully decorated. There is a hard tennis court that guests may use.

✉ 8 Gorteade Road, Upperlands, Co. Londonderry, BT46 5SA ☎ 028 7964 4490 🛏 Double £130–£180 🛎 8 🚗 Take the A29 towards Coleraine; after 3km (1.9 miles) take the B75 for Kilrea through the Upperlands. Pass the W. M. Clark and Sons sign and take the next left

PORTAFERRY
THE NARROWS

www.narrows.co.uk

This delightful hotel is on the shores of Strangford Lough. Some of the bedrooms have sea views but all are comfortable. The public areas include an appealing restaurant and the Ruffian bar.

✉ 8 Shore Road, Portaferry, Co. Down, BT22 1JY ☎ 028 4272 8148 🛏 Double £90 🛎 14 🚗 A20 to Portaferry and continue down to the shore; turn left to hotel

Right *Many rooms at The Narrows offer harbour views*

PRACTICALITIES

Practicalities gives you all the important practical information you will need during your visit from money matters to emergency phone numbers.

WEATHER

WHEN TO GO

» Although Ireland is temperate, there are several factors which can help you to decide when to go. In winter some visitor attractions close until spring, and be prepared for total darkness by 4pm in December.

» In July and August it doesn't get completely dark until about 11pm. For the best chance of sunny weather, come in May or June, and for the highest temperatures, July and August, though these two months are the height of the tourist season so you should reserve accommodation in advance, and be aware that there will be more volume of traffic on the roads will be greater too.

» Dublin and Belfast are great cities to visit in any season with attractions open all year round.

CLIMATE

» Ireland does not have extremes of temperature owing to the influence of the Atlantic Ocean and the Gulf Stream. Temperatures of below 32°F

(0°C) or above 86°F (30°C) are rare. The average daily temperature is about 50°F (9°C) across the country. The coldest months are January and February with a mean temperature between 39° and 44°F (4° and 7°C), and the warmest months are July and August, although even then average inland temperatures are only between 64° and 66°F (18° and 20°C). The sunniest months are May and June, while December has the fewest hours of sunshine.

» Despite being mild, Ireland is a very wet country. Irish skies are completely covered by cloud approximately half of the time. You can, and should, expect rain at all times of the year, although the summer is generally not as wet as winter. The parts of the country that receive most rainfall are the west and the hills. In terms of wind, the north and west coasts are two of the windiest areas in Europe.

WEATHER REPORTS

» For weather forecasts, look up www.met.ie (The Irish

Meteorological Service Met Éireann), which gives regional forecasts for the island. The Meteorological Office in the UK (www.metoffice.com) also gives forecasts for the Republic and Northern Ireland. The BBC website (www.bbc.co.uk/weather) gives 5-day weather forecasts, useful if your plans are weather-dependent.

» The Irish Times, Irish Independent, The Belfast Telegraph and Evening Herald newspapers all have detailed weather forecasts.

DOCUMENTS

PASSPORTS

» When planning your trip to Ireland, remember that the Republic of Ireland and Northern Ireland (which is part of the UK) may have different passport and visa requirements. Check what applies to you before you leave your home country.

» Take a photocopy of the relevant pages of your passport with you, so you can leave your passport in your hotel safe. Keep a note of your passport number in case you lose it.

DUBLIN
TEMPERATURE

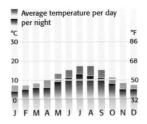

BELFAST
TEMPERATURE

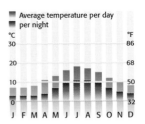

CORK
TEMPERATURE

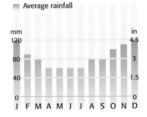

RAINFALL

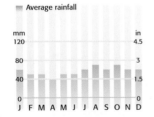

RAINFALL

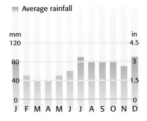

RAINFALL

If you do lose your passport, contact your embassy without delay.

Northern Ireland
» Non-UK nationals must have a passport that is valid for at least six months at the date of entry into Northern Ireland. UK nationals will need photographic identification. You are strongly advised to take your passport as identification anyway, because ferry companies and airlines have their own rules as to what constitutes an acceptable form of 'photographic identification'. Clarify the situation before you travel.

Republic of Ireland
» EU nationals should take a valid passport.
» Non-EU nationals must have a valid passport or national identity card as appropriate.

VISAS
» Entry requirements differ depending on your nationality and are also subject to change. You should always check the requirements prior to a visit and follow news events that may affect your situation.

Republic of Ireland
» EU citizens and nationals from the US, Australia, Canada, New Zealand and South Africa do not need a visa. Visitors from all other countries should contact their local Irish Embassy/Consulate before visiting the Republic. The website of the Irish Department of Foreign Affairs (www.irlgov.ie/iveagh) is useful.

Northern Ireland
» If you have a passport from the US, Canada, Australia, New Zealand or South Africa, you do not need a visa for stays of up to six months. You must have enough money to support yourself without working or receiving money from public funds.

Those who wish to stay longer than six months and nationals of certain other countries require a visa. To check this see the UK government's website: www.ukvisas.gov.uk

TRAVEL INSURANCE
» Insurance is recommended for loss or theft of your personal possessions and for medical costs. If you are robbed, report it to the police and keep all receipts for expenses. For details of health insurance, ▷ 328.

CUSTOMS
Visitors to Ireland from the UK and other EU countries do not need to make a customs declaration on

CUSTOMS

From another EU country

The following are guidelines for the quantity of goods you can take into Ireland without paying further taxes or duties, provided you accompany the goods and they are for personal use.

3,200 cigarettes	10 litres of spirits
400 cigarillos	90 litres of wine (of which only 60 litres can be
200 cigars	sparkling wine)
3kg smoking tobacco	20 litres of fortified wine (such as port or sherry)
110 litres of beer	

For the purposes of visitors' allowances, the Canary Islands, Gibraltar and the Channel Islands are regarded as non-EU countries.

Note: Limits for tobacco products are lower if you are travelling from some EU countries. Check before you travel.

From a country outside the EU

200 cigarettes or	2 litres of still table wine
100 cigarillos or	1 litre of spirits or strong liqueurs over 22%
50 cigars or	volume;
250g of smoking tobacco	or 2 litres of fortified wine, sparkling wine or
60cc/ml perfume	other liqueurs
250cc/ml eau de toilette	Up to €175 worth of all other goods per adult

GALWAY
TEMPERATURE

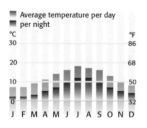

Average temperature per day
per night

RAINFALL

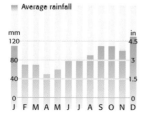

Average rainfall

PRICES OF EVERYDAY ITEMS

ITEM	EUROS (REPUBLIC)	POUNDS STERLING (NORTHERN IRELAND)
Pint of Guinness (pub)	4.00	2.50
The Irish Times	1.80	0.85
Postcard	0.50	0.40
Stamp for postcard to England	0.82	0.36
Cup of tea or coffee	2.00–2.70	1.50–2.00
Packet 20 cigarettes	6.00	4.50–5.00
Litre of unleaded petrol	1.30	1.20
Bottle of water (in café)	2.00–2.25	1.70–2.50
Takeout sandwich	3.00–4.00	2.50–3.00
1 hour city parking (Dublin/Belfast)	2.00	1.50

arrival. However, certain goods are restricted or prohibited for environmental and health reasons—restricted goods include meat and poultry.

VAT REFUNDS
Value Added Tax is generally included in the price of goods and services. If you are from outside the EU, you can obtain a VAT refund on goods you purchase to take home. Some stores will deduct the VAT (from large purchases) at the point of sale. Otherwise, get a tax refund form from the store and keep your receipts. When you leave the country go to the Customs Office to have your receipts stamped before you check in. You will need your passport or other identification to do this.

MONEY
When you are planning a visit to Ireland, remember that the Republic of Ireland uses the euro, while Northern Ireland (which is part of the United Kingdom) has pounds sterling as its currency. Pounds are not accepted in the Republic, although occasionally some establishments in Northern Ireland (particularly in Belfast) accept euros. For example, in Belfast some telephone booths accept pounds and euros. However, you should not rely on this, and plan to take pounds sterling to the North, or change money when you get there.

A useful website for converting currency is www.xe.com/ucc/

THE EURO
The euro was introduced as the unit of currency in the Republic of Ireland on 1 January 2002. Euro notes are identical across the euro zone, while euro coins have one side dedicated to their country of origin. For some reason, Irish euro coins have become quite collectable and many are bought for higher than their real value by collectors.

BANKS
Ireland has no shortage of banks. Many have a foreign exchange desk where you can change money; look for bureau de change signs. Standard opening hours in the Republic and Northern Ireland are 9.30 or 10am to 4pm Monday to Friday, although some banks also stay open until 5pm one day a week (often Thursday). Banks are closed on Saturdays, Sundays and on public holidays.

AUTOMATIC TELLER MACHINES (ATMS)
These are widely available across the country and accept most credit and debit cards. Remember that your credit card issuer may charge you a fee for a cash advance by credit card. You will need a four-digit PIN (comprising four numbers, not letters) from your bank to use an ATM.

CREDIT CARDS AND TRAVELLERS' CHEQUES
Visa, MasterCard and American Express are widely accepted in Ireland. You'll see credit card symbols displayed in the windows of many shops, hotels, restaurants, car rental companies and fuel stations. If you have another credit card, ask in advance if it is acceptable.

You can cash travellers' cheques at most banks and bureau de change offices in Ireland. Remember to bring some identification with you.

CHANGING MONEY
Larger branches of major banks have money-changing facilities and there are many bureau de change kiosks, for example at airports, at the Busáras bus station in Dublin and in the Belfast Welcome Centre on Donegall Place. The commission charged at bureaux de change, which have longer opening hours than banks, may be high so do try to shop around. One option in Northern Ireland is to change your money at a post office, although only larger branches offer this service. The post office does not charge any commission, although the exchange rate may not be as competitive as that offered at banks. You can pay by cheque, cash, Visa, MasterCard, Switch/Maestro, Delta, Solo or Electron and you may be asked for identification, so bring your passport. The post office also has the advantage of opening on Saturday mornings.

WIRING MONEY
In an emergency, money can be wired from your home country, but this can take a few days and is expensive. You can send and receive money using Western Union (www.westernunion.com) or MoneyGram (www.moneygram.com). You can do this at Busáras bus station in Dublin and also at the bureau de change kiosk in the Dublin Tourism Office on Suffolk Street.

VAT REFUNDS
▷ 327 for VAT refunds.

TIPPING
In restaurants, check your bill to see if a service charge has been made. If it hasn't, add 10–15 per cent if you

MAJOR BANKS
These banks have many branches across Ireland. Some main branches in Dublin and Belfast are listed.

NAME OF BANK	ADDRESS AND TELEPHONE NUMBER	WEBSITE
Bank of Ireland	6 Lower O'Connell Street, Dublin; tel 01 878 7870	www.bankofireland.ie
	4–8 High Street, Belfast, BT1 2BA; tel 028 9024 4901	
National Irish Bank	66 Upper O'Connell Street, Dublin; tel 01 484 0040	www.nib.ie
Allied Irish Bank	37 Upper O'Connell Street, Dublin; tel 01 873 1188	www.aib.ie
Ulster Bank	11–16 Donegall Square East, Belfast, BT1 5UB; tel 028 9024 4112	www.ulsterbank.com

are satisfied with the service. You don't have to tip taxi drivers, but if you would like to do so, about 10 per cent of the fare is probably about right. For hotel porters about €1 (Republic) or 50p to £1 (NI) per bag is the norm.

HEALTH

The Republic and Northern Ireland both have a national health service which works alongside the private sector.

EMERGENCY	
Phone Numbers	
Police, fire, ambulance, mountain rescue, cave rescue	
Republic	999 or 112
Northern Ireland	999

BEFORE YOU GO

» Make sure you have full health and travel insurance.
» British visitors to the Republic of Ireland should bring an EHIC card, which entitles them to reduced-price urgent medical treatment, from a public hospital or from a doctor participating in the General Medical Service Scheme. In Northern Ireland, you are entitled to receive medical treatment as in mainland Britain.
» If you are from another EU country (not Britain), you may be entitled to a certain amount of free health care, including hospital treatment. You must complete all the necessary paperwork before you travel.
» If you are from a non-EU country, private medical insurance is essential; bring the policy document and a photocopy with you.
» Australia has a reciprocal agreement with Ireland, which entitles Australian passport holders to receive emergency public hospital treatment. However, they still have to pay a nightly in-patient charge and an Accident and Emergency fee.

WHAT TO TAKE WITH YOU

» If you are taking medication, bring enough for the length of your stay.
» A first-aid kit should include plasters (Band-Aids), sterile dressings, cotton wool, antiseptic cream, pain relief tablets, remedies for constipation and diarrhoea, antihistamine tablets, wet wipes and bandages.

IF YOU NEED TREATMENT

» Admission to hospital in Ireland is usually arranged by a doctor. However, in an emergency, call 999 or 112 for an ambulance or go to the casualty department (emergency room) of a hospital.
» The following hospitals in Dublin have an accident and emergency department:
Beaumont Hospital, Beaumont Road (tel 01 809 3000)
Mater Hospital, Eccles Street (tel 01 803 2000)
James Connolly Memorial Hospital, Blanchardstown (tel 01 821 3844)
St. James Hospital, James Street (tel 01 410 3000)
St. Vincents Hospital, Elm Park (tel 01 221 4000)
» In Belfast there are several hospitals with an accident and emergency department:
The Belfast City Hospital Trust is on Lisburn Road (tel 028 9032 9241)
Mater Hospital is on Crumlin Road (tel 028 9074 1211)
The Royal Hospitals are in the west of the city, on Grosvenor Road (tel 028 9024 0503)
Ulster Hospital is east of the city in Dundonald (tel 028 9048 4511).

PHARMACIES

» For minor ailments, you may want to consult a pharmacist before speaking to a doctor. Many pharmacies in Ireland have a flashing green cross outside and most are open Mon–Sat 9–5.30 or 6. In Dublin, several city branches of the O'Connell's chain stay open until 10pm. In Belfast, some pharmacies stay open until 9pm on Thursdays.

DENTAL TREATMENT

» Dentists are listed in telephone directories or, for Northern Ireland, use the British Dental Association's online service at www.bda-dentistry.org.uk
» Check that your health insurance policy covers dental treatment.

OPTICIANS

» If you wear glasses or contact lenses, pack a spare set and bring your prescription in case you lose or break them. Opticians are listed in the Yellow Pages (NI) and Golden Pages (Republic), including such chains as Vision Express (RI and NI), Boots (NI) and Specsavers (NI).

WATER

» Tap water is safe to drink.
» Mineral water is widely available.

HEALTHY FLYING

» Visitors to Ireland from as far as the US, Australia or New Zealand may be concerned about the effect of long-haul flights on their health. Deep vein thrombosis, or DVT, is misleadingly called 'economy class syndrome'. DVT is the forming of a blood clot in the body's deep veins. The clot can move around the bloodstream and could be fatal.
» Those most at risk include the elderly, pregnant women and those using the contraceptive pill, smokers and the overweight. If you are at increased risk of DVT see your doctor before departing. Flying increases the likelihood of DVT because passengers are often seated in a cramped position for long periods of time and may become dehydrated.

To minimize risk:
» Drink water (not alcohol). Don't stay immobile for hours: Stretch and exercise your legs periodically.
» Do wear elastic flight socks, which support veins and reduce the chances of a clot forming.

Other health hazards
Other health hazards for flyers are airborne diseases and bugs spread by the plane's air-conditioning system. These are largely unavoidable but if you have a serious medical condition seek advice from a doctor.

ESSENTIAL INFORMATION | PRACTICALITIES

BASICS

CLOTHES
The amount of rainfall in Ireland makes rainwear essential. For city visits an umbrella may be enough, but for windy coastal areas and the hills pack a waterproof jacket. Pack sweaters as well as lighter clothes, whatever the time of the year.

ADAPTORS
The standard electricity supply is 240 volts AC in Northern Ireland and 230 volts AC in the Republic of Ireland. Sockets take 3-square-pin plugs, as used in the UK, so visitors from Europe and the US will need an adaptor for any electrical equipment. A plug adaptor necessary to convert 2-pin plugs to 3-pin plugs can be bought at electrical stores.

OTHER ITEMS TO PACK
» Details of emergency contacts.
» Driver's licence or International Driver's Licence (if your licence is not in English).
» First-aid kit.
» Glasses or contact lenses and solution, and prescription details.
» Photocopies of passport and insurance (or send scanned versions to an email account such as Hotmail).
» Travellers' cheques and/or credit cards, and some cash in euros (Republic) or pounds sterling (Northern Ireland).
» Credit card numbers and registration numbers of expensive items.

PUBLIC TOILETS
Hygiene standards in public toilets vary. Newer buildings also have toilets for people with disabilities and a baby-changing room. Some signs may be in Irish. *Mná* means 'women' and *fir* means 'men'.

LAUNDRY
It may be worth checking when you reserve accommodation whether the hotel or guesthouse has a laundry service and how much this costs. Otherwise, if you prefer to do your own washing, most towns have self-service laundrettes. Look under 'Laundries' or 'Dry cleaners'

in Golden Pages (Republic) or the Yellow Pages (Northern Ireland).

PLACES OF WORSHIP
Tourist Information Offices can advise you on places of worship in their area

DUBLIN
Christ Church Cathedral
www.cccdub.ie
✉ Christchurch Place ☎ 01 677 8099
🕐 Sunday: 11am Sung Eucharist and sermon, 3.30pm Choral Evensong, 5pm Eucharist in Irish on 4th Sunday of the month. Weekdays: 10am Morning Prayer, Noon Peace Prayers, 12.45 The Eucharist, 5pm (Mon, Tue, Fri) Evening Prayer, 6pm Choral Evensong (Wed, Thu, Sat, Sun)

Jewish Progressive Synagogue
✉ 7 Leicester Avenue, Rathgar
☎ 01 285 6241

Islamic Cultural Centre of Ireland
✉ 19 Roebuck Road, Clonskeagh, Dublin 14
☎ 01 208 0000

St. Mary's Pro-Cathedral
www.procathedral.ie
✉ Marlborough Street ☎ 01 874 5441
🕐 Mass: Sat evening 6pm, Sun 10, 11, 12.45, 6.30, weekdays 8.30, 10, 11, 12 .45, 5.45. Confessions: Mon–Fri after 8.30 and 12.45 Mass.

St. Patrick's Cathedral
www.stpatrickscathedral.ie
✉ St. Patrick's Close ☎ 01 475 4817
🕐 Choir sings at service Mon–Fri 5.45.

BELFAST
Belfast Islamic Centre
www.belfastislamiccentre.org.uk
✉ 38 Wellington Park, BT9 6DN
☎ 028 9066 4465

Belfast Synagogue
✉ 49 Somerton Road ☎ 028 9077 5013

The Cathedral Church of St. Anne
www.belfastcathedral.com
✉ Donegall Street 🕐 Sunday Services: 10am, 11am, 3.30pm. Weekday Services: Mon–Sat 1pm. Holy Communion: Holy Days, Saint's Days and Wed 1pm. Healing Service, Fri 1pm.

St. Peter's Roman Catholic Cathedral
www.stpeterscathedralbelfast.com
✉ St. Peter's Square
☎ 028 9032 7573

LOCAL WAYS/ETIQUETTE
Talking to strangers
Irish people are friendly, and will spontaneously chat to you in a pub or at a bus stop. If you look as if you are lost, someone may try to help you. Unless you are directly asked for your opinion, it's wise to listen rather than join in when politics and/or religion are on the agenda. Sensitivities can run close to the surface and you don't want to cause offence inadvertently. It is also best not to bring these subjects up if you are initiating a conversation.

Buying your round
There is a tradition in Ireland (and also in Britain), that if you are in a group of friends in a pub, each person in the group takes a turn in buying drinks for the others in the group. This is called buying a round. If you find yourself in this situation, it is better to offer to buy drinks for your companions rather than to be prompted. If you are not sure, ask 'Whose round is it?'

Joining in with music
In pubs, particularly in rural areas, people may pull out a fiddle, *bodhrán* or penny whistle for an impromptu musical session. This can be a wonderful experience to listen to, and you may be invited to join in if you have an instrument with you. As long as you feel comfortable and confident in your musical ability, play along.

Smoking
In both the Republic of Ireland and Northern Ireland smoking is prohibited in all enclosed public places including hotels, restaurants and pubs.

FINDING HELP
PERSONAL SECURITY

» In general, crime rates are fairly low in Ireland, although you should be careful in Dublin and Belfast, and take the normal precautions.
» Keep valuables in your hotel safe.
» If you are visiting as a couple or in a group, split money between you.
» Make a note of the numbers on any travellers' cheques and keep it separate from the cheques.
» Park your car in an official, covered parking area and keep the ticket.
» Never leave valuable items in your car and leave nothing on view.
» Avoid walking in deserted streets at night.
» Be aware of who is standing behind you when you are withdrawing money from an ATM.
» Keep a tight hold of your bag (purse), particularly in crowded streets, and on buses and trains.

POLICE
Republic of Ireland

» The national police force in the Republic of Ireland is the Garda Síochána, known as Garda or Gardaí. Officers wear dark blue uniforms, peaked caps and have the word 'Garda' on the back of their jackets. The Gardaí offers an Irish Tourist Assistance Service (ITAS) which aims to provide assistance to tourists who are victims of crime. ITAS is based in Dublin but can provide assistance anywhere in the country. The service includes use of telephone, fax and email facilities and help with language difficulties, replacing stolen travel tickets and cancelling credit cards. The service does not include financial assistance or legal advice. If you are a victim of crime, contact Irish Tourist Assistance Service, Garda HQ, Harcourt Square, Dublin 2; tel 01 478 5295; www.itas.ie. It's open Monday to Saturday 10–6 and on Sunday and national holidays 12–6.

Northern Ireland

» The Police Service of Northern Ireland (PSNI) is the police force. If you are a victim of crime in Northern Ireland, contact the local police station by calling 999 or 0845 600 8000. Once the PSNI have taken details of the crime, they will refer you to the nearest tourist information office, where staff will try to help you. www.psni.police.uk

CALLING AN EMERGENCY NUMBER

» You should call the emergency numbers 112 and 999 only in a genuine emergency. State clearly which service you need and wait to be connected to that service. When you are connected, say where you are and what the problem is.

LOST PROPERTY
Republic of Ireland

» For lost property in Dublin contact the Garda (police) or tel 01 666 0000. For items lost on buses contact Dublin Bus, Earl Place, Dublin 1, tel 01 703 1321, Mon–Fri 8.45–5; www.dublinbus.ie

Northern Ireland

» The Lost Property Office in Belfast is at Musgrave Police Station, Ann Street, tel 028 9065 0222.

EMBASSIES IN DUBLIN

If you lose your passport or are arrested, contact your embassy.

COUNTRY	ADDRESS	CONTACT DETAILS
Australia	2nd Floor, Fitzwilton House, Wilton Terrace, Dublin 2	Tel 01 664 5300; www.irelandembassy.gov.au
Britain	29 Merrion Road, Dublin 4	Tel 01 205 3700; www.britishembassy.ie
Canada	3rd Floor, 7–8 Wilton Terrace, Dublin 2	Tel 01 234 4000; www.canada.ie
New Zealand	The Embassy of New Zealand for Ireland is in London. See chart below for details.	
South Africa	2nd Floor, Alexandra House, Earlsfort Centre, Earlsfort Terrace, Dublin 2	Tel 01 661 5553
US	42 Elgin Road, Ballsbridge, Dublin 4	Tel 01 668 8777; www.dublinusembassy.ie

EMBASSIES IN BELFAST AND LONDON

COUNTRY	ADDRESS	CONTACT DETAILS
Australia	Australian High Commission, Australia House Strand, London, WC2B 4LZ	Tel 020 7379 4334; www.australia.org.uk
Canada	Canadian High Commission, Macdonald House 1 Grosvenor Square, London, W1K 4AB	Tel 020 7258 6600 www.canada.org.uk
New Zealand	New Zealand House, 80 The Haymarket, London SW1 4TQ	Tel 020 7930 8422; www.nzembassy.com
South Africa	High Commission for the Republic of South Africa, South Africa House, Trafalgar Square, London, WC2N 5DP	Tel 020 7451 7299; www.southafricahouse.com
US	US Consulate General, Danesfort House 223 Stranmillis Road, Belfast, BT9 5GR	Tel 028 9038 6100; www.usembassy.org.uk

OPENING TIMES AND TICKETS

TICKET CONCESSIONS

Student and youth cards

International Student Identity Cards (ISIC cards) entitle students to concessionary rates of admission to museums and visitor attractions as well as discounted transport tickets (▷ 54). A Euro Under 26 card is available to visitors who are under the age of 26, and provides similar discounts to the ISIC card. These cards can be obtained from student travel agencies and youth hostels.

Seniors

Senior citizens, usually those aged over 60 or over 65, can benefit from reduced rates at a number of attractions and places of interest as well as on public transport. You will need to carry some form of identification with a date of birth as proof of age.

Heritage Cards

The National Trust (in Northern Ireland) and Dúchas (in the Republic of Ireland) are both heritage organizations which manage such properties as stately houses and gardens, prehistoric sites, cathedrals and national parks. Admission to these is free to holders of an annual ticket, and this can save you money as long as you are doing a lot of sightseeing. Annual tickets are available at any of the sites managed by the relevant organization: membership of the National Trust (www.nationaltrust.org.uk) costs about £82 for a family and £46 for an adult—special offers are available online. A Dúchas Heritage Card (www.heritageireland.ie) costs €55 for a family and €21 for an adult.

OPENING TIMES

Banks	Mon–Fri 9.30 or 10–4	Some banks are open until 5pm one day a week, although the day varies from town to town (in Dublin and Belfast this is Thursday). Banks are closed on Saturday and Sunday and on public holidays.
Shops	Mon–Sat 9–5.30	In villages and towns there is often a grocery store which stays open until 10pm. In Dublin most shops are open until 6pm Monday to Saturday and late-night opening (until 8 or 9) in Dublin and Belfast is Thursday. Shopping malls often open Sunday 12–5 or 6. See www.4ni.co.uk for Northern Ireland.
Pubs	In the **Republic** closing time is 11.30pm midweek, about 12.30am from Thu–Sat and 11pm on Sun	There's half an hour drinking up time. Pubs shut on Good Friday and Christmas Day. Nightclubs and late-night bars serve drinks until 2.30am.
	In **Northern Ireland** when a pub closes depends on its licence	Many close at 11pm Monday to Saturday, 10pm on Sunday, although some Belfast bars close at midnight during the week and at midnight or 1am on Friday and Saturday. Nightclubs close at about 3am, although owing to a legal anomaly, you can't buy an alcoholic drink after 1am.
Post offices	Mon–Fri 9–5.30	Some post offices also open on Saturday 9–1. In Dublin the main post office on O'Connell Street is open 8–8 Monday to Saturday and 10.30–6 Sunday. In Belfast the main post office on Castle Place is open Monday to Saturday 9–5.30.
Pharmacies	Pharmacies are generally open from 9–5.30 or 6	In Dublin, several central branches of O'Connell's stay open until 10pm. In central Belfast no pharmacies open late, except on Thursday, when some stay open until 9pm.

NATIONAL HOLIDAYS

1 January	New Year's Day
17 March	St. Patrick's Day
March/April	Good Friday (Northern Ireland)
March/April	Easter Monday
May (first Monday)	May Holiday
May (last Monday)	May Holiday (Northern Ireland)
June (first Monday)	June Holiday (Republic)
12 July	Orangeman's Day (Northern Ireland)
August (first Monday)	August Holiday (Republic)
August (last Monday)	August Holiday (Northern Ireland)
October (last Monday)	October Holiday (Republic)
25 December	Christmas Day
26 December	St. Stephen's Day/Boxing Day

Good Friday is not a public holiday in the Republic, but many businesses observe it, so expect to find some offices, restaurants and pubs closed on this day.

COMMUNICATION

TELEPHONES

The main phone company in the Republic is Eircom (www.eircom.ie) and in Northern Ireland, British Telecom (ww.bt.com/ni). Both companies are efficient with reasonably priced calls and a large number of phone boxes (phone booths).

PUBLIC PHONE BOXES (PHONE BOOTHS)

Republic of Ireland

Eircom call boxes are the most widespread. Some accept coins only (minimum €0.50), while others accept coins, Eircom call cards and some credit cards. The display instructions are in a choice of languages (English, German, Irish, French and Spanish). You can buy €7, €10 or €15 Eircom call cards in newsagents, shops and post offices.

Northern Ireland

British Telecom (BT) call boxes are widespread. To call within Northern Ireland or other places in the UK costs 40p for the first 20 minutes, 10p for every subsequent minute and call boxes accept cash (coins only), some credit cards, debit cards and BT chargecards. Call boxes accept incoming calls. For free operator assistance dial 100 (UK) or 155 (international). See also www.bt.com/payphones

MOBILE TELEPHONES

If you want to use your cell phone in Ireland, only phones with GSM subscriptions and a roaming agreement will work. Check with your phone provider before you leave home.

CALLING IRELAND

» To call the Republic from abroad or from Northern Ireland, dial 00 353, then the area code (without 0), followed by the local number.

» For calls within the Republic, dial the area code (including the first 0), then the local number.

» To call Northern Ireland from abroad, dial 00 44 then the area code (without 0) then the local number.

» To call Northern Ireland from the Republic of Ireland, dial 048 then the area code (without 0) then the local number.

» Calling Northern Ireland from the UK or from within Northern Ireland is the same. Dial the area code including the first zero, then the local number.

» All codes within Northern Ireland are 028.

POST OFFICES

» AnPost (www.anpost.ie) runs mail services in the Republic and post boxes here are bright green. Royal Mail (www.royalmail.com) covers Northern Ireland and their post boxes are red.

» The main post office in Dublin is in a beautiful neoclassical building on Lower O'Connell Street and is open 8am–8pm Monday–Saturday and also 10.30–6 on Sunday and holidays, but only for stamps and bureau de change. The main post office in Belfast is on Castle Place and is open from 9–5.30 Monday–Saturday. You can change money at both.

» Post offices across the country are generally open from 9–5.30 Monday–Friday; some open 9–noon or 1 on Saturday. You can buy stamps here or at newsagents and shops.

» Postal codes in Northern Ireland are a combination of letters and numbers, for example, BT1 5AD; the Republic doesn't have a postal code system. Dublin has a simple numbering system, with numbers 1 and 2 indicating the middle of the city.

AREA CODES WITHIN THE REPUBLIC OF IRELAND

Cork	021
Dublin	01
Galway	091
Limerick	061
Sligo	071
Waterford	051

INTERNATIONAL DIALLING CODES

Australia	00 61
Canada	00 1
Germany	00 49
Italy	00 39
New Zealand	00 64
Spain	00 34
UK	00 44
US	00 1

MAILING RATES FROM THE REPUBLIC OF IRELAND

The prices below are all for a letter or postcard which weighs up to 50g

Standard to Britain	€0.82
Standard to Northern Ireland	€0.55
Standard to Europe	€0.82
Standard to rest of the world	€0.82

FROM NORTHERN IRELAND

First class within the UK	up to 60g	£0.36
Second class within the UK	up to 60g	£0.27
Airmail Europe	postcard	£0.48
	letter 60g	£0.90
Airmail USA, Canada,	postcard	£0.54
South Africa, Middle East	letter 60g	£1.58
Australia	postcard	£0.54
	letter 60g	£1.74

USEFUL TELEPHONE NUMBERS

WITHIN:	NORTHERN IRELAND	THE REPUBLIC
Emergency	999	999 or 112
Directory enquiries	118 500	11850
International directory enquiries	118 505	114
Talking Pages to find a number	0800 600 900	1 618 8000
(Yellow Pages directory in NI and Golden Pages directory in the Republic)		

BOOKS AND FILMS
BOOKS

Ireland has a long literary history and a list of the world's best known writers would surely include several Irish names. To get you in an Irish frame of mind before you go, read from the selection below.

» James Joyce's literary masterpiece *Ulysses* (1922) is set in Dublin on one day in 1904 and provides an insight into Ireland and its people, although it is long and can be confusing. Other works by Joyce include *Finnegans Wake* (1939) and *Portrait of the Artist as a Young Man* (1916). Jonathan Swift (1667–1745) was Dean of St. Patrick's Cathedral in Dublin and his best-known work is probably *Gulliver's Travels* (1726). If you prefer poetry, try any work by Sligo poet W. B. Yeats.
» Ireland has also produced many noted playwrights. Oscar Wilde's wit is legendary and some of his best-known plays include *The Importance of Being Earnest* (1899) and *An Ideal Husband* (1899). George Bernard Shaw, who won the Nobel Prize for Literature in 1925, wrote *Pygmalion*, and the best-known play by Samuel Beckett (1906–89) is the absurdist *Waiting for Godot*.
» Ireland has also produced its fair share of women writers. Novelist Edna O'Brien's trilogy of *The Country Girls* (1960), *The Lonely Girl* (1962) and *Girls in their Married Bliss* (1964) paints a picture of life in the countryside of West Ireland. Iris Murdoch (1919–99) won the Booker Prize for her novel *The Sea, The Sea* (1978).
» For something more recent, try a collection of poems by County Derry poet Seamus Heaney, (who won the Nobel Prize for Literature in 1995), such as *The Spirit Level* (1996). Two of Roddy Doyle's novels *The Commitments* (1987) and *The Van* (1991), which are set in working-class Dublin, have been made into films. Frank McCourt's gritty depiction of his childhood in Limerick in his novel *Angela's Ashes* (1996), won him a Pulitzer Prize, and the book was made into a film in 1999. If you prefer travel writing, read County Waterford-born Dervla Murphy's account of her journeys around Northern Ireland by bicycle, *A Place Apart* (1980).

FILMS

» Several recent films have been made about well-known Irish figures. *Michael Collins* (1996) depicts his cause, an independent Ireland. *Nora* (2000) is about James Joyce and his wife Nora's exile in Italy, starring Ewan McGregor. *Iris* (2001) is about the writer Iris Murdoch's life, focusing on her loving relationship with her husband John Bayley.

» For a whimsical look at Irish ingenuity, watch *Waking Ned* (1998). It's the story of a village's attempt to collect the lottery winnings of a man who had a winning lottery ticket, but died before he could collect his money. For lovers of soul music *The Commitments* (1991) is the tale of a group of working-class Dubliners who decide to form a band.
» The Troubles in Northern Ireland are the background to *Some Mother's Son* (1996), which stars Helen Mirren. *In the Name of the Father* (1993), which stars Daniel Day Lewis, tells the true story of an IRA bombing in England.
» *Once* (2007), an Irish musical film, is set in Dublin and stars Glen Hansard. It won an Oscar for the soundtrack.
» Though not about Ireland, *Braveheart* (1994) and *Saving Private Ryan* (1997) merit a mention as they were both filmed on the island. To find out where a movie was filmed, look up www.movie-locations.com
» Many Irish actors have made it big in Hollywood, such as Pierce Brosnan (James Bond movies), Liam Neeson (*Rob Roy, Schindler's List*), Colin Farrell (*Minority Report*) and Gabriel Byrne (*The Usual Suspects*).
» There are film festivals in Cork (October), Galway (July), Dublin (March) and Belfast (March/April; see www.belfastfilmfestival.org).

MEDIA

TELEVISION

» National television and radio stations in the Republic are operated by Radio Telefís Éireann (RTÉ). RTÉ has four radio and two TV channels, funded by a licence fee and advertising.

» In Northern Ireland, the British Broadcasting Corporation (BBC) has BBC1 and BBC2, both non-commercial channels. The main commercial channel is UTV which has a similar schedule to ITV1 in England. There are also some independent regional channels such as Channel 9 (C9TV) which broadcasts in the Derry area.

RADIO

There are several independent, regional radio stations in Ireland.

» The national independent radio station in the Republic is Today FM (100–100.3 FM). It has music and talk shows. www.todayfm.com

» For Irish speakers, there is the RTÉ channel Radio na Gaeltachta (92.5–96 FM).

» RTÉ Radio 1 (88–90 FM) has music, news and chat shows.

» 2FM (90.4–97FM) plays pop music.

» Lyric FM (96–99FM) plays classical music.

» BBC Radio Ulster (92–95.4 FM) has news, weather reports and travel bulletins.

» BBC Radio Foyle (93.1 FM) has news, sports and talk shows with phone ins.

NEWSPAPERS

In the Republic

There are four daily papers available in the morning in the Republic:

» *Irish Independent*

(www.independent.ie) the biggest selling daily paper in Ireland.

» *The Irish Times* (www.ireland.com).

» *The Irish Examiner* (www.irishexaminer.ie).

» *The Irish Daily Star* (www.thestar.ie).

The Republic's evening papers are:

» *The Evening Echo* (www.eecho.ie).

» *Evening Herald*.

There are also several Sunday papers. The two weekly newspapers in Irish are *Lá* and *Foinse* (www.foinse.ie).

In Northern Ireland

» The *Irish News* (www.irishnews.com) has a nationalist slant.

» *News Letter* (www.newsletter.co.uk) has a Unionist perspective.

» The capital's main 'evening' paper, *The Belfast Telegraph* (www.belfast-telegraph.co.uk), has two editions, one in the morning.

BRITISH NEWSPAPERS

» There are plenty of British papers to choose from in Ireland, some of which are available in Irish editions. Some examples are quality broadsheets such as *The Daily Telegraph* (www.telegraph.co.uk), *The Times*

(www.thetimes.co.uk) and *The Guardian* (www.guardian.co.uk). There are also tabloids such as *The Daily Mail* (www.dailymail.co.uk) and *The Daily Mirror* (www.mirror.co.uk).

MAGAZINES

» The main British magazines are available across Ireland. *RTÉ Guide* (www.rteguide.ie) is the most popular TV and radio listings magazine (although daily newspapers also contain TV and radio schedules). There are also What's On guides, which list the current things to see and do.

» Dublin Tourism produces several guides to the city, although they are not free. These include *Where to Stay in Dublin*, *Top Visitor Attractions and Tours*, *Where to Eat* and *Rock 'n' Stroll-Music Walking Trail*. You can buy all of these guides at Dublin Tourism on Suffolk Street, O'Connell Street and the airport.

» The Belfast Welcome Centre has a range of free guides produced by the City Council (www.belfastcity.gov.uk/guides) which include *72 hours in Belfast*, *Belfast Shopping Guide* and *Belfast on a Budget*.

» The best music magazine in Ireland is *Hot Press* (www.hotpress.com) which is published every two weeks.

TERRESTRIAL CHANNELS	
In the Republic	
RTÉ 1	Similar to BBC1 in Britain, although unlike the BBC, it has advertisements. Soaps including British *Eastenders* and the Dublin-set *Fair City*, main evening news at 9pm. *The Late Late Show* is a popular chat show. www.rte.ie
RTÉ 2	Mostly showing films, documentaries, Australian soaps and *The Simpsons*. www.rte.ie
TV3	National independent commercial station showing mostly American talk shows *(Oprah, Rikki Lake)* and British soaps such as *Emmerdale* and *Coronation Street*. www.tv3.ie
TG4	Irish language channel. www.tg4.ie
In Northern Ireland	
BBC1	Soaps, chat shows, shows for children, drama and documentaries. The main evening news shows are at 6pm and 10pm, with regional news and weather reports immediately afterwards. www.bbc.co.uk
BBC2	This channel has documentaries, comedy and cultural/arts shows. www.bbc.co.uk
UTV	This commercial channel has children's shows in the afternoon and soaps, drama, movies and entertainment shows in the evenings. www.u.tv
Channel 4	Some American shows, such as *Will and Grace* and repeats of others, including *Friends* and *Sex and the City*, documentaries, quality movies and comedy; news at 7pm Mon–Fri. www.channel4.com
Five	Lots of movies, Australian soaps; news at 5.30pm and 7pm Mon–Fri. www.five.tv

TOURIST INFORMATION

There are various organizations which promote tourism in Ireland. Tourism Ireland (which covers Northern Ireland and the Republic), promotes Ireland abroad, while Fáilte Ireland is Ireland's main tourist authority. The Northern Ireland Tourist Board covers Northern Ireland including Belfast, while Dublin Tourism promotes the capital of the Republic.

TOURIST INFORMATION OFFICES IN THE REPUBLIC OF IRELAND

Aran Islands (Oileáin Árann)
Kilronan, Inishmore, Co. Galway
tel 099 61263, fax 099 61420

Cork
Áras Fáilte, Grand Parade, Cork City
tel 021 425 5100, fax 021 425 5199;
www.discoverireland.ie/southwest

Donegal Town
Quay Street, Donegal Town
tel 074 972 1148, fax 074 972 2762;
www.discoverireland.ie/northwest

Dublin City
Dublin Tourism Centre, Suffolk Street,
Dublin 2
tel 01 605 7700;
www.visitdublin.com

Galway
Áras Fáilte, Forster Street, Eyre Square, Galway
tel 091 537700, fax 091 537733;
www.discoverireland.ie/west

Kilkenny
Shee Alms House, Rose Inn Street, Kilkenny tel 056 775 1500,
fax 056 776 3955;
www.discoverireland.ie/southeast

Limerick City
Arthur's Quay, Limerick City
tel 061 317522, fax 317939;
www.discoverireland.ie/shannon

Northern Ireland Tourist Board
16 Nassau Street, Dublin 2
tel 01 679 1977; fax 01 679 1977
www.discovernorthernireland.com

Sligo
Áras Reddan, Temple Street, Sligo
tel 071 916 1201, fax 071 916 0360;
www.discoverireland.ie/northwest

Waterford
Waterford Granary, The Quay, Waterford City
tel 051 875 823, fax 051 876720;
www.discoverireland.ie/southeast

Wexford
Crescent Quay, Wexford
tel 053 23111, fax 053 41743;
www.discoverireland.ie/southeast

IN NORTHERN IRELAND

Belfast
Belfast Welcome Centre,
47 Donegall Place, BT1 5AD
tel 028 9024 6609,
fax 028 9031 2424;
www.gotobelfast.com

Fáilte Ireland, 53 Castle Street,
BT1 1GH
tel 028 9032 7888,
fax 028 9026 5515;
www.discoverireland.com

Derry
44 Foyle Street, BT48 6AT
tel 028 7126 7284,
fax 028 7137 7992;
www.derryvisitor.com

TOURISM IRELAND OFFICES ABROAD

Australia
Tourism Ireland, 5th level,
36 Carrington Street, Sydney,
NSW 2000
tel +61 2 9299 6177,
fax +61 2 9299 6323;
www.tourismireland.com/au

Canada
Tourism Ireland, 2 Bloor Street West,
Suite 1501, Toronto, M4W 3E2
tel +1 800 223 6470,
fax +1 416 925 6033;
www.tourismireland.com

New Zealand
Tourism Ireland, 7th Floor, Citibank Building, 23 Customs Street East, Auckland 1010 tel +64 9 977 2255,
fax +64 9 977 2256;
www.tourismireland.com/nz

UK
Tourism Ireland, 103 Wigmore Street, London W1U 1QS
tel 0800 039 7000, fax 020 7493 9065; www.tourismireland.com

US
Tourism Ireland, 345 Park Avenue, New York, NY 10154 tel +1 800 223 6470, fax +1 212 371 9052;
www.tourismireland.com

USEFUL WEBSITES

AIR TRAVEL
www.dublinairportauthority.com Information on Dublin, Cork and Shannon airports
www.aerlingus.com
www.ryanair.com
www.aerarann.com
www.easyjet.com

BICYCLING
www.ctc.org.uk Cyclists' Touring Club of Northern Ireland
www.sustrans.org.uk Maps of Northern Ireland
www.cyclingsafaris.com Accompanied bicycling holidays

BUSES, TRAINS AND FERRIES
www.dublinbus.ie Timetables and prices for Dublin buses
www.buseireann.ie Long-distance buses in the Republic
www.irishrail.ie Train timetable and fares for the Republic
www.irishferries.com Ferries to Ireland
www.translink.co.uk Information on all public transport in Northern Ireland

DRIVING
www.aaroadwatch.ie Up-to-the minute traffic reports
www.aaireland.ie Automobile Association of Ireland
www.trafficwatchni.com Traffic bulletins for Northern Ireland, particularly Belfast
www.theAA.com Become a member, buy motor insurance or order maps, atlases and travel guides

GENEALOGY
www.groireland.ie Office of the Registrar General for information on births, deaths and marriages in the Republic
www.proni.gov.uk Public Records Office, for help in tracing ancestry in Northern Ireland
www.nli.ie For the National Library's Genealogy Service
www.irishgenealogy.ie The origins of Irish surnames

GENERAL INFORMATION
www.anpost.ie The site for the postal service in the Republic
www.postoffice.co.uk Postal services in Northern Ireland/UK
www.goldenpages.ie Business directory for the Republic
www.yell.com Yellow Pages Business directory for Northern Ireland

HERITAGE
www.nationaltrust.org.uk The Trust owns many grand houses and gardens in Northern Ireland
www.heritageireland.ie Dúchas, Irish heritage service responsible for protecting historic sites, castles, houses and national parks
www.heritagetowns.com A directory of Heritage Towns, listed for their architecture

HORSE-DRAWN CARAVANS
www.irishhorsedrawncaravans.com
www.horsedrawncaravans.com

NEWS AND SPORT
www.ireland.com *The Irish Times*
www.belfasttelegraph.co.uk Belfast's evening newspaper
www.bbc.co.uk News, weather reports and listings BBC channels

TOURIST INFORMATION
www.failteireland.ie
www.tourismireland.com
www.visitdublin.ie
www.gotobelfast.com
www.discovernorthernireland.com

VISITORS WITH DISABILITIES
www.nda.ie (Republic)
www.disabilityaction.org (NI)

WALKING
www.irelandwalkingcycling.com
www.walkireland.ie

WEATHER
www.met.ie
www.metoffice.com

KEY SIGHTS QUICK WEBSITE FINDER

Sight/Town	Website	Page
Aran Islands	www.visitaranislands.com	206
Ards Peninsula and Strangford Lough	www.strangfordlough.org	276–277
Belfast	www.gotobelfast.com	280–287
Blarney Castle	www.blarneycastle.ie	160–161
Brú na Bóinne	www.meathtourism.ie	116–119
Bunratty	www.shannonheritage.com	208
The Burren	www.theburrencentre.ie	210–211
Connemara	www.connemara.ie	212–215
Cork	www.cork-guide.ie	164–165
Derry	www.derryvisitor.com	289
Dingle Peninsula	www.dingle-peninsula.ie	166–169
Dublin Castle	www.dublincastle.ie	74–75
Galway	www.discoverireland.ie/west	218
Kildare	www.kildare.ie/tourism	126–127
Kilkenny	www.discoverireland.ie/southeast	128–130
Killarney	www.killarney.ie	172–173
Limerick	www.limerick.com	174
Lough Erne	www.fermanagh-online.com	298–299
National Museum	www.museum.ie	84–85
Powerscourt	www.powerscourt.ie	132–133
Sligo	www.discoverireland.ie/northwest	222–224
Strokestown Park and Famine Museum	www.strokestownpark.ie	258–259
Trinity College Library	www.tcd.ie/library/	90–92
Ulster American Folk Park	www.folkpark.com	303
Waterford	www.waterfordtourism.org	178–179

SHOPPING

Celtic jewellery, Ulster linen, Irish lace, Aran sweaters, Irish whiskey, Connemara marble, musical instruments, Waterford crystal—there are countless unique items you can buy in Ireland, and usually at considerably lower prices than you would pay outside the country. Many are available nationwide, though the best choice is naturally at the place of origin. Lots of shops display the 'Tax Free for Tourists' signs. Ask at any of them for details. Non-EU citizens can reclaim the VAT (currently 21 per cent in the Republic, 17.5 per cent in Northern Ireland) by presenting the refund forms at the airport on departure.

CLOTHES

Irish tweed is top quality and you can buy it as lengths of fabric or in ready-made items such as jackets, trousers, shirts, skirts and caps. Knitwear, especially Aran, is also good value. Plenty of the sweaters are factory made, but there are handmade ones too. You can usually tell by the price.

CRAFTS

Irish jewellery is exceptionally good, in particular the work of jewellers who incorporate traditional Celtic designs into rings, brooches, ear-rings and necklaces. Look for Claddagh rings, a design dating from the 17th century which incorporates a heart, a crown and two hands and is worn as a sign of fidelity. Celtic themes are also used by painters and print-makers.

Belleek porcelain is uniquely Irish and appeals to those who like basket-work and floral designs. More modern styles of simple, but striking ceramics are produced by the increasing numbers of young potters.

Irish lace and Ulster linen are of exceptionally good quality if hand-made, and if you just want a small souvenir you can find inexpensive items such as place-mats. Rugs are popular too, including ones made of tweed, and, like all bulky items, can be shipped.

FOOD

Smoked salmon is one of the most popular buys, but check that it is wild, not farmed salmon. The farmed variety can be fine but never tastes as good. If it doesn't say wild, assume it isn't. Irish cheeses are also worth seeking out. You only have to look at the green and healthy Irish landscape to know that they must be good. Whiskey-based products abound, including fruit cake, mustard and honey.

GLASS

Everyone knows the quality of Waterford Crystal, available all over the country and internationally, but there are other manufacturers of fine glassware too, such as Tyrone Crystal, and several regions have their own glassmakers so don't let your glass shopping start and stop with the name of Waterford.

MODERN STORES

Irish communities are smaller than in most other Western European countries, and chain stores are not as common, apart from the types you find anywhere, such as chemists, bookshops and department stores. There are some names you won't recognize, like the Avoca Handweaver shops and Blarney Woollen Mills. Dublin and Belfast are the best places for modern stores, with Cork, Limerick and Galway not far behind.

MUSIC

Few people can visit Ireland and not be touched at some point by the country's wonderful music. Its stars are famous around the world but there are many incredibly talented musicians whose fame has not necessarily spread beyond Ireland's shores, including artists whose work you can hear and buy only in their home region. Many produce CDs to sell when they're playing.

Musical instruments, too, are on sale everywhere, whether you know how to play them, aspire to play them, or simply see them as an attractive ornament. You don't need to spend the earth. Tin whistles are inexpensive and often come with tutorials. Much more costly are unique instruments such as the harp or *uillean* pipes (you may have to join a waiting list to buy one). The *bodhrán*, a hand-held drum covered in goatskin and beaten with a small stick, is in the mid-price range.

WINES AND SPIRITS

There are several brands of Irish whiskey (note the spelling, with an 'e'), which tastes different from Scotch—if you don't like Scotch, try a good Irish brand such as Bushmills or Jameson's. You might be pleasantly surprised. The choice is less bewildering than in Scotland. Do ask questions if you're thinking of buying, and tell the assistants what you like. They tend to know their product! You can also buy whiskey-based liqueurs, the most popular being Bailey's Irish Cream, combining cream with whiskey, and a concoction called Irish Mist, a blend of whiskey, honey and heather.

REGIONAL SHOPPING

While most goods that appeal to visitors can be bought nationwide, there are always local shops where you can find unique items, such as books, music, food, crafts and clothing, that are special to a particular town or region.

DUBLIN

The Republic's capital has the best choice of shopping, from food and flea markets to designer fashions. If you're only visiting Dublin you won't miss out on the chance to buy the best regional products too, as there are branches of stores such as Avoca, the Crafts Council of Ireland, Claddagh Records and the Kilkenny Shop, bringing the nation's best goods to the city. There are shopping malls, including St. Stephen's Green and Powerscourt Townhouse, as well as traditional department stores Brown Thomas and Arnotts.

THE EAST

The Kilkenny Design Centre, in Kilkenny (www.kilkennydesign. com), is one of the best places to buy the work of craftspeople from all over Ireland. It sells jewellery, clothing, glass, ceramics, metalwork and many other items. In Avoca in Wicklow is the original from which the chain of Avoca Handweavers shops sprang (www.avoca.ie).

THE SOUTH

Waterford is the place for crystal—Waterford Crystal, of course. Glass-making here goes back to 1783, and a tour of the factory is enlightening. Don't expect any bargains—anything that is slightly flawed is destroyed. Cork and Kinsale are two of Ireland's main gourmet centres, so explore the local markets and food shops for the best regional produce.

THE WEST

Galway is the home of the Claddagh ring, and good jewellery stores in Galway City sell original rather than mass-produced examples. This is also a literary city, where you can browse second-hand bookshops

for hard-to-find Irish titles. For Aran sweaters, there's no better place than the Aran Islands, off the west coast. Many are hand-knitted by local women. You will pay more, but they will last much longer than machine-made sweaters.

Just north of Galway City is Connemara, where the marble is quarried. It's on sale everywhere in a huge range of items, and it's just as easy to find an inexpensive little souvenir as a costly gift.

Farther north, Donegal is the place to buy tweeds, especially in Donegal town itself. Tweeds here are made on traditional hand-looms and the quality is second to none. You can buy them elsewhere in Ireland, but a rewarding part of the shopping experience is buying items direct from the maker.

THE MIDLANDS

In this rural area of Ireland, woollen items are a good buy. Look for farm shops as you travel—you may find bargains buying direct from farmers who process fleeces as well as selling home-grown foodstuffs. The best shopping is in such towns as Athlone and Mullingar, although the range of local crafts is not as great as in other parts of Ireland.

NORTHERN IRELAND

Northern Ireland is home to Bushmills whiskey (you can tour the distillery) and Belleek Pottery, which has a Visitor Centre explaining how ceramics inspired by the Greek island of Paros came to be made in an Irish village. Other great buys are linen, for which Ulster is noted, and lace.

Right *There's a huge range of shops and merchandise in Belfast*

ENTERTAINMENT AND NIGHTLIFE

The Irish have a long and fine tradition in the performing arts, especially as musicians, dancers and storytellers. The great emphasis on the popular culture in the bars and on the streets should not detract from organized performances. You will find world-class theatre, dance and opera in Dublin and Belfast, and in regional artistic cities such as Galway and Cork (European Capital of Culture in 2005). Daily papers are the best sources of information, along with weekly listings magazines in the major cities.

There has never been any lack of good nightlife in Ireland, from the smallest village to the largest cities. In the past it has mostly focused on music sessions in bars, a tradition that's as healthy as ever. However, there has been a big increase in the number of more sophisticated types of entertainment, particularly in Dublin, Belfast, Cork, Limerick, Galway and other major towns. In smaller places, though, you might find that nightlife consists of the cinema or the pub, with the latter being as lively as you're likely to find anywhere else in the world. If live music is on offer in one of the bars, the musicians will usually just pass the hat round for a contribution. If it's in a separate bar for music only, you may have to pay a small entrance fee. Both the Republic of Ireland and Northern Ireland have banned smoking in all places of entertainment, including pubs, so if you want to smoke you will have to step outside.

THEATRE

Dublin is the major focus of contemporary and classical drama. It has theatres such as the Abbey (opened 1904, www.abbeytheatre. ie) and Gate (opened 1929, www.gate-theatre.ie). Belfast also has several theatres, and cities such as Galway, Limerick, Waterford and Cork have much to offer, such as the Galway Arts Festival, which is a major event taking place in the summer. There's a Theatre Festival in Dublin in September/October.

CINEMA

There are few parts of Ireland where movies haven't been made—*The Quiet Man, In the Name of the Father, Braveheart, The Commitments, Michael Collins*. You will find several cinemas, including multiplexes, in the main cities, and at least one in most of the major towns, with just as much interest in art movies as in Hollywood blockbusters. There's also a film festival in Dublin in late February/ early March, and another in Cork in October.

DANCE

Ireland has no resident ballet or major contemporary dance company, but visiting groups can often be seen in the cities and at the major arts festivals around the country. Traditional dance boosted by the international success of *Riverdance*, is on a high and can be seen at traditional music festivals. The large hotels put on shows for tourists.

OPERA

The major opera houses are in Belfast and Cork, while in Dublin opera fans can see shows at the National Concert Hall, and at the Gaiety Theatre in April and November when the Dublin Grand Opera Society perform. The main event on the opera calendar is the Wexford Opera Festival in late October/early November, focusing on rarely performed works. The Waterford International Festival of Light Opera is in late September/early October.

CLASSICAL MUSIC
In Dublin the National Symphony Orchestra appears at the National Concert Hall, while Belfast has its Ulster Hall for a variety of cultural events. One series not to miss is the June festival of Music in Great Irish Houses, with concerts around the country. Bantry House in Cork hosts the West Cork Chamber Music Festival in June and July.

TRADITIONAL MUSIC
The best traditional music nights are the impromptu sessions in a bar. Ask around, and be guided by local advice on the best venues. There are pubs in almost every town and city.

RESERVING TICKETS
Credit card reservations by phone or online are taken by most venues. In Dublin, tickets can also be reserved at the Tourist Information Office

Opposite *The Club Milk in Belfast*
Below *Belfast's Grand Opera House*
Right *The violin is an integral part of traditional and classical music*

on Suffolk Street, Celtic Note on Nassau Street or at Ticketron inside the main shopping centres.

DRESS CODES
Informal clothes are fine on most occasions. You may wish to wear smarter clothes for evening concerts, but only the grandest events would require formal clothing.

PUBS AND BARS
The old-fashioned pub is alive and well in Ireland. Few pubs are all-male domains, and women are welcome. Young children too, for the most part, but no one under the age of 18 is allowed to stay after 9pm. In the Republic of Ireland pubs open at 10.30am (12.30 Sundays) until 11.30pm Monday–Thursday, until 12.30am Friday–Saturday and until 11pm on Sundays. In Northern Ireland the hours are 11.30am–11pm Monday–Saturday and 12.30pm–10-pm Sundays.

More stylish bars are also found in the big cities, especially Dublin. Here the Octagon Bar at the Clarence Hotel (which is owned by members of the rock group U2) is a fashionable hang-out.

CLUBS
Don't expect to find sophisticated nightclubs outside the big cities. Clubs can stay open until 2am, with some of the more hardcore dance clubs such as Buck Whaleys in Dublin open until 4 or 5am. The Pod on

Harcourt Street is a long-established and well known club that draws Dublin's young movers and shakers.

CASINOS
Casinos are not big business in Ireland except in Dublin where there are several, including the Merrion Casino Club on Merrion Square (www.merrioncasinoclub.com) and the Fitzwilliam Card Club, Clifton Hall, Lower Fitzwilliam Street (www.fitzwilliamcardclub.com). Amusement City on Westmorland Street is Dublin's biggest casino. Opening hours vary, but are usually from about 6–9pm until 6am.

COMEDY
The Irish are known for their natural wit and ability to tell a tall tale, and comedy clubs in the cities continue to enjoy huge popularity in the wake of comedians such as Ed Byrne, Ardal O'Hanlon and Dylan Moran, who are leading lights on the international circuit.

GAY AND LESBIAN SCENE
Ireland was quite repressive until comparatively recently, and even now it is not considered acceptable to flaunt homosexuality in public. The atmosphere is more relaxed in Dublin, Belfast, Cork and Galway, where there are more open gay nightlife scenes. To tune in to what's happening, you can get a copy of the free monthly *Gay Community News*.

SPORTS AND ACTIVITIES

Ireland is a sports-mad nation, and anywhere in the country, at any time of year, there are sporting events, big and small, taking place. Try seeing one of the nation's home-grown sports, such as Gaelic football or hurling.

With its fabulous landscapes and small population, Ireland is justly popular with people who like to get outdoors for walking, bicycling, horseback riding, golf and almost any other sporting activity that can be enjoyed in the open air. Its waters also attract visitors who prefer fishing, kayaking, surfing and going to see, or swim with, dolphins. You have to be prepared for the weather, so take your waterproof gear, whatever you're doing. But wet or dry, everyone loves the active side of Irish life.

BICYCLING

There can be few countries better suited to bicycling than Ireland. Rural roads are generally quiet, although there can be as much traffic as anywhere else when you're bicycling in or near the big cities. Most drivers are respectful of bicyclists, however. The one drawback can be the weather, although that applies whatever you are doing. Make sure you're equipped for rain and cold.

Part of Ireland's appeal is that there are many places where the mountains sweep down to the sea, providing views of hills and ocean at the same time, though it does mean that you have to bicycle up those hills. The west and southwest areas are particularly good for bicycle routes, including outstandingly beautiful places such as the Dingle Peninsula, the Ring of Kerry and the Sheep's Head Peninsula.

CAVING

The opportunities to go caving are on the increase in Ireland, and the main places are in counties Clare, Cork, Kerry, Fermanagh, Leitrim and Sligo. For detailed information contact the Speleological Union of Ireland (www.cavingireland.org).

CRICKET

The summer game of cricket has never been as popular in Ireland as in England, but it is widely played in Northern Ireland and increasingly in the south. A national side has recently been competing against some English county sides, and winning. There are currently around eight grounds of international standard, which include two in Dublin and others in Belfast, Bangor, Waringstown, Eglinton, Comber and Cork. Check in the local papers or the local tourist information office for details of fixtures.

CRUISING

While the beauty of Ireland's coastline is renowned, less appreciated are the delights of its inland waterways. Taking a small boat along its rivers and canals, and pulling up at night at a pub or restaurant where you might be the only visitors, is hard to beat. Not for nothing do they call it the Ireland of the Welcomes, and when you've arrived on the water you've earned your place at the bar or the table.

The River Shannon is the prime cruising location. It's the longest river in the British Isles at 354km (220 miles), and most of that distance is navigable. There are numerous companies offering boating trips, in craft ranging from basic to luxury. Almost as popular, and certainly just as beautiful, is Lough Erne and the waterways around it, known as the Lakes of Fermanagh. The Shannon–Erne Waterway that links them means you can enjoy both, and you can rent a boat to do a one-way trip.

DOLPHIN-WATCHING
There are opportunities to watch and swim with dolphins off the west coast. These are concentrated in the West Clare area, and Dingle (An Daingean) is another place with trips.

FISHING
Fishing attracts many visitors to Ireland. In the Republic coarse fishing is permitted all year, but for other types of fishing you will need to check locally, as seasons vary within regions and sometimes even according to the river. Day permits (available from angling shops) are reasonably cheap, as are the licences for salmon and sea-trout fishing. These can be bought in advance from some Irish Tourist Board offices overseas, or from Tourist Board and Fishing Board offices, from government-run fisheries and from angling shops within the Republic. In Northern Ireland, consult the Northern Ireland Tourist Board (www. discovernorthernireland.com) or a local angling shop, where you can buy permits. For sea fishing the south and west coasts are the best, with Kinsale popular for several species, including shark. The Irish Tourist Board (www.discoverireland. com) publishes information for fishermen, as does the Central Fisheries Board (www.cfb.ie).

GAELIC FOOTBALL
The most watched sporting event in Ireland is the All-Ireland Football Final, held in September at Croke Park stadium in Dublin, the climax of a season that starts in February. The game is a unique cross between rugby and soccer.

GOLF
Ireland claims to have more golf courses per head of population than any other country except Scotland. It is an incredibly popular pastime, and while its courses may not match Scotland's best in terms of their reputation, they rival them for stunning settings and unique challenges. The Royal County Down (www. royalcountydown.org) and Royal Portrush in County Antrim (www. royalportrush.com) are two of the best. Costs remain comparatively inexpensive, and courses less busy, although in summer you would be advised to reserve in advance. You should also carry your handicap certificate. The Irish Tourist Board (www.discoverireland.com) and Northern Ireland Tourist Board (www.discovernorthernireland.com) publish guides for golfers.

GREYHOUND RACING
Watching greyhound racing has been popular in Ireland since it was introduced to the country in 1927. There are 20 tracks in the country, from Derry in the north to Cork in the south, with a concentration of courses in the south and east. Dublin has two courses, at Shelbourne Park and at Harold's Cross. More information and details of all the stadia and fixtures are available from the Irish Greyhound Board (www.igb.ie).

HORSE RACING
A day at the races is an incredibly popular pastime in Ireland, for all ages and walks of life, with 25 race tracks scattered around the country. Steeplechasing (also called National Hunt racing) takes place all year, while the flat racing season is from March to November. There's great fun to be had at the smaller courses, but the big events are the Irish Grand National, held on Easter Monday at Fairyhouse, County Meath, and the Irish Classics run at the Curragh track in County Kildare.

HORSEBACK RIDING
Ireland is ideal riding country, and riding stables can be found almost everywhere. The Wicklow Hills south of Dublin are particularly good, and there are numerous places in Northern Ireland and on the west coast too. Contact the Irish Tourist Board (www.discoverireland.com) and Northern Ireland Tourist Board (www.discovernorthernireland. com) for information.

HURLING
Peculiar to Ireland, this sport is an older version of both hockey and lacrosse, and is popular everywhere. The season starts in summer and builds up to the All-Ireland Hurling Final at Dublin's Croke Park at the start of September.

Opposite *Bicycle power on a sunny day near Lough MacNean*
Below *Rugby matches are played all over Ireland*

KARTING

There are karting tracks all over the country. The largest indoor track is Kylemore Indoor Karting in Dublin (tel 01 626 1444; www.kylemore-karting.com). You can try 15 minutes on its two tracks for €20.

RUGBY

If you are in Dublin in spring, you might be lucky enough to get a ticket for a home game in the Six Nations Championship at Croke Park (while Lansdowne Road is being redeveloped) in Dublin. Rugby is as popular here as in the rest of the British Isles, with games played weekly all over the country through winter into early summer.

SAILING

There is hardly a part of Ireland's coastline where a sailing club cannot be found. It's an immensely popular pastime. To locate a club in any area contact the Irish Sailing Association (www.sailing.ie).

SOCCER

Soccer is almost as much of a passion in Ireland as in the rest of Europe. The Republic's national stadium is at Croke Park (while the Lansdowne Road stadium is being

Below There are many sailing clubs along the Irish coastline

redeveloped), Dublin, and there are teams in virtually every town, with most games taking place at weekends. The season is now virtually all year round. Check local papers or at the local Tourist Information Office.

SURFING

Hawaii it's not, but there are dozens of beaches where you can surf, most in the west and southwest, with some on the north coast. Conditions can be wild, however, and few beaches have tuition.

WALKING

Wherever you go in Ireland there's good walking, so it would be impossible to single out any regions in particular. Tourist Information Offices will be able to provide information.

HEALTH AND BEAUTY

Ireland might not be the first country people think of when they consider a health and beauty break, but it's fast catching up and new spas are opening all the time. Most of the major hotels feature health and beauty facilities, and there are retreats dedicated to personal pampering everywhere, often in some of the country's loveliest and most secluded and peaceful locations.

SPA TOWNS

There are only two spa towns in Ireland: Enniscrone in County Sligo and Lisdoonvarna in County Clare. The latter has Ireland's only working spa, the Spa Wells Health facility, although there are some other natural springs of the water, which has a strong mix of sulphur, iron and iodine. There are several Victorian bath-houses in Enniscrone, where a mix of sea water and seaweed is used. A seaweed bath is often available in hotel spas, especially in this corner of Ireland. Many of the larger hotels offer a range of health and beauty treatments.

HEALTH FARMS

Ireland enjoys a multitude of healthy spas, spread all over the country and in some spectacular, remote

locations. Information about these establishments can be found on the Irish Tourist Board website www. discoverireland.com.

FOR CHILDREN

There's no shortage of things for children to do in Ireland. Attractions, although not always highly sophisticated, certainly don't lack good, simple fun. There are numerous outdoor activities, as well as beaches to enjoy. You're more likely to find a farm to visit than a theme park but there's a warm welcome for children everywhere.

BEACHES

Ireland may not have the best climate for a beach holiday, but it has many long golden beaches, usually with room for children to run and play, and explore rock pools. Look to the west coast, southwest and Donegal, but there are also excellent beaches in Antrim and Wexford, and some surprisingly close to Dublin.

FESTIVALS AND FAIRS

In addition to many of the events listed opposite, children will particularly enjoy the old-fashioned fairs that travel the country and can turn up anywhere. There are also events like the Connemara Pony Show in Clifden, County Galway, where semi-wild ponies are sold and raced, and the Auld Lammas Fair in Ballycastle, County Antrim, both held in August.

FESTIVALS AND EVENTS

The Irish are renowned for getting the maximum enjoyment out of everyday life, but when a special day comes along they really celebrate, and it's a safe bet that music will be involved. In big towns and cities events are usually more organized than they tend to be in rural areas. Wherever you are, strangers are welcome to join in the fun. For Ireland's national holidays, ▷ 332.

RELIGIOUS
St. Patrick's Day is celebrated everywhere on 17 March, with parades and parties sometimes eclipsing the religious element.

ARTS
Admirers of James Joyce come to Dublin on 16 June for Bloomsday, re-enacting parts of *Ulysses*, with a smaller celebration in Belfast too. Summer sees Galway's Arts Festival, while in Dublin there's a Theatre Festival in October/November and the Winter Opera Season in November/December. Music festivals abound: classical in Dublin in April, jazz in Bray in May, closely followed by a Choral Festival in Cork and the four-day Fleadh Nua of traditional Irish music in Ennis in County Clare at the end of May.

FOOD AND DRINK
Cork in the South is renowned for its food, with the Bantry Mussel Fair in May and the big Kinsale Gourmet Festival every October. September brings the International Oyster Festival in Galway.

TRADITIONAL
Romance plays a big part in traditional festivals, with an International Bachelor Festival in Ballybunion, the Rose of Tralee beauty pageant in County Kerry in summer, and the Matchmaking Festival at Lisdoonvarna in County Clare in September. Then there's food, music and fairgrounds in the Auld Lammas Fair held at the end of August in Ballycastle in County Antrim, which also hosts the old Horse Ploughing match on St. Patrick's Day. The Puck Fair at Killorglin in County Kerry in August is as traditional as they come, with a wild goat being crowned king.

Opposite *Children enjoying a pony ride*
Below *Horse traders at the Auld Lammas Fair in Ballycastle, County Antrim*

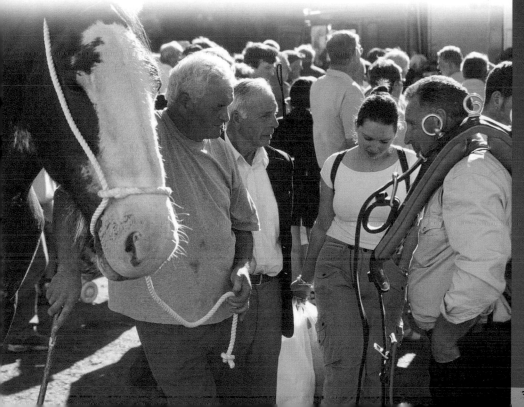

PRACTICALITIES WHAT TO DO

EATING

Ireland has some of the world's finest natural food resources, but for many years didn't seem to know what to do with them. The land is fertile, the air is healthy and the seas and rivers are clean and pure. Yet for centuries the diet was mainly potatoes, meat and vegetables. Bread and cheese were always good, but now a demand for finer foods has brought out the best in Irish chefs and you can dine as well here as anywhere in the world.

CURRENT TRENDS

Styles are slow to change in the countryside, although there is an awareness that more diverse eating options are needed, such as healthy eating, vegetarian and vegan choices and more sophisticated dishes. The major cities follow European trends, whether it be for fusion cooking or tapas bars, and new twists on native Irish dishes—New Irish Cuisine— remain popular.

SMOKING BAN

A strict law prohibiting smoking in the workplace has been introduced throughout Ireland. This includes all bars and restaurants, though outdoor areas may be set aside for smokers.

PRICING

Ireland is not an especially expensive country, and restaurant prices are broadly similar to those in most of western Europe. It is expensive by American standards, but less so in rural areas, and cities have such inexpensive options as cafés and pubs, where bar food can be a good bargain.

MEALTIMES

Breakfast may be served any time from 7am until 10am, depending on the establishment, and is sometimes later at weekends. Lunch is usually from about noon until 2 or 2.30pm. An increasing number of places stay open all day, and some pubs serve food all day, but this isn't the norm. Dinner is served quite early, from about 6pm, and might stop by 10pm, or even earlier in rural districts. In the cities, places will stay open later, principally the Indian and Chinese restaurants.

RESERVING

Ireland is a casual country and reserving isn't usually necessary, unless you're planning to dine in one of the finer restaurants. In smaller towns it might be advisable to check in advance, simply because there may not be other options nearby.

DRESS CODE

As with most things in life, the Irish take a very laid-back approach to dress codes. Casual attire is fine in all but the most expensive restaurants and some of the more stylish hotel restaurants.

LICENSING LAWS

In the Republic of Ireland pubs are open from 10.30am to 11.30pm Monday to Thursday, 10.30am to 12.30am Friday and Saturday and 12.30pm to 11pm on Sunday. In winter they close 30 minutes earlier. In Northern Ireland pubs may open at any times, but are only permitted to sell alcohol from 11.30am to 11pm Monday to Saturday and from 12.30pm to 10pm on Sunday. Extensions may be granted for special occasions.

The minimum drinking age is 18, and 18–20s must carry proof of age. Under 17s are banned from licensed premises after 9pm, unless attending a private function with a large meal. At other times under 15s must be with an adult.

VEGETARIAN

Being vegetarian in Ireland isn't easy but is far from impossible. The Irish diet has traditionally been meat-based, but today hosts are more aware of the particular needs of vegetarians and vegans, and suitable options will often be available. If staying and dining in a small or country house hotel, you might find it helpful to telephone ahead with any specific dietary needs.

For more information, look for a copy of *Dining in Ireland,* a free publication by the Irish Tourist Board.

BREAKFAST

The traditional breakfast, in Northern Ireland known as an Ulster Fry, consists of fried bacon, sausages, tomatoes, eggs, black pudding, white pudding and perhaps several kinds of bread (frequently home-made). Lighter options are available.

LUNCH

If you indulge in the full fry-up, you might feel the need for a lighter lunch. Picnic supplies include the very tasty and unusual Irish breads and local cheeses, which are two of the country's best products. Pub lunches are often excellent value. It may not be gourmet cuisine, but it is usually good, simple fare like fish and chips.

SNACKS

It's an Irish tradition to feed people well, and in some places, particularly guesthouses, you'll be faced with a plate of scones or sandwiches and a cup of tea or coffee, whenever you walk through the door, be it in the middle of the afternoon or late at night, when you have probably just returned from having dinner.

DINNER

Dinner itself can be anything you want it to be. The big cities offer everything from expensive restaurants to inexpensive ethnic cafés. Choice will be more restricted in smaller towns, but standards have improved vastly in the last 10 years or so, and Ireland has food to be proud of.

ALCOHOLIC DRINKS

Ireland is famous the world over for several of its alcoholic beverages, and also for the part played by the local pub in the social culture. Irish whiskey is popular everywhere and

can be drunk anytime, not merely as a post-dinner tipple. Many prefer it to Scottish whisky, and Bushmills, Powers and Jamesons are popular brands. Ireland has one vineyard, the most northerly in the world, near Mallow in County Cork, but Californian, Australian and European wines are widely available.

There isn't as much variety in beer as there is in some countries, as the Irish tend to prefer dark stouts over lager or bitter beers, and generally call them porters rather than stouts. These beers can be too heavy for some, but no one should go home without drinking a glass of Guinness, or its rival Murphy's. Guinness is said to get better the closer you are to the River Liffey, and therefore is at its best in Dublin. Remember to order it in good time, as bartenders take great pride in knowing how to pour a Guinness: very slowly and with a pause half-way through.

Opposite *Fresh soda bread*
Below left *Fruits of the sea*
Below *There's an art to pouring a pint of Guinness*

PUBS

Ireland hasn't yet quite had the explosion of so-called 'gastro-pubs' (pubs priding themselves on their restaurant-quality food) as has happened in mainland Britain, but nevertheless the standard of pub food in Ireland has increased immensely in recent years. In some instances pubs can provide a way of getting restaurant-type food at less expensive prices, and in other cases the pub is simply a place to find a good, hearty and affordable meal.

Some pubs in the main cities will serve food just about all day, but the vast majority will serve hot meals from around noon to 2 or 3pm, and again in the evenings from about 6 until around 9 or 10pm. At other times you may be able to get a basic bar snack, such as a sandwich.

A number of pubs do have proper, dedicated restaurant areas in addition to their bar food, so make enquiries about what the eating options are. In the restaurant area you may get a wider menu than if you eat in one of the bars—and slightly higher prices.

In rural areas the food on offer probably won't be quite as sophisticated, or the menus as extensive, though that's not to say it won't be good. The dishes on offer are more likely to be traditional Irish recipes rather than cutting-edge cuisine. The hours food is available may be shorter too, but it's not unknown for a landlord or landlady to rustle up a meal for visitors outside of the stated hours, if they're not too busy.

FAST FOOD

There is as much variety of fast food to be had in Ireland as anywhere else in the western world. Few places are without a fish and chip shop, a Chinese or Indian takeaway, or somewhere selling kebabs, fried chicken or burgers. In the cities you may find that some streets will have all these and more.

Various ethnic cuisines are popular in Ireland, and for an inexpensive and quick meal you should seek out one of the numerous Indian, Chinese, Italian or Mexican restaurants.

TEA AND COFFEE SHOPS

In Ireland the café, like the pub, is often a place to meet as well as eat. In the cities you will find a wide variety to choose from and, depending on the establishment, you'll be able to enjoy a range of meals and snacks from all-day breakfasts to cakes and other delicacies. Some cafés also open in the evenings when they might serve more elaborate meals.

There are still plenty of the old-fashioned working-men's cafés around, known as the 'greasy spoon' from the greasy fried food they traditionally serve, but these days in the main cities there are just as many sophisticated continental-style cafés too. In the smaller towns and rural areas it is more likely to be the old-fashioned kind you will find, which are fine for a quick cup of tea or coffee, or a cheap and filling plate of fried food if you're really hungry.

BACON AND CABBAGE
usually boiled ham rather than fried bacon, served with cabbage and potatoes. A hearty, country dish

BARM BRACK
a fruit loaf with a very doughy, yeasty texture

BLACK PUDDING
pork, pigs' blood, oatmeal, breadcrumbs and other ingredients producing something like a sausage, which tastes better than it might sound

BOXTY
potato cakes, sometimes served stuffed with meat, fish or vegetables

BROWN BREAD
infinite varieties, made from wholemeal flour and sometimes buttermilk

CHAMP
potatoes puréed with butter, milk and spring onions

COLCANNON
cabbage and spring onions (scallions) mixed into mashed potatoes. Leeks and kale might be used instead

CRUBEENS
pigs' feet, usually slowly cooked in stock

DRISHEEN
a County Cork version of black pudding, using mutton instead of pork

DUBLIN BAY PRAWNS
huge, slightly sweet and highly sought-after prawns, which are the same as langoustines, or scampi

DUBLIN CODDLE
potatoes and onions slowly cooked with meat, usually ham, bacon and/or sausage, which is traditionally served late on a Saturday night

IRISH COFFEE
a mix of coffee, a double whiskey, sugar and cream, the proportions varying according to the maker. You can always ask for a weak one, or one without sugar

IRISH STEW
a casserole of chunks of lamb with onions and parsley, topped with sliced potato

PORTER CAKE
a very filling cake made with dried fruit such as sultanas and raisins, a porter, usually Guinness, and spices

POTATO CAKE
not quite bread, not quite potato, made from a mixture of flour, butter and mashed potatoes

POTEEN
an illegal home-distilled strong liquor, usually made from potatoes

SODA BREAD
bread, which can be white or brown, raised with bicarbonate of soda instead of yeast

SODA CAKE
a little like soda bread, but with raisins

SODA FARL
a cross between a bread and a cake, made with soda and buttermilk

STRUISÍN GAELACH
Gaelic for Irish stew

UISCE BEATHA
Gaelic phrase from which the word 'whiskey' derives, meaning 'water of life'

WHEATEN BREAD
Northern Irish version of brown soda bread

WHITE PUDDING
Black pudding without the blood

PRACTICALITIES | EATING

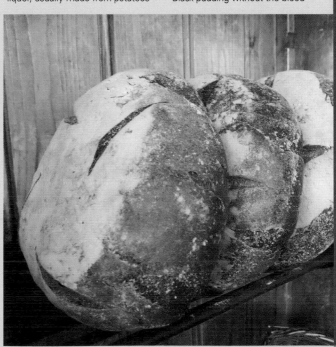

STAYING

In Ireland you can stay in anything from a castle to a horse-drawn caravan. The variety of accommodation is tremendous, and there's something to suit every budget. But whether you choose a manor house or a working farm, a city hotel or a country cottage, you'll receive a warm welcome and hospitality second to none. Most local Tourist Information Offices will have a bed reservation service or can advise on accommodation.

RESERVATIONS

It's always a good idea to make reservations in advance, especially for Dublin and if you're visiting in peak season. Prices are listed either as a room rate, usually without breakfast, or as bed-and-breakfast (B&B) per person based on two people sharing a room. Single supplements are often charged. Prices are quoted in euros for the Republic and in pounds sterling for Northern Ireland.

Within Ireland, tourist offices offer a reservation service, charging a small fee to cover phone calls and a 10 per cent non-refundable deposit. You can reserve online via the Bord Fáilte website www.discoverireland. com. The reservation services below cover accommodation in all price brackets. You may pay a small fee.

Gulliver (www.gulliver.ie) operates a reservations system throughout the Republic and Northern Ireland. All properties are approved by the Irish Tourist Board. You can reserve online at www.goireland.com or via the following toll-free numbers: within Ireland: 1-800 369 87412; from the UK: 0800 783 8359; from Europe: 00800 369 47412; from the US: 1-888 827 3028. Lines are open Monday to Friday 9am to 8pm.

The Irish Hotels Federation (tel 01 497 6459) publishes Be Our Guest, a directory of approved hotels and guesthouses in the Republic, available at tourist offices or by calling 0800 039 7000. Or reserve online: www.discoverireland. com. The Northern Ireland Hotels Federation (tel 028 9077 6635; www.nihf.co.uk) publishes a free guide, available at tourist offices or from the Northern Ireland Tourist Board, 59 North Street, Belfast BT1 1NB, tel 028 9023 1221. Or reserve online at www.nitb.com.

HOTELS

Properties which display the shamrock symbol have been inspected by the Irish Tourist Board or Northern Ireland Tourist Board.

Prices average around €80 for a two-star hotel, €145 for three-and four-star, and €225 for five-star. Some of the large chain hotels in major cities may offer discounted rooms at the weekend. Others may offer special packages.

In resort areas, four- and five-star hotels may have sports and leisure facilities. In smaller towns, a hotel with a good bar may be the hub of social activity. Our listings indicate where hotels have extra facilities or activities available.

Throughout Ireland, converted castles, manor houses and country house hotels are generally set in beautiful rural surroundings and offer sophisticated dining, some of the finest in the country. Fishing or horse-riding may also be available.

Above Duvane Farm guesthouse, Clonakilty

Hidden Ireland (tel 01 662 7166, www.hiddenireland.com) is a collection of private houses with character and fascinating history. Guests often dine with their hosts.

Ireland's Blue Book (tel 01 676 9914, www.irelands-blue-book.ie) gives details of some of the top country house hotels in the country.

Manor House Hotels and Irish Country Hotels (tel 01 295 8900, www.cmvhotels.com) have accommodation in castles, manor houses and family-owned country hotels.

Most hotels charge dearly for drinks and snacks from the mini-bar. You will also pay high rates for using the telephone line in your room for making calls or using the internet. International calls can be exorbitant. Check the rates in advance if they are not already posted in your room.

Tipping is not generally expected, even at the larger hotels. Services such as carrying bags to your room or serving drinks are considered part of the hospitality. The exception is hotel restaurants: Unless a service charge is added to the bill, waiters should be tipped 10 to 15 per cent.

GUESTHOUSES

Guesthouses have more rooms than a B&B, but the atmosphere is friendly and informal, with an emphasis on personal attention. The hosts may or may not live on the premises. You'll often be served afternoon tea and scones on arrival, and a generous Irish breakfast is assured.

Prices are higher than a B&B, reflecting a higher level of comfort and amenities. Some can be as expensive as a top hotel.

Associations with properties of character include Premier Guest Houses of Ireland (tel 01 205 2826, www.premierguesthouses.com) and Irish Country Inns (tel 01 660 7975, www.tourismresources.ie/fh).

BED-AND-BREAKFAST

Bed-and-breakfast accommodation is in family homes, with generally one to four private rooms reserved for guests. Furnishings are simple, but rooms are clean and pleasant

and usually have private bathrooms. There are B&Bs in nearly every town and village, and while advance reservations are always wise, another attraction is that accommodation can usually be found for those visiting without a fixed schedule. Average prices start from around €30 per person, including a full Irish breakfast.

Farmhouse B&Bs are particularly popular in Ireland. They are an excellent way to experience the countryside at first hand and make contact with local people. Good fresh food and a warm welcome are an added feature. Prices start at €28 per person, including breakfast.

Associations specializing in B&B include: Family Homes of Ireland (tel 091 552 000; www.family-homes.ie); the Town and Country Homes Association (tel 071 98 22222; www.townandcountry.ie); Irish Farmhouse Holidays (tel 061 400 700; www.irishfarmholidays.com); and the Northern Ireland Farm & Country Holidays Association (tel 028 8284 1325; www.nifcha.com).

HOSTELS

For those on a budget, there are more than 200 hostels in both cities and the countryside. In addition to dormitory beds, most now have private rooms, including family rooms, some with private bathrooms. Many offer meals and activities. Prices range from €12–€25 for dormitory beds and €12–€60 for private rooms.

For affiliated hostels, contact An Óige, the Irish Youth Hostel Association (tel 01 830 4555; www.anoige.ie) or Hostelling International Northern Ireland (tel 028 9032 4733; www.hini.org.uk).

SELF CATERING

You can rent traditional houses, cottages, apartments (or even a castle with butler and housekeeping staff), usually on a weekly basis. Cooking utensils and bed linen are generally supplied, though you may want to bring extra towels. Prices range from €100–€700 per week (£65–£455 in Northern Ireland). You may pay extra for electricity and gas.

Gulliver (▷ 350) lists more than 2,500 approved properties. In the Republic, contact Irish Self Catering Federation (tel 0818 300186; www.iscf.ie) or Irish Cottages and Holiday Homes Association (tel 01 205 2777; www.irishcottageholidays.com). In Northern Ireland try Northern Ireland Self-Catering Association (tel 028 9043 6632; www.nischa.com) or Rural Cottage Holidays (tel 0870 236 1630; www.cottagesinireland.com).

CAMPING AND CARAVANNING

There are more than 200 camping and caravan parks in Ireland. Many sites have motor homes that can be rented by the week. Prices range from €6–€15 for a small tent and from €6–€22 for a motor home, according to location and season.

The Irish Camping and Caravan Council (tel 098 25970; www.camping-ireland.ie) lists parks in the Republic on its website. In Northern Ireland, contact the tourist board for a list of approved sites. You can obtain permits for camping in forest areas from the Northern Ireland Forest Service (tel 028 9052 4480; www.forestserviceni.gov.uk).

HORSE-DRAWN CARAVANS

For a slow but adventurous journey, you can rent a horse-drawn caravan. Wagons can accommodate four to five people, and you spend the nights in the country or on the grounds of a rural pub or country house. A short break costs between €330 and €600 in the off season, while a week in the peak season starts at €750. You'll pay around €15–€20 for overnight parking. See www.irishhorsedrawncaravans.com.

CABIN CRUISING

You can rent a barge or cruiser sleeping two to ten people; you don't need a licence, and you will be given instructions. Cruisers are usually rented on a weekly basis and prices range from €800–€2,500 or more. Contact Waterways Ireland (www.waterwaysireland.org) or Inland Waterways Association of Ireland (www.iwai.ie).

IRISH LANGUAGE

Irish is the official first language of the Republic of Ireland. Spoken everywhere on the island until the early 19th century, it was subsequently relegated to the fringes until its revival in the 20th century. And while English—the official second language—is the dominant tongue today, the Irish language is an important symbol of national identity. All official documents are printed in both languages, making Ireland a bilingual nation.

A CELTIC TONGUE

Irish is the purest of the Celtic family of languages which once ranged throughout Europe. It was introduced by the first Celtic migrations to the island during prehistoric times. Irish is the correct name for the language, though it is often called Gaelic, as it is related to, but different from, Scottish Gaelic, Breton and Welsh. Old Irish is the earliest of the Northern European languages in which extensive writings still exist. Irish bards took the language to poetic heights, and the Norman aristocracy adopted it. Until the early 16th century, the country remained Irish-speaking. But with English conquests and plantations, Irish culture was systematically destroyed. English became the language of government and town, though Irish continued to be spoken in rural areas. Death and emigration during the Famine years took a heavy toll on the Irish-speaking community, and it became further associated with poverty. By 1891, more than 85 per cent of the people spoke only English.

REVIVAL

In the late 19th century, two forces spawned an Irish language revival: literature and nationalism. Writers such as W. B. Yeats and J. M. Synge found inspiration in the old Irish storytelling tradition. Douglas Hyde founded the Gaelic League in 1893 and promoted the return of Irish lessons in schools. It became associated with the rise of the republican spirit.

Today, Irish is a compulsory subject in schools in the Republic, and a requirement for university entrance. Figures vary, but some 35 per cent of adults claim to have a knowledge of Irish. English remains the official language of Northern Ireland.

THE GAELTACHT

Areas where Irish is spoken as the main tongue are called the Gaeltacht. They are largely rural regions on the western seaboard, in counties Galway, Mayo, Donegal, Cork, Kerry and pockets of Waterford, separated from each other. People from other parts of the country send their children to board with Gaeltacht families during summer holidays to learn Irish. But the Gaeltacht regions are largely remote with poor economic prospects compared with the rest of the country, and as a result young people tend to move away, so the number of Irish speakers is threatened. People in the Gaeltacht are bilingual, although the road signs are mainly in Irish only.

SPEAKING IRISH

The Irish language is difficult for the beginner. Words are often pronounced quite differently from the way they are written. Most vowels are short, not long. The 'craic' is pronounced 'crack' and 'fáilte' is pronounced 'fawl-ch'. There are many unfamiliar combinations and silent letters; for example, 'bh' is usually pronounced as 'v', as in the name Siobhan ('Sh-vawn') and 'sidhe' is pronounced 'she', with the 'dh' silent. 'Si' or 'se' is pronounced as 'sh', while the combination 'gh' is pronounced as an 'h', as in Gallagher ('Gal-a-her'). To complicate matters, there are different Irish dialects and spellings in different regions.

Here are a few basic words you may find useful:

fáilte	welcome
tá/sea	yes
níl/ní hea	no

PLACE NAMES

IRISH ROOT	ENGLISH MEANING	IRISH PLACE NAMES
ar, ard	height	Ardmore, Ardgroom
áth, atha	ford	Athlone, Athy
bal, baile, ballya	town	Ballycastle, Ballyhack
beg, beag	small	Beaghmore Stone Circles, Lough Beg
carrig, carrick	rock	Carrick-on-Shannon
cashel	castle	Rock of Cashel
drom, drum	a ridge	Drombeg Stone Circle, Drumsna
dun, dún	a fort	Dundalk, Dún Laoghaire
glen, gleann	a valley	Glenveagh, Glencree
innis, onnis	island	Enniskerry, Enniscorthy
kil, kill, cil	a church	Killarney, Glencolumbkille
knock, cnoc	a hill	Knocknarea Mountain, Knockferry
lis, liss, lios	a ring fort	Listowel, Lisdoonvarna
mor, mór	big or great	Aranmore, Lismore
rath	a ring fort	Rathfarnham, Rathdrum
slieve	a mountain	Slieve Bloom, Slieve League
tra, trá, tráigh	a beach or strand	Tramore, Tralee
tul, tulagh	small hill	Tullamore, Tullynally Castle

JAMES JOYCE (1882–1941)

Joyce was born in Dublin but wrote his greatest works when living in Switzerland, Italy and France. He first achieved fame with his 1916 novel, *A Portrait of the Artist as a Young Man*, a semi-autobiographical account of his early life in Dublin, but it was the two later monumental works that confirmed his place as one of the leading novelists of the 20th century: *Ulysses* (1922) and *Finnegans Wake* (1939).

EDNA O'BRIEN (1932–)

Born in County Clare, Edna O'Brien qualified as a pharmacist in Dublin. Her first novel *The Country Girls*, published in 1960 after she had moved to London, became the first in a trilogy following the lives of two Irish girls. The trilogy was among several of her books that were banned in Ireland for their sexually explicit passages. She has also produced a play about Virginia Woolf (1981), a biography of James Joyce (1999) and the non-fiction *Mother Ireland* (1976). She has won several awards, such as the Kingsley Amis Award for fiction in 1962 and the Los Angeles Times Book Prize in 1990.

KEY FIGURES IN IRISH LITERATURE

SAMUEL BECKETT (1906–89)

Born in Foxrock, near Dublin, Beckett was one of the late 20th century's most influential dramatists. He won the Nobel Prize for Literature in 1969, one of four Irish writers to do so. His best-known work is *Waiting for Godot*, summed up by one critic as 'nothing happens, twice'. Like James Joyce (for whom he once worked as secretary), he achieved his fame in exile, in Beckett's case in Paris, where he is buried.

BRENDAN BEHAN (1923–64)

Dublin-born and as famous for his personal life as for his writing, Behan joined the IRA at the age of 13. His later experiences in reform school and prison produced work such as *Borstal Boy* and *The Quare Fellow*.

RODDY DOYLE (1958–)

Probably the most prominent of contemporary Irish writers, Doyle's background growing up in, and teaching in, one of the poorer parts of Dublin helped to shape novels such as *The Commitments* and *Paddy Clarke Ha Ha Ha*, which won the prestigious British Booker Prize for Fiction.

SÉAMUS HEANEY (1939–)

Born in County Londonderry, the son of a farmer, Heaney is a well-liked and well-respected poet. He lectured at Queen's College, Belfast, before receiving the Nobel Prize for Literature, in 1995. He has also taught at Oxford and at Harvard. His work often deals in subtle ways with his rural childhood, Irish mythology and the modern political situation in Ireland.

GEORGE BERNARD SHAW (1856–1950)

Dublin-born Nobel Prizewinner (in 1925), Shaw was one of those writers seemingly blessed with boundless energy. He wrote more than 50 plays for the stage, thousands of letters, a few novels, a vast amount of journalism and became regularly embroiled in political matters. He was an early vegetarian, a campaigner for women's rights, a naturist and an advocate for, among many other things, the simplification of English spelling. His plays include *Mrs Warren's Profession*, *Arms and the Man*, *Man and Superman*. His best-known work, *Pygmalion*, was

Clockwise from left to right *George Bernard Shaw; Seamus Heaney; Roddy Doyle*

adapted into the stage and film musical, *My Fair Lady*.

BRAM STOKER (1847–1912)

Born in Dublin, Stoker worked for a time as a civil servant at Dublin Castle, turning to writing in later life, though it was a long-held dream. He is best known for *Dracula* (1897). Less well known is his volume of children's fairy tales, *Under the Sunset* (1882) and several other works of fiction.

JONATHAN SWIFT (1667–1745)

Like Oscar Wilde two centuries later, Swift was born in Dublin, studied at Trinity College and went on to outrage society—though not for quite the same reasons. Swift came from an eminently respectable family, and after an English education he returned to Dublin and took holy orders. He also began writing, and became known as one of the sharpest satirists of his day. His suggestion that the Irish poor sell their children as food to the rich was not always seen in the savage way it was intended. His great work, *Gulliver's Travels*, was another satire on the society of his time. In 1713 he became Dean of St. Patrick's Cathedral, where he is buried.

OSCAR WILDE (1854–1900)

Wilde was born in Dublin and studied there at Trinity College, before moving to Oxford in England, where his Bohemian nature and his literary talents began to manifest themselves. He is as much remembered today for his lifestyle and his wit ('I have nothing to declare except my genius,' he is said to have told a New York immigration official) as his writing, but he wrote several successful plays, including *Lady Windermere's Fan* (1892), *A Woman of No Importance* (1893) and *The Importance of Being Earnest* (1895), as well as his only novel, *The Picture of Dorian Gray* (1891). He was persecuted and jailed for his homosexuality, illegal in the UK at the time, and died in exile in Paris.

W. B. YEATS (1865–1939)

Yeats was the first Irish writer to win the Nobel Prize for Literature, in 1923, and one of the many fine writers to have been born in Dublin. His interest in philosophy, religion, Irish legends and the occult influenced his poetry enormously. He also wrote plays and short stories. He was a great promoter of Irish literature, and was manager of the Abbey Theatre for several years, as well as helping found the theatre and Dublin's National Literary Society. Some of his best-known poems include *Easter 1916*, about the Easter uprising, *The Lake Isle of Innisfree* and *Under Ben Bulben*. The poet is buried in a graveyard in the shade of Ben Bulben mountain, in County Sligo, where he spent much of his childhood.

TRACING YOUR ANCESTORS

After the mass exodus of the Famine years, the Irish diaspora spread throughout the world. But emigrant ties to the old country have always remained strong, passing down the generations to the present day. People of Irish descent are proud of their roots—witness the exuberant St. Patrick's Day celebrations in America—and it's no wonder that tracing ancestors has become a popular pursuit among visitors to Ireland.

STARTING YOUR SEARCH

Every Irish person is descended from an old family sept, or clan, and even if you can't go further back than your grandfather, it's fun to learn the archaic spelling of your family name and whether your ancient kin were bards, warriors or high kings. Many books and websites can tell you the regions where particular names were prevalent. However, you will need to know more than your surname if you're serious about tracing your roots. Do some basic research at home before your visit,

so you can make the most of your time in Ireland.

First, pinpoint where your ancestors lived, not only the county but preferably the name of the parish or townland (an ancient land division, unique to Ireland, and now the smallest recognized sub-division). Build up a profile of each ancestor you want to trace: the year he or she emigrated, the age, marital status, names of spouse (including maiden name), any children, and their port of arrival. Knowing their religion and occupation can also be useful in deciding which parish registers, directories and legal records to consult. If you can't find out from relatives or family records, you can search various public records such as marriage and death records or passenger lists.

RESEARCH IN IRELAND

In Ireland, a good place to start is the Genealogical Office in the National Library in Dublin (tel: 01 603 0200; www.nli.ie). Staff here can help you to access the library's many information sources, including Catholic parish registers, land

valuation records, estate records, newspapers, and trade and social directories. The service is free and especially helpful for beginners. There is also a list of genealogists who will undertake research for a fee. The Genealogy Advisory Service is open Monday to Friday 9.30am–4.45pm and Saturday 9.30am–12.30pm. No appointment is necessary.

Every county has a genealogical or Heritage Centre. These are listed on www.irishroots.net. Although the available data and search facilities vary, these places should be able to help you access parish rosters and other local records. General advice is usually given free, but professional researchers will charge a fee for their services, so always ask before you begin a search. The Irish Tourist Board publishes a booklet, available at tourist offices, listing resources for tracing ancestors in Ireland. To trace ancestors in Northern Ireland, contact the Public Record Office (tel: 028 9025 5905; www.proni.gov.uk). Admission is free and the website gives advice on using its records to trace your family tree. The Centre for Migration Studies at the Ulster American Folk Park (▷ 303, tel 028 8225 6315; www.qub.ac.uk/cms) is another excellent resource. Its Irish Emigration Database has primary source documents on emigration to North America, including letters, newspaper articles and family papers as well as records.

Unfortunately many census records and Church of Ireland parish registers were destroyed when the national public records office in Dublin was burned down in 1922. But many Roman Catholic parish registers have survived, as have other sources. The Office of the Registrar General (tel: 090 663 2900; www.groireland.ie) is the central archive for records of births, marriages and deaths in the Republic. Check online for samples of records held and how to read them. You can also search records in the National Archives (tel 01 407 2300; www.nationalarchives.ie). In Northern Ireland, contact the General Registrar Office (tel 090 635 4423; www.groni.gov.uk). In addition to civil records, clues can be found in census, church and property records.

ANCESTOR HUNTING ON THE WEB

With the development of the internet, genealogical research has become infinitely easier and more accessible. Many types of public records are now available online, and there are a number of websites which offer advice on how to trace your ancestors. They also have links to sources in your home country where you can access data and start your background research. Many of these services are free. The following is a list of useful websites to get you started:

www.genuki.org.uk
This self-styled virtual reference library has excellent advice for beginners in how to get started in researching your family history; it gives recommended publications, books and other sources for tracing your Irish roots from abroad.

www.ireland.com/ancestor Part of *The Irish Times* website, this site has basic surname and ancestor information to whet your appetite, and for a fee you can access their database searches.

www.genealogy.com
A wealth of practical articles on researching your family history, some specific to Irish ancestry; also free online lessons in tracing your ancestors.

www.genealogy.about.com
Useful site with online Ireland databases, articles, tips, lessons and documents for tracing your Irish ancestors.

www.familysearch.org
The Church of Latter Day Saints in Salt Lake City, Utah, keeps the largest family history library in the world; the website gives advice on searching their vast collection of records.

www.irelandseye.com/irish/traditional/names/index.shtm
Good advice on beginning your genealogical research.

www.ancestry.com
Online collection of US and UK databases including passenger and immigration lists, census data, newspapers, periodicals, civil and other records.

PILGRIMAGE SITES IN IRELAND

Pilgrimage to Ireland has been in high profile since the opening of Knock's international airport in 1986 to deal with the massive annual influx to the shrine at the town of Knock. This amazing County Mayo site draws a massive 1.5 million (approximately) pilgrims every year. The story began on the evening of 21 August 1879, when 15 people witnessed for 2 hours a clear and detailed apparition on the gable of the church featuring the Virgin, St. John the Evangelist and St. Joseph. As a result, this is now an international pilgrimage site, has a new Church of Our Lady, Queen of Ireland (dedicated 1976) with a capacity for 10,000 people, and was visited by Pope John Paul II in 1979.

There is evidence of pilgrimage to Irish religious sites since at least the 12th century, when a European knight called Owen is known to have visited St. Patrick's Purgatory on an island in Lough Derg, County Donegal. Here devout pilgrims—about 3,000 every year—go through an austere regime of fasting and barefoot penance over three days at the place St. Patrick is said to have visited for prayer more than 400 times.

Croagh Patrick mountain (▷ 216) in County Mayo, is where St. Patrick is said to have fasted for 40 days and nights in AD441. Thousands of people come to climb to the top—many in bare feet—during the summer, but the big day is the last Sunday in July, when more than 20,000 pilgrims make the ascent.

Opposite *Graveyard at Powerscourt*
Below *Statue of St. Patrick on Croagh Patrick*

anticlockwise......counterclockwise

aubergine..........................eggplant

bank holiday.......... a public holiday

bill (at restaurant) ....check

biscuit (sweet).................... cookie

biscuit (unsweetened)....... cracker

bonnet............................hood (car)

boot................................trunk (car)

bowls........................ lawn bowling

busker ....street musician

caravan.............house trailer or RV

car park ....parking lot

carriage ....car (on a train)

casualty .... emergency room (hospital department)

chemist ....pharmacy

chips ....French fries

coach .... long-distance bus

coach (train)..............................car

coaching inn pubs or hotels dating from 17th–19th centuries, located on main travel routes

concessions .... reduced fees for tickets, often available to students, children and elderly people

corn (field)...................wheat (field

coriander..........................cilantro)

courgette ....zucchini

crèche.............................. day care

crisps ....potato chips

directory enquiries.......... directory assistance

draughts (game)..............checkers

dual carriageway.............two-lane highway

economy/tourist class (plane)...... coach

en suite .... a bedroom with its own private bathroom; may also just refer to the bathroom

football...............................soccer

foyer ....lobby

full board.................... a hotel tariff that includes all meals

garage .... gas station

garden .... yard (residential)

GP .... doctor

half board............... hotel tariff that includes breakfast and either lunch or dinner

handbag ....purse

high street .... main street

hire .... rent

hoarding (noun) .... billboard

inland ....within the UK

jacket potato ....baked potato

jelly ....Jello™

jumper, jersey....................sweater

junction ....intersection

layby .... rest stop, pull-off

leader (newspaper) ....editorial

level crossing.......... grade crossing

licensed ....a café or restaurant that has a licence to serve alcohol (beer and wine only unless it's 'fully' licensed)

lift ....elevator

lorry ....truck

main line station ......a train station as opposed to an underground or subway station (although it may be served by the underground /subway

maize ....corn

market garden) .... truck farm

nappy ....diaper

note (currency) .... bill

off-licence ....liquor store

pants .... underpants (men's)

pavement ....sidewalk

petrol..gas

plaster .... Band-Aid or bandage

pony trekking ...... horseback riding

post ....mail

power point ....socket/outlet

primary school .... grade school

public school ....private school

pudding..............................dessert

purse .... change purse

pushchair ....stroller

return ticket............roundtrip ticket

rocket ....arugula

roundabout... traffic circle or rotary

saloon (car) .... sedan

scone .... biscuit

self-catering..........accommodation including a kitchen

single ticket ....one-way ticket

solicitor .... lawyer/attorney

stall (market) ....stand

stalls (theatre) .... orchestra seats

surgery ...... doctor's/dentist's office

swede.................................... turnip

tailback...........................traffic jam

takeaway ....takeout

taxi rank ....taxi stand

ten-pin bowling.................bowling

terraces, terraced houses....... row houses

tights ....panty-hose

T-junction.....an intersection where one road meets another at right angles (making a T shape)

toilets ....restrooms

torch ....flashlight

trainers............................. sneakers

trolley ....cart

trousers..................................pants

underpass .... subway

verge (of a road)...............shoulder

vest .... undershirt

way out ....exit

windscreen ....windshield (car)

wing (car)............................ fender

IRISH FLOOR NUMBERING

In Ireland the first floor of a building is called the ground floor, and the floor above it is the first floor. So an Irish second floor is a US third floor, and so on. This is something to watch for in museums and galleries in particular.

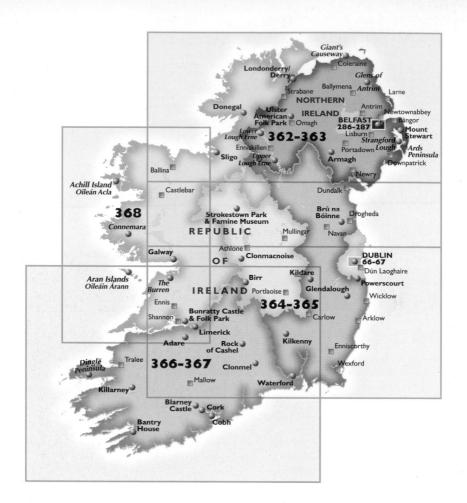

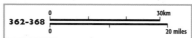

362-368

| 0 | 30km |
| 0 | 20 miles |

Toll motorway (Turnpike)

Motorway (Expressway)

Motorway junction with and without number

National road

Regional road

Other road

Motorway / Road under construction

Railway

International boundary

County boundary

City / Town

Built-up area

National Park

Featured place of interest

Airport

621 Height in metres

Viewpoint

MAPS

Map references for the sights refer to the atlas pages within this section or to the individual town plans within the regions. For example, Roscrea has the reference ✚ 364 E6, indicating the page on which the map is found (364) and the grid square in which Roscrea sits (E6).

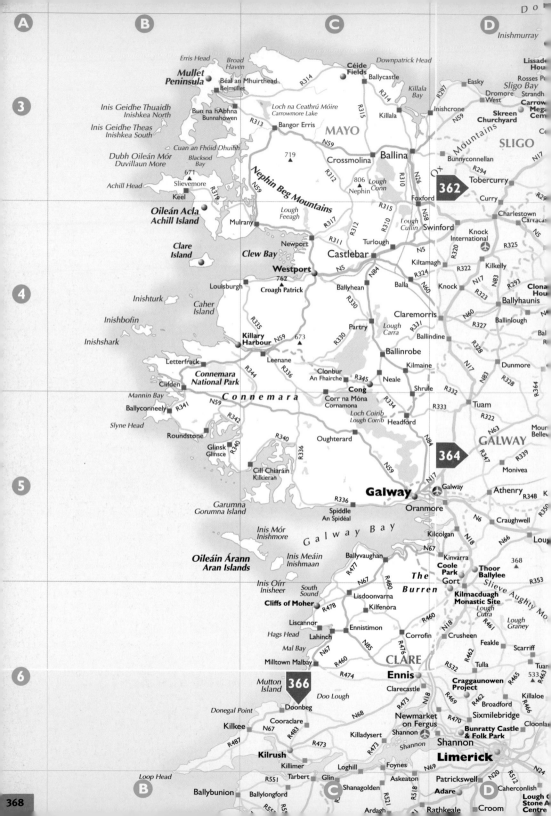

MAPS INDEX

371

PICTURES

The Automobile Association would like to thank the following photographers, companies and picture libraries for their assistance in the preparation of this book. Abbreviations for the picture credits are as follows: (t) top; (b) bottom; (l) left; (r) right; (c) centre; (AA) AA World Travel Library.

2 AA/S Whitehorne;
3t AA/S McBride;
3ct Belfast Visitor and Convention Bureau;
3cb AA/J Blandford;
3b AA/L Blake;
4 AA/G Munday;
5 Photolibrary Group;
6 AA/J Blandford;
7 National Trust/John Lennon;
8 Irish National Stud and Japanese Gardens;
10 AA/M Diggin;
11 AA/S McBride;
12 AA/C Jones;
13 © Reuters/Corbis;
14 Northern Ireland Tourist Board;
15t AA/S Day 15c Crispin Rodwell/ Rex Features;
15b Stuart Wilson/Getty Images;
16 David Rogers/Getty Images;
17l Mayo Naturally;
17cr Scott Halleran/Getty Images;
17br Stockbyte;
18 AA/S McBride;
19t AA/C Coe;
19b AA/C Coe;
20 AA/C Coe;
21tl AA/C Coe;
21tr © Geray Sweeney/Corbis;
21b © Peter Titmuss/Alamy;
22 AA/S McBride;
23t David Levenson/Getty Images;
23c Justin Williams/Rex Features;
23b AFP Photo/Robyn Beck/Getty Images;
24 Stockbyte;
25t AA/C Hill;
25c AA/S Day;
25b Failte Ireland Dublin Horse Show;
26 Cork – European Captial City of Culture 2005;

27 AA/S Hill;
28l Mary Evans Picture Library;
28r AA;
29l AA/M Diggin;
29r ;
30 AA/S Hill;
31t MS 57 fol.21v The Man, symbol of St. Matthew the Evangelist, introductory page to the Gospel of St. Matthew, Irish, from Durrow, County Offaly (vellum),/© The Board of Trinity College, Dublin, Ireland,/The Bridgeman Art Library;
31b AA/M Short;
32l AA/C Coe;
32r AA;
33t AA/M Diggin;
33c AA/M Short;
33b AA;
34 Mary Evans Picture Library;
35tl AA/S Day;
35r AA;
35cl AA;
36 AA/G Munday;
37t AA;
37c AA/S Whitehorne;
37b AA;
38 AA;
39l Keystone/Getty Images;
39c AA/S Day;
39br Illustrated London News;
40 AA/C Coe;
41t AA/C Coe;
41c Norm Betts/Rex Features;
41b Mary Evans Picture Library;
42t AA/C Coe;
42b Belfast Visitors and Convention Bureau;
43 Photodisc;
45 Digitalvision;
47 AA/C Jones;
48 AA;
49 AA/J Blandford;
52 Translink Trains;
53 Irish Rail;
54 AA/C Jones;
55 Aer Arann;
56 AA/C Jones;
57 AA/M Diggin;
59 Belfast Visitors and Convention Bureau;
60 Belfast Visitors and Convention Bureau;
62 AA/D Forss;
63 AA/C Coe;
64 AA/L Blake;
70 AA/S Day;

71 AA/S Day;
72 AA/S Whitehorne;
73 Image courtesy of Dublin Tourism;
74 AA/S Whitehorne;
75l AA/Slidefile;
75r AA/M Short;
76l AA/S McBride;
76r AA/S Day;
77 Guinness Storehouse;
78 AA/M Short;
79l AA/M Short;
79r AA/Slidefile;
80 AA/S McBride;
81t AA/S McBride;
81b AA/S McBride;
82 AA/S Day;
83 AA/Slidefile;
84 AA/S Whitehorne;
85t The Tara Brooch, from Bettystown, County Meath (cast silver with glass, enamel & amber), Celtic, (8th century)/National Museum of Ireland, Dublin, Ireland,/ The Bridgeman Art Library;
85b AA/S Day;
86t © Adrian Wilson/Beateworks/ Corbis;
86b © Werner Foreman/Corbis;
87 AA/S Day;
88l AA/Slidefile;
88r AA/S Whitehorne;
89 AA/S Day;
90 AA/Slidefile;
91 MS 58 fol.291v Portrait of St. John, page preceding the Gospel of St. John, from the Book of Kells, c.800 (vellum), Irish School, (9th century)/© The Board of Trinity College, Dublin, Ireland,/The Bridgeman Art Library;
92t AA/S Day;
92b AA/S Day;
93 AA/S Day;
94 AA/S Whitehorne;
95 AA/S Day;
96 AA/S McBride;
98 AA/M Short;
101 AA/S Day;
103 AA/S Day;
104 AA/C Sawyer;
107 Finnstown Country House Hotel;
108 ImageState;
109 ;
110 AA/S Day;
112 Stillorgan Park Hotel;
113 The Merrion Hotel;
114 AA;

IRELAND

ACKNOWLEDGEMENTS

ACKNOWLEDGEMENTS IRELAND

116 AA/M Short;
117 AA/C Jones;
118 AA/P Zollier;
119t AA/C Jones;
119b AA/C Coe;
120 AA/C Jones;
121 AA/M Short;
122 AA/C Jones;
123t AA/Slidefile;
123b AA/M Short;
124 AA/M Short;
125 AA/M Short;
126t AA/S McBride;
126b AA/S McBride;
127t AA/M Short;
127b AA/M Short;
128l AA/S McBride;
128r AA/C Jones;
129 AA/P Zollier;
130 AA/M Short;
131l AA/C Jones;
131r AA/C Jones;
132 AA/L Blake;
133 AA/M Short;
134 AA/C Jones;
135 AA/S Day;
136 AA/C Jones;
137l AA/M Short;
137r AA/C Jones;
138 AA/I Dawson;
139t AA/I Dawson;
139b AA/I Dawson;
140 AA/C Jones;
141l AA/C Coe;
141r AA/C Jones;
142 AA/L Blake;
144 AA/C Coe;
146 ImageState;
149 Tinakilly Country House & Restaurant;
150 Nuremore Hotel & Country Club;
153 Stockbyte Royalty Free;
154 AA/J Blandford;
156 Richard Cummins/Corbis;
157 AA/S Hill;
158l AA/C Jones;
158r AA/S Hill;
159 AA/S Hill;
160 AA/S McBride;
161 AA/S Hill;
162 AA/C Jones;
163c AA/D Forss;
163b AA/C Jones;
164 AA/S McBride;
165t AA/C Jones;
165b AA/C Jones;
166l AA/M Diggin;

166r AA/C Jones;
167 AA/C Jones;
108ll AA/C Jones;
168tr AA/J Blandford;
168b AA/J Blandford;
169l AA/J Blandford;
169r AA/C Jones;
170 AA/C Jones;
171 AA/J Blandford;
172 AA/J Blandford;
173 AA/S McBride;
174 AA/P Zollier;
175 AA/C Jones;
176 AA/S McBride;
177t AA/D Forss;
177b AA/S Hill;
178 AA/C Jones;
179t AA/C Jones;
179bl AA/C Jones;
179br AA/C Jones;
180 AA/C Jones;
181 AA/J Blandford;
182 AA/S McBride;
183 AA/S Day;
184 AA/C Jones;
186 AA/P Zollier;
187 AA/C Jones;
189 AA/J Blandford;
190 Puck Fair Festival;
191 Puck Fair Festival;
192 © Gerry O'Carroll;
194 Sheen Falls Lodge;
195 Ballyrafter House;
196 Longueville House Hotel;
197 Photodisc;
198 AA/C Jones;
199 Garnish House;
200 Sheen Falls Lodge;
201 TongRo Images Stock/Alamy;
202 AA/S McBride;
204 Photolibrary Group;
205 AA/L Blake;
206 AA/S Hill;
207l AA/C Coe;
207r AA/C Jones;
208 AA/P Zollier;
209 AA/S Hill;
210t AA/M Diggin;
210b Nature Photographers (Brinsley Burbidge);
211 AA/M Diggin;
212 AA/C Jones;
213 AA/D Forss;
214l AA/C Jones;
214r AA/C Jones;
215t AA/C Jones;
215b AA/L Blake;

216t AA/L Blake;
216b AA/C Hill;
217 Photolibrary Group;
218 AA/S McBride;
219 AA/M Diggin;
220 AA/I Dawson;
221 AA/C Jones;
222 AA/C Hill;
223 AA/C Hill;
224 AA/I Dawson;
225 AA/L Blake;
226 © William Manning/Corbis;
227 AA/I Dawson;
228 AA/C Jones;
229 AA/C Jones;
230 Mayo Naturally;
231 Mayo Naturally;
232 AA/E A Bowness;
233 AA/R Ireland;
235l AA/J Johnson;
235r AA/C Coe;
236 AA/L Blake;
238 Drumoland Castle Restaurant;
239 Park House Hotel;
241 The Abbey Restaurant, Castle Grove Country House;
242 AA/C Jones;
243 Atlantic Heights;
244 Castle Grove Country House Hotel;
246 AA/M Short;
248 AA/L Blake;
249 AA/L Blake;
250 AA/C Jones;
251t AA/S McBride;
251b AA/L Blake;
252 AA/L Blake;
253 AA/C Coe;
254l AA/C Coe;
254r AA/M Short;
255t AA/S McBride;
255b AA/C Coe;
256 AA/L Blake;
257 AA/M Short;
258t Strokestown Park and Famine Museum;
258b Strokestown Park and Famine Museum;
259l Strokestown Park and Famine Museum;
259r Strokestown Park and Famine Museum;
260 AA/S Day;
261 Irish Image Collection/Axiom;
262 AA/L Blake;
263l Irish Image Collection/Axiom;
263r AA/M Short;

264 AA/P Zollier;
267 AA/M Short;
268 Left Bank Bistro;
269 Wineport Lodge;
270 AA/L Blake;
271 Hodson Bay Hotel;
272 AA/I Dawson;
274 AA/G Munday;
275 AA/G Munday;
276 AA/I Dawson;
277t AA/D Forss;
277b AA/M Diggin;
278 AA/G Munday;
279 Northern Ireland Tourist Board;
280 AA/C Coe;
281 Belfast Visitors and Convention Bureau;
282t AA/C Coe;
282b AA/G Munday;
283t AA/G Munday;
283b AA/I Dawson;
284t AA/I Dawson;
284b Belfast Visitors and Convention Bureau;
285 Belfast Visitors and Convention Bureau;
288 Northern Ireland Tourist Board;
289 AA/C Coe;
290 AA/I Dawson;
291 AA/I Dawson;
292 Northern Ireland Tourist Board;
293 Northern Ireland Tourist Board;
294l AA/C Coe;
294r Northern Ireland Tourist Board;
295 National Trust/Roger Kinkead;
296 AA/I Dawson;
297 AA/G Munday;
298 AA/G Munday;
299t AA;
299b AA/C Coe;
300 AA/M Diggin;
301 AA/I Dawson;
302 Northern Ireland Tourist Board;
303 Northern Ireland Tourist Board;
304 Northern Ireland Tourist Board;
305t AA/I Dawson;
305b AA/I Dawson;
306 AA/M Diggin;
308 AA/I Dawson;
309l AA/I Dawson;
309r AA/I Dawson;
310 Belfast Visitors and Convention Bureau;
315 Photodisc;
316 ImageState;
319 Shu, Belfast;
321 AA/C Sawyer;

322 AA/I Dawson;
324 The Narrows;
325 AA/I Dawson;
331 AA/C Jones;
332 AA/S Day;
333 AA/G Munday;
334l © FoxSearch/Everett/Rex Features;
334r Everett Collection/Rex Features;
335 Belfast Visitors and Convention Bureau;
336 AA/S Day;
339 Belfast Visitors and Convention Bureau;
340 Belfast Visitors and Convention Bureau;
341l Belfast Visitors and Convention Bureau;
341r AA/SlideFile;
342 Northern Ireland Tourist Board;
343 Belfast Visitors and Convention Bureau;
344t AA/S Whitehorne;
344b Mayo Naturally;
345 Northern Ireland Tourist Board;
346 AA/M Short;
347l AA/S Hill;
347r AA/C Coe;
348 AA/S McBride;
350 Duvane Farm;
352 AA/S McBride;
354 Time Live Pictures/Mansell/Time Life Pictures/Getty Images;
355l Geoffrey Swaine/Rex Features;
355r Johnny Eggitt/AFP/Getty Images;
356 AA/M Short;
357 AA/L Blake;
358 AA/C Jones

Every effort has been made to trace the copyright holders, and we apologise in advance for any accidental errors. We would be happy to apply the corrections in the following edition of this publication.

CREDITS

Managing editor
Marie-Claire Jefferies

Project editor
Lodestone Publishing Ltd

Design
Drew Jones, pentacorbig, Nick Otway

Cover design
Chie Ushio

Picture research
Vivien Little

Image retouching and repro
Sarah Montgomery

Mapping
Maps produced by the Mapping Services
Department of AA Publishing

Main contributors
Chris Bagshaw, Donna Dailey, Lyn Gallagher,
Mike Gerrard, Isla Love, Daniel Mccrea,
Penny Phenix, Christopher Somerville,
Jackie Staddon, Ann Stonehouse, Hilary Weston

Updaters
Jackie Staddon, Hilary Weston

Indexer
Marie Lorimer

Production
Lyn Kirby, Karen Gibson

See It Ireland
ISBN 978-1-4000-0773-8
Third Edition

Published in the United States by Fodor's Travel and simultaneously in Canada by Random House of Canada Limited, Toronto.
Published in the United Kingdom by AA Publishing.
Fodor's is a registered trademark of Random House, Inc., and Fodor's See It is a trademark of Random House, Inc.
Fodor's Travel is a division of Random House, Inc.

Color separation by Keenes, Andover, UK
Printed and bound by Leo Paper Products, China
10 9 8 7 6 5 4 3 2 1

Special Sales: This book is available for special discounts for bulk purchases for sales promotions or premiums. Special editions, including personalized covers, excerpts of existing books, and corporate imprints, can be created in large quantities for special needs.
For more information, write to Special Markets/Premium Sales, 1745 Broadway, MD 6-2, New York, NY 10019
or e-mail specialmarkets@randomhouse.com
Important Note: Time inevitably brings changes, so always confirm prices, travel facts, and other perishable information when it matters. Although Fodor's cannot accept responsibility for errors, you can use this guide in the confidence that we have taken every care to ensure its accuracy.